Praise for *Salesforce.com® Secrets of Success*

"Cloud computing is changing everything. David Taber has written the definitive guide to navigating this transformation. Every functional vice president should read this book in order to understand how to get maximum value from Salesforce.com, integrate social media into operations, maximize sales and profits, and become a truly customer-focused company."

—Dave Kellogg, CEO, Host Analytics

"David Taber maps out our dreams for SFA/CRM, its technical and adoption challenges, and real-world executive strategies for managing the organizational/political work of a Salesforce.com implementation. His guidance is masterful, and this book captures it."

—Rich Mironov, CEO, Mironov Consulting

"I have reread David Taber's *Salesforce.com® Secrets of Success* more than a few times now, and I open this book first when I start a new project. Somehow I always seem to find the perfect tips to save me time, strategies to deliver a better project, and anecdotes to make me look good in front of customers.

Salesforce.com® Secrets of Success is my go-to guide for accurately framing a problem, avoiding disaster, and explaining the best solution to my project sponsor.

Read this book, and benefit from David Taber's extensive experience with the Salesforce.com platform while you enjoy his intelligent and witty navigation through the politics and pitfalls of project delivery."

—Dan Weiss, Senior Consultant, Appirio

Salesforce.com® Secrets of Success

Second Edition

Salesforce.com® Secrets of Success

Best Practices for Growth and Profitability

Second Edition

David Taber

PRENTICE
HALL

Upper Saddle River, NJ • Boston • Indianapolis • San Francisco
New York • Toronto • Montreal • London • Munich • Paris • Madrid
Capetown • Sydney • Tokyo • Singapore • Mexico City

Many of the designations used by manufacturers and sellers to distinguish their products are claimed as trademarks. Where those designations appear in this book, and the publisher was aware of a trademark claim, the designations have been printed with initial capital letters or in all capitals.

Sales*Logistix*, the SFA Maturity Model, and "Perfectionism Doesn't Pay" are trademarks of Sales*Logistix*, Inc. All rights reserved. Nothing in this book is to be construed as legal advice.

The author and publisher have taken care in the preparation of this book, but make no expressed or implied warranty of any kind and assume no responsibility for errors or omissions. No liability is assumed for incidental or consequential damages in connection with or arising out of the use of the information or programs contained herein.

The publisher offers excellent discounts on this book when ordered in quantity for bulk purchases or special sales, which may include electronic versions and/or custom covers and content particular to your business, training goals, marketing focus, and branding interests. For more information, please contact:

U.S. Corporate and Government Sales
(800) 382-3419
corpsales@pearsontechgroup.com

For sales outside the United States, please contact:

International Sales
international@pearson.com

Visit us on the Web: informit.com/ph

Library of Congress Cataloging-in-Publication Data

Taber, David, 1956-
  Salesforce.com secrets of success : best practices for growth and profitability / David Taber.—
Second edition.
       pages   cm
  Includes index.
  ISBN 978-0-13-351739-2 (pbk. : alk. paper)
  1. Customer relations—Management. 2. Sales management. I. Title.
  HF5415.5.T32 2014
  658.8'10028553—dc23

                                        2013031832

Copyright © 2014 Pearson Education, Inc.

ISBN-13: 978-0-13-351739-2
ISBN-10:   0-13-351739-X
Text printed in the United States on recycled paper at RR Donnelley in Crawfordsville Indiana.
First printing, November 2013

Editor-in-Chief
Mark L. Taub

Acquisitions Editor
Laura Lewin

Development Editor
Michael Thurston

Managing Editor
John Fuller

Full-Service Production Manager
Julie B. Nahil

Copy Editor
Carol Lallier

Indexer
Ted Laux

Proofreader
Denise Wolber

Technical Reviewers
Todd Cawthron
Daniel Weiss

Publishing Coordinator
Olivia Basegio

Cover Designer
Alan Clements

Compositor
CIP Group

To my wife, Jennifer, who makes everything possible.

Contents

Acknowledgments

If it takes a village to raise a child, it takes a lot of colleagues and good friends to write a book. I have a lot of people to thank for this one. Before I do, I have to apologize to Jennifer, Andrew, and Nicholas for my absenteeism as a parent and husband these past months.

First and foremost, I have to thank the team at Prentice Hall. Laura Lewin helped me throughout the second edition process and got the update of this book approved. Trina MacDonald, my original acquisitions editor, helped me sell the book idea in the first place. Michael Thurston, my development editor, helped shape my writing for the needs of the reader. Carol Lallier, my copy editor, had to deal with my endless punctuation errors. Denise Wolber proofed the galleys and found hilarious examples where the automatic spell-checkers had made silly substitutions. Finally, Olivia Basegio kept the draft organized and on schedule.

As this book covers a lot of ground, the text contained a ton of ideas that had to be organized and balanced. A raft of people helped me by bullet-proofing arguments and reviewing chapters from the perspective of different enterprise organizations. To Todd Cawthron, Geraldine Gray, Erin Kinikin, Bo Laurent, Patricia Menadier, Steve Messino, Rich Mironov, Deepa Patel, Roger Solin, Craig Stouffer, Michal Wachstock, and Chuck deVita of the Growth Process Group, thanks.

Thanks to my technical reviewers who read the whole manuscript and provided valuable input: Todd Cawthron at Persistence Group and Daniel Weiss at Appirio.

I am indebted to industry analysts and gurus who publish survey results that I used to substantiate my points. In particular, Aberdeen Group, AMR Research, CSO Insights, GoToMarket Strategies, Inside CRM, and Sirius Decisions have provided valuable perspectives on the best interactions between sales and marketing departments.

I also owe a debt of gratitude to the readership of *The Taber Report* for their feedback and positive arguments about controversial marketing and sales topics. Thanks, too, to my Sales*Logistix* customers for providing the technical and organizational challenges that were my inspiration for this book. I also want to acknowledge Meredith Rudof Weiss and Daniel Kushner for not saying anything bad about the content.

Finally, Dave Korba deserves special mention here as a comrade, source of inspiration, and friend.

Thanks to you all.

About the Author

David Taber is an internationally recognized marketing and management consultant in the IT industry, with more than 20 years' experience in real (non-consulting) companies, including 10 years at vice president or above.

When he first used Salesforce.com back in 2000, David saw the system's potential even in that early version. His company, Sales*Logistix*, is a certified implementer of Salesforce.com solutions, with clients in the United States, Canada, Israel, and India. He has personally worked on hundreds of Salesforce.com implementations, from early-stage startups to larger companies such as EMC and Cisco.

David's experience as a marketing VP in publicly traded companies—working with the sales organization, engineering, customer, support, finance, and corporate management—gives him unique insight into the habits and needs of the executive suite. Additionally, his background in IT makes it easy for him to translate insights into language that both business and technical people can understand.

As an accomplished writer and speaker, David has created and delivered presentations to audiences in 10 countries, and he coaches CEOs on VC pitches. He teaches at the Haas School of Business at University of California at Berkeley. In addition, he has taught the Product Marketing class at the University of California Berkeley extension, and has been a guest lecturer in marketing at Carnegie Mellon University.

David is a fourth-generation Californian who still hasn't figured out how to leave the Bay Area.

More information about David is available on LinkedIn (www.linkedin.com/in/davidotaber/).

Introduction

Everybody sells.

—Thomas Watson

Salesforce.com (SFDC) is the world's leading cloud-based system for salesforce automation (SFA), customer relationship management (CRM), and support operations.
Used by more than 100,000 businesses worldwide, the SFDC community includes
100,000 external developers and 2 million end users. This community has doubled over the
last 4 years. SFDC is the 800-pound gorilla in the CRM market.

Paying Off on the Promise of CRM

From recent industry analyst reports and surveys, it's easy to see why SFDC is growing:

- According to CSO Insights, successful CRM customers see a 10% increase in sales
  representatives achieving quota, a 10% improvement in win rates for forecasted
  deals, and a 10% better conversion rate at every level of the waterfall (the more
  stages you have in your waterfall, the bigger the "compound interest" effect provided by SFDC).

- According to Aberdeen Group, 86% of CRM customers following "best practices"
  saw an average 24% increase in annual customer revenue. Nearly the same
  number of firms saw an increase in sales contribution margin, with the average
  increase being 25%.

- CSO Insights surveys show a 25% reduction in sales rep turnover rate with use of
  a good CRM system. Consequently, companies see fewer "learning curve effects"
  and an improvement in overall spending effectiveness, which translates into a
  deal or two more per rep per year, easily paying for an SFA/CRM system in a
  few months.

These are the generic industry data. In reality, SFDC has been able to achieve much better
outcomes than these numbers, with its customers typically achieving industry-leading
results.

Avoid Death in the Board Room!

It's week 12 of the quarter, and the board is wondering if you're really going to make your number. What's worse, your company is going to need some more capital soon, so you need the financial picture to look as solid as possible for investors.

You're sweating a bit as you prepare for the meeting because the forecast has been jumping around from week to week. Two weeks ago, the pipeline looked thin—there was no way to make the quarterly number. You chewed out your sales team, and they came back with a bigger forecast. But how could this extra business suddenly appear? Are the reps just trying to make you feel good? Is this forecast any more realistic than the last one?

The guys and gals in the factory are telegraphing that they don't believe the sales goal is reachable. They haven't shifted the production schedule because they don't see the orders yet. If they manufacture too much product, you'll be sitting around the first week of next quarter with a bunch of inventory to drag down your profits.

Terrific.

This is one of the nightmares that a solid CRM system will help you avoid. A CRM system won't necessarily make your business grow fast enough to make your investors happy, but if the system is done right, you'll always know where you are, and you'll have confidence indicators that will help you sleep well—even in week 12 of the quarter.

There's only one problem with this rosy picture: most CRM customers fail to get meaningful results from their system. This isn't an SFDC problem but rather an issue that's endemic to the whole CRM industry. Take a look at what industry analysts have said recently:

- AMR Research surveys indicated that 35% of CRM implementations faced serious user adoption issues. This percentage was down from 47% of CRM customers in 2002, but it is still higher than what customers expected.

- In surveys by CSO Insights and GoToMarket Strategies, respondents indicated that the average CRM customer had adoption rates of less than 75% among members of its sales team, with even lower percentages among its marketing and customer support personnel.

- These two firms' surveys confirmed that only half of CRM customers are achieving significant sales performance improvements or believe they can get real-time information from their CRM system. Most customers use the system only for contact management and pipeline management; only 30% use it for forecasting.

- Approximately 75% of prospect business cards will never make it into the SFA system, according to CSO Insights.

- According to Inside CRM surveys, only half of sales managers who do use their CRM system for forecasting and opportunity management believe the system is effective.

- According to *Software* magazine, only 30% of companies that deploy CRM systems report significant increases in sales performance (e.g., shorter sales cycles, better win rates, or overall revenue increases).

These issues don't arise because of a technology or product problem. They're caused by *people*, *policy*, and *process* issues. These issues are the reason I wrote this book.

Achieving the Promise of SFDC

The promise of SFDC is increased profitability *and* increased customer satisfaction at the same time—a pretty tall order—as shown in Figure I-1.

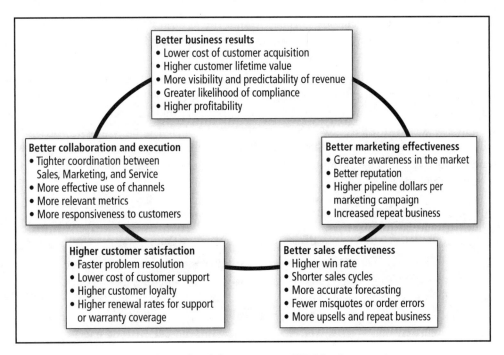

FIGURE I-1   Benefits that can be realized from a proper SFDC implementation

The key success factor for achieving any of these benefits is early and deep user adoption; everything else flows from that source. When the users naturally turn to the SFDC system because it makes them more efficient, they will fill the system with more credible data. Those data make reports more meaningful—and so the availability of good information attracts more users to the system. We discuss how to encourage this virtuous cycle throughout the book.

The promise of SFDC cannot be achieved just by buying some new software. Some change also is needed in business processes and user behaviors. Most customers discover months *after* they buy an SFDC system that, to achieve real improvement in sales and operations, they must be more disciplined, develop new processes, and apply best practices. Just slapping automation on top of an outdated business process merely makes you execute errors faster.

Real SFDC success depends on three factors:

1. **Products** that extend SFDC and integrate it with other systems so that the users can get a complete view of the customer's situation and do the right thing as smoothly as possible

2. **People** who are fully indoctrinated on how to use SFDC to more quickly solve customer problems

3. **Business processes** that are "tuned" so that the *natural* way people work supports company objectives, best practices, and regulatory compliance

Getting optimal results from SFDC is hard. Big SFDC customers spend boatloads of money on consultants to extend the functionality, integrate the system, redesign business processes, and indoctrinate the users. Of course, smaller companies can't afford the time or money to follow this path. Most SFDC customers need shortcuts, "canned" procedures, and best-practices-in-a-box so they won't flail around and be frustrated. This book was designed to give you the information you need quickly and without a lot of Web searching or head scratching.

HOW TO BLOW UP TWO CAREERS AT ONCE!

A friend of mine was a VP of marketing at a startup, and she walked into a board meeting ready to present her group's results for the quarter. She was walking into an ambush.

The VP of sales hadn't made his number, and at the start of the board meeting he had made a long presentation about why the sales representatives *couldn't* make their numbers. They didn't have enough leads, and the ones that they did get were garbage. Marketing wasn't doing its job—that's why sales underachieved.

The board of directors confronted the VP of marketing, who was totally blindsided. Once she heard the complaint, she asked to be excused for 5 minutes. She went back to her office, pulled together some numbers, and came back to the board meeting. It turned out that marketing had delivered eight times as many leads as sales had said—and 95% of those leads had never been contacted, not even *once*.

The board got it, and the VP of marketing was off the hook.

Actually, no. The board ended up firing both the VP of sales and the VP of marketing. The twin functions—which really need to feed each other—were too disconnected, too dysfunctional.

This company had a basic SFA system. But all the *business processes surrounding its core system* were broken. Nobody agreed on the definition of a lead or what it took for a lead to be qualified. Poor-quality data made reports misleading. Sales and marketing weren't communicating through the system. Politics were rampant. The business leverage just wasn't there.

Sometimes, the only way to fix a CRM problem is to fix the *people and the processes*. That's what this book is all about.

Do You Need an SFA System or a CRM System?

Industry analysts often treat SFA systems as a different product category than CRM systems. This book makes the case that the SFA/CRM distinction is really a continuum of functionality and business practices. It also argues that SFDC can be used very effectively as *either* an SFA system or a CRM system: it all depends on how you invest and which behaviors your team takes on.

The term *sales force automation system* is really a misnomer, because these systems don't automate the sales function. They *can* prevent things from falling through the cracks, streamline processes, accelerate the sales cycle, and provide clear metrics, but sales is still a very human process. From an image perspective, the SFA category is badly named: no sales rep wants to be automated. Even so, the SFA moniker stuck. What the SFA marketers in the 1990s should have insisted on was "sales funnel acceleration"—a far more user-friendly positioning of what these systems actually do.

SFA systems typically start out as software for direct sales or telesales people, providing simple contact and account management. Small companies tracking calls and managing lead maturation may be able to use Microsoft Outlook, Microsoft Excel, ACT, Goldmine, or Zoho without a problem. Over time, however, those simple tools tend to run out of gas as the sales organization tries to manage opportunities and the pipeline. These customers may use SalesLogix software or another computer-based tool to provide this level of SFA functionality, but they're better off using SFDC.

All of these "SFA-only" systems are driven by the sales team and are basically stand-alone products. Consequently, they cannot fundamentally improve sales efficiency. To make a real difference in efficiency and follow-through, the business must start to integrate its SFA system into the rest of the enterprise. The first area for system expansion is the marketing function, as it is the source of the leads, programs, and collateral that feed the sales cycle. The next natural area for expansion is quoting and contract approval, because the objective of any sales team is to close deals faster. Given that this functionality is usually handled by other systems, the natural expansion strategy is to integrate the quoting and digital signature screens into the SFA system. This incremental integration is a natural evolution for SFDC customers, and they tend to take this route at their own pace.

Of course, as the reach of the SFA system expands, sales reps' behaviors and business processes have to evolve as well. Marketing has to confer more frequently with sales to make sure that the lead flow has both the quality and the quantity necessary to generate a sufficient pipeline. Marketing starts to work with sales to select and "tune" upcoming campaigns. In a similar way, as the sales reps begin using the system to create quotes, quote approval needs to be handled in a different way. For example, sales reps do *not* need to send out quotes until the discounts have been approved, and they should *not* modify quotes once they've been approved. These process changes, although obvious, often take months to become standard operating procedure. Unfortunately, process failures in these areas are often blamed on the SFA system. This book shows you how to completely avoid the most common and troublesome problems and rapidly recover from any process failure that knocks things off the rails.

The next expansion step is for the SFA system to be used by the customer support team. Because the customer's contact information and purchase history are already in the system, bringing the service and support folks into the SFA system is a natural step. By the time the customer support team has adopted the SFA system, they have moved it incrementally toward becoming a CRM system—that is, the focal point for acquiring, retaining, and growing profitable customer relationships.

CRM systems have a loftier set of goals than just sales productivity: the system should help convert your company's content (expertise) into customer conversations,[1] thereby moving customers into shared experiences (and common values), proceeding to transactions, and producing lasting relationships that create a long-term revenue stream after the company has been established as a trusted advisor to the customer. A full CRM system touches the customer from several angles: sales, distribution channels, marketing, service, support, training and consulting, Web community, and even accounting (for contracts, invoicing, and accounts receivable). Further, a modern CRM system needs to

---

1. If you've never read the classic *The Cluetrain Manifesto,* which explores the concept of commerce as a conversation, I recommend it. An abridged version is available for free at http://manybooks.net/titles/variousother05cluetrain.html.

be linked with digital marketing, brand-reputation engines, and your Web site. Clearly, serious CRM must inevitably be integrated with several existing systems.[2] A full-blown CRM system also demands process and policy improvements to avoid misuse and user dissatisfaction (discussed in Chapters 8 through 13).

SFDC is one of the very few systems that can grow incrementally from a straightforward contact manager (`group edition`) to an SFA tool (`professional edition`) into a serious CRM system (`enterprise` and `unlimited editions`). Thanks to its technically solid and flexible platform, SFDC can be extended with partner products and integration tools (discussed in Chapter 7) to achieve a wide array of functions, from public relations to human resources. Indeed, at the end of the system evolution, SFDC may not only provide a 360-degree view of the customer but also become the central executive application for managing the entire business.

Only you can decide whether you want an SFA system or a full-bore CRM. Here are some ways to think about the distinction at a high level:

- Do you want to monitor sales rep behavior (SFA) or customer behavior (CRM)?

- Are you trying to manage the transaction (SFA) or grow lifetime value (CRM)?

- Are you worried about quarterly revenue (SFA) or annual profitability (CRM)?

When Salesforce.com Is the Best Choice—and When It Isn't

SFDC is the pioneering CRM delivered in a hosted *software as a service* (SaaS) cloud-computing model. Recent industry data from CSO Insights and other sources indicate that dramatically better outcomes can be achieved with cloud-based CRM systems than with on-premises products:

- Much faster time to value

- Fewer budget overruns

- Higher end-customer satisfaction

- Better sales productivity

SFDC is the best-of-breed cloud CRM system. It's reliable, it's secure, and it performs well from anywhere in the world.[3] It offers the best compromise of features, flexibility, and

---

2. For all intents and purposes, there is no such thing as a standalone CRM system.

3. You *do* have to have a decent Internet connection, as there isn't an on-premises version of SFDC. Although the system can be used with an Edge Wireless connection (<100Kbps), that is just not a good way to live.

usability. It can be quickly set up, and it's accessible from BlackBerry, Android, and iPhone devices. SFDC is an ideal choice for companies that need to get their feet wet in an SFA system, try it out in one department, and ultimately expand use of the system to other areas. SFDC lends itself to incremental usage in terms of both the number of users and the features enabled, giving your organization time to learn and optimize the way it uses the system.

It's important to understand that SFDC out of the box is a fairly skeletal CRM system. As discussed in Chapter 1, SFDC's standard features cover the basics of what sales, marketing, and support need for lead generation, pipeline management, and customer service. But to get beyond the basics in almost any area, SFDC must be extended with plugins, custom coding, or integration with outside systems. Fortunately, SFDC has the industry's widest array of add-on products, and there are more ways to integrate outside systems with SFDC than any other CRM system on the market. If it turns out that you don't like the available third-party products, the SFDC system provides a full-blown development and deployment environment that lets you build custom applications that leverage the core system data. There might be no other product that can match it in this area: no matter where you are on the continuum of needs, SFDC offers several strategies for efficiently satisfying them.

That said, there are some situations in which SFDC may not be the right approach:

- If you're a smaller company doing a "greenfield" implementation that needs to include SFA, professional services automation, accounting, and inventory/distribution—all at once—a unified system from a single vendor could serve your purposes better. It can reduce finger-ponting and give you more of a known quantity out of the box. No incompatibilities.[4] If you like the cloud model, this probably means NetSuite (but not Microsoft). If you prefer the on-premises model (in which you own the software and it runs on your servers), this probably means Microsoft, Oracle, or SAP (but not NetSuite). Be aware that a single-vendor strategy will almost never provide best-of-breed options, and you'll still need third-party add-ons and customization.

- If you're a large company with very complex requirements and you want to leverage your IT team's development skills for CRM, there are two on-premises alternatives. If your team has significant PHP skills, SugarCRM is written in PHP throughout. On the other hand, if your team has deep C# skills, the componentry and API richness of the on-premises version of Microsoft Dynamics CRM provide a solid foundation for developers. With either of these strategies, however, your team really has to know what they are doing with the platform and be self-supporting over time. You'll need to tightly manage the long-run costs of coding, documenting, and maintaining these home-brew modules, as they can overwhelm

---

4. "No incompatibilities" is only a rhetorical advantage. Which is worse: incompatibilities *between* products or bugs *within* the single-vendor product you just bought to avoid incompatibilities?

the short-term advantages of this approach. And of course, don't forget the costs of buying, running, and managing servers over time—plus the support and upgrade fees you'll pay to your software vendor.

- If you're a large company, you may already have several CRM systems in place and they cannot be removed, so adding yet another system to the mix is unlikely to improve the situation. That said, having a strategic plan to consolidate multiple CRM systems onto SFDC usually makes a huge amount of sense. Just be aware that getting everything right in a multi-CRM environment—including external system integration, business process changes, and user behavior modification— takes a while and requires serious effort and tight management. This goes double if one or more of your incumbent systems is of the home-brew variety.

- If you're a small company and all of your users need the system for a single, narrow task (e.g., personal contact management), you don't yet need a full CRM system. Like most SaaS products, SFDC charges by the user, and you won't get much of a discount unless you're buying hundreds of user licenses. If you find an on-premises product that satisfies your basic needs, you may strike a better deal for your current needs with a perpetual-license, on-premises product (particularly if you already have a strong internal IT function and more than 90% of your users are in a single building or campus).

- If you're a corporation that has a mandated enterprise application suite such as that offered by SAP or Oracle, getting another system in the door (even if it's "in the cloud") can be a bureaucratic and technical nightmare. In this case, your only practical solution may be to use the suite vendor's CRM module. Generally speaking, the suite vendors' cloud offerings are quite weak: you'll probably install their on-premises version—which the users will hate.

- If you're a large company with a lot of low-cost talent, in IT as well as in the user organizations, an open-source SFA system can be a reasonable choice. As long as you budget time for the inevitable administrative and development work that is involved with these "free" SFA systems, open source matches the cost sensitivity and technical culture in developing countries such as China and India. Even in low-cost areas, though, businesses must be highly competitive. Cost control is too limited a perspective: growth is what increases company profitability.

Rather than focusing on which vendor to buy from, the better strategy is to focus the discussion on maximizing the business value of your CRM system. A CRM without grass-roots adoption is an empty shell and will be considered a failed project. Better to focus on starting the CRM down the path of the virtuous cycle: user adoption → data quality → usability → business value. Put user productivity, collaboration, and profitable growth at the center of your SFA and CRM decisions.

How to Use This Book

Do not read this whole book. Seriously. Read the pages that are immediately relevant to your current problems, using the index as your starting point. If a chapter intrigues you, start at the last page and read the summary. Then, look back in the chapter if one of the summary bullets is intriguing.

This book is organized to provide specific answers for decision makers and users at every level of SFDC user organization:

- CEOs, presidents, and board members ("What's possible?")

- VPs of sales, marketing, and support ("Which direction should we set?")

- IT, finance, and operations people ("How do we get it done?")

- Sales reps, sales managers, support personnel, and marketing folks ("How do *I* do it?")

Focus on the chapters that are immediately relevant to your role and those sections that answer questions pertinent to your immediate situation:

- If you are an executive, read the Executive Summary and the one chapter between Chapters 9 and 13 that comes closest to your job title. You might also want to scan Chapters 5 through 8 for topics that are relevant to you.

- If you will be part of an SFDC implementation team, read Chapters 1 through 4, focusing on those sections that are most relevant to where you are now. You also should scan Chapters 5 through 8 looking for interesting topics.

- If you're a future user of SFDC, you'll want to understand how the system is best deployed across your organization. Read the one chapter between Chapters 9 and 13 that matches your role in the organization—so you can see what we've told the boss to do. Scan Chapters 5 through 8 to understand the people, products, politics, and process issues surrounding substantial SFDC implementations.

In case you thought that this book isn't long enough, there are over 500 pages of supplementary materials, templates, and extra goodies at www.SFDC-secrets.com. It's all free to you, so check it out!

—David Taber
Palo Alto, California

Executive Summary

> *Don't solve problems: pursue opportunities.*
>
> *—Peter Drucker*

This executive summary is the distillation of the best practices presented throughout the book, reframed from the perspective of VPs and CxOs (e.g., CEOs, COOs, CFOs, and CMOs) of a company that plans to implement a Salesforce.com system or radically expand an existing one. We designed it to be the only part of the book that every executive needs to read. *If you're not an executive, skip this executive summary*, as you'll find the more detailed information you need in later chapters that cover your specific organization.

Why should you bother reading this chapter?

How about competitive excellence? Lower customer churn? Higher win rates? Visibility? This chapter wasn't written to sell you Salesforce.com (SFDC), but it will convince you that customer relationship management (CRM) can make more of a difference to your profitability than any other type of enterprise software. How much more profit can you get out of your supply chain optimization going forward? Do you really think that your accounting or HR package is going to give you a couple of extra points of margin and several more points of revenue growth?

CRM can. Done right, CRM can transform your marketing effectiveness, improve sales win rates, and increase customer loyalty—all at the same time. Although a CRM system's impact is more about revenue increases than cost reductions, it can do both.

Problem is, "done right" is rare. This book exists because killer CRM systems are counterintuitive, with projects that look nothing like traditional IT.

What Every CxO Needs to Know about Salesforce.com

SFDC is *the* right choice for most companies who want an easy-to-use and flexible salesforce automation (SFA) or CRM system. Here are seven things *you* need to know about it:

- **User adoption is everything**: If it doesn't hold solid data, the SFDC system is an empty shell. More users mean more data in the system, and more data mean a

1

better view of the customer situation. So your *first* job is to make sure that users adopt the system. Communicate verbally and through behavior that *you* will be relying on the system to make management decisions—and you expect people at every level to do the same. A key success factor for your SFDC implementation is the way employees perceive how *you* use the system and value its data. If they sense you don't care about it or don't believe in it, neither will they. Provide rewards for early adopters, and use the system yourself.

- **Bad data entries are your nemesis:** Duplicates, low-quality data, and lost entries are to be avoided at all costs, as they hurt user adoption, undermine system credibility, and can even undermine *your* credibility. The key here: don't skimp on data migration, integration, and automation projects that stop bad data at the source. Set aside a serious budget to get as much customer-relationship data as possible stored in SFDC, or at least make it accessible from there.

- **Visibility is your first benefit:** Once users are really on the system, SFDC provides you much more visibility into what's going on with prospects and customers. It gives you better early warning signals for forecast, pipeline, and customer satisfaction problems. It also gives you clear metrics and real-time dashboards for achievement versus goals. Invest in the integration that gives you a 360-degree view of the business. Provide incentives for predictability.

- **Management by exception is your goal:** The best way to manage your time is to use management by exception (MBE). By taking the "normal" for granted, you can focus on the variances where you can make a difference. SFDC provides dashboards, alerts, workflows, and approval processes that facilitate compliance and managing to a plan. Set realistic goals, relevant metrics, timely thresholds, and clear employee incentives that match the desired behavior. Once you have a reliable, accurate base of information to work with, you can streamline and accelerate business processes—and then manage to them. Reward autonomy so that your organization learns that management by emergency (the "squeaky wheel" effect) is *not* how you're running the company anymore.

- **Strategy is the crown:** Who are your most profitable customers, and why? Which products do they buy from you, and what are the reasons they prefer doing business with you? Where do you need to be investing more, and where can you economize on marketing, selling, and support efforts? These questions can be answered only when you have a database of customer purchase patterns and a history of behaviors. The answers will be just guesses and gut feelings until your CRM system serves as the foundation for strategic analysis.

- **Be careful about what you say:** Everyone in your organization will be on the alert because CRM systems come with a bit of political baggage—the "Big Brother" effect. Sales reps aren't asking to be automated, and nobody wants to be micro-managed. If your staff senses that your real goal is to more tightly monitor *them*, all the good things that a CRM system can do for your company will be delayed or even nullified. Even though the following words may have the same abstract meaning, what your people will *hear* from the two lists is drastically different:

Do talk about:	*Don't* talk about:
Bigger deals	Higher productivity
Happier customers	Tighter management
Less wasted effort	Automation or cost control
Improved business processes	Job elimination
Easier goal achievement	Leverage
Tools employees need	Comprehensive system

If employees sense that you're using the SFDC system to unify your company and make it more coherent and coordinated, they will follow your example. But if they sense that you're going to use the system to lay blame or fuel political battles, they will subtly sabotage the system as they would any enemy.

- **Publicize the good news:** It's been proven many times that the organization will follow your lead in regard to the SFDC system. Post on `chatter`[1] daily. Really. Celebrate the good things that the system is doing for the business every quarter while it's being built and extended. Tell the board about your successes, tell your peers about the benefits, and tell your subordinates about the customer wins made possible by SFDC. Get the news out about how CRM is reshaping your business and giving your team a strategic advantage.

Why Are You Looking at an SFA or a CRM System?

You don't need me to tell you that the "good old days" of selling are gone—the easy money has already been made. Customers expect a much higher level of sales rep knowledge, tighter execution, and deeper postsales support. Also, customers expect your Web marketing, sales, and support to seamlessly reinforce what you do in person and on the phone—whether your operations are ready for it or not. If you want to achieve higher customer lifetime value, your sales, marketing, and customer support teams must collaborate much more effectively than they did in the past. Think about how you want to give the revenue engine a tune-up.

---

1. We talk about `chatter` later in this chapter—for now, think of it as an instant messaging system baked into SFDC.

Typically, a company's most unreliable business process is revenue generation. This unreliability shows up as erratic forecasts, spotty rep productivity, one-off contracts, excessive discounting, rocky customer satisfaction ratings, weak profitability, and other unamusing issues. You wouldn't let your production line be that unreliable. It's time to make your revenue process a consistent, predictable engine—one that's firing on all cylinders. While you're at it, make sure you replace the old carburetor of spreadsheets with the modern fuel injection of SFDC.

The business case for CRM is all about *profits*. Those profits will come mainly from *revenue* increases: bigger deals, higher conversion ratios, more repeat business, and improved customer loyalty. Although CRM systems can also lead to cost reductions, putting the emphasis there starts the project out on the wrong foot.

Every executive in your company who reads this chapter needs to agree on the high-level business objectives you are trying to achieve with CRM before you make the investment. Although each company has unique goals, some precepts are nearly universal for SFDC customers:

- The whole point of a CRM system is to get the most return from the amount you invest in marketing and sales (e.g., salaries, programs, travel, and customer dinners). The purpose of the system should be *maximizing customer life-cycle profitability*, which entails a lot more than just "getting more sales."

- Although growth may come from getting new customers, *profit* definitely comes from milking existing ones. It is 3 to 10 times more expensive to acquire new customers than it is to upsell and expand existing accounts. *Of course* you need new customers, but SFDC can help you do that while also getting more profit out of every customer you ever won. This is why enabling the support and services team with CRM is so important.

There are dozens of good reasons why investing in an SFA or a CRM system can make a decisive difference in company performance—take a look at the following list. It's a compelling list, but **the temptation to say "let's do it all" is a recipe for failure.** Every one of these business objectives is within reach, but in most cases you will **achieve only three or four** of them in the first year of SFDC system operation. And to really get them, you have to keep the team focused *consistently* on those three or four objectives until they are actually achieved. So choose wisely and stand by your prioritization.

Higher Profitability

- Lower costs for finding and closing new customers
- Faster sales cycles and improved conversion rates

- Larger order sizes
- Higher profit from existing customers
- Improved marketing and promotional effectiveness
- Faster customer uptake of new products and services
- Much better leverage of Web, partner, and distribution channels
- Higher service margins by leveraging service, support, and training partners
- Fewer erroneous orders and product returns
- Lower customer service and support costs

Better Visibility, Better Decisions

- Deeper, broader view of customers and operations
- More realistic and real-time metrics of the customer relationship
- Greater ability to see and predict customer behavior
- Better product design decisions
- More measurable business processes
- Better pipeline and inventory forecasts
- Greater visibility into product, market segment, and regional performance
- Better partner and channel visibility
- Smoother, faster collaboration across organizational boundaries
- Tighter controls and improved compliance
- More effective business processes
- Tighter controls and improved compliance

Improved Competitiveness

- Better competitive intelligence
- Better leverage of social media such as LinkedIn or Facebook
- Greater ability to spot and react to market trends faster
- Faster, more effective responses to competitive threats
- Faster growth in new markets and geographies

- Quantifiable improvement in market reputation

- Improved customer satisfaction, loyalty, and repeat business

Keeping the Big Picture in Focus

As desirable as the business goals discussed are, before you even think about an investment in a CRM system, you have to think through how you want your organization to change. Putting in an SFDC system without optimizing the sales, marketing, and support business processes means missing a huge opportunity to transform your business. Instead, you need to consider broader organizational, people, and process goals.

Change Management

Like business-level goals, business process changes must be prioritized because you can make only a few real changes during a year's time. Business process changes have too many organizational repercussions if you overdo them—so don't try to fix too much at once.

The first step for changing the business process is to perform triage:

- Which two or three business processes will be replaced or rebuilt[2] from the ground up?

- Which business processes will be modified in small ways?

- Which business processes (the vast majority) will be kept the same?

The next step is to make sure that the people below you and in different organizations are committed, *before* you begin, to making improvements to the two or three business processes that will be undergoing major surgery. Passive-aggressive resistance can destroy the chances of success, so deal with the political issues up front!

Next, establish baseline metrics of the business process's performance in terms of both the things that basically work today (e.g., number of transactions or cost per transaction) and the areas that aren't working well (e.g., error rate or number of executive escalations). Don't skimp on these "as-is" metrics, as they become the baseline for your project's return on investment. If you don't know how much the broken process is costing your company, you can't really know if some extra investment is a good business decision. See, your CFO isn't crazy.[3]

---

2. Consolidated, eliminated, or automated.
3. If you want to understand the CFO's perspective better, check out the first couple of sections in Chapter 12.

Next, define *achievable* and *meaningful* metrics for how the business process needs to perform. State these "to-be" metrics in terms of both absolutes (e.g., 30 transactions per hour) and percentage improvement (e.g., 50% more transactions with existing staff), as each form dramatizes the required change in a different way.

Why Is Social CRM Such a Big Deal?

Everybody knows about Facebook, Twitter, and other social networks, but most businesses don't pay much attention to them beyond LinkedIn and Yelp. So why are you hearing noise about social CRM?

Because in businesses large and small, leveraging social networks as part of your sales, marketing, and support strategies can have huge payoffs in little things like profitability. Here are the main drivers:

Social Marketing

- As you can read about in Chapter 10, CRM is the tool that helps marketing become more effective and more measurable at the same time. If you spend significantly on advertising, the single biggest improvement you can make is to improve the relevance of your message to your target audiences. Social media is the next wave of the digital marketing revolution, every bit as powerful as Google.

- Marketing to your community of interest—the customers and prospects who really care about your products and services—is the single most cost-effective way to increase customer *awareness*, *interest*, *desire*, and even *action*. Get through the "A-I-D-A" sequence faster and more reliably using social media techniques that are managed through the CRM system.

- The brilliant company name "Reputation Defender" says it all. You need to have a 24 × 7 social media monitoring system, and you need to be able to act on brewing firestorms before they flame out of control on the Web. The CRM system needs to be "mission control" for real-time monitoring of customer/prospect sentiment and the foundation for automated responses going forward.

Social Selling

- For any significant purchase, people buy from people. Where and when you communicate can be just as important as what you communicate, so getting to the prospect *where they already are* and *when they are going to be most receptive* can make the difference between listening and deciding. Consequently, incorporating social media conversations into the CRM is just as important as capturing email threads and voicemails. For the U.S. market, social media is just as effective a sales tool for business-to-business (B2B) as it is for business-to-consumer (B2C). We all have plenty to learn from leaders like Amazon, TigerDirect, and PriceLine.

- If there's one critical success factor for CRM projects, it's the depth and speed of sales user adoption, because it starts a virtuous cycle. More users mean higher-quality data, which begets more usage, still more users, and a more complete picture of the customer relationship. Early on, though, your salespeople will whine that they don't have time to type prospect and pipeline data into the CRM. But those same sales reps seem to have no problem writing Tweets, sending an email, and jumping onto their social networks. When social networking and communications are done right—fully threaded through the rest of the CRM object model—they quickly add to the depth of data in the system. SFDC's `chatter` is a social medium that will start the virtuous cycle for your CRM system.

- Sales reps learn best when they see another rep do something that wins a deal. So formal training isn't as important as *natural collaboration* and competition across your sales teams. All CRM systems help with this effort, but SFDC is unique with `chatter`, a social media tool focused on collaborative problem solving. Used right, `chatter` helps the teams figure out what the competition is really doing and come up with a winning response. It also helps reduce internal email by up to 25%, saving *everyone* serious amounts of time (check out "What's All This Noise about Chatter" in Chapter 13).

Social Service and Support

- Access to service and interaction with support should be easy. Why make customers more frustrated than they already are with their problem? You want to get to the support situations in whatever medium the customer is in, and respond in full view of your community. So keep up with the support Web sites, the email addresses, and the phone lines. But make sure that your product's Facebook page or service's LinkedIn page aren't just billboards. In most industries, speed and style of first response can be more important than thoroughness or time-to-resolve. Social CRM will make your support staff more effective and decrease the likelihood of an online customer revolt.

- Self-support really works—so make it work better. Many organizations depend on customer self-support, as the user community is "on the air" 24 × 7 and often provides answers faster than your support team can. Even if the user base can't provide the answers, they can certainly generate the widest range of test cases and real-world workarounds. Use social media to make the "customer experts" an active part of your knowledge base, and use the CRM system to measure and improve community dynamics.

- Support is the new sales. We all know that a single disgruntled customer can undo the positive effects of 10 happy customers, and we all know that upsells and renewals are much more profitable than new customer wins. Whether you work for a large enterprise or a small company, over the long haul your support team will be in touch with customers more often than your sales team will. And they can be much more effective—not just cost-effective—at selling if they have the tools and the information they need to get that renewal or upsell. That's what leaders in every industry have discovered with their social CRM initiatives.

Social CRM is visionary stuff, and it's still so new that it's hard to make the business case for a new CRM initiative solely on its benefits. If your marketing, sales, and support strategies *are already based on social media*, you can make the case today. If not, the items listed should be viewed as upside and leverage potential for the future.

Setting Metrics of SFDC Success

The metrics of success for your SFDC project will be a mixture of business process improvements and overall business performance. As a member of the executive team, you need to document these goals for the first year of the SFDC project *before* the project starts—and commit to not changing those goals:

- **Business performance:** A list of three to four measurements, such as average deal size, customer retention rate, or cost per order.

- **Business process improvements:** A list of perhaps three metrics for business processes that will be upgraded during the year.

- **New capability or system functionality:** A *short* list of big-picture items to be added from a business (not technical) perspective, such as "95% of quotes to be reviewed and generated automatically" or "all orders conform to discounting rules." Make the criteria as quantitative as possible.

Each of these goals should be envisioned as providing go/no-go criteria for the acceptance of the SFDC system. If the goals aren't sufficiently clear, change the statement of metrics so they become black and white. Note that some goals may work against each other (high growth versus high profitability, profit of support versus customer satisfaction), so make sure that your goals aren't self-contradictory.

It's a best practice for the executive team to also set *nongoals:* things you want to avoid, as well as things that you acknowledge aren't economically feasible in the short term. Nongoals will be surprisingly useful to the team—and to you—in project reviews months down the line.

Your Role in Driving Project Approval

Before the SFDC project even begins, you'll be asked for money and political sponsorship. You need to directly participate in the process or else appoint a delegate with decision-making power and some budgetary authority.

Championing

Industry analysts universally agree that executive championship is a key success factor for any CRM project, even while the business case is being prepared. Of course, not all executives are equally effective in filling this role. The best formula is to have the COO/VP of sales be the champion and driver of the SFDC project. Nevertheless, if the CEO feels very strongly about SFDC, he or she can be an effective champion as well. See Chapter 6 if you want to understand more about the choice of champion.

To make an SFDC system successful across the layers of a company, *every* executive must take on the following *personal* action items:

- When investing in CRM functionality, always give the users something that is intrinsically valuable—something that saves them time or makes *them* look smarter—before you ask users to put additional effort into the system. If individuals (particularly sales folks) don't get anything directly in return, they'll view the system as a burden and a tax—and, not surprisingly, the amount and quality of the data in the system will decline.

- Focus on system *credibility* over system functionality. The fanciest features in the world won't make any difference if they're based on garbage data. Be ready to put some serious time and money[4] into data quality, migration, and integration. It is almost impossible to spend too much on ensuring data credibility.

- Provide more reasons for users to stay in the system and fewer reasons for them to work outside it. Make sure to identify key user groups, and keep the project team focused on tailoring the system to their needs. The goal is to make outboard spreadsheets and "insurance policy" steps disappear because they're a waste of effort and they prevent you from really seeing what's going on in the

---

4. In most SFDC implementations, data massaging accounts for 20% to 50% of the total system cost—and a much larger percentage if you have a lot of messy historical data spread across several systems.

organization. Push for the system to embody *all* of the steps and data for the business processes it is supporting.

- Plan to build the system incrementally, with features coming in phases rather than being delivered as a "Big Bang." In the implementation project, start small with a tight team and quick wins. Grow incrementally, delivering value to the business at least every 60 days. You'll be asking users to change some of their behaviors for handling customer interactions. Putting these changes in place will be for the better, but it will still take time. Users need time to learn and modify their behaviors if they're going to be really effective SFDC users.

- As an executive, you need to do five things for the SFDC team:

  ➡ Set the business priorities.

  ➡ Define the metrics of success.

  ➡ Provide funding and dedicated staff.

  ➡ Remove organizational obstacles.

  ➡ Promote system usage and celebrate system users.

- As an executive, you need to keep the project and your organization paying attention to the right things:

Don't focus on:	Do focus on:
Technology for its own sake	Business process improvement
Excessive measurement	Change management
Cost control	Revenue/profit increase

The Business Case

The business case for SFDC is pretty straightforward, at least on the cost side of the equation. On the benefits side, the tricky things to quantify are *opportunity costs*—expenses you can avoid or lost deals you could win. The SFDC project team will need your help answering questions like these:

- How much more revenue could you realistically get if you could close the trickiest 1% of customer deals? What about the trickiest 5%?

- What would be the impact of shortening the sales cycle by one week? What if sales reps could do a better job of qualifying prospects? Would that mean more revenue or simply reps with more time on their hands?

- What would it mean to the bottom line if marketing could divert 10% of its programs from people who aren't likely to buy and instead spend that money on people who are more likely to buy?

- What would it mean for customer support profitability if the team could handle each customer issue with one less phone call?

- What would it mean for your bottom line if customers were 5% more satisfied with your product or service? What would it mean if you achieved a 1% better upsell rate?

- How would it change your business if you could predict customer behavior better? How much more profitable would the company be if the sales forecast were 5% more accurate?

Of course, none of these improvements will be achieved the first day the SFDC system is running. Nevertheless, you want to think about the big picture to ensure that the team is pointed in the right direction and the business case for your CRM investment is tightly tied to solid business objectives.

SFDC: THE GOLDILOCKS INVESTMENT

Enterprise software has been bedeviled with high costs, delayed deployments, and a surprising amount of outright failure. While nothing is perfect, SFDC is an amazing step forward for successful CRM deployments.

SFDC is a game-changer not because of features[5] but because of its *incremental development model* that lets you invest *just enough* to make business progress quickly. Once you've done a lightweight initial implementation, you can put the SFDC system into production and measure its initial results. From there, you'll rapidly discover the next area where some additional functionality will make a business difference. SFDC incremental improvements can happen in a matter of weeks, so you might be able to identify and measure initial benefits in the same quarter you paid for the changes.

This *Agile* style of development and investment gives your investment horizon a shorter range: it's a "by-the-drink" model, with lots of little releases that are prioritized on the most current needs of the business and preferences of the users. In contrast, last-century IT focused on creating a one-shot requirements bible and managed projects as "bet-the-farm" investments that took a year or more to bear their first fruit. Beyond making for a simpler business case, using Agile's incremental style means you avoid investments that weren't

---

5. SFDC's sales reps curse me when I say this.

really needed in the first place. You also get increased business flexibility at every stage of the system's life.

However, Agile's "Goldilocks investment" requires three behavioral changes on your part:

- Investment in CRM isn't a one-shot, fire-and-forget-it deal. Instead, only build the things that are absolutely essential right now—**bigger is not better**. Making the project as small and simple as possible lowers the chance of overruns and schedule slips. But that means you need to be more attentive over time to the need for incremental investment as new priorities arise.

- Don't ask for a cast-in-concrete feature roadmap. Decisions are made all along the way with Agile's incremental approach, so priorities, schedules, and expected results will change on at least a quarterly basis. Also, don't expect big requirements documents: they tend to be a waste of effort (and you won't read them anyway). If you're really keen on getting a specific feature, the way to make sure it happens sooner is to invest some of your own budget in it. Check out Chapters 4 and 12 if you want to know more about this topic.

- Don't make decisions based on lowest cost. That works for air conditioners and server hardware but not for something that evolves the way a good CRM system does. Since the whole point here is to transform your business and customer relationship, your focus has to be on maximizing business value.

Requirements and Priorities

The majority of SFDC customers make significant modifications to the off-the-shelf system before it becomes truly effective for their business. The larger your company and the more complex your products and sales cycles, the deeper the modifications need to go. SFDC makes most modifications really easy to implement and maintain, but don't be fooled: you need to invest time and money in the implementation.

While detail-level requirements aren't collected up front, you need to provide overall direction and priorities for the SFDC project. Which CRM problems do you need to solve? Which functional areas of the system will your team be using first? How many people will be on the system? Which other systems will need to be integrated with SFDC?

In stating requirements, do not telegraph a sky's-the-limit perspective. Be incredibly clear about the "nice to have" features versus the real priorities for the short term. The biggest enemies of a successful CRM implementation are vague or inconsistent priorities.

During the formative stages of the project, you should identify a few archetypal users to be interviewed so that the system is designed around the needs of real people. It is imperative that the SFDC team interview people at "the bottom" of the organization. There's no one like a few sales reps, a person from order operations, and a customer service rep to make the system requirements reflect the real priorities of the business. This means that the project must involve cross-functional operational teams and must not be another project driven by central IT.

In addition, the team should ask you to participate in some brainstorming around reports and dashboards that you *personally* need. At the early stages, nobody is trying to design the specifics; they're just trying to see the big picture of what you need to drive the ship. This session—maybe 45 minutes huddled around a whiteboard—is intended to help the team understand what you manage to and what information you need to see on a daily or weekly basis.

THE EXECUTIVE VIEW

What do you need from the SFDC system—*personally*? What is the *one critical report* you need to do your job, and what are the five to seven pieces of information you need (whether in the current system or not) to make key decisions? Here are example questions to think about:

- How often do you look at the SFA/CRM information?
- Why do you look there, and what are you trying to measure?
- How do these data affect the things that *you* are measured on?
- What actions or decisions do you make on the basis of the data?
- What incentives have you established for the people below you?
- If you question the data, how would you validate them? What would you compare the data to?
- If you found an error in the data, whom would you talk to about getting the problem fixed?
- Which other items of information would be useful for you (i.e., what would actually change your behavior or alter a decision)?
- Which comparisons (e.g., historical or comparative to industry norms) of these data would be meaningful?
- How would you access this information (e.g., on a phone, a tablet, a laptop, an office PC, or [shudder] a print-out)? Or would you just call your administrative assistant to read the answers to you?

Don't spend any time trying to figure out the answer to the question "What would be a useful addition?" You don't need more items or cool new ideas—it's the few critical pain points that we're after. The goal is to understand what features will *really* make a difference to the decisions you will make.

Terminology and Semantics

As part of your company culture, you have your own terminology for customer interactions, sales management, marketing campaigns, and support programs. One of the key factors for successful SFDC usage is establishing a common vocabulary and a well-understood set of semantics for the sales process. Although the executive team shouldn't get bogged down in any of the details, it's amazing how much time can be wasted in a meeting when there isn't a common understanding of the words *customer* and *deal*. So before the CRM project is even approved, it's a best practice to get everyone on the same page on "obvious" issues like these:

- What's a *lead*, a *contact*, a *sales cycle*, and a *customer*?

- When is a customer no longer a customer?

- What's a *partner*? What are your *channels*?

- What are the stages of the sales cycle?

- What are the stages of the customer support cycle?

- What are the trigger events or conditions that move a prospect from one stage of the sales cycle to another, or a customer from one support status to another?

- What is the difference between *booked deals* and *recognized revenues*?

- What are the main product lines and service categories the company offers? Which services do you offer in the form of a product?

Make sure that these definitions are nailed down and agreed to by *all* departments early in the SFDC project.

Resource Commitments

When the management decision is made to go for SFDC, the company will be committing money to the project. *Every executive* who has any plans to leverage the system will need to dedicate some of his or her staff's time throughout the life of the project to make sure that the system actually meets the organization's needs. Great systems happen only with the participation of people who care and are empowered to make binding decisions about the following tasks:

- Clearly spelling out the details of requirements and understanding the repercussions of decisions and tradeoffs

- Making sure that data are properly interpreted and prepared for the new system

- Identifying business rules and thinking through business processes to make sure they are unambiguously documented

- Reviewing user interface screens to make sure they're clean, clear, and usable

- Helping design reports and dashboards that highlight the issues management really cares about

- Participating in acceptance testing of the system while paying particular attention to the meaning and accuracy of results

Make sure the right people on your team are assigned goals and that they dedicate time—your entire organization will benefit dramatically from the right level of participation. Of course, some of *your* time is required as well, to handle escalated issues, budgets, and political battles.

Your Role Once the Project Is Under Way

As soon as the SFDC project starts, the team will come to you asking for your department's time—including some of your own time. The sections that follow cover things to expect during the project (particularly during the first quarter or two).

Detailed Requirements

Throughout the project, the SFDC team needs access to knowledgeable individuals in your organization to drill into the detailed requirements and rules of the road for the system. Fortunately, the team won't be asking for a bunch of time or effort—and every hour you invest will have *very high leverage.* You will get a better system sooner if you make this small investment to ensure the team is building the things your organization really needs.

The implementation team needs three kinds of input, usually from three different levels in your organization:

- **Business process and policy knowledge:** This information lies at the heart of how your company does business, and the SFDC team will sometimes need to know the *why* behind a procedure or a tradeoff. This level of information is usually best obtained from a fairly senior manager in your organization.

- **Details about how things really work or how they need to change:** These data consist of the standard operating procedures, the wrinkles, and the exception-handling procedures that make everything really work. This level of information usually comes from people who have been around a while but who work near the bottom of the organization.

- **The meaning and behavior of data:** This information consists of knowledge about data models, semantics, interactions, and integrations among systems. This level of information is best known by quasi-IT people (employees or consultants) in your organization, with titles such as business analyst, system administrator, data specialist, or application architect.

Business Process Changes

Don't think of SFDC as being solely focused on automating sales or marketing. In fact, SFDC can be the basis for making business process improvements in nearly every customer-facing aspect of your business. An SFDC system doesn't just speed things up; it helps you change the *way* you do business. Done right, SFDC can become the basis of competitive advantage and industry leadership.[6]

In thinking about business process changes, it's important to push the implementation team to follow these best practices:

- **Focus on things that matter to the customer:** Emphasize issues that slow down the sales cycle or hinder customer interactions. Combine individual steps to make the process more sensible and systematic. The goal is to eliminate activities that are clumsy, out of order, patchwork solutions, or workarounds.

- **Work on a few high-leverage processes that are naturally linked:** Don't try to "boil the ocean." Fix things that are naturally related, not disparate elements from across the organization.

- **Validate business rules:** First, make sure the rules are still relevant and meaningful. The *single most highly leveraged thing* you can do in business process reengineering is eliminate obsolete or redundant rules, policies, or standards. If you must have a complex set of rules, make sure they provide something of beauty or value *to the customer* rather than just avoid a hypothetical negative.

- **Remove paper from the process:** As innocent as paper might appear, it is nearly always indicative of wasted time, increased error rates, and manual labor. Many organizations still use manual data entry—from data on paper—to link data across business processes. Replacing paper with on-screen steps and system integration will lower costs, save time, and increase professionalism. The on-screen updates will make the workflows much easier to monitor, measure, and improve over time.

---

6. The SFDC sales reps love it when I say this. And it's true.

- **Increase information sharing:** While being mindful of security and compliance issues, sharing information is the first step to effective collaboration. Better collaboration means faster identification of problems and unintended consequences, while creating more meaningful measurements at every level of the organization.

- **Bake in measurements and thresholds:** You can't fix what you don't measure. If there is a clear metric that is meaningful to the customer (e.g., "number of hours before we got back to the customer about a problem"), add thresholds, alerts, and automatic escalations to the new process so that management can see problem areas before they boil over.

- **Minimize manual exceptions:** Although human judgment is what sets great businesses apart, you want to minimize the judgment calls. And even exceptions need to be handled in a methodical way in your business processes. MBE forces you to systematize and streamline how you handle up to the 97th percentile[7] of the business process. Not every step of the exception-handling procedure can be automated, but the entire exceptions process should still be systematized and measured so that the organization doesn't spend too much time on the unusual cases.

- **Optimize globally:** Keep your eye out for suboptimization and siloed thinking. Discourage "over-the-transom" behaviors because they don't help anybody and they usually hurt the customer. The point is to make the *entire system* (your company) work better, faster, and more pleasantly for the customer. That said, expect to find significant business process variations in your international operations, and know that the SFDC system will need to be modified to accommodate them.

- **Keep it practical and immediate:** Even though business process engineering has to consider big-picture effects, focus your energy on improvements that can be measured in the here and now. Don't let tasks get ridiculously complicated or let perfectionism creep in.

- **Ask for workflows; look for diagrams:** The whole point of business process improvement is streamlining and workflows. By having a clear delineation of business processes, you establish metrics and thresholds for what's normal and what's a variance. In the SFDC system, business process workflows may be triggered by deadlines, customer actions, and thresholds. These workflows free up people from the mindless tedium of repetitive actions and allow them to start managing by exception. Workflows also make the important parts of your business more measurable.

---

7. The 97th percentile value represents a two-sigma standardized process (representing the cumulative proportion of the Gaussian distribution up to $+2\sigma$). In sales and marketing, anything beyond that level of automation almost always involves ridiculous investment, so the best bang for the buck in SFDC-relevant business processes is to allow about 2% of cases to be handled manually.

HOW TO BLOW UP AN AGILE PROJECT

In the spirit of David Letterman's "Top 10 Lists," here's an itemization of the worst practices that can make even the best Agile team melt down:

Number 10: Start a crash project with a big budget

The idea behind Agile is to break down communication barriers and have software engineers work on what the users really need (rather than what somebody is willing to push through a committee and transcribe in a big document). Crash projects that throw all the resources in at the beginning don't allow anybody time to think or plan (yes, you do that in Agile), so the team tends to whipsaw for the first few weeks. If you really have a crash project, start it with a small team of architects and developers who've worked together successfully before, and add team members only as they ask for them.

Number 9: Demand requirements tomes, data dictionaries, and Six-Sigma/SLCM/ITIL/ISO 9001 processes

These management artifacts are terrific for hardware projects and monolithic applications (such as application packages or network switching systems), but those aren't the kinds of projects where Agile thrives. Most business applications are incremental extensions and integrate with existing functionality. Although Agile projects involve careful thinking, Agile has no use for big documents or heavy processes—they only get in the way. The *clean code* folks take it one step further: they don't want any comments in the code (partly because they are often misleading, partly because commented code is an invitation for people who don't really understand the workings to break code by trying to improve it). User cheat-sheets and recorded WebExes are fine—but you'll notice they too are short.

Number 8: Demand fixed price, fixed schedule

The cornerstone of Agile builds on the old joke "Price, schedule, features, and quality: pick 3." By doing software in a fundamentally different way—user-centered, tests first, require-ments constantly negotiated/reprioritized—Agile dramatically reduces waste, because the stuff you really don't need never even gets started. But an Agile project that is given a fixed set of goals—with an inflexible budget and immovable schedule—is an oxymoron. And the only behavior you'll get out of the team is friction.

Number 7: Demand monthly waterfall metrics

Agile has its own style of management, which is fairly inward-looking. It's based on the rugby scrum (aka football huddle), and it's not focused on producing management reports. Further, since outside managers don't really know what's going on hour by hour, they can't add a lot of value to the efficiency or effectiveness of the Agile team. Of course, if you're the budget holder, you want to see dashboards and flowcharts. Try to resist this tendency, as preparing those translations of Agile's native project mechanisms (cards, stories, integrations, and burndown rates) won't make the team any more efficient. In effect, by demanding waterfall formalities, you're just adding a tax.

Number 6: Don't let your users participate until the very end

The reason Agile projects are so effective is that they allow direct and continuous contact between the developers and the users. It's not just user-centered design: it's intimate connections with the business processes, team know-how, and continuous user testing that help avoid the bugs and the real-world gotchas that plague most application projects. Although some managers say that they can't afford to put a user on the team, it's like building a custom house without being willing to actually visit it during construction. Nobody would do that with their own home—so why would you let it happen with your IT investment?

Number 5: Start and stop the project frequently

Agile allows developers and users to innovate quickly and become high-functioning teams. But the success of such teams depends on the continuity of effort and objectives. Sure, detailed priorities may change continuously, but if the global purpose of a project shifts frequently, the good effects of Agile will never take hold. Same thing if there are interruptions of more than a couple of weeks—the flywheel never really gets going. For a number of human-factors reasons, restarting a project that's been stalled for a month is almost worse than starting from scratch.

Number 4: Don't give teams access to test resources until beta

What could be duller than testing? It's a chore for the users, a bore for the compliance guys, and besides, the test labs can't afford to be available all the time. You'll hear these kinds of arguments, and you have to overrule them. You don't have to be a card-carrying member of the *test-first* crowd to know that the economics of software defects is all about catching them early and fixing them cheaply. Here's the Agile answer: if you do testing throughout the project, you don't need a beta at all. The software just migrates into production when pilot users say it's ready.

Number 3: Use politics for leverage

You know the drill: find and exaggerate catch-22 situations, exploit optics and rhetoric, use threats, shuffle the team around, promote and demote people randomly, or install a czar (preferably someone who knows nothing about software but is an I'm-in-charge-here, get-it-done, take-no-prisoners kind of leader). These tactics all work wonders to break down internal trust and external communication and are even more effective when used in combination.

Number 2: Don't put your best players on the team

One thing is for sure: the folks who conspired to write the Agile Manifesto are smarter than the average bear. Way smarter. Agile tends to work best when you have users who are articulate and know their business processes cold. Agile developers are usually wicked smart. It's not just soloist brain power, though: the team members must respect each other. If they don't, communication will not be quick and smooth. It's also best if the team members are within shouting distance (if not in the same room). Location matters: it's almost impossible to have great productivity if the team is spread across multiple time zones.

And the Number 1 way to blow up an Agile project: Use the element of surprise

The Agile effect comes from trust (the team is deputized and empowered to make key decisions on their own), close communication, and relentless focus on the highest-priority goals. If you frequently surprise the team with new mandates, unstated top priorities, an uncertain budget, political crossfire, decision overrides, unexpected forcing functions, secrets, or just a simple lack of trust—well, it's hard to imagine anything more damaging to both morale and productivity. So go ahead, surprise them and watch them melt!

The Touchy Side of Business Processes

Ideally, the SFDC team focuses on improving a small number of business processes rather than fostering a wholesale replacement. Refining or streamlining an existing business process involves a lot less stress and uncertainty than starting from scratch. Plus, if you are upgrading a business process that exists, it is easier to establish valid (and achievable) comparative metrics (e.g., 20% fewer errors or 10% decrease in labor costs).

There can be a lot of politics involved with a big business process change. In some cases, you'll be changing the daily tasks of workers—or even changing their jobs entirely. The uncertainty inherent in this kind of change can lead to a lot of questions, endless meetings, and user resistance—even if the workers are given orders from on high. You may even want to include HR issues in your thinking if jobs are going to be redesigned in a big way.

Sponsorship and Escalation Path

Probably *the* critical success factor in any CRM project is strong executive sponsorship—from day one—that propels the implementation team and the end users into action.

When prioritizing and trading off requirements, the SFDC project leader needs a set of executive sponsors who can act as champions for the project when political and resource issues arise. For project success, the champions *must* include the VP of sales but will also usually include the VP of marketing, the VP of support/service, the CFO, and perhaps even the CEO. Championship is about making sure resource commitments and policy changes happen, so this responsibility can't be delegated very far down the organizational hierarchy. Fortunately, filling the champion role probably requires only a couple of hours per month for the key VPs.

As the project champion, you'll also need to break logjams on escalated issues. Because the SFDC implementation team works fast, it will make a big difference whether you resolve issues this week versus next. Team members won't ask for your intervention often, but when an issue is escalated your way, you must respond quickly.

Management Council

Corporate VPs cannot afford the time to personally participate in the SFDC project, but the team needs access to some senior knowledge and judgment on a regular basis. You need to deputize a senior person on your staff to be a regular participant in the SFDC implementation team. The SFDC project leader will form a management council of these deputies to make priority calls, policy decisions, and tradeoffs. For simplicity of voting, the team needs to be small and contain an odd number of people (including the SFDC product manager). A small management council would include representatives from sales and marketing plus the project leader. A larger council might add representatives from finance, customer care, international operations, professional services, channel operations, and business analytics. This council will need to hold *brief* meetings on a weekly basis.

The management council will probably handle most escalations. With luck, at least 80% of escalated issues can be decided there, but sometimes budgetary or policy variances require the intervention of the sponsoring VPs.

Team Members

Some of your staff members will need to devote significant time to the tasks mentioned in the section "Getting the Right Resources Committed" in Chapter 1. These team members will be charged with delivering documents and making binding decisions at a detail level, so you'll want to assign individuals who know their stuff. Their effort on the team must be part of their "day jobs," so you need to dedicate a portion of their schedule and allocate some of their personal goals (MBOs) to this endeavor.

Agile Project Reviews

As an executive, you've been trained to look for a budget that's firm and a schedule that has a clear end date. Unfortunately, large systems projects don't fit that model too often. High degrees of command and control just don't work with software projects. Also, Agile project management—which focuses on quick cycle time and high-quality delivery of only the features that are really needed—can create a frustrating uncertainty about exactly what will be delivered when. You need to give the project leader some wiggle room so that he or she can deliver what matters, sooner.

CRM systems and processes must be highly adaptable to evolving business needs, so they are *never* implemented with a predetermined and fixed architecture the way a building would be constructed. Focus your attention on the cutover (go-live) date for the features your organization needs, and emphasize the absolute minimum acceptance criteria that must be met to achieve the go-live goal. Most significant SFDC implementations are replacements for previous systems, and it should be fairly straightforward to identify the criteria needed for the new system to be good enough to support the switchover. It is important to use terms like "good enough" or "acceptance criteria" to communicate the understanding that the system will continue to improve after the go-live date. In many areas, the company will need only 50% of the SFDC functionality on day one to support the business.

WHY CFOs SHOULD LOVE AGILE PROJECTS

Agile projects on the surface may look disorganized and chaotic. But let's face it: *all* large software projects tend toward disorganization and chaos—the Agile methodology just surfaces that reality. In doing so, Agile projects also make for *more efficient spending* for the following reasons:

- They don't make big, long-term resource commitments. They spend in small chunks on the things that are most highly valued by the business at the time.

- Because Agile delivers in time-boxed increments, the higher-priority items quickly percolate into view rather than being buried on page 87 of an impenetrable requirements document. Even better for your budget: stuff that really isn't important quickly fades from view.

- Less-certain elements fail fast rather than mushrooming into cost and schedule nightmares. If something isn't going to work out or won't be worth the effort, you'll know sooner; as a consequence, investment in that wasteful area will be abandoned earlier than with traditional software models.

- Agile projects give visibility sooner to the real costs and real benefits of a project or feature.

- Agile projects ruthlessly avoid features for which there is no passionate user or customer. Nice-to-have features are implemented only when they will be *used*. Perfectionism is almost unheard of in Agile projects.

As always, perfectionism does not pay. By focusing the discussion on what is *really* needed to support a given business process on a day-to-day basis, you can make realistic decisions and tradeoffs. For example, it might be a great idea to *manually* approve orders for the first month of operation as a double-check of the system's automatic order approval rules.

Agile Project Deliveries

Agile projects focus on frequent delivery of functionality so that **something of value is made available to the business twice a quarter.** That doesn't mean that *your* organization will get wonderful new features all the time, but *somebody* in the corporation will get an important improvement on a regular basis.

When a new feature is being delivered to one of your groups, it's important that employees participate in its final testing (to make sure they're getting exactly what they need) and receive appropriate training. The training sessions will be short and nondisruptive, and they will save your employees a lot of time and misunderstanding. Make *sure* your organization knows that training is mandatory.

Of course, SFDC is still software, which suffers from the "iceberg phenomenon": the toughest work in the project relates to infrastructure and data cleanup that has no visible feature, no immediate "win" for any department. Nevertheless, this infrastructure effort (particularly at the beginning of the SFDC project) lays the foundation for the features that will benefit the company as a whole. Solid, reliable data—which will give you visibility and automation you need—don't come for free.

THE ENEMY: SCOPE CREEP

Scope creep is one of the most dangerous things that can happen to any software project, and the danger grows with the size and length of the effort. The problem occurs whenever a requirement is stretched, an assumption is made that "we can fit that in," or an executive proposes an *even better idea.*

The key warning sign of scope creep: the requirements list grows while the project is under way. Because items aren't removed from the list, the number of deliverables grows even though the budget and schedule remain unchanged. When the project runs into trouble and needs a schedule or budget extension, there's a particular temptation to load up the requirements even further, even though it should be obvious that the project is already well on its way to underdelivering.

Your behavior as an executive is a critical part of the solution for scope creep. Do not let your staff propose new requirements without demoting or eliminating some existing requirements. If you sense that some other VP is letting new requirements creep in, call him or her on it.

Your Role in the Adoption Cycle

The historical success rates for CRM systems have been quite low: most industry analyst surveys show that less than 50% of CRM projects are deemed a success by management. A core reason for this low percentage is that any CRM product—even if perfectly implemented—is only a tool with little intrinsic value. Without users and accurate data, the CRM will remain just an empty shell.

The single most important thing for you to do is to stimulate adoption and usage of SFDC, getting people on the bandwagon so that the system becomes a valuable data asset.

Your *personal* behavior over the entire deployment sequence really counts. Everyone must get the unambiguous message that SFDC is important to *you* and the way you want to do business. Your team knows you and can read your nonverbal messages about what you *really* think. A few words carelessly thrown around when you're stressed out can set SFDC adoption back by months.

In addition to your consistent personal support, there must be a proactive "good news" campaign touting the SFDC system almost from day one. Post something relevant on `chatter` every day. Move the "Monday Sales Update" email to a `chatter` post so everyone gets the message. If you don't have time for that, have your admin do it for you.

Executive Mandates

As delivery of SFDC features begins, put some mandates in place so that your organization gets the right big-picture orientation about the system:

- The SFDC system is what executives will use as their only source for information about customer relationships. If other systems contain customer data (such as warranty registration), they'll need to be integrated with SFDC over time so that the company achieves a 360-degree view of the customer.

- SFDC is *not* to be used as a spying machine or micromanagement tool. You will not listen to people who try to use it that way or who are trying to game the system for personal or political gain.

- The SFDC system is to be used as the command center or virtual war room for winning accounts and keeping customers happy. The data entered into the system need to be good enough to drive real decisions and allocate resources at every level of the organization.

- SFDC is supposed to eliminate excessive emails, data reentry, and forgotten action items. Show users that requests made via email are given lower priority than requests made through the SFDC system.

- Paper reports and spreadsheets generated outside of SFDC will not be acceptable for use in management meetings. It's acceptable to "pretty up" the format of SFDC data, but it is not okay to prepare external spreadsheets independently of the official, system-of-record data.

- The organization will move toward an MBE policy, which means routine decisions should be handled "in process." People should be able to handle more than 90% of the work without invoking manual workarounds or unusual decisions. SFDC's alerts, thresholds, workflows, and reports should be used to handle normal situations and to automatically flag or escalate the unusual cases.

- The company is to be a learning organization, and you expect things to improve incrementally and consistently. SFDC follows that philosophy by delivering changes in increments and adapting to feedback along the way. If problems occur, you expect feedback to be delivered candidly to the SFDC team so that they can adjust and do better. Sniping does no good for anyone.

ADOPTION SEQUENCE

In an SFDC system rollout, there is a preferred sequence of user adoption that may seem counterintuitive: inside sales, support reps, and marketing first, outside sales last.

Even though the phasing of the rollout is fairly fast (almost always within the same quarter), you're probably wondering why the executive suite and other high-priority roles in the company come so late to the SFDC system. Why aren't they first?

The answer: data credibility and reliability are the foundation for adoption of SFDC. Anything that undermines system credibility—including having a user work the system before it's ready—must be avoided. When you've got a new system (or a cutover from an old, unreliable one), the quality, completeness, and relevance of the data in the system just aren't good enough during the early stages of the implementation. It takes a while for the data assets in SFDC to ripen to the point where you can bet the farm on them.

So hang on. You'll be getting the cool new stuff as soon as it's got the solidity you expect.

Adoption Metrics

The executive team should set up adoption metrics early on in the project so that the organization can know how well the system is being accepted. Make sure that the metrics you establish are *meaningful to the business* rather than being trivial data points (e.g., the number of people who logged in to the SFDC system last week).

Here are examples of meaningful adoption metrics that should be used to judge SFDC acceptance and success:

- Number of times the average person logged in during the week

- Percentage of deals that have any meaningful data attached to them

- Percentage of deals that have complete data attached to them

- Average length of time since deals had an update to the data

- Percentage of error-free records

- Percentage of fields that are erroneous

- Percentage of users who are "totally into the system," "average users," and "Luddites" (resistors)

- Percentage of executives who trust the data in the system versus those who distrust the data or think the data are meaningless or misleading

The Politics of System Adoption

Unfortunately, some people will inevitably look for any excuse not to use the SFDC system. They will jump at the chance to criticize it and will point to others' criticism as the basis for not bothering to log in. Your support is a key success factor in overcoming resistance.

Use both carrots and sticks to motivate the users. If you are an SFDC executive champion, clearly articulate why the system is important to the way you do business.

Champions

The champions of the system are the single most important force in driving SFDC usage, because it is their will and budget that make the system happen in the first place. It is also their organizational clout and enthusiasm that drive *fast* adoption.

Champions must act consistently about SFDC, and their behavior should demonstrate that they will be depending on the system for their success. They need to say how often they'll rely on its data and reports to run management meetings. They need to have a dashboard named after them and have that dashboard appear on the home screen of their organization. See Chapters 9 through 13 for more best practices in this area.

Each champion should create a sequence of milestones for meetings that will depend on SFDC data and reports. For example, if the system will initially go live in January, the sales champion should ask that all lead reports used by executive staff be based on the system by March, that all opportunity lists be driven off the system by April, and that all forecasting and pipeline reports be based only on SFDC data by May. As the year unfolds, the sales champion should issue an email stipulating that no deal will be discussed at any level of management review unless it is in the SFDC system first. Later, an email from this executive should clarify the requirement that deals won't be reviewed unless their SFDC data have been updated within the last 2 weeks. By *incrementally* and *repeatedly* emphasizing the importance of the system to every level of the management chain, the champion cements the right kind of thinking and behavior about SFDC.

It's incredibly important to maintain the illusion of the inevitability of system usage. It takes only a few negative or ambivalent words from the champion to halt SFDC's positive momentum. When misinformation shows up in a report or dashboard, the champion must have the discipline to say, "This information is no good. I rely on my team to keep the data in SFDC accurate and timely, and I don't want to see this happen again." If in a moment of frustration the champion says something like, "This system is no damn good—I can't use this garbage," the champion will be setting back SFDC adoption by months. Rumors fly fast.

Setting Expectations for System Performance

SFDC is a cloud application, which means that none of the computing work is done within your company. SFDC spends millions every year to make sure its systems are reliable and perform on a 24 × 365 basis.

Although the SFDC production systems have had virtually zero *unplanned* downtime for the last 6 years, there are planned (and carefully preannounced) maintenance windows. These windows are typically 1–4 hours long and occur during weekend evenings once every 10 weeks or so. Almost all customers have no problem coping with these maintenance windows, because only parts of the system are unavailable. If you have eCommerce or other supporting systems that need to get SFDC data 24 × 365, you must make provisions for these interruptions.

SFDC's system responsiveness is consistently very good around the world, and the company proves it by publishing the measurements right on its Web site (http://trust.salesforce.com). Although Google's pages may show up faster, that company isn't trying to do the customer-specific complex calculations that SFDC has to perform on every page.

However, if your network is busy, SFDC's screen updates may seem to take forever. If you hear noise from users along these lines, upgrading your company's internal network is the quick and easy fix. In most cases, you really needed to make that upgrade anyway, and SFDC usage just becomes the forcing function.

Sticks

Upper management always has the power to issue mandates. Of course, if you issue overly grandiose management commands or use sticks too early, the risk is that workers will dismiss them as "another thing those executives will forget about next month." Obviously, this you need to avoid.

Because the SFDC system will be delivered incrementally, "sticks"—commands and requirements—should also be doled out gradually. In the very early days of the SFDC project, the system will not be functionally complete and—worse—it won't contain much interesting data. The trick is to get users on the system doing *something* that will add to the system data asset as a *natural part of their jobs*. The user representatives on the implementation team will find a part of the business process to serve as the beachhead for SFDC users. Once this step in the business process is identified, management should mandate that the users change to the new behavior on a specific date. After a few weeks, more user steps should be added to the mandatory SFDC activity.

Only after SFDC has the required functionality, data volume, and data quality to be a reliable asset should the big sticks come out. Any penalties (such as "No commission on deals will be paid unless . . .") should *not be even hinted at* for the first 6 months of system usage.

Carrots

"Carrots" are positive incentives for people to use the SFDC system. Carrots are typically more powerful and reliable than many of the sticks described in the preceding section.

The first carrots come from organizational incentives: procedures or activities that are more easily performed by using the system than by not using it. For example, if your sales team needs loaner equipment or travel authorization, make it easier to get these resources approved through the system than by using the old way. Management should make it clear that action items presented to them as SFDC tasks will be handled sooner and more predictably than requests presented by email or voicemail. Not surprisingly, users will rapidly acquire new habits when they realize you stick to your guns.

The next carrots come from rewards. After the first few weeks, you can start contests with rewards and recognition for the users with the best data, the most frequent logins, and the most complete customer records. Make these contests and incentives as relevant to your business objectives as possible—awards for meaningless system metrics are about as lame as the ones for "tidiest office cubicle" or "most recycled coffee cups."

The last bunch of carrots comprises the benefits that are intrinsic to SFDC system usage: the users discover that doing things through the system saves time and streamlines onerous tasks. These carrots become more important as the system becomes more functionally complete and has workflows, integrations, and data that make it *the* optimal way to carry out a task. When you discover some good news in this area, make sure to send out emails touting these highly leveraged behaviors so that people can see the effects on their personal productivity. If your field sales and support people don't already have iPads or Android tablets, these devices are nice rewards and really can make a difference in the customer's perception of your service.

Your Role after Deployment: Using SFDC to Help Drive the Ship

Once the SFDC system's data asset has become solid thanks to greater usage, it will serve as a key management tool. In addition to delivering good metrics on internal activities, it represents the repository for your customer intelligence. The system can be the command center for customer relationships—and here are best practices for how to use it in this role.

Be Careful What You Ask For

In a system with as much data and reporting as SFDC, it's easy to ask for things and get a nice-looking dashboard in short order. Unfortunately, you could ask for lots of meaningless data on this dashboard, and subordinates aren't likely to say no to your requests.

For example, it's easy to ask for the number of leads each week. But leads are like Web site traffic: they are better indicators of visibility and vague interest than they are of a solid pipeline. Further, activity management indicators (such as "number of dials" or "customer support call volume") are very easy to "game," and the numbers won't mean anything to the business.

Here are the best indicators of business health, particularly when compared over time:

Marketing

- Number of fully qualified or converted leads
- Number of converted leads accepted by sales
- Percentage of leads converted
- Percentage of free trials that converted
- Percentage of nonresponsive or stale leads

Sales

- Percentage of reps logging in on a weekly basis
- Number of sales cycles started
- Number of quotes issued

- Average time in stage (or, conversely, number of stalled deals)
- Percentage of wins, losses, and no-decisions
- Number of new customers
- Average deal size for new customers versus repeat customers
- Percentage of repeat business
- Percentage of renewals/retained customers

Pipeline

- Forecast sales versus quarterly goal
- Actual bookings versus weekly expected achievement[8]
- Percentage of opportunities "moving backward" (decreasing in size or probability, or moving out in time)
- Number and dollar value of disappearing opportunities (deals dropping out of the quarter, plus losses and no-decisions)
- Forecast accuracy
- Number and value of unforecasted deals

Customer Support

- Number of new problems identified
- Number of problems solved
- Customer-perceived "time to resolve"
- Percentage of satisfied customers
- Percentage of problems solved through your knowledge base
- Number of highly dissatisfied customers

Customer Base

- Cost of customer acquisition
- Percentage of revenue coming from repeat business

---

8. For example, this statistic tells management something like, "By week 4 of the quarter, we normally expect 20% of the total target to be closed; this quarter, we have only 15% closed."

- Percentage of customer base that's still active/current

- Customer lifetime revenue

- Customer lifetime profitability[9]

- Customer loyalty (upsells, renewals, and repeat business)

THINK ABOUT USERS BEFORE ASKING . . .

It's easy to ask for reports that you won't actually use, but it's *dangerous* to ask for reports that you *will* use to bad effect.

Before you ask the reps to enter any more data (which they'll view as a tax and an intrusion), figure out what you would really *do differently* if you already had the report in front of you. Which decisions would you *actually* change? If you're just curious or not sure what you'd do differently, *don't ask* the reps to enter anything new.

If you ask the reps to do something new, walk a mile in their shoes first. Top-down edicts with measurements and incentives practically guarantee attempts to game the system, particularly if the edicts have clear penalties or rewards. If you're going to lay down the law, make sure that gaming the system carries the biggest penalties of all.

When reps game the system, it not only undermines SFDC's credibility (and data integrity) but also insidiously undermines *your* authority. Don't open the door to this behavior.

Don't get too fancy with the analytics too early. They scare the employees, and besides, half the time the data aren't any good early during the system implementation process. Gradually add a new report, dashboard, or analytic every 6 weeks or so.

SFDC also has a set of dashboards that can give you a great personal overview of the data. There's one key caveat: *any time* you see a Refresh button on a dashboard screen, click it! Dashboards are the only part of the system that do *not* display data in real time, so the *information will be misleading* if you haven't refreshed it recently.

Forecasting

SFDC is a real-time system that allows forecasts to be run at any time. For most companies, a weekly forecasting cycle is all that's needed. The forecasting cycle typically starts on Thursday evening (when the individual reps put in their commit numbers) and

---

9. It is important that you look at this figure over time, not as a snapshot. If you decide to get rid of your least profitable customers without making changes to your company's overhead, you'll instantly create a new batch of customers who look unprofitable.

continues with a multilevel review and refinement process that culminates in a consolidated forecast ready for executive review on Monday morning. As discussed at length in Chapter 9, it is imperative that *all* qualitative and quantitative information about the forecast be stored in SFDC, and *only* in SFDC.

SFDC is the natural place to run sales forecasts, and there is no reason to look outside the system for *bookings* forecast information. When it comes to accounting data (adhering to generally accepted accounting principles [GAAP]) and *revenue* forecasts, however, you must look to the financial system for the best data. Only that forecasting system has the revenue recognition, inventory allocation, reserve accounts, and other special logic and calculations needed to prepare an accurate worldwide forecast of all channels' revenues.

We recommend that this bifurcation of forecasting roles be maintained: the SFDC system for bookings (which is usually what sales and marketing use to manage things) and the financial system for revenues (which is what the executive staff and the board need to see). Of course, the SFDC bookings forecast must feed into the revenue forecast, but the financial forecast should *not* be pushed back into the SFDC system. In addition to keeping things simpler, this division of roles ensures that only those with a need to know have access to the corporate financial forecast.

Executive Meetings

No one will ever run an executive staff meeting exclusively from an SFDC screen. Nevertheless, it is a best practice to have a couple of dashboards and reports that are available for executives first thing on Monday morning.

Many executives have trouble reading the fine print of an HTML report. For ease of reading and nice formatting, SFDC reports should typically be exported to Excel, where they can be made far more legible using simple macros. Although it may take a while to get everything just right, these reports can be reproduced by clicking two buttons every week. Make sure that a lucky executive assistant knows where to find those two buttons and is made responsible for printing the spreadsheets in preparation for your management meeting.

If the executive staff meeting generates minutes, any sales or customer-related items should be documented in SFDC records. SFDC's `notes` area allows for notes to be made private so that prying eyes won't see confidential remarks.

Compliance

Although SFDC is almost never the system of record for accounting or other auditable and regulated data, it may hold sensitive information and feed business processes that draw government and legal attention.

For publicly traded companies, the Sarbanes-Oxley Act mandates business process documentation and enforcement of information controls and revenue forecasts. SFDC has very fine-grained access controls to make sure that only the right people can see certain fields and that an even narrower group of people can make changes to sensitive data. SFDC also has workflows that can be configured to assure that forecasts are modified by authorized people only and that closed deals cannot be modified by anyone except individuals in the finance organization.

For companies that work in health care, financial services, higher education, and other regulated markets, there are industry-specific mandates about customers' private information and required audits. SFDC has passed the regulatory requirements in virtually every industry, so the platform is solid. But the devil is in the details of how you use the system, so make sure that the implementation team has "locked the system down" from day one.

As a matter of best practices, you should deliberately discourage anyone in the organization from sending pipeline-related internal emails with any real content. The critical information should reside in the SFDC system, which serves as the central repository of all things customer—for all the authorized people to see. Emails have no inherent controls for what's in the message, when the email will be read or acted on, or who will see the email (via random forwarding). SFDC's controls and workflows guarantee that only the right people will have access to all the key data, while reducing the amount of internal email about current deals and customer situations.

Essential Tools for the Executive

Most executives want to see reports, dashboards, and scorecards for their organization. When sophisticated reports and analytics are desired, SFDC reports will typically be supplemented by outboard systems such as data warehousing, business intelligence, and scorecarding systems. It will take several months for SFDC's underlying data, integration process, and outboard databases to sufficiently mature to make such analysis worthwhile. Talk to your business analysts about when you can get the reports and summaries you need.

If you are a hands-on executive and want to be quickly able to get information while you're on the road, there are a couple of nice tools for you. SFDC's `mobile edition` lets you find key information right on your smartphone (iPhone, Android, BlackBerry, and Microsoft Mobile devices) in real time. You can look up almost anything, and you can even enter new data (if your fingers are nimble). There's also a mobile version of `chatter`, which lets you see the internal collaboration around any topic, company, or customer issue. There's nothing like `chatter` for getting an issue escalated and resolved in real time. In addition to the instant access these tools provide, the mobile tools have great "wow value" with customers.

GETTING THE MOST FROM SFDC

- Keep the project consistently focused on a few *high-level* goals.
- Think small and simple: do not try to boil the ocean.
- Work incrementally, delivering something valuable every 6 weeks.
- Use Agile so you don't overinvest in customizations.
- Focus first on user adoption and quality data (everything great about CRM flows from these).
- As an executive, your job is to be a champion—so stay involved *and live in SFDC yourself!*

FOR SMALL COMPANIES

- Identify one key problem to solve this quarter, and set up a three-person team to get it done.
- Probably, your first-phase work will focus on the handoff from marketing to sales ("conversion").
- Set the example by really using the system as soon as the data is good.

FOR LARGE ENTERPRISES

- Identify the business process issues that are getting in the way of leverage.
- Focus the business case on revenue increase and improved margins; it's about leverage, not cost control.
- *Enterprise CRM* means integration with other systems—so engage with other VPs and IT folks from day one.
- Change management is a key success factor!

PART I

Planning and Implementation

CHAPTER 1

Planning Ahead

"Intangible results" is just another way of saying
"poor planning."

—Anonymous

T his chapter is intended for executives, decision makers, business analysts, and
project leaders who need to make decisions; set expectations properly; and budget
the time, money, and people for an SFDC project. Readers will learn how to make
planning decisions that give them the best chance of success and the quickest possible
failure recovery.

A truly effective Salesforce.com (SFDC) system can dramatically improve your business
results in terms of customer satisfaction, executive decision making, smooth partner/
channel interactions, a better social media reputation, more effective marketing, and, of
course, sales. But the benefits of increased visibility, streamlined operations, and faster
cash-to-cash cycles are anything but automatic. The whole reason for this book is to
guide you through a series of choices and actions to get you the best results with the least
amount of cost, delay, and risk.

One of the key success factors in any salesforce automation (SFA) or customer relationship management (CRM) project is strong executive sponsorship that propels the implementation team and the end users. You'll want to check out Chapter 6 to learn about the
best sponsors for your company's situation—but here we'll assume that you already have
an executive with fire in his or her belly.

Peter Drucker wrote that the most important part of solving a business problem is a
well-formed question. The same is true here: the best way to achieve results quickly is
to clearly articulate and prioritize problems to solve and goals to achieve. This chapter
focuses on understanding the requirements, schedules, and costs that are involved in
completing any SFDC project successfully. You'll want to make sure the entire team
understands the business drivers and the tradeoffs that shape your SFDC implementation,
its integration with surrounding systems, and the instantiation of business processes that
streamline the way your business runs.

Developing a Model of Your Customer Relationship

SFA and CRM applications are designed to improve the speed of acquiring new customers and to achieve the highest amount of revenue or profits from accounts, thereby raising the customer lifetime value. Before you start detailed planning for any CRM project, you need to develop a model for how your organization works, showing the basic organizational ownership for each stage of the customer cycle. Figure 1-1 depicts the customer cycle, showing how a company converts the initial investment in marketing and sales to a completed, invoiced order. In developing the customer cycle for your company, you need to identify which groups are responsible for each stage. Make sure the relevant groups have basic agreement on *who does what* to double-check your model.

Note the dashed lines at the qualifying, delivering/servicing, and upselling stages: these lines are meant to indicate where the current customer cycle "breaks"—where conversion or retention ratios tend to be too low or where organizations squabble and opportunities fall through the cracks. It is very common to have breakage points in these three

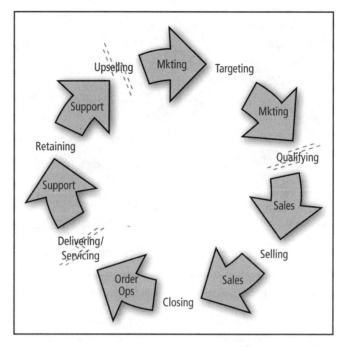

FIGURE 1-1   Example customer cycle (Source: Sirius Decisions and DOTnet Consulting)

stages, but every organization is different and you should identify the perceived breakage points for your organization as early as possible in the project.

The right side of the customer cycle is the sales cycle in which sales and marketing activities generate all your company's revenues. You need to have a detailed model of what the sales cycle stages are, who "owns" them, how long they take, and what the conversion ratios at each step are expected to be. Figure 1-2 illustrates an example sales cycle for a business-to-business (B2B) direct sales operation.

The sales cycle may be viewed as a "waterfall" showing the conversion steps for each stage of the cycle. The diagram shows who owns each stage, what the expected conversion ratios are, and how long each stage takes. Make sure that both sales and marketing executives concur with the basic data and relationships within this waterfall early in the project. Find out which stages represent the biggest problems and where the executives believe the CRM can help them the most.

The left side of the customer cycle is the service and support cycle that builds customer loyalty to a renewal or upsell transaction. Although there typically isn't a structured waterfall for the service and support cycle, it is critically important that the VPs of sales and customer service have a solid rules of engagement document (it can be as simple as

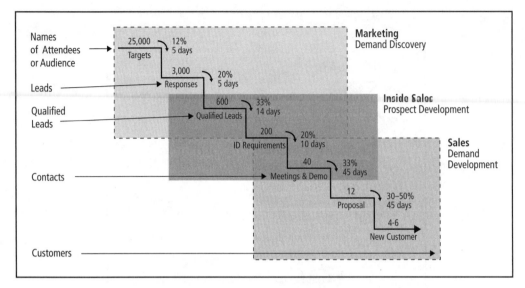

FIGURE 1-2   Example direct B2B sales cycle (Source: Sirius Decisions and DOTnet Consulting)

one PowerPoint slide) that indicates who handles the customer at every stage of service, and when the motivated customer is handed off between the customer support representative (CSR) and the account manager in sales. Make sure that the order operations and finance people are totally in sync regarding how renewal and upsell orders are handled in terms of pipeline management, forecast, and the close process.

Setting Goals at the Business Level

Before you drill down into any of the details, it's important to define a set of business goals that transcend individual requirements. These goals are best stated as numeric performance objectives[1] that are not currently being achieved but are easily communicated to executives, such as these examples:

- Improving calls-per-day to 55
- Shortening the sales cycle by 2 weeks
- Increasing the conversion or close rate by 20%

---

1. Avoid vague or overly qualitative goals such as "improve collaboration" or "gain visibility." This kind of goal statement is too mushy to drive a business decision.

- Lowering the cost of customer acquisition by 15%

- Increasing the average order size by $10,000

- Increasing revenues by 20%

- Lowering the number of service calls (truck rolls) by 10%

- Lowering the cost of customer problem resolution by 20%

- Increasing gross profitability by 10%

- Raising customer retention to 80%

- Raising customer lifetime value by 10%

- Decreasing customer service complaints by 30%

- Decreasing incorrect orders to 1%

Of course, you can't have everything. Keep the list as short as politically feasible. But no matter how many metrics there are, upper management *must* prioritize them (with no two goals having the same priority). These figures of merit are important touchstones for prioritizing the features and process changes that will be done in the course of the SFDC implementation.

Setting CRM Requirements: Who, Where, What, and Why

To make the business case for the SFDC project, you need to identify and prioritize system requirements at an overview level. Even though the details of many individual requirements can't be known until several weeks or even months after the project go-ahead, you need to have enough information to scope the cost and assess the benefits. **You can't sell the project to management without identifying specific, concrete pain points and potential advantages.**

The first step in requirements setting is to identify who will (and who won't) need to use the future SFDC system. It's easy to say "everybody," but that decision can mean big implementation, training, and ongoing costs. Worse, it means trying to make "everybody" happy, even if those people aren't critical users. In most companies, only a few departments directly touch the customer every day, so many people will not need direct access to the SFDC system. It's far better to have a narrow list of users, at least initially.

Create a spreadsheet with a list of user names, including the user's organization, job title, location, contact information, and expected SFDC interactions. From this list of users, group the people who are expected to have similar SFDC interactions. Each type of user represents an *actor* (sometimes called a *persona*) in the system. For each archetypal actor, create a one-page description that provides overview information about the actor: location, level of mobility/road-warrior-ness, educational level, job title, job responsibilities, other actors they must interact with, preferences, work habits, language, and so on. Almost any SFDC implementation will involve at least four actors, but this number will multiply quickly in large companies. To keep the number of actors to a reasonable level (more than 25 can be unmanageable), you'll probably need to generalize across similar actors. Descriptions of actors should cover their general *role and goals* in using the system: how often (and how long) they are expected to be on the system, what they are trying to achieve, which parts of the system they use, what they need to avoid, and what they expect in terms of usability (e.g., users might need to do their job on a smartphone while they're on the road).

Later in the project, team members will want to interview representative actors to get detailed requirements and feedback on the system. For now, however, these one-page summaries help provide some reality and context to the planning process. It's a good idea to give each actor a nickname and include a small photo on the description page to make the user seem more real. Log on to the *Salesforce.com® Secrets of Success* book Web site (www.SFDC-secrets.com) to download a template Actor document.

Going beyond the list of people who will actually touch the system, it's important to create a list of people who will indirectly depend on the system. These individuals may never log in, but they will depend on some report or data flow that comes from the system. You don't really need to create a full persona description for these individuals (or roles), but it is important to understand which requirements they have for the system (e.g., a distribution center manager who might need the system to be fully operational on Saturdays, even if no users are logged into the system).

Get management involved early in the decisions regarding "how far we want to go"— not the detailed requirements but the general objective. Identify the executive champion, and engage that person in the process (see Chapters 4 and 5 for more on this topic). Use the SFA Maturity Model™ level descriptions from Chapter 5 to guide this decision, which will provide an overall "scoping" of the project investment. Also go through the SFA Maturity Model questions in Chapter 5 to understand your organizational readiness, and note which actors are part of particularly advanced or immature organizations. In your project planning, avoid overreaching! It kills both budgets and the likelihood of project success.

Once the objectives and the actors are settled, develop the *scenarios* (also called *use cases* or *user stories*) for each of the ways the actors will use SFDC. For example, actors in order operations will be entering and reviewing orders all day long, but they may also need to approve exceptional discounts or other special cases every day or so. Assuming that the approval process involves different thinking and actions from ordinary orders,

DO YOU NEED TO CALL IN OUTSIDE HELP?

This chapter assumes that the reader is part of a team that will be doing the project on its own. Many companies choose this path, but you should consider whether you need advisory help early on to prepare the business case, prioritize requirements, understand the implications of alternatives, and give guidance. The right advisor can save your company a bunch of time and money by avoiding blind alleys.

Consider an outside expert if you're feeling uncomfortable with the topics here or are looking for industry best practices from day one. An outsider can help you answer the following types of questions:

- What are your competitors doing with SFA and CRM?
- What capabilities do your customers expect from sales reps or field support?
- Which departments should be using the SFA/CRM system, and which ones really shouldn't?
- What are the high-payoff business processes to streamline, and which should be left alone? (See Chapter 8 for more on this topic.)
- Should you try to enhance your existing CRM system, or should you do a wholesale replacement of it?
- What are the quantitative payoffs for your industry peers of a solid CRM system?
- What are the lessons learned and pitfalls to avoid in CRM projects for a company like yours?

Before you engage an outside consultant, check with the members of your own information technology (IT) team. They may have a list of preferred vendors and, at the very least, can help screen consultants for competence and value.

approvals must be described in a different scenario. The same person may need to do sales forecast reports to support executives, again requiring a different scenario. These scenario write-ups should *briefly* describe what the actors are trying to achieve, the data they need to see and modify, the approvals they need to proceed, and the other actors or business processes they need to interact with. Make sure to note whether the scenario requires direct access to the system or could be handled through indirect means such as interacting with another application (e.g., the accounting system) or viewing a Web page, spreadsheet, or report. Log into www.SFDC-secrets.com to see an example scenario. Expect to develop an average of three to five scenarios for each actor. From the scenarios, the team needs to distill a set of system requirements. In many cases, the scenarios will have overlapping needs that are stated from different perspectives. A key step is to identify and consolidate the near-duplicate requirements and to map them to the features provided by SFDC and related systems. For example, one sales scenario is to create a quote for an opportunity. This is fairly similar to the sales operations' scenario of updating a quote as well as to the sales manager's scenario of reviewing and approving a quote. All these scenarios depend on the requirement to edit opportunity, forecast, and quote information in real time (with the proper access controls to protect privileged information).[2] This requirement maps to stock features in SFDC's `enterprise edition` but adds the requirement to integrate quote approval with the accounting system. It's a smart idea to create a correspondence table showing which scenarios need each requirement. Check out www.SFDC-secrets.com for an example of this kind of mapping.

Many users (particularly executives) don't really think in terms of discrete requirements. Instead, they simply visualize what they need to make a decision or take an action. For this reason, it's a good idea to do mock-ups of a few reports, forms, approval screens, and dashboards (using Excel, PowerPoint, or even pen and paper) and do a "day in the life" walk-through of people's jobs to get them thinking. Creating these paper mock-ups can rapidly elucidate hidden—and difficult—requirements. You'll be surprised how often a user will say something like, "Of course, I have to be able to see the customer's order history to make my decision." To make sure you're being realistic, run through a couple of the exercises described in Chapter 2.[3]

WATCH OUT FOR INTERNAL CONTRADICTIONS

Sometimes the requirements of different teams will slightly (or even thoroughly) contradict the stated goals of other departments. This is always dangerous to system credibility, so it's important to flag these contradictions before you run off to build them into a system.

There's no way for the SFDC team to resolve misalignments or contradictions among goals: that has to be done by a meeting of the minds at an executive level. One side or the other will have to subordinate its objectives for the good of the whole.

Resist the temptation to speak in terms of product feature lists. Each requirement should be stated in terms of the business need (i.e., a step in a business process with a measurable result) rather than as a technical description (how a feature might work). Each requirement description should be as brief as possible, and each should be stored in

---

2. Of course, there are nuances, details, alerts, and exceptions, but the team will deal with all that in the implementation cycle. Don't get bogged down in that: for now, ignore the details and keep things at a summary/overview level.

3. SFDC will have no problem complying with all these requirements, but you need to know about them so the system can be properly configured from day one.

a separate document. (If your company is really into paper, the requirements document should be placed in a three-ring binder, with individual pages being inserted or updated on at least a monthly basis.)

In addition to user-driven features, make sure to cover your organization's "taken for granted" system characteristics, such as the following:

- System availability (e.g., 7 A.M.–10 P.M. EST five days a week)

- System response times (e.g., 1 second during operating hours)

- Administrative response times (e.g., 1 hour during operating hours, 4 hours on weekends)

- Thresholds for data error (e.g., zero defects in records A, B, and C, but 4% in all other records)

- Cost thresholds (e.g., no document shall cost more than $1 to store over the life of its use)

- International language support

- Multicurrency support

- Unusual fiscal periods

- Other "environmental items" that you discover from your requirements gathering

In a large company with complex business processes, the scenarios and requirements multiply quickly: their sheer number soon become overwhelming. The best way to handle this issue is to create a short overview spreadsheet that organizes and summarizes the requirements in a hierarchical fashion and helps the team visualize them from a "top-down" perspective. This high-level spreadsheet should not provide the details of any one requirement but rather should show how the requirements fit together to form the big picture of the project. (Check out www.SFDC-secrets.com for an example requirements overview spreadsheet.) The requirements spreadsheet needs to make it obvious to team members (and executives) why each line item is there, its scope, its schedule, its cost, its sponsor, and the line item(s) it could be traded off against.

Organizing and Publishing Project Documents

Even before the project begins, best practices call for storing, publishing, and organizing the project's documents online. Put them in an intuitive hierarchy, with all the project-related documents in one place that is scanned by an internal search engine or a desktop index (such as Google's free desktop search or X1's indexer) and is backed up regularly.

You can store these documents in a shared folder on a file server, but even better is to have them in an intranet site. Best of all would be a wiki[4] that's accessible to all team members (including contractors). Your top-level wiki "article" should include pointers to the project schedule, the current phase's goals and nongoals, project personnel, news, discussion forums, blogs, and user tips on the system. The wiki should also provide a hierarchical library that includes all of the requirements documents, discussions, rationales for priority calls, and the project requirements phasing spreadsheet.

An alternative approach—actually a best practice—is to store the project documentation in the cloud. Google Drive is a solid way to collaborate around the narrative requirements documents and summary spreadsheets. It has the benefit of being sharable with any vendors or contractors you need to work with during the project, and it can send you notifications when a document has been updated. Cool, intuitive, and free if you do it right.

Whatever mechanism you choose, these shared documents should be "Information Central" for the project from the moment it's just an unapproved idea. Any relevant information should be available there, including team members' contact information, email aliases, email/discussion archives, cheat sheets, training materials, podcasts, WebEx sessions, screen cams, and internal success stories. By making it really easy to get to and find all the current project information, you'll be on the road to clearer communications, better expectations management, and a much lower chance of confusion throughout the project.

Once you have even the earliest system prototype, you should also put a link to the shared document area in the SFDC system when you first get it turned on. Promoting the available information allows any interested user or project team member to quickly become better informed.

It's usually best that these documents be editable Word files, with Track Changes turned on. For Excel files, the first page of the spreadsheet should include a revision history indicating who changed what and when. The files should be downloadable by any authorized user but should be *updatable* only by sending the changes through the project manager. In this way, the project manager can filter and prioritize input and manage the evolution of the requirements and other documents (which inevitably change throughout the project).

Documents should never be deleted. Obsolete documents should be marked as such and moved to an archive directory.

---

4. What's a *wiki*? Time to catch up on your jargon! A wiki helps you present information in a *kiosk model*—where users are given information only when they care about it. This approach stands in contrast to a broadcast model such as email—where users are given information at a time when the *originator*, rather than the receiver, thinks it's relevant. Using a wiki properly can save dozens of emails, phone calls, and even the occasional status review meetings. To find out more, read the article on the topic of wikis at the granddaddy of them all, wikipedia.org.

Prioritizing Requirements

One of the toughest tasks throughout the life of the project will be understanding the ramifications of requirements and making priority calls among them. With a system of any size, some requirements will have to be delayed or may even have to be abandoned as too expensive. Making these decisions can get interesting when interdependencies among the requirements exist, and things get even juicier when political overtones and competition among the requirement sponsors complicate matters.

Although this complexity sounds scary, there's a counterbalance. The overriding principle of prioritization for any CRM project is that **it doesn't matter how many requirements you've delivered on if the users aren't adopting the system in droves.** This is because the *value* of a CRM system—to sales, marketing, support, and executives—grows in proportion to the amount and quality of data the system holds. The number of features doesn't matter: the data does. Make priority calls that cause users to get quality data in the system sooner and that persuade users to get on the system more often, and the rest will follow. Instill this overriding principle in the project sponsors as much as you can so everyone pulls in the right direction.

One way to guide prioritization discussions is to use the short list of the specific business problems that the executives defined earlier in this chapter. These improvement goals should be specific, unambiguous, and quantified—"reduce customer support response times by 20%," not "improve brand value." Estimate how the major features will affect these business goals, and from that estimation, calculate the return on investment (ROI) for the feature: lowering costs, increasing revenues, or both. This overview page will help keep things in perspective as you try to make priority calls.

Like all complex decisions, the tough calls are made in meetings where there is insufficient information. Your requirements summary spreadsheet is the tool the team will use to make those tradeoffs and priority calls. The goal of the project leader is to channel the discussions during these meetings down paths that are rational: all of the choices are achievable, and the final choice optimizes ROI.

PRIORITIZATION TOOLS AND TECHNIQUES

www.SFDC-secrets.com describes several tools that help prioritize requirements. Give at least one of them a try to find out which tool is most natural for your team and produces the most credible priority rankings.

The two groups that usually get the highest weight in the prioritization are sales representatives and executives. Things that are of direct, immediate benefit to them are assigned a lot of points. The specific points you give to other departments and user types are up to you, but a CRM implementation team that forgets who's the boss does so at their own peril.

There isn't a universal formula for prioritizing requirements: it mostly depends on the specifics of your company. For example, should the requirements from highly sophisticated users (as identified in Chapter 5's SFA Maturity Model) be prioritized *higher* than others (because those users can gain the most) or *lower* than others (because those users will be better able to cope with an incomplete feature set)? The answer to this question inevitably depends on your company, its management style, and the internal political environment.

You'll want to carefully plan out who will start using the system and when, as the sequencing of user group migration affects priorities. Put simply, the timing and order in which you deliver SFDC functionality and extensions can have a *big* impact on the total project cost and schedule. Some functional areas go together very easily; others can involve a lot of controversy, meetings, and rework. Although the order of functions is fundamentally your choice, a good rule of thumb is to bring users onto SFDC in the order listed in Table 1-1.

TABLE 1-1   General Sequence of Bringing Users into SFDC

Organization	Activity	Business Priority	Political Priority	Phase
Telesales/inside sales	Orders	High	Medium	I
Order operations	Approvals	High	Medium	I
Sales development	Appointments	High	Low	I
Telemarketing	Cold calls	High	Low	I
Marketing	Lead generation	Medium	Low	II
Sales analysts	Executive support	Medium	Medium	II
Product marketing	Purchase analysis	Medium	Low	II
Sales VP and marketing VP	Management, forecasting	High	High	II
Executive team	Management	High	High	III
Legal	Contracts	High	Low	III
Sales engineers, consultants	Deal support	High	Low	IV
Shipping/receiving	Distribution	Low	Low	IV
Customer support	Customer care	Medium	Low	IV
Finance	Business analysis	Medium	Low	IV

TABLE 1-1   General Sequence of Bringing Users into SFDC (*Continued*)

Organization	Activity	Business Priority	Political Priority	Phase
Field sales managers	Sales management	High	High	V
Partner/channel manager	Channel management	Medium	Medium	V
Individual sales reps	Selling	High	High	VI
International operations	Selling	High	High	VII

Almost always, the revenue-focused business processes conducted at headquarters are implemented first. Later, other headquarters processes are brought online. Usually, business processes done in the field happen a bit later.

You might wonder why the executive suite and other high-priority roles in the company seem to come so late to the system. **Why aren't the big-wig requirements satisfied first?** Because you get only one chance to make a good first impression. Chapters 3 and 4 provide a more elaborate answer: the quality, completeness, and relevance of the data in the system just won't be good enough early on. Any reports or dashboards an executive wants won't be reliable, and they could even provide misleading information that would lower the credibility of the system. It's a big mistake to bet the farm on SFDC data assets before they are ripe.

Add groups and adjust priorities on the list in Table 1-1 to fit the realities of your business. No matter what the order selected, use the sequence of delivery to help prioritize requirements. Requirements coming from teams that will be coming on board early should be treated as having a higher priority (so they get done early).

A key issue in prioritizing requirements is the "squeaky wheel" phenomenon, whereby a noisy or politically powerful proponent causes great emphasis to be placed on a requirement that, on balance, isn't really critical. All too often, a significant proportion of the effort in large projects is devoted to requirements that are "nice to haves" but that ultimately waste time and effort. Consequently, *the* highest leverage thing a project leader or business analyst can do is identify and deprioritize the uncritical. While avoiding confrontation, smoke out dubious requirements using gambits like these:

- "How much of *your* budget would you be willing to dedicate to solving the problem?"

- "Can you quantify how much waste this problem has been causing for you on a monthly basis?"

- "How much profit increase would the company see if this were done?"

- "How much more work could your team do if the problem were solved?"

- "Which other department needs this feature?"

- "How have you been able to succeed without this so far?"

- "What's the forcing function—the deadline beyond which we can no longer do business the current way?"

- "Which of *your* other requirements would you be willing to put on the back burner to get this one done?"

Avoiding Happy Ears

Whenever a new system is being developed and people are interviewed about what they need, users start to hear hints about how things will work. Nearly everyone will assume that if they've *heard* about an issue, it's going to be solved by the new system. They'll even extrapolate, imagining all the wonderful new features that will become available to make their job easier. It's human nature to be optimistic, and that goes double for sales and marketing folks. But this "happy ears" phenomenon leads to spiraling expectations and scope creep that can kill a project.

Project leaders, and especially project sponsors, must continuously push to **lower user expectations** even if they haven't yet seen overt signs of happy ears. The project goals must be simple—even minimalist—for the first phases, and the "great ideas" must be explicitly pushed off to later phases. Even when things are going okay, *undersell* and be tentative about making the schedule. Even if the team has a way of delivering "something great," consider delaying it (ironically, see "The Art of the Quick Win" later in this chapter). When you *do* deliver this great thing, *do not publicize it until it's delivered and tested* so that you can provide pleasant surprises to users.

In prioritizing and trading off requirements, the project leader will need a set of executive sponsors who can act as champions for political and resource issues. For SFDC project success, the champions *must* include the VP of sales but usually include the VP of marketing, the VP of support and services, the CFO, or perhaps even the CEO. As these key supporters cannot afford the time needed to participate in the project, they'll need to deputize a senior person on their staff to be a regular participant[5] on the SFDC implementation team. The project leader should form a management council of these deputies to make priority

---

5. As we discuss later in this chapter, *participant* means an active worker who is charged with the task of delivering documents and making binding decisions. Participants' effort on the team needs to be part of their "day job," so their boss needs to dedicate a portion of their schedule and allocate some of their personal goals (major business objectives [MBOs]) during the months of their project involvement. Their effort needs to be measured and rewarded!

calls, policy decisions, and tradeoffs. For simplicity of voting, the team needs to be small and contain an odd number of people (including the project manager). A small management council would include representatives from the sales and marketing departments, plus the project leader. A larger council might add representatives from the finance, customer care, international operations, professional services, channel operations, and business analytics departments. This council will need to have *brief* weekly meetings (probably a Web conference), and it should devote a significant amount of time to analyzing business processes. Because a key factor in ensuring project success is the availability of the right people for this team, get their (and their bosses') commitments early.

The challenge for the project leader is to keep one (and only one) priority list that encompasses everyone's needs, while clearly limiting the number of items that are "must do's" for each phase. Maintaining a consistent, clear, tightly enforced requirements priority list is an invaluable tool for the project leader, and its existence will help fend off countless arguments during the project.

When Requirements Should Bend

It is common for requirements to be stated as absolutes, with intricate detail being provided about the way things must be done. But these "requirements" are often an interpretation of a business need, an executive's preference, or even a legal regulation. Sometimes, the literal requirement is a poor interpretation of the underlying business need. It's important to be as creative as possible in requirements statements so that you don't overspecify or get locked into one particular approach. Identify alternatives and different ways of achieving the underlying goal. Sometimes, it is even possible to sidestep requirements entirely via limiting assumptions or tiny changes to a contract.

For example, the finance department may have an edict that an order cannot be shipped without a manual approval, so the requirement is stated as a mandatory human approval cycle. But if the approval cycle is there only to apply a set of strict rules, maybe the *manual* approval cycle isn't the real requirement. By restating the requirement as "no shipment will be made without applying the following rules," it becomes possible to have a fully automated approval, saving time and cost on every order.

Look for opportunities to restate requirements that are overspecified or arbitrarily complex. Requirements should be statements of business goals and criteria rather than strict step-by-step procedures.

In some cases, the best path forward is to change the business process rather than invest in automation of a silly or obsolete practice. In particular, look for opportunities to improve the process by making subtle changes to the sales and marketing processes. Some of the most doctrinaire CRM requirements miss key opportunities for leverage. The CRM system will give sales reps and managers information and tools they never had before. Because the whole point of the system is to make it easier for the reps to make their numbers, why not take the blinders off? For example, better qualification of leads can mean fewer pointless sales calls and shorter sales cycles. Likewise, marketing personnel should be encouraged to think outside the box, looking for entirely new ways to plan campaigns and execute events. Of course, you need to get the executives' approval before you formally recommend process changes or restate the requirement, but it's well worth the effort.

Bending and restating requirements in this way can make the system much easier to implement, easier to use, and more beneficial to the business over time.

Knowing Your Boundaries

One of the most important issues when setting requirements is determining the "edges" of the system—that is, the boundaries beyond which users must log in to a different system if they want to do something. All users would like the system to encompass all of the things they need to access for their particular jobs, but it's impractical to deliver a single system that covers every business function for every employee.

If you install SFDC without any add-on products, it has the following functional boundaries:

- **Marketing:** Leads, contacts, campaigns, and email interactions are well handled within SFDC. Almost all of the details having to do with email blasts, marketing events, advertising, or other marketing initiatives, however, will be in your email blasting, marketing automation, or content management system, not in SFDC. For example, SFDC tracks the outcomes and history of campaigns, but the detailed mechanics of actual campaign management are external to the system.

- **Advertising and social media:** Salesforce.com has a sophisticated set of tools for running social advertising campaigns and monitoring social media, but they are fairly specialized. General-purpose social media monitoring and advertising will be handled outside of SFDC.

- **Web portals and eCommerce:** Salesforce.com has a set of optional portal features, particularly for customer self-service and channel partners. However, these tools typically work as an adjunct to your main corporate Web properties. Your overall Web content and eCommerce functionality will be managed in external Web content management systems and eCommerce frameworks.

- **Order entry:** Anything having to do with bookings, invoices, or payments is in your order-management, accounting, or enterprise resource planning (ERP) system, not in SFDC.

- **Order management:** Anything having to do with shipments, order status, returns, or exchanges will be in the order-management, distribution, or ERP system, not in SFDC.

- **Customer assets, inventory, and licenses:** Almost anything having to do with the customer's order history, shipments, downloads, or licenses will be in your accounting, ERP, or other corporate databases. SFDC has a very limited view of assets.

- **Defect reports or bug tracking:** Anything having to do with technical problem resolution will be handled by a defect management or bug-tracking database; most companies already have an entrenched system for this purpose. SFDC can be configured to integrate with these systems, but out of the box it's really focused on "cases" or "incidents."

- **Consulting projects or training classes:** Although SFDC is often configured to have projects and training as quotable "products," the system doesn't have any functionality to help with the planning, scheduling, or delivery of these services. Those details will be handled in external professional services automation (PSA) or learning management systems (LMS).

- **Documents:** Almost anything in your sales literature, marketing library, Web site content, proposals, customer specifications, or contracts is already stored outside of SFDC, often in a file system or in content management products. Although SFDC has some very useful content management and delivery features, they are usually used to supplement rather than supplant the existing external systems.

- **Business analytics:** Although SFDC provides an excellent set of built-in reports and dashboards, almost any business analyst will need to go beyond these features and use an external database and business analysis tool.

For a detailed view of business systems that touch on SFDC, see Figure 1-3. As shown in the diagram, several add-on products may be tightly integrated with SFDC to improve its functional coverage (see Chapter 7 for a discussion of these products). These extensions and external products are a huge strength of SFDC because they allow the core system to be simple and easy to use, yet flexible and scalable enough to handle much broader requirements. Further, SFDC has a very open and well-documented set of external interfaces, presented as Web services. These application programmer interfaces (APIs) allow programmers to connect, integrate, and extend SFDC to almost anything.

Even though you *could* integrate SFDC with any external system, it's easy to overshoot the mark by trying to do too much in the initial implementation. In evaluating and prioritizing requirements, it's important to identify when a requirement crosses over into an

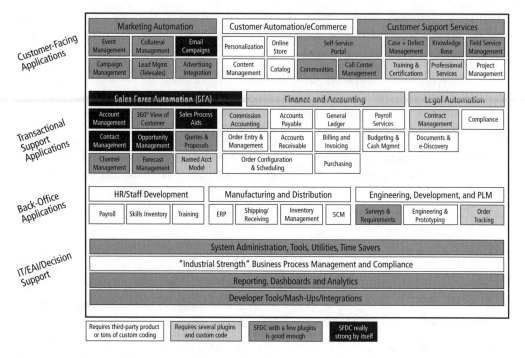

FIGURE 1-3   SFDC and the application landscape

external system. **Any requirement that involves spanning systems is inherently more complex and risky, so it should be assigned a lower priority** than requirements that are entirely within SFDC's native functionality. Read the section on integration in Chapter 7 before you deal with any requirements for integration.

Thanks to the modularity of the SFDC architecture, almost all internal functions can be turned on in phases at the time of your choosing. For example, turning on the Campaigns or Forecasting function can be done the day you bring up the system or, alternatively, months later without involving significant rework. Many external add-ons act in the same way, allowing a very flexible deployment schedule. However, some of the more sophisticated add-ons (such as Eloqua marketing automation or Intacct accounting) involve significant changes to your data, the user interface, and user behaviors. Consequently, the timing and sequence of deploying the more complex and expensive add-ons cannot be taken lightly.

As with all requirements, the extension of SFDC via add-ons and integration with other systems should be prioritized with a keen eye toward schedule and risk. Even though basic integration is of the "plug-and-play" variety, the interaction among systems and databases can cause subtle data corruption problems that won't be discovered for

WHEN OTHER PROBLEMS MUST BE SOLVED FIRST

In large organizations, the political drivers for installing or replacing the existing CRM system will be executive visibility, customer reporting, or uneven execution of business processes. Unfortunately, merely upgrading to SFDC will not help in many of these situations. In large organizations, other problems need to be solved *before* the new system will function properly, let alone resolve any deep issues.

The project manager should analyze the requirements and problem statements to understand which of them are actually caused by bad data, disconnected systems, unclear business rules, inconsistent business processes, and other "environmental" or infrastructure issues. These problems are typically scattered across several databases or applications, and fixing them will be a prerequisite to any successful SFDC deployment.

If you discover this situation, it is important to get a project team started on analyzing and remedying those external problems even before your SFDC work starts. That project team should be chartered to work with your SFDC team, but typically it should be managed separately. If this team is chartered to work under the SFDC team, make sure that its focus doesn't become too broad (e.g., "rework this entire outside system") or distract the main SFDC implementation team.

several weeks. Consequently, it is usually a good idea to deploy basic SFDC functionality without external integration, get the users comfortable using it, and get some real data flowing through the system (even if only manually) in the early weeks. Later, new functional add-ons and integrations should be deployed one at a time on top of a stable baseline system, so that users can gradually become used to the new features as the system expands. External integrations (particularly with complex systems such as accounting, ERP, and marketing automation) should be started early for testing purposes but should not be turned on for full two-way data transfer until later phases.

www.SFDC-secrets.com provides example requirements for both a small company and a large company. Of course, every company's needs and priorities are different, but the examples show the level of detail that you need (not much, at this stage) and the kind of interdepartmental prioritization you must think about when preparing your company's list of requirements.

The SFDC system will almost certainly be implemented over several quarters, with only the first two phases as "hard priorities." Later requirements will be reordered depending on perceived business priority after initial usage; it is inevitable that technical issues and needed process changes will be discovered during the project.

More important, perceived business needs are likely to change over the life of the project.[6] The whole point of the Agile project management methods we advocate throughout this book is to minimize the negative consequences of those priority changes. If your company decides to not use Agile techniques, any major shift in priorities will cause delay and wasted efforts. Communicating this point clearly but pleasantly is one of the amusing challenges for the project leader, because the executives are as vulnerable to "happy ears" as anyone else.

Making the Business Case

Most companies require a formal business case for an investment in SFDC. Even if yours doesn't have a formal review meeting for the decision, it's a good idea to go through the exercise of cost, benefit, and ROI analysis so that the team understands the financial implications of what it is doing. Underestimating the costs—both in terms of your effort and the outlay to outside firms—is altogether too common and dangerous an error for SFDC project teams. Understanding the things that really make a big financial difference—and the things that really don't—helps everyone make better decisions throughout the life of the project.

Estimating Costs

When evaluating cloud (aka software as a service [SaaS]) systems such as Salesforce.com, it is tempting to think that cost analysis isn't critical. After all, it's just a monthly fee, and you pay only as long as you're receiving value . . . right? That's what the salesperson wants you to think, if only to make you stop thinking. Life just isn't that simple.

The big three cost areas are procurement, implementation, and ongoing user expenses. We deal with each of these in turn.

Procurement

Procurement costs for SFDC, like most cloud products, consist of a monthly fee. The fee varies on the basis of the following factors:

- The number of users (e.g., internal sales cloud, service cloud, and marketing cloud users; platform users; mobile users; external partner users; and customer users)

---

6. If you doubt this, answer the following questions: Do you think that your users will state their requirements with such thoroughness and precision that you won't misunderstand them? Do you believe you understand your data, business processes, and cross-system integrations so well that there won't be any surprises? Do you expect that the users won't change their minds about details and priorities during the course of the project? Do you think your channels and competitive environment won't change during the life of the project? Will you foresee all the government regulations, customer contractual stipulations, and internal standards you'll need to comply with? In the immortal words of Clint Eastwood, "Do you feel lucky?"

- The version you buy (most readers will purchase the `enterprise edition`, but many will also want the `sandbox` or other extra-cost items)

- The amount of storage you'll need—SFDC charges for these items can become important if you don't have many users

- The length of the contractual commitment (1 year is the minimum; more than 3 years seems to make little difference to the discount)

- The date of the purchase (end-of-month gets less of a discount than end-of-fiscal year)

- Your willingness to prepay (prepaying 1 year makes a difference, but longer pre-pays seem to make less of a difference)

WHO SHOULD PAY?

The best decisions happen when the departments that *benefit* the most *pay* the most for the system. This typically means sales should pay at least 50% of the total, with marketing and support sharing the remainder of the cost. Of course, this split depends entirely on your company's organizational structure and system usage.

Another funding formula is to have the project be financially sponsored by the executive suite—at the corporate or business unit level, which shows the executive team's level of commitment.

The only funding model that *doesn't* work is to have central IT foot the bill. Although this approach works with infrastructure, in cloud applications—and particularly those that directly benefit only a part of the company—this model doesn't work in either the short run or the long run. Check out Chapter 6 for more on this topic.

Because you will be delivering the system in phases, make sure to activate only the number of seats you will actually use at any one time. In the negotiations for a large deal, this aspect of incremental deployment may save your company a significant sum.

Include third-party add-on products (see Chapter 7 for more on this) in your procurement cost estimates, thinking through phasing effects that will affect the number of users and the timing of activation for each product separately. Most add-on products for SFDC also use a cloud model, but a few are on-premises products with hardware requirements and perpetual licenses. For those products, don't forget to include the cost of hardware procurement.[7]

---

7. For both security and performance reasons, you'll almost certainly want any on-premises add-on products to run on dedicated servers.

Don't expect steep discounting: cloud vendors have less negotiating room than traditional software companies do, particularly when there are fewer than 50 users.

Do not neglect support fees. The basic support level that's included in cloud products will be insufficient for at least your first year. You'll need speed of access to in-depth expertise that is available only through premium support. Your team members (particularly developers and system administrators) will also need technical training classes (typically $2,500 each) to become rapidly productive. Developer support—deep technical assistance that's akin to consulting—is typically not included in premium support. Do *not* negotiate for these items piecemeal if you want the best discount.

If your company will have more than 100 users, the annual fees for cloud products can be a surprise. While it's true that you aren't paying for upgrades, patches, hardware, and operating staff, total SaaS fees can easily exceed $100,000 per year, and the amount climbs to megabucks (literally) per year for the very largest deployments.[8] Don't assume that you'll have a lot of bargaining power once the deal is signed: once you're on board, the only way you can get a better discount is to buy even more or to commit for an even longer period. Downgrades are not allowed except at renewal time. The vendor knows you don't have a credible threat of changing the system, as the real cost of a changeover can be quite large even with the flexibility provided by the cloud's Web services technology. As your users grow accustomed to features and your developers become experts at using SFDC's APIs, you will be just as locked in to the vendor's technology as you would be with any Microsoft product.

To get a significant discount on the procurement, you need to get a budgetary allocation for the multiyear commitment. Work with your finance department to develop the business case, making sure those personnel understand that the number of users will go up over time even if the per-seat price is stable.

Implementation

In contrast to procurement costs, implementation costs for SFDC and other cloud systems are one-time fees. For a project of any size, you will need some help from your IT team—even if it's just permission to proceed without their interference. Do not assume that your internal IT people are interested in SaaS projects or that they have the required skills and experience (but you might want to check out the discussion in Chapter 13 anyway). You will almost certainly need consulting and other services required to convert legacy data, integrate with other systems, write custom `APEX` and `Visualforce` code, test the system, deploy it, and train the user community.

---

8. Discounts on cloud deals have been gradually improving as the vendors become more competitive. Discount levels for the very largest deployments (10,000 users or more) and the most strategic accounts are a well-guarded secret, but we've heard about some significant discounting. If you have knowledge about the negotiated price of a large SFDC deal, feel free to email me at david@SFDC-secrets.com.

Some of the implementation costs are easy to identify and are "fixed fee" in nature (e.g., training classes). Most of the big elements of implementation, however, are highly customized and can be brought to a fixed-price bid only after significant analysis by your vendor. Of course, every finance department will want a fixed price, but there is *significant* gamesmanship in fixed-price bidding. It is very easy to get caught up in the engineering change order (ECO) trap, where fixed-price contracts create an avalanche of overruns.[9]

WHEN THE PRICE ISN'T RIGHT

At the beginning of a project, all you can see is price. At the end of the project, all you'll remember is the value of benefits, the quality of the work (or lack of it), the pain (or lack of it), and the overruns (large or small). It's easy to be penny wise and pound foolish. **It is far more important to choose a vendor that you can trust than to pick one that bids low.** You need to see proven experience, skills in project management, actionable communication, and references from other customers.

One of the advantages of the phased deployments we recommend in this book is that the vendors can give you a more accurate bid for the immediate phase (which will be very tightly defined) than they can for the project overall (which may suffer from scope creep and extensions). *Best practices are to use hourly rates with a tightly managed cap rather than fixed-price engagements* because this practice exposes the scope creep that hurts overall chances of project success; avoids the bickering, administrivia, and gamesmanship of fixed-price change orders; and prevents vendors from hiding large margins in their bid.

Explore your consultant's willingness to work using performance incentives. If they are designed properly, these types of contracts can yield the best possible deal for you because your goals and metrics are tightly aligned with the consultant's. As wondrous as pay-for-performance contracts are, they're equally rare. But give it a shot.

The first step in quantifying the implementation costs is drawing up the statement of work and the development/integration requirements for each of the projects. The more homework you can do yourself, the more accurate the vendors' bids will be. Some of the project areas will require analysis that you can't do, and the bidding vendors will have to perform this analysis themselves. The vendors are unlikely to do enough drill-down analysis for free, but there is good news here: the initial scoping project will be short and *should* be fixed-price. This is money well spent before you make a large commitment. Some vendors will do this scoping project only *after* you have signed on with them for the main project. My own experience with this kind of vendor is not good, but don't treat that issue as a show-stopper. If the vendor is very well qualified and you trust the individual consultants, proceed.

---

9. For more on this, check out the essay "WorkingAgile.docx" at www.SFDC-secrets.com.

Note that the cost of implementation talent for serious SaaS projects isn't much different from the corresponding costs of conventional on-premises software packages. If anything, the cloud sharpshooters are more expensive. Skills and deep experience in cloud implementations are still fairly rare (particularly outside the United States), and fees can be $300/hour or more for the best people. It is not uncommon for overall implementation costs to exceed the software fees paid to cloud vendors in the first year. Although the first-year cloud fees are significantly lower than customers paid for classic enterprise software (where implementation was typically projected to be 1.5 or more times the cost of the software licenses), the implementation costs can come as an unpleasant surprise if proper allocation for it has not been arranged.

WHAT IF NO EXTERNAL PEOPLE WILL BE USED?

During initial setup and particularly in the out-years, every once in a while, important people will have great ideas for improving the SFDC team. Their ideas allow no external resources, though.

So how do you make sure you don't get burdened with a huge project load (that's "free" for the requesters)? If your company uses internal transfer costs, find out what the hourly rate is for your IT team and use that to generate the chargeback estimate. That'll slow down many of the frivolous requests. If that doesn't work, estimate the calendar time that the project requests will take—and be realistic about testing, deployment, and training implications. In addition, estimate the number of weeks that the project will delay some other preexisting high-priority request. The requesters may have no idea that their "simple little requests" may involve hundreds of man-hours. Since they can rarely relate to man-hours, focus their attention on the calendar.

If there are other externalities (knock-on effects) that will result from the project, make sure to quantify them in the same way as the direct costs. When presented with the "total bill," the requesters may quickly decide to simplify or even eliminate their demands as being "not worth it to the business."

Do your cost estimating only for the initial implementation, but know that the happier your users are, the more likely they will be to ask management for further system enhancements later on. It is not uncommon for companies to have multiyear engagements before they reach the management nirvana of the 360-degree view of the customer.[10]

---

10. The 360-degree view refers to the ability to see all customer interactions with your company from all angles, from Web site visits to social media to orders to payment history to letters of complaint. This visibility lets management see which accounts are the most valuable versus which customers are noisy but just not profitable enough. While this 360-degree visibility is very powerful for marketing and management personnel, it involves extensive integration and changes to business processes that can take years to come to fruition.

Don't forget to include the costs of your internal people. It's not unusual to have five people be involved on a full-time basis in an SFDC implementation (even with consultants), plus another five involved intermittently. Even though these people's salaries are already budgeted for, the effort they put into SFDC will be time that *won't* be available for other company priorities.

Ongoing Costs

After estimating total first-year costs—first-year fees, add-on procurements, and implementation expenses—the ongoing costs for cloud services are basically the annual subscription fees. There may be some one-time costs in the out-years (such as a data recovery exercise or temporary use of SFDC's `sandbox`), so put a placeholder in those budgets. The more interesting ongoing costs are related to people: follow-on implementation or expansion work, training costs for new users or administrators, travel and fees for "power users" attending technical conferences (a good investment), and time for any consultants working on the system.

As with any large system, data pollution is an inevitability, and it's poisonous to SFDC's credibility. Business analysts and others will discover corrupted or duplicate data creeping into the system over time. Whether you use a temporary coder, a data-entry clerk, or overtime hours of internal people, set aside some budget for a health check and cleanup session at least once a year. You'll almost certainly want a deduping or data cleansing tool, which will cost about $100 per user per year, but is still money very well spent (see Chapter 7 for discussion). Furthermore, identifying the source of the data pollution problem, rectifying it, and cleaning up the data are often tasks carried out in collaboration with contractors.

These ongoing costs are likely to be most pronounced in year two of the system, but some budget should be set aside every year after the initial deployment.

The total costs for SFDC will be lower than you'd expect for equivalent on-premises software packages, particularly up to year three. Generally speaking, we recommend that you use a 3- to 5-year time horizon for your cost model: anything longer is not realistic given the nature of most sales, marketing, and channel organizations.

Quantifying the Return and Getting to Hard Numbers

Any project this size has to be justified with improvements to the bottom line. The two components of achieving this goal—lowering costs and increasing revenues—are easy to imagine but hard to quantify. But they can at least be modeled to provide a credible SWAG.[11]

---

11. Scientific wild-ass guess.

Lowered Costs

To counterbalance all of the costs outlined previously, it's important to identify areas of cost saving. Because SFDC is a salesforce *automation* system, you'd expect to find some economies. But that's rarely the way it works—after all, many of the expense areas are sunk costs that cannot be recovered or labor that is taken for granted. You may have to be a good detective to ferret out the labor savings.

The first obvious place to look is cost avoidance for the system SFDC is replacing. It won't be much, but at least it can be immediately quantified. Next, look at ancillary systems that can be decommissioned because SFDC makes them less relevant. For example, you may have a large number of spreadsheets for the marketing group with macros that won't need to be maintained or extended any more. Those product or consulting costs can add up.

The next place to look is wasted labor. Whether the waste takes the form of contractors or employees, the hours and the hourly rate should be quantified. Here are example areas where wasted labor can be avoided:

- System administrators or sysops who now maintain software and hardware that can be retired. This will probably amount to at least 32 hours per month; for large systems, it can be much more.

- Sales administrators who—even in small companies—may spend 8 or more hours per week preparing, rolling up, and reconciling the weekly pipeline forecast.

- Order operations people who spend dozens of hours per week on order entry, correction, and reconciliation.

- Business analysts who spend huge chunks of time trying to piece together spreadsheets from fragments of customer data that are spread across several systems.

- Order fulfillment people (license generation, shipping, distribution, and expediting) who may spend their entire day doing things that could be 80% automated.

- Customer support people who can easily waste 10 minutes per call trying to find data, correct erroneous entries, or fix problems that could have been avoided by automation and a good support console. They may also be wasting easily half of their time on customer issues that could better be solved with a good knowledge base and customer self-support community.

- Trainers or consultants who waste hours each week emailing back and forth with clients. If the information were centralized and available in a customer portal, this task could be avoided.

- Everyone in the company who deals with too much email. (Pay attention to this one—McKinsey estimates that office workers spend about 25% of their time just on email—think of how many hours could be saved!)

- Executives (or at least their assistants) who may be wasting hours per week trying to find information before taking a difficult customer call.

These areas of direct waste add up, as they occur every week and may become much larger in the closing weeks of the quarter. Even though employees' time is a "sunk cost," quantify the savings as if those workers were paid by the hour.

See Table 1-2 for an example cost-savings matrix for a small company (as always, check out www.SFDC-secrets.com for free downloads of Excel spreadsheets and other files that you can use on your project).

TABLE 1-2   Potential Cost Savings and Efficiency Improvements

Cost Savings	Units	Savings/Year
Hard Cost Savings		
Ongoing license fees for existing SFA/CRM system	n/a	n/a
Support fees for existing SFA/CRM system	n/a	$ 2,000
Hardware maintenance and support costs for SFA/CRM system	1 server	$ 1,500
Auxiliary software products for existing SFA/CRM system	3 licenses	$ 3,000
Potential Cost Savings/Efficiency Improvements		
Tradeshow and related travel expenses reduced	1 tradeshow/year	$30,000
Advertising and other marketing expenses reduced	n/a	$20,000
Avoiding unproductive onsite sales calls/ demonstrations	1 meeting/year	$ 2,000
Avoiding low-probability proof-of-concept projects	1 POC/year	$ 2,000
Improved product marketing and engineering decisions	n/a	$10,000
Improved executive decisions	1 decision/year	$25,000
Internal Labor Savings		
System administration time for existing SFA/CRM software and hardware	16 hours/month	$20,000
Sales administrator time reconciling orders	32 hours/month	$30,000
Sales administrator time rolling up forecast	32 hours/month	$30,000
VP time investigating/adjusting weird forecast numbers	12 hours/month	$12,000

Continues

TABLE 1-2   Potential Cost Savings and Efficiency Improvements (*Continued*)

Cost Savings	Units	Savings/Year
Missed Opportunities		
Lower cost of customer acquisition by 5%	50 new customers/year	$100,000
Prevent one lost sale*	1 new customer/year	$ 50,000
Ability to do one more upsell*	1 upsell/year	$ 20,000

* This should be the revenue from the average first sale to new customers. Sophisticated finance types will tell you that this is an overstatement and will try to get you to use the *profit* from a new customer instead. Don't do it: your fallback position should be the **contribution margin** value from an *extra* transaction.

Opportunity Costs

The larger cost savings are more difficult to quantify because they involve missed opportunities or avoidance of wrong decisions.

- What would it mean if the cost of customer acquisition were 5% lower?

- How would it lower costs if the sales cycle were a week shorter?

- What would be the impact of reducing sales representative turnover by just *one rep* per year?

- What percentage of marketing dollars is spent on marketing to the wrong people or participating in the wrong events?

- How much could be saved if you could quantify which marketing activities really produced revenue rather than just "visibility"?

- How much travel expense and labor could be saved by avoiding just one unproductive tradeshow, sales call, proof-of-concept project, or truck-roll?

- If you knew more about which prospects were (or weren't) going to yield the most profit, how much better would your targeting and profitability be?

Focus on quantifying **external waste** that could be reduced rather than on internal jobs that could be eliminated, as the latter will bring the project nothing but political strife. You'll need to interview people in sales, marketing, and presales support to make this determination. Nevertheless, as you develop an effective model for estimating the cost savings, the amount saved can turn into big money.

There is also value to the risk reduction that SFDC will bring. Hits to customer reputation, knocks to brand value, and even Wall Street embarrassment all cost the company money—and all can be improved by a solid CRM system. **Avoiding just one unreliable** forecast or a few irate customers can save enough to pay for the whole of SFDC. The problem, of course, is justifying this quantification.

HEAD'S UP!

Watch out for finance groups that try to use your estimates as a justification for cutting the budget of other departments. They may say, "Well, if you do such a great job detecting unproductive marketing activities, we'll just cut their budget by 10% now to make sure you actually achieve that goal."

This kind of budgetary reasoning can get poisonous in a hurry, so always couch cost savings as potential and as a way of increasing the leverage of the money that needs to be spent anyway. In other words, describe the change in terms of improved ROI or getting more value for the company's money, not in terms of spending less money.

Increased Revenues

The flip side of lowering costs is increasing revenue. To develop credible estimates, it's important to interview several sales and channel managers, discounting the opinions of people who are not directly responsible for revenues. **It is political suicide to present your revenue conclusions without having first reviewed them with the sales VP.**

Take a look at the section "Why Are You Looking at an SFA or CRM System?" in the Executive Summary of this book. Develop a spreadsheet that shows the value of extra deals that could be closed with the aid of better prospect and customer information, better lead quality, tighter qualification, and higher conversion/win rates.

- What if a hot prospect never fell through the cracks?

- What would be the value of the extra deals you could do if the sales cycle were shorter?

- How much bigger a deal could you close if your sales teams were armed with the best intelligence and technology?

- What kind of extra revenue might the channel produce if leads were handed off and managed more effectively?

- What would be the value of doing one additional upsell per year or of closing a deal with one more customer?

- What if your customer loyalty or retention rate increased by 10%?

- How much larger could your consulting projects be if your initial sales were 10% larger?

For the sake of credibility, keep these estimates conservative.

It's also a good idea to identify opportunities to increase sales leverage—that is, to get more yield from the same cost structure. How would it change the company if a sales rep could manage twice as many deals without slip-ups? Or if a sales manager could manage 50% more sales reps? How would the company operations change if the forecast were *really* reliable in week 10 of the quarter? These issues could mean better scalability for the company and the ability to respond to market changes more quickly. These speed and scalability advantages increase both the profitability and the value of the company.

DREAM ON

If you read the "Social CRM" sidebar in the Executive Summary, you have to face the fact that social media are sexy, and they might even do your business some good someday. There are already real success stories in social CRM, but how do you quantify the benefits for your company's business case?

The success stories are usually pretty specialized and hard to extrapolate in a way that a skeptical CFO would believe. If your company already spends heavily in social media, has very large audiences (particularly in B2C markets), and has already built infrastructure and expertise to repeatedly benefit from social advertising, marketing, selling, and support—well then, you're just too cool. You can probably come up with a defendable upside and cost saving from social CRM. Otherwise, you have to value the benefits as icing on the cake and not as the core of your business case.

Beware of politics surrounding revenue estimates. It's tempting to say something like, "We could increase revenue 10% if only. . . ." Sales executives will be very sensitive about this topic, and ornery finance executives might say, "We'll approve this project only if the sales department is willing to increase its quota by 10%." To avoid this downhill spiral, focus your estimates on quantifying the *increased probability* of making the revenue targets the company already has. This approach is a less direct way of making the business case for SFDC, but it avoids the political traps and still makes the point.

Finally, beware of blatant double-counting of cost savings or revenue improvements. Although some double-counting is almost unavoidable, if it's too obvious, it simply lowers your credibility (note that the example in Table 1-2 shows just "the right amount" of double-counting).

As with the cost analysis, the benefit analysis of the system should be looking at no more than a 3-year time horizon. Too many things will change for a longer time horizon to yield credible data.

Developing a Straw-Man Schedule

Part of making the business case for SFDC involves answering the question, "How soon can we get the benefits?" Once the project is approved, the schedule will be the single most visible aspect of managing the implementation. Although SFDC and other cloud systems can be turned on in a day or so (the SFDC sales reps will have made *sure* to publicize that), the standard system that is delivered will be of no practical use until it is configured (the SFDC reps may not have emphasized this point). The time to configure the system may be short, but the time required to think through and test precisely how you need the system configured will be just as long as it would be with enterprise software. And the biggest cost and schedule elements—integration and data import—are just as large and uncertain as they would be with a conventional system.

In large companies with a sophisticated IT department, allocate time in your schedule for initial review meetings: even though SFDC is a hosted system, security and compliance reviews will be required before you're allowed to go live. Given that unexpected delays—no matter what the source—may be tagged as "project failures" by upper management, estimating the schedule and setting executive/sponsor expectations appropriately are key success factors for delivering the project.

As with any complex project, the SFDC schedule estimate will be based on a reasonable best-case scenario: you assume that you won't make wrong decisions, that the right resources will be available when needed, and that there won't be any unpleasant discoveries along the way. To counteract this structural optimism, buffer elements must be added to the schedule during the riskiest tasks (such as development of a new software element or integrating an external system). Buffer elements must also be added during weeks that are critically constrained for sales personnel and executive management (e.g., sales managers are unlikely to be responsive to an action item during weeks 12 and 13 of the quarter, and no executive can be expected to attend an SFDC management review during weeks 1 and 2 of the quarter due to quarterly financials and the board meeting).

One of the first things a project manager should do is collect the calendar of "blackout periods" for each key resource. Immediately after completing this task, the project manager should identify "forcing functions"—external events with firm deadlines—that will likely drive the deployment calendar. For example, an annual sales meeting will be an ideal time to roll out new functionality and do user training.

Ironically, one of the major areas of schedule uncertainty is in requirements setting and prioritization. A common problem of large IT projects is to overspecify at two levels: at the high level, creating requirements that have questionable or unknown business value, and at the microscopic level, specifying things in too much detail. At both levels, overspecification creates a lot of extra work and often engages employees in a level of perfectionism that has limited payoff.

GANTT CHARTS, PERT DIAGRAMS, AND OTHER MANAGEMENT DELUSIONS

While developing the schedule *estimate*, it really helps to use a Gantt charting tool such as Microsoft Project. This kind of software is fairly straightforward to learn, and during the planning phase, its nice charts can help persuade busy managers about resource commitments.

By contrast, it is a very rare project that actually *uses* the Gantt charting tool during the life of the actual work, because maintaining the data and updating the schedule charts require a tremendous amount of effort. Unfortunately, few project participants will be willing to update their own information, so maintaining an accurate Gantt schedule usually falls to the project manager. (There are some new cloud collaborative scheduling tools from Atlassian, Clarizen, and others that can work nicely.) Most of the time, the real-world schedule takes the form of a spreadsheet. Set expectations with management accordingly.

That said, when a new project phase starts (or, less optimistically, when a major rework of the schedule is required), it is a good idea to redo the Gantt charts. Store backup copies of the original chart files for comparison purposes, but develop new ones that show the expected work breakdown structure at an overview level. You can have hours of fun comparing the original schedule with reality and develop lessons learned for later phases of the project.

The idea behind "value engineering" is to make sure that a requirement is going to be *worth* satisfying before you spend the resources to implement it. The best possible investment you can make as a business analyst or project manager is time spent vetting and validating requirements, because every hour you spend can save days of effort later. **Allocate double the amount of time you think you'll need for interpreting and prioritizing requirements, as smoking out a marginal or bogus requirement can cut overall wasted effort in half.**

Although the iterative process of an Agile project (described in Chapter 4) helps to contain the risk, any significant project will require a large number of meetings to discover what the requirements really are, how to prioritize and sequence them, and what they really mean for the system implementation. Sorry to condemn you to this fate.

The sequence of phases can be as important as the amount of effort applied to the project, because the sequence of features determines which system benefits are visible to the users and sponsors. Unfortunately, even with SFDC some amount of effort will be required for enablers—infrastructure, integration, data cleansing, analysis, and testing—that don't deliver any specific feature (even though no feature would be possible without the invisible items). The resource for this infrastructure work needs to be planned first, before the visible-feature work is planned. However, always have *something* for the users.

THE ART OF THE QUICK WIN

From the outset, it's important to develop a wide collection of user-visible features that can be liberally sprinkled through the schedule to maintain the perception that progress is being made and that the project is delivering business value on a frequent basis. This "quick win" list gives the project leader a tool to manage expectations and counteract a known negative (e.g., "For the next two weeks, you can't do X, but we've given you this cool new feature Y to make your day go better"). Sometimes, the quick win prevents a problem from ever occurring again. At other times, it creates an alert to automatically flag unusual situations or adds a new "toy" that keeps users interested.

The quick win doesn't have to involve a lot of technology—the less, the better—and it should *never* involve a lot of work. It can be something as simple as a "mashup" with a traffic map so reps can figure out which route to drive to get to their appointments. Fortunately, SFDC's AppExchange has more than 1,500 free add-ons that provide features for users. Early in your project, do a survey of the AppExchange to see which freebies you can drop into the system during the implementation. Create a calendar of the "goody drops" and reschedule them as needed during the project.

The project leader needs to creatively identify other opportunities for quick wins. Sometimes, just putting data in one place can create several opportunities for wins. For example, if you put all your employees' contact information into SFDC, which kind of reports could be generated? How about a mailing list for HR or a birthday list for the administrative employees? These featurettes may take 10 minutes to implement, but each one can give you a week's worth of breathing room.

A project that devotes more than two-thirds of the effort to things without visible results will have a tough time surviving in most organizations.

The project phases should start with the core of SFDC and then add system extensions, external data, and external system integrations on top of a stable base. This order is preferred for two reasons: technical simplicity and user training. Users rarely have patience for training sessions lasting even an hour, so the amount of change you present to them during each session must be fairly small. You want users to become proficient with the core of the system that's immediately relevant to their jobs before you focus them on the fancier parts. Chapter 5 provides much more detail on the best practices in training.

The early schedule for a deployment will look something like Table 1-3. Note that this schedule is realistic *only for a very small implementation of SFDC and a proficient implementation team.*

TABLE 1-3   Schedule for Small- to Medium-Sized Company SFDC Project Phases

Phase	Description	Start Date	Completion Date	Current Status	Business Processes	Affected Departments
1	Lead capture and routing	3-Mar	17-Mar	Done	Pipeline formation	Marketing, Sales
1	Campaigns and Web site integration	3-Mar	24-Mar	Done	Pipeline formation	Marketing
1	Historic lead import, 1 year	3-Mar	1-Apr	Done	Pipeline formation	Marketing
1	Lead scoring and qualification	18-Mar	7-Apr	Done	Pipeline formation	Marketing, Sales
2	Opportunity creation	8-Apr	15-Apr	Done	Pipeline formation	Sales
2	Basic forecasting reports	15-Apr	22-Apr	Done	Pipeline management	Sales
2	Opportunity aging and backtrack alerts	15-Apr	29-Apr	Done	Pipeline management	Sales
2	Advanced forecasting	23-Apr	5-May	In progress	Pipeline management	Sales, Finance, Executives
2	Order-level quoting	1-May	15-May	In progress	Quote to invoice	Sales, Finance
2	Line-item-level quoting	16-May	1-Jun	Not started	Quote to invoice	Sales, Finance
3	Historic opportunity import, 1 year	16-May	15-Jun	Not started	Quote to invoice	Sales, Finance, Support
3	Historic opportunity import, 3 years	16-Jun	16-Aug	Not started	Quote to invoice	Sales, Finance, Support
3	Contract import, 1 year	16-May	15-Jun	Not started	Support and renewals	Sales, Finance, Support
3	Contract import, 3 years	16-Jun	16-Aug	Not started	Support and renewals	Sales, Finance, Support
3	Support ticket integration	16-May	1-Aug	Not started	Support and renewals	Support

TABLE 1-3   Schedule for Small- to Medium-Sized Company SFDC Project Phases (*Continued*)

Phase	Description	Start Date	Completion Date	Current Status	Business Processes	Affected Departments
3	Advanced forecasting reports and alerts	16-May	15-Jun	Not started	Pipeline management	Sales, Finance, Executives
3	Advanced campaign reports	16-May	15-Jun	Not started	Pipeline formation	Marketing
3	Dashboards	16-May	1-Jun	Not started	Executive management	Executives

Following are some guidelines to use as a sanity check on your schedule. Note that these recommendations are *minimums*, so it's fine if your schedule assumes slower progress. Many of these tasks can be carried out in parallel, so they may overlap on the calendar.

- Initial SFDC bring-up, including basic configuration of users, roles, profiles, page layouts, territory assignments, security, and basic user training: 4 person-weeks per 100 users or operating country.

- Integration with your company's Web site and Web advertising campaigns: 1 person-week for a simple static system; 4 person-weeks for a full content-management system.

- Integration with external email blasting or marketing automation systems: 1 person-week per system, but bugs and testing may make this much longer.

- Preparation for data import/migration: 2 person-days on the learning curve for each data source.

- Lead information import, including data cleansing, deduping, reorganizing, and enrichment: 1,000 to 10,000 records per person-day depending on what kind of shape your data is in.[12]

---

12. Data need to be cleaned of errors (typos, bad entries), normalized (e.g., state names changed to ISO-standard codes), and validated (e.g., checking that the postal code corresponds with the state or province name). These tasks are trivial if all relevant data reside in one system and your existing processes automatically clean data as those data are used. Of course, the more data you have, the more different ways it can be messed up (particularly if the data have been imported from one system to another over several years). The worst-case scenario is having to cross-check system data with paper records or unstructured files (such as email, Word, or PDFs), as often happens with contracts. You may need to hire student interns to help with this process. In these cases, it's important to import only the essential data and to carefully assess the business value of processing another year's worth of historical records.

- `Account` import, including account renaming and hierarchy creation, deduping, and enrichment: 500 to 5,000 records per person-day depending on how many sources of "accounts" you have and the shape of the data.

- `Contact` information import, including data cleansing, deduping, reorganizing, and enrichment: 500 to 5,000 records per person-day, depending on what kind of shape your data is in.

- `Lead/contact activity` and `campaign history`, including data cleansing, deduping, reorganization, and enrichment: 500 to 5,000 records per person-day depending on what kind of shape your data is in.

- `Opportunity history` import, including creation of historical `accounts`, `contacts`, `notes`, and `attachments`, as necessary; data cleansing; deduping; reorganizing; and enrichment: 40 to 5,000 records per person-day depending on what kind of shape your data is in.

- `Price list`, product structures (SKUs), and quoting rules: 20 to 200 line items per person-day depending on the complexity of your products, pricing models, business rules, and update history. Due to the nature of price lists, integrating the full price list may require several weeks of additional analysis and restructuring.

- `Contract history` import, including data cleansing, deduping, reorganizing, and enrichment: 50 to 500 records per person-day depending on the shape your data is in. Many companies actually have to scan or key in data from paper contracts, which obviously means even lower productivity than indicated here.

- Customer `asset` inventory import (such as serial numbers, license keys, and other purchase history info): 500 to 5,000 records per person-day depending on what kind of shape your data is in.

- Support "ticket," "`case`," or "customer incident" data import, including creation of historical `accounts`, `contacts`, `notes`, and `attachments`, as necessary; data cleansing; deduping; reorganizing; and enrichment: 40 to 5,000 records per person-day depending on what kind of shape your data is in.

- Internal `reports` and `dashboards`: 1 person-week for the initial "toy" versions, although just the meetings to decide about the reports and modify them can take that long. Note that reports and dashboards will continue to evolve, so expect this effort to require several person-weeks of work over the first year of system use.

- External `reports`, data analysis, and business intelligence: Several person-weeks, although it may take much longer depending on the amount of data to be analyzed and the tools used.

- Workflows, alerts, and basic automation: 1 person-week for the initial set, although the meetings you'll need for making decisions about policies and business rules can often take much longer. There is often a surprising lack of clarity about sales territories, compensation plans, business rules, and other automation essentials.

- Integration with external systems: No estimate is possible without a technical analysis of the two systems. Even though several SFDC partners provide out-of-the-box connectors to scores of external software packages, in most cases significant extra work is required after the initial connector is installed. Often, the two systems cannot be perfectly synchronized, so extensive data manipulation may be required to reconcile the two systems' data sets.

It is almost impossible to budget too much time for data cleansing and integration projects. Don't cheap out on this—it will only hurt the project in the long run.

Agile Project Metrics

Agile projects aren't a marathon: they are a series of short sprints that are focused around a short-term deliverable that's visible and valuable to the business. Agile projects are not managed like conventional waterfall projects, and they can't be measured with simplistic check-the-box and compare-the-numbers metrics either. In preparing the business case and early project plan, the following lists represent the key success factors for each sprint:

- Sprint variances from stated schedule:
  - Did feature development stop on time?
  - Was code integration done every night?
  - Did the final tests start on time?
  - Did the sprint complete on schedule?
- Sprint compliance with coding standards:
  - What percentage of new variables have data definitions?
  - What percentage of the classes or modules have unit tests?
  - What percentage of lines of code were covered by tests?
  - How many test records did the tests use?
  - How many outcomes (variations on expected results) were evaluated by the tests?

- Sprint variances for stated budget (or level of effort):

  ➥ Did the sprint consume unbudgeted resources such as staff developers, contractors or test resources?

  ➥ Did it not consume budgeted resources that could or should have been allocated elsewhere?

- Sprint compliance:

  ➥ Did the sprint break any deployment or security rules?

  ➥ Did the release go through the required audits and reviews?

  ➥ Did the release generate any items that need to be remediated in future sprints?

- Sprint business value:

  ➥ How many value points were supposed to have been delivered by the sprint, and how many actually were?

  ➥ How much of the sprint effort was infrastructure and refactoring to keep the code flexible to accommodate business needs in an upcoming sprint?

- Sprint repeatability:

  ➥ Can the team continue to do sprints in this way without team burnout or other side effects of heroic effort?

  ➥ Has the team created a brief postmortem document and lessons learned on personnel, organizational, and technical issues?

Avoiding the Big Bang Project

Throughout the process of "selling" the Salesforce.com project, getting the budget, and allocating the staff, expectations are being set about all the problems that will be solved. During this process, expectations are being set about the schedule as well—and often a fixed date (usually the first day of a fiscal quarter) emerges as an important corporate milestone. Finally, management develops expectations about the nature of the deployment, usually focusing on a system cutover, where users switch from the old way of doing things to the new system. And almost always, **all of these expectations will prove to be wrong.**

This story is as old as the computer industry itself. Fred Brooks's classic *The Mythical Man Month* (Addison-Wesley, 1995) describes how the larger the systems project, the more likely it is to be late. Even better, the further a project is into its schedule, the more likely it is that increasing the staffing and investment would make it *even later.*

The complete-system launch, sometimes called a Big Bang project, just doesn't work for software. It can work when there is military-style command and control: the Manhattan project, Operation Desert Storm, and the Apollo program are shining examples. But in business systems, it's hard to find examples where a Big Bang was a big success. Businesses don't have tight military hierarchies, and IT has a culture of trying to accommodate new business requirements during the project. This accommodation and tendency toward scope creep—particularly in software—is a poisonous cocktail. The Standish Group, an IT consultancy, published a series of studies that extensively analyzed failed IT projects. *The Chaos Reports* concluded that overblown requirements and overzealous adherence to large, monolithic deliveries were key warning signs of failed projects.

We discuss this issue in detail in Chapter 4. For now, be aware that the most important thing the project team can do before any project work begins is to warn executives and **avoid three things:**

- Fake, vague, or overstated requirements

- Infrequent project milestones

- Large, complex, monolithic project deliverables

Scope Creep Is the Enemy

Scope creep is one of the most dangerous things that can happen to a project, and the danger grows in tandem with the size and length of the effort. This problem occurs whenever a requirement is stretched, an assumption is made that "we can fit that in," or an *even better idea* is proposed by problem-solving executives.

The chief symptom of scope creep: the requirements list grows while the project is under way. Because items aren't removed from the priority list, the number of deliverables grows even though the budget and schedule are unchanged (or worse, are being overspent by the project). There's a particular temptation to load up the requirements even further whenever a project needs to get an extended schedule or extra budget, even though it should be obvious that the project is already at risk of underdelivering.

The only solution for scope creep is vigilance among everyone on the project team, regular management reviews to root out new creepy requirements, a very persuasive project leader, and consistency on the part of executives. The project leader must develop political skills to escalate scope-creep issues without angering the people who are proposing the additional Great Things for the project.

Even if the project has been sold with a lofty set of goals and tight Big Bang deadlines, it is important to quickly move to a phased approach. This isn't just because of the IT laws of physics; it's also human nature. Put simply, change management and confidence building take time. For even small companies, reset executive expectations by making the following arguments:

- We all know what the desired end-state is going to be, and those goals have been agreed to. But until the project is fairly far along, we can't know which problems we'll find in our data, precisely how business processes need to change, or exactly what every user will need.

- Given this inevitable uncertainty, the best way to achieve our goals is to rapidly deliver a small part of the project that is big enough to *provide value to the business*. This first delivery will give users a chance to learn the system and provide real-world feedback that will improve later system deliveries.

- Delivery after the first phase should be incremental, with each cycle providing a new element of value to the business. Having small, frequent deliveries makes it more likely we'll have happy users and low risk while meeting budgetary and schedule goals.

In making these arguments, the trick is to find the right "cornerstone functionality" to deploy for each phase, paired with the internal constituency you want to leverage. This decision making is profiled in detail for each phase, as described in Chapter 4, but as part of selling the project, you need to establish the constituency for the first phase's subsystem right now.

The best way to select the subsystem is to answer this question: Which system element could be deployed the soonest and deliver real value to a meaningful constituency? By producing a quick win, you earn credibility for the project as well as users for the system.

Outsourcing

Almost inevitably, you will need to use some outsource resources to assist in the project implementation, and you'll want at least budgetary placeholders for them. There are many tasks that your internal team *shouldn't want to get good at*. Even so, you cannot outsource everything—your team must be involved in defining business rules, performing data extraction, reviewing prototypes, validating data conversion, doing acceptance testing, and, of course, managing the project. One thing to insist on is a full "technology transfer" from any consultant you use, so that your team becomes self-sufficient in any area of ongoing development, maintenance, and administration.

In evaluating and choosing vendors, follow these rules of thumb:

- The cloud vendor's consultants will know more about the *internal* workings of their product than any partner consultant can. They will also have direct access to product engineering and will have several back-door tricks that can save time and make their prices a bargain. For internal extensions, customizations, scripting, rule setting, query design, and other deep-dive projects *directly* related to their own products, the vendors' consultants are likely to be the best choice. However, they are less likely to be the right people for external integrations or business process design.

- A specialist system integrator with a practice dedicated to SFDC or other cloud product is likely to know best how to do external work that integrates across applications. However, these individuals' level of knowledge and skill regarding business processes vary dramatically. In fact, many firms that are fully qualified at the technical level have zero capability when it comes to understanding and optimizing business processes. Check references before you make specific task allocations!

- A technical "coding shop" typically will be very good in its particular domain (e.g., enhancing a CMS-driven Web site or an external order-management system), but the individuals who bid on your project may not have experience with Web services and high-speed integration using SOAP, ReST, or JSON.[13] Even though most cloud applications use Web services for integration, every vendor uses the core technology a different way. For this reason, it's important to check the vendor's experience with SFDC's APIs and any AppExchange products you're planning to use. As always, references are more meaningful than vendor claims.

- A consultant who already works with your company has a natural advantage over outsiders. In addition to already being "connected" in your organization, the incumbent consultant is much more likely to know a lot about your technical environment and at least something about your business processes. Check with your IT organization to find out who is already under contract. If you've got only

---

13. Many readers won't know what these APIs are, but that's okay because they're a great litmus test for system integrators. Ask them to explain it to you: if they don't know that SOAP stands for "Simple Object Access Protocol" or ReST stands for "Representational State Transfer" or JSON stands for "JavaScript Object Notation" and that these are the ways to join applications (or Web services) together in a light-weight, loosely coupled fashion, maybe you should look elsewhere. SFDC has a rich set of these Web service APIs that let you securely access and manipulate almost any SFDC data from other applications. Ask would-be integrators which version of the APIs they've used (if they aren't up to version 28 or so, they probably aren't up to snuff).

a few person-months of work to do, the incumbent's learning-curve advantage may be a decisive one.

- Data cleansing and enrichment houses can be very economical (using tools and offshore resources unavailable to you), but this part of the project must be done *correctly and completely* to be at all meaningful. Check whether the vendor has done work on your size database in an SFDC project: most have not, and they'll experience a serious learning curve. Check references carefully to confirm the details, because offshore data cleansing/enrichment operations tend to overstate their capabilities and are very *in*efficient at learning to do new things.

- Management consultants, sales process consultants, and organizational design specialists understand the human side of your business processes better than any other vendor type. Large organizations typically need to use these consultants to optimize business processes, redesign sales procedures, and set policies. However, these consultants are rarely in a position to do implementation work, because they don't understand the inner workings of SFDC and other systems well enough. They also have a tendency to make recommendations that are technically very difficult or even unfeasible to implement. So absolutely include them on your team to design best practices and increase the speed of user adoption—but do not expect them to implement much in SFDC.

No matter which kinds of vendors you use, it is essential that you have a positive, cooperative relationship with them. Adversarial relationships just don't work—in terms of price, quality, or schedule. That said, it's essential that you manage each vendor relationship tightly. Although you don't manage a vendor in the same way you do an employee, vendors are every bit as important to project success and budget as any other team members. Weekly checkpoints and monthly scorecards are essential for all vendors. This goes double for offshore providers.

Generally speaking, there are several areas that you *don't* want to outsource. It typically doesn't pay to have an outside team learn the peculiarities of your old homegrown systems. An outsourcer should not be making policy and process decisions for your company (they can make recommendations, but *you* have to own the decision).

Even if a major technology is implemented by outsiders, your internal team needs to have ongoing capability and knowledge. For example, you'll want to be able to make simple system modifications without calling in a vendor, and it's a good idea to be able to make minor changes to cope with the inevitable upgrades of external systems or minor updates to business rules. In your resource allocation, think through which of the tasks *must* be done internally, which would be best done through a vendor, and which should be done jointly.

Setting Executive Expectations

Executives have been trained to see a business case that's firm and a schedule with a clear end-date. Unfortunately, large systems projects don't fit that model too often. And Agile project management, which is designed to make quality deliveries of only what's really needed in the shortest amount of time, creates a frustrating uncertainty with executives. They want to see a nice, tidy roadmap—and it's really asking for the wrong thing. The project leader must figure out how to bridge that gap.

The first step is to convince the executives that CRM systems and processes must be adaptable to evolving business needs, so they are never completed the way a building would be. The next step is to focus attention on the initial cutover (or go-live) date, including the absolute minimum criteria that must be met to achieve this goal. Most significant SFDC implementations are replacements for previous systems, so it should be fairly straightforward to identify the criteria for the new system to be good enough to support the switchover. It is important to use terms like *good enough* or *acceptance criteria* to communicate that the system will continue to evolve after the go-live date. Some functional areas need to be only at the 50% level at cutover time to support the business.

As always, perfectionism does not pay. By focusing the discussion on what is really needed to support a given business process on a day-to-day basis, you can get realistic objectives and feedback on which tradeoffs could be acceptable at the go-live date. For example, it may be okay to *manually* approve orders for the first month of operation, so as to make sure that the automatic order approval rules accurately reflect your business policies.

The executives need to know that functionality will be delivered incrementally and that their staff will need to play active roles in assuring quality over several phases. Executives also need to know when the key business processes affecting their specific departments will be done. Consequently, we recommend organizing the presentation of the schedule in two ways: chronologically, for the overview perspective, and organizationally, for each executive. Keeping the schedule in a spreadsheet (which can be generated from your Gantt charting tool) allows rapid creation of these executives' views, as shown in Figure 1-4. In this view, many tasks are repeated so that each executive can see the impact on his or her specific organization without having to refer elsewhere.

One of the biggest challenges of setting executive expectations is the iceberg phenomenon: the toughest work in the project is in infrastructure and data cleanup that has no visible feature, no immediate win for any department. Most executives don't have patience for these intricacies of the project, and the best way to talk about them is in terms of "laying the foundation" for the features they want to see. Foundational work typically continues throughout the project, and it's often best to depict it during all phases. Even so, every single phase needs to deliver *some* interesting feature to at least

Phase	Description	Start Date	Completion Date	Current Status	Business Processes
Executives					
2	Advanced forecasting	23-Apr	5-May	In progress	Pipeline management
3	Advanced forecasting reports and alerts	16-May	15-Jun	Not started	Pipeline management
3	Dashboards	16-May	1-Jun	Not started	Executive management
Sales					
1	Lead capture and routing	3-Mar	17-Mar	Done	Pipeline formation
1	Lead scoring and qualification	18-Mar	7-Apr	Done	Pipeline formation
2	Opportunity creation	8-Apr	15-Apr	Done	Pipeline formation
2	Basic forecasting reports	15-Apr	22-Apr	Done	Pipeline management
2	Opportunity aging and backtrack alerts	15-Apr	29-Apr	Done	Pipeline management
2	Advanced forecasting	23-Apr	5-May	In progress	Pipeline management
2	Order-level quoting	1-May	15-May	In progress	Quote to invoice
2	Line-item-level quoting	16-May	1-Jun	Not started	Quote to invoice
3	Historic opportunity import, 1 year	16-May	15-Jun	Not started	Quote to invoice
3	Historic opportunity import, 3 years	16-Jun	16-Aug	Not started	Quote to invoice
3	Contract import, 1 year	16-May	15-Jun	Not started	Support and renewals
3	Contract import, 3 years	16-Jun	16-Aug	Not started	Support and renewals
3	Support ticket integration	16-May	1-Aug	Not started	Support and renewals
3	Advanced forecasting reports and alerts	16-May	15-Jun	Not started	Pipeline management
Marketing					
1	Lead capture and routing	3-Mar	17-Mar	Done	Pipeline formation
1	Campaigns and Web site integration	3-Mar	24-Mar	Done	Pipeline formation
1	Historic lead import, 1 year	3-Mar	1-Apr	Done	Pipeline formation
1	Lead scoring and qualification	18-Mar	7-Apr	Done	Pipeline formation
3	Advanced campaign reports	16-May	15-Jun	Not started	Pipeline formation
Finance					
2	Advanced forecasting	23-Apr	5-May	In progress	Pipeline management
2	Order-level quoting	1-May	15-May	In progress	Quote to invoice
2	Line-item-level quoting	16-May	1-Jun	Not started	Quote to invoice
3	Historic opportunity import, 1 year	16-May	15-Jun	Not started	Quote to invoice
3	Historic opportunity import, 3 years	16-Jun	16-Aug	Not started	Quote to invoice
3	Contract import, 1 year	16-May	15-Jun	Not started	Support and renewals
3	Contract import, 3 years	16-Jun	16-Aug	Not started	Support and renewals
3	Advanced forecasting reports and alerts	16-May	15-Jun	Not started	Pipeline management
Support					
3	Historic opportunity import, 1 year	16-May	15-Jun	Not started	Quote to invoice
3	Historic opportunity import, 3 years	16-Jun	16-Aug	Not started	Quote to invoice
3	Contract import, 1 year	16-May	15-Jun	Not started	Support and renewals
3	Contract import, 3 years	16-Jun	16-Aug	Not started	Support and renewals

FIGURE 1-4   Executive's overview of deployment phases

one department, so the executives don't become frustrated with the amount of effort expended on "invisible stuff."

Getting the Right Resources Committed

At some point, there will be a meeting to make the decision to move forward. Usually, these meetings focus on the immediate expenditures. Unfortunately, the commitments for ongoing expenses and effort are assumed away or quickly forgotten—and that's dangerous.

For a truly successful large-system implementation, the following funds must be assigned to the project *at the initial go/no-go meeting*:

- Initial procurement funding for the system, add-on products, and any hardware or IT resources required

- Ongoing funding for the recurring fees, added to the budget for at least 2 years

- Fees for consultants and service providers needed to configure, extend, integrate, and deploy the system

- Fees for training courses and user-group sessions offered by the vendors

- Dedicated personnel, typically in the form of a time allocation *with specific measured goals or MBOs*:

  - Make ongoing priority calls about requirements and schedules

  - Decide policy issues and business rules

  - Design approval cycles, exception handling, and workflows

  - Do actual work on the SFDC system, including data cleansing, record imports, and other housekeeping tasks

  - Work on external systems such as data modeling, data dumps, enabling external interfaces, doing testing, and other tasks

  - Assist with IT infrastructure tasks (security audits, installing wiki software, server deployments, and so forth)

  - Do technical tests of the SFDC system and validation of its external integrations

  - Do user testing of the system

  - Run final acceptance tests

- Regular (brief) intervals of executive time to escalate issues, break logjams, reallocate resources, and do final approvals

Surprisingly, most executives tend to focus on the top of this list. In reality, the items near the bottom tend to cause the biggest issues with projects over time.

At the meeting, you'll also need to set general expectations—preferably quantitative metrics of success and criteria for a successful deployment—for the first phase. Without these objective measurements, executives tend to remember only the date for the first phase deployment, which tends to put people in happy-ears mode. Make sure to start the project off on the right foot, with documented budgets, schedules, and success criteria.

GETTING THE MOST FROM SFDC

- Focus the project on a few meaningful business goals.
- Orient requirements around user archetypes and business processes: don't get bogged down in feature-itis.
- Ruthlessly prioritize. Use Agile so you don't overinvest in customizations.
- Don't overdocument. Keep things at the PowerPoint level for now.
- Plan to work incrementally, delivering something valuable every 6 weeks.
- Focus the delivery plan on user adoption and quality data (everything great about CRM flows from these).

FOR SMALL COMPANIES

- Identify one key problem to solve for sales, and set up a team of three to get it done this quarter.
- Focus the business case on revenue.
- Use AppExchange add-ons liberally.
- Try to avoid custom code.

FOR LARGE ENTERPRISES

- Identify the business process issues that are getting in the way of leverage.
- Base the business case on both revenue upside and improved leverage.
- Look for cross-departmental efficiencies and leverage.
- Dedicate serious time for your staff to handle business process, policy, and compliance issues throughout the life of the CRM project.
- Make sure to develop internal capacity to maintain and enhance the system over time.

CHAPTER 2

Reports and Data

> *A man's judgment cannot be better than the information on which he has based it. Give him the truth and he may still go wrong, but give him no news or present him only with distorted and incomplete data . . . and you destroy his whole reasoning process.*
>
> —*Arthur Hays Sulzberger*

Reports are, for many users, the most relevant part of a CRM system. Reports are the first way that users approach the data, measure business activity, and monitor the business processes. Reports thus need to be meaningful and based on accurate data. The first part of this chapter explains how to use report design to elicit requirements from the executives who will be using the system. The rest of the chapter focuses on the underlying data because no one will believe the reports or use the system if the data are confusing or a waste of time.

For many users, the way they understand a system is through the presentation of data. Users don't care about how a feature works; they care about what the dashboard looks like or what the report tells them. To users, *data* means "visibility."

In Chapter 1, you analyzed system requirements at a general level—that is, as high-level functionality supporting business processes. That perspective is fine for the abstract thinkers in your company, but people don't usually think in terms of business processes. To understand what business users *really* need, work with them to describe the reports they need to see or the charts they use in presentations and meetings.

This chapter describes how to scope detailed system requirements through report and screen design. This process needs to be done early to uncover the needs for remote system access, object relationships, and data quality *before* any of the project work begins. Even if a specific need won't be satisfied for several months, it's important to understand the need and make provisions for the required data now to avoid painting yourself into a corner later.

> ### START WITH WHAT YOU HAVE
>
> Almost any SFDC implementation is a replacement for some other system. If your company uses Outlook and Excel for all of its CRM needs, or even if your only tools are a blackboard and a legal pad, SFDC will replace your current "system." Start the process by identifying which information is currently visible and reported on. Almost invariably in the existing system, there is some way of interacting, viewing, and reporting on the following items:
>
> - Prospects (`leads`)
> - Customers (`accounts`)
> - Sales representative activity (`tasks`)
> - Pipeline and forecast (`opportunities`)
> - Revenue (closed `opportunities`)
> - Contracts (`contracts`)
> - Support issues (`cases`)

The Executive View

Start at the top of the CRM-using organization, looking for the highest-level person who reviews these data on at least a monthly basis. Typically, that person is the VP of sales, but the specific job title of the individual who fulfills this role depends on your organization. Interview that person and find out the *one critical report* he or she needs to do the job, and the five to seven pieces of information the individual needs (whether those data are part of the current system or not) to make key decisions. Here are example questions to ask:

- How often do you look at the information?
- Why do you look there, and what are you trying to measure or control?
- Which decisions do you make on the basis of the data—and what actions do you take?
- How do these data affect the things that *you* are measured on?
- What incentives are in place for the people below you to do well according to the data?
- If you question the data, how would you validate it? What information or other source would you compare it to?

- If you found an error in the data, who would you talk to about getting it fixed?

- Which other items of related information would *actually* change your behavior or alter a decision?

- Which comparisons (e.g., to history, industry norms) are meaningful for these data?

Don't spend too much time trying to figure out what the executives would also find useful in an ideal world. The hard reality is that many an executive's thoughts on extra reports and data are nearly impossible to implement and wouldn't be as meaningful as that manager might think (since he or she has somehow survived without having the extra information until now). Even so, it's worth investigating executives' answers to set helpful context about the system behaviors and data requirements.

Next, ask a few questions about the usage occasions and the look and feel of the data— the data *presentation*:

- For information that is ad hoc or a quick lookup:

  ⟶ How do you find this information: through a search (by name or keyword), a view (e.g., "today's leads" or "New York deals"), a bookmark (e.g., "the things I was looking at yesterday"), or something else?

  ⟶ How long does it take you to find the information? How many attempts and false starts are involved?

  ⟶ What is the next step you take (e.g., once you've found the person/account/ deal/case you're looking for, what do you do next)?

- For information that is for personal review or analysis:

  ⟶ Which form is most convenient for looking at this information (e.g., a report, an Excel spreadsheet, or a chart)?

  ⟶ What's the occasion (is this a weekly meeting with the boss or an annual strat- egy review)?

  ⟶ Which decisions are being made because of reported data? What is the real business objective of the report or analysis?

- For information that is for daily or weekly "health checks":

  ⟶ Which parts of this information need to be found on a graphical dashboard or a scorecard, and which parts need to be shown as a listing that can be easily manipulated?

➥ If the executive favors management by exception, which exceptions are being monitored? Which kinds of alerts are useful (e.g., automatically page me if a quote is for more than $100,000)?

- For information that is intended for presentation to management:

➥ What is the occasion, and what are the key success factors that need to be presented? Which decisions are being made?

➥ Which formats are being used (e.g., spreadsheet, pie chart, bar chart, time series graph)?

➥ In the preparations for these management meetings, which kinds of data problems need to be avoided? Can political fallout occur if the data is questioned? How is the management report or presentation validated and bulletproofed?

After completing this cycle with the head of the sales function, repeat the questionnaire with his or her executive peers who (should) have access to and interest in the CRM data: the head of marketing, VP of customer support, VP of consulting and training, and perhaps the CFO and CEO. Each set of answers should be recorded separately but must be reconciled against the other sets and budgetary realities. For example, if the CFO and VP of sales disagree about the meaning or consequences of data, it's important to get them talking to resolve the internal contradiction before any implementation begins. This area may require some political delicacy or even escalation to the SFDC project champion.

The View from the Trenches

The next step is to identify the 5 to (at most) 10 system users who will be looking at and interacting with SFDC data most intently on a daily basis. These people will likely be near the bottom of the organization, but they are on the front lines of lead generation, customer capture, shipments/fulfillment, customer support, and transactional truth. Ask these operational users the following questions:

- Which data screens or data views do you look at most often?

- Which actions or decisions do you take on the basis of the data?

- Which of your actions are triggered by changes in system data? What portion of your decisions or actions could be part of an automatic workflow?

- Which other items of information (i.e., data items or trend information) would actually change your decisions and actions?

- Which kinds of alerts or exception conditions need to be in force for your job? Which kinds of CRM data need to be monitored on at least a daily basis?

- Which reports do you run on a daily or weekly basis? Which data are being monitored by these reports?

- Which ad hoc reports or dashboards do you run? When are the standard reports or screens insufficient, and why?

- Which kinds of reports do you run to satisfy your immediate boss? What is the boss trying to measure or assess by running these reports?

Answers from each of the people surveyed should be recorded separately and analyzed for internal contradictions and gaps. If someone needs data that are not found in the system today, you need to figure out where those data will come from and who is going to enter and update them in the future.

New Things You Need to Measure

Businesses are measuring the business processes covered in CRM with increasing depth and detail. They have to: in many businesses, sales and marketing represent the single largest part of costs. So tiny improvements in efficiency and effectiveness drop straight to the bottom line.

It is critical that SFDC not be viewed by users as a Big Brother system that executives use to micromanage and punish workers. So it's important to not just measure the right things, but measure them the right *way*. Just because you can measure something or calculate a ratio, it doesn't make the result meaningful. That means avoiding measuring how busy you are (because that is easily gamed) or how lucky you are (because that is out of the worker's control). We'll go into this in Chapters 9, 10, and 11, but it's important to get this principle right at the very start of the project.[1]

Let's go through the ultimate cash-to-cash business process: from marketing campaigns to closed deals. You'll note that at the end of each list is an item called DO NOT MEASURE. Heed this advice.

Marketing—The Top of the Funnel (Chapter 10)

- **Campaigns:** The percentage of leads from purchased lists (should be 0.0%), the percentage of leads that are not tagged with a `campaign` (should be 0.0%), the percentage of lead actions (e.g., downloads) that are not tagged with a campaign (should be 0.0%), the total cost of executing each campaign, the number of new leads, the number of existing leads and contacts that were "retouched," the total

---

1. This section is full of highly opinionated, perhaps even cynical, material. You will find in these later chapters lots of text (*lots of text*) that explains the rationales that probably seem abrupt here.

number of converted leads, the total value of pipeline created, the total value of pipeline influenced, the total value of pipeline closed.

- **Lead management:** The number of hours between first lead capture and routing to the correct rep (in most cases, the "correct rep" is no one: it's the marketing automation system's job to robotically follow up on initial leads), the percentage of leads that are completely bad data and could never be used, the percentage of leads that were scored as marketing qualified (MQL) but were subsequently rejected as unqualified.

- **Lead nurturing (assuming that this is marketing's responsibility):** The average number of "touches" a lead receives in the first 30 days after initial capture, the total number of actions the lead has taken (e.g., collateral downloads, free trials), the number of total touches for each lead prior to conversion, the percentage of unsubscribes, the percentage of "hard bounces" (where you can no longer contact them), the percentage of nonresponsive leads (where there has been no activity for, say, 90 days).

- **DO NOT MEASURE:** The number of collateral pieces mailed, ad impressions, emails sent; the total number of leads; the cost per lead (all are misleading, if not just meaningless).

Account Development Reps—The First Line of Defense (Chapter 9)

- **Responsiveness:** The average length of time that leads sat in a queue or were assigned but sitting in open status, the percentage of dead leads that simply went stale (no action for, say, 7 days).

- **Communication:** The number of significant conversations with `leads` or `contacts` in which the call lasted more than 15 minutes in a given month.

- **Quality:** The percentage of `converted` leads that were rejected by sales as unqualified or that did not result in the creation of an opportunity.

- **Throughput:** The total value of pipeline created, the total value of pipeline influenced, the total value of pipeline closed.

- **Assists:** The total value of pipeline in which the account development rep helped move the deal along during the close process; the total value of pipeline actually closed by the rep, including renewals and upsells.

- **DO NOT MEASURE:** The number of dials, number of emails, average length of time on the phone, and so on (almost always misleading to management and demeaning to account development reps).

Sales—The Bottom Line (Chapter 9)

- **Adoption:** The percentage of reps logging in on a weekly basis.

- **Volume:** The number and value of sales cycles started (`opportunities` opened), the number of `quotes` issued, the number of `contracts` signed.

- **Velocity:** The average time in stage (or, conversely, number of stalled deals).

- **Results:** The percentage of wins, losses, and no-decisions; the number of new customers; the average deal size for new customers versus repeat customers; the percentage of repeat business; and the percentage of renewals/retained customers.

- **Forecasting:** The quarter-to-date (QTD) sales versus quarterly goal, actual bookings versus weekly expected achievement,[2] the number and value of unforecasted deals, and forecast accuracy.

- **Pipeline management:** The percentage of opportunities "moving backward" (decreasing in size or probability, or moving out in time), the number and dollar value of disappearing opportunities (deals dropping out of the quarter plus losses and no-decisions).

- **DO NOT MEASURE:** The number of dials, number of emails, number of meetings, average length of time on the phone, and so on (almost always misleading to management and demeaning to sales reps).

Customer Support—The Customers You Keep (Chapter 11)

- **Volume:** The number of new incidents created per week, the number of new defects/problems identified per week, the number of cases closed per week, the number of problems solved/solutions generated per week.

- **Responsiveness:** The customer-perceived time to resolve, the number of escalations, the number of service level agreement (SLA) violations.

- **Efficiency:** The percentage of problems solved (okay, deflected) through your knowledge base, the percentage of problems solved on the first call.

- **Satisfaction:** The percentage of case participants who were offered a survey, the percentage of participants who responded to the survey, the percentage of satisfied customers (as indicated by survey), the percentage of highly dissatisfied/at-risk customers (as indicated by complaints and case reopens).

---

2. This statistic tells management, "By week 4 of the quarter, we normally expect 20% of the total target to be closed; this quarter, we have only 15% closed."

- **DO NOT MEASURE:** The number of dials, number of emails, number of meetings, average length of time on the phone, and so on.

Social CRM and Customer Reputation (Chapter 9)

- **Audience size:** The number of followers in each social network you participate in; the number of likes, thumbs-ups, plus 1s, and so on.

- **Interaction:** The number of times prospects or customers contacted you via each social medium, the percentage of presales interactions handled in each social medium, the percentage of postsales/support interactions handled in each social medium.

- **Influence:** The number and value of pipeline deals influenced through a social media interaction (should be tagged with a `campaign` event).

- **Reputation:** The overall audience sentiment, customer audience sentiment, percentage of thumbs-down versus thumbs-up postings.

- **DO NOT MEASURE:** The total number of tweets, total number of ad impressions, unfiltered aggregates of exposure, and so on.

Business Model—Aggregating the Big Picture (Executive Summary)

- **Cost of customer acquisition:** The total advertising, marketing, presales consulting, sales, fulfillment, and collection costs of acquiring a new customer. (This is a surprisingly big number, often guaranteeing no profit in the first sale.)

- **Percentage of revenue coming from repeat business:** The percentage of revenues generated from existing and prior customers. (This should be your most profitable revenue.)

- **Percentage of customer base that's still active/current:** The number of accounts that have done business with you in the last year as a proportion of the total number of customers in the company history.

- **Customer lifetime revenue:** The total revenue spent per customer (whether active or not) over the entire company history. This includes all upsells, renewals, and repeat business.

- **Customer lifetime profitability:**[3] The total profits (*not* contribution margin) per customer over the entire company history. (Some of your biggest, most loyal customers by revenue will be unprofitable.)

---

3. It is important that you look at this figure over time, not as a snapshot. If you decide to get rid of your least profitable customers without making changes to your company's overhead, you'll instantly create a new batch of customers who look unprofitable.

Scoping the System via Report Mock-Ups

After completing these interviews, the business analyst should create a composite of the reports that will be needed. Using some fake data, a set of management reports should be mocked up in Excel and given to users to review. Likewise, key management dashboards[4] should be mocked up (either in Excel spreadsheets, Visio diagrams, or PowerPoint drawings). Make sure to include in the review cycle at least one highly quantitative/analytical person from both the marketing and the finance groups to make sure that their product, promotion, pricing, program, and profitability questions can be answered from the system's data. The layout and format of the mock-ups are not important, but the *content* of the mock-ups is critical to understanding the system requirements.

Check out SFDC's internal list of precanned reports (there are dozens of them in the system's `report` tab and dozens more freebies available for download in the AppExchange), and select the top 20 or so most relevant ones to your company. Use these templates as starting points for your mock-ups.

While preparing the report mock-ups, capture the information listed in Table 2-1 in the Comments area of Excel or in the Notes area of PowerPoint slides.

TABLE 2-1   Data Attributes

Semantics	What is the meaning of the data item, and what do changes in value signify to the rest of the business?
Data source and timeliness	What is the source of each data item? If the data elements come from outside the system, how "fresh" must the data be (e.g., daily refresh versus continuous update)? Can the data be updated by SFDC user entry (i.e., are the data read-write or read-only)?
Response/ reaction time	Which information must be acted on quickly, and what's the deadline? Which data are just reference or background information?
Accuracy	How accurate or detailed do the data need to be for each data item (e.g., does the report just need total units shipped to the customer or all specific model or serial numbers)? For example, it may not matter if an address is missing or erroneous, but it's usually a big deal if the company name or price is wrong.
Ownership	For the data native to the system,* which department is responsible for entering the data items? Which incentives and measurements need to be in place to make sure those personnel enter data quickly and accurately enough?

Continues

---

4. Often, users will describe dashboards that cannot be created with SFDC. Even so, the process provides important information about the kinds of reports and underlying data that are needed for a successful system rollout.

TABLE 2-1   Data Attributes (*Continued*)

Access	Which people should have access to the reports? Is there a need for access controls to hide certain pieces of sensitive information from certain people? Are any special controls needed on the reports for compliance reasons?
Thresholds	What is the threshold for "interesting values" for each data item? For example, transactions involving less than $1,000 may be handled according to one set of rules, those between $1,000 and $50,000 based on another set of rules, and those involving more than $50,000 by a different set of rules.
Trends	What are the trends or perspectives that need to be captured or communicated? How long can a trend go on before it changes a decision?
Alerts and triggers	For the fields that trigger alerts or start workflows (e.g., executive reviews or approval cycles), what is the triggering value? What is the function of the trigger, what alert should be issued, and what workflow (e.g., escalation, approval) should be started (if any)?
Supporting detail	When looking at a dashboard, which supporting "drill-down" data do users need to support investigation and understanding?
Significant relationships	What are meaningful relationships among data items? For example, if the average deal size is decreasing, but the total number of deals is increasing, is that a positive indicator for the business or a negative one?
Exports	Which `data` or `report` exports are needed from the system? Which spreadsheets need to be created on a regular basis, and who gets them? Which users should be authorized to get exports? Are any special controls needed on exports for compliance reasons?

*   These data are originally entered by hand into SFDC; they do not include information integrated from an external system feed or a historical import.

Once the `report` and `dashboard` needs have been captured for headquarters, it's important to get feedback from one of the international sales operations. The feedback from international staff will probably differ in important details, such as the required accuracy for the data or the meaning of specific thresholds. It's no problem for international users to interpret SFDC data differently, but you want to detect and document situations where they are looking at *different* data or would make *very different decisions* than the U.S. people would, given a specific situation or set of data. As before, you're looking for contradictions or gaps that need to be resolved before the CRM work begins.

The Crux: Semantics

Each of the international variations needs to be assessed for its impact upon the system screens, reports, and overall data design. Thanks to SFDC's sophistication, screens can be customized by user `profile` (including considerations like their business function and location), and reports can be tailored to almost any individual need. But SFDC's data model—which fields are each object, what they represent, what they mean—is singular and must hold true for *all* users and situations. So the data model is a big deal, and we discuss it later in this chapter.

To avoid confusion later, spend the time upfront to ensure a common understanding of the meaning and behavior of data. Be on the alert for data items where the clarity of the definitions *decreases* the more people ask about it. The ambiguities become really important when a data item is stored in two different systems and called by two different names. To get the complete meaning of these hydra-headed data items, you may have to survey a wide range of people—not only up and down the organization but across organizations.

Spend significant effort to understand the meaning and semantics of business-critical data so that no questions arise about such issues as the following:

- What does it mean to be a qualified `lead`?

- What are the criteria for `lead` conversion (that turns them into a `contact`)?

- What triggers the creation of an `opportunity`? Who does that?

- What are the stages an `opportunity` needs to go through to become a closed sale?

- What are the trigger events or conditions that move a prospect from one stage of the sales cycle to another, or a customer from one support status to another?

- How can we tell that a `quote` has been approved by management?

- Under what conditions would someone reopen an `opportunity` that was marked as lost?

- What is the definition of a customer?

- When is a customer business unit a division versus a separate `account`?

- When is a bundle of products a new `product`, and when is it just a promotional price?

- What are the vendor-specific objective evidence (VSOE) conditions that trigger revenue recognition?

- How do you reopen a `case` that was falsely closed?

- What items require special `approval processes`, and why?

- How do we handle customer `entitlements` for postsales support and warranty coverage?

It's amazing how much time you can waste in a meeting when there isn't a common understanding of the words *customer* and *deal*.

YOUR DATA DICTIONARY

As you collect all of the requirements for data items—both in SFDC and in other systems—you need to document the characteristics of each piece of data. Your data dictionary should be done either as an Excel spreadsheet (if you've got a fairly simple implementation), as a highly structured Word document (with change bars on so everyone can see the revision history), or as a Google Doc. It should contain most of the items indicated in Table 2-1, plus the following elements:

- **Meaning:** What is the data item's field name, description, and user prompt ("help bubble")?

- **Technical metadata:** What are the data type, number of characters/digits, allowable values, correlations/connections to other data items, rules/constraints about the data values, and so on?

- **Data ownership and security:** Who owns the data, who is allowed to see it, who is allowed to change it, and so on?

- **Provenance:** What is the original source of the data? How do we know the data in this item are correct and authoritative? Where are the data stored, and which systems modify the data values? Which audit trails are (or need to be) maintained?

- **Data quality:** What are the known issues with the quality of data in this field? Which kinds of interactions or changes could degrade the data quality?

The data dictionary file(s) should be posted to the project's wiki or Google Drive directory.

Reports—Inside versus Outside

SFDC has a powerful Web-based reporting system that is intuitive and useful for most initial data inquiries. Dozens of predefined reports come with the system, designed for marketing, sales, administrators, and executives. The reports can be generated quickly, are real time, are fairly intuitive, and produce charts that are at the core of dashboards. The report wizards let you access nearly every record in the system and modify the layout and filters in real time. It's practically the definition of what's possible in a Web-driven reporting tool.

A NOTE TO THE READER

Surprise! SFDC's notes *object can be very useful, but you can't report on them (or even view them as a list) from the standard system screens. The only way to get a compendium of* notes *is to export the data from SFDC and join them with their referring objects in an external tool. If that last sentence is nonsense to you, jump over to Chapter 7 and check out the "Essential Tools for Analytics" section.*

Unfortunately, SFDC's reports cannot be made very pretty, and the large ones are hard to read. To achieve good format control and fast data scanning, even the simplest reports should be exported to Excel (either using the `export details` button or via SFDC's `Office connector` plugin, which allows pulling down of reports from within Excel). For all executive meetings and external presentations, use Excel for report reformulation, formatting, and arranging. There are also some nice report formatting engines that run on top of SFDC, and they aren't very costly.

More importantly for the data junkies, most SFDC reports can fully explore only a couple of objects[5] at a time. Although several reports join data from three or even four objects (e.g., `opportunities` with `products`), and `custom report types` provides amazing flexibility in the wizard system, it's all too common for product marketing and business analysts to need complicated object joins. You are almost certain to find at least one executive asking for a report that *cannot be created* in SFDC's internal report system.

To create these more sophisticated reports, there are five approaches. Any of them will work, but different project teams tend to gravitate to only one of them.

- Export the raw data to Excel, and use `VLOOKUP` formulas to create the joins and `Pivot Tables` to design the views that are needed. The advantages here are intuitiveness for Excel users, the ability to rapidly create charts and exports that are easily used by the rest of the organization, and the power of VB macros. Note that this strategy does not work for data tables involving more than a million rows[6] and is quite slow for tables beyond 100,000 rows.

---

5. Object-oriented purists can ignore this footnote. SFDC is fairly object oriented, and it organizes all data in a small number of hierarchical business objects. For example, almost all of the information about people is stored in either the `lead` or `contact` object. Information about deals is stored in `opportunity`, `assets`, and `contract` objects. SFDC's internal reports usually provide information on just one or two of these objects, so if you want to know about all people in the system, you have to write at least three reports (for `leads`, `contacts`, and `users`).

6. Although modern versions of Excel can handle lots of rows, SFDC's Excel connector cannot deal with any more than 32,000. Using SFDC's `data loader` instead, Excel can be filled to the rafters with records, but the spreadsheets take a long time to open and can be amazingly slow to manipulate. You can speed up Excel by turning off auto-calculation in Excel before you load big spreadsheets.

- Export the raw data to Access or your business's favorite desktop relational database, and use that tool's database view design and join capabilities. The advantages here are power, speed, programmability, and intuitiveness for Access users. Access can easily crunch a million rows or more, and for purely relational problems, it's more straightforward than working in Excel. (Of course, Access and Excel can be used together, particularly for formatting and chart generation, but be mindful of problems with CSV files discussed in "The Joy of Regex" in Chapter 3.)

- Use a plugin reporting engine (such as Conga or DrawLoops) that supports more complex queries and nice formatting (producing Excel, Word, PDF, or even Power-Point files). These engines pull all the data from SFDC on demand, so there's no data extraction or external database to think about and manage. The advantage here is relatively low cost and nicer output than the previous two approaches.

- Export the raw data to an analytics engine, particularly for reports that need to be generated on a regular basis. These report engines are typically optimized for creating a large number of reports, but they can also be used for powerful one-time-use reports on an ad hoc basis. Several report engines are available in SFDC's AppExchange, but these engines can be expensive and require user training.

- Export the raw data to a data warehouse or business intelligence (BI) tool. The advantage here is speed and analytical power: for ad hoc what-if and multi-dimensional analysis, no other option can come close to this strategy. Although these tools are expensive and require extensive user training, they can illuminate issues and make discoveries better than any other approach. They also can generate graphics that can silence any debate about the validity or relevance of the data.

REPORTING ON OLD DATA

SFDC's reports are real time and cannot realistically report on last week's view of the data. Although you can create `analytic snapshots` *to give summaries of history, you have to set them up so they can start recording what you want to report on over time. Even with that, reporting on data that are more than 12 months old can be quite tricky in SFDC—data disappear from view if you don't ask for that information in exactly the right way.[7] If you routinely need to do a lot of historical analysis, you probably want to dump a copy of the old data into a data warehouse or BI tool database.*

---

7. Using the Data Loader's `Export All` button or the API's `QueryAll` SOQL verb.

You'll notice that none of these strategies include the idea of *modifying* the report data outside of SFDC. That's because it is a sublimely horrible idea. The goal is to have SFDC be the system of record for much, if not all, of the customer relationship. Although it's okay to *filter and summarize* data outside the system, actually *changing* values in the external reporting system would be—in the immortal words of Harold Ramis in *Ghostbusters*—"very bad." If you find data that mess up external reports, fix the data at their origin—whether in SFDC, in an external system from which SFDC pulls source data, or in a business process that is causing data pollution. If instead you make the data fixes in an external reporting system, you are unlikely to document what you did or to replicate those changes in the original source. As a consequence, the external reports will no longer agree with SFDC's internal reports and dashboards, undermining the credibility of the system *and* the data analyst at the same time.

BIG DATA

Generally speaking, CRM systems aren't likely to produce Big Data. Sure, your Web site and marketing automation system (MAS) can, but it's very unlikely with SFDC. Although SFDC can easily store and process tens of millions of records, it's unlikely to do so unless you're in a serious B2C business. Are you really going to have 5 million leads or 1 million accounts?

That said, SFDC may hold a ton of data about your interactions with prospects and customers. It's not unusual to have millions of tasks *and* campaign *members, particularly if you've integrated your MAS into SFDC. If you're tracking all the outbound emails from a MAS, you may also have millions of* email *records and* chatter *posts. These can all be reported on in SFDC or in outside engines, but you have to wonder about the signal-to-noise ratio in that mountain of data. Follow Einstein's dictum: the database should be as complicated as it really needs to be but no more complicated.*

All that said, external reports (particularly in a data warehouse) can rapidly expose contradictions and ambiguities in the SFDC data. Data warehouse and business intelligence tool users should be encouraged to report discrepancies in data they analyze and to notify members of the data architecture review team (discussed in Chapter 3) so they can understand the problem and examine corrective measures.

Scoping the System via User Screen Design

Now that you've done a "reverse engineering" of data requirements from reports, you should use a similar tactic to capture the system's functional requirements by designing user screens. As before, create mock-ups of the key user screens in PowerPoint, Visio, or Excel. This time, however, you also need to create storyboards that describe the customer interactions and business situations that are the very reason the SFDC users are working on the system. For example, a storyboard could describe an irate customer who is trying to get an exchange for defective merchandise. Check out www.SFDC-secrets.com for example storyboards and screen mock-ups.

Create mock-ups and storyboards for each of the following elements:

- **SFDC screens:** For most installations, SFDC basically has one main screen for each internal object: `leads`, `campaigns`, `contacts`, `accounts`, `opportunities`, `quotes`, `orders`, `contracts`, and `cases`. On each screen mock-up, make sure to show the `related lists` that users need to be able to see when looking at a record. Identify any screen design requests where the users want to make edits that straddle SFDC objects, as these will require `VisualForce` or other coding tricks.[8]

- **External system screens:** Assuming that the external systems will be integrated with SFDC, the typical approach is to use `tabs` (for dedicated external screens) or `VisualForce` (for external system frames embedded in an existing SFDC screen). The mock-up needs to show whether the external system has its own screen (via a new window pop-up or dedicated tab), is visible through a subwindow (via frames or mashups), or is represented as new custom data fields in an existing SFDC screen. Each of these approaches is equally valid, but each also means a different user experience and a different level of effort.

- **Views and searches:** A view is a mini-report that quickly guides the user to a subset of data (e.g., "deals I've edited today"); in contrast, a search is a way of rapidly getting to relevant individual records. Itemizing the views and searches—navigational aids—helps the implementation team see how the users think about the system, and it may uncover misunderstandings and imprecision related to the data semantics. Each view should be mocked up as a spreadsheet, and each type of search should be described in a text document.

- **Interactions:**[9] Each class of user will use the system to complete some business process interactions (the more sophisticated the user, the more interactions he or

---

8. These are more difficult requirements to satisfy; you'll want to push back on the user pretty hard to make sure it's a real business need. Typically, the cross-object data entry screens come in a later sprint, after the initial functionality is deployed as a single object.

9. *Interactions* here are defined as any decisions, transactions, or activities that users engage in beyond simple reading and updating of data. Interactions are typically part of a larger business process. For example, it's not an interaction to update a user's phone number, but it *is* an interaction to cancel an order because of a bad payment history.

she will have). These interactions should be documented as PERT charts, process-flow diagrams, or checklists. Although almost any tool can be used for text, the diagrams are best created in Visio or a similar tool.

- **Alerts and workflows:** The system probably needs to trigger automatic workflows or issue alerts for exception handling. For example, management will need to approve large discounts or unusual payment terms. These management-by-exception aids should be documented as PERT charts or process-flow diagrams, with special attention being given to the trigger criteria, escalation conditions, approval delegation, and process routing exceptions for large backlogs or "emergency" conditions.

WHAT ABOUT UML, BPML, AND OTHER STANDARDS?

The nice thing about standards is that there are so many to choose from. The un-nice thing is that many (okay, almost all) business people don't know markup languages, find them hard to follow, and fundamentally don't care whether they are used. To be honest, they don't want them being used. They prefer simpler, less rigorous diagrams. If you are more effective with tools leveraging the formal markup languages, fine—but expect to have to recast their output as simpler, less rigorous diagrams when talking to the users. So go ahead, knock yourself out.

While preparing these mock-ups and storyboards, the business analyst should capture the following information in the comments area of Excel or in the Notes area of PowerPoint slides. In addition to the items listed in Table 2-1, find out about the following data characteristics:

- **User resistance:** Which kinds of information do users resist updating? Which kinds of things are they trying to hide (or hide from)?

- **Clutter:** For the frontline users (telesales, sales, and customer support), what is the *absolute minimum set of data* they need to see to do their jobs? Which fields, screens, and steps can be hidden from various users to make the system easier to use?

- **Format/layout:** What sets of fields need to be in a special layout that isn't supported by SFDC's native two-column layout?[10] What fields need special fonts or symbols?

---

10. SFDC's default user interface supports simple two-column layouts for fields, with almost no flexibility. If some fields need special formatting or layout (e.g., quarterly financial information or other tabular data), annotate the number of columns and rows that will be needed. This will involve special `VisualForce` coding that needs to be specified up front.

- **Ownership/visibility:** Who owns this data in the organization? If it's from another department, can those users block the data from being integrated into SFDC (or would they)? Are there situations where a Chinese Wall must be maintained for some users?

- **Required fields and default values:** What are the (very few) required fields? For all fields, what is the appropriate default value? For which fields do we need to establish `validation rules`[11] to enforce data quality standards (e.g., ZIP+4 for U.S. addresses)?

A Guided Tour of the SFDC Object Model

To understand how to map all the data requirements into the system design, you need to understand how all the data are organized in SFDC. This is not an abstract exercise: you need to develop a list of which data are a standard part of SFDC, which data need to be added as `custom fields` or `custom objects`, which data should be a discrete field and which should be pointers to other records, and which data need to be migrated from outside systems versus pulled in on an as-needed basis.

Business software such as SFDC includes a complex set of internal data tables that represent the business objects you work with—`opportunities`, `contracts`, `cases`, and so forth. Although it is not necessary to understand the internals, you *do* need to understand some of the basics and the relationships among the largest components of the system. This knowledge is particularly important when designing reports and user screens because, much of the time, standard reports or screens can interact with only one of the system's objects at a time.

Salesforce's object model involves relatively few tables (entry-level systems use less than 10) and the tables have only a few pointers to other tables in the system. SFDC's basic design principle is "one table is one object." In contrast, a system like Microsoft Dynamics or SAP involves hundreds of relatively narrow tables to achieve equivalent application functionality.

So let's start with the basics: What is an *object*? The easiest way to think about this concept is as a tab in SFDC's user interface: `leads`, `contacts`, `accounts`, and `opportunities` are all examples of high-level objects. Objects are typically hierarchical, with parent–child relationships (e.g., the parent account field in the `account` object may point from a division up to the headquarters office).

---

11. `Validation rules` are an SFDC mechanism to prevent bad input at a field-by-field level. Although you will start with them, as the system gets more sophisticated, they start to cause irritating bugs. If your requirements are pushing toward a lot of validation rules, it's probably best to use `VisualForce` and JavaScript from the very beginning to provide a gentler but more robust mechanism.

If you look at an `account` (or any of the SFDC objects that has its own tab), the top part of the page is called the `account` detail. This is the only part of the page you edit directly, and it's where a subset of the data and attributes of the `account` object are presented. Below the detail area of the page are a series of `related lists`—for example, `contacts`, `contact roles`, `open activities`, and `activity history`. These related lists show an overview of the children of the main object you're examining. In many cases, the parental relationship is unique: for example, an `account`'s `contacts` can't be attached to any other `account`.

In some cases, the items in the related list are inherited[12] from one or more children. For example, a contact may have an `open activity` (and if you looked at that contact's record, the `activity` would show up in the `related list`), but when you look at the `contact`'s `account`, you see that the same `open activity` shows up there as well. This inheritance doesn't always occur for all objects, but when it is helpful to see the "roll-ups" of things like `activities`, SFDC presents them.

With all these parent–child relationships, what's the "top of the family tree"? From the system's perspective, almost everything attaches one way or another to `accounts`,[13] as shown in Figure 2-1. But instead of explaining this concept in an abstract, top-down way, it is more intuitive to talk about the object model in a more chronological way.

For most users, the first time they interact with the system is to look at a `lead`. Leads are people who have declared some level of interest in your product or service—they registered on a Web page, attended a seminar, or stopped by your tradeshow booth. We don't know much about leads,[14] other than basic contact information and some level of interest.

There is an amazing amount of confusion about what a `lead` is and how it should be treated. We explore the best practices for sales and marketing in Chapters 9 and 10, but here we simply talk about what the objects are and how they are related. A person stays as a `lead` for as long as that individual is just curious—wanting information but not wanting to start a sales cycle with us. A person can remain a `lead` for 5 minutes or for 5 years. For a number of reasons, even if a person walks up to us and immediately asks to buy, that individual should be initially entered into the system as a `lead`.

---

12. This is the reverse of the normal definition of "inherited," but these usages were invented by software engineers who, frankly, didn't get out much.

13. Of course, there are dozens of exceptions, but I'm trying to keep things simple here. For a thorough technical explanation of the SFDC object model, check out the AppExchange and DeveloperForce for presentations, white papers, and free tools, such as the Object Explorer and EasyDescribe.

14. The sales folks and executives will use the word *lead* as the person they're about to sell to and *contact* to mean a person they know but aren't currently doing business with. Just to make things entertaining, Salesforce does it the other way around. In SFDC, `lead` is pretty low value and isn't attached to a deal or even an account: `contacts` are who you sell to. And no, you can't really reverse it. So expect loads of confusion about these two words when talking to executives!

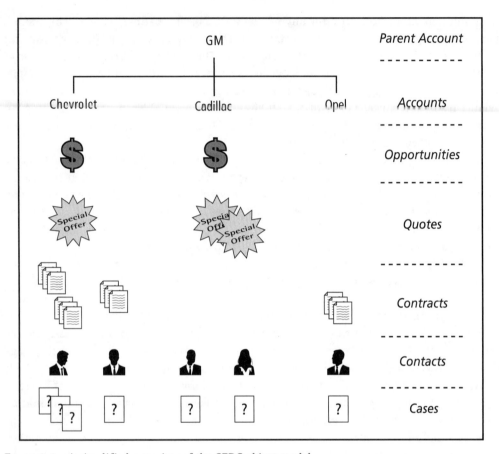

FIGURE 2-1   A simplified overview of the SFDC object model

As soon as a person starts to express interest in doing business, the lead needs to be converted to a contact. Contacts are people who are attached to accounts (companies) and are considering doing a transaction with us. The possible transaction is called an opportunity. A specific contact can be attached to only one account (his or her employer) but may be involved in several opportunities. It's easiest to see a contact as a grown-up lead, but this is not quite true and causes some confusion. Think of it more like a caterpillar and a butterfly: they're the same animal but with very different characteristics at different stages of life. Once the butterfly emerges, the caterpillar is gone. When someone is a lead, we don't know much about the person beyond his or her topic of interest and maybe the purchase timeframe. When the lead grows up to be a contact, we know more about him or her as an individual, but the information about the product interest and purchase timeframe has been stripped away. That information isn't a permanent characteristic of the person—his or her interest and purchase intentions will change over time—so in the conversion process, that information is removed from the lead and put in a new opportunity record.

Conversion is a one-way process: contacts can never devolve into leads.[15] The conversion process involves the transformation of a lead into a contact, the creation of an account (or the attachment of the contact to an existing account), the creation of an opportunity (the purpose of conversion is to signal the start of a sales cycle), and the creation of a follow-up task (to make sure that things move forward).

A lead and a contact are the only two objects in the system that describe a prospect, customer, or channel partner. Every bit of contact information and personal information can only be stored either in a lead record or a contact record. All other objects in the system describe abstractions (a corporation, a contract, a purchase decision) or events (a service call, an action item, an email exchange). So a lead (a person) cannot evolve into an opportunity (a thing). Even though you'll hear people say that leads become opportunities, don't let their misunderstanding of these concepts confuse *you*. (Leads become contacts who participate in opportunities.)

Once the conversion has occurred, the sales rep should interact mainly with the opportunity record—that's what will become a deal, and that's where the most relevant information about the pending transaction is kept. Off the shelf, the opportunity detail information is fairly sparse: the expected amount and close date of the deal, its current status, and maybe information about the competitors. But opportunities have a lot of related objects: the account; the contacts that are relevant to this opportunity; the roles (such as purchasing agent) of each contact; the products that are being considered; the forecasts that have been made; and the open activities that represent action items, meetings, and other next steps.

When the sale is made, the opportunity is closed out and a contract is linked to the account. The contract typically contains a small amount of unique information (such as a term, renewal date, and payment schedule) but is used to determine eligibility for support, to trigger renewal marketing, and to foster other administrative activities.

The last major object from the user's perspective is the case, an incident reported to the customer support organization. Cases contain customer issues and resolutions, and their solutions can be summarized in the knowledge base used by customers for self-support.

---

15. This is stated from a user's perspective. A system administrator can actually turn contacts back to leads again, but it's a very complex process that is done en masse to correct erroneous user actions (fake conversions, usually done to game the system metrics that their bosses see).

There are two other objects we must mention, but they don't fit neatly in this narrative overview:

- `Activities` (aka `Tasks` and `Events`) are the places where action items, calls, and historical notes are kept. They can reference up to 10 people (contacts or leads) and one nonperson object (such as a company or a case).[16]

- `Chatter feeds` are the place where users collaborate around information-gathering, problem-solving, and other interactive discussions. A `chatter feed` can be established around nearly anything in the system and provides a real-time forum for exploring topics and documenting solutions.

These core objects point to one another in subtle ways to make relationships. For example, a `contact` may be involved in multiple `opportunities` in different ways. Each of those `contact-opportunity` relationships (called a `contact role`) is tracked separately. By combining these objects, relationships, and states, SFDC creates its native applications. Each application shares the same data but presents it from different perspectives to support

- Sales force automation

- Channel management and partner portals

- Call center automation

- Marketing campaigns and social media

- Community management

- Customer self-service portals

- Support automation and knowledge base

SFDC makes it very easy to extend the data model, object model, and applications on your own or via plugin applications in the AppExchange (see Chapter 7 for a discussion of these free and low-cost products). Of course, the extensions you put in need to be consistent with the underlying object model because the data will be shared with other applications. Any `custom fields` or `custom objects` added into the system reinforce and extend the object model. The trick, of course, is to avoid redundant extensions to the data model, as these will only complicate things and confuse developers and users alike.

---

16. The `activity` object has lots of ifs, ands, and buts, so you'll find that it is not very flexible or extensible the way most SFDC objects are. Beware optimistic assumptions about `activities`—always check the documentation and do a quick prototype to avoid gotchas!

Let's take a look at some common misconceptions:

- Information about competitors may legitimately *start out* in `leads`, but competitive information learned in the course of a sales cycle needs to be added to `opportunities`. Competitors are situation specific, so "what's the competitive product" should not be attached to the `contact`, the `account`, or even the `contract`.

- Information about the customer's project team (such as the number of team members) we're working with in a deal should be attached to the `opportunity`, but users often ask for the data to be attached to the `contact` or the `account`. Project teams are transitory and aren't an attribute of the company—so they shouldn't be described in the `account` record. Project teams comprise more than one person, so the project team information shouldn't be part of a `contact` record. Also, even when looking at the `contact` who is the project leader, that role is transitory. The best way to summarize a project team is to add its members into the `contact roles` related list for the relevant `opportunity`.

- The current state of a deal should always be stored only in the `opportunity` record. If a particular person is acting as our champion in the deal, that information needs to reside in the `opportunity` record (as a `contact role`), not as a field in the `contact` or `account` record.

- Phone calls and `tasks` related to an `opportunity` should be attached to that deal rather than to the `account` records related to the deal. The `tasks` still indicate the name of the person involved, but it's important to attach the `task` in the most relevant, visible place.

- That said, an `activity` indicating a casual social meeting with a purchasing agent—not tied to any specific deal but describing generalities about account management—should be attached to the `contact` record. However, if there is discussion about a new purchasing policy or an organizational budgetary cap, that information is relevant at the `account` level and should be attached there.

- In SFDC, the worst problems with extended objects occur where there isn't any extension at all: users simply scribble information they want to save in random text fields, such as `description`, `comments`, or `notes`. Although the users may be consistent enough in this practice to make the information easily digested by humans, the resulting data is so unstructured and irregular that it can't be reported, summarized, or used as the basis for triggers or alerts. Although it's best to keep the number of visible fields to a minimum, if you discover users adding data randomly to long text fields in SFDC pages, it's a sure sign that at least one additional field is needed in that object's data model.

Because there isn't room here for more than a quick orientation, we're just scratching the surface. If you want to understand any of these areas in more detail, SFDC has the full object model nicely documented at www.salesforce.com/us/developer/docs/api/Content/data_model.htm.

Before we leave this tour of the object model, though, we have to hit on one of the biggest areas of misunderstanding—the security system. SFDC provides very fine-grained control of user access to data, way beyond the "user/group/world" model of Linux or the access control lists of the PC. What you need to know now is that every record in SFDC has a single `owner`, and every user has a single `role` and a `profile`. The system uses a `role hierarchy` which is used to exclude `users`, and `sharing rules`, `account teams`, `sales teams`, and `sharing lists` that override the hierarchy to add reinclusions.

The system supplements this hierarchy with `profile`-level privileges for what you create and see for each kind of record. This sounds abstract and complicated because it is: you may find that you need to create dozens—or even hundreds—of roles, profiles, sharing rules, record types, and page layouts. This can turn into a manageability nightmare: one 40-user system we worked on had nearly 4,000 different items that could be adjusted for security, access controls, and user privileges. Obviously, this topic is much too complicated to cover here, but try to keep the security and access model as general and open as possible, avoiding complex logic and special situations. These will turn into a never-ending make-work project for some poor underling.

What's in a Namespace?

A namespace is the formal way to refer to all the allowable words (or numbers) you are allowed to use when identifying or describing something. A namespace is thought of as a rigorous naming convention.

The easiest example of a namespace is a pick list: all the allowable names (or values) are there for users, and they can select only from the list. As only an administrator inserts new names into the list, there's no way for a user to accidentally enlarge the namespace with irrelevancies or cause a confusing duplication.

Real-world namespaces are a lot more difficult to maintain because nobody knows in advance what the names will be—yet you have to think through at the beginning so that you'll have a paradigm to handle all possible names that your business might need.

In the case of people (`leads` and `contacts`), you don't have to come up with a namespace—society did that for you. Most of the time in SFDC, the namespace for people is the first name and last name. If you have a serious number of people in the system, it's best if you add the middle initial or some other identifier to distinguish John A. Smith from John B. Smith. If you don't have the middle initial, consider using a state as a placeholder (like this: John [MI] Smith for the John Smith that registered from Michigan). If you have an unbelievable number of names (millions of consumers), you may need to put a serial number or date stamp in the bracketed area of the example above.

In contrast to people's names, the names for `accounts`, `opportunities`, `campaigns`, `contracts`, `products`, `pricelists`, `cases`, `documents`, `folders`, `reports`, `dashboards`, and several other objects are entirely under your control and have to be carefully designed. If you don't choose them correctly, you'll either confuse yourself, lose things, or confound SFDC processing. This becomes a really big issue as you scale your system.

Names in a namespace must be easy for a human to unambiguously understand and be mechanically parsable by the system (for `reports`, `filters`, `validation`, `triggers`, and so forth). SFDC may have no problem with a product called 234-xy-593.23-US, but it's not likely to be very user friendly. At the other extreme, a product called "today's special" will cause endless problems in screens, reports, and external integration—and it is so ambiguous that it's likely to frustrate the users as well.

For example, you might have an account in your system called "DOTnet Consulting" in the United States. Suppose you start to do business in Germany and find an identically named account there. The U.S. and German companies are unrelated and need to be handled separately. So you might add a country identifier to your namespace so that all account names are unique. In this example, "US–DOTnet Consulting" is different from "DE–DOTnet Consulting." Naming accounts this way makes it really easy to filter by country and ensure that the two companies are never confused by humans or system reports.

To design a good namespace for each object, think about the following issues:

- What is the range of items that the namespace will need to encompass over the next three years? For example, a product namespace might need to include new product lines, seasonal promotions, industry-specific packages, customer specials, upgrade items, and replacement parts. How will the namespace indicate this year's upgrade product versus next year's? Will the names be unique so that they can't be confused by the system or users?

- Will the names be easily grasped by humans? What shorthand (nicknames, aliases) will they use instead of the formal name? Consider using a "street name" field on objects that people refer to all the time, as the system-generated identifiers are typically useless over the phone or in meetings.

- For the other systems that already deal with these same items, what do they currently call them? Could there already be more than one naming convention in your organization? Might one of the existing namespaces be usable in SFDC, or will you need to create a new namespace and have a correspondence table to map between the two? If so, is there any reason why the correspondence will *not* be unique (i.e., one-for-one)?

- If you are integrating your internal systems with external systems that need to refer to your new namespace, are those external systems technically able to accommodate all of your names? For example, are the external systems able to handle uppercase letters only, with no numbers, spaces, lowercase, punctuation, accents, or other diacritics? For example, will they be able to deal with names of only 20 characters (no more, no less) or just abstract numbers (931-3492087-001)?

- How will you need to use the names? Will they appear only in an SFDC record, or will they be used outside the system? Can they be easily searched for in SFDC or in your company's intranet search engine?

- How will the names look in a list or report? Can the names be sorted alphabetically and still convey meaning?

- How will the names look to people outside the United States? Can the namespace accommodate foreign character sets (e.g., to handle a European company's name)? Will sorting the names using international sorting standards cause confusion?

- Do the names refer to individuals in your company? If so, could they be replaced with their function's name? For example, instead of a name like "Joe's territory," can you use "Northwest U.S. mid-market territory"? A few quarters from now, Joe is inevitably going to move on and be replaced by Sam.

- How will the names look in captions that may be automatically generated in charts and dashboards? Will people quickly get their meaning even if the names are truncated?

SFDC's Data Requirements

In the course of developing all of the mock-ups, you will almost always discover significant implications about the data that will be involved to achieve the required function. The system needs three categories of data: internal, external, and historical. As the difficulty and cost of each of these types of data vary widely, we discuss them separately.

Internal SFDC Data

Internal SFDC data are collected and entered directly in SFDC, involving almost no interaction with outside systems. For example, `lead` data may enter the system from the Web site and spreadsheet imports; `opportunity` data may be entered by sales reps and sales administrators. For purposes of this analysis, the internal data do *not include any histor-ical*[17] *system data:* they consist of only the data collected from the go-live date onward.

Generally speaking, you should keep the number of fields to the absolute minimum. Resist the temptation to add lots of nice-to-have fields because every one of them has to be entered and interpreted by someone. If a field is going to be empty 25% of the time and wrong another 25% of the time, leave it out: it will only be an irritant for the person entering the data and a detractor of system credibility for anyone trying to use it. It's very easy to add new fields at any time later—but properly *removing* spurious fields (particularly pick lists) can involve a lot of data crunching.

Whenever you want to modify or add a field, always create a new custom field. Leave the system-standard fields alone, as they are much less flexible than the ones you define yourself—not only in terms of the initial system setup, but also in terms of the advanced functionality you'll want later. Overall, there may be a dozen system-defined fields that you *must* use,[18] but you should use a custom field any time you can.

On any data entry page, a few items must be filled in before the page can be saved. Keep the number of required fields to the absolute minimum, as they irritate users. I can't remember the last time I saw a page requiring more than five items to be filled in, and even that was a debatable decision. Keep all the required fields "above the fold" on the page layout, so you don't have off-screen fields that block the save button from working.

Special attention must be given to any user data that has legal status "personal infor-mation."[19] The clearest examples are credit card, Social Security, insurance policy, and financial institution account numbers: avoid these items like the plague. Storing this kind of personal information in SFDC may make the system subject to PCI, HIPAA, FERPA, or other compliance audits, and it may even incur the wrath of regulators. If your company already stores these data in other systems, *leave the data there* and specify that SFDC integrate with those systems of record via an arm's-length relationship (e.g., using a "mashup" window to view the data that are always stored in the original system).

SFDC's internal data comes almost entirely from human data entry, which is the most costly and error-prone source. To the maximum degree possible, avoid free-form typing: use pick lists (pull-downs), lookups, and check boxes instead (see Figure 2-2 for examples).

A pick list allows selection of allowable values. Even though pick lists must be main-tained as the system evolves, they speed up error-free data entry. Using pick lists means planning (oh darn . . .) but has big payoffs over the life of the system. Here are consid-erations for pick lists:

---

17. If SFDC is a replacement for an existing SFA or CRM system, all of the current system's data is considered historical for the purposes of this section.

18. Such as `opportunity stage`, `probability`, and `amount`.

19. When working with citizens of the European Union, you need to be attentive to their privacy laws (95/46/EC) and almost certainly go through Safe Harbor certification.

Figure 2-2   Pull-downs and lookups versus free-text fields

- A pick list should be kept to fewer than 20 items whenever possible, and longer lists should be broken into categories or hierarchies that lend themselves to dependent fields (e.g., "job title" should be a dependent field of "department" to avoid presenting invalid choices to users).

- If a pick list has only two or three items, use check boxes instead.

- When creating pick lists, leave out items unless you're sure you need them from day one. It is very easy to add pick-list values later, but removing those values can involve some careful data decisions and costly data crunching.

- When a number to be entered doesn't need to be precise—for example, if it lends itself to a range or a band, such as number of employees—consider using a pick list instead of a number field. However, if the bands or ranges will not be consistent (e.g., a midsize company in the United Kingdom is 1,000 employees but in the United States is 5,000 employees), either define the bands vaguely (e.g., small to medium business), use record types, or stay with a number entry.

In contrast to a pick list, a look-up field allows selection of only allowable values, but it doesn't need to be maintained as the system evolves. However, because look-up fields present a list of items to choose from, they involve a pop-up window and extra mouse-clicks.

A free-text field is infinitely flexible, but it doesn't give any clues as to format or allowable values. It virtually guarantees typos and requires offline cleansing or correction. For items that must be left to free-entry fields (e.g., D-U-N-S number or SIC code), think through the range of reasonable values to see if there's a way to "type"[20] the free-entry data.

- When possible, assign the field to a specific type, such as date, phone number, or number. This is the first step toward trapping bad data at the source.

- If there are strong patterns in the data (such as phone numbers or ZIP codes), assign `validation rules` to flag bad data before they are entered (e.g., a ZIP code is 5 or 5 + 4 digits, an international postal code is 1 to 7 alphanumeric characters). SFDC provides data-entry `validation rules` for numbers and text to ensure that each field's entry is within acceptable ranges.

Data `validation rules` can be fairly complex formulas that ensure the correspondence of key fields. For example, validation can make sure that the state code entered is valid for the country code entered. Even though `data validation` works fine for individual data items, it can't trap "silly" entries (such as the address 123 Cherry Lane, Anytown, IL, 60609 or the email address asdf@fubar.com). As we discuss in Chapter 13, system administrators need to create data quality reports that highlight unexpected trends in records and implement an ongoing bad-data removal process.

Long-text fields are almost always a bad idea. Over time, they will be filled with nothing, long narratives that are better stored as attachments or `tasks`, or weird "overloaded" data that should have been stored as one or more numerical fields. In any case, long-text fields are almost impossible to search or report on, which renders them only marginally useful. All too often, long-text fields hold incidental information that is ignored by humans and systems alike. For situations where long text really is required, it's usually best to store those data as `notes` attached to the main record.

If certain combinations of data in a record are significant, consider creating a new field that captures the significant combination. For example, companies with more than 1,000 employees in the United Kingdom may be flagged as major accounts, whereas as companies in the United States might require 5,000 employees to qualify for this status. Due to this ambiguity, adding a check box for major account to the record is very helpful to users looking at the screen and makes it much easier to write reports. If the significant

---

20. Data types are a way of structuring fields to behave in a consistent way. "Number," "currency," and "phone number" are example data types in SFDC. Typed fields are inherently easier to search, validate, and maintain than "strings" or free-text fields.

combinations are simple and routine enough, they can be automatically indicated using SFDC's `formula` fields or `workflow field updates`.

As discussed earlier, it's important to add any custom fields into the correct part of SFDC's object model, particularly with respect to `leads`, `contacts`, `opportunities`, `contracts`, `assets`, and `cases`. It's very common to put new fields onto the wrong object, and fixing these errors can become very expensive down the road.

That said, sometimes it's helpful to denormalize data by including (partially) redundant entries in different parts of the object model to make it easier to find and report on relevant data.[21] Continuing with the major account example, the check box normally is visible only if you're looking at the `account` object. It may be very helpful to add that check box to the `opportunity` and `contact` records as well. This can usually be accomplished with a clever `formula`, workflow `field update`, or a bit of `APEX` code. But denormalization always has a cost: either you must write some code to keep this duplicated data up to date, or you must have a person who updates the redundant copy of the data and cleans up others' errors.

SPLIT BRAIN

At first blush, you might expect the SFDC database to hold everything having to do with prospects and customers. But sophisticated organizations often use a split-brain approach that separates the *marketing* database from the *sales* database. Organizations take this tack for two reasons: they often have a large number of low-quality `leads` (really, they're little more than names—see Chapter 10) that aren't relevant to the sales folks, and they use a marketing automation tool or service that needs to operate from its own copy of the data.

What's involved with the split-brain approach? The marketing pool of names is managed in a separate database, and the transaction history of `campaigns` and responses is managed there. When a name starts behaving more like a `lead` (as reflected in its internal `lead` score), it is promoted from the marketing pool to the sales `lead` area. Its data are deactivated in the marketing names database and (semi-)automatically entered into SFDC as a hot `lead`.

`Leads` also migrate in the other direction. When a `lead` has been unresponsive, has lost interest, or has been demoted by sales,[22] it is deactivated in SFDC and reactivated in the

---

21. Database purists will cringe through this paragraph, but despite their rantings, there are practical situations where denormalization is a valid choice. Just know the costs and risks, and engineer for automatic updating of denormalized fields.

22. Sales demotes `leads` either by disqualifying them or by ignoring them for so long that they go cold. You don't want to know how often the second reason is the cause of `lead` demotion.

marketing names database. Neither `leads` nor names should ever be deleted from either SFDC or the external database (to prevent duplication and to maintain history), but the inactive ones should carry flags marking them as such. There are several mechanisms you can use to hide these inactive records.

By keeping these databases separate, the metrics and operations of marketing can be tuned more finely without interfering with the natural way that sales works. However, the split-brain model has a side effect: sales will not be able to easily see *all* of the interactions of a large `account` because some of the action will be taken by `leads` and some by names. This can cause a bit of a blind spot.

If you're already using a marketing tool—such as Eloqua, Marketo, Vertical Response, or ExactTarget—you're probably on the split-brain path. If you aren't using these kinds of tools, you have an architectural choice to make now. Do you need to have all your `leads`—regardless of quality—in one place, or do you want to create a category of `leads` that are of such low quality that they're handled externally? Although there's no overwhelming cost advantage to going in either direction, changing your path after deployment will involve considerable one-time costs and changes to the workflows and automation surrounding `leads`.

So, choose now. Adding the marketing names database will add another integration point, but it will also allow for more sophisticated marketing operations over time.

There's an analogous issue with SFDC `cases` and bugs that may be stored in external defect tracking systems. SFDC should be tracking all the customer incidents and related `entitlements` and `solutions`. But engineering almost always prefers that defect tracking be managed in an outside system that they use. This is another integration point (with required cross-reference pointers) but leads to more natural and effective use of both systems.

Self-Healing Data

It is important to apply the principle of self-healing data: in the course of the project, you want to make changes to systems and processes to continuously improve the resilience and health of SFDC data over time. Whenever system modifications are made in SFDC, its integration adaptors, or surrounding systems, a portion of the implementation team's effort should go toward improving code and supporting processes that can enhance data quality and validation. Through an incremental improvement strategy, data quality can painlessly become better over time.

The most highly leveraged part of this work is making sure that new data flowing into the system is high quality and meaningful. Aside from human input applied directly into SFDC screens, the main sources of new data into SFDC consist of the following streams:

- **Leads** and **contact** updates from the Web site, email marketing system, and imports from internal and external sources

- **Account** and **opportunity** updates from order management, accounting, eCommerce, or channel management systems

- **Case** updates from Web and email inputs as well as engineering's bug tracking system

We address each of these sources in turn.

The Web site registration pages should whittle the number of fields down to what's really essential and reduce user typing as much as possible. Use pick lists ("pull-downs") for job title, state, and country. Use JavaScript to validate the format of phone numbers and postal codes. Use mail-response loops to validate that the email address is valid and active. The Web site data feed should use deduping code from either your own developers or from products such as RingLead or DemandTools. Most larger SFDC implementations have multiple landing pages on the Web site, and it is important to assign a unique identifier to each page (usually, a **campaign** code) to make it easier to troubleshoot page-specific data problems.

The email marketing system may be directly integrated into SFDC: make sure its deduping features are always on. If your email blaster operates as a separate silo, follow the guidance in the next paragraph.

For **lead** imports, most companies use Excel spreadsheets. Beware CSV file corruption, particularly from external sources (check out "The Joy of Regex" described in Chapter 3). Create templates for these imports, using formulas and macros that clean bad entries, validate formats, and normalize data (e.g., translating state and country names into ISO codes, fixing ill-formed phone numbers) to trap bad data before it's imported into the system. The spreadsheet imports should be done through products such as RingLead and DemandTools with the goal of stopping duplicate records at the source.

Account and **opportunity** updates occur via integration with outside systems. The single most important data pollution control measure here is prevention of duplicate **accounts, opportunities,** and **contacts.** The first line of defense is the use of unique keys and duplicate-detection code in the integration layer. Unfortunately, with outside systems such as eCommerce or channel ordering systems, it may not be possible to have a unique key that works in all situations. Develop a proxy identifier to make sure that **accounts** and **opportunities** are not double counted. If for policy reasons a somewhat redundant **account** *does* need to be created in your system, make the new one be a child of the existing SFDC **account.** The second line of defense is to integrate as few fields as possible: the fewer the fields, the lower the chance of data corruption.

Case records are updated by **web2case** and **email2case** features in SFDC. Use the same ideas we discussed a few paragraphs ago about Web site registration pages, and configure your `email2case` code so that it converts ill-formatted or denormalized data at the source. Use field validation rules. The good news is that you don't have to worry about deduping cases the way you do with leads. `Case` records may also be updated by your bug tracking system. Make sure that the integration strategy you use (either an off-the-shelf adaptor or custom code) normalizes data and prevents duplicate creation (of either `cases` or `contacts`).

For *all data records*, but particularly in name, company, and address fields, foreign character sets must be properly handled and transferred.[23] Fix problems in this area by reconfiguring or upgrading the outside source to be Unicode compatible.

Migrating Historical SFA/CRM Data

Your company likely has some or even most of the data mentioned earlier in existing systems—for example, SFA, CRM, or Outlook—and it's important to understand how these data will be transitioned into SFDC. Here are the alternative scenarios:

- The data will be imported and expunged from the old system (or the old system will be decommissioned outright). The key issues to understand: how "dirty" is the data, how many duplicate (both fuzzy and hard) records exist, and how recently have the data been updated? Generally speaking, B2B contact information rots at a rate approaching 10% per quarter, so data more than three years old might have less information value than the cost of cleansing, deduping, and enriching the records. Check out the discussion in Chapter 3 to see how much fun this process can bring to your life. As always, the old data shouldn't be completely deleted but rather should be archived into a relational database after import to SFDC.

- The data will be partially imported into SFDC, but some of it will continue to live in the current system. In addition to the issues outlined earlier, a key decision will be synchronization.[24] Generally speaking, it's best to have either SFDC or one external system be the system of record for any particular field in a database (e.g., mailing address). In this way, all fields are unambiguously owned, and there's no issue of replication or synchronization conflicts. This is a complicated topic—read the integration section in Chapter 7 before you make firm commitments on this front.

---

23. SFDC has no problem dealing with properly encoded foreign character sets using UTF-8 Unicode. Unfortunately, some external systems simply produce the wrong codes, creating gibberish in the system for Asian and most European languages. As we discuss in Chapter 10, one best practice is to create an Anglicized search-friendly version of foreign characters in addition to the original names. The implementation team needs to implement these ISO Latin-friendly versions of fields for name, address, city, and company in the `lead`, `contact`, `account`, and `contract` objects.

24. Our recommendation is almost invariably to avoid the requirement for full two-way synchronization. It's a slow, error-prone step that usually adds unneeded complexity.

- The old data will not be imported into SFDC at all but rather will be kept in the original system and accessed via a mashup or other read-only mechanism.

There may be some data you've identified that must be migrated from other systems that aren't CRM but are nevertheless important to the customer relationship. For example, your order management system may contain important historical information that really should reside in SFDC going forward. You have to make decisions for these data on the same issues you've just handled for the historical CRM data.

Aside from the cost of migrating quality data into the system, there's the ongoing cost of data maintenance. SFDC charges for data and file storage beyond a per-user quota, and Big Data also means Big Backups that have to be stored somewhere. As always, it's a matter of business value: if you're not sure who's going to use historical data that is more than a year or so old, prioritize that part of the data migration lower.

External System Data

External system data are collected, entered, and maintained in some system outside of SFDC and are available within the system only via integration. For example, partial-shipment data may need to be viewable from the SFDC `account` screen, but the system of record would be the company inventory management system. For the purposes of this section, these data do *not include any historical system data;* rather, they comprise only the data collected in other systems from the SFDC's go-live date onward.

The defining characteristic for external data is that SFDC users and administrators have no direct control over the quality or form of the data, and they may have limited control over the format and editing of the records. Most of the time, the users have to take what they can get from the external system. So the task here is to itemize which data items:

- Need to be seen, by whom, and under what conditions.

- Need to be edited, by whom, and with which controls.[25]

- Can be aggregated for ease of use (e.g., SFDC users care about a flag called "customer on credit hold" but shouldn't care about which specific payments are late).

The cardinal question here is "What is the minimum set of data that is required for the users to do their job?" With each request for external data comes a decision. Will it be resolved through complex and expensive integration code, or can the issue be bypassed by simplifying or restating the requirement?

---

25. Almost always, only a small portion of the external system data is fully editable from the SFDC screens.

As before, the first step in analyzing the requirement is to map the external systems' data into the SFDC object model. The team needs to identify which SFDC object the field should be associated with (e.g., credit holds should be part of the `account` object, not the `opportunity` or `contact`) and which reports the data should be included in. If you're lucky, there's little to map because the external system has unique data that will never be stored in SFDC. But in the cases where SFDC's data fields *do* map to an external system, you have some decisions to make:

- What will be the universal key that identifies critical objects across the systems? At the very least, you'll need keys to identify `account`, `contact`, and `order` records; it's likely you'll need keys for `product`, service incident, and bug (defects or RMAs) records as well.

- How will you handle apparent duplicate or redundant entries from the external system? If there are two cases of ABC Corporation, which one should be presented? For display purposes only, should certain parts of ABC Corporation's records actually be consolidated? If it's better to show only half the data, what will be the rule for selecting which half?

- Does the external system have a data hierarchy, such as price list bundles, bill of material (BOM) structures, or account–division–site distinctions? You will need to decide how to map these structures into SFDC.

- What will be the strategy for searching through and presenting foreign character sets (particularly foreign characters or accents in people's names, company names, and addresses)?

For example, if the requirement is just a read-only view of a customer's order history, this can be presented as a few rows in SFDC's `account` page. But if a fully editable view of the order history is needed, it should probably be a dedicated `VisualForce` page (and perhaps even a `tab`) in SFDC's user interface. For each data item, the team needs to specify how current the data must be (e.g., read-only address data may be updated only weekly, a data edit concerning a warranty claim can be delayed until a nightly refresh, and a data edit about inventory may require real-time synchronization), whether it's writable from SFDC, and the rules for handling data conflicts.

For any items that users will edit via the SFDC interface, it's important to inquire about the field constraints (data formats and allowable values) and other data validation that are expected by the external system of record. We need to know what SFDC is expected to do before the data is transferred and how errors will be handled by the two systems.

Sometimes the external system represents data in a way that is counterintuitive to SFDC users, and that may not fit well with the SFDC object model. For example, SFDC has an `account` object and a `partner` object but no customer object (because a customer in SFDC is just an `account` with a closed/won `opportunity`). Your accounting system probably has a customer object, but no partner or prospective customer object to match with SFDC's `account`. Because SFDC probably has many more `accounts`[26] than the accounting system has customers, some way of coordinating the two is needed (in this example, using the `account`'s `type` pick list to flag customers and partners is a likely strategy).

Two areas deserve special attention because they're so essential and so challenging to implement: customer purchase histories and price-list entries. Both of these data sets exist somewhere in your external systems, and both probably need to continue to be held in these systems of record. SFDC will probably need its own representation of these data, and synchronizing the two will be a challenge.

Customer and Account Data

Customer data—from company name to order history and payments—is almost certainly needed by some SFDC users. The first issue is customer identification:

- What is the unique key that can be used to cross-reference customer information between SFDC and the external system(s)?

- Is every customer consistently referred to by a single key, no matter which country the customer is in or which product division the customer ordered from?

---

26. This is particularly true in a named account model of selling where the sales organization may create hundreds of accounts before the company has ever done business with the customer. Although this is a best practice for sales management, it causes confusion with the accounting and finance types who view these prospective accounts as bogus. See Chapter 9 for more discussion of this topic.

- If the customer is a large conglomerate, how are different divisions noted in your company's systems? For example, Japan's Mitsubishi and South Korea's Hyundai both comprise hundreds of operating divisions that make everything from transistors to cars to entire steel mills. How do your company's systems refer to Mitsubishi's television division versus its electrical machinery division? And how do those systems refer to the electrical machinery division in the United States versus the one in Canada?

It is important to clarify these company nomenclature issues early so that you don't have ridiculously complicated requests of the integration team or make unachievable promises to your users.

The next issue is, "How many external systems need to be referenced for a given SFDC object (such as `account`)?" Every additional system that is integrated (particularly with synchronization) brings with it a huge increase in cost and complexity.

The final issue is, "Exactly how much customer information will be required from the external systems?" Usually a customer's order history is needed for a full SFDC system but at what level of detail? Will any SFDC user really need to know the line-item details on every order?

THE IMPORTANCE OF UNIQUE KEYS

One of the toughest problems in IT boils down to Shakespeare's classic query, "What's in a name?" Whenever two systems or databases need to be integrated, the team must find a universal identifier that reliably and uniquely indicates "this is the record you're looking for" in both systems.

In some cases, these keys are strings (such as "GM Corp HQ"), but usually they're unique numbers. In Web and marketing systems, the key may be the email address with which the customer registered. In accounting systems, the key may be the customer's tax ID number.

Unfortunately, almost no company has a unique, universal key that works across all systems. For each system you need to integrate with, you'll need to identify and understand its available external keys. You will almost certainly need to add several external keys to SFDC's records, one key for each system you need to integrate with. In exchange, SFDC's external keys (18-character alphanumerics) should be stored in each of those external systems.

Depending on the quality and breadth of the data in the system you're trying to integrate with, several viable strategies for matching keys may be available. If you're lucky, you will be able to use a reliable third-party identifier for matching records, such as a D-U-N-S number or FEIN tax ID number.

Most of the time, this strategy handles 50% to 80% of the historical records of a given type. For the remainder, it'll be rougher going. You will need to use some sort of tricky matching strategy, such as data fingerprints or scoring-based matching (e.g., a record is deemed to match if data from seven of nine fields match). Another matching strategy is based on historical activities (i.e., if the order history is identical, it is deemed to be the same customer). The problem comes, of course, with those records where the fingerprint is blurred by typos, foreign character sets, duplicates, and other data problems. The dirtier and noisier the data, the tougher the matching will be.

What if you can't find a direct matching strategy for your SFDC records? You may have to make the correspondence through a third system that acts as a Rosetta stone for customer or order identifiers.

In the worst case, you won't have any reliable way of making the correspondence between systems. In that situation, all you can do is simply say "no history available" and record the external keys in SFDC on a going-forward basis.

Price List

Price-list line items (also known as stock-keeping units, or SKUs) are needed for most advanced SFDC installations to support quoting, forecasting, and automated order entry. Your company's relevant price list may be printed in one document or available as a spreadsheet. In large multidivisional companies, however, the price list is often implemented in several different order management systems. Finding the system of record for all the company SKUs can be a serious exercise, as you may find that the price list is partitioned across several systems. SFDC may need to be integrated with each of those systems.

Each of the external systems may have data quality issues of its own, and integrating with more than one of those systems may surface even more data quality and consistency issues. Further, different systems use different structures for the product and price-list items, and some of these (particularly bundles and BOM structures) do not translate easily to SFDC.[27] These problems must be understood early, before any promises are made about the speed and depth of external system integration.

The good news is that price lists don't change very often, even if your firm does frequent promotions. Usually, price lists can be updated with simple file imports or spreadsheets forwarded over email on a weekly or monthly basis.

---

27. SFDC uses a hierarchy of tables for its price lists, starting with the product master, the list of price lists, and the item-level prices for each currency. SFDC does not have tables for discount schedules, product bundles, or upgrade paths—those must be implemented via custom objects and custom code.

Historical External Data

Historical external data comprise any data stored in some external system of record but are presented in the SFDC user interface. For the purposes of this section, historical data are defined as anything that was collected before *SFDC's go-live date*.

Although it's easy to understand how users would need last year's complete data, in most businesses users do not need to see data that are more than 3 years old. Use of historical data comes at a significant cost because a three-step process must be completed. First, these data must be located. Second, they must be integrated. Third, they must be adjusted to make the historical data meaningful and comparable with today's data.

For example, if 3 years ago a customer ordered Promotional Package 35, it's unlikely that this specific promotional package still exists. The records describing the package may be sketchy, and the package may have gone through several variations in different countries. In many cases, the original people who entered the data will have had context and knowledge that was "in their heads"—and they may have moved on. The farther back in history you go, the more expensive this kind of reinterpretation becomes.

When specifying historical data for integration, keep the request as shallow (for a short period) and as narrow (as few fields or records) as possible. In many cases, all that's really needed is a summary field ("here's the total dollar value of orders in the last 3 years") that can be generated or approximated in several ways, using alternative sources. These "roll-up" fields can save significant integration work without losing any real information.

The Days of Future Passed

Data stored in SFDC are, by default, available indefinitely in the future. While some older records may be harder to see, they are still there.

For larger companies, an important aspect of your system's data and report design is a data retention policy. Our recommendation is that users should *never* have the ability to delete records, and administrators should *almost never* use their privilege to do so, even if the records are erroneous or misleading. Such records should be hidden (via a change of ownership or a bad data flag) for analysis and correction and should be stored for comparison with future error records (to identify a recurrence of an error source or pollution-generating process).

Even though data should never be deleted, it's perfectly legitimate to archive old or inactive data. The question is the time horizon. In some industries, a record that's been inactive for more than a couple of years may not seem interesting. By comparison, when you are trying to run reports and comparative analysis, it is valuable to have at least 5 years of data. Further, regulators in some industries may want to look back 7 years—and generating reports from archived data can be amazingly difficult.

As a matter of principle, `account` records should never be archived. Unless you have millions of records, we seldom recommend archiving SFDC's objects before a 5-year horizon. When the objects are archived, they should be stored as relational tables for easy analysis and recovery. See Chapters 7 and 13 for more on this topic.

There's an important caveat about SFDC historical data: if you don't touch a `task` or `case` record for 12 months, it may be transparently moved into a kind of SFDC limbo. The old data *will* show up in all standard user screens, but they *may not* show up in reports or exports. If you need to always see those old data, you'll have to avoid using reports. Instead, you'll need to use the API's `QueryAll` operator and filter out deleted records (when SFDC says "all," it means *all*).

When it comes to documents, SFDC has four different models[28] for storing them—each with its own lovely security attributes. When your document-retention policy indicates "time to go," leave the metadata describing the document in SFDC and pull the actual file out. If your policy is to destroy the document, do so. If your policy is to retain documents in a special privileged archive, put it into an indexed file server.

Finally, there's `chatter feeds`, which can be quite voluminous and cumbersome to manage. However, for legal and regulatory reasons, it is wise to archive these feeds. Check out Archive for Chatter, Compliance Locker, and other AppExchange products for this purpose. Unfortunately, these products are so new that we can't advise on best practices here.

---

28. Documents may be stored as `Attachments`, `Documents`, `Content`, or `Files`. Going forward, you should focus most of your storage in the `Content` and `Files` areas.

GETTING THE MOST FROM SFDC

- Reverse-engineer the data model and many requirements from existing spreadsheets and reports.
- Use screen-design storyboards to get more details on the data model as well as core business process requirements.
- Make sure the team understands the core of SFDC's object model.
- Spend time early on getting agreement about semantics surrounding leads, contacts, opportunities, and cases.
- Develop naming conventions for important things (particularly companies, deals, and support incidents). Don't overcomplicate: focus on data that will actually make a difference!

FOR SMALL COMPANIES

- Focus on the VP of sales and his or her team's needs. Get a copy of whatever spreadsheet the VP is using.
- Focus on contacts, accounts, and opportunities. Keep screens simple.
- Work with marketing to design the leads so they fit with your registration pages. Avoid collecting lead data that won't be migrated during conversion.

FOR LARGE ENTERPRISES

- Interview every VP or CxO who will be using SFDC—get their report needs!
- Spend serious effort understanding data held in outside systems that must be integrated with SFDC. What data are available? What are their limitations?
- Develop a defendable horizon for the historical data to be imported.
- Develop a strategy for analytics and BI. Will you leverage an existing data warehouse? Will SFDC produce all key reports?

CHAPTER 3

Preparing Your Data

*Okay kids, everybody get out your EBCDIC
decoder ring!*

—Johnny Quest

T his chapter focuses on the underlying data itself because no one will use the system
if the data are confusing or a waste of time. This chapter is intended for anyone on
the original implementation team because first, data preparation, conversion, and
import are the most costly and time-consuming parts of any SFDC implementation; second, data are the basis for all reports, which is what most people use to judge the project
success; and third, data are the basis for system credibility, which is the single biggest
determinant of system usage and effectiveness.

From 1936 until 1969, water pollution was so bad in Ohio's Cuyahoga River that it occasionally caught fire. Data can become every bit as polluted as that water, with equally
spectacular effects.

Because the credibility of SFDC depends on having data that are meaningful and valuable, before any implementation work begins, a "project 0" should be started to assess the
health, cleanliness, and value of the data that will be flowing into the system. Fixing data
quality and meaning will be much harder than programming or system configuration—so
put the best people on this task from the beginning. If your company has experience
with data warehousing and extract, transform, load (ETL) tools, try to recruit one of
those people to be on your team—if nothing else, to be trainers and mentors for the tasks
outlined in the rest of this chapter.

As mentioned earlier, it's almost impossible to overestimate the cost and time involved
with data cleansing, import, and integration. You're about to see why.

Getting the Lay of the Land

It's very easy to get lost and disoriented in a large data migration project, so it's a great
idea to have a roadmap explaining which data items come from where, what they need

to be reconciled against, and how data will be transformed and cleansed *before* you start the effort. Here are the overall steps to creating this roadmap.

First, understand how much of the data really needs to be migrated. There are two axes to this determination:

- **The appropriate time horizon:** Does anyone really need to know what a customer's `cases` were from 3 years ago now that that company is no longer a customer?

- **The breadth/depth:** Do you really need to have access to all of the attachments and artifacts of a file, or just a few of the columns?

Scoping the data migration down along both axes can dramatically lower both the effort and the error rate of your work.

Next, double-check that migration is the best approach: with some kinds of operational data, leaving the data in its current home and doing an integration to make it accessible in SFDC—rather than a migration of data into the system—will yield better results.

Take an inventory of all data fields you need, and then map them (in a diagram or a spreadsheet) to the possible sources. If there is more than one source for an item, create two lines on the chart and annotate positives and negatives about each source. Annotate technical aspects of the data sources (e.g., "FTP server, but we don't have secure access to it"). Identify *unused* items in your data sources that could be used to corroborate or otherwise validate the data that you will be migrating.

This chapter assumes that you don't already have a "customer master" database that would allow a clean, single-pass import. Instead, we deal with the more common situation where you need to migrate up-to-date but flawed data from existing systems. Essentially, the goal is to find "the best of the worst" information and improve its quality during the migration process.

As a first step, get the external data exported (typically into a CSV file) and stored on your migration-staging servers. For most systems, this is a straightforward task involving a few tables, but we have seen cases where hundreds of tables had to be painstakingly exported to build a complete CRM data set from the current systems.

PERFECTIONISM DOESN'T PAY

In importing, integrating, or migrating data, it is tempting to want a squeaky-clean system with 100% data quality—at least on day one.

This temptation must be resisted because it can really kill your budget and your schedule. Removing impurities from data is similar to other industrial processes: it's asymptotically expensive. The first standard deviation (68%) of errors is cheap to remove, the next standard deviation (17%) costs about twice as much (even though you're only fixing one-fourth the total number of errors), the next standard deviation (4%) costs about four times as much to eliminate (even though you're fixing only one-fifteenth as many errors), and so on. Getting to Six Sigma purity (99.9998%) in data carries an astronomical cost. Even if you find a magical way to get all of the data right, new data errors will start to creep in from the first day of system operation anyway. So lighten up.

Instead of focusing on the purity of the data, optimize for correctness of meaning *from the customer's perspective*. If you can save half the effort by using limiting assumptions or even outright guesswork to get the meaning of the data "close enough," that's the shrewd path to take. For example, if you don't really know which products customers paid for, assume they bought the most expensive one and have them tell you when you've assumed wrong. If you sell IT products, assuming the most expensive product means that you get to charge higher support fees—which would be a major source of crocodile tears for our clients' sales folks.

Unless there's something very special going on in your company, error rates of 2% are usually unnoticeable, and an error rate of 5% is often quite acceptable as part of a manual exceptions-management process. Obviously, some parts of the records (e.g., customer number, amounts paid) must have a zero-tolerance policy—but does it really matter if there is a misspelling in a comments field?

Bottom line: data quality is both valuable and expensive. Make a sound business tradeoff here because the costs of the next increment of quality improvement typically increase faster than the benefits.

Migrating Data from an Existing SFA or CRM System

Here, the big task is to process the data from the existing SFA or CRM system(s) for migration into the system in preparation for cutover time. For the sake of simplicity, this section describes the situation where only one existing system is being retired; if there is more than one system (whether a different brand or multiple instances of the same brand), the work in this section multiplies quickly.

In migrating data into SFDC, it's important to understand the big picture of the data model. Figure 3-1 gives a partial overview of the standard SFDC object hierarchy. (If you want more detail on this, check out SFDC's free "Force Explorer" in the AppExchange.) Of course, SFDC is so flexible that your system will have more objects and more relationships than are shown in the figure. It is because of these interrelationships among data items that the sequence for importing should almost always proceed as follows:

1. `Accounts` have few data elements but typically have the most pointers to other records. Given that `accounts` appear at the top of the SFDC information pyramid, there will be relatively few of them.

2. `Contacts` typically have the most data elements for cleansing and enrichment as well as a couple of pointers to other records (e.g., `accounts` and `opportunity contact roles`). Typically, `contacts` are the number three population of data records in the system.

3. `Opportunities` have only a few data elements but have the most interesting time sequences for update history. You'll need to process both current (open) `opportunities` and historical (closed) ones.

4. `Products, product line items`, and `price lists` are highly static and don't represent many records. You'll have to make sure that all of the `product's` attributes (such as pricing models, terms, multiple price lists, discount schedules, and revenue recognition schedules) are represented in the SFDC table.

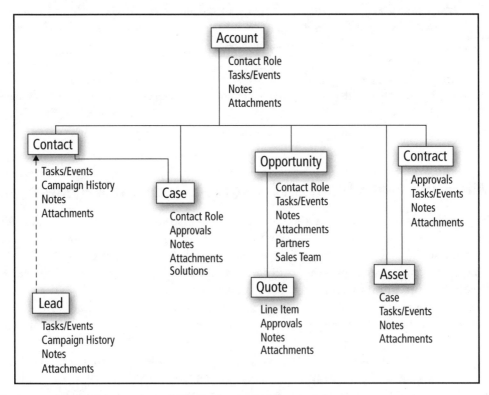

FIGURE 3-1   A partial overview of SFDC's standard object model

5. Leads may have many data elements to clean and enrich but do not have many pointers that need to be correlated with other records. Typically, leads are the number two population of data records in the system.

6. Campaigns are typically a few hundred historical descriptions of marketing outreach activities. Each holds a few data items but may have large attached files.

7. Campaign members are the history of all leads and contacts the company has touched. They hold a very small number of data items but can consist of a very large number of records.

8. Contracts are typically a few hundred or few thousand records associated with closed opportunities. Typically, there aren't many fields in these records, but they may have important attachments that need to be imported.

9. Customer assets represent the history of customer purchases. Usually, the assets are just the summary of purchases, with little or no detail about the purchase history. These asset summaries typically have to be generated from roll-up tables stored in external systems. Although there is rarely a big data cleansing task here, processing of the customer purchase roll-ups needs to avoid double counting of inventory.

10. Cases typically contain relatively few data items but often contain pointers to other data records and attached files. You may have a lot of cases to process.

11. Solutions are solved cases and contain few data items but have important long-text fields that need to survive even if they have hidden non-ASCII characters. Solutions also typically have attachments that need to be linked to the proper record in SFDC.

12. Contact roles (for accounts, opportunities, and cases) contain almost no data, as they are just pointers to other data in the system. But they are important to show connections and indications of political influence in companies and deals.

13. Activities are fairly simple records, typically about 2KB each. But they have three pointers (to a user, a person, and a thing in the system) that require solid external-key references. In the comments area of the activity, the system may have appended text from emails—these can be long. If the source system(s) are connected to email blasters or marketing automation systems, Activities comprise the single largest record count in the system—sometimes representing more records than all the other tables combined. (This is an area for judicious pruning during the import cycle.)

14. `Notes`, `documents`, `content`, and `attachments` typically have few data elements, but several types of corruption are possible in the fields. Clean the fields but don't be so aggressive as to remove the text formatting (tabs and carriage returns) embedded in them.

Now it's time to plan and do the data conversion. You'll want to follow the conversion and import cycle described below for *each of the data objects in the preceding list*. Before you even start, ask users of the existing CRM system to flag as many duplicates and bad records as possible in the current system. The best way for them to do so is to mark the records with a unique, searchable marker (such as ###dedupe### or ###junk###) in a seldom-used field. Storing the record identifiers in a spreadsheet dedicated to listing duplicate or garbage records works as well.

The first step of your process is to create a staging area in SFDC to test migration procedures and results. A free `developer instance` will work initially, but its 2MB storage limit will soon get in your way. Ideally, you should use an SFDC `Sandbox`,[1] which gives you an area for testing and debugging that won't interfere with the normal working[2] system. If your company can't afford a `sandbox`, you'll have to do frequent system backups and work very carefully in your operational system.

Next, export a subset of the data you're trying to import and look at the results in Excel. Visual inspection is important because there's no faster way to see incomplete records, missing fields, gross data corruption (such as an email address stuffed into a phone number field), and trash data (such as a text field filled with 2,500 characters of a foreign character set). Get your mind around—and fix—these gross problems first.

The next thing to do is look at the data model of the old system and map it to SFDC's object model. If you're lucky, this task will involve a straightforward, field-by-field mapping. Of course, this task is quite likely to be a lot more complicated than that, requiring joins of disparate fields to create the SFDC objects (one memorable example from my firm involved manipulating 180 different tables to migrate the data out of a single system). Note any cases where a join with data from a third system is required because these situations probably require special attention. At the other extreme, all of the data you're trying to work on may be in one giant table or in flat files, requiring several passes through the data to synthesize the objects and events needed for SFDC. In any event, it is critically

---

1. SFDC's `Full Sandbox`—the one you need for data migration—is an extra-cost item that provides a complete staging system with duplicated code and data. Because it can hold all of your data records simultaneously, the `sandbox` gives you an area to do comprehensive development, testing, and validation away from the prying eyes of users.
2. The system may not be working yet, but the main area of the system will be where prototypes and mockups will be. You don't want to step on other teams' toes.

important to understand the format, meaning,[3] provenance, and acceptable range for each field. Create a checklist of steps in your mapping procedure to account for these issues.

Decide whether you will import all of the historical data into SFDC. In most cases, all of the data will come over. If you have hundreds of thousands of records that haven't been active for 5 years, however, you may choose to put the older data into an archive and bring over only the last few years' worth of data. If you have a million `leads`, each of which has 10 `activities`, you will quickly outgrow SFDC's storage space—and expansion is expensive.

After this migration storyboard has been completed (using essentially no real data), a small data set (maybe 10% of the total) should be exported from the old system to do a trial migration into an SFDC developer account. Working with a subset of the real data, the team will discover lots of complicating factors and real-world problems that can be corrected with corrective spreadsheets, SQL queries, UNIX utilities, and other tools. The basic corrective sequence—which you may do yourself or hire a contractor specializing in data migration—is outlined here:

1. **Incompletes:** Validate that all the records you expected to migrate have, in fact, shown up in SFDC. Investigate any missing records to find out what prevented them from being imported, and fix that issue.

2. **Trash characters:** Look for nonprinting characters (which may just show up as a space) that may cause the record to not be transferred. These nonprinting characters often appear in long-text fields, where a user has copied and pasted text from an email or other outside source, but they can also occur because of improper foreign character translation. To preserve the formatting of these long-text fields, the best approach is to use UNIX text utilities (such as `tr`, `sed`, `od`, or `awk`) and regular expression formulas to substitute acceptable characters in the fields. Excel formulas using the `CHAR`, `SUBSTITUTE`, and other string manipulation operators work as well.

3. **Column swaps:** Look for rows that have swapped columns. In data sets that have been in place for a long time, any number of actions may have caused columns for certain rows to have been offset or swapped. Phone numbers may show up in country fields, street addresses in ZIP code fields, and countries in state fields. Find these patterns, group the affected rows together in your data correction tool (typically Excel), and correct the columns.

---

3. Semantics are almost certain to be misleading or misunderstood for at least one data item, no matter how small the data set you're working with. Do not assume that *phone* means "business phone" or that *amount* means "total discounted revenue amount for this transaction." Assumptions kill productivity.

4. **Foreign characters:** Foreign character sets often become corrupted (e.g., a French é showing up as e# or whatever), and they may appear in any text field. This is particularly true of email body text that may have been pushed into `long-text` fields. Create a list that maps the corrupted text to the original characters, and then use either UNIX text utilities or Excel `substitute` formulas to correct the characters. For non-European characters, you'll need someone with the foreign language skills, and someone with knowledge of Unicode, to help you set up the character correction tables.

5. **Alphas in numerics:** Numbers that include alpha characters (such as "ext" in phone numbers) need to be cleaned; this can often be done with Excel `substitute`, `left`, `right`, and `concatenate` formulas. If a field is supposed to be all letters and includes a number, apply the same tricks.

6. **Bogus numbers:** Numbers that are out of range should be analyzed to understand the patterns. Are the units wrong (e.g., $ rather than $M)? Was the number originally a date (and corrupted into the "number of days since 1970" or "number of minutes since the beginning of the year")? Are numbers simply transposed between fields (part numbers are substituted for price)? Are numbers transformed into scientific notation (as occasionally happens with phone numbers and SFDC ID numbers)? Are leading zeroes removed (really annoying for New England ZIP codes)? Are dates messed up by Y2K problems (yes, I've seen this in SFDC data migrations)? You can have hours of fun understanding these error patterns and correcting them.

THE JOY OF REGEX

In many cases, the tools you'll use to do data conversion, correction, and enrichment are low-level goodies you already have on your PC. Although they're no cost and familiar—which saves on the learning curve—they also have some foibles you need to be ready for.

If you're trying to clean up text, *never* use Microsoft Word. It will corrupt even the most innocent-looking text in a hurry. Instead, use a low-level text editor (like HTML Pad or even MS-DOS's edit function) to make sure that carriage returns and other nonprinting characters are preserved. If things are really hairy, you may need to use `awk`, `sed`, `tr`, or other UNIX/Linux tools to keep things clean.

If you're trying to clean up a table, Microsoft Excel is the most commonly used tool—and it works well if you really know how to use it. Master the `VLOOKUP`, `format`, `clean`, `concatenate`, `left`, `right`, and other string-manipulation commands. Excel is usually not case sensitive, but SFDC *is* (particularly with record ID numbers), so be careful when doing searches and matches. Use copy down mouse actions with care: if the thing you're copying is a number, Excel will magically corrupt your data by incrementing the value by one in each new row. Be really careful when using the `sort` function—if you don't highlight all of the columns of the table before you perform the sort, the entire data set will be corrupted.

Beware working with the CSV file format—if you're not careful, Excel "auto-mangles" phone numbers, SFDC ID numbers, or any other large integers by turning them into scientific notation or suppressing leading zeroes. One trick for avoiding this problem (on Windows-based systems) is to *not* double-click on .csv files to open them. Instead, rename them as .txt files before opening them. Then, use Excel's `Open` menu item, which will invoke an import wizard that allows you to assign the number columns as *text*, which (perversely) solves these number-smashing problems. Then, save the workbook as a .xls file before you start working on the contents. CSV files also have interesting problems with foreign character sets and illegal character sequences that can cause columns to be thrown out of alignment or can cause a single field to be split into several subfields. After a while, it gets to be kind of entertaining.

Also be aware of Excel's structural limits: certain operations limit the effective cell size to 255 characters, and the product handles only a million rows per worksheet. Even with the expanded row limits in the latest versions of Excel, functions such as `VLOOKUP` slow down dramatically beyond 64K rows. This warning goes double if you're using SFDC's Excel connector, which simply won't handle more than 32K rows.

7. **Country codes:** Country names should be transformed into ISO-standard two-character[4] country codes. Yes, do all 239 of them—you won't save any time by leaving out country names. In case the country field is blank, you can use other information (i.e., phone number, state, and city) to synthesize the country code. In the case of `accounts`, you can use the local version of Corporation (e.g., "Gmbh" for Germany or "Pty" for Australia) to identify the country. Leave as few country fields blank as possible because they are needed for several SFDC rules. Note that every user in the system will need a cheat sheet for these codes, so make sure to create one of these on card-stock paper and as PDFs in the project wiki and SFDC's documents section.

8. **State codes:** State names (at least for the United States and Canada, plus Brazil, Germany, France, Russia, India, and China if you do business there) should be transformed into ISO-standard two-character state codes. For other countries,

---

4. You may want to use three-character codes; decide on which system to use, and be consistent from there forward. Note that SFDC has new country and state pick-list fields which automatically map to two-character codes (ISO 3166-1 alpha-2).

leave the state fields as they are—they won't do any harm and you may decide to transform them into state codes later. As with the country codes, everyone will need a cheat sheet for the state codes.

9. **Postal codes:** ZIP/postal codes need to be checked for format (five or nine digits in the United States, six digits in the United Kingdom and Canada, five digits in France, and so on). They should also be checked for geographic correspondence (the postal code should match the state code, city name, or phone number's city or area code) if possible. There are some nice third-party tools that do this kind of checking in Excel, and there are some others available for fixing addresses after the data has been imported into SFDC.

10. **Phone numbers:** Phone numbers need to be checked for several issues. U.S. phone numbers are completely regular and should be in the format AAA-EEE-NNNN (where A is the three-digit area code, E is the three-digit exchange code, and N is the four-digit line number). But watch out: many North American companies have cute alphanumeric versions of their phone numbers like 1-800-EAT-BEEF. These must be replaced with pure numeric versions prior to import. International numbers are much more variable but should be in the format +CCC AAA NN NN NN NN (where C is the one-, two-, or three-digit country code; A is the one-, two-, or three-digit city code; and N is the six-, seven-, or eight-digit line number). Frequently, users will omit the +CCC part of the number and insert a 0 in front of the rest of the number. Because the range of formatting and content problems on international numbers is fairly wide, you'll want to analyze your specific symptoms before designing corrective formulas. Part of your corrective strategy should be checking the phone numbers against the state and country codes of the address, which can help disambiguate number problems. In the United States, number portability and Voice over IP (VoIP) have dramatically decreased the efficacy of geographic/area code validation.

11. **Extensions:** Some phone numbers include extensions or access codes. These should be split off from the phone number field and stored as a separate `custom field` in SFDC's `lead`, `contact`, and `account` records.

12. **Email addresses:** Email address formats should be corrected (to xxxx@yyy.com/biz/mil/edu/gov in the United States and xxx@yyy.co.cc or mailto:xxx@yyy.cc in all other countries). Watch out for the external system's email opt-out flags—they may not exist where you would expect them to appear. Ask about external systems (such as email vendors) where this flag may be stored. We recommend that records of people who have opted out have their email addresses corrupted (e.g., joe.blow@abc.com.nospam) so that the addresses will be automatically bounced in case they are accidentally used.

13. **Pick lists:** Pick-list values in the exported data set will need to be checked to make sure that they are (or are mapped to) a verbatim (character-by-character) match to the pick-list norm in the SFDC data model. Pay particular attention to the `type`, `status`, `stage`, `industry`, and `source` fields on any object where they occur. Watch out for leading and trailing spaces! Also make sure that dashes are not confused with minus signs, hyphens, or em dashes. In cases where you are transforming a free-form entry (plain-text or number field) from the outside system into an SFDC pick list, you need to create a sorted list of all the free-form entries (e.g., using Excel pivot tables) and normalize them to the pick-list values.

14. **Booleans:** Boolean values will need to be normalized to `TRUE` or `FALSE`. Remember that in some data sets manipulated by Microsoft code, -1 means `TRUE`. In cases where you are transforming a free-form entry (plain-text or other fields) from the outside system into an SFDC Boolean, you'll need to do a sorted list of all the free-form entries and normalize them to the Boolean values.

15. **Required and default values:** Verify that SFDC's required fields are populated in all cases. If you discover instances where a required field is empty or has an unreasonable value, go back to the original source data to make sure something in your process isn't corrupting the data. If the required field is empty in the original system, assign the default value (if applicable) to it, or see if there is a way to synthesize the real value from the available data. If there's no way to do that, but the record is still valid, fill the field in with a unique value, such as "DummySynthesized-031208@14:15:47" to enable the record transfer.

16. **Ownership:** In SFDC, every record needs to have an owner—this is the core of its security model. Ownership of every single record needs to be assigned to a current user[5] in the system. Each record needs to be checked against the sales rep's (or, with `case` data, customer support rep's) territory assignment. Because representative turnover and territory definition changes occur fairly frequently, ownership for many records in your migrating data set will be incorrectly assigned. Fixing this problem can be a simple matter when the territories are geographic and large (by state and country) but can become very complex indeed when overlays exist or territories are defined by industry, company size, revenues, street address, or even company name. Territory definitions can be surprisingly difficult to get from sales management—just push until you get the territory descriptions or maps, and pray that they aren't too ambiguous.[6] In the end, you'll need to

---

5. If you have to deal with historical records whose original ownership needs to be maintained, create a hidden field in SFDC and import the original owner's name there verbatim, in addition to the standard ownership that will be used by SFDC.

6. Check out the discussion of territory management in Chapter 9 for more on this issue.

construct a series of rules that (we hope) will automatically do the reassignment of ownership. Keep those rules as simple as you can: you know you're in trouble if the description of the rules processing strategy takes more than a few pages of narrative or diagrams. Because of security and access control issues, ownership needs to be correctly set for every single record in the system: it's as big a deal as it is a pain in the neck.

17. **Dates:** Record creation dates should be transferred from the old system to SFDC. If the external system has more than one `create date` for a record, use the oldest one for SFDC's `create date`. A funny thing happened a few years ago—Y2K rollover—that in some cases may mean dates on old data need to be transformed. SFDC uses full four-digit years, so look for any date kludges that may have been done in the existing system and perform transformations on them as part of the import process. During the trial imports, you will not have historical date insertion enabled in SFDC, so the `create dates` you see on the first passes will always be "today."

18. **Old pointers or ID numbers:** Most systems will have existing ID numbers for each data record. Although these numbers/strings are system generated and cannot be used by SFDC, they should be imported as hidden fields into the system. If the old ID is a pure number, you should either set the External ID attribute or store it as a `text` data type in SFDC (to prevent leading-zero suppression). Further, pointers between old records (e.g., old parent–child or master–detail relationships) should be imported as well. This strategy allows the implementation team to backtrack and validate the provenance of each record during the testing cycle.

19. **Record histories/audit trails:** If your data source keeps a record (history) of changes made to fields over time, it is possible to recreate most of that information in SFDC. It is an arduous task, however, and we certainly recommend that you try to negotiate your way out of this job.[7] Note that change-history records are stored for an 18-month horizon (i.e., any historical record referring to a change made more than 18 months ago), and `stage history` (opportunities) and `case history` (cases) cannot be imported at all.

20. **Duplicates:** Duplicate records are a major pain because they're deadly to both system data quality and user credibility. What makes dupes tough to eliminate is that they're almost never literal duplicate records—the matches are fuzzy, and judgment is required to do the right thing. Some of the deduplication must be

---

7. In most situations, importing these audit-trail records will be something of a kludge and will only really be useful for troubleshooting and ad-hoc analysis. Our general advice here is to export the audit trails from your to-be-retired system into an external SQL database for your analysis and not import those data into SFDC.

performed during the importing cycle (typically using the email address as the unique identifier) to make sure that the process itself isn't creating duplicates (this possibility is a particularly vexing issue when data must be drawn from more than one outside system). That said, we've never come across a situation where all of the deduping *had to be done* before the data was imported into SFDC.[8] We recommend doing as much of the deduping *in* SFDC as you can (using tools from companies such as RingLead and CRMfusion), which makes it easier to see the impact of what you're doing. By contrast, if you identify a truly prodigious number of dupes, it's important to understand which system or process is creating them. Once you've identified the culprit, make the get-well project one of your highest priorities because delays cause an exponential rise in correction cost.

21. **Consistency reports:** After all of the preceding steps have been completed, a series of reports should be run on the data to make sure that the record count is correct and that major statistical characteristics of the original data set have been preserved. For example, if the original data consisted of 12% of records coming from California and 0.1% from South Dakota, it would be an unpleasant surprise to find the Dakotans representing 53% of data at the end. Trust me, this kind of problem happens. The data consistency reports should scrutinize the heuristics and statistical character of every column to make sure that the conversion process hasn't corrupted the data set. If you find prodigious errors, it would be a real judgment call whether to fix the data in SFDC versus reimporting a subset of data from scratch.

DATA ENRICHMENT

The art of adding value to data by merging it with outside sources should almost never be done as part of the data migration cycle. Although such a merge could be done at this stage, I've not seen a case where it would yield any better results than doing the merge later, after the import has been validated and all of the data have been stabilized. The data migration cycle is stressful enough on its own—there's no reason to add the risk and hassle of more tasks to this process.

Once you've completed the trial migration, you'll need to do a full pilot migration. For this operation, you'll need access to `enterprise edition` account. Talk to your SFDC sales rep; he or she can probably get you temporary access for testing purposes,

---

8. If you face this situation, tools that plug in to Excel and Access are available. In addition, ETL tools used for data warehousing and business intelligence may be used for deduping purposes. We discuss the deduping procedures later in this chapter.

even if you haven't yet purchased the system. During the complete pilot migration, you will almost certainly discover problems that occur only when you are working with the entire data set. As mentioned earlier, if you're using Excel, you'll probably need to break up Big Data sets into manageable chunks. Make sure the partitioning and reaggregation of the data are done correctly—it's easy to make procedural errors because of the complexity of this issue alone. To check the validity of the results, do extensive comparative reporting and analyze the data set for unexpected changes to the statistical "shape of the data"[9]—staying cognizant that you can afford to spot-check only a few hundred records in detail.

All of these corrective steps need to be carefully documented, put into a script, or configured as an ETL program workflow because it may be several weeks before the final data migration occurs. When that happens—usually in the first wave of implementation—there won't be any spare energy for discovery or refinement.

Migrating Data from Other Systems

You may have to migrate data from other systems that aren't SFA or CRM but still hold important customer data. For example, your order management system may have important information that really should reside in SFDC going forward.

The first step in this process is to make sure that the data *should* be moved—that the system of record should be SFDC from now on. Moving data out of an established system—rather than leaving it there and integrating SFDC with the existing system—can mean important improvements in performance, existing code, and user access.[10] As part of that decision, be sure to read the "Who Owns the Data Now?" section in Chapter 6.

Once the decision to move the data is made, go through the data cleansing sequence outlined in the previous section. Although the general strategies will be similar for every system from which you migrate data, the checklist and procedures will be different every time.

Your Big Weekend: Doing the Import

Up to now, you've been doing test import cycles into developer accounts, the Sandbox, or temporary SFDC instances. Now it's time to import data directly into the main system,

---

9. The heuristics should include such items as record count, mean, median, range, and modality.

10. Once the data is moved into SFDC, it will be directly accessible only by SFDC users. Some existing users of the external system may feel disenfranchised—in this case, create a report that delivers an Excel spreadsheet of the data they are currently used to.

which may already be in use. Ideally, all of the discoveries, practice cycles, and checklists presented earlier will pay off in a smooth data import.

The data import session should occur at a time when there are very few users on the system and when the exporting systems can be taken offline or put in read-only mode. Almost without exception, this operation should be scheduled as a weekend session that begins on Friday evening at 7 P.M. or so in the company headquarters' time zone (or whichever time zone contains the most SFDC users).

BE PREPARED—THAT'S THE BOY SCOUT'S MARCHING SONG . . .

At least 1 week before your Big Weekend, open a case in SFDC's support system requesting historical date insertion—the ability to create records with `create` `dates` *other than "today" (the system default). Once your support request for a data migration/history audit dates is logged as an SFDC support system case, call your SFDC sales rep and have that case escalated. There is no way to do your Big Weekend tasks unless this feature is enabled. Typically, SFDC leaves this feature enabled for a week or two, but ask for even more time so you can rework the portion of the import that didn't make into SFDC the first time.*

Before you actually start your migration cycle, perform a *complete* backup of your production SFDC instance. Although SFDC does provide automatic backup of all your data for free, data recovery is time consuming and expensive. Any time you plan to muck with SFDC data in bulk, it is vital that you **do a complete backup to a local hard drive**. Leverage the system's `weekly export service`—it's free with the `enterprise` and `unlimited editions`, and it's the fastest way to perform a complete backup. Unfortunately, you can use this strategy only once (because you're only allowed to use it weekly, and your import cycle better take a lot less time than that). You *will* need to do a subsequent full-system backup, but complete that task using SFDC's Data Loader or another bulk export tool.

If you're lucky, all of your Big Weekend tasks can be done in one pass and one day. Of course, matters rarely go that smoothly, particularly if you have to import or migrate data from more than one external system. Consequently, it's important to have a disciplined, repeatable process and take careful notes with each pass. If a large or distributed group is doing the import tasks, you'll need to carefully coordinate the group members' activities, even to the point of having a coxswain for the team. Otherwise, you may do a complete system import, only to discover later that the data do not behave properly or that one of the steps was done incorrectly or out of order. You may then have to use SFDC's Data Loader tool (or even heavier-duty tools, as discussed in Chapter 7) to erase a bad import—and you may discover you have to erase more than you wanted to because of data dependencies and pointers. Rinse. Lather. Repeat. It's okay: you get faster and better at it with each pass.

There's Got to Be a Morning After: Deduping Records

Once data have been successfully migrated into SFDC, the very first thing you should do is a *complete* system backup (yes, including attachments). Once the system is backed up, it's essential to deduplicate records before users start working with the system. Duplicate records are irritating to users who will be tempted to engage in these dangerous behaviors:

- Deleting records.

- Incorrectly performing record merges, which delete or corrupt data.

- Scattering data across duplicates, which results in data being lost.[11]

- Lowering data standards because "It's a mess anyway."

- Lowering their opinion of the system.

At the time the system is brought up, shoot for less than 2% duplicate records. Identify and remove as many of these buggers as you can because users will notice them from the first moment.

Duplicate records can appear in any SFDC object but occur most frequently in `leads` and `contacts`. Although fixing these redundancies is important to system credibility and usability, duplicate `opportunities` and `accounts` are more likely to cause the most problems. Accounts are particularly difficult because they are at the top of SFDC's data model and are pointed to by so many other objects.

Accounts

Duplicate `accounts` occur for three reasons: first, some system users just won't follow the best practices you taught them[12]; second, an imported data set or integrated system generates the duplicates as a result of faulty code or suboptimal business policies; and third, business process problems that systematically create duplicates. Let's look at user-created `account` dupes first.

Users are supposed to `search` for `accounts` before creating them, and they should be looking for existing `account` names before they `convert leads`. In most SFDC installations, a few bogus `accounts` are created each week by sloppy users. The tell-tale

---

11. In fact, the data are not lost—but finding the information can be so irritating that impatient sales reps and executives simply give up. This is *not* their problem: it's the system's problem, and the team needs to prevent it from occurring.
12. Some people might say they're lazy, but we'd never put *that* in print.

signs of these bogus `accounts` are the `account` was created by the `account owner`, there is some relevant manually entered data in the `account` fields, and there may be an open `opportunity` or a follow-up `activity` associated with the new `account`. When you first look at the SFDC system, run a report (or use a deduping tool's diagnostic mode) to identify these human-created dupes, and merge or subordinate them with the master `account` as described later in this chapter.

You'll want to do this kind of housekeeping on an ongoing basis, once every week or so. Wait for a system "quiet time" when users won't be updating records. That would be nights and weekends, with Friday from 7 P.M. Pacific time to Sunday 2 A.M. being primo hours. This is why data administrators do not go out on dates much.

User Accounts for External Integration Code

SFDC is quite good at tracking who created and updated records, and it can be configured to keep detailed audit trails for important data changes. Any code external to SFDC, including integration, data migration, and externally hosted code elements, must log in to the system before it is permitted to interact with the data. For a number of reasons, it's a best practice to have an SFDC user account dedicated to each major external subsystem (the user name is usually the friendly name of the IT system it runs in) so that updates are marked as having been performed by code rather than people.

If your system has more than one complex bit of code outside of SFDC, consider having each program run under a different user account. If your external integration needs to access opportunities, cases, campaigns, or other advanced objects, it will have to be an `enterprise` or `unlimited` license. If, however, the external application needs to get to only a few tables, you may be able to use a less expensive `single-application force.com` license. Either way, you'll save much more than what it costs whenever you're trying to debug a data corruption problem. Plus, you'll get some extra SFDC storage that you can allocate to real users.

More interesting is the case of `accounts` that have been generated by code, which almost always result from a data migration or integration gone awry. What code should do is compare existing `accounts` in SFDC with the new `accounts` being migrated or integrated into the system. Otherwise, errant code (or import procedures) will simply create new `accounts` with nearly identical information to accounts already in SFDC. The first step in this situation is to stop the bogus `account` generation by using a universal key or by using a search method to find the best match in the existing SFDC `accounts`. Once this problem has been fixed, you'll probably find that the duplicate `accounts` in SFDC can't be simply deleted: they have to be merged with the good data.

More interesting still (at least to this author's pitiful worldview) is the situation where the `accounts` are created because of a business process problem. These can be hard to identify and even harder to rectify because business process problems are the organi-zational equivalent to neurosis.[13] If you can't stop the creation of the dupes, use your knowledge of the business process to automatically generate an alert message whenever a dupe has been generated.

INSTEAD OF DEDUPING ACCOUNTS . . .

Although other system data really *have* to be deduped, there is another option for near-du-plicate `accounts`: create parent–child relationships. The basic strategy is to leave the multiple `accounts` in place and make them children of the master `account`, as shown in Figure 3-2.

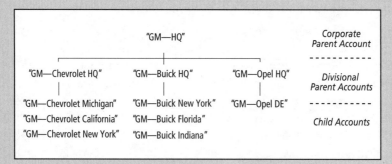

FIGURE 3-2   Example account hierarchy

Using this strategy, none of the child `account` information is lost, and the people who are searching for the right division of ABC Company can quickly find the relevant information.

Deduping involves finding record sets that should be merged, designating one of them as the master copy, and moving all of the related list items (e.g., `tasks`, `contacts`, `attachments`, `notes`, and `opportunities`) to the master record.[14] Only when the

---

13. The old saw "What makes a behavior neurotic is that you're proud of it" comes to mind here.

14. If you're reading closely, you'll note that all the related list items survive, but some of the fields in the non-master records will be thrown away. For example, for an account's Web site, there can only be one surviving value. If you need to make sure that the field entries from the lost records survive, you'll need to do some very clever preprocessing of the data. This is essential for fields such as owner, status, email, and phone in nearly any record you want to merge. The procedure is tricky, so check out www.SFDC-secrets. com for the how-to checklist.

duplicate records are emptied of good data are they deleted. This process can be highly automated using products from RingLead, CRMfusion, and others. Even so, the effectiveness of the automation depends on *reliably and consistently* identifying which is the master record.

In the case of `accounts`, deduping won't be simple. Using first created or last updated rules will yield inconsistent results, which can be disastrous because there's no ability to undo a record merge.[15] You'll need to run a report on the `accounts` that appear to be duplicates, showing the `create date`, `modified date`, `owner`, `created by`, and `modified by` fields. Also look at patterns in the `account` data and related lists to indicate which record should be the master. If your integration code is smart enough to put the universal key (which identifies `accounts` across all of your IT systems) into the record, any record holding a universal key is automatically defined as the master. It is usually a good idea to create a custom field on the object that can be populated with markers that indicate "this is the master."

Once you've identified the rules that consistently identify the master, set the marker field. Now that the masters are clearly identified, you can use the last updated rule as the default for the merge/deduping tool. If the tool has an option to have filled fields in an old record trump empty fields in the newer record, use that option. Unfortunately, the deduping tools seem to delete the duplicate `accounts` automatically[16] rather than marking them as obsolete.

Opportunities

`Opportunities` aren't as thorny as `accounts`. Because `opportunities` exist both in SFDC and in your company's order management and accounting system, however, they need to be handled carefully. Because a closed `opportunity` means revenue, it's important not to have double-counting here.

The secret here is proper naming and identification of `opportunities`. An external key is needed to keep SFDC's data properly synchronized with the order management system. Typically, the systems will share a quote number, which will be transformed into an order number when the transaction closes. SFDC should be configured to hold the external system's quote and order numbers, and the integration software should keep the data synchronized on a near real-time basis.

I know of no tools for deduping `opportunities` internal to SFDC; instead, this task must be done using external tools. If you have to do it manually, the master

---

15. This is why the *first thing you do* after the system goes live is a complete backup.
16. Although this is not the right thing to do from a purist's perspective, these tools save so much time and effort that it's worth the risk of losing the data associated with depleted duplicate records. That said, the duplicate records can be reconstituted from your backup files.

opportunity's record is where quote and order numbers are stored; all duplicate `opportunities` will have to be compared (either in a spreadsheet or visually using two Web browsers), and any unique data in the duplicates should be manually copied into the master record. All `contact roles`, `tasks`, `activity history`, `attachments`, and other related items need to be transferred from the duplicate `opportunities` to the master `opportunity`—and all of these transfers are usually done manually in the UI. Even after a duplicate `opportunity` is emptied of all unique data, it should not be deleted.[17] Instead, it should have its `stage` changed to duplicate opportunity and its probability percentage changed to zero.

Any `opportunity` for new business that has not been the subject of any updates for a year should also have its `stage` changed to closed/lost. (Note that renewal `opportunities` may be valid in the system for as long as 3 years, depending on your business practice.)

Contacts and Leads

The nice thing about duplicate `contacts` and `leads` is that there are so many ways they can occur, and there are such dramatic ways to collapse them. But in collapsing these items, it's important not to lose important historical data. Although the data deduping tools will automatically append most of the history from underlying `leads` (e.g., `activities` and `campaigns`), they may not faithfully consolidate the entire audit trail of changes (`Field History`) and by themselves, they can't do the right thing with the `lead source`. You have to take some steps first.

Most of the audit trails will be properly concatenated by the deduping tools or the SFDC merge function, but there will be cases where some subtleties will get lost, perhaps because of overlapping or contradictory updates in the multiple `lead` and `contact` records. If you really need to have a complete audit trail for forensic reporting, the best course of action is to dump the `history` data for all `leads` and `contacts` into an archival file prior to performing any deduping.

With the `lead source`, the problem is that this standard field can have only one value at a time, but reality is sometimes better reflected by a series of values (e.g., Web site registration, download, Webinar). The right approach is to create a series of well-structured `campaigns` that mirror each `lead source` value. Each `lead` should then become a member of its appropriate `campaign` *before* the deduping process, so that the tools you use can properly append and transfer the `campaign memberships` during

---

17. Deletion just isn't the right thing to do. For both Sarbanes-Oxley Act compliance and for general data hygiene, records should never be deleted because all audit trails would be deleted along with the record. Keeping duplicate `opportunities` will use an infinitesimal amount of storage, yet will provide evidence for any forensic audit or business process analyses in the future.

the deduping cycle. It's really important to get this right, even though it may take some serious time. Check out Chapter 10 for a deeper discussion of `campaigns`.

Documents and Emails

It is not at all uncommon to discover that documents have been redundantly stored or that an email conversation has been copied into the system multiple times. Unfortunately, I know of no SFDC tools that identify—let alone correct—this situation. There are tools in the storage management arena that help find these redundancies, but they will have to be used entirely outside of SFDC. The specific techniques used for deduping documents and emails are well outside the scope of this book, but the general idea is to export the documents (and their reference pointers), remove them from SFDC, dedupe the exported copies externally, and then reimport them into SFDC.

DON'T LEAVE FOR HOME WITHOUT MAKING ANOTHER BACKUP

Do another complete system backup of any data you have deduped. Save each backup under a different name, and archive the old ones so you can backtrack if necessary. Even after you think the project is finished, keep these files around. You may discover a subtle corruption weeks later, and these interim files will provide forensic data to reconstruct the crime . . . and, one would hope, rebuild the data.

The Morning After the Morning After: Enriching Data

This section could have been called *The Poseidon Adventure II,* but that would have been too obscure a reference. So I didn't do that, and we just move on to the next step.

Now that the initial deduplication has been done, it is time to perform data enrichment: adding outside data into SFDC to provide more complete information about `leads`, `contacts`, and `accounts`. The enrichment process uses the data already in SFDC to match up with the external data and then imports these "fatter" records back into the system.

For example, with `leads`, the one part of the record that can be validated as correct is the user's email address. Everything else in the record may be bogus or have typos, but with the right systems in place,[18] at least the email address will be correct. Using a

---

18. For example, when users register at your Web site, the site should not grant access to the requested documents or resources without sending an email to the user's address; the email should contain a link that directs the user to the requested resource(s). By clicking the link, the user is uniquely identified and the email address validated. Of course, some people use single-use email addresses, but they usually represent an extremely small percentage of the total number of visitors. See Chapter 10 for further discussion on this topic.

reverse lookup, enrichment vendors can provide such information as the person's name, company name, title, phone number, address, and information about the company they work for. SFDC's data.com service (previously known as Jigsaw) is the de facto standard for this data cleansing and enrichment process, but there are external services that offer more depth in certain vertical industries and countries outside of the United States. This enrichment process typically costs about $1 per record and takes a day or two to complete. Depending on your specific audience, these enrichment services may get a hit rate as high as 50%—but don't be surprised if 20% or less of the records match (particularly for international demographics).

`Contact` records typically have better data intrinsic quality because someone in your organization has communicated with those people to qualify them for `contact` status (see Chapters 9 and 10 for more on this topic). Of course, you can use the email address enrichment strategy as you did with `leads`, but you can also buy business databases on CD-ROM or from online services. These databases provide a range of information about the `contact`, including title, professional certifications, and other information—in some industries there is an amazing amount of information available. When using one of these databases, though, it is essential *not* to dump its entire contents into SFDC (that is the most wanton kind of data pollution), but instead to perform a `join` that simply expands the scope of data for the records you already have in the system.

The final area for enrichment is `accounts`. In SFDC, `accounts` are at the top of the information hierarchy, so enriching this information can prove quite valuable. `Account` enrichment is particularly appropriate with the Named Account model of selling (see Chapter 9), which tries to penetrate a small number of high-value customers without relying on lead generation. A named account sales rep is always hungry for more information about new `account` prospects. Two data-enrichment alternatives exist: databases on CD-ROM and online services (in particular, data.com, which now includes the Dunn & Bradstreet database of companies). Each source can have valuable data about the `account`'s business, organizational structure, vertical industry, purchasing patterns, and other useful information. As before, it is essential *not* to indiscriminately import large amounts of data into SFDC. In the Named Account model, it is reasonable to import as many as 1,000 `accounts`' worth of data but almost never more. As always, make sure that you're not creating duplicate `account` names when you perform this data enrichment. See Chapter 10 for a fuller discussion on best practices for this process.

The Ultimate Job Security

You may be old enough to remember the TV ads that proclaimed, "There will always be a future in computer maintenance." It didn't quite work out that way, but I'm here to tell you that there *will* always be a future in data maintenance.

Because CRM credibility depends on the volume and value of the data in SFDC more than any other factor, data quality is the lifeblood of ongoing SFDC operations. There are three levels of data maintenance—architectural, manipulative, and administrative—and they each need to be staffed as ongoing processes.

Architectural

The SFDC data model is clean and well organized, and it is important that additions to it (custom fields and custom objects) do not introduce redundancy and chaos. As discussed in Chapter 4, if your company is doing any significant degree of customization and integration, you will need to have an architectural review board to review all changes. The review board needs to set system policies, procedures, standards, and training requirements for everyone—from administrators to end users.

The following areas are the most dangerous to data quality:

- Wanton and sloppy data imports.

- Lack of control over new-record creation (tons of duplicates).

- Redundant or underutilized data fields.

- Creation of custom fields attached to the wrong point in the data hierarchy (e.g., competitors attached to the `account` or `contact` object).

- Too-lax `field access` rules.

- Missing `validation` rules.

- Improper `ownership` of records, or mass transfers to the wrong owner.

- Uploading of huge attachments (wasting space), which are then attached to the wrong objects.

- Failure to remove the `delete` and `merge` privilege from user account `profiles`.

- Sloppy or uninformed usage of administrator tools, such as the Data Loader, Excel Connector, or deduping products.

- Mass conversion of `leads` to `contacts`, or entering `leads` as `contacts`.

- Integration of external data sources without the proper deduping logic.

- Creation of phantom records to deal with uncontrolled external systems (particularly from partners or the channel).

- Uncontrolled use of the `Salesforce for Outlook` connector.

- Sloppy or untrained administrators.

- Too many people with administrator privileges, even if those individuals are well trained.

- Uncoordinated development and administrative effort (change control tools exist for a reason!).

As the first line of defense for data quality, the architectural review board should review business process changes, administrator training levels, and all proposals for significant system changes. Initially, meetings will need to occur frequently, but a monthly cycle should be sufficient over time.

Manipulative

Marketing users, sales operations personnel, and support managers typically have some special access privileges in SFDC. They can see more data, and they can manipulate it in special ways. These users need to be trained to use their privileges properly to avoid data damage.

Important risk areas for data quality reside in the marketing arena because marketing users often perform bulk operations that can go wrong in a hurry. `Lead` imports, creation of `campaign` lists, and interaction with email blasters or marketing automation tools (such as ExactTarget, Vertical Response, Marketo, or Eloqua) are everyday tasks that must be done correctly. Training, templates, and very thorough cheat sheets are absolutely essential for these users. We also recommend specific incentives (both spot bonuses for consistent good work and somewhat public embarrassment for errors) to ensure as few defects in this area as possible.

Another area also deserves some attention: survey design. When marketers or support people design a survey with the intent of putting the survey results into SFDC records, it is essential that the survey answers/values map verbatim to SFDC records (particularly for pick-list values). If the survey is designed or executed incorrectly, some of the data will have to be thrown out—and in some cases an entire column of data (all the answers to a question) may have to be excluded or reprocessed prior to import into SFDC.

Administrative

Each SFDC administrator has a lot of power to enforce the right behaviors and to provide insurance against Big Messes. In an operation of any size, the administrator's main duty is to say "no" to requests that don't fit with best practices and haven't been approved by the architectural review board.

In the course of an administrator's day-to-day duties, he or she does a lot to preserve and improve data quality. For example, on a weekly basis the administrator should perform these tasks:

- Run deduping tools.

- Run administrative reports on data quality.

- Update record ownership to reflect sales staff and territory changes.

- Run a full system backup (although it's usually not practical to back up attachments more often than once a month, or even once a quarter).

- Undo erroneous imports.

- Undelete records (using the system's recycle bin).

Check out Chapter 13 for a broader discussion of administrative duties.

Creating a Cost Model for Clean Data

Given the amount of effort that goes into data cleansing, correction, enrichment, and deduping, it's a good idea to create a model of the *cost of a good record* in SFDC. Even if the `lead` or `contact` never produces any revenue, there is a cost—and a value—in creating and maintaining it. In your model, estimate the business value of a fully qualified lead (a few hundred dollars), an unqualified lead (a few dollars), and a name (zero). With this cost and value model, you can make rational choices about the next marketing campaign that will generate 100,000 new (but essentially worthless) leads or the wisdom of importing that CD promising 13 million email addresses.

Because the perceived value of SFDC largely depends on the cleanliness, timeliness, and relevance of the data in the system, it's a good idea to put data quality and maintenance objectives on several individuals' MBOs.

GETTING THE MOST FROM SFDC

- Identify your main sources of data pollution early in the project.
- Pay attention to data quality throughout the project because it will be the cornerstone of system credibility. That said, perfectionism in data quality doesn't pay.
- Data migration from existing systems—CRM or other—will be a multi-step process you'll need to plan for and document carefully. After you've proven the basic steps, set aside a weekend for the big migration.
- After migration, you'll need to do deduping and will probably want to do data enrichment. These all require care and repeatable processes.

FOR SMALL COMPANIES

- Focus on leads, contacts, accounts, tasks, and opportunities.
- You probably don't need to migrate more than a year's worth of data.
- Buy data.com for enrichment and CRM-fusion or RingLead for deduping.
- Use the Excel connector or Data Loader for ETL work.

FOR LARGE ENTERPRISES

- Understand the data (and error patterns) of each external system you need to migrate data from.
- Set up Full Sandboxes for trial data imports and staging areas.
- Set up Dev Sandboxes to use as test systems for developing data migration and dedupe strategies.
- Develop a set of standards around account naming that makes it easy to identify divisions and operating units of multinational customers.
- Create an architectural review board for extensions to the SFDC data model.

CHAPTER 4

Implementation Strategy

Official Project Stages:
1. Uncritical Acceptance
2. Wild Enthusiasm
3. Dejected Disillusionment
4. Total Confusion
5. Search for the Guilty
6. Punishment of the Innocent
7. Promotion of the Nonparticipants

—Anonymous

This chapter is for all implementation team participants, technical or not. Team members need to understand the project from the "top down," even though their day-to-day perspectives will be detail oriented (seeing the project from the "bottom up"). Readers will understand how they fit in, who depends on them, and the rules of the road.

Companies tend to treat SFDC implementations like they do other projects: they obsess about budgetary variances and the go-live date. One of the lessons learned from a decade of CRM projects is that the technology improvements *by themselves* are meaningless unless users adopt the system. Without interesting, relevant data, the SFA tool is just a toy. So the go-live date really doesn't have much meaning. It's the *start* of the process of creating business value—not the conclusion. The key metric of success is user adoption of more than 50%, not the go-live date.

Further, although budgetary variances are important, they are not decisive factors. An overspend rate of 20% (a significant amount) will be dwarfed by the productivity increases you're trying to achieve in sales, marketing, and support. If you come in on budget, but sales still loses deals due to sloppy execution and measurement, you haven't made the right business decision. The focus needs to be on revenue achievement rather than budgetary containment.

Before you begin the project, make sure that your executive champion and the leaders in the sales, marketing, and service departments not only are supportive of SFDC but are also explicitly targeting organizational improvement to accompany the new system. The automation and capabilities of SFDC are most powerful when they become the foundation of better business processes. The executives should identify the process changes for each of their organizations. Check out Chapters 6 and 8 through 11 if you haven't done so already.

Big Bangs and Waterfalls

If you've ever done a "knock-down" remodel of a house, you can believe the statistic that 38% of these Big Bang projects blow up, causing a divorce among the homeowners.[1] Why does this occur?

As discussed in Chapter 1, Big Bang software projects—which tend to feature major chunks of functionality delivered all at once—are more likely to suffer budget overruns and schedule slips than smaller, more incremental projects. Although this phenomenon was first documented in the 1960s, the evidence continues to the present day:

> Technology projects bear a striking resemblance to home renovations. Both are surrounded by wildly high hopes at the start and often end up causing financial and emotional heartache. Even now, 50% of projects suffer budget overruns and 62% have experienced delays, according to a new report by Tata Consultancy Services.
>
> —Elizabeth Bennett, in *Baseline Magazine*

There are many reasons for this tendency. Like a home remodeling project, big IT projects involve solving problems whose scope cannot be truly known until the project is under way. It's only as you rip away the veneer of patches in presentation logic that you discover the dry rot of loopy data structures underneath. It's only when you actually try to install the new fixtures of user interface that you understand the creaky logic in data pipes that were hidden before. With each new problem comes the recommendation to "fix the architecture," which can only add to short-term cost and delay. As was said so eloquently in CRMsolution's executive guide[2] for avoiding SFA implementation pitfalls, "A majority of businesses embarking on an SFA solution make the fatal mistake of implementing too many features too quickly."

As the go-live date for a Big Bang project starts to slip, it's common to justify and resell the project by adding more features. This leads to scope creep—the expansion of project deliverables with little regard for budgetary, scheduling, or logistical realities.

---

1. The American Institute of Architects is too embarrassed to have ever published these numbers, but the Construction, Restoration, and Planning organization conducted a survey and published it on its Web site, www.crap.com. (Okay, it's true, I made this number up.)
2. You can read this very worthwhile document online at www.crmsolution.com/crm-blueprint.html.

Decision makers often miss the logical folly of statements such as "We promised to give you x in 90 days and weren't able to do that—but now we've found a way to give you $1.5x$ in 120 days!" Of course, in the end the project delivers $1.1x$ in 180 days, if you're lucky.

Big Bangs backfire because of long timelines, uncertainty, poor project sizing, changes to scope, false expectations, and wandering executive attention. The executives approving the project want a fixed price, a fixed schedule, and a guaranteed set of features. Meeting these criteria would be a snap with perfect command-and-control, but even in the Defense Department project overruns are legendary.

Most Big Bang projects use a waterfall model of project management. Symbolized by Gantt charts, the waterfall theory starts with requirements being thoroughly documented at the beginning and then delivered through a linear process of design, coding, testing, and deployment. There are three problems with this theory: first, it doesn't work in software; second, it ignores the reality of requirements discovery and business change during the project; and third, it doesn't work in software. What really happens is that users give engineers a big spec and a budget, and then are told to go away for 11 months. After the coding work is done, the project is presented in test mode to users, who are often shocked by the developer's lack of quality control, taste, and ESP.

A clear antidote is to change the constraints and assumptions to reflect software reality, and to improve the performance and flexibility of software teams:

- Remove one of the constraints: keep the schedule and budget fixed but allow variation in the requirements delivered.

- Focus on the end state rather than the delivery style: instead of delivering "everything" as a package at the end, allow the team to deliver functionality in small chunks over several rapid iterations.

Although these choices may seem scary, when properly managed, they provide less risk, less trauma, and a higher likelihood of delivering what *actually matters to the users and the business* without breaking the bank. If you do it right, you will have near zero waste (that's very unusual in software) and users who actually like the system (that's nearly unheard of).

The Agile Manifesto

In 2001, some of the industry's most innovative and productive software development organizations met to propose a new method of managing and delivering software. They knew from experience that the waterfall model and Big Bang projects—which virtually mandated long meetings; bureaucratic behavior; and long, boring specifications—simply didn't pay off. Their proposal, argued by gurus such as Martin Fowler, Kent Beck, and

Roy Singham, was to turn software project management on its head. The Agile Manifesto argued for an iterative style of thinking and delivery: peeling off the layers of the onion. Their idea was that requirements can't really be set in stone at the beginning—even if they are, during the 18 months of the project, economic or internal business changes invalidate many parts of the "stone tablets." Fifty years of software experience has shown that users and executives alike *don't really know what they want until they see an example of it.* So why pretend? Instead, set requirements dynamically as the project goes along. Why not start with a prototype (or storyboard) with a business test ("Don't ship to customers while they're on credit hold") rather than some abstract document of features?

If the requirements can be set incrementally, why shouldn't testing be done at every stage? Instead of keeping everyone in the dark about quality issues until the very end—when problems are most costly to fix—why not expose as many quality problems as possible early on? At the extreme, you might even use a test-first development style, where you don't allow software to be developed until you've created the test it must satisfy.

If satisfying the users is the end goal, why shouldn't they be involved in the prototyping and testing processes? They know more about what's important to the business and natural for the business process than an engineer ever could. This Agile idea took user-centered design to the next level.

The Agile Manifesto and follow-on writings argue for an adaptive style of software development and project management that molds itself to the business need:

- Projects should be optimized for frequent delivery of value to the business.

- Project teams should make decisions as late as possible because it's not really clear what's *truly* important—or the degree of difficulty involved—until you're in the midst of the work.

- Project teams should focus on being as responsive as possible, thereby ensuring they deliver working software that provides a competitive advantage.

- Projects will be more efficient and effective if they avoid large bureaucratic meetings, heavy documentation, and static waterfall scheduling.

- Projects should have predictable time cycles and budgetary impact, but allow freedom regarding the feature set delivered.

- Projects should include frequent testing with the twin goals of exposing unforeseen design issues and lowering the cost of defect correction.

- Projects should work with rapid prototyping and frequent user feedback to make sure that *only the essential features are being worked on.*

The user organization should perceive an Agile IT project as being like a subway system: everyone knows how much the journey will cost and how long it will take, but they don't know (or really care) which specific train they're going to be on. As members of the organization become more confident that "the next train" will arrive very soon, they'll be less upset if their favorite feature didn't happen to make *this* particular train. Executives will resist the temptation to pull political strings to accelerate their pet feature at the expense of others or push for scope creep.

As outgrowths of the original Agile Alliance, software development shops such as ThoughtWorks, product management consultants such as Enthiosys, and software houses such as Rally and Atlassian have created tools and methodologies to make Agile development more accessible to IT teams and more reliable for management. Like the Japanese auto industry, which focuses on flexible manufacturing and repeatable processes to gain speed and profitability, the Agile methodology focuses on trying to "get lean"—changing the rules to improve quality and deliver better value to the customers. Unlike the Japanese auto industry, however, software doesn't have the statistical or procedural rigor of the Deming methods.

You Really Have to Plan: Agile Development Is Not Enough

Although, in theory, Agile methods allow for rapid productivity, in the real world, Agile works best when developers are serious wizards and users are highly motivated and engaged. The engineers frequently ask the project leader and user representatives detailed questions and tricky priority calls, and they typically need to get their answers in a few hours to avoid wasting development time. Agile development demands a lot from the team members, and most CRM projects don't have the luxury of perfect human resources.

Other issues have also emerged since the Agile Manifesto was published: Agile methods are highly focused on the needs and behaviors of engineers. Nontechnical managers don't receive the tomes of documents and project plans that they're familiar with, so they find it tough to figure out the real status of the project. The pointy-haired bosses (PHBs) of *Dilbert* lore want to see project milestones that are fixed, are measurable, and have deliverables defined well in advance—and Agile development won't provide any of these. The bean counters get nervous about the chaos and uncertainty around costs.

Agile projects can appear to be very chaotic, with tasks and resources seeming to jump around on a weekly basis. For the participant as well as the observer, the flexibility that is the hallmark of Agile projects—and the basis of their effectiveness—can also prove to be very stressful.

Further, Agile projects can become defocused if the teams work items off the backlog in the order they appear on the list, rather than in the order that is needed to satisfy all the dependencies and prerequisites of a complex feature set. Intricate, big-picture features seem to be delivered in fragments.

Even with these thorny issues, the economic, quality, and productivity advantages of Agile development are hard to deny. The technologies of SOA and cloud systems cry out for an incremental, prototype-oriented style of development. Even SFDC uses Agile methods in developing the system. Because SFDC is delivered as a set of modules and components, why not run the project in the way that leverages that technical foundation?

What if there was a way to impose a little more structure on top of Agile development?

Wave Deployment

In small organizations, it's easy to get everyone around a table and come to agreement on which features need to be developed and which users will transition to the system at each deployment stage. In some cases, deployment can all be done at one step, and the system can remain in a steady state for 6 months or more. Done.

But in larger organizations, there's no way to get all the users productive at the same time, even if the functionality could be delivered all at once. With larger, more complex SFDC systems, it's important to deploy the functionality in phases to waves of users—groups who will value the functionality that is being released in each phase. The trick is to identify the prioritized features and the most appropriate group of users at the same time.

It's traditional in CRM to have users adopt features in an iterative style, as illustrated in Figure 4-1. But our experience with SFDC is that users in one department want to absorb features at a different time—or even in a different order—than other departments. Building on these lessons, my firm[3] has developed the Wave Deployment methodology

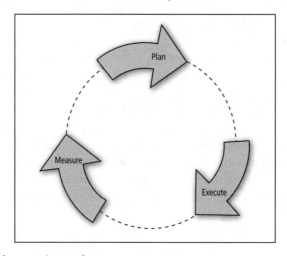

FIGURE 4-1   The implementation cycle

---

3. Sales*Logistix*, a specialist SFDC consultancy.

for SFDC implementations. Thanks to the modularity and "instant" provisioning of SFDC features and the varying needs of users in different functional groups, waves provide a natural way to evolve the features and the user base at the same time.

The downside of Agile project management is that you can't predict at the outset precisely when any individual feature will be delivered. The beauty of adding waves is that you can predict both the *order* of delivery and the groups to which features will be delivered, so that you'll have a logical story to tell even before the work has begun.

A *wave* refers both to the features—the *business deliverable* for a deployment cycle or increment—and the group of users it's intended for. Each wave starts out as a loosely defined set of features (typically fitting on a single page) scheduled for delivery. In a small company, the wave description would be something as simple as, "telesales will get call-center-lite automation by May 15." The functional description must be kept deliberately vague because the specific feature list will change throughout the course of the wave.[4] Although the wave may actually include a bunch of other features for other users, the description should focus on the *main theme of value* that will be delivered to the business. Check out www.SFDC-secrets.com for an example high-level wave description.

Waves should typically occur twice per business quarter.[5] No single user group should be the focal point of two waves in a row. When the features (and the required training) are distributed in this kind of "round-robin" fashion, no one group has to deal with the disruption of a new learning curve more often than once per quarter. Generally speaking, waves should not be delivered during the first week or the last 2 weeks of the quarter to minimize the disruption on sales, order entry, and accounting. If a piece of functionality must be "turned on" at the first day of a new quarter, training sessions should be done before week 12 of the previous quarter.

What's in a Wave?

The trick in planning, of course, is to define what's in the wave and which groups will be part of the wave at the same time. Sometimes it's easier to start with the features that are "doable" and define the target users; in other cases, it's easier to start with the affected user groups and figure out which features they'll value most.

---

4. Remember that the innovation of the Agile methodology keeps deadlines and budgets fixed, but the actual deliverables variable. This counterintuitive method is what makes for flexibility, productivity, and quality.

5. If the teams are good, waves could happen every couple of weeks. But users won't be happy dealing with that much change: they need time to get used to the technology, see how it affects the way they do business, and gain experience before they give feedback. There's nothing wrong with delivering a new report or improving some feature overnight in response to user requests—but the plan for rolling out big chunks of functionality should be more measured.

> ## Deployment: Push versus Pull
>
> To get the highest-quality (and, in the end, the fastest) adoption of the system, avoid over-selling SFDC or overzealously pushing people to use it before they are motivated to do so.
>
> The dream situation occurs when the next group of users is asking—even begging—to be let on the system. In this ideal situation, you want to create a sense of exclusivity where "the chosen few users" are allowed to get on the system early. Use your early adopters—technophile cowboys—to create an aura of coolness around the system. Have an early access program where users have to be nominated to get in on the latest features. Remember what Gmail did with its "by invitation only" group of pilot users? Try to get some of that same energy going with your users.
>
> SFDC's `chatter` is a very useful tool for building that energy so that users build on each other's learnings and ideas. Collaboration will be maximized if you set up groups and hash-tag topics that are immediately relevant to pilot users. Their natural interactions will become an important part of your internal FAQ and `knowledge base` for the general deployment cycle. Check out Chapters 6 and 13 for more discussion of this topic.

In defining waves, it's important to keep these seeming contradictions in mind:

- All users need to feel that some value is being delivered to them whenever you ask something new of them, *but* no user can absorb a really big chunk of new functionality more than once every 6 months or so.

- The project has to be able to show delivery of value to some part of the business at least once (and preferably twice) per quarter, *but* the most significant features will take longer than 6 weeks to implement.

- Few significant features can be completed without some infrastructure, integration, or data scrubbing, *but* no user values infrastructure, integration, or data scrubbing per se.

- The most aggressive early adopter users may have the most to gain from deploying a new feature, *but* the most conservative, technophobic users must be cooperative if new features are to be deployed successfully (even though the latter user may perceive that they receive little immediate, personal gain for their extra effort).

Planning the Sequence of Waves: WaveMaps

In Chapter 1, we discussed development of a pro forma schedule and roadmap that can be used to sell the project to upper management. Like all convenient fictions, this one needs to be reworked to expunge hidden diabolical minutiae.[6] It's time now to create a schedule that is based on better information and real details.

Many companies want to see an overview of the project deliverables for a year or more because managers have set aside portions of the budget for the project. The job of the project champion and team leader is to set reasonable expectations for the end state of the system and try to give themselves enough wiggle room to succeed. In an Agile world, things need to move around.

Things get a little thornier when an executive wants to know in which quarter his or her pet feature will be deployed. Maneuver the conversation to focus on the end state and try to avoid committing to specific delivery dates: at the beginning of the project, you simply don't know how long it will take to make that pet feature a successful reality because you don't yet know how hard it really is. If you are pressed, make commitments that are contingent, such as "We'll get that up for pilot users 2 months after the Enterprise Service Bus is selected."

All that said, you do need to have a roadmap and a sequence of feature sets. A Wave-Map is a roadmap with a "third-dimensional" overlay showing the user groups deploying the functionality of each wave. One of the best ways to visualize this third dimension is to have the background of the WaveMap be your company's department-level organization chart. On top of this background, overlay the "local version" of the Wave timeline. (See Figure 4-2 for an example.) If your org chart is "flat" and this approach doesn't work, try using a geographic map (U.S. or globe) as the background instead. As you can imagine, WaveMaps tend to be fairly large, and they work nicely when displayed on a wall (with feature timelines pinned up on the map so they can be easily read and updated).

Assume that during the year you will complete seven waves,[7] and allocate the requirements priority list you developed in Chapter 1 across them. It is critical that you communicate in writing and in person that these are *not* promises or commitments—rather, the WaveMap is a logical sequence of features that *could* be deployed. The details will inevitably change as the timeline unfolds to fit most efficiently and logically with the facts and resources that become real during the project timeline.

---

6. The devils that are in the details.
7. Generally, we recommend unleashing two waves per quarter. Usually, the team has trouble delivering one of the waves, either during the Christmas season or at the fiscal year-end. If you plan for completing only seven waves and then complete the eighth, you'll be guilty only of underpromising and overdelivering. Pray for such problems.

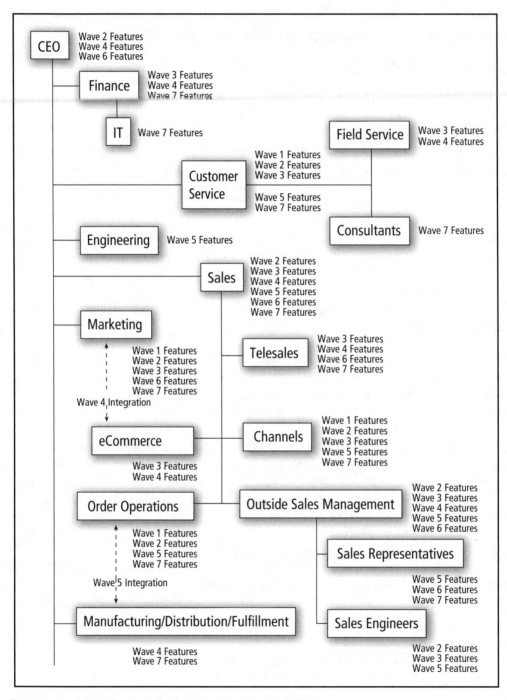

FIGURE 4-2   A WaveMap overlaid on an organizational chart

OUR INTERNATIONAL FRIENDS

A great example of Wave development is the delivery of features to international users because it clearly shows the interrelationships among users and functionality. International users may have differences in the following areas:

- On-screen language
- Data-entry character sets and keyboard layout
- Mobile device support
- Currency
- Address and phone number formats
- Pick-list values and defaults
- `Sales processes`, page `layouts`, and `record types`
- Time zones
- Business hours and days (particularly for the Middle East)
- Business rules
- Business processes
- Legal requirements, compliance issues, and customer-privacy regulations
- Training and documentation

Make sure to put extra time into the schedule to accommodate significant international requirements because collecting them, understanding them, implementing them, and testing the features is guaranteed to take longer than the corresponding efforts for domestic users. Although SFDC is *very* international friendly, third-party products and externally integrated systems may not be. Further, you may find that international rules and business processes may be quite opaque—even hidden from the local workers.

Multiple-currency operation requires special attention, owing to its effects on the system. If you have doubts about the need for `multi-currency` in SFDC, keep your system all in one currency as long as you can. You can never go back once you've turned the `multi-currency` function on. But if you know for certain that you must have `reports` and `forecasts` in local currencies, you might as well activate these capabilities sooner rather than later (as the transition may break `reports`, `validation rules`, `dashboards`, custom code, and `workflows` that you have set up).

Of course, the highest-priority, lowest-effort items should come first, right? Not quite. Three big-picture issues need to be considered in sequencing the features across waves: technical dependency, legal approvals, and user readiness.

Technical Dependency

The first issue is technical dependency: some SFDC and add-in features have a significant number of dependencies and prerequisites. As a consequence, some SFDC functions have to be delivered in a specific order. The evolution of SFDC functions will almost always follow this sequence:

1. Cleaning, deduping, normalizing, and enriching existing data is the first step for any significant SFDC deployment. It's hard to know which is worse: deploying a feature with no legacy data at all, or deploying it with crummy data that will be cleaned up "later." Either approach undermines system credibility and makes the system harder to use. If you didn't read it already, check out Chapter 3 for guidance on the best way to handle the data preparation and migration.

2. Do not attempt to integrate everything at once. It is best to delay integration as long as possible and do it incrementally so that you introduce potential destabilizing elements on top of a solid base of data and system functionality.

3. `Contacts` and `accounts` have to be in place before any other SFDC features can be sensibly used.

4. `Activities` (mainly `tasks`) need to be populated for at least a month before any activity monitoring reports are used.

5. `Opportunities` have to be solid before `forecasting` makes sense.

6. `Leads` and `campaigns` should have at least 6 months of good, deduped data before any marketing effectiveness dashboards are deployed.

7. The `products` and `price` lists have to be in place before `quoting` or `contracts` make sense.

8. The `products` and `assets` have to be enabled in SFDC before the new system is integrated with an outside license management, inventory management, or distribution system.

9. `Cases` and `solutions` need to be in place (with data imported) before it makes sense to implement the `knowledge base` or `customer portal`.[8]

10. Most of the items above need to be set up and relevant partners entered into the system as `contacts` before you implement the `partner portal`.

11. The `sandbox` needs to be in place before serious work begins on integration or `multi-currency` operation.

---

8. If you haven't already implemented the customer or partner portal in your SFDC instance, it is no longer available to you.

There are too many detailed prerequisites to capture all the possible permutations here. As you investigate a feature set in SFDC and add-on products, keep close tabs on the dependencies so you can analyze their effects on the feature-deployment order. *Do not* fall into the trap of leaving the uncertain (or least-known) things until the end of your agenda. Do just the opposite: put the riskiest items at the beginning where you have room to "discover."[9]

Legal Approvals/Review Committees

As is discussed further in Chapter 6, large companies have a lot of moving parts with abstruse functions and interlinkages. SFDC is an information system that may touch on internal policies, business processes, and regulatory stipulations. Be realistic about how required review and approval cycles will affect the deployment schedule. A single security or compliance review could take weeks.

It's a good idea for the project manager to take a quick inventory of *all* your company's internal review committees and figure out which ones might want to review part of the SFDC plan. Contact the committee chair, and if he or she seems uninterested, ask that individual to write an email to the effect that this SFDC project does not need to go through that committee's review process. These emails will prove to be invaluable later on in your project.

User Readiness

The third issue that helps determine the ordering of feature sets is the users themselves. Some groups of users are much more likely to love and leverage SFDC early on and will naturally take to using the system. Having close working relationships between your implementation team and end users is a key success factor for any SFDC implementation. In using the system, those individuals will populate SFDC with valuable data that make it a more attractive asset for other users. For example, customer support personnel are always on the phone with customers, and they naturally come across information that is valuable to the salesforce. Having members of the customer support team store their notes about happy or unhappy customers, upcoming renewals, and possible upsell opportunities in SFDC—something that's relatively painless for them to do—will make the system more interesting to the sales reps (who are always hungry for information about their accounts).

Figure 4-3 illustrates the sequence in which user groups typically adopt SFDC. Almost always, the people manning the phones are the first users: the contact management and reminder features of SFDC make their jobs immediately easier, and they are no-brainers

---

9. Aka "fail."

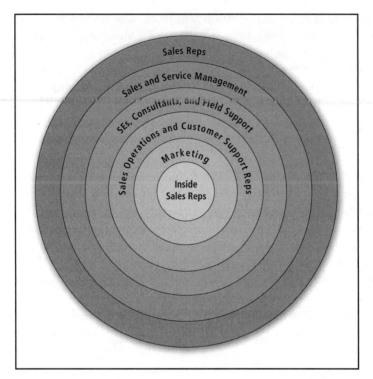

FIGURE 4-3   Typical sequence of SFDC user adoption

to learn. The business development reps (BDRs)[10] work naturally with the system, and the team manager quickly figures out how to get the metrics he or she needs on reports and dashboards. Tactical marketing personnel (particularly the people who do lead generation programs) also tend to adopt the system very early. These two groups provide a bedrock of `leads`, `contacts`, and `opportunities` that are useful to others.

Typically, the next group to switch to the system is sales operations people who must work with reps to push deals through. The sales operations group is typically a centralized function that doesn't ever "touch" customers, but team members do expedite quotes, orders, and paperwork through the bureaucracy. Because they are involved with deals as they progress through the sales cycle, it's natural for these employees to use SFDC to keep tabs on deals and provide reminders for follow-up.

The next likely user group consists of the presales engineers and postsales consultants or service people who "touch" the customer. Because SFDC already contains the

---

10. This group does initial lead prospecting and qualifying. "BDRs" is a bit of a misnomer because these representatives don't actually close any deals; instead, their job is to cultivate and prep the prospects to the point that they want to take a meeting with the company's sales reps. At different companies, this group may be called telemarketing, telesales, inside sales, sales development, account development, or lead cultivation.

account, contact, and opportunity information, these groups will constantly be looking up data in the system and making notes on their specific projects. The ability to attach documents to deals (closed opportunities) and to put in auto-reminders for tasks and action items makes SFDC a natural way for these teams to collaborate. Even though these employees may have used email and their personal calendars as collaborative tools for years, the shared access and visibility inherent in SFDC make the system a better way for teams to collaborate.

At this point, sales management will have been using the system for a while, albeit usually for simple monitoring and reporting on pipelines and activities. Only as the system grows to include a significant amount of customer data do sales managers start to use the system as a personal resource. For example, if the CEO wants to know what's going wrong with a deal and the sales rep doesn't answer his phone, the sales manager can look in the SFDC system to see the "state of play" at the account. Eventually, sales managers will do mini account reviews based on SFDC data, and they will start running their regular forecast review meetings through the system. These changes in management behavior will send a signal to the individual reps that it's time to get serious about using the system.

Perhaps surprisingly, the last users to wholeheartedly endorse the SFA or CRM system—which is supposed to improve a sales rep's efficiency—will be the sales reps themselves. Generally speaking, the more senior the rep, the longer it takes for that person to really leverage the system. Of course, these senior reps are often the rainmakers in the organization, so it's not a great idea to push them too soon.

As the sequence of waves starts to take shape in your requirements spreadsheet, you should identify a *theme* for each wave's features as well as the principal user group that will benefit from it. Although waves frequently include random features that happened to make the cut, discussing each wave in terms of the theme and the target users will make it much easier to sell across the organization. When you have an initial complete draft WaveMap, review it with your main project sponsors. They may have forcing functions or other real business issues that change some of your assumptions and accelerate or delay the need for a feature set. The larger the company, the more likely the roadmap of waves will resemble a patchwork quilt: there will be rationality to every decision, but there won't be a simple checklist with one department's needs being clearly fulfilled in a given quarter. This scattershot effect is almost unavoidable, and SFDC's inherent flexibility and responsiveness should be sold as a benefit.

SWEETEN THE POT

When looking at the contents of a wave, make sure to cast the features in terms that the user can understand. Don't be abstract—avoid feature-itis. Instead, talk about the ways that a set of features will save users 5 minutes a day, every day.

It's important that management not perceive WaveMaps as being cast in stone: they are a forecast of the best use of company resources given *current* information. As you'll see, the WaveMap's overview will be adjusted to reality (e.g., shifts in priorities, staffing changes) at the beginning of every quarter. This tinkering can save your company substantial engineering and staff resources, and it gets extra mileage from your budget.

What If Management Just Says No to Agile Development?

Some organizations just don't believe that they have the intensity or talent to use Agile project styles. Some organizations even mandate the use of more conventional development methods.

If your organization fits this description, apply as many of the principles outlined in this chapter as you can to your approved project management methods. For the configuration of SFDC features, involve the users and do frequent prototyping and review sessions. For the installation of third-party modules, use the vendor's suggested implementation cycle. In the case of integration—the most complicated part of any SFDC project—keep the requirements as minimal as you can and test frequently to make sure no data are being corrupted.

If your company advocates a waterfall management style, have as many small, independent deliverables as you can to minimize the risk of Big Bangs and scope creep.

No matter which project management and deployment techniques you use, optimize the results for the users: give them features that really matter, that really work, and that increase the credibility of the data in the system.

Collecting Resources for a Wave

Waves have an interesting characteristic: you always know when they'll start and how long they'll last. As a consequence, resources can be scheduled with tight end dates, which is a good thing for getting commitments. Of course, resources also have to be scheduled with firm commitments on start date and level of effort—a sometimes challenging feat to achieve.

Every wave requires technical people to configure, develop, integrate, and deploy functionality. Usually, the overall technical team is in place over several waves, but the individual task assignments (and subgroups) may change with each cycle.[11] On the technical side, it's a matter of allocating available talent to the specific needs of the wave.

---

11. The IT people need to read up on SFDC's API as well as the project wiki content. They also need the right tools: a free SFDC developer account for prototyping and testing, the SFDC developer tools (Force Explorer, Data Loader, and Eclipse plugin), and (if possible) access to an SFDC Sandbox.

STAFFING: CONSULTANTS OR EMPLOYEES?

Although the decision whether to use in-house personnel or external resources for carrying out an SFDC project will depend entirely on the specific needs and availability of talent at your company, there are clear best practices for staffing waves.

Generally speaking, internal staff should do 80% to 90% of the work in the overall implementation. Even if your staff is extremely constrained, no part of the work should be done entirely by outsiders because your organization will need internal capabilities to manage the system going forward. SFDC will continue to evolve every 6 months or so after the completion of your WaveMap—either needing expansion or readjustment of the system to meet changing business realities—so you'll need to have internal competence.

That said, it's not a great idea to have major parts of the project done without *any* outside input. There are certain parts of the project that you don't really want to get good at: technologies that provide you no particular leverage, or processes (such as data cleansing) that are incredibly boring or time consuming. Also, consultants bring valuable lessons from other implementations, and they can help you develop best practices in areas such as sales processes or Agile project management. If you haven't already done so, read the sidebar in Chapter 1 dealing with consultant selection.

Most waves will require a business analyst to think through process and business-rule issues. Although business analysts are rarely "in the trenches" and seldom know the details of individual customer situations, they bring valuable perspective to requirements definition, acceptance criteria, political issues, and final testing. Depending on the area of specialization and overall organizational size, the business analyst may change from wave to wave. Nevertheless, maintaining continuity of business analysts over several waves will cut down on learning curves.[12]

Every wave also requires dedicated time from one or more users representing the target audience for the wave's main theme feature set. The next step is to identify the best team participants to represent the users. Choosing the right users—those with a keen business sense and high energy level—is a key factor in your Agile team's success. People who are too high in the organizational hierarchy have neither the time nor the day-to-day knowledge needed for this phase of deployment; people who are too low in the organizational structure do have the time and the day-to-day knowledge, but they don't understand the reason for the business process or the changes that management may have in store. Most

---

12. The business analyst needs to know the basics of SFDC and should read up on materials in the project wiki or Google Drive area. He or she will also need to understand the basics of any external system relevant to the business processes being targeted. The business analyst will use Word, Excel, PowerPoint, and perhaps Visio or Project to do his or her job.

wave development teams can work well with one user from each affected user department, but more complex (or politically charged) areas of functionality may require more users. These users will typically be involved in the project for an hour every few days during much of the wave, plus several hours per day at the beginning[13] (for requirements translation) and at the end (for testing and validation) of their project area.

Every wave also needs an assigned champion—that is, an executive to whom issues and controversies can be escalated. The assigned champion should come from the department that represents the target audience of the main-theme feature set. In an ideal wave, the champion should not be needed to break logjams—but in the real world, escalations may happen every week or so.

Everybody on the Same Page

Everyone on the wave development team—and particularly the sponsor/executive champion—should clearly understand the implications of Agile projects and time boxing. They need to agree that making the deployment deadline is more important than delivering any particular detail in this wave.

Team members need to not only prevent scope-creep behaviors in other members of the team but also resist the temptation themselves. They need to avoid making specific promises about features because the project needs freedom in the feature list so that it can meet its binding promises related to schedule, quality, and budget.

Maintaining these behaviors can be hard, particularly for old-guard IT people. But the benefits of going Agile—particularly for an SFDC implementation—are just too important to ignore.

Every wave will need some IT resources: system access, lab access, data, review committees, and so forth. In small companies, the necessary resources may simply amount to a developer's PC or access to a database. By contrast, in complex environments, SFDC is integrated with other hosted solutions, databases, servers, and on-premises applications. Even though SFDC is an externally hosted solution, its integration interfaces may need to be reviewed for conformance with company architecture, standardized products, network security, data access policies, and even Sarbanes-Oxley Act compliance. In large companies, these IT review resources may need to be scheduled well in advance of the start of the wave and, in some cases, will change the ordering of projects on the WaveMap. If

---

13. The user representatives will need to learn the basics of SFDC, in addition to the systems that they already know. They should read up on the project wiki or Google Drive area and should have access to the same Microsoft Office tools used by the rest of the project team.

you have not already done so, at least skim Chapter 13 to understand how and when to engage your company's IT team.

Most waves will need special resources for testing. In most cases, these resources will consist of copies of databases (or an SFDC Sandbox), staging servers, test code, and test personnel. Although these test resources are used most intensively at the end of the wave, they are useful early on as well. Particularly if large amounts of data must be cloned for a test database, make sure to request these resources early enough so any delay in obtaining them doesn't impinge on the wave schedule.

In Agile projects, documentation is a by-product rather than a first-class deliverable. Even so, documentation needs to be the responsibility of every team member. SFDC encourages you to annotate many of the changes you make with its internal help bubbles and description fields, but that doesn't obviate the need for documenting the following items in the project wiki or Google Drive area:

- Rationales for decisions

- Assumptions made

- Rationales and "owners" for business rules

- Business process diagrams

- Storyboards

- Data cleansing and conversion procedures

- Technical approaches to integration

- Code comments

- Test setups, data sets, and sequences

- User checklists and cheat sheets

- Administrative checklists

- User training materials

ALLOCATION OF EFFORT

Agile projects have to be flexible, but they tend to follow patterns. About 10% of the project effort will be involved with requirements collection, prioritization/tradeoff meetings, architecture, and preconstruction analysis. About 40% should be reserved for testing, deployment, and user preparedness (aka training). Only about 50% of the effort goes into the actual construction of features, but with SFDC, this tends to go a long way.

Finally, deployment and training resources need to be scheduled. Mostly, these personnel will consist of internal resources who are already on the project, but in large organizations, dedicated "train the trainers" sessions may be required. In any case, the trainees and users form a critical path resource as well: it's important to work out the training venues and nail down the training time early to prevent stress as the deadline approaches. Check out the discussion on this topic in Chapter 5.

The final resource you need to think about is optional only when the project is small. Every project needs an incentive or a way to celebrate completion of the task, particularly when you're trying to engage users in the system development process. Each wave needs to have a *tchochke* for the team participants, though these items don't need to be expensive to be effective. T-shirts are the classic give-away, but they work only if people will wear them to help spread the word about the project. Coffee mugs and baseball caps work as well. Talk to the marketing people who do events at your company; they'll be able to come up with dozens of inexpensive ideas, from cell-phone skins to mouse pads to henna tattoos—the choice depends on your company culture.

WAVE DEPLOYMENT PERIODS

In larger organizations, there's no way to get all users productive at the same time, even if the wave's technical deployment is straightforward. People and energy levels throttle deployment speed. In large companies, a wave may be affected by

- Different departments with different agendas and priorities.
- Departments in the midst of organizational or political turmoil.
- A range of user types, from early adopters to technophobes.
- A range of locations, including users who are on the road all the time.
- A range of languages, currencies, and business practices.

Because many significant waves involve installation of a bit of software[14] on the user's PC, just the wave's deployment and training cycle may take several weeks to complete in larger organizations. Some groups may even defer using a new SFDC feature for several months in an effort to accommodate external issues.

---

14. Although the core system of SFDC is totally hosted and doesn't require so much as a browser plugin, several popular third-party features require libraries, plugins, and applications to be installed on the user's PC, iPad/Android, or smartphone. As a result, beyond the initial stages of SFDC usage, there is often software to be deployed (at least on the power users' systems).

Starting the Wave

Once the roadmap has been negotiated and stabilized, the detailed requirements for the current wave must be scoped. In the Agile methodology, we don't really dig into the details of any requirement until the work begins: essentially, the details of the requirements are developed in tandem with the functionality itself.

The first step of the detailed requirements cycle entails validating that the business still values the requirement and is willing to spend the resources to satisfy it. This validation becomes increasingly important in later waves because business priorities may shift over the months following the start of the implementation.

THE IMPORTANCE OF NONGOALS

Goals and requirements, everyone gets. I'm here to extol the virtues of nongoals. They are the things that you not only won't get done but also have no intention of even starting.

In any wave, having nongoals helps manage expectations by setting the boundaries of the things that you do intend to work on. Publishing nongoals during a wave is a great way to counteract scope creep and happy ears.

In stating your nongoals, it's important to not come across as whining. Don't complain about lack of resources, time, organizational support, data quality, or anything else. Nongoals should simply be bullets that briefly and simply state what's out of scope and *won't* be worked on.

The next step is to scope the detailed requirements so that they can become tasks for the wave development personnel. In the context of a wave, the first step of scoping is setting the business's acceptance criteria for the requirement (usually in the form of a test, a transaction, or a trained group of users). Next, the teams need to transform each requirement from a business requirement (completing a measurement, event, or step in a business process) into a technical one. Work with the user representatives to make sure that each business requirement is stated in the best way, and then ask questions about different ways to satisfy the requirement.

For example, sales personnel may have stated that they need to see current order status for all customers, which implies a technical requirement for real-time integration between SFDC and your company's order management system. On investigation, however, you may discover that order status doesn't change more often than twice a week, and the salespeople won't really mind if the data are updated only weekly.

Instead of a real-time update system for SFDC, then, a weekly batch update via Excel spreadsheets will serve the business requirement. Simplifications such as this one can save the project staff weeks of time and avoid unnecessary purchases. Consequently, analyzing each business requirement for technical alternatives can pay for itself quickly. Check out Chapter 7's discussion of integration before you try to implement any integration feature.

For any interesting functionality, one key attribute is access control—that is, who should be able to see the data or use the feature. SFDC allows very fine-grained access control, but every security element added to the system makes it more difficult for people to access and share information they may need. Start with an assumption of minimal controls and maximum access, and employ more restrictive measures only in the situations where there is a clear and specific reason to do so.

Strive for simplicity and minimalism in all features. SFDC makes it very easy to incrementally add complexity and elegance *after* you've got the basics in place.[15] By focusing on the essentials, you simultaneously reduce workload, technical risk, and training requirements. Once the users start working with the system, if they *beg* you to add more complexity and clutter, give it to them—but not before some serious pleading takes place.

Once the technical feature requirements have been written down, the next step is to identify the steps required to implement the functionality. From this list of tasks, the level of complexity, resources, and level of effort can be estimated.

Each business requirement and its associated technical implementation tasks should be summarized in a spreadsheet for the wave development team. This spreadsheet doesn't need to be continuously updated, but an initial pass geared toward filling out its content needs to be completed early in the wave. The spreadsheet should be posted in the wiki or Google Drive area describing the wave, but it needs to include boldfaced warning messages indicating that these are the goals and *initial intention* of the wave development team, not the current work plan.[16]

The final step before initiating tasks is to prioritize the tasks within the wave. Even though you have already prioritized the requirements at a macro level *across* the Wave-Map, the tasks now need to be prioritized in a different context. *Within* a wave, priority is generally given to those tasks that have a higher probability of success, require less

---

15. Interestingly, it can be a bigger pain to remove features and data items from SFDC than it was to create them in the first place. In a few cases, it is impossible to remove SFDC complexity once you've used it for the first time. For this reason, you should start with a streamlined list of features and build out from there only as needed.

16. To the frustration of linear thinkers everywhere, in an Agile project the current work plan is almost invisible—it tends to live in the minds of the team members, on blackboards, on sticky notes, and in indecipherable spreadsheets. Resist the temptation of over-documenting because it wastes time. If management, finance, or IT types insist on using a project management tool, avoid Microsoft Project or equivalent tools—instead, choose a tool like Atlassian's JIRA or ThoughtWorks' Mingle, which are designed to be a natural fit with the way Agile teams work.

effort, or have fewer dependencies (i.e., prerequisites for success or repercussions of failure). At the same time, the killer macro-priority tasks are given priority because they're the theme of the wave. This prioritization will be reevaluated several times during the course of a wave, particularly if a task is completed earlier than expected or runs into a technical problem or logistical delay.

WHEN A REQUIREMENT IS TOO BIG FOR A WAVE

Most functional requirements can be implemented quite quickly in SFDC: it's a matter of configuring a feature, adding some `custom fields`, using `record types`, installing a plugin, creating a `custom object`, or quickly writing a `VisualForce` page.

Other requirements require deep work: integrating the system with a new external database, cleaning and enriching data, and developing serious code. These tasks just won't fit in a 6-week cycle, particularly if the requirement itself needs some business analysis and restatement. What to do?

These longer projects need to be decomposed into smaller components of less than 6 weeks' duration. Each component is treated separately (but in proper order) on the WaveMap, with expected deliverables for each wave those components reside in. For example, integrating a data warehouse into an SFDC installation might involve the following sequence of components:

1. Analyze data flow requirements to and from SFDC; specify frequency and size of ETL cycles.

2. Identify data cleansing, transformation, and remapping required for each data extraction; identify and evaluate appropriate ETL tools.

3. Do a proof of concept with ETL tools, and validate that they can complete the data warehouse load operation in the desired time window.

4. Purchase and install ETL tool(s); write control programs, scripts, and procedures for users.

5. Write initial reports for the data warehouse.

Each of these five component projects can be done during the 6 weeks allocated to a wave, though not all of them can be finished in a single wave. But there's another issue at work here: the teams won't be delivering much value to the business until the last component is completed. As with infrastructure projects, keeping the business users happy and engaged means interleaving the early "nothing in it for me" components with quick wins and other projects that do deliver business value as part of the wave.

As a Wave Takes Shape

Once the wave is under way, the team starts to work on the requirements—refining them while trying to implement them—and they will make discoveries. The small discoveries about technical or business details are briefly documented in the wave development wiki. The bigger discoveries relate to the way users actually work or the characteristics of the data the team is trying to import into the system. These discoveries may influence the overall wave plan.

"I THINK YOU SHOULD BE MORE EXPLICIT HERE IN STEP TWO."

Sciencecartoonsplus.com

Earlier in this chapter, one potential wave was initially described as "telesales gets call-center-lite automation." Let's explore what that means, including how it might evolve during a wave as discoveries are made.

The business requirement might be stated as follows: "The 15 telesales reps need to be able to complete 60 outbound dials per day, including 15 live conversations. Each of these contact attempts needs to be facilitated and documented (with some fields automatically filled out in SFDC). Email activity needs to be recorded for each of the contacted prospects. The telesales manager needs to be able to monitor and analyze activity and call-success rates for each individual and to summarize the results by sales region on a daily basis with weekly summaries."

The initial list of technical features might be as shown in Table 4-1. During the wave, the team discovers several things:

1. The real-time lead flow from the Web site may not be ready at the time it's needed for this wave. As a consequence, this feature is bumped down the priority list; later, it is pushed off to the next wave when the Web site changes are further delayed.

2. The auto-data-fill function using Skype is a cool feature that could save a lot of time, but it requires a complicated setup that might be incompatible with other features that have already been deployed. As a consequence, this requirement is transformed into a research project for one of the team members. When he or she reports back to the team about compatibility and workarounds, this feature will be rescheduled (either in this wave or the next one).

3. It is discovered that a lightweight Skype dialer is available, and it takes almost no effort to install. This item is added to the list as a substitute for the more meaty Skype features that were postponed. The lightweight Skype dialer is helpful to every user, not just the telesales people.

4. Autodial using the PBX is another time saver. It's discovered early in the phase that this feature is fully compatible with the company's existing phone system. Even though this one feature is hard to complete, it's pulled up in the priority list.

5. The automatic upsell reminders and automatic scripting are cool features that could fit in the wave, but marketing can't decide exactly what the customer segments are or what the rules for detecting them or selecting appropriate messages are. Also, customer support has some political arguments and wants to send out these reminders themselves. Because no automation can be built for renewals or the scripts until these issues are resolved, this task is pushed off to a later phase of the project.

TABLE 4-1   Initial Feature List Example

Description	User	Difficulty	Dependency	Priority
Custom screens for reps	Telesales	Easy	None	High
Real-time lead flow from Web site	Telesales	Easy	Web site	Medium
Deduped lead flow from programs	Telesales	Easy	Install tool	Medium
Autodial and data fill via Skype	Telesales	Medium	Install tool	Medium
Outbound email recorded	Telesales	Medium	Install tool	Medium
Inbound email recorded	Telesales	Hard	Install tool	Low
Custom screens for managers	Manager	Medium	None	High
Automatic renewal reminders	Telesales	Medium	Renewal data	Medium
Autodial using PBX	Telesales	Hard	Buy plugin	Medium
Automatic upsell reminders	Telesales	Hard	Rules and scripts	Medium
Automatic scripts and cues	Telesales	Hard	Scripts	Low

In a similar manner, the team may discover that some target groups defined for a wave may not really be ready to adopt the features making up the wave. For example, a business process may not have been defined, a reorganization may not have been completed, or other business priorities may be taking precedence.

The list of features, target groups, and priorities needs to "roll with the punches" as the project progresses. The priority list—including current status and staff assigned—should be updated (typically weekly) and posted as a new file in the project wiki or Google Drive area. By continuously publishing the current status of items and showing the change from the previous week, the project will earn confidence in the user community. Transparency pays off in credibility.

THE U PATTERN OF CHANGE

The amount of change in a priority list seems to follow a U pattern as the SFDC wave evolves: high degree of change at the start, lower in the middle, and rising again toward the end. This kind of change in priority lists over the course of a phase may seem chaotic, but it's what makes for the flexibility and opportunistic productivity that are hallmarks of Agile project management.

Dirty Little Secret: The Data Are Everything

Okay, I admit it: I've buried the most important concept in the middle of the book. Bully for the careful reader—and for skimmers, tough!

Like any CRM system, the value of SFDC depends on the amount and value of the data it holds. The system's credibility and usage levels depend on good data being presented to users.

Data quality is a shared responsibility that starts with the implementation team who should do their duty in the following areas: design, import, reports, and data ownership. In designing and configuring SFDC, the team will make dozens of choices about the way data are entered and organized. Refer back to Chapter 3 during the implementation, and take its lessons to heart!

In the course of testing and early system operations, it's important to assign someone to own data quality. This person is tasked with making sure the current data don't become corrupted and detecting new sources of data problems and rectifying them before a wave's features are deployed. The data quality owner should turn on `History`

`Tracking` for all SFDC objects[17] and weekly `data exports` from the first day to help identify and troubleshoot data problems. He or she should also create reports that help identify flaky data entries (exporting the report details to Excel and using pivot tables is one of the fastest ways to find subtle problem data). This individual should periodically run data quality reports and use SFDC's data quality dashboard to measure the number of duplicate records, nonconforming data, and outright corruption. The data quality owner should also designate an area for corralling bad or questionable data: it's never a good idea to delete records because deletion merely hides the process problem that created them. Use the crummy records to analyze and rectify what went wrong with the data. Further, the data quality owner needs to establish a unique key (typically a hash based on a combination of data points) that acts as a fingerprint for identifying duplicates when they occur across multiple systems.

During the Wave: Real-Time Scheduling

The core of Agile project management[18] is to deliver in a flexible way in inflexible constraints. The wave needs to utilize the time, people, and dollars budgeted but no more. The team needs to deliver on time, repeatedly. The features delivered have to work, can't corrupt data, and must include user feedback.

Where the project manager has flexibility is in "exactly which features are delivered." Instead of delivering a complete feature list late, the Agile methodology focuses on delivering a scaled-back feature list on time and with the required quality. Further, Agile teams test throughout the development cycle: both with users (for feedback) and with test code (to ensure that the acceptance criteria are being met). Whether the immediate task is designing a screen or integrating with an outside system, some level of testing should be done every week. Although the daily or weekly tests may be brief, it's important to reserve the time and external resources for testing so test results are available when needed.

The art of wave development project management is the practice of *time boxing*: breaking down the project into tasks with fixed, short deadlines. The task team does a sprint to its deadline, delivering the most useful core features first and adding refinements and

---

17. `History Tracking` provides an audit trail for as many as 20 fields for each object (almost every table in SFDC is eligible for this feature). In large systems, 20 data items per object isn't enough—but that's all there are, so you have to choose the highest-priority items to track. By default, the audit trails last 18 months: they can be extended on request.

18. In small projects, there is only one project manager. In larger projects, there may be a program manager overseeing managers for individual tasks. For simplicity's sake, in this chapter, I refer to the project manager as if he or she were a single person, even though the role may take the talents of several individuals. See www.SFDC-secrets.com for an example project manager job description.

extras only if time permits. In some business quarters, the time boxes can be defined arbitrarily by the project manager. In other quarters, key dates on the calendar create forcing functions for time boxes. For example, the calendar might include a holiday, a user group meeting, or an internal training session whose date is known well in advance. The time-boxing deadlines should simply be organized around these fixed dates, thereby ensuring that the team gets the most productive days out of the calendar.

BUILDING TRUST WITH USERS BUILDS SYSTEM CREDIBILITY

A CRM system is just a shell unless the users use it. Persuading users to adopt the system is a critical success factor for increasing sales productivity, service effectiveness, and business results. For this reason, building credibility of the system (and the data in it) is job one for everyone on the implementation team.

The wave development methodology starts this process before the system is even delivered. By producing something of business value on a regular basis, waves foster trust among users. Even if a particular feature is missing from this wave, users trust that the next wave will deliver something even better.

In the early waves of a project, the team needs to work like crazy to deliver a component of business value and then showcase it. This approach is particularly effective when a feature solves a high-profile problem or just makes a highly visible irritant go away. To create a buzz for system credibility, encourage important or highly connected people to send out emails about how they use the new feature. Check out Chapter 6 for more on this topic.

What makes time boxing work is short tasks with frequent (typically weekly) milestones. The project manager wants to know about any task that is in trouble as early as possible so that adjustments can be made. The manager can make the following adjustments to bring a task back on schedule:

- Add an extra resource or buy a tool, component, or service.

- Pare down the expected feature by simply leaving off refinements or nice-to-have attributes.

- Implement a feature in a radically simplified way (thereby delivering a "temporary hack" that will be upgraded during the next wave).

- Push the feature out of the wave (see "Kicked Out of a Wave" later in this chapter).

In some cases, a feature will go off schedule because of business issues, such as undecided business rules, political arguments, less-than-committed team members, resource hoarding, or delayed approvals. The project manager needs to wield the scalpel of escalation with skill—using the political pull of the wave sponsor early enough to make a real difference but infrequently enough to avoid becoming an irritant.

Inherently, waves and time boxes discourage scope creep. In an Agile project, resources do not remain slack for long—in fact, they're supposed to be 100% utilized at all times. Even so, everyone needs to be vigilant, particularly if a feature has been kicked out of a wave and the teams implementing surviving features in a wave ask for a few more resources. Reassigning resources is never a friction-free process, so it should be avoided unless a specific reason exists to do so. If a feature is on the borderline of missing its milestone, of course it makes sense to redirect slack resources to it. Beware the situation in which a feature is basically on schedule yet asking for resources: this is practically an invitation to expand the feature's scope. Given the short intervals of waves, any expansion in scope—even with the extra resources—is almost guaranteed to cause schedule slippage.

SCOPE CREEP WARNING SIGNS

Scope creep comes in many forms, and some of the most dangerous ones come from inside the project itself. The blatant request from an outsider is easy to detect. But watch out for these subtle internal appeals:

- "Since we're in there anyway . . ."
- "This code is not maintainable; I need to rearchitect . . ."
- "Let's refactor this . . ."
- "It'll work even better if . . ."
- "I figured out how to do ___ a better way"
- "In the long run . . ."
- "The way it really should work is . . ."
- "We should upgrade to a new version of . . ."

These phrases aren't always indicative of scope creep. But no matter how well intentioned, they can lead to perfectionism and make-work projects that add risk and delay the overall plan.

The ultimate scope-creep weapon is the WaveMap—specifically, those requirements that have survived several rounds of prioritizing. When someone asks to expand one of the requirements or features, the project manager needs to ask, "Which of the things on this priority list should be kicked out of this wave to accommodate your new request? I'll reshuffle everything the minute that you get the project champion for the requirement you propose deferring to agree." That will usually stop the discussion dead unless something important really has changed in the business.

MANAGING THE FEATURETTES

In old movie houses, in between the feature movie showings, the projectionist would throw in a featurette—a 10-minute, short-subject film about some interesting topic. The audience never knew which featurettes would be shown each week, but they would be disappointed if they weren't there, thrown in as fillers. Essentially the same management technique is used here: the project manager throws in an appropriate featurette or two in each wave.

Earlier in the book, the terms *quick wins*, *eye candy*, and *user toys* were introduced. These are all pretty much the same thing—simple additions to the system that make it more easy and fun to use but don't really cost the project anything. They're too small to explicitly schedule, and the whole point of having them is to "sweeten the pot" of a wave in an effort to make it more appealing to users.

Thanks to the size of SFDC's user community, more than 1,500 plugins and add-ons for the system have been developed, and half of them are available for free. In addition, SFDC's newsgroups and user forums have lots of hints about simple links and mashups that can provide a lot of raw material for featurettes.

At the start of the project, one task should be to survey all the freeware that's available in the AppExchange and elsewhere on the Web. Make sure to download and save everything you can about the featurette when you discover it because these mini-apps tend to change URLs over time and can become very hard to find again. Create a spreadsheet summarizing the basic featurette, the URL it came from, the GoogleDoc discussing it, the estimated implementation time (typically a couple of hours), and a best guess about which departments would value the featurette.

As the wave progresses, the project leader should identify a few featurettes to be thrown in. Typically, the three featurette audiences warranting the most attention are the target users for the main theme of the wave; the "squeakiest wheel" group (particularly if they aren't getting much that's interesting in this wave); and, most important, any group that is likely to feel put upon or upset because of a change, delay, or extra work they're going to have to do.

Kicked Out of a Wave

Due to unforeseen problems, items may need to be pushed out of a wave. Perhaps the requirement is ill defined (e.g., no one can agree on what the acceptance criteria are), the requirement depends on a purchase that isn't budgeted, or the implementation has failed testing. One of the benefits of Agile management is its bias toward a "fail fast" attitude— one that identifies problems sooner so waste is decreased.

Of course, every attempt will be made to keep the highest-priority components of a wave going—but in the face of resource diversion intended to complete that high-priority component, something will have to go. Once the project manager makes the decision to push an item out of the wave, he or she also has to determine whether that item's team members should be reassigned to another task in the wave. If they can't contribute effectively to another task, the team can continue working on their task, even though it will not be delivered until the next wave cycle. If, however, the team members can be effectively reassigned in the wave, the project team should stop its original task. Because no one knows when they'll restart that task, members of this team need to carefully document where they left off and then put the work in mothballs. They'll need to estimate the remaining work and dependencies, and insert their task into the prioritization cycle for the next wave.

Wave Endgame

Even though every team has been doing component-level testing throughout the wave, the wave itself concludes with a final test cycle that works at two levels: technical and business.

The technical tests entail fairly straightforward validation of functionality and data manipulation. For features that are built and configured entirely within SFDC's environment, testing can be fairly light because there's seldom a risk of data corruption. For features that are written in `APEX`, `VisualForce` that leverages Ajax, or connectors that integrate with outside systems and hosted services, testing is needed for the following issues:

- Functionality
- Security and access control
- Crashes, lockups, and race conditions
- Performance and timeouts
- Error handling
- Data corruption

If a feature fails the technical tests, it should be disabled in the system until it is fixed.

Given that some of these tests may require a significant amount of data, it's important to allocate lab system time for creating and analyzing the test data sets. If the data sets are not properly set up, resetting them to rerun a test may take longer than conducting the test itself. The use of `APEX` code requires that initial unit tests be developed and executed in the `Sandbox` before the code can be brought into the product system. This is a very good thing, but that test code is just the beginning—plenty more real-world tests will be required on the running system, and their completion will take time out of the schedule.

The business tests don't require as much in the way of technical resources, but they often take longer to carry out than the technical tests. The good news is that the business tests can often be run in parallel with the technical tests. The first part of the business test is usability. This issue should have been addressed throughout the wave development with an increasingly wider range of users looking at the system as work on the feature progressed. The second part of business testing is validating the business acceptance criteria. In other words, does the transaction clear, can the business process proceed, and can the users do their jobs with the new feature? Usually, the business test passes at *some* level, though it might not be complete, or it might involve a few too many mouse clicks. Even so, armed with a cheat sheet and some training, the users can usually work around business-level defects until the next wave.

Conversely, if the function doesn't work at all or actually does the wrong thing (e.g., falsely approving an erroneous `quote`), the feature must be disabled in the system until it is fixed. If the fixes cannot be completed and retested by the deadline, that feature will have to be kicked out of the wave.

The final step of the wave is user training. As discussed in Chapter 5, best practice consists of short, task-oriented, "day-in-the-life" training that involves users "driving the mouse" during the training session. Training sessions should be an hour or less in duration, and at least one of the live sessions should be captured either as video or as a WebEx session for subsequent replay when users try to use the feature and have forgotten their training. Podcasts are also a very effective on-demand way of getting training to the users. For most users, it's also very helpful to create a laminated cheat sheet with annotated screenshots explaining the procedures for their most common tasks. Given that each department will need a different set of cheat sheets, it's best to post the entire library of these aids on the project wiki, organized by user department.

Deployment

No matter how small the feature, it needs to be put into the operational system. And the act of deployment is never complete without communicating to the users in advance:

- What's new

- What's in it for them[19]

- When it's coming

- Where to find their cheat sheet

- What to do if the new feature gives them trouble

SFDC is a hosted solution, so the deployment of native features and system configurations is almost a nonissue: the system simply starts behaving differently once you've put the customizations in. During a wave, however, there may be so many changes that it's best to keep the new customizations hidden (using `screen layouts`, `VisualForce`, `record types`, the `Sandbox`, and other techniques) until they are done. At the end of the wave, the veil is removed, and in a few minutes the new features become available to everyone.

More complex features and integrations do need to be formally deployed. In many cases, add-ins or products may need to be installed on the user's PC. Servers will need new connector modules installed. Implementation of these features will require a more deliberate deployment strategy, particularly if their full development spans more than one wave.

In the case where the new feature set simply provides access to something new or does read-only operations, the deployment is a matter of software logistics. Somehow, the new software modules will need to be packaged and sent with instructions on how to install the various components. Because prepackaged installers from several vendors are often involved, the installation cycle can't be fully automated, and users will need to have really foolproof instructions.

The foolproof instructions *must* include an uninstall procedure and a phone number to dial in case of problems. Make sure to test those foolproof instructions with an executive or other appropriate personnel during the wave's main test cycle. Usually, the software is small enough that it can be sent out as a download link, but even if it's large enough to require a download from a server, put a copy of the software and instructions on the project's wiki or Google Drive area (typically in the "What's New" section) and mention it in the project newsletter or podcast.

The most difficult deployment case is when a CRM system is already in place and is being replaced by SFDC. These deployments are so tough because the chances for data corruption are higher, users may get confused or even rebel against using the new features, and the waste involved in a failed deployment can make it highly visible. In these situations, it pays to have a set of cutover criteria (covering technology readiness,

---

19. Why they should give a damn.

> ### The Virtual Help Desk
>
> For really significant deployments and large organizations, it's a good idea to have a user support "war room." Of course, you should have an FAQ and troubleshooting guide on the wiki, but you have to be ready for people who don't read these documents or who are clever enough to discover problems you didn't anticipate.
>
> The war room is not really staffed, and it's not really a room. Instead, it's an email address and a voicemail box that are checked very frequently. Ideally, these support duties will be handled by one person who really has time; if no one has time in their schedule, the task should be handled as a rotating duty shared by several team members. At any one time, one person should be responsible for talking with the user and another person should stand ready to handle escalations. The duty roster should pass hands once or twice a day at predictable times (like, noon). It is simply amazing how much better the users react to a confusing or buggy system when you are *really* responsive on the phone and in email.

business readiness, and user readiness) with a formal go/no-go meeting to make sure there's management buy-in.

Transition Type: Slash Cut versus Parallel Play

In a slash-cut transition, the old system is turned off forever (typically on a Friday night), and the new system is used first thing the next business day. Slash cuts involve some logistical complexity—all the moving parts have to line up—and a significant amount of time pressure. The implementation team may be pulling 18-hour days over the weekend to get all the data in shape and imported into the new system. If there's a problem on Sunday night, the new system may not be ready for business on Monday morning. However, slash cuts give users a quick, decisive transition, and they don't have to do duplicate data entry. Further, reports, alerts, and dashboards are more likely to be correct with this strategy.

In contrast, the parallel-play strategy keeps both old and new systems up for a transition period (usually from a week to a month). Users must enter data into both systems (almost always in different ways with different error patterns). Although it's painful, this strategy allows for deeper testing and debugging with less risk (only the old system contains real, live data during the parallel play period). Further, if major problems are found, the new system deployment can be postponed (temporarily ending the extra effort of parallel play), lowering business risk. During the parallel-play period, many reports, alerts, and dashboards in SFDC are likely to contain bogus data, but they are invaluable debugging aids and provide visible indications of system progress during the parallel-play interval.

Generally speaking, smaller SFDC projects go with slash-cut transitions. But the larger, the more complex, and the more revenue-critical the SFDC deployment, the more appropriate parallel play may be.

Go/No-Go Criteria

In theory, go/no-go decisions are simple: the criteria are met or they aren't. These kinds of risks really should be dealt with on a zero-tolerance basis:

- Data corruption

- Lost revenue transactions

- Severe compliance or security problems

- Unplanned business interruption (for longer than a coffee break during the day)

In real-world, high-stakes decisions, however, you have to leave room for gray areas and interpretation. It's a matter of assessing and trading off business risks. These are example subjective risks that beg the question of "acceptable levels":

- Transactions requiring manual workarounds

- Misleading reports

- Data that seem to be lost but are actually just hard to find

- Data ownership and visibility issues

- Incomplete user training

- Calculations having to be done in outboard spreadsheets

A good rule of thumb for assessing deployment readiness is to judge business impact: if the new functionality is deployed, does it actually make something worse? Can any errors be corrected and problems be recovered from later on? As long as the rework is not prohibitively expensive, *correctable* short-term issues should not stand in the way of a feature deployment.

Getting Ready for the Next Wave

Once the deployment is done, the team needs to engage in two important but brief meetings.

The first meeting checks the WaveMap for the upcoming wave. Have things changed? Does the map need to be readjusted to reflect tasks that were kicked out of the just-finished wave or business priorities that have changed? Although it's never mandatory to change the WaveMap, it is important that the map reflect reality at the beginning of every quarter (every other wave).

The second meeting is a 30-minute postmortem discussion to capture learnings about the following topics:

- What were the budgetary and schedule variances? What were the root causes of the three to five worst offenders? What were the positive surprises?

- What worked technologically? What didn't work technologically, and why?

- Which resources will need to be in place to make things even better in the next wave?

- Which means of communication with the users worked, and which didn't?

- Which means of team communications worked, and which didn't?

- Which organizational/political issues came up, and how might they have been avoided or circumvented?

- Which team interactions were effective, and where was the team operating ineffectively?

- What (specifically) do we need to do differently in the next wave?

The postmortem meeting *must* include a member of the user community (someone who wasn't part of the wave implementation team) and should include the wave's executive sponsor as well as a quorum of the actual worker bees. The postmortem minutes and resolutions for future waves should be put in the project wiki, particularly for the benefit of future team members.[20]

Postimplementation Implementation

Due to the flexibility of SFDC and its plugin products, expect that there will be modifications and extensions to the system every quarter or so. Even if business requirements do not evolve, organizational roles will likely change over time. Further, the more third-party products plugged in to the SFDC system, the more frequently upgrades will be needed and will require slight modifications to the system.

---

20. While the project team's composition will remain largely stable over several waves, typically 20% of the team members will be new with each wave. This is particularly true for the business analysts and user representatives, who will benefit greatly by learning from previous waves' experiences.

All this activity will occur if the system is only a moderate success. If the system is a real hit, there will be a flood of change requests that must be managed. Most of these minor changes—extra fields, reconfigurations, and so forth—will be so small that they can be done without starting up a wave team. You should just log them into a spreadsheet, which should be posted on the project wiki or Google Drive area. These should be managed and traded off just like any other wave requests, as "maintenance" can take just as many cycles as a new feature request.

Once the system is really in "steady state," you'll want to set up a change management system to track feature requests, approval cycles, and deployments. After an initial review of the proposed change to make sure it won't break anything or contradict any company policy, the task can be approved and assigned to the technical people for quick implementation. Once they are done, there should be another approval cycle to track acceptance of the result by users.

Don't overcomplicate things, though. There's a free version of a light change-control system for SFDC in the AppExchange—look for the ChangeIT plugin.

ARCHITECTURAL REVIEW

For a system of any size or complexity, sometimes the most innocent-sounding changes can have huge negative repercussions. We recommend that your system have a three-member architectural review board to evaluate proposed changes in the system and surrounding processes. The job of the board members is to make sure that the business and the users experience only progress, avoiding anything that will undermine system credibility or cause costly rework.

The board should have fairly stable membership, with each architect having at least a 1-year term and not allowing more than one change in board membership per 9 months. The three members of the board should fit the following criteria:

- **Application/process architect:** Typically an engineer or a business analyst who understands all the moving parts of SFDC, its plugins, and your custom code. This person's area of specialization focuses on understanding the interaction among these software elements as well as the system's impact on business processes and corporate compliance standards.

- **Data/integration architect:** Typically an engineer or a business analyst who understands all of the external data sources with which SFDC interacts. This person's purview is understanding the potential for data corruption and the amount of "data massaging" work that would be involved in changing the data model.

- **System administration/user architect:** Typically an SFDC system administrator or power user who understands how the system is used on a day-to-day basis. This person's bailiwick is understanding the potential for user disruption or interference implied by a proposed change. If this team member is not your SFDC data steward (see Chapter 13), he or she needs to at least confer with the steward on a regular basis.

The architectural review board should examine almost any system change and should vote on the changes before they are slated for implementation. The initial vote can be conducted by email (with the conclusion posted to the project wiki or Google Drive area). If the vote is unanimous, no further action is required. If there is a dissenting vote, the dissenter needs to write a brief opinion about why he or she objects to the change, including a rough estimate of the potential for disruption or rework.

Sometimes there is an executive mandate to make a system change: if the members of the architectural review board object to this dictate, they should email the sponsoring executive about the potential for problems and the budgetary impact if things go awry. Of course, the executive can still enforce the mandate—but at least he or she will have been properly apprised of the risks.

See the discussion in Chapter 3 for more about the architectural review board.

If we achieve our real goal—broad user adoption and optimization of business processes—there will be calls for expanding the system beyond the areas originally desired. For example, quoting may be expanded to full order operations. For these significant expansions, reestablishment of a wave team is required, giving the reader a wonderful excuse to reread this chapter months from now.

GETTING THE MOST FROM **SFDC**

- If at all possible, avoid Big Bang projects. Instead, leverage SFDC for its towering strength: incremental deployment and smaller, lower-risk projects.
- Ruthlessly prioritize, and make tradeoffs that focus on delivering business value. Don't get trapped in feature-itis.
- Involve users at every stage of the project to improve usability, perceptions of quality, and adoption. Think about the sequence of users you're going to deploy to: surprisingly, field reps may be the last ones on board.
- Focus on credibility, for the system and the team. Don't over-document, but do overcommunicate. Seriously consider using `chatter` as an enthusiasm-building tool.

FOR SMALL COMPANIES

- If you're lucky, you can just skim most of this chapter.

FOR LARGE ENTERPRISES

- Get your IT types to read the Agile Manifesto. Meet with the chairperson of any review boards or compliance committees to brief them on the iterative nature of your deliveries.
- Make allowances in your schedule for several cycles of internal reviews, user testing, and external system integrations.
- Set up an architectural review board early, and get it staffed.

PART II

People, Politics, Products, and Process

CHAPTER 5

People and Organizational Readiness

Automation doesn't eliminate human error, it merely replaces operator errors with design errors.

—IBM

This chapter should be read by the executive sponsors to set the right high-level goals but is actually intended for everyone on the SFDC implementation team; it will help team members gauge the state of user readiness. While users in small organizations can skim this chapter, members of larger, more complex organizations need to understand it in detail for a successful deployment across multiple divisions.

Before starting the implementation, project leaders need to understand their organization's CRM maturity and state of readiness so as to better appreciate which benefits are within reach for their organization. During the implementation and adoption phases, users need to appreciate what other departments need from them to make the overall organization successful. Everyone needs to appreciate cultural issues that can form barriers to adoption.

Salesforce.com is a fine product that can be configured as an excellent sales, marketing, and customer service system. It can be integrated with accounting, licensing, and inventory systems to provide a full 360-degree view of your customers.

But only if people use it.

People will rapidly adopt new technologies and methods if there's something in it for them: functionality that actually makes their job easier, improves their productivity, or eliminates waste and duplication. SFDC *can* provide these benefits for anyone in sales, marketing, support, and the executive suite, but people on those teams may not perceive it that way—and perceptions drive adoption and usage.

Getting utilization rates up—not only overcoming user resistance and learning curves but also making the users highly motivated to use the system—is *the* challenge for any CRM system deployment. SFDC's ease of use, as well as the incremental deployment style recommended in this book, make it easier to achieve this goal. But a successful launch of an SFDC system is not just a matter of product and features: it's a matter of getting the interactions with people right.

You need to understand the perceptions of the user community to get the most out of your interactions with them during the project. These interactions will come at various phases of the project:

- Interviews and surveys at the start of the project

- Validation of screen designs and data in the middle

- Chatter interactions among pilot users

- Testing and business validation near the end

- Training sessions at deployment time

If communications with the users fail during any of these key interactions, the break-down can cause significant schedule and credibility problems for the SFDC project.

Using the SFA Maturity Model

There's almost always a gap between where the organization really is—how it really does business—and where it needs to be to make optimal use of SFDC. My firm developed the SFA Maturity Model to measure where client practices and processes really are so that we can guide companies and design projects with a high probability of success and user adoption.

The SFA Maturity Model assesses an organization's needs, sophistication, and state of readiness for SFDC features and business processes. The first part of the model helps identify the level of SFDC functionality that fits the organization's top-down goal. The second part of the model scores users to indicate which level of SFDC functionality each department is currently ready for.

The SFA Maturity Model must be used before the project begins as well as whenever a deployment phase includes a department that has not been involved with SFDC before. For example, if you're extending an SFDC implementation to include a new division, subsidiary, or foreign operation, you need to survey the new business unit and score it against the Maturity Model. Only by doing so can you ensure that your goals are realistic and achievable with minimum friction.

The output of this model is a set of scores that indicate the current state of readiness for each department evaluated. In most cases, the level of SFDC usage should be targeted at slightly above the median[1] score of participating departments so that users see value but are not overwhelmed by complexity and change.

---

1. The median is the *middle score*, which is different from the average score. Because of the small number of user scores in a typical SFDC survey, the median is usually more reflective of organizational readiness than is the average. You'll be targeting SFDC functionality that is near the median score for each department to which the system will be deployed.

The SFA Maturity Model is meant to provide guidance about the scope of the project and *general* readiness, but it doesn't take into account organizational politics or specific user adoption issues. As you'll see later in this chapter, before making deployment decisions about any specific group, it's important to do a detailed survey of its users that goes beyond the model.

Part I: What Does Management Want to Achieve, and How Hard Will It Be?

SFDC needs to be thought of as more than just a tool. SFDC has its most positive impact when it changes the way people allocate their time, complete business processes, and make the company money.

That said, having too-ambitious goals for an SFDC implementation will not pay off. Overshooting an organization's readiness—requiring user actions that have limited business value, relying on data that cannot be easily collected, or requiring big changes in behavior—can be quite counterproductive.

Although SFDC could simply be mandated in the organization—the way organizations sometimes do with a sales process or marketing vendor—best results happen when the system capabilities are a good match for the organization's people and those employees are intrinsically motivated to use the new system.

In using the model, it's important to *not* reach premature conclusions about deployment timing or sequence. Indeed, for many organizations it's best to do some of the levels "out of order."

The SFA Model's Five Levels[2]

Although small companies can happily use SFDC in a fairly simplistic way, the demands of larger companies mean they must use the system at more sophisticated operational levels. This part of the SFA Maturity Model defines the levels (or modes) in which organizations use SFDC, as illustrated in Figure 5-1. In an ironic twist, smaller companies can implement the highest levels of the model more easily than larger companies can.

Let's take a look at the five levels of the SFA Maturity Model:

I. **Contact Management and Basic Pipeline Development**

This level entails using SFDC as if it were ACT, Goldmine, SalesLogix, or even Excel. All Web leads are automatically entered into the system. Leads and

---

2. The SFA Maturity Model is stated in terms of the needs of a multichannel sales organization. Later in the chapter, we discuss the needs of SFDC users that *aren't* sales organizations at all (e.g., venture capitalists, fundraising organizations).

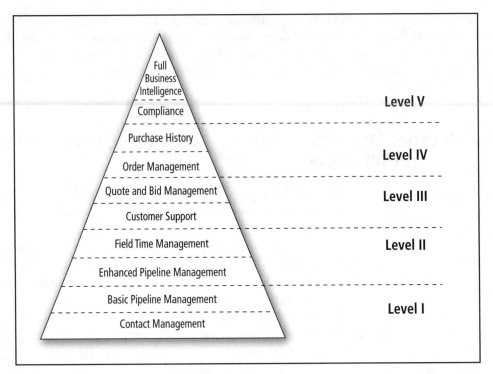

FIGURE 5-1   SFA Maturity Model levels

contacts are put in the system only by marketing, are refined by a sales development group,[3] and are passed to the sales reps for action.

Once a sales rep receives a lead or contact, he or she qualifies the prospect. An unqualified lead is rejected (but never deleted!) from the system. A good prospect is converted into an opportunity, but from that point forward there aren't many updates. Often, the rep won't put meaningful updates into the opportunity until the deal closes.

There are basic marketing and telesales reports, but they aren't consistently used (or believed). At this level, forecasting and account reviews are done entirely outside the system, typically in monthly phone conferences. Level I of the SFA Maturity Model is achieved by nearly all companies.

---

3. These groups qualify and cultivate leads to ready them for the sales reps. In some cases, they may set appointments for the reps, or they may do low-level pitches and demonstrations themselves. These groups are sometimes called telemarketing, telesales, business development, account development, inside sales, sales development, or lead qualification—and part of the function may be outsourced.

II. Enhanced Management of Activities, Pipeline Development, and Forecasting/ Quotas

By using `tasks`, `campaigns`, Outlook integration, and PBX/VoIP adaptors, sales, service, and marketing, users gain enough trust in the system and its information to use it to track their action items, prioritize their work, and manage their schedule.

At this level, there are enough credible updates to the data to permit real pipeline management, `forecasting`, and `quota` management. `Leads`, `contacts`, and `opportunities` are never deleted from the system, and the reps are more diligent about updating `opportunity` information to signal the rest of the organization about what's needed to close the deal. All reps' quotas are in the system; `territories`, overlays, `sales teams`, and splits are defined; and dashboards or reports compare the state of achievement with the sales reps' goals. Reports and dashboards show key workflow metrics in lead generation, lead cultivation, appointment setting, opportunity development, and close ratios.

At Level II of the SFA Maturity Model, all forecasting and most account reviews are based entirely on SFDC. The data in the system is accurate on a weekly basis, and reports are used consistently. Sales and marketing VPs use the SFDC data to drive their teams. This is the level that companies need to achieve when they have more than 20 reps.

III. Quoting, Deal Management, and Customer Support

This level makes it possible to develop and manage all quotes in the system. SFDC's Products module has been turned on, price lists have been populated, and approval workflows have been implemented to handle unusual deals. `Quoting` has been integrated with order management. An outside commission management system—whether a series of spreadsheets or a product (such as Centive, QCommission, or Xactly)—may have been integrated, and sales policy now states that commissions will not be paid unless a deal is in the system for at least 2 weeks prior to closing. At this level, all employees who take outside phone calls will have the SFDC screen up before they even think of answering the phone.

Although presales engineers may have been using the system for a long while, Level III adds postsales customer support to the SFDC user base. Postsales support (which may span the customer care, warranty, technical support, training, certification, and consulting functions) is a key point of customer contact that should be visible to everyone who interacts with prospects (particularly the sales reps). Within SFDC, the `Knowledge Base` has been turned on and populated with solutions, and the `Customer Portal` has been turned on.[4] The company's Web site CMS, survey, and email blasting systems have been integrated into SFDC so that a history of all customer communications is visible to all users. Reports and dashboards are in place to monitor customer support responsiveness in real time.

Management now has a 360-degree view of *the sales and marketing team*. Level III is the level that companies with more than 30 reps need to achieve.

IV. Order Management and Purchase History

This level integrates access to the accounting/enterprise resource planning (ERP) system for order entry, tracking, and management purposes. Within SFDC, quotes can be converted to orders and invoices as soon as they have completed the approval cycle. If the company uses eCommerce, that order flow has been integrated and is visible to SFDC users. All quotes, orders, contracts, invoices, and supporting documents (such as RFI and RFQ responses) are stored and available from the SFDC user screens. SFDC's `Partner Portal`[4] is available to users and allows for effective management of leads and deals that are being handled through the channel. At this stage, all bookings can be seen in real time, and even members of the finance department can use SFDC as an authoritative source.

In addition, the history of customer transactions is available to authorized users. Within SFDC, the `contracts` module is being populated with Terms and Conditions and periods of service. Through integration with ERP, license management, and other systems, a customer's purchase history (including specific line items, serial numbers, license keys, shipment manifests, and returns) is presented on the SFDC screens. Through integration with accounting, a customer's payment history, current credit status, and discount eligibility are available for the sales reps. Level IV is the level companies need to achieve when they have more than 50 reps and have established a multichannel organization. At this level, executives will have a 360-degree view of *customers*.

V. Compliance, Controls, and Business Intelligence

Through SFDC's fine-grained `security` mechanisms, `audit trails`, `workflow` system, and real-time integration, this level adds the ability to apply controls on critical user activities—even those that may be initiated from systems outside of SFDC. Workflows and alerts are extended from the first moment a quote is generated, through the closing of the order and issuance of the invoice. Revenue recognition triggers are put in place, and true revenue forecasts are

---

4. If you have not already enabled the `customer portal` or `partner portal` in your instance of SFDC, it is no longer available for you. It has been replaced by `chatter communities`.

shown on SFDC screens. Opportunity data, bookings, and revenue forecasts are locked down in the system to promote Sarbanes-Oxley Act compliance.

In addition, SFDC (in conjunction with other enterprise systems) is used as a key driver of analysis at every level of management and planning. By adding BI tools or a data warehouse, analysts can examine customer profitability, cost of customer acquisition analysis, product release planning, and other strategic issues. Companies should achieve this level of visibility and integrated operations before they go public. At Level V, members of the executive staff are using SFDC information to drive the business on a daily basis, and it is a foundation for a 360-degree view of *the business*.

What Is Your Overall Goal?

Different types of organizations need to achieve different levels of SFDC functionality. Not everyone needs to achieve Level V, and some organizations can do just fine operating only at Level III.

In this section, we explore the different kinds of SFDC user organizations and consider which level of the model each will likely need to reach.

Direct Sales Complexity Categories

Companies have different levels of sales and channel complexity. Generally speaking, the longer the sales cycle, the more complex the organization must be to handle it, and the greater the leverage that can be provided by SFDC.

For the purposes of SFDC implementation and adoption, it's important to understand where the company is positioned along the complexity continuum, from a single geographic direct sales organization to a highly complex multichannel organization. Typically, the amount of time it takes to implement and adopt the system will be a multiple of the Sales Organization Category. For example, a typical Category 2 organization will take twice as long to get to Level V as a typical Category 1 organization will. And make no mistake about it, large direct-sales organizations *will* need to achieve Level V.

Category 1 sales organizations have the following characteristics:

- The company has a single type of sales organization with few (if any) channel or territory overlays.

- Only one type of representative can take an order (e.g., only outside reps take orders—an inside rep's main role is to facilitate outside reps' productivity).

- The company has limited eCommerce, original equipment manufacturer (OEM), or indirect business (typically representing less than 10% of the company's total dollar volume).

- Repeat business, upsells, and long-term contracts represent approximately 33% of total company volume.

- The sales team works as a single business unit (product lines are closely related; every sales rep is able to sell all the company's products and services).

Typically, a Category 1 sales organization can get away with Level I SFA usage. **Category 2** sales organizations are slightly more complex:

- The organization has a mix of geographic, vertical, and named-account territories, and there are some overlays.

- Both inside and outside reps can take orders; there are thresholds and criteria for who takes different kinds of orders.

- Most territories are exclusive, but the basis of exclusivity can be complicated and cause for argument.

- Revenues from eCommerce, OEM, and indirect business are becoming important (representing as much as 40% of the company's total dollar volume), and managing customer relationships across channels is becoming a bigger issue.

- Repeat business, upsells, and long-term contracts may represent 50% of overall company volume.

- There are multiple business units and product-line specialists; many reps do not sell all of the company's products.

Typically, a Category 2 sales organization is operating at Level I of SFA usage, but it will need to achieve Level III as it grows.

Category 3 sales organizations are more complex and need to coordinate to fully service customer accounts:

- The organization has a complex array of geographic, vertical, and named-account territories; the company also has some global account managers for its top accounts.

- All channels can take orders, and there are complicated rules of engagement regarding how to hand off orders and accounts across sales teams and out to the channel.

- Few territories are exclusive, except for global strategic accounts; most exclusives are temporary (a year or two) and account transition is a key success factor for ongoing revenues.

- The eCommerce, OEM, and indirect channels handle more than 50% of the company's transactions, and they may produce 50% of total company revenues.

- Repeat business, upsells, and long-term contracts may represent 66% of overall company volume.

- The company may have multiple salesforces, each focused on a different product or service line.

Almost always, a Category 3 sales organization must be operating at Level III or IV of SFA usage, but there is frequent backsliding. When the system is replaced, the team will typically have to start over at Level I.

Category 4 sales organizations are fully integrated, multichannel, multinational operations:

- The organization has a complex array of geographic, vertical, and named-account territories in each major selling country; the company also has a department of global account managers for its top 250 accounts.

- All channels can take orders, and there are complicated rules of engagement regarding how to hand off orders and accounts across sales teams and out to the channel. International channel conflicts must be managed.

- Few territories are exclusive, except for global strategic accounts; most exclusives are temporary (a year or two) and account transition is a key success factor for ongoing revenues.

- The eCommerce, OEM, and indirect channels handle 70% of the transactions, and they may produce 60% of total company revenues.

- Repeat business, upsells, and long-term contracts may represent 75% of overall company volume.

- The company has dedicated salesforces for different business units.

Category 4 sales organizations need to be operating at Level IV or V of SFA usage. As with Category 3 organizations, these companies experience frequent backsliding as CRM systems fail or are not properly maintained. Due to the complexity and depth of interactions, cleaning up a Category 4 organization and restarting the SFA system can take several painful quarters.

SFDC Sales Teams That Aren't Pure Direct

What if your team isn't a direct sales organization? It's important to understand what kind of an organization your users are in,[5] because different organizations look for different things in SFDC, measure themselves along different lines, and optimize their operations differently:

- **Indirect Sales:** Indirect sales teams work through channels, distributors, dealers, resellers, or partners to make business happen, and they do not sell directly to customers. Leads generated by the marketing group are typically handed over to channel partners to pursue. Indirect teams are typically much smaller than direct teams, and they focus on managing the health and productivity of their partner accounts. Indirect selling organizations are worried about channel loyalty and are competing against many other vendors for the partner's attention. These channel management teams will typically need to reach Level II of the SFA Maturity Model, and they almost always need to add SFDC's Partner module.

- **Outbound Call Center:** Call center teams tend to work a large number of lower-priced deals for consumers or small- to medium-sized business customers. They emphasize the number of calls made, the number of transactions, and tight activity management. Call center operations typically have weekly or even daily metrics, so they typically use SFDC to more tightly manage their teams for the highest short-term productivity. These teams will typically need to achieve Level III or IV in the SFA Maturity Model, although they won't need a lot of functional depth because their sales cycles are so short and the average deal size is fairly small.

- **eCommerce:** Vendors that are able to complete the majority of their transactions via the Web have a very different sales focus. Because their customers use an automated system, the overall number of transactions is higher even than for a call center, and the average selling price (ASP) may be $100 or even less. Typically, the sales personnel for eCommerce operations are inside reps who assist customers with transactions that don't work in the "Web store" or that comprise repeat, renewal, or upsell business. eCommerce-driven users of SFDC tend to be very focused on real-time features because the customer will be in the store for only a few minutes. These organizations need to operate up to Level IV of the Maturity Model but have light needs in Levels I and II.

- **Inbound Call Center:** Inbound call center teams usually focus on customer support, from troubleshooting eCommerce problems to expediting shipments, to

---

5. In a small company, there's no question which kind of an organization the user is in. But in a large multinational company—let's say, General Electric—different divisions will have employees who fit each of the profiles listed here.

handling product problems, to authorizing returns and refunds. Their emphasis is on the number of calls handled, the speed and expense of problem resolution, and tight activity management. Inbound call center operations typically have weekly or even daily call-handling metrics, and they will use longer-term customer-satisfaction metrics based on surveys. Organizations that fall within this category will typically need to achieve *only* Level III or IV in the model.

- **Venture Capitalist, Private Equity, and Investment Banker:** In this kind of organization, the user is not a salesperson at all but rather an investment professional who is trying to prospect, evaluate, and monitor high-value investment opportunities. Even though such organizations may do only a few deals a quarter, their personnel need to cull through thousands of candidate companies each year and track entrepreneurs long after the initial meeting. These kinds of organizations use SFDC as a collaboration and tracking tool rather than as a selling system. The emphasis here is on achieving the easiest data entry and gathering the most valuable information with the least amount of effort. Typically, these organizations need to operate at Level I of the SFA Maturity Model.

- **Fundraising/Not-for-Profit Organization:** This kind of organization is a cross between a venture capitalist and a call center user—the employees are not trying to sell but rather are trying to track and contact a large number of people. These personnel work extensively over the phone to cultivate relationships and motivate donors. This kind of team uses SFDC as a prospect database and activity management tool to make sure that all persons on the phone bank are meeting their "dials per hour" objective. Typically, the organization needs to operate at Level I of the Maturity Model.

Part II: Is Your Organization Ready for Its Target Level?

It's important to understand where your users are today, because different levels of CRM readiness require different kinds of SFDC deployments. Without an analytical framework to assess the readiness of key user departments, the project will be lost in a sea of opinions and the project team members will likely misjudge the deployment requirements.

Organizations with lots of users who have used SFDC before in previous jobs will have a series of expectations from their previous experiences. They will immediately ask for bells and whistles that the more junior members of the organization won't even understand the need for.

At the other extreme, organizations with little experience with any CRM system will need to have a much slower rollout of the system, allowing time to acclimate to SFDC concepts, metrics, and practices. These organizations will tend to be far more resistant to

> ### FIND THE EARLY ADOPTERS, BUT DON'T FALL IN LOVE WITH THEM
>
> No matter which kind of organization you work in, people will vary in their willingness to adopt new technologies and processes. You need to identify the risk takers—the early adopters—because their willingness to put in a little extra effort to adopt new technologies will be very helpful in your prototyping, testing, and deployment stages.
>
> Although you need to leverage their enthusiasm, energy, and domain expertise, don't rely on the early adopters too much for providing "typical" feedback. They're usually so far ahead of the pack that their input will be misleading. In your surveys, review sessions, and testing, include a representative sample of users that includes several "average" users and even the occasional hardened Luddite.

adopting the system (particularly if they like to keep secrets), and their employees may complain for months that the system is getting in their way.

My firm has developed a 500-question survey to measure the state of readiness for each of the major groups in a CRM organization. In our interview process, we try to capture as many subtleties as we can, with the goal being to avoid surprises later in the project.

Of course, you don't have to perform that kind of detailed survey to get a feel for your own organization's readiness for an SFDC system. The goal is to understand the gap between the target level and the organization's current operations. Briefly interview two or three people in each of the organizations discussed in the remainder of this section, asking the 20 questions that are relevant to their role.

Sales Organizational Readiness

The following questions are intended for members of the sales organization, assuming your company uses a direct sales model at least to some extent.

1. Are all leads and contact information stored natively in the existing SFA system? Have all employees stopped using their "little black books" to manage their sales contacts?

2. Are all leads routed automatically, and are queues are in use? Do sales reps know where to find their new leads, and do they know the difference between a lead and a contact?

3. Do the telesales/telemarketing/inside sales/sales development reps use the SFA system on *every* call?

4. Is there a clear delineation of responsibility for all phases of lead handling (e.g., marketing does lead generation and imports, sales development does lead cultivation/qualification/appointment setting, and sales does lead conversion and pipeline development)?

5. Are there clear phases or stages that define the sales cycle through which *every* deal progresses, and does the SFA system reflect these stages?

6. Is every deal in progress stored as an opportunity in the SFA system? Even renewals and upsells?

7. Does everyone in the sales organization know how to enter a deal and see its current status?

8. Are qualification criteria "baked in" to SFA screens and usage patterns?

9. Are there leads, contacts, accounts, or opportunities stored outside the SFA system?

10. Are all forecasts based only on data in the SFA system?

11. Do reps use contact roles to show the customer politics involved in a deal?

12. Does the SFA system accurately reflect territories, overlays, quotas, splits, and sales teams?

13. Is the company's sales methodology incorporated into SFA screens and workflows?

14. Do sales executives and sales administrators see the SFA system as their key information resource?

15. Does sales management see the SFA system as the first point of inquiry when trying to find out about a customer situation?

16. Are all orders either placed via the SFA system or visible from it?

17. Are all quotes and orders seeking exceptions subject to automatic approval cycles?

18. Do reps use the SFA system as *the* way to organize their time and do their account planning?

19. Are customers' order history and current credit status visible from within the SFA screens?

20. Are commission calculations based *only* on SFA data so that deals that aren't properly in the system don't earn a commission?

Marketing Organizational Readiness

The following questions are used to score your marketing processes—and it doesn't matter whether those processes are performed by employees or contractors. Again, the questions assume that your company sells at least partially via a direct sales model.

1. Are market segments and target customers defined and prioritized in a fairly stable way, or do they jump around quarter after quarter?

2. Do marketing and sales personnel jointly design and select outbound activities for each quarter?

3. Do marketing personnel handle all aspects of lead processing and management (e.g., automatic lead input for Web-generated leads, importing all leads, performing deduping, enriching, and correcting lead information before it is imported into the SFA system)?

4. Are leads automatically "aged out" so that untouched leads more than 60 days old are pulled back from sales and maintained in the marketing database?

5. Are all leads assigned to at least one campaign?

6. Are all email blasts done in conjunction with, and measured by, the SFA campaign system?

7. Do marketing personnel work in conjunction with the sales staff to define qualification criteria, conversion criteria, and telesales scripts, and is lead qualification baked in to the SFA system?

8. Does each major campaign have its own landing page on the Web site?

9. Are leads scored or prioritized based on data and systematic rules? Are marketing tactics "tuned" using scoring data from previous campaigns?

10. Is marketing running proactive social media campaigns, and is it measuring messaging effectiveness and audience sentiment on a regular basis?

11. Is the marketing department using a marketing automation system and follow-up "drip email" campaigns to make sure that each and every new lead is automatically contacted several times?

12. Is each search engine marketing (e.g., Google AdWords) ad campaign linked to its own landing page on the Web site, with separate measurements for conversion ratio and cost per conversion?

13. Do marketing and sales personnel use the same metrics and terminology for lead development, lead qualification, and pipeline development?

14. Are telemarketing/lead cultivation operations (i.e., phone people whose effectiveness is measured on numbers of appointments made) managed separately from inside sales (i.e., reps who have revenue targets)?

15. Is the effectiveness of marketing campaigns measured by the number of sales cycles those campaigns have directly affected?

16. Has the marketing department developed campaign influence reports and dashboards that link marketing tactics to the pipeline?

17. Does the marketing department have a model for the lead waterfall showing the expected time in stage and the conversion ratios at every stage?

18. Have marketing personnel put all customer reference information into the SFA system?

19. Have product marketing personnel put all customer survey data into the SFA system, and do they use the SFA data for product planning and feature prioritization?

20. Does the marketing department evaluate itself by measuring the cost of customer acquisition and the *profitability* of running campaigns?

Services Organizational Readiness

The following questions score the technical support and professional services organization for the company. The customer support people who are focused on expediting orders, handling credit card refunds, or collecting payments should not answer these questions.

1. Does the customer support/customer care team use the CRM system for tracking customer calls, cases, incidents, and customer interactions?

2. Does the customer support/customer care team use the CRM system for tracking bugs, product defects, and product returns (return to manufacturer authorizations [RMAs])?

3. Does the professional services group use the CRM system for storing basic customer information?

4. Does the professional services group use the CRM system for storing basic project information (e.g., bids/quotes, statements of work [SOWs]/work breakdown structure [WBS] documents, specifications)?

5. Does the professional services group use an automatic tool for time cards, measurement of progress against milestones, and project invoicing?

6. Does the company send automatic reminders that notify sales reps and customers when a support contract is about to expire?

7. Is the service team leveraging social media, particularly to intercept rapidly growing problems?

8. Has the customer support/customer care team established response times that it measures itself against?

9. Does the customer support/customer care team have automatic escalation rules to ensure that the company lives up to contractual stipulations or service level agreements (SLAs)?

10. Does the customer support/customer care team measure itself on SLA compliance?

11. Does the customer support/customer care team measure itself on support profitability?

12. Does the professional services team measure itself on profitability?

13. Are the customer service and professional services teams viewed as a collaborator in the sales cycle?

14. Is the CRM system viewed as a key resource for measuring and understanding customer satisfaction?

15. Is the CRM system viewed as a key resource for understanding customers' total purchase history, customer assets, and other characteristics?

16. Is the CRM system the core of a public knowledge base and customer self-service portal?

17. Does the service team have a real-time chat system integrated into both the public Web site and the CRM system?

18. Does the CRM system have alerts and workflows that enforce approval of unusual consulting projects?

19. Is the CRM system viewed as a key resource for understanding customers' total consulting, training, and certification history?

20. Are CRM system reports and dashboards used for measuring and planning support and professional services offerings?

Finance and Legal Organizational Readiness

In most cases, members of the finance and legal departments are very far away from adopting SFDC; in many cases, they may still run everything on Outlook and Excel. Even so, you need to understand where their processes are today and how amenable they are to integration with SFDC.

1. Are all legal documents scanned and stored in electronic form?

2. Are all legal documents stored with naming conventions and access controls so that any lawyer can quickly find needed documents without having to call another person?

3. Does the accounting system(s) used by finance have external interfaces that can "talk" to other software packages?

4. Are commissions calculated in an automated way that is driven by accounting system data (invoices)?

5. Has the finance department's customer list, contact information, and price list been correlated to information in the CRM system so that the two could be synchronized in the future?

6. Has the legal department reviewed the Web site, SFA, and email blasting system for CAN-SPAM Act and European Privacy compliance?

7. Has the finance department set up revenue recognition rules and vendor-specific objective evidence (VSOE) thresholds that could be triggered by automated means?

8. Has the finance department set up approval cycles that include delegation (in case of absence) that could be handled by automated means?

9. Does the legal department store the sales-related documents (e.g., SLAs, licenses, contracts, letters) in a way that can be accessed through the CRM system?

10. Does the finance department "own" the revenue forecast but expect the sales department to own bookings forecasts?

11. Do finance personnel derive the bookings forecast off of CRM data (no credit if they use it only as a reality check for their revenue forecast)?

12. Have finance/legal personnel set up contractual approval and "paperwork generation" (e.g., licenses, signature pages) in such a way that those tasks could be handled by automated means such as DocuSign?

13. Does the finance department pay commissions only if the deal is in the CRM system prior to quoting?

14. Has order entry been integrated between the accounting and CRM system, and are data locked down once a deal has been closed?

15. Are approvals for bids, quotes, and orders approval handled through automatic workflows?

16. Is the customer's order history fully synchronized between the accounting and CRM systems?

17. Do legal department personnel use SFA reports to forecast the amount of contractual work that will be required during a given month?

18. Has the legal team developed a retention policy for documents stored in the CRM system, and are there need-to-know rules for CRM pipeline data?

19. Have the finance and legal departments survived a Sarbanes Oxley, HIPAA, FERPA, or similar audit thanks to CRM controls and workflows?

20. Do finance personnel use SFA data as the basis for marketing/sales budgeting and customer profitability analysis?

> ### KNOWING THE SCORE
>
> *Each "yes" answer above represents ¼ point toward achieving the levels described earlier (e.g., if a person answers yes to 14 of the above questions, his or her department is currently operating at about Level III of the SFA Maturity Model). The Web site www.SFDC-secrets.com provides some example score sheets for an organization.*

IT and Web Team Organizational Readiness

For the IT organization and the Web site team, a checklist doesn't make as much sense as a discussion about the skills, prerequisites, and training these personnel will need to succeed. Essentially, any IT or Web team can achieve any of the CRM levels—the higher levels simply mean more effort (or more contractors). But it's a good idea to let them know what you'll need and ask them to quantify what it will take them to be ready for adoption of the SFDC system.

There are two basic questions that—believe it or not—have to be asked:

- Is the user hardware there? SFDC does all the server stuff, but every SFDC user will need access to a PC, laptop, iPad/Android tablet, or smartphone. If you're dealing with a mobile workforce, make sure they have a 4G-capable device. Don't start an SFDC implementation without these items being in place.

- Is the culture there? If your company is fundamentally uncomfortable leveraging technology (e.g., everyone really uses paper Day-Timers), moving overnight from "nothing" to a highly integrated CRM system is not a realistic goal.

Make sure that somebody in IT reads Chapter 13 as soon as possible—yesterday is not soon enough. SFDC and other cloud-based products can be almost invisible to the internal IT team: the software is hosted externally and places few requirements on IT infrastructure. Even so, it's a good idea to invite a member of the IT team to the early planning meetings for your project. The IT team needs to identify corporate issues (such as security, external access, information protection, password policies, and user access controls) and make SFDC consistent with the rest of the company policies. Achieving this goal may mean a full-scale review of SFDC—although the SFDC product has been so widely deployed that it should be able to quickly pass any internal review. If the IT team has never worked with a large-scale cloud product, the architecture and deployment/ operations groups will have a small learning curve (as discussed in Chapter 13).

The internal IT organization also needs to be involved with integration between SFDC and internal applications using a service-oriented architecture (SOA, via SOAP, ReST, and other Web service protocols). The IT team probably has the generic skills needed to handle this responsibility but must learn SFDC's specific APIs and data structures. To smooth the way, SFDC has developed over 10,000 pages of documentation, some great self-training tools, and a vibrant self-help community for developers—all for free.

Sophisticated customers need to go beyond SFDC to round out the functionality, so the IT team must deploy those new products (which may involve on-premises hardware and software) and integrate them with existing systems. Deploying those packaged products doesn't require any specialized skills, but it still takes time on the IT calendar.

The internal help desk needs to know enough about SFDC to respond to basic user questions and administrative requests. For example, these personnel need to know how to let users back into the system when they forget their passwords. SFDC offers a wide range of classes, but most help desks use a "train the trainer" model that means only one person needs to attend the full course. SFDC systems administrators (who typically work in IT, sales operations, or marketing) end up answering a fair number of user questions themselves.

The Web site team will have interactions with SFDC at several levels. Web site registration pages will require some new HTML and JavaScript. If the Web site is based on a content management system, the content download pages will need to interact with SFDC and your marketing automation system to some extent. All of these tasks can be handled via off-the-shelf adaptors, a server-side scripting language, or .Net/Java to invoke Web service APIs. Typically, the Web site teams won't have the technical depth needed to write these "SOAP" calls, but members of the central IT team will. Fortunately, these skills are needed only temporarily, so the Web site team can get by with using contractors.

Part III: How Big Is the Gap?

How do you know whether the gap between the users' current level and the desired levels of CRM execution can be realistically crossed? How do you tell if the goals have been set too high?

As mentioned earlier, a good rule of thumb is to target the expected CRM level at slightly above the median score of the affected department. But this criterion really applies only with a fairly large user population that can go through several cycles of capability improvement. In smaller organizations, you have to make the judgment on an intuitive—rather than a quantitative—level.

If users are anxious about the scale of change or are scared about learning the new system, a more incremental goal is highly advised. For example, if the current user population uses no SFA or CRM system at all or is going through a "crash program," the users will be required to make significant jumps in sophistication and changes in their behavior. Expect this process to require some effort and political capital (see Chapter 6), such as:

- Incentives and personal measurements that give users unambiguous signals about how and what they need to change

- A deeply committed upper-management champion (who almost always has to be a sales VP, service VP, or COO)

- Several cycles of user training, with scoring and "certification"

- Extensive documentation, cheat sheets, and other content on the project wiki

- An identified group of early adopters who are tasked with using the system from the first day of deployment to identify system areas for streamlining[6]

- A long-running program of internal marketing, including `chatter` groups

As with any change management project, measuring progress frequently, managing expectations, and listening to users are key determinants of success.

---

6. This "advance group" can become the basis for some positive internal competition in the organization. Because membership in the advance group is by invitation only and connotes more sophisticated users, users may be enticed by the "extra toys" that members of the advance group get to use in their jobs. If this happens, do not expand the advance group too quickly: users who really aren't ready will become frustrated and waste time on unproductive system usage. Even worse, because of their lack of knowledge, they may corrupt or destroy data in the system.

Understanding the Next Wave of Users

As discussed in Chapter 4, in a large multidivisional organization, each wave of features may involve new users with different organizational affiliations, work habits, and functional interactions. Prior to each implementation cycle, you need to understand enough about the new user groups to avoid adoption and internal politics problems. Check out Chapter 6 for further details on adoption.

Who Are the Users?

In Chapter 1, you created personas that are archetypes of users. Now it's time to understand the specifics of the *real* users you'll be working with—their state of mind, their goals, and their readiness.

First, assess the users' initial beliefs about SFDC. Have they had good experiences in the past with *any* SFA or CRM system? Do they believe that a good system can make their jobs easier by saving them time, preventing dropped balls, or earning them more commissions? Can they see how putting more information into SFDC would cut down on emails and phone calls? Do they perceive the goals of the project to be reasonable, or is there disagreement about what the problem *really* is?[7] Are they suspicious that SFDC is a Big Brother monitoring system to put the squeeze on people? If the users have strong preconceptions, it can make deployment very tough.

HOW WELL DO YOU HAVE TO KNOW THOSE PESKY USERS?

In a small organization at a single location, you can probably answer all the questions in this section yourself.

But in larger organizations with many departments and locations, you need to have a feel for the people you are working with. For each major constituency, make contact with at least three people who are representative of the organization. After you've met them initially, keep track of their contact information (as you may need to communicate with these individuals more than once during the project).

---

7. If there is widespread suspicion that the *real* reason the project is being done is to "satisfy the bozos in marketing" or "find the bad reps" or "help the execs do CYA maneuvers," the CRM team needs to escalate this issue immediately! Your executive champions need to make other members of the organization believe that the goals of the SFDC project are to make everyone more successful, lower stress levels, and improve customer satisfaction.

Next, find out about the users' level of organizational trust. Do they make decisions individually or in groups? Do they share information with other departments, or do they tend to carefully manage the flow of information (and even keep secrets)? Do people tend to trust the information they get from management (taking it literally), or do they tend to interpret (and even second-guess) it?

Next, understand the users' work habits. Are they locked in to their computer screens all day long? Do they carry their iPads or laptops with them to internal meetings? Do users tend to use paper printouts in analyzing problems or reconciling data, or are they more comfortable working online? Do they use Excel spreadsheets, or are they comfortable with an Access database or even a business intelligence tool?

It's particularly important to understand how users in the sales department currently handle their tasks now. Are they using paper (notepads, Day-Timers, or sticky notes) for managing their callbacks and action items? Do they carry their laptops with them on sales calls, and do they have 4G access? Do they use a spreadsheet for forecasting, or are a series of spreadsheets passed around by email? Do these users tend to manage their tasks, reminders, and action items in Outlook? Do they use a file server for document storage, do they file stuff in their own PC's folders, or do they just leave documents attached to email messages?

The good news is that SFDC can be easily configured to work well in any of these user environments. But you can't know how to optimize (or which potholes to avoid) until you've interviewed the users.

Why Should Users Change?

When you implement SFDC, you will ask groups of users to change the way they do their daily tasks. You will also ask them to attend training, deal with a new user interface and, in many cases, add an extra step to something they have to do already. Some people may be willing to perform new steps purely for the sake of achieving a better process or a more efficient organization—but that is rare. Most people—and particularly those in sales and marketing—are *not* process people.

So, what's in it for them? It's your job to figure that out.

When planning each major deployment phase, you must identify which groups of users will be the most significantly affected by the changes and survey them so you can anticipate and counteract issues that could cause user resistance.

You'll need to identify benefits that can offset the costs of change *from the individual's perspective*. Make sure to identify and highlight situations where the *current* way of doing things could cause problems *for that individual*. For example, if employees will get into trouble if they divulge confidential information, but they regularly email a spreadsheet containing confidential data, it's only a matter of time before the "address auto-complete" feature in Outlook accidentally sends the spreadsheet to someone—inside or outside the company—who isn't supposed to see it. In another example, if a key document is stored only as an attachment in an individual's Outlook file, it's only a matter of time before a PST file corruption causes the permanent loss of that document. Because no one wants more exposure to risk or more manual steps, highlight cases where the new ways of working through SFDC will benefit the users directly.

There are four categories of benefits for individual users:

- **Making it easier for that user to make his or her number or achieve that bonus-laden quarterly goal:** Sales reps are coin-operated, and everybody wants to make it home for dinner.

- **Getting new features that will make the user's job easier or better right away:** Sometimes, these features are small things. It's important to clearly promote these direct benefits without overselling the system.

- **Making the boss happy by complying with a mandate:** For mandates to be effective, they must be genuine. It's important that the people at the top of the organization be vocal and consistent supporters of the system and show that *they* will be using the system to manage the organization. Even if penalties are proscribed for not following the mandate, if upper managers hint that they won't be using the system at all or that they won't be paying attention to CRM reports for guiding the business, their attitude will set user adoption back by several months.

- **Providing things that will make the user's job easier at some point in the future:** The problem with deferred benefits is that users have to wait for the system to become more powerful, for the data to be more comprehensive, or for other users

CARROTS, STICKS, AND TOYS

You're asking users to change their behavior, so you need to clearly illustrate the benefits that the user will experience. The more personal and direct, the better. Managers already know how to use both carrots and sticks to motivate behavior. With SFDC, we can add "toys" to the arsenal.

Each major functional expansion of the system typically involves some new complexity and some incremental behavioral changes. Best practice is to *give* users something new—even if it's just minor eye candy—any time you're asking them to *do* something new. As discussed in Chapter 1, "featurettes" and "quick wins" are one key way to do this.

To the degree you can, time the deployment of a featurette to match the appearance of a new "tax item" you're asking the user to do. Giving users a quid pro quo reduces user resistance and makes them feel that they aren't being taken for granted. You'll want to plan a series of these user toys, clustering the most attractive ones around the more annoying (but inevitable) tax items.

to change their behaviors to realize these rewards. These are the most tenuous benefits because the user has to pay the taxes *now* without getting any personal result until some vague point in the future. Although some people will make changes simply because it's the right thing to do, that group will almost never amount to a critical mass of users.

Communicating with the Users

Throughout the project, you need to communicate with the user community—surveying them for input, notifying them of upcoming changes, describing new policies or procedures, and alerting them about training sessions and other events.

To do so, you need to figure out the most effective and pain-free way of communicating with users. Will they actually read a paper version of a CRM newsletter? Will users read blogs for internal Q&A? Do people pay more attention to unofficial emails and IMs from colleagues, or do they sit up when they receive official emails from corporate headquarters? Can you get a section on the company's podcast? Survey the user base, and tailor the medium and style of your communications to match their preferences.

THE MEDIUM IS THE MESSAGE

Part of the deployment cycle is the "broadcast" of good-news stories that illustrate how much better life is becoming thanks to the SFDC project. To be effective, these broadcasts need to be put through the channel(s) that are most frequently seen and readily believed. Putting a notice up on the wiki or sending out a lame internal newsletter won't cut it.

All too often, an email that starts with a person low in the organization and spreads outward is taken more seriously than official propaganda. Think about using guerrilla marketing techniques for getting the word out . . . and believed. `Chatter` is also a great way of spreading the news among the cognoscenti—the lucky few who've been allowed on the system early.

For more on this, see Chapters 6 and 13 and check out www.SFDC-secrets.com.

User Training

As it gets to be time to deploy each major area of new functionality, you need to engage affected users in training or even indoctrination. Generally speaking, classroom-style training is not effective for most business users. Typically, too much information is delivered all at once, and the information isn't very relevant to the audience at the time it's delivered. By the time the situation comes up in the real world and the users actually *need* that information, they will have forgotten it. Even if they have been given a full user's manual, they are likely to forget that they ever received any training on the topic.

You need to assess your users before deciding which kind of training to provide. Do they like classroom settings, or can they be effectively trained with self-paced, Web-based courses? Does your company use videoconferencing for training? Does the company already use podcasts for training and internal "newscasts"?

Generally, the shorter and more task-oriented ("day in the life") the training, the better. Try to keep training sessions to less than an hour, and do training in stages (with sessions separated by a couple of weeks and extending as long as they are needed) to make sure that users have *really* learned the basics before giving them more advanced material. It's best to have the training include real examples from the users' daily tasks and to have users "drive the mouse" during the session.

No matter which kind of training sessions you hold, record them! This step is particularly important for worldwide implementations of SFDC systems and for organizations

---

CLASS . . . CLASS . . . CLA-AAAA-ASS . . . WAKE UP!

Training is always tricky—everyone says that employees haven't had enough training, but nobody wants to sit through yet another class. To make the most of the training time that you can get, here are three formulas that work well for effective, memorable training:

- A classroom setting where every student (or pair of students) has a computer with full network access and can run through exercises relevant to their jobs during the class. These sessions are the most expensive to do (particularly in a company with many locations), but this approach is the best way to ensure uniformity and depth of training.

- A meeting-room setting where students bring their laptops, using WiFi or 4G connections to run through the exercises on SFDC and internal systems. These sessions are easier to schedule and set up (because they are closer to the users' workspace), but they are also more vulnerable to interruptions and delays as people drift back to their desk during breaks.

- A "live" Webinar training session, where users take the "class" while sitting at their desks and using their own computers. These sessions are logistically the easiest and can save considerable travel costs, but it's impossible to know whether students are paying attention to you or their Angry Birds game. If Webinars or other computer-based training are used, students must be tested before they have completed the training requirement—and they must know that they will be tested *before* they start the session.

See www.SFDC-secrets.com for an example training syllabus.

that experience frequent turnover. Don't bother using a videocam: they're not good enough to capture any detail, they make boring sessions even duller, and they record in a format that won't be usable outside of North America. Instead, the preferred recording medium should be internationally portable, allow editing, and be fed by a good microphone and screen-capture software. We've had good luck just recording sessions via WebEx or GoToMeeting. Make the recordings available to all as files on the project wiki or Google Drive area.

Podcasts are also a very effective way of getting training to users on demand. In some cases, you can just strip the audio track from some of your longer sessions—but you'll almost certainly need to edit the sessions down so the listener doesn't fall asleep and drive off the road.

It's also very helpful to create a laminated cheat sheet with annotated screenshots explaining the most common tasks for each user type. Some people will want an entire user guide in paper form as well. These hard-copy documents should also be stored in PDF in the project wiki or Google Drive area and in SFDC's documents area.

What User Readiness Means for Deployment

Not all departments in a large organization will be equally ready to make the move to SFDC. The marketing department might be urgently waiting, the sales department somewhat ready, and finance/legal nearing Luddite levels of resistance. So the deployment of each wave of functionality should proceed at a pace that's matched to the individual department's needs. Don't mistake naive enthusiasm for readiness, particularly in Luddite groups. Those employees may have a positive attitude about using the new features, but they may have a vacuum of skills and ingrained habits that will get in the way of achieving real productivity with SFDC.

For organizations that are truly eager to adopt SFDC systems, deploy features quickly with user tips for maximum productivity. Make training about standards, practices, and nuance, and consider making it self-paced. You don't have to worry about confusing or intimidating users, so the more toys for power users you can offer, the more they'll like it.

For organizations that are only somewhat ready to make the switch, features should be deployed at a slower pace and training sessions should be more deliberate. Make sure that some kind of user toy (e.g., eye candy) becomes available as a featurette every release or so, but don't overdo it.

Organizations that are populated with Luddites need to have the technology deployed more carefully, with full training and assurances before users actually have the freedom to do anything life threatening. These folks can take two to three times as long to truly absorb new technology, let alone be truly productive with it. In such organizations, it's important to release cheat sheets and good-news stories (look how SFDC helped avoid this potential disaster!) on a monthly basis. New toys and eye-candy features may merely serve to confuse these users with screen clutter, so use SFDC `record types`, `page layouts`, and `VisualForce` to keep the screens simple for them.

Postdeployment User Frustration

Aside from training issues and forgetfulness, there are a few things to watch out for when working with any new group of SFDC users. Every security feature in SFDC is there to protect your data from being seen by the wrong eyes and to keep the bad guys out. But this mandate translates into ongoing issues for users, so system operations needs to have a range of strategies to handle the inevitable issues. Check out Chapter 13 if you want to know more about the technical details, but here are the three big ones for developing corrective procedures:

- **Users often forget their passwords and lock themselves out:** The system has password-strength screening, which is a good thing. Unfortunately, stronger passwords are harder to remember. Plus, most organizations will configure the system so that the password "ages out" every 60 to 90 days, requiring the user to come up with a different hard-to-remember password before they really memorized the last one. Best of all, most security-conscious clients turn on the system lockout feature that temporarily disables an account that has been subject to repeated failed login attempts.

  The first thing you need to do is place a detailed explanation of this behavior and its rationale—along with your company's corrective policies and contact information—on the project wiki or Google Drive area. The second thing you need to do is to set up a special phone number and voicemail box to assist people who've been locked out. **This voicemail needs to be checked at least hourly, and it's even better if the account (or an email address) automatically pages the on-duty SFDC administrator.** For global companies with mission-critical usage, the SFDC administrator role needs to be covered on a 7 × 24 basis.

- **Users may log on from a different location or from a different PC:** SFDC has a feature that authenticates not only the user, but also the computer and network he or she is working on. The first time a user tries to log in from home, or on a different computer, or even from a different network while on the road, the system will not let the user in until s/he is re-authenticated. This authorization is a necessary evil taking only a couple of minutes, but it's a pain for users.

  As always, the first line of defense is information and solution checklists on the project wiki or Google Drive area. You could even have this as a "help line" hint while they're waiting on hold for the system administrator. The authentication cycle can be completed by email or by phone, and really isn't that hard.

- **Users may not be able to see or modify a record:** SFDC has very fine-grained controls for user access to records. The essential rule is that a user can see only those records that he or she owns or that the user's subordinates own. When there's a change of territories, transfer of `accounts` or `opportunities`, or reorganization, users may suddenly not be able to change records, or even see them at all.

The main remedy here is to have very well-thought-out and communicated access hierarchies, and to let users know they'll be losing some access before the change is made (the wiki/Google Drive makes for a wonderful CYA resource in these situations). In cases where a sales rep needs to see or manipulate records that are not part of the rep's hierarchy (this happens frequently when there are overlay territories such as partner managers or global account managers), use SFDC's `sales team` feature to give the users access to the specific `accounts`, `contacts`, and `opportunities` that they need so see. Of course, there are numerous solutions to this problem, but all of the other strategies involve carefully manipulating security levels.

How Many Administrators Does It Take to Screw In a Light Bulb?

A classic question in SFDC deployments is "How many administrators do we need for the system?" SFDC's software and data are professionally managed by the Salesforce.com staff, and they have an exemplary record for system uptime and (with one exception) security.

Every customer instance of SFDC will need to have at least one administrator, whose routine tasks include user management, data import, system backup, and other thrilling duties. The administrator role is usually a part-time job, and the person who fills it usually works in marketing, sales administration, customer service, finance, or IT. It is *strongly* advised that your system administrator take SFDC's administrator course and become certified. Although this will burn 5 days of time and currently costs $3,800 plus expenses, an administrator course will save significant wasted time and hassle for your users.

For any serious SFDC installation, however, there should be one administrator per continent (really, North America, EMEA, and Asia/Pacific) so that the administrative duties can "follow the sun" for 7 × 24 support. For industrial-strength SFDC installations, it is fully justified to have six administrators with a range of talents (e.g., IT, familiarity with external systems, reporting, or political acumen). But each of these administrators needs to have an *explicit* reason for being, and duties must be assigned using consistent rules. Further, their job roles and process hand-offs must be fully documented to pass Sarbanes-Oxley Section 404 and 409 audits, plus any other process audits for HIPAA, FERPA, USDA, and so on. Check out the discussion in Chapter 13 to learn more about the duties and desirable profiles for administrators.

Almost inevitably, there will be power users in sales, marketing, and services (usually first- or second-level managers) who have worked extensively with SFDC in the past. Some of these users will ask for full administrative powers so that they can "do their jobs better." While they may have genuine issues, *beware of these requests and almost always deny them*. Thanks to SFDC's security system (which is both powerful and fine-grained), there is almost *always* another way to solve these power users' problems. Typically, you can grant users delegated or temporary authority to access exactly and only what they need. Their issues are usually a pretext designed to get them system powers beyond what's needed for his or her position, or otherwise game the system to their advantage. In addition to causing morale and data quality issues (e.g., deleting records that show weak performance), these superfluous administrators are typically cowboys who are bound to cause security and compliance issues.

Just say no.

Getting the Most from SFDC

- Adoption is everything. Don't try to push your organization farther than its real readiness for CRM and behavioral change.

- Examine your company for its SFA and CRM maturity.

- Score the main user departments (sales, marketing, service, and legal) for their level of sophistication.

- Understand the users you're working with, and figure out what will motivate them to welcome SFDC (hint: make it easier for them).

- Be smart about internal communications and training. `Chatter` and WebEx/ GoToMeeting work best in most organizations.

For Small Companies

- If you're lucky, you can just skim most of this chapter.

- No more than three system administrators are needed.

For Large Enterprises

- Identify the government and industry standards you'll need to comply with.

- Spend some time evaluating the target level of CRM maturity and sales organization you need going forward.

- Survey the affected teams and quantify the gap between where you are now and where you need to be. Don't overreach.

- Consider bringing in a change-management consultant. In large organizations, sociology and politics matter.

CHAPTER 6

Working the Politics

Practical politics consists of ignoring facts.
—Henry Adams

This chapter is for all SFDC users, because they need to understand the political environment surrounding SFDC. Because budgets and system adoption are creatures of company politics, "working the system" is a key success factor during and after the implementation.

Technology is not the problem. According to a recent report[1] by industry analyst Forrester Research, the problems of "aligning business strategy" and "managing change" were each twice as important as "technology" and "integration" in CRM projects. Even the problem of "executive commitment" was more important than any of the technology or product issues.

In other words, getting the technology right isn't enough.

In other, other words, succeeding with politics is a key success factor of any CRM project.

From the very beginning, you need to work politics to get the proper budget and get executive authority to proceed. Even when the project is firmly underway, you need to be working politics at every level to manage expectations and achieve the adoption that's required to make the system truly effective.

It's Not Just Big Organizations

Let's face it: the larger and older the organization you work for, the more that politics enter into nearly every decision the organization makes. But even small organizations can have their share of friction. And when it comes to the topic of sales productivity, political strife can get pretty thick no matter how young the organization is.

---

1. "How to Get Business and IT Executives to Agree on CRM Priorities," William Band, Forrester Research's Principal Analyst for CRM strategy.

The whole job of a sales rep is to manage information and to leverage emotions to his or her advantage—so sales organizations are going to be pretty adept at framing and managing political issues. Because sales folks are very sensitive about quotas, commissions, territories, leads—well, practically everything that's going to be held in the CRM system—expect them to engage in a sometimes fractious debate when it comes to SFDC tradeoffs and priorities.

But it's not just the sales personnel who may be worried. A lot of people have job security and bonus payments at stake:

- Marketing personnel will be concerned about the cost-effectiveness of their campaigns, the quality of leads, and the marketing metrics that will determine their bonuses.

- Customer support personnel will be anxious about how many cases will be filed, how quickly they'll be handled, how frequently they need to be escalated, and the number of SLA violations. They may also be worried about outsourcing or automation that could affect their careers.

- IT personnel will be concerned about the development work they probably *won't* be doing and the budget they'll probably be losing (the cloud lowers centralized procurement budgets). They'll also be concerned about the tricky integration and data migration work they will need to do as part of the SFDC implementation.

- Manufacturing personnel will want to make sure that all orders are shippable configurations, and they won't want an inventory squeeze at the end of the quarter.

- Finance and legal personnel will want to ensure that unapproved quotes never reach the customer, and that orders and forecasts fully comply with SEC and industry regulations.

You can't ignore these realities, which inevitably affect SFDC projects from their first inception to their ongoing management and upgrades. Politics will drive budgets, priorities, schedules, and staffing—it can't be assumed away.

Who's the Champion?

So let's start with your key political resources. The champion is the person who drives the SFDC decisions and creates the consensus in the organization to buy a system and modify business processes. The champion typically has to get the budget for the initial procurement (as described in Chapter 1) and will probably have to bear the brunt of ongoing fees.

But the champion also has to be the arbiter of priorities and the creator of deadline pressure to get things done. The champion will almost certainly be an executive with the political clout to remove obstacles and give orders. For the initial system, the champion can be any one of the roles described in the following subsections. Notice that if the champion *isn't* in the sales organization, he or she will need to have some very special characteristics.

Chief Financial Officer

The finance organization is usually quite interested in getting the most leverage out of corporate assets, and its denizens are often surprised by how much sales, marketing, channel (partner), and customer support departments cost. The financial gurus are typically tightly focused on sales productivity and improving measurements (usually because the sales folks are busily trying to obfuscate those very numbers).

It is possible for the finance organization to be the initial champion of the SFDC system, particularly if this department owns the group that handles order processing and commissions payments. The CFO may also be able to succeed if he or she is a trusted advisor to the CEO, and if the company's board of directors has specific concerns about sales costs and effective yield.

The problem with having the CFO lead the charge toward SFDC is that it virtually guarantees an adversarial relationship with sales management. Even if the VP of sales is supportive, everyone on the sales team will know that the initiative is really coming from the bean counters. The individual sales reps will assume that the main purpose of the system is to give upper management a way to spy on their activities, micromanage them, and punish them for weak productivity. *Consequently, almost nobody in the sales organization would see SFDC as being in their personal interests.*

The individual reps will not view SFDC as a tool to help *them* manage their time, accelerate deals, or make their quota. Typically, this would virtually guarantee low system utilization, empty records, low system credibility, and very limited leverage. Upper management will get "visibility," but the numbers they receive won't be very meaningful.

There's a further issue: the CFO will make his or her decisions based on purely financial data. Because SFDC has several benefits that are invisible in the "big numbers"—less friction, better collaboration, fewer emails, happier customers—the CFO will tend to miss important values of the system. Consequently, the company will tend to underinvest in the SFDC system, and it will miss opportunities to make the sales, marketing, and service teams more effective.

Bottom line: having the CFO as the initial champion for the system is very unlikely to succeed. It's far better to have the CFO coax someone else to take the reins.

Chief Marketing Officer

The VP of marketing or CMO is usually quite interested in making a CRM system happen because it fits his or her analytical nature.[2] The marketing folks are responsible for producing leads, and they're curious about why many campaigns produce leads that go into a black hole and are never seen again. Even though marketing's leads don't seem to generate much pipeline, sales reps keep closing deals: the people they're selling to *had* to hear about the company and its products somehow. Everyone in the marketing department privately wonders what the sales department is actually doing and whether the reps are changing the records to make themselves look good—and to make the marketing staff look like a bunch of bozos.

The VP of marketing might just be the most competent person in the whole organization to run the system, but there's a problem: in most companies, there's a distant (if not difficult) relationship between the sales and marketing organizations. They don't really trust each other, and they don't spend a lot of time together. At an emotional level, they're competing organizations—and marketing almost never wins this game. Even if the VP of sales is supportive of SFDC, everyone on the sales team will know that the initiative is really coming from marketing. The individual sales reps will assume that the system will be used to glorify marketing, spy on sales reps, and hold them accountable for a bunch of metrics that don't mean anything to the business. The members of the sales organization won't see what all the urgency for the SFDC system is about, and they are unlikely to see it as helping *them*.

There's another problematic issue: most marketing organizations just don't have a sense of urgency about revenue.[3] They don't have the end-of-quarter panic *in their bones*, and everyone in sales knows it. Even if the marketing folks work long hours, they are rarely perceived as being responsive to field needs. They don't know what it takes to drive a deal home, or how bad it feels to lose a deal.

Even worse, most marketers just *love* data. They'll ask for boat-loads of it. They'll churn out tons of reports and PowerPoint presentations. And most of this output is just meaningless to the sales representatives in the field. Marketers will generally fill up the SFDC system with dozens of fields that won't be filled in and reports that will never be used. Even though these data-junkie behaviors won't be viewed with suspicion (the way they might be if they originated from the finance department), they'll still be a low-grade irritant to the sales team.

---

2. Generally speaking, the difference between marketing and sales people is their relative strength of IQ versus EQ. Marketers love to think (about selling) for a living. Salespeople love to sell for a living.

3. Even though my background includes 20 years as a card-carrying member of marketing, this section has to be as candid as the rest of the book.

In most organizations, having someone from the marketing department champion the SFDC system is a harbinger of—you guessed it—marginal system utilization, empty records, low system credibility, and limited leverage. The individual sales reps will not view SFDC as a tool to help them manage their time or accelerate deals. Marketing will get its analytics, upper management will get visibility, but sales productivity—the whole point of the system—will likely remain elusive.

One way to successfully have the marketing department own the system from the beginning is if the marketing team reports to the head of the sales department (or the other way around). In this situation, the marketing folks are viewed as being on (almost) the same team, with the head of marketing having a close relationship with the head of sales.

Chief Operating Officer

The sales VP or COO is *the* natural champion for an SFDC system—after all, it's called *Sales*force.com. The VP of sales has his or her neck on the line to make the numbers, so this executive needs to be able to manage the sales managers and see what the individual reps are doing.

The VP of sales won't be the person who actually owns the system over time—sometimes, no one in the sales organization really wants that role—but it certainly makes sense for the VP to be the champion. When SFDC comes out of his or her budget and is on the agenda at sales staff meetings, it subtly reinforces the message that the SFDC system is a genuinely important initiative. Even if the reps and managers don't like the system, they'll know the boss cares—and that's a powerful motivator. They may not agree with the metrics or policies being put in place for the new system, but they will not be able to ignore them.

But there's another issue: if the sales VP is the driving force behind the adoption of SFDC, reps will actually try to use the system and talk about how the tool helped them close deals. Their ultimate goal may be to butter up the boss, but their open discussion of SFDC will stimulate other reps to get on the bandwagon. It might all be baloney, but it can be *effective* baloney.

The only time it *doesn't work* to have the VP of sales champion the system is when that person is on his or her way out of the organization. Sponsorship by a loser VP or a lame duck is never the way to inspire confidence in an SFDC system. In this situation, the system start should be delayed until a new sales VP comes in, or sponsorship should be kicked upstairs.

VP of Customer Support, Services, or Success

There seem to be loads of euphemistic titles for the head of the customer service team, just as there's a wide variety of their duties. In many SFDC clients, the initial driver for the system is not revenue per se—it's execution, fulfillment, and customer onboarding. Typically, these companies have more support, service, success, and client relations people than they have sales people, and they may have large call centers or field service agents. If this sounds like your company's situation, the VP of customer support may be the best initial champion for the system.

When the VP of customer support is in the driver's seat, the system evolves with the service cloud first, where most of the features are focused on efficiency, responsiveness, self-service, and cost control. SFDC has a rich feature set in these areas, and in the early days, few (if any) of the sales team will be interested. But all the managers in the customer support organization will be deeply involved, and the customer support reps will be avid early adopters. In our experience, there is less political baggage to deal with when the initiating organization for SFDC is support, and that happy situation continues even as the system evolves toward the sales cloud later on.

The Chief Executive Officer or the Board of Directors

Most of the time, a CRM system is too small an issue for a CEO or board committee to care about or sponsor. Those executives have bigger fish to fry, and they won't spend enough quality time to make the judgment calls or push the action items.

But it *does* make sense for the highest levels of management to drive the system if, as mentioned earlier, the sales VP is a lame duck or if there's been a significant "blowup" of the forecast, and the company missed its numbers due to limited visibility.

The second situation makes for system priorities that are very different from those associated with the normal SFDC project. In this case, the issue isn't marketing effectiveness or even sales effectiveness—it's making sure that the forecast is reliable and bulletproof and that *closing*[4] the sales cycle is streamlined.

Having the CEO or the board champion the SFA system is fine for securing the budgets, making priority calls, and having clear deadlines (almost always, the next board meeting). Once the budgetary allocation is made, however, the sponsorship needs to be deputized down at least one level so that it can be executed. Almost without exception, the head of sales or customer service should be deputized for making the system happen.

---

4. Most SFA implementations focus more on the *beginning* of sales cycles and on keeping reps busier with more prospects. In contrast, board-level, forecast-driven implementations tend to focus on the *end* of the sales cycle—that is, on revenue achievement and accurate forecasts.

> ### SPONSORSHIP AND CHAMPIONING LATER PHASES
>
> One of the hallmarks of CRM systems is that they continue to evolve long after they are installed. Either they are expanded to cover more organizations, or they are modified to more completely address new business needs.
>
> Once an SFDC system is in place and being used by sales reps, upgrades can be successfully achieved when they are sponsored by nearly any part of the organization. The key indicator of success is the answer to the question, "How ardently do the reps use the system?" If there's any wavering or grumbling from a group of users, the upgrade is better championed by the head of that organization.[5]
>
> As the system matures and touches more parts of the business, it will be more likely for operations or finance personnel to become champions of expansions. The key, no matter who serves as the champion, is to make sure that the users of the new functionality have an *inherent reason* to use SFDC as part of their normal way of doing business. If new users don't care from the first day that the new feature is put in place, your investment in technology will be undermined by user reality.

Who Pays for the System Implementation?

By its nature, SFDC spans many departmental budgets. And many groups will benefit: if the system really does its job, every stockholder wins. Of course, somebody has to pay for the implementation, the ongoing fees, and the expansion of the system.

In almost any company, the 5-year costs of SFDC will be in the hundreds of thousands or even millions of dollars. Budgets have to be put in place indefinitely, as most SFDC costs are recurring expenses. Even though budgeting processes are highly political and vary by company, a few generalities apply:

- **SFDC fees:** All the fees paid for the system (SFDC licenses, implementation project, and training/indoctrination) come from the sales budget. This approach is recommended because it reflects reality—but also because it brings ongoing attention from sales executives that this is *their* system and they should be getting the most out of it.

  ➥ While users may be in several other departments, typically 75% of the total user count comes from sales, channels, order management, and related sales

---

5. Most of the time, the grumbling will come from sales personnel. But not always! Listen carefully and act accordingly.

support roles. If the nonsales user count is very high, set up a chargeback through your finance group.

- **Third-party fees:** Any add-on item or project (including associated consulting fees) is paid for by the department that asked for it or that benefits the most from it. For example, if corporate finance personnel want a fancy reporting engine or a data warehouse, let those users put their money where their mouth is. If it turns out they don't need that feature after a year, this system add-on should be turned off unless someone else needs it enough to pay for it. This practice not only conserves budget but also keeps system complexity under control.[6]

- **Infrastructure costs:** Integration, data migration, and incidental costs are paid out of IT, G&A, or other overhead budgets. Many different items fit into this category, and it's important to not neglect them because they're often the motor oil that keeps the car from blowing up:

  ➥ System administrator, developer, and business analyst training fees

  ➥ Record deduplication tools

  ➥ Lead enrichment tools

  ➥ Sandbox fees

  ➥ AppExchange tool/product fees (unless the product was specifically requested by a single department)

  ➥ Cost of disk drives/servers for storing documents, system backup snapshots, wikis, and so forth

- **User costs:** Headcount costs are paid out of the budgets for those employees' departments. Typically, the only people who are really devoted to the system are working on a part-time basis as part of their other roles: sales system administrator, marketing system administrator, support system administrator, and IT administrator/data architect. Even if a person is devoted full-time to SFDC, that individual's salary should be paid for out of his or her management chain's budget. The good news is that you won't see large incremental headcount once SFDC is up and running.

---

6. One of the biggest lessons in conventional IT is that, all too often, functionality really isn't required. "Nice-to-have" subsystems become institutional albatrosses. The cloud's cost structure helps tamp down this problem.

Who Will Own the System?

While the best practices for championing, sponsoring, and paying for SFDC development are pretty clear, ownership and ongoing operations of the system are a bit more ambiguous. Ideally, the system owner shouldn't change more often than every 3 years.[7]

That said, a successful SFDC system will evolve every 6 months or so as a result of the following factors:

- New users

- Changes to the company's products and services (such as new product lines, prices, or promotions)

- Incremental business rule or organization changes (e.g., accommodating a reorganization, new policy, or new business unit)

- The need to leverage new features that have come in subsequent SFDC releases[8]

- Expansion of SFDC to new user groups (e.g., telesales, a new product division, or overseas operations) or business functions (e.g., field support or legal/contracts)

- Changes in the systems to which SFDC connects (e.g., ERP version upgrades, external system expansions, or a new data warehouse)

- Integration of SFDC with a wider range of systems (e.g., ERP, distribution, or a call center)

The system owner acts as the ultimate gatekeeper, having to balance the needs of ongoing operations against these new system developments. System ownership is also important because "ownership is nine-tenths of the law": the owner is in the position to set and enforce system policies that will affect everyone. In this section, we discuss who should own the system in the first year and who should own and run the system in the subsequent years.

---

7. In a perfect world, no unplanned personnel turnover would occur. Whenever a key person in the SFDC operations team moves on, it's a natural time to review who should own and run the system going forward.

8. In the cloud applications, the product will be upgraded on the vendor's schedule, whether you ask for it or not. You don't have to *use* the new features, and they won't interfere with what you already use, but there's no such thing as a "system lockdown" as there was for on-premises enterprise software. See Chapter 13 for further discussion of this topic.

Chief Financial Officer

Although the finance organization should almost never be the initial champion for SFDC, it *is* a good owner/operator of a mature system. The CFO and the operations people have the right attitude to invest in process and data quality, and they have to touch the system to do their jobs.

The issue with having the CFO, sales operations, or other numbers-oriented groups running SFDC is the risk that they will be overbearing or micromanagers. Either of these tendencies will put off end users of the system, which means system utilization can suffer somewhat. If this problem occurs, the amount, credibility, and relevance of the data in the system will decline. Since these are all key success factors for a good SFDC system, it's important to monitor for these possibilities and head off these issues before they grow into real problems.

Chief Marketing Officer

People on the marketing team will need to touch SFDC on a daily basis. These folks understand metrics and may be comfortable with report writing and spreadsheets. And they can relate—at some level—to people in the sales organization.

Unfortunately, marketing talent is often very thinly stretched (the people with real skills are pulled in a dozen directions), and some of the ongoing obligations of running SFDC would represent a problem for them. Further, the *individuals* in marketing who need to touch the system on a daily basis—such as the folks who do events and campaigns—tend to be weak on consistency and process (at least when it comes to running SFDC).

Although in theory the CMO can be the owner and the marketing department could be a great place for running SFDC, in practice it often represents a workload and political burden for the organization.

Chief Operating Officer

Most of the members of the sales organization have neither the interest nor the skills to run SFDC. Even having a contractor to manage SFDC under most sales managers is ill advised.

That said, people in order operations, sales support, or sales operations do have the right attitudes and aptitudes to run an SFA system. They already deal with process, numbers, reports, and spreadsheets. The real question is, Do these people have the time or interest to take on another complex, stressful task?[9]

---

9. In actuality, running SFDC should be neither complex nor stressful. But at the end of the quarter, when everyone is trying to get those last orders in, even the smallest incremental work will appear to be a burden. If the sales operations group has some spare capacity, consider it as a viable candidate for SFDC ownership.

VP of Customer Support, Services, or Success

If the system is properly focused on the sales cloud, the VP of support has someone on the team with the aptitude and incentive to make the system run well and expand smoothly. This is particularly true when there is a process-focused team in the organization or if there is a consulting group wanting to develop software as a service (SaaS) skills.

The CEO or the Board of Directors

I have yet to find a situation where the CEO, members of the board of directors, or any similar senior executive should be charged with running the SFDC system. Anything's possible, but assigning long-term ownership of SFDC to the board room seems misplaced in any organization.

Chief Information Officer

Even though the IT department should never be the initial champion of SFDC, having IT personnel handle ongoing operations of the system would not be a bad plan. IT people have the skills and attitudes to do the operational and maintenance work.

Larger companies are typically structured to include a centralized IT group as well as some IT people within business units. The IT people in business units can be a good choice for owning and operating SFDC, if they have the time available. The other option—the centralized IT department—is usually disconnected from the user community, and SFDC users tend to be an opinionated and impatient lot. If a centralized IT department will own and operate the SFDC system, it will need to be closely tied to the sales, marketing, and service departments to keep the IT personnel responsive and aligned with ongoing user needs.

Smaller companies typically don't have a real IT department—just a system administrator or contractor who handles IT responsibilities. Thus, IT ownership of the SFDC system won't be a viable choice for them.

Mixed Team

Our recommended approach is to separate who holds the ongoing SFDC operational budget (almost always the sales or finance department) from the management responsibilities of running the system (a departmental IT or a sales/marketing/support team). The governance team can be very small and use lightweight processes—emails and Google Docs—for most issues, with short monthly meetings for tricky problems or policy changes.

By default, the SFDC administrators fit this governance role quite well. They are very familiar with how the system actually works, they already deal with users and SFDC issues in the normal course of their jobs, and they don't have any political agenda.

However, system admins are often politically disconnected, so they will need to have a management person (typically at the director level) to escalate issues to. The specific choice of "escalation manager" depends entirely on the company and the personality and interests of the individual, but the key is that the manager must be able to effectively drive decisions to resolution. Waffling or inability to get needed resources just makes the entire SFDC team look ineffectual.

Who Owns the Data Now?

Who owns the data now is a deceptively simple question, which is naively answered with "IT" or "everybody." Almost never does that answer suffice for real-world SFDC projects.

In smaller companies, everyone has access to any data they can see on the network, and there are few, if any, onerous process controls. But in most small- and medium-sized businesses (SMBs) and all larger companies, information is kept in silos that are protected (technically and politically) from uncoordinated or unauthorized use. All publicly traded companies and most firms working in the medical, financial, education, and defense industries may face legal sanctions if they don't keep their data from prying eyes. Data access can be a big deal.

The real issues here are these:

- Who enters, handles, or controls the data?

- Who dictates policies about the data, such as access, ability to modify, ability to delete, ability to copy, and ability to report/summarize?

- Which controls and audit trails must be enforced?

- Which integration methods or approaches are acceptable or encouraged?

- What are the semantics of the data? Who knows what it's supposed to mean? What are the naming standards and pick-list values?

- What is the provenance of the data? Who knows which parts of it are authoritative (system of record) versus informational (replicated or transferred from some original source)?

- Who controls or invests in the quality of the data?

- What legal stipulations or compliance standards apply to handling the data over time?

Each of these issues can add significant bureaucratic inertia to an SFDC project—either initial implementation or subsequent integration/extension—so they must be well understood *before schedule commitments are made.*

The first area to explore is the current and historical CRM system data that will be migrated to SFDC. Ownership of these data must be "taken over" by the new SFDC champion and owner organizations. This data stewardship usually entails a fairly light responsibility, along the lines of the Hippocratic oath ("At least, do no harm"). But if the existing SFA or CRM system holds significant corporate history, there can be some interesting obligations. For example, many companies need to keep order history available for as long as 3 years, and in financial services there may be requirements for a full 7 years' access. The data do not necessarily need to be available online, but they do need to be readable and consistently reportable without requiring ridiculous effort. As always, several ways of satisfying the basic requirement exist, but the point of this paragraph is the system owner needs to *know* what the requirements are before taking over the data.[10]

The other areas to explore are the data sources with which the SFDC system will need to be integrated. Each of these information sources will have its own characteristics in the previously given bulleted list, and there will sometimes be significant sensitivity regarding information sharing. Don't be surprised to hear the information-owning organizations present all kinds of fabulous and complicated issues—if you're lucky, these stories will have the telltale odor of bureaucratic origins.

Although each of the following examples has good motivations behind it, these objections are usually off-point and easily dealt with:

The auditors say that nobody can have access to this data.

> On the face of it, this assertion is at least an exaggeration. Even in government classified projects, *somebody* with the right qualification can have access to sensitive data. Of course, some data do need to be protected and must not be altered after the fact. These mandates are part of all accounting disciplines and the Sarbanes-Oxley Sections 404 and 409—but they are intended to prevent creation of bogus records or the alteration or deletion of legitimate ones.

> In most cases, SFDC integrations require only read access. Further, SFDC provides very fine-grained access controls, allowing administrators to manage exactly who can see exactly what. Get the person who throws this objection to specify which auditor made this stipulation. Then talk to that person (or company) and have the auditor identify who can see which data and for which purposes. From this discussion, you can develop an access control plan that meets the specific needs of the auditors.

---

10. In the inevitable game of bureaucratic "hot potato," 2 weeks after an organization relinquishes control of data, its members will have no recollection of where anything came from or how to access, use, or interpret the data—and the new owner will be left high and dry. When dealing with historical data, pay careful attention to the task of getting knowledge transfer *prior to* responsibility transfer.

SEC or other regulations say this data can be made available only to specific individuals on a need-to-know basis.

SEC and other agency regulations are specific about who should be able to read data that will affect stock prices—privileged "insider information" about sales, revenues, collections, and profitability *in the aggregate*. Visibility into the bookings or revenues for the whole company is, indeed, highly restricted. In contrast, SFDC users typically need to have access to this information only for a few customers, not in the aggregate.

By integrating the external data into the system at the individual record level and linking it into custom SFDC fields, the external system's aggregate reports would be hidden from all SFDC users. Further, SFDC's internal access control facilities can ensure that only the right people have access to each customer record and that the aggregate views and roll-up reports are made available only to executives with the need to know.

Our legal policy is that this customer data must be kept private and cannot be shared with any other division that didn't originally collect those data.

Although the legal requirements may have been interpreted this way, in my opinion it is a fairly inane contortion of privacy policy. The way to work through this objection is to describe the actual business process that involves sharing these data. For example, if the purpose of sharing the data is to prevent the creation of duplicate records (i.e., "Don't create a new `account` record in SFDC if that company is already a customer of another division"), the only way that SFDC would be accessing the foreign system's data is when the customer already exists in both systems. In other words, the customer has already given consent twice, and by implication the sharing of the personal data is authorized.

Of course, there may be some cases where sharing the data would be a violation of the customer's privacy. In particular, watch out for wanton email blast requests from sales, marketing, or customer support sources.

European privacy laws say that we have to store and process these data only in Europe.

There is indeed an EC Directive (95/46/EC Chapter IV) that effectively requires European citizens' personal information to be processed and stored in the European Union.[11]

---

11. Strictly speaking, the EC Directive requires that personal data be transferred, processed, and stored only in countries that have the data security and privacy regulations that comply with EC laws. The Directive was written in the early 1990s, and it does not mention the words *Internet*, *Web*, and *eCommerce*. So you can tell it's *tres au courant*. Some EC member states, such as Germany, have implemented national laws that are even more restrictive than the EC laws. These variations are a lawyer's dream and a practical nightmare.

Like all laws, it is open to interpretation—and the most rabid interpretation would make much of electronic commerce and even email nearly impossible. The good news is that there are several strategies to comply with the law's requirements. You must check with your attorneys for legal advice on these strategies—this book provides only technical alternatives that *may* be compliant. You may need to use more than one of the following strategies to be fully compliant.

The first strategy is to have your instance running on one of SFDC's "EU" clusters dedicated to European clients. This works well if most of your users are in Europe, the Middle East, and Africa (EMEA) but has a performance penalty if your users are mainly in the United States or Asia-Pacific. This approach can be done in one of two ways: first, by running the whole company's system on an SFDC[12] European instance; or second, by partitioning the customer base and using two SFDC instances (the EU one for use by European employees and customers and the main one in the United States for use by everyone else in the world). Neither of these approaches will cost any more in terms of SFDC licenses, but both will involve some interesting complexities in implementation and operations. You'll definitely want to use the `Salesforce to Salesforce` feature if you choose this approach.

The second strategy is to go through the Safe Harbor certification process via your internal legal counsel. This process can be quite involved but is done regularly by global companies. Because other systems inside your company may have already dealt with this issue in the past, extending your company's existing waivers to SFDC might be a relatively minor procedural matter.

The third strategy is to have your lawyers include specific verbiage that confers user permission to process personal information outside the EU as part of all your European contracts and nondisclosure agreements. If your company is a pure business-to-business marketing and selling organization, your lawyers should also argue that it isn't collecting personal information for "a natural person." The information being collected in this case isn't personal information, such as home phone and private email, but rather *business* contact information (e.g., business phone numbers and email addresses). In this context, your lawyers may be able to argue that the regulation is moot.

The fourth strategy—and it can't hurt to apply this one in any case—is to specifically ask European users for permission to process and store their personal

---

12. This approach requires that any add-on products or integrated systems within the company follow the same geographic partitioning strategy for any data deemed "personal." The larger the company, the more logistically complicated it becomes to use this approach.

information outside the European Union. If you get the person's "unambiguous permission," either before the individual provides his or her personal information or as part of subsequent email/reregistration cycles (analogous to opt-in sequences), you should be able to avoid almost all of the burden imposed by this regulation. In using this strategy, you want to store more than one level of opt-in and opt-out information in SFDC. Even if your company has a content management system or email blaster that manages individuals' subscriptions and preferences, the key check box data need to be integrated into SFDC so that the system enforces users' preferences before you attempt to communicate with them.

The final strategy is technically more complex but has some nifty advantages. The starting point is to store only the "insensitive" parts[13] of personal data in the SFDC U.S.-based system. The sensitive portions of personal data (e.g., email address, postal address, Social Security or other tax identification number, phone number) would be stored in your company's European offices (e.g., in an Exchange contact folder, an LDAP directory, or DBMS). This strategy would typically involve the use of `VisualForce` to allow viewing and updating the European data from within the SFDC user interface. The first step in this approach—which isn't a bad idea in any case—is to document which customers' information needs to be viewed and manipulated by which specific users. This approach would cause some annoyance for internal users and add a bit of complexity, but it would allow your company to use a single, U.S. instance of SFDC.

Corporate network administrators have put limits on the bandwidth requirements for replicating the data. You can have only 1,000 records per day.

Bandwidth constraints are almost unheard of in the United States. In international markets, however, data links may be very slow and expensive—so this objection is not completely ridiculous. But it's close. From a business perspective, does it make sense to force users to be less productive and limit sales effectiveness just to save $10 on monthly data fees?

Even from a technological perspective, this argument makes little sense. In a cloud-based application, every SFDC keystroke and screen refresh comes over the Web, using some of the most verbose mechanisms available (HTTPS, XML, and SOAP). If it makes sense for the business to use network traffic to support end users, why not devote another 0.1% of network traffic to keeping the data current and relevant?

---

13. These data elements would consist of just a person's name and a cross-reference number to other company records.

Finally, if the point of integration is between two outside sources (e.g., SFDC and another cloud application or SFDC and your Web site), the integration traffic will not need to go through your company's network at all. Thanks to integration adaptors from companies such as Dell (Boomi), Informatica, and Actian (Pervasive), integration can be handled entirely in the cloud, so SFDC integration traffic will not count as company network traffic at all.

IT security mandates forbid software elements inside the company's firewall from communicating directly with SaaS applications on the open Internet.

This objection is more profound and reasonable than the previous ones. SFDC, as a cloud application, stores and processes all its data in highly secure data centers in the Web. Communication between SFDC and users occurs over the encrypted Secure Sockets Layer (SSL, as denoted by the use of *https:* in the URLs). On the user's desktop, SFDC in the browser passes muster with security departments around the world. Communication with user applications (such as deduping tools) and with plugins (installed in Microsoft Outlook or Excel) takes place over SSL and SOAP, and the security risk is rarely viewed as significant.

But when it comes to integrating the cloud with your company's internal systems, the integration adaptors need to communicate with third-party services via the Web. The fact that your company's data will have to punch through the firewall, out to a third party whose security infrastructure is not well known—and then on to SFDC out in the cloud—can cause conservative security personnel to take notice. They will probably require a specific review of *which* data are needed, *why* they are needed, and the *scope of damage* that might result from a loss of data or control.

This kind of scrutiny is okay—after all, it's their job. SFDC has done an exemplary job with its security infrastructure, which has passed hundreds of tough security reviews both in the United States and overseas. Getting the third-party integration service providers approved may take a while, but it can also be accomplished without major surgery.

The best way to deal with this situation is to set up a *very* lightweight integration at the outset (e.g., read-only access, using one-way file transfer on a monthly or weekly basis), and then add more elegant, automated integration over time as the security personnel complete their review processes. This interval also provides time for user requests to build, becoming more urgent and eventually counteracting internal resistance to the SFDC integration.

Dealing with Review Committees

In the immortal words of Clayton Christensen,[14] "Form doesn't follow function: it follows failure." Review committees usually exist because something yucky happened, and they often have the important function of keeping people in the company out of hot water in the boardroom—or the courtroom.

Early on in the SFDC project, the project manager must go through the exercise of inventorying *all* of your company's review committees and figuring out which ones might conceivably be interested in approving the SFDC work. The most likely candidates include the following committees:

- IT security

- Network security, architecture, or identity

- IT architecture or applications

- Compliance and audit

- Financial controls

- Risk management

- Customer privacy

- Marketing practices

- Web site systems

On each of these review boards, the project manager should befriend at least the committee chairperson to get this individual's cooperation in ensuring a speedy, lightweight review process. If committee members view your project manager as an annoyance, they can slow down SFDC implementation progress significantly. All they have to do is withhold a little bit of information, or not open a loophole, or postpone the discussion when the meeting runs out of time.

Everyone has to maintain the right frame of mind about these review committees and processes. They exist to protect you and others from pain and damage, and they will save you time—no matter what the people pestering you to "skip that" tell you. In talking with the committee chairperson, ask for examples of other projects that ran into trouble by doing the wrong thing and see if they have a list of common mistakes to avoid. You'll

---

14. From his great work, *The Innovator's Dilemma: When New Technologies Cause Great Firms to Fail* (Harvard Business School Press, 1997), but he may have been paraphrasing Petroski's book *The Evolution of Useful Things* (Alfred Knopf, 1994).

find that this level of question often gets the chairperson in the mood to suggest positive things you can do—ways of presenting the information, safeguards to enquire about—that will help your project sail through the review cycle.

Identifying and Dealing with Opposition to the Project

Most of the direct opposition you will encounter during the decision-making process was described in Chapter 1. However, even after the system is deployed, you may run into opposition when the company is making a significant decision to expand SFDC. The opponents may be focused on derailing the choice of SFDC, or limiting its scope, or simply trying to stop a new job requirement.

The easiest opponents to spot are those who simply don't want to spend the money. Whether they work in finance or sales (which will have to bear most of the budgetary brunt), the argument usually takes the form of "We're going to be spending $X00,000 per year *forever,* and for what? To do something that Outlook and Excel already take care of!" These rhetorical arguments need to be silenced by the members of upper management—the VP of sales and the CEO—who are the SFDC champions. The issue isn't the size of checks the company will write but the size and number of checks the company will *receive from its customers.* The crux of the counterargument is "Give sales personnel the tools they need to do their jobs better, the tools that every one of our competitors already has, and that will pay the bill in a month."

The next opponent group will be those people who don't want a CRM system at all or who dislike change in general. They are usually fairly vocal, and their main issue is typically that the new system will bring them more work yet yield little in the way of perceived benefits. The crux of their objection is that there's nothing in it *for them.* For these folks, the prospect of a new SFDC system is about as attractive as a tax increase. The best way to deal with this group is to find something that *will be* in it for them. Whether it's a process that can be automated, a new report, or a new CYA mechanism that shows who is (and isn't) accountable, discover or create something that *will* be in their personal interests—and put it in a highly visible spot on the feature list.

The next opponents are those organizational members who do want a CRM system but want a different one. In some cases, they'll be quite straightforward about what they're advocating. When you see a competitor's "slam sheet,"[15] you'll know what you're dealing with. The way to handle this objection is to keep the comparison a realistic one and to keep the comparison criteria as simple and easy to understand as possible. Keep

---

15. Slam sheets are talking points that highlight the problems with one product and the comparative benefits of a competitor's. While often shrouded in "white paper" format, the telltale sign of slam sheets is their exclusive emphasis on the negative points of the competitor's product and their overfocusing on marginal or obscure issues that no real customer would ever notice.

the discussion focused on the *business objectives* rather than on some abstract set of requirements. As most businesses prefer fast time to value, ease of use, low entry cost, and extensive customer references, SFDC will win hands down nearly every time.

The most sophisticated strain of opponents to the SFDC system will not mention a competitor's product at all. Instead, their tactic is to broaden the system requirements to cover an impossibly wide spectrum. By extending requirements into the "boil the ocean" range, the opponents hope to bog down the entire process. If they can make the decision process start over from scratch, all decisions that have been made in the process will be invalidated. The way to handle this situation is to treat it as a giant case of scope creep. Highlight the new "requirements" that are dealing with problems that don't really exist yet, or don't have ROI, or simply don't have a specific champion. Focus attention on the wastefulness of proposals that smell of pork-barrel politics. Bring the conversation back to the business basics—keeping things simple, quick to deploy, and easy for users to adopt. Promote the idea of incrementalism, where *extensive features shouldn't be added* until users are actively using the core system and the data asset is growing in value.

The Politics of System Adoption

Success rates of CRM systems are quite low: most industry analyst surveys show that less than 50% of CRM projects are deemed a success by management. A key reason for this poor rating is that any CRM system—even if perfectly implemented—is a tool with little intrinsic value. The business value of any CRM system is the improved effectiveness for sales, marketing, and support teams thanks to the following changes in the way the company operates:

- Better collaboration

- More complete customer information

- Fewer dropped action items or missed opportunities

- Better metrics and visibility

Every one of these factors depends entirely on data entered by users as part of their touching customers. If the data aren't there, none of the business benefits can happen. Clearly, getting users happily on board—and developing the value of the information asset—is more important than installing any particular set of CRM product features.

From the moment the system project has been approved, job one for the implementation team is getting users interested in the system. Involve users in requirements gathering, storyboards, anything you can think of. Use `chatter` as a way of spreading the word even before any other part of the system is deployed. Set up a proactive "good news" campaign touting the system almost from day one.

Unfortunately, some people inevitably look for any excuse to not use the system. They jump at the chance to criticize it and point to others' criticism as the basis for not bothering to log in. To counter their objections, the project team needs to leverage every avenue for support: top down, bottom up, and inside out.

Top Down: Champions

The champions of the system are the single most important stimulants for system usage, because it is their will—and budget—that makes the system happen in the first place. It's their organizational prestige and personal enthusiasm that will drive fast adoption of SFDC.

It is incredibly important for the champions to act consistently about SFDC and to show people through their behavior that they will be depending on the system for their own success. These advocates need to say how often they plan to use the SFDC data and reports to run management meetings. They need to have a dashboard named after them and have that dashboard on the home screen of their organization. See the Executive Summary and Chapters 9 through 13 for more best practices in this area.

The champion should create milestones for a sequence of meetings that depend on SFDC data and reports. For example, if the system will initially go live in January, the champion should ask that all `lead` reports presented at executive staff be based on the system by March, that all `opportunity` lists be driven off the system by April, and that all `forecasting` and pipeline reports be based only on SFDC data by May. As the year unfolds, this individual should continue to issue emails stipulating that no deal will be discussed at any level of management review unless it is in the system first. Later, the champion should send an email clarifying the requirement that deals won't be reviewed unless their SFDC data have been updated within the last 2 weeks. By incrementally and repeatedly emphasizing the importance of the system to every level of management, the champion cements the right kind of thinking and behavior about SFDC.

As the VP of sales is usually the SFDC champion, it's incredibly important for this person to not break the illusion of the inevitability of system usage. It takes only a few negative or ambivalent words from the champion to neutralize the system's positive momentum. Rumors fly fast, and any frustration expressed by the champion will get around the company overnight. When misinformation shows up in a report or dashboard, the champion must have the discipline to say, "This information is no good—I rely on my team to keep the data in SFDC accurate and timely, and I don't want to see this happen again." If in a moment of frustration the champion instead says something like "This system is no damn good—I can't use this garbage," he or she will set back user adoption of the SFDC system by months.

Top Down: Sticks

Upper management—whether the individual is an SFDC champion or not—always has the power to mandate things. Of course, it is reasonable to make requirements, do indoctrination, train, and enforce standards. But it is all too easy to issue overly grandiose management commands or to use sticks too early, only to have them be dismissed by workers as "another thing they'll forget about next month." This is the kind of thing SFDC team members need to avoid.

Because the system will be delivered incrementally, the use of mandates and requirements should also be applied gradually. Early on, the system will not be functionally complete and—worse—it won't contain much interesting data. The trick is to get users on the system doing something that will add to the system data asset as a *natural part of their job*. Consequently, the user representatives on the implementation team need to find a part of the business process to serve as the beachhead for SFDC users. Ideally, it won't require duplicate data entry even though it will inevitably involve some change for users. Once this step in the business process is identified, management should mandate that the users change their behavior just in that area by a specific date. After a few weeks of data entry this way, more user steps should be transitioned into SFDC activity.

Only after SFDC has the required functionality, information value, and data quality to be a reliable asset should the big sticks come out. For example, any penalties (such as "no commission on deals will be paid unless . . .") should not be even hinted at for the first 6 months of system usage. See Chapters 9 through 13 for organization-specific best practices in this area.

Inside Out: Heroes and Mavens

In sales and marketing organizations, what the boss is saying about SFDC is always a little suspect. Users think the system is at least partly there to spy on their activity, monitor them, and be the basis for endless pestering and measurement. Consequently, some of SFDC's credibility will depend on the experience of users: word needs to get around about how the system helped Sally close a deal faster or prevented Joe from forgetting a customer request. These stories are an important part of system folklore, and they need to be encouraged.

As discussed in Chapter 4, the implementation team will seek out early adopters to provide input into the system design. Exactly who they choose for this role should depend in part on the individual's maven quality—his or her "connectedness" throughout the organization. No matter where this person appears on the organizational chart, a maven has an informal following and a very large Rolodex.[16] Ideally, the maven should also be

---

16. Of course, it's not one of those antique Rolodex thingies—it's probably an Outlook contact list. Mavens have contacts by the thousands, so their name is widely recognized across organizational lines.

a blabbermouth. During the system rollout stages, it's important to coddle mavens and make sure they have great experiences with the system. By making them happy, the word will spread that the system is easy to use and saves time.

Heroes are a bit different from mavens in that they're manufactured. A hero is someone who does something great as a consequence of using SFDC and who will be "promoted" by indirect means. For example, if a customer support rep is able to convert an irate customer into a happy one thanks to SFDC, a congratulatory email may be sent across the organization highlighting the "win." These emails need to be written subtly, though, to avoid sounding like crass boosterism or a bad newsletter.

Within the sales organization, the hero emails or verbal announcements need to be even more subtle because, well, sales reps know a bad pitch when they hear it. The sales hero is a rep who closed a bigger deal or did a faster upsell—people expect to hear about that kind of news overtly. But the sales hero also has to have a "secret to success" that most reps don't know about. News of this special technique (involving, of course, SFDC) needs to come directly from that rep—*not* from management or the SFDC team—almost in the form of bragging. All of this subterfuge may seem contrived and childish, but sales reps only listen to other sales reps (particularly the ones who are more successful than they are).

CHATTER, EMAIL, AND GETTING THE WORD OUT

We all know about email, and it will forever be a key internal communication mechanism for implementation teams.

Salesforce `chatter` is a different way of getting people to collaborate and interact, and it has the important ability to draw people in to SFDC (because that's where all the action is). You can have an almost unlimited number of `chatter` users for free, and the relevant chats are all visible in one place, organized by topic and by user. (Check out the "What's All This Noise about Chatter?" section in Chapter 13.) Pretty cool stuff, if orchestrated well. But a real source of glop if not well orchestrated.

Use `chatter` almost from day one with your system design team and the users who will be reviewing the system. Initially, limit it to that small community and conduct a mandatory training session on how to use `chatter` properly. During the course of the project, you'll develop your company-specific "chattiquette." Document that, and share it with all new users.

As new users come on board with each Agile sprint, expand the scope of the training and the chattiquette to "just enough." For a starting point, go to www.salesforce.com/chatterguide/start-here/practices.jsp and https://www.facebook.com/Chatter..., or just Google "chatter best practices" for articles all over the Web.

Bottom Up: Technogeeks

At the bottom of the organizational chart are the worker bees who actually get stuff done. And in most organizations, this is the level where many technogeeks live. Whether they are sales engineers or customer support reps, marketing analysts or product managers, accounting specialists or order expediters, they have great PC skills and are known for tricks, techniques, and toys that others haven't mastered.

Having a few technogeeks on your side helps drive adoption of the SFDC system because it shows that there's a cool side to the system, some tricks that save time, and maybe an element of fun. Technogeeks spread the positive word though IMs, water-cooler talk, and after-work beers—the informal channels that can really count.

It's largely for the technogeek that the implementation team will put in toys and eye candy, the featurettes that might otherwise seem trivial. These things give people something to talk about, so a system that could be as dull as a spreadsheet has an element of fun. In geek-speak, plant Easter eggs.

In addition to deploying the featurettes, you can encourage geekthusiasm through postings on the project wiki, little contests with T-shirt giveaways, and similarly nerdy exercises. Sounds dumb, works great.

System Out: Carrots

Carrots are positive incentives for people to use the system, and they can be more powerful and reliable than many of the mechanisms described in the preceding subsections. Three types of carrots exist, and all should be used as soon as they are available.

The first carrots are the featurettes: little things that make life a bit easier but are unavailable elsewhere. For example, you can implement a tool to automatically draw an organizational chart of the customer account or an SFDC button to automatically dial Skype or your desk phone. These convenience and gee-whiz features can be positive reasons to use the system almost from day one.

The second set of carrots takes the form of organizational incentives: procedures or activities that are more easily done through the system. For example, your sales team may have loaner equipment for use in sales cycles. If management makes it easier for these personnel to get loaner equipment or gives preference to the loaner applications that are made through SFDC, you will provide a positive reason for people to use the system. In another example, if management makes it clear that action items presented as SFDC `tasks` will be handled sooner and more predictably than requests presented by email or voicemail, users will rapidly acquire new habits. After the first few weeks, you can add contests with rewards and recognition for the users with the best data, the most frequent logins, the most complete `opportunity` records, and the most informative `cases` or solutions. Make these contests and incentives as relevant to the business objective as possible—awards for meaningless metrics are about as lame as the ones for "tidiest office cube" or "most recycled coffee cups."

The last bunch of carrots comprises the ones that are intrinsic to system usage: by doing things through the system, the user saves time or streamlines an onerous task. These carrots take the form of `workflows, alerts, automatically emailed reports`, or business process aids in SFDC. This bunch of carrots becomes more important as the system becomes more functionally complete and has workflows, integrations, and data that make it *the* optimal way to do a task.

Identifying and Dealing with Adoption Problems

Adoption of the SFDC system is so critical that it needs to be measured and managed during the first several quarters of the system's life. Some adoption problems arise because of technical issues, lack of time for training, or organizational stresses unrelated to SFDC. These issues aren't a major worry. Instead, you need to be on the lookout for adoption problems that are caused by interorganizational politics and systemic people issues, as they can really stymie overall success.

Active versus Passive Resistance

Overcoming active, overt user resistance is relatively straightforward. These critics self-announce their objections, and they will make overt arguments.

Things are a little more difficult with passive resistance, because it's more difficult to identify the individuals who are dragging their heels on SFDC adoption and pinpoint their issues. The first way to identify problem organizations is to hook into your company's rumor mill. If your company has administrative assistants, start there. Also talk with worker bees in the order operations or sales administration area. You're trying to find out both what the issues are and who is raising them.

If you hear an issue that's just plain wrong, you need to publicize the correct information quickly. Putting "the right answer" up on the wiki is not enough. Outreach strategies—at least an email plus an internal podcast—are essential to overcoming the subterranean grumblers.

When the issue isn't completely erroneous, you need to highlight the good things that will be coming to users of the SFDC system. The passive resisters will be much more likely to listen to heroes, mavens, and technogeeks, so make sure there's a constant stream of emails and hallway conversations from these informal sources.

WHAT WE'VE GOT HERE IS A FAILURE TO COMMUNICATE

In many cases, the root of active or passive resistance is hard to find because people don't *want* to communicate about the real issue. They'll invent a never-ending series of problems to slow things down, looking for ways to undermine progress.

Many of the objections will be smoke bombs that are set off to misdirect attention. If totally false arguments are being raised, you can deal with those issues head on. But as soon as you get rid of one objection, another will be raised because the emotional energy—the *real* reason for the objection—hasn't been dealt with. Try to figure out what the real issue is and why the naysayer doesn't want to talk about it. The underlying worries typically focus on the following issues:

- SFDC will cause too much change (having to learn new complexity; having to change the way the job is done; losing one's job to automation).
- SFDC means being monitored closely (overmeasured, micromanaged).
- SFDC means being exposed (making errors; shown as being incompetent, useless, or boring).
- SFDC means extra work, with no real payoff.
- SFDC will make the critic's part of the organization look bad or unprofitable . . . because it *is*.
- SFDC will make it harder to get the real job done.
- SFDC represents a step backward in functionality or integration (particularly when it is replacing a system that was highly customized to the needs of a few pet organizations).
- SFDC represents a significant new learning curve, particularly for people who need to write, modify, and interpret reports.

Most of these issues will be temporary, so you can counteract them with discussions about future enhancements and temporary workarounds. Sometimes, just talking through the issue dissipates a lot of its power. You may not be able to do anything about these troublemakers directly, but at least you can talk with their managers so they can work on the negative individuals offline.

Dealing with Luddites

Luddites are people who just don't want to participate at all. They want to keep all their sales information on paper, trusting a Day-Timer more than a laptop. They also tend to hide information from everyone[17] and may be quite worried about being micromanaged.

---

17. Their customers, their subordinates, and, most of all, their bosses.

They can view the tiniest request for data entry with outright hatred, and they seem to enjoy getting the entire sales team riled up as a mob to oppose something that actually is there to *help* them. These guys (and it usually is the male of the species) eat nails for breakfast, listen to talk radio, and make their living by emotional persuasion and dogged negotiation. They can be tough.

But at least they're easy to identify: even if they're not openly vocal, you can spot Luddites as the people who never log in to the system. SFDC has a couple of simple ways to report on users' login history, and the telltale sign of a Luddite is two or fewer logins per month.

The cardinal rule of sales management is, "If you're making your numbers, you're golden." So don't try to force the issue with a successful Luddite. But the moment he *doesn't* make quota, bring the situation to the attention of the Luddite's boss and make sure SFDC usage is part of the rep's "plan."

Aside from using sticks, the only real solution to this problem is for Luddites to become aware of what a real CRM system can do for *them*. If they can see the results in their pocketbooks, very little conversation will be required.

Indoctrination

Indoctrination isn't training. Training—we covered that in Chapter 4. Indoctrination is about religious fervor and application of best practices. Chapters 9 through 13 provide dozens of recommendations about best practices, but many of them involve—surprise!— some extra work. So it's important that users be indoctrinated about *why* they need to take on these new and different ways of doing their job.

The easiest indoctrination comes from memories of pain. Associate best practices with ways to avoid repetition of painful experiences and grunt work in previous systems. This approach can quickly galvanize worker bees in marketing, order operations, and even telesales as they scurry to avoid revisiting a painful past. Even at the executive level, an embarrassment in front of the board or an investor's meeting can be a powerful motivator.

The toughest people to indoctrinate are the individual sales reps. They aren't personally exposed to the negatives of "worst practices"—the aftereffects are somebody else's problem (and the "somebody else" isn't their boss). The only way to inspire religious fervor in these workers is for them to see results: faster, bigger sales that mean commission checks and membership in the President's Club. The only thing that will really get them going is hero stories from other sales reps. The internal email chatter about bigger commission checks is the ultimate motivator.

The Politics of Restriction

SFDC is a very powerful system. If it is integrated effectively with other systems, it can give users access to virtually any customer or product information within seconds. For this reason, its use must be properly restricted to keep users from seeing or modifying things that must be controlled for legal and financial reasons. If the users aren't very sophisticated, they typically don't know what they're missing and won't notice the restrictions that have been properly put in place.

Oddly enough, the more sophisticated the user, the more you may need to restrict his or her freedom. Power users will instinctively know what they're missing, and they are likely to object to limits on their behavior in a fairly vocal manner. They will try to convince their bosses they need administrative privileges or should have access to records that are outside of their purview.

As discussed in Chapter 5, it is important to keep the number of SFDC administrators to a bare minimum (typically three people). When obstreperous users ask for this level of access, the conversation quickly degenerates. Your best weapon is the CFO, who wants to keep things controlled and has solid, specific business reasons why access must be regulated. Your second-best weapon is the corporate attorney, who will be able to invent dozens of reasons why the user access should be limited. Wow—I just knew attorneys were good for something.

Getting the Most from SFDC

- Adoption is everything. Politics will get in the way.
- Use a combination of carrots (from day one) and sticks (applied gradually) to drive the right behavior in users.
- Use both email and chatter to get the positive feedback loops going early.
- Choose your executive champion wisely. It's almost certain to be the COO/VP of sales or the VP of customer service.
- Sales will probably pay for all the initial system implementation.
- Enhancement/expansion projects will probably be paid for by the department that benefits most from them.
- Over time, the system will probably be owned by finance, IT, or customer support.

For Small Companies

- If you're lucky, you can just skim most of this chapter.
- Seriously, you think your company is free of politics? Maybe you are out of the loop.

For Large Enterprises

- Before you start the project, identify all the review boards that will want to review SFDC. Buddy up with the chairs of those committees.
- Figure out the chargebacks you're going to need for the implementation and ongoing costs. Get the budgets set aside.
- Data ownership is a big deal. Make sure you've identified and dealt with the stipulations and regulatory concerns of the data owners before you try to integrate or migrate it.

CHAPTER 7

Products You Will Need

*If you have built castles in the air, your work
need not be lost; that is where they should be.
Now put the foundations under them.*

—Henry David Thoreau

For a company whose slogan is "no software," there sure are a lot of software products available to add on. This chapter is for decision makers and project managers, who need to know about the third-party tools and products that can really make a difference with an SFDC implementation and foster solid user adoption. Although specific products aren't reviewed here, the categories of important products (and their selection criteria) are discussed in depth.

SFDC is a fine CRM system out of the box, with five applications in the `enterprise` and `unlimited` editions:

- Sales and Telesales

- Marketing

- Customer Support (Call Center)

- Community

- Collaboration (Chatter)

These basic applications expand into four main product lines: Sales Cloud, Service Cloud, Marketing Cloud, and Platform. SFDC also has several optional products that tend to span the Clouds, for such "horizontal" features as communities and mobile editions. SFDC's price list is actually pretty complicated and seems to constantly evolve, so you'll just have to hit their Web site or take a call from one of their reps if you want to understand specific features and pricing.

You may need functionality that goes far beyond the essentials, as shown in Figure 1-3. And that's where SFDC's real advantage comes in: **SFDC is a platform, not just a product.** SFDC's platform allows you to build your own powerful apps, integrate with hundreds of cloud and on-premises software packages, or buy third-party add-ons and plugins.[1] SFDC's AppExchange currently has more than 1,500 add-ons that provide feature-level improvements ("point functionality") as well as full applications that provide brand new functionality. For example, the following categories of applications and tools are available in the AppExchange:[2]

- **Collaboration and user productivity:** `Chatter` tools, email tools, calendar management, gamification, mass editing, document/content/file management, Web conferencing/event management, mobile tools, external data sources, geo-location, equipment location tracking, project management, idea and community management

- **Education/training:** Recruiting/admissions, enrollment, administration, student scheduling, digital media management, learning management, school management

- **Finance:** VC deal tracking, M&A tracking, wealth management, asset management, banking/capital markets, insurance, mortgage, accounting packages, expense tracking, fleet management, payment management, billing, compliance, venture and private equity info feeds

- **Government:** Local government permits, code enforcement, law enforcement, mass transit, grant management, asset/fleet management, membership tracking

- **Medical/healthcare/life sciences:** Clinic management, treatment monitor, physicians' CRM, pharma CRM, claims management

- **Human resources:** Payroll, recruiting, vacation tracking, learning management, appraisals and evaluations

- **Manufacturing:** ERP, order management, warehouse management, service/call center management, TPM, configuration management, supply chain management, inventory management, shipments management, semiconductor CRM, textile CRM

- **Marketing:** Lead generation, lead cultivation, email blasting, marketing automation, document/content management, PR/analyst relations, CPG marketing,

---

1. In this chapter, I'm using *add-on* as the generic term for all third-party products, services, plugins, and amendments that can be installed on top of or around SFDC. Most of these add-ons are found in SFDC's AppExchange, but a good portion are available only directly from vendors or open-source projects. As discussed later in this chapter, it's important to understand the consequences of using these different sources.
2. I've organized these add-ons in a different way than the way SFDC does it in the AppExchange to make it easier to spot relevant applications.

product management, conference/speaker/event management, surveys, Web site integration, landing-page generation, social networking, deduping/data cleansing, search marketing, report engines, Web sites, marketing analytics

- **Media:** Advertising sales, advertising campaign management, PR management

- **Nonprofits:** Fundraising, volunteer management, donation/grant management, program management, political campaign management, payment processing

- **Professional services:** Time tracking, project/task management, PSA, recruiting

- **Real estate:** Real estate broker management, property management, portfolio management, mortgage origination, hospitality property scheduling, appraisal

- **Reporting, analytics, and document generation:** Data warehousing, business intelligence, dashboarding, scorecarding, document generation

- **Retail:** eCommerce, promotion management, order entry/management, shipping management, sample management, UGC/recommendations

- **Sales management:** Sales rep productivity/scorecards, forecasting, territory management, sales methodology enablement/enforcement, account profiling/ enrichment, incentive/commission management, mobile sales/field force tools, eCommerce, channel management, program management, configuration/quote management, order/contract management, document generation, sales operations, telesales scripting, sales analytics

- **Service and support:** Agent productivity, community management, eLearning, field service, mobile enablement, help desk/knowledge base management, quality assurance, surveys, telephony integration, service analytics

- **Software:** Bug tracking, Agile tools, developer tools, integration tools, connectors, servers

- **System administration:** Integration, ETL tools, data cleansing, mashups, issue management, change control, systems development, single sign-on, security management, knowledge bases, forums, telephony integration, developer tools, object model profiling, system administration

Nearly half of the AppExchange packages are free, so there is an embarrassment of riches here.[3] Here's the irony: most SFDC customers don't use more than a handful of

---

3. Look for add-ons created by Salesforce Labs—they're all free, and they have solved some real customer problems.

these add-ons. This means that neither the customers nor the authors of these add-ons are benefiting as much as they could.

Don't Overdo It

Even though hundreds of add-ons may be relevant to every customer situation, you should go easy on them for a number of business, human factors, and technical reasons. *Initially, deploy fewer than five add-ons. Even as the system grows, try to keep the number to fewer than a dozen or so.*

The first reason is business value: do not add things to SFDC that don't add obvious business value. This book is full of warnings and advice about removing unnecessary complexity, and installing too many add-ons will undo the streamlining you achieved elsewhere. Add-ons typically put more items on the screen—tabs, reports, fields, buttons—which can lead to confusion and clutter. Also, many add-ons are unsupported and have sparse documentation, so you'll have to figure out how to use many of them and train your users. If the add-on stops working the way you expected, there may be no recourse with an unsupported application other than to uninstall the add-on. In the end, the "free" app may cost you more than the value it brings.

The second issue is complexity and uncertainty. Although each of the apps goes through architectural review and unit testing, there is no way to test for all the possible interactions among all of them. With 1,500 add-ons available, there are more than 10^{4115} different combinations. Even though these apps are generally of high quality and have little potential for harm, understanding the interactions among the software features—even when they work as intended—can make for a delightful learning experience. The more add-on apps you use, the more moving parts—which means more bugs, weird system behaviors, and wasted time.

The third issue is dependency and the data "roach-motel"[4] effect: once you start using the add-ons, they typically store some extra data in SFDC `custom fields` or `objects`. If you stop using one of them, the special data they stored may be nearly inaccessible or useless to you, even though that information is safely in the system. If you want to uninstall an add-on, the system may ask, "What do you want to do with the data?"—and there may not be a good answer other than exporting it to a series of spreadsheets and archiving it. If the data aren't worth dumping into a spreadsheet, this is a pretty solid indication that the add-on wasn't that important in the first place.

The fourth issue is system limits on the number of `custom objects`, `tabs`, `workflows`, `fields`, lines of `APEX` code, and `applications` for unmanaged

---

4. Also known as the Hotel California effect: you can check in anytime you want, but you can never leave.

packages.[5] Even SFDC's `unlimited edition` has limits, and large organizations will bump into limits in the `enterprise edition` if they install too many add-ons.

Finally, there's the issue of timing. Chapters 1 and 4 admonished you to take advantage of featurettes to obtain quick wins and to motivate users. These are important tricks, but you want to use them in a *timed sequence* for maximal effect. Even if you know of 10 add-ons that your users will love, don't install them wantonly: dole the new features out as a continuous drumbeat of goodies to counteract user agitation, impatience, or frustration.

There's a further issue of timing and sequencing: system stability. If you introduce add-ons following, say, a monthly schedule, you'll have a defined, stable baseline to work with. You should be using the `sandbox` as a staging area to test all add-ons first, but some issues simply won't show up until you move to production. If anomalies show up only after a couple of weeks of use, it will be much easier to troubleshoot and recover from them. Be sure to read the "Monthly Activities" section of Chapter 13.

First, Seek to Understand

An add-on is not an add-on. Some of them consist of five lines of scripting or a couple of reports that present no danger to your data or users. Others are huge hosted software applications that cost a bundle and can rock your world if used incorrectly. Some vendors deliberately try to confuse you with terminology in their promotional materials to hide weaknesses of their add-on product or service. So you should understand several aspects of add-ons before you start evaluating and using them.

Differences between Add-On Technologies

SFDC has gone out of its way to make its system easy to extend with very different technical approaches. The solid platform and rich API explains why so many add-ons have been created in such a short time (none of SFDC's competitors come even close on this front).

The smallest and lightest-weight add-ons are called native apps, because they do their magic entirely within the Salesforce application. All the buttons, tabs, and interactions feel as if they're seamlessly part of SFDC because, well, they are. In some cases, native apps don't even contain any code: they're just configurations of `objects`, `fields`, and `reports` that provide useful new functionality. If you're curious, you can look under the covers to see how these add-ons work, creating additions and extensions to them to suit your specific needs. You can also modify things like `formulas`, `thresholds`, and

---

5. Some add-ons are open source and delivered as unmanaged packages. Managed packages, which are what you'll find with nearly all paid-for products in the AppExchange, don't count against these limits.

`workflows` of the apps (although you'd better know what you're doing on that front). Native apps are always installed from `packages` that are stored in public or private areas of the AppExchange. They can be installed or uninstalled in a matter of minutes, particularly if they don't store any special data. Many of the freebies in the AppExchange are native apps, and these are what you'll be using for most featurettes.

SFDC's platform provides the ability to write in three browser-side languages (HTML, CSS, and Javascript) and two server-side languages (`VisualForce` for presentation layer and `APEX` code for business logic, system functions, and database queries). `APEX` code allows for the creation of serious magic in a high-performance and safe environment that is seamlessly part of the SFDC user experience.[6] You can create your own `APEX` code right in the system or in external IDEs, but be aware that `APEX` requires skills similar to those used in Java programming, knowledge of database queries, and expertise in object orientation. To make this kind of code safe for a multitenant environment (where a Sales-force server cluster may be shared by 10,000 customers or 150,000 users), the system imposes governors to prevent resource hogging and requires that all code go through unit tests before it can be deployed from your development `sandbox` to your production instance. `APEX` add-ons can be quite small and easy to install (delivered in packages with their own test code, just like other native applications), and a few of them are free in the AppExchange.

SFDC also works with apps that invoke external applications and services, and the AppExchange is full of examples of these add-on products. Although most of the code in these products doesn't run in your SFDC instance, it is tightly and securely integrated. The first category of these external products runs on a user's (often, the SFDC admin-istrator's) PC.[7] These add-ons are often geared toward data management functionality:

- Data exchange with Microsoft Outlook, Word, Excel

- Email and contact interchange with IBM Notes or Gmail

- Bulk-data loading tools

- Data cleansing and deduping tools

- Data analysis and business intelligence tools

The second category of external add-ons runs on one of your servers (almost always a server run by an SFDC administrator). These products are almost never free, and they are likely to provide high-value, data-driven functionality:

---

6. `APEX` functionality is included in the `enterprise, unlimited,` and `developer editions` of SFDC and is available as an option in the `professional edition`.

7. Almost none of the external add-on products are available for Macintosh or Linux-based computers.

- Report engines

- Data warehousing and business intelligence

- Data integration with other applications (such as accounting or ERP)

That last bullet requires some clear thinking when it comes to your internal security group, as these personnel need to understand exactly where the data flows to and from will be if they are to make the correct decisions about the product's deployment. If you have a data integration adaptor that runs on your server, and the adaptor connects SFDC (via HTTPS or SSL) directly to your internal application on the same server, your network security team ought to feel relatively good about the technical risk. The alternative approach is discussed in just a bit.

The next category of add-on is a hosted service that runs on a third-party cloud but interacts with the SFDC screens in an interesting way. The external hosted service typically has a direct connection with SFDC (for things like single sign-on and data interchange) and some level of integration with the SFDC screen that runs in the user's browser. In the loosest integration, there's just a link or a button in an SFDC screen that starts up a new browser tab (or even a new instance of the browser). This level of integration is not very useful because users may have to re-enter data or handle interactions that aren't natural or coherent with the rest of their SFDC interactions. Such half-baked integration is often offered by vendors who are trying to worm their way into the SFDC customer base without investing much in technology or support. These add-ons may be valuable, but they are not preferred.

Another form of hosted service is fully integrated with SFDC's user interface but provides functionality beyond what's possible in SFDC alone. The vendors that offer such add-ons take one of two approaches: `S-controls`[8] and `VisualForce` pages that make the add-on app behave in a coherent and natural way with the rest of SFDC, or deep integration using `custom objects`, `APEX`, `VisualForce`, and `AJAX` code. While achieving this level of integration takes more effort (i.e., more time for the vendor to write) and may be a bit more expensive, these add-ons will pay off for you with lower training costs and happier, more productive users.

Business Models for Add-On Products

In the software business, getting customers in the midmarket (SMB/SME companies with revenues of $100 million to $1 billion or so) has always been a challenge, so the SFDC

---

8. Although `S-Controls` were officially deprecated by SFDC years ago, a surprising number of products still use them. Be very careful when modifying `S-Controls`, as you may inadvertently disable them in an irreversible way.

customer base is a hugely desirable target. Now that SFDC has more than 1 million users, it is not surprising that software vendors and system integrators are looking for ways to leverage the AppExchange for their own growth.

Why do you care? First, you want to know before you buy how the vendor plans to charge you for its products and services. Pricing models are often obscure, and it's good to know exactly what the pricing scheme is before you commit yourself to a product. Second, you want to be able to spot the "flash in the pan" vendors that won't be around for long to support your product.[9] If you depend on an add-on that is later orphaned, everybody loses.

The first business model to examine is open source. Although there are more than 500,000 open-source projects in the world, commercial open-source products are a fairly tricky area (you can read up on the issues in the article I wrote[10] in Wikipedia). An SFDC add-on that adheres to the open-source model is an almost unqualified good: the code is available for all users to see and modify as they see fit, so even if the sponsoring vendor abandons the effort, the code will live on and be maintainable. Open-source products are free by definition, but vendors frequently offer a feature-filled (and more desirable) version available and supported only as fully chargeable software. Read the product description carefully to determine whether you can live with just the open-source version's narrowly proscribed features (and self-support model).

The other unsupported category of software is freeware or shareware—that is, software that doesn't carry any charge but whose code is inaccessible to you. Freeware and shareware products are often created by individuals, and the risk to you is that their creators will lose interest in maintaining or extending the products over time. Even if they are interested in moving the freeware product forward, they may be too busy doing their "day jobs" to effectively support users (it is, after all, a labor of love). Freeware and shareware are therefore riskier than open-source products over the long term because you never have access to the code and can't maintain it yourself.

Of course, freeware and shareware strategies are often used by large, reliable vendors that give away a free version of a feature-stripped product in the hopes of upselling users to more feature-rich, paid versions. These freemium add-ons should be viewed as if they were commercial products, except that no support is available without the upgrade.

Over half of the goodies in the AppExchange follow open-source and freeware/shareware/freemium models. Virtually all of the add-ons written by SFDC fall into these categories.

Vendors that charge for their products in the AppExchange have to go through design reviews and compatibility testing, and they have to pay fees to SFDC for participating in this system. Consequently, they need a certain level of sales just to break even on the

---

9. The only support available for plugins will be from the third-party vendor.
10. http://en.wikipedia.org/wiki/Commercial_open_source_applications.

AppExchange investment. Some vendors also sell products that are *not* offered via the AppExchange as a way of circumventing those fees. These products should be scrutinized very seriously, if not avoided altogether, because the AppExchange's compatibility and architectural reviews provide important protections for you, the customer.

Different Pricing Models in the AppExchange

As mentioned earlier, most of the add-ons found in the AppExchange are available for free. For those that are not free, you'll notice in the product description area a field for pricing that provides you some hints about the cost of the add-on, but in most cases you need to contact the vendor's friendly sales rep to get an accurate price quote.

Many of the chargeable products in the AppExchange follow the model of a per-seat fee as part of a recurring revenue model whereby payments continue for as long as you use the product or service. One of the questions to answer is, "How many seats do you need?" Some products charge for the total number of users in the system, and others charge for specifically identified users. A few products have supplementary charges based on usage metrics (such as database size or number of accounts).

Some products deliver value to all users, but the value is sensed only when the product is being actively used by a narrow group of users. For example, email blasters, printing engines, proposal generators, and contract management systems may be priced on a per-usage basis, with the customer prepurchasing a block of usage "chits" for the year. Customers that go over their prepurchased block may be charged heavy premiums, creating an incentive for purchasing more usage units than the company actually needs (analogous to mobile-phone usage plans).

A few products use a mixture of these pricing models, but vendors try to keep matters as simple as possible to close sales more quickly. In evaluating alternative pricing, use a spreadsheet to keep all the details straight—but remember it's more important to have the product that really works for you rather than a marginal version that saves a few bucks per month. Changing out add-on products such as email blasting or commission systems can be an *amazingly* painful experience—and don't let the vendors' sales reps persuade you otherwise.

There aren't many gotchas in the AppExchange pricing mechanisms, other than annual commitments and automatic renewals of contracts. Try to negotiate those provisions away—though unless you're a really big customer, you won't have too much luck. Make sure that you've thought through the storage and compliance implications of your add-ons: if a prodigious amount of data will be stored in SFDC records, SFDC surcharges can really pile up.

Calibrate the Level of Effort and Reward

Some add-ons are trivial and involve virtually no risk or effort—and modest rewards. Others require a substantial amount of cash and time to really pay off. For the really

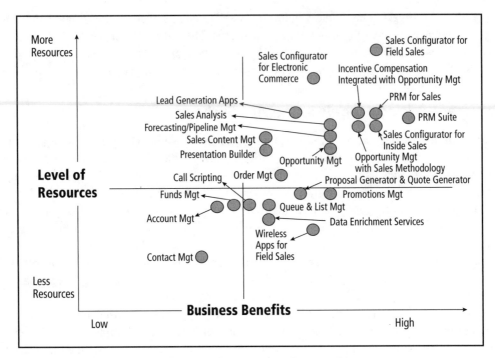

FIGURE 7-1   AppExchange product matrix (Source: Salesforce.com)

big stuff, a behavioral and business-process change will be required on your part. If your organization is not up to that task, you can rapidly disqualify several of the heavier-weight add-ons as possible extensions to your SFDC system.

Figure 7-1 shows an analysis (done by Salesforce.com) of add-on product categories for the sales and sales support functions. Although SFDC hasn't published corresponding analyses for marketing, support, or other business process areas, products in those domains lend themselves to similar kinds of categorization.

Next, Weigh Your Options

With trivial add-ons such as featurettes, there really isn't much thinking to do. You'll find two or maybe three apps with roughly the same functionality: choose the one that offers the best mix of features and ease of use. With the weightier add-ons—such as data warehousing, marketing automation, commissions, accounting, or order management—you need to think a bit more deeply.

Integrate Rather Than Extend

First think about whether the add-on functionality needs to be part of SFDC at all. Would it really kill you to have a second browser or application up on the user's screen? If the application is used only by a small percentage of the user base (and for the heavy-weight add-ons, that's often the way it works out), why burden all the users with another SFDC tab and set of features to ignore? Even though most of the unusual stuff can be hidden from the user base with `page layouts` and hidden `tabs`, each substantial add-on will make for some added complexity somewhere (particularly in administrative tasks).

Using the two-window approach can actually have benefits, particularly if the other application has busy periods that make its response time unpredictable. Some third-party applications may even freeze the entire browser under some conditions, so having a separate window means the user can be productive with SFDC even if the other app is "busied out." Further, not every user of the external application will need to use SFDC, so you can avoid adding some SFDC user licenses if you follow the two-window approach.

Of course, even though you'll have two "systems," you'll almost certainly want to maintain the illusion of a *single-system view* of the data they operate on. In this scenario, you almost certainly need to have some level of two-way integration of the underlying back-end data even though the user interfaces of SFDC and the other system remain separated. This integration cost can be substantial—if no off-the-shelf adaptor is available from Actian, Boomi (Dell), Informatica, Jitterbit, SnapLogic, Tibco, or other vendors, custom integration may be even costlier than the SFDC add-on application fees. Using the two-window approach requires some careful thinking about how users need to interact with the systems, what double entry may be required, and what process control steps may need to be added. Don't skimp on that analysis before making the purchase decisions.

Here are the alternatives for integration, in order of increasing risk:

- Read-only pop-up window[11]

- Read-write pop-up window

- Read-only, with batch file import

- Read-only, with batch file import and export

- Read-only, with continuous one-way data flow

- Read-only, with continuous two-way data flows

- Read-write, with continuous one-way data flow

---

11. This window may be a browser pop-up using `VisualForce` or JavaScript, or it may be implemented as an SFDC `tab` or an `iFrame` mashup.

- Read-write, with continuous two-way data flows

- Real-time replication/synchronization of fields

Of course, integration brings some important architectural issues to the fore:

- **Depth of integration:** Does the user really need real-time, two-way synchronization of records? Much of the time, read-only integration or periodic update is all that's actually needed. The risks and costs go up dramatically with deeper integration.

- **Tightness of integration:** Does the user need to have continuous access to the external system data with transaction locking? This is rarely a hard requirement, and inexpensive workarounds (such as logging in to an external system via a pop-up window) may get the job done. Tight integration must take into account timeouts (usually temporary, caused by a noisy network rather than SFDC), planned SFDC downtime (typically a couple of hours twice per business quarter), and incompatibility windows (may last several days, caused by patches to external systems that have unintended consequences). You may need to use a message-buffer architecture to queue up transactions during the downtime intervals; this architecture makes debugging, audit trails, and compliance much easier, so it is recommended for all large SFDC installations.

- **Federating the system of record:** If systems are integrated, what is the system of record for each object? In many cases, the system of record needs to be identified at the field level, as SFDC will be the authoritative source for parts of an object, whereas the accounting system may be a more authoritative source for other parts.

Integration is a nearly universal requirement in sophisticated SFDC systems (particularly for customer support and service use cases), but it's not well enough understood. With off-the-shelf packages (such as accounting software), if at all possible use an *off-the-shelf integration adaptor.* There are two main types: the first is a software module or integration appliance that runs inside your own server complex (connecting to SFDC via SSL and SOAP or ReST through your firewall), and the second is a hosted service that connects to SFDC and the third-party applications via SSL and SOAP or ReST directly "across clouds." Each approach has advantages, and the good news is that integration adaptors for SFDC are less expensive than the offerings of enterprise application integration (EAI) vendors of the last century. The hosted-integration model has become increasingly popular over time.

INTEGRATION TODAY, INTEGRATION TOMORROW, INTEGRATION FOREVER

The alternative to migrating data into SFDC is to leave the data where it currently lives and use data integration to access and update the required records. Indeed, in many cases this is the only viable approach.

SFDC's APIs, `workflow`, `outbound messaging`, and `APEX` capabilities support very flexible integration strategies for outside systems, including closed-loop and real-time integration. With the addition of third-party integration adaptors, SFDC can be integrated with almost anything.

The business benefits of integration can be astounding. Integration is what lets an SFDC user look at inventories, available-to-promise dates, and payment history. It forms the backbone of business process automation, and it enables your company to streamline operations and improve compliance. It's what makes the 360-degree view of the customer possible.

Unfortunately, integration is not without its costs. If the system being targeted for integration is old or poorly documented, your implementation team or consultant will spend a surprising number of hours just learning how the data behave and which integration strategies are even feasible. You may have to develop code within the SFDC system, in the integration server layer, and in the external system. And, of course, anything you develop must be documented, tested, internationalized, and maintained over time. **In most serious CRM implementations, integration is more expensive than the CRM system itself and is second only to data transformation/cleansing in terms of its overall cost and schedule impact.**

Carefully evaluate the off-the-shelf adaptors for five things: security, freedom from duplicate creation,[12] flexibility/configurability, complexity of code that you might be required to write, and up-time/long-term reliability. Do *not* believe vendor claims on any of these decision points without verifying them: talk with references, and test the behavior of the adaptors in a pilot project with your specific software configuration.

The final strategy is to develop your own integration code using AppExchange tools and libraries. This strategy provides the highest degree of control and flexibility, but it requires serious in-house development skills and should be considered only if (1) there is no off-the-shelf adaptor that will work for your use case, or (2) you need very low-level, fine-grained control to integrate an existing home-brew application (such as order operations) with SFDC.

---

12. By its very nature, application integration without the right design can cause the prodigious creation of spurious or duplicate records (particularly `accounts`, `opportunities`, and `quotes` but also `contracts`, `contacts`, and `assets`).

Buy AppExchange Add-Ons

Using AppExchange add-ons is the path that most companies take, and in many instances it's the only sensible option. Because of the user training and technical implications of add-ons, we recommend that the SFDC system be brought online with only one or two of them enabled and that subsequent add-ons be introduced incrementally (as part of waves).

To counteract the testing and compatibility risks, we recommend that system administrators who want to try new add-ons do so only in their sandbox instance. With this approach, normal system operations will not be affected by errors related to the add-on products.

FINDING GOODIES IN THE APPEXCHANGE

The AppExchange currently houses over 1,500 products, and the number of new and revised/renamed/repurposed products grows every day. So in this section, we don't give you the specific names or URLs to look for. Things change too fast for that (this book is on paper, after all). Instead, we give you generic product category names that will get good results as keywords in the AppExchange's search bar.

You may need to look beyond the AppExchange listings, as some goodies are not listed there—you'll have to Google them. Heed the warnings in the "Where Does All This Free Stuff Come From?" sidebar, later.

Extend with Your Own Add-Ons

If you have specialized needs—driven either by your organization's business model, corporate structure, regulations, or other reasons—none of the off-the-shelf apps will pass muster. SFDC's technology platform is robust, well documented,[13] and rich enough to build almost any business application either natively or with some outboard code running on your company's servers. If you have a strong IT department or a specialist integrator who really understands the guts of SFDC, this approach can get you exactly the functionality you need with no unnecessary clutter or complexity. This approach can also give you strategic advantage and lower risk.

Of course, with this approach comes engineering costs, both now and in the future. Make sure to have your IT folks or consultants read Chapter 13 before you start. Its effectiveness depends on how savvy your company's software developers are. For example, companies such as Google and Microsoft virtually forbid the purchase of software from outside. If your company's technology culture belongs to the DIY or only-best-of-breed camp, building your own add-on is a sound choice.

---

13. Now weighing in at over 10,000 pages.

THE COSTS OF BUILDING IT YOURSELF

There's nothing like a home-brew application to get exactly the features you want. Good implementers can make features that are easy to use, fast, and exactly fitted to your business environment.

In the short run, developing something initially may look cheaper than paying some vendor an annual per-user fee. But the long-term costs can bring some big surprises in the following areas:

- **Testing and rework:** The creation of test code, test cases, and test procedures. All your tests must be run at least four times a year to prepare for new SFDC versions. Even if your organization's needs don't evolve, ramifications of external technological changes can still require rework of your code.

- **Internationalization:** Deciding which languages will be supported for user input and UI elements, and then doing those translations. Internationalization may include currency support, local holidays, and English/metric unit selection.

- **Performance tuning:** Developing performance test cases and profiles, then running them and optimizing code to optimize response time and throughput.

- **Documentation:** Writing and maintaining user cheat sheets, developer reference docs, and FAQs/wikis for administrators and users.

- **Self-support:** Some vendors will no longer support the "main system" if your add-on is running.

- **Feature expansion:** If your development is successful, users will have ongoing requests that a purchased product might have taken care of—but you'll have to develop for yourself.

Take this route with your eyes open!

Before you commit resources to building in-house software products, check the SFDC product roadmap and SFDC's *Ideas* area (https://success.salesforce.com/ideaHome) to make sure that you aren't working on an area in which SFDC itself will implement a solution.[14] Even if you built a highly tailored, fully customized application, it would be really frustrating (and expensive) to deploy your own nonstandard version of a feature only to find it in the standard platform 3 months later.

---

14. For a number of legal reasons, SFDC will never tell you exactly what they're working on. They drop serious hints at their annual DreamForce conference, but the Agile model means even they don't know when the feature will be delivered. When looking at `Ideas` postings, know that most of them are ignored, and it's rare for anything with a score of less than 2,500 points to make it into the product.

If you do pursue in-house development of SFDC add-ons, in your prototyping stage (you should be following the Agile development style described in Chapter 4), use the free apps in the AppExchange as starting points for storyboards and UI examples. There's no point in reinventing the wheel entirely.

If you are going to build functionality, make sure to use a language that has solid libraries supporting the SSL, XML, and SOAP or REST protocols and UTF-8. No matter which language you use, you will almost certainly use the Eclipse developer toolset. SFDC's version of Eclipse makes code deployment a snap and facilitates import and export of metadata and setup configurations.

To develop functionality that actually runs on SFDC's servers, you use `VisualForce` or `APEX`. For functionality to run on your own servers,[15] most developers use PERL, PHP, Python, Visual Basic, Ruby/Rails, or another scripting language. For the more adventurous, it's C# or Java. Although every vendor will claim that its products are fully compatible with SFDC, the ease of working with Web service protocols varies widely. Further, even Web-savvy technologists can run into trouble with international character sets, network timeouts, and other error conditions. For the latest information, have your developers check out the DeveloperForce (www.salesforce.com/developer) bulletin boards and SFDC user groups.

Essential Toys: Featurettes

The featurettes—useful but simple add-ons, eye-candy, productivity aids—mentioned in Chapters 4 and 6 are an important mechanism for wooing users into adopting the system. Several featurettes don't even rate add-ons from the AppExchange: they're just special links, `formulas`, `rules`, `buttons`, `Javascript` hacks, and mashups that do cute little things that are valuable to users. For example:

- A button on the `lead` or `contact` pages that automatically dials the phone number on the page, via Skype

- Maps showing the location of a `contact`, `lead`, or `account`, along with local restaurants in the area

- Data `validation rules` that trap bad entries before the record is saved

- An organizational-chart drawing tool that creates a graphic from the `accounts` and `contacts` in the system at the click of a button

---

15. Or on an execution environment such as AWS, Heroku, or Rackspace. If you choose one of those cloud environments, make sure to dedicate time in your project schedule to familiarizing yourself with the setup and administrative worlds that they entail. Also, don't try to be cheap: you're going to need to have serious error-logging and replication/redundancy servers for any kind of serious application.

- A report link that creates a `campaign members` report for each campaign

- A `report` link that shows all the `tasks` you've assigned to others

- Maps that show all your customers and `leads` in a city

These tiny features do not count in the recommended number of add-ons because almost all of them are just clever uses of SFDC and HTML that don't consume constrained SFDC resources.

WHERE DOES ALL THIS FREE STUFF COME FROM?

If you look in the AppExchange, you'll discover an amazing array of free stuff. About half of the goodies you can download are available for free, and many of those were written by SFDC engineers.

Of course, because almost all of the free stuff is completely unsupported, you might wonder about the quality and origins of the add-ons. Most of the free stuff that isn't from SFDC comes from companies like mine, which are in business to deliver products and services to the SFDC user base. Companies that put modules in the AppExchange worry about their reputations, so they will not risk putting junk out there. If they did, user ratings of the product would rapidly demote garbage products to near-oblivion. And their company's reputation along with it.

Further, all the products added to the AppExchange go through a formal review of their security and architecture and an informal review of their usefulness.

In contrast, lots of goodies available in the developer forums have not undergone any type of review whatsoever. Although I've never seen any malicious or risky code posted, there's no explicit mechanism to stop it—so be a little more wary of those unofficial goodies in the wild.

Fortunately, developers rarely post junk in any forum, and when they do, community dynamics (peer reviews) rapidly push the garbage and the contributor to the sidelines.

The bottom line is that there's not much risk of truly bad things happening with this freeware. If you want to be extra careful, just don't use any `VisualForce` or `APEX` code without thorough code reviews and `sandbox` testing.

The best way to find out about these things is to go to SFDC's developer blog and discussion boards, searching for features you might like (although sometimes, it's more effective to just Google "Salesforce <feature>"). Joining your local SFDC user group can unearth a wealth of current information on these tricks, and these groups increasingly have `chatter` or LinkedIn discussions and meetings. Because there are too many featurettes to mention here, the fastest way to find these add-ons is to go to the AppExchange, look in the left navigation area for your domain (say, "Marketing"), and then look in the subcategory "Free Components." Some featurettes have real power and should be introduced into your SFDC instance as users start to push against the edges of the system:

- Connectors to Microsoft Outlook mail client to synchronize emails, contacts, and calendar entries

- Connectors to Microsoft Office to facilitate mail merges, spreadsheet updates, and other Office–SFDC data interchange

- Connectors to Gmail and Google Applications, which foster easy collaboration with employees and interaction with customers

- Any of over 200 dashboards tailored to the needs of nearly any industry or function

Essential System Administrator Tools

Because system administrators have to try out and install every add-on that is ever put into their systems, we thought it fitting to talk about the tools they need for themselves.

Most of the administrator's tools consist of desktop applications that run outside of SFDC but communicate with the database via SOAP or ReST. Probably the first tools they need will facilitate data import, export, and maintenance. SFDC's Data Loader is a freebie that allows your PC to perform high-speed data loads and dumps, with solid features and a good user interface. It also has a command-line interface that supports batch mode operations. Unfortunately, Data Loader doesn't work on Macs or any SFDC edition lower than the Enterprise version. In that case, you may have to use the slower and buggier[16] Excel Connector (which is also free). Watch out, because the Excel Connector comes in two (incompatible) versions: one for the SFDC `professional edition` and the other for the `enterprise edition`. Although the Excel Connector has some nice behaviors (particularly when you're just learning about the system), most administrators will rapidly move to the Data Loader for its speed and reliability.

Informatica and others have released data loader tools and services that go far beyond the capabilities of SFDC's version. These services can connect SFDC to Excel and popular relational databases, have some very fancy functions and filters, and support scheduled and repetitive uploads or downloads of data. Another helpful tool for learning about the SFDC system is the `Force.com` Explorer, which easily browses the SFDC object model, showing object relationships and metadata.

---

16. The tool has some bugs that are literally charming, once you get used to them. It's open source, so you can contribute fixes if you like. But the toolkit that it depends on is closed source and frozen at API 16, which means most of the juiciest objects introduced into the system over the last 3 years are inaccessible.

Finally, administrators with a developer bent will want to download SFDC's version of the Eclipse development environment. Although Eclipse is a fairly complex application, it has tools and features that the more sophisticated administrator won't want to live without.

Nearly 200 free add-ons for administrative housekeeping can be found in the AppExchange's application category "IT & Administration" and subcategory "Admin & Developer Tools." For example, ChangeIT, FieldTrip, EasyDescribe, Draggin' Role, Print Anything, the User Adoption dashboard, and the `chatter` dashboard are freebies that my firm uses all the time.

But with real value comes real pricing. The SFDC administrator should expect to budget some money for more comprehensive tools:

- **Deduping tools:** Duplicate `accounts`, `contacts`, and particularly `leads` are a significant issue from the first day of real system usage. If you're migrating data from other systems, you need tools to handle the potential for duplicates even before you bring the system up. You need tools (or hosted services) that dedupe data in place, data imports, and data coming from Web site registration pages (via replacement for SFDC's standard `web2lead` feature). The best tools let you dedupe `leads` against `contacts` as well as `leads-leads`, `contacts-contacts`, `accounts-accounts`, or any other table against itself. The tools should provide a range of matching fields and algorithms, including "fuzzy" matches and character reversals. The most advanced tools include phonetic matches or spell-check algorithms to find the tricky "almost dupes" (think "Cold Jim" versus "Gold's Gym"). As there is no "undo" for merging records, misusing these tools can be dangerous. Using them is something of an art form, so make sure to check out the discussion of their use in Chapter 13 and the how-to guide at www.SFDC-secrets.com.

- **Data cleansing/quality/enrichment:** A hosted service typically goes through the SFDC `leads`, `contacts`, and `accounts` to improve data quality or enrich it with more fields. These services can correct phone numbers, fix addresses, and add parametric data about people (e.g., title) and companies (e.g., D-U-N-S number) that can be derived from public sources or proprietary databases. Several of these services are good at populating and enriching `account` data, but only a few of them are very good at improving the data for individuals below the vice president level. The best services use data derived from both proprietary and public sources (specifically, the Web), but the services are rarely able to enrich data associated with people who have only a commodity email address (such as an MSN or Gmail address). Use of these services should be coordinated closely with the marketing department, so skim Chapter 10 for a discussion of this topic. Data cleansing and enrichment tools can be expensive, but you must weigh their cost against how much has been spent to collect and maintain the data up to now. Worthwhile data are always more expensive than the system that stores those data. The most popular of these services is SFDC's own `Data.com`, but several other specialized services deserve your consideration.

- **Documents and content management:** SFDC now provides 11GB of file storage with every account, and this quota grows by 612MB[17] with each additional user for whom a license is purchased. Although this amount of storage is more than sufficient for many SFDC instances, the use of attached documents from emails or large files can quickly consume all of this space. SFDC's additional storage is relatively expensive, so customers often look for alternatives to storing documents in SFDC. A number of alternative approaches exist, but the key comparison point must always be, "Will the users like it?" Ease of use—and particularly the addition of documents via drag and drop—is the number-one evaluation criterion. It's important to ensure that the documents stored externally to SFDC can be "seen" by the correct users, whether they are working in the office or on the road. Do some real-world testing before you implement your document/attachment solution in SFDC, as each approach may involve storing the documents in different ways from how you do things now. In addition, check with your company's network security group to make sure they're comfortable with the technology before you buy it. Note that externally stored documents are *never* searchable by SFDC, so consider setting up a search engine on any file system where you store documents.

- **Sandbox:** This SFDC product has two forms: a freebie that duplicates just the system configuration and a paid version that duplicates all the user data. Both of them are among the most useful tools for administrators and developers, as they provide safe havens for testing integration adaptors, code, business processes, third-party products, and data manipulation strategies. The `sandbox` may seem expensive, but it will save your life (and your weekends). Most customers purchase a single `full sandbox` (which can be filled with all of their system's data) and a `configuration-only sandbox` that holds their schemas, customizations, and code. Very large customers may need a second complete sandbox for very intricate integration projects. These additional applications can be purchased for quarterly periods, so don't buy one until you know it's absolutely necessary.

- **Backup, archive, and ETL tools:** The AppExchange has several free tools to download (and upload) records into nearly every part of the system. These come from SFDC and third-party stalwarts such as Informatica. In addition, there are tools that create special archives and data replicas for compliance, system integration, and data warehousing use-cases. Not surprisingly, the most powerful tools are not free. A frequently overlooked requirement is the backup of metadata (the system configuration, object model, and code). The most user-friendly approach to

---

17. This figure is for everything except the Personal and Developer editions.

that is the SFDC sandbox, but the most powerful approach is the use of the Force. IDE, an Eclipse-based tool that keeps an XML backup of the system metadata for analysis, editing, and redeployment if necessary.

- **Inspectors and controllers:** These are tools that the administrator uses to understand the system configuration, troubleshoot problems, and quickly make changes. There are too many of these to cover, but some popular favorites are Draggin' Role, Force.com Explorer, and Easy Describe.

Finally, if the company purchases an add-on product or decides to integrate its SFDC system with an external application, the system administrator must investigate additional tools for managing these other applications. Almost certainly, those administrative tools will *not* be listed in the AppExchange. You'll need to Google the application name, and with luck you will find at least some postings in online forums from your compatriots. Unfortunately, outside of the AppExchange, the information won't be well organized.

How Good Are the Vendors?

If you're buying—and relying on—products from the AppExchange, you want to make sure that the vendor will be around for a while. Because all the strategic AppExchange products are real products—not freebies—you'll need to have a way of comparing vendors as well as products.

Here are some factors to consider beyond the product attributes (features, ease of use, ease of administration, scalability/performance, quality, and price) when considering a purchase:

- How long has the vendor been offering products in the AppExchange?
- How many votes have been cast in the AppExchange listing (anything less than 5 is an issue), and how high are the votes (pay more attention to the number of low votes, not the average)?
- Are any irate or negative reviews posted in the AppExchange? Has somebody lost data? Note that you can typically reach out to the reviewer if you want to know the gory details.
- What portion of the vendor's business comes from the AppExchange?
- Can the vendor provide solid customer references for this AppExchange product?

Although none of these issues should, by itself, be the tipping point, all of them are indicators of vendor commitment and viability in the AppExchange. Approximately 30% of your evaluation should focus on the vendor situation and 70% on the product attributes. Put simply, if the vendor is in the market for the long haul, its product is more likely to be of long-term value to you.

Essential Add-Ons for the Marketer

Even though the marketing department will not have the most users on the SFDC system, and those personnel will not necessarily be part of the first wave of system users, the marketing folks are going to be interacting with larger amounts of data and more intense operations than any other department.[18] For many marketing departments, SFDC is the only marketing automation system they really have. So let's look at the elements that nearly every marketing department needs:

- **Duplicate blockers and deduping tools:** Duplicate `leads` are a significant issue from the first day of real system usage, and few problems will drive sales personnel crazy faster. Every time you do a `lead` import, there's a chance to create yet another almost-identical copy of a `lead` or `contact`. Read the material on deduping tools for system administrators found earlier in this chapter. Also, check out Chapter 10 for a discussion of using `campaigns` and `activities` to really solve the problem of automatically generated duplicates.

- **Marketing automation and email blasters:** Whether it is doing mass emailings or vertical "drip marketing" campaigns, almost every marketing team needs a real email blasting service. Using Outlook or Salesforce for these purposes is just wrong for any serious organization. SFDC's recent purchase of ExactTarget and Pardot signals that in the long run, these are the favored email blasting systems. That said, it's not a slam-dunk, and nearly a dozen email blasters and marketing automation system (MAS) tools claim to be compatible with SFDC. Don't take that at face value—there are some amazing differences in features and integration depth. Evaluating these systems on price alone is a fool's errand. The better MAS products are really content management systems in disguise—if you don't have at least five PDFs per campaign/messaging theme, figure out how you're going to get that content created first. The MAS can be quite complex to set up and use, so don't buy a bigger product than your staff is prepared to manage.[19] Assess the product by three key points of comparison: first, how well the email functions and statistics can be integrated with SFDC `campaigns`; second, how realistic and flexible the `lead` scoring and internal nurturing algorithms are; and third, how well the email blaster's model of campaigns matches with what your company actually needs to do. Some products, for example, keep `campaign` data private so that one marketer cannot see another's campaigns. Although that may make sense

---

18. If your company's IT department isn't deeply involved in SFDC, the marketing team will need to take responsibility for the "tools for the system administrator" outlined earlier.
19. The industrial-strength products may require half of a full-time employee on an ongoing basis if your company is doing several blasts per week.

for some marketing organizations, for others it's impractical. If the product isn't tightly integrated with SFDC, administration tasks such as keeping opt-out lists fully synchronized are a pain. Do not buy any email blaster until you've gone through a real-world trial for at least a couple of weeks; many vendors make you pay for that trial, but that will be money well spent.

- **Campaigns:** For almost any business-to-business (B2B) company, SFDC's `campaigns` module is a must. Even though it's free in the `enterprise` and `unlimited editions`, this feature isn't used often enough and is the root cause of much `lead` and `contact` duplication. Even if you have to pay extra for it, the `campaigns` module is a must.

- **Social media:** For almost any business-to-consumer (B2C) and many B2B businesses, social media such as LinkedIn, Facebook, and Twitter are key elements of the brand strategy and reputation management. There are several free add-ons to harness social media, and some of the paid ones (e.g., for LinkedIn) are well worth it. Of course, your social strategy should also include community development, which almost certainly will include `chatter`. For blog and discussion group/forum marketing, take a look at HubSpot's offerings. More advanced social strategies require the message testing and media features of SFDC's `social media marketing product` and the reputation and buzz metrics of `social media monitoring`.

- **Google AdWords:** Google AdWords has become the most relevant form of advertising for most B2B firms and some B2C companies. Unfortunately, `Salesforce for Google Adwords` was not particularly wonderful at managing AdWords from within Salesforce. It is officially discontinued, and even though it's still available on a grandfathered basis, marketers should look to other solutions. Most MAS tools enable much better answers for AdWords, but configuring all your landing pages appropriately is a nontrivial effort.

- **eCommerce/payments clearing:** For any B2C company and most B2B companies with a multichannel strategy, an eCommerce system is a must-have addition to the firm's Web site. Since the first edition of this book, over a dozen products are available in the AppExchange. Unfortunately, most customers find that they need to do custom integration and custom code for the best customer experience in the storefront, catalog presentment, recommendations engine, payments processing, and fulfillment/expediting. The word *custom* appears twice in that sentence, and that means real money. Sorry. That said, Intuit, Zuora, and others now have billing and payments processing products nicely integrated with SFDC.

- **Public relations/analyst relations:** If your firm has a PR function, SFDC can be configured to handle reporters and analysts as "customers" of PR "campaigns."

The PR/Analyst Relations module is free, but it is really useful only if the company's PR people reside in several locations (e.g., employees in different countries or an internal PR person who works with an outside agency). If you install this add-on, you need to implement some very tight naming conventions for `campaigns`, `accounts`, `contact types`, and a few other fields. But you can't beat the price (nothing!), and this add-on is certainly a more effective collaboration tool than emailing an Excel spreadsheet in a round-robin fashion.

- **References and surveys:** Nothing is more powerful than the recommendation of a customer, so you want to cultivate and manage references as a key asset. There are several add-on products now that do a good job of collecting and digesting surveys, cultivating and managing references, and integrating the results into reports that can be used by executives and product management alike.

- **Reporting and analytics engines:** In most organizations, the finance and marketing personnel are the ultimate number crunchers. SFDC includes a powerful yet simple reporting engine, but the multidimensional data analyst will quickly run out of gas. SFDC reports and dashboards can now be scheduled to run regularly, and the system has added analytic snapshot capabilities. Even so, executives who want detailed, nicely formatted reports pushed to their mailboxes at 8 A.M. on Monday morning can quickly become frustrated. A number of reporting engines, analytical tools, and data warehouse options are available for SFDC, with prices ranging from free to very expensive—and feature variations to go with those price tags. If you missed it, check out the section in Chapter 2 entitled "Reports—Inside versus Outside." For marketing, though, there's a special class of analytics focusing on the life cycle of a lead. Marketo's Revenue Lifecycle Analytics product deserves close inspection, as do Birst, Cloud9, Good Data, and other specialty offerings. When evaluating these engines, use these evaluation criteria: first, will you really use the features they offer? Second, are they missing something you actually *do* need? Third, are they easy enough for users to comprehend? And fourth, what are the long-run organizational costs of using the system (particularly, the cost of a data analyst to build the really clever reports)? You'll notice that initial procurement prices for these tools may not look enormous, but they can be overwhelmed by the long-run costs.

Essential Features for Sales Management

SFDC was designed with the sales rep and sales manager in mind, but sales managers inevitably ask for lots of extras. Although it's important to keep the system as streamlined as possible for the first few months, it's very natural for extra add-on products to be integrated into the system as managers demand them.

- **Email to Salesforce:** This is a built-in (free) feature of the system that is too often overlooked. Send an email from any phone, PC, or other device, and Bcc: a special email address. SFDC picks up the email and attaches it to the `lead`, `contact`, or even `opportunity` that's relevant to the email recipient. It can even store the email attachments for you (although, for a number of reasons, we recommend that you keep that feature turned off).

- **Chatter:** This is an invaluable way to improve internal collaboration, stay on top of the latest news about the pipeline, and communicate with the troops. `Chatter` is part of the SFDC UI, but there's also a desktop app and a mobile app for when you're not logged in to SFDC. What most people overlook is that `chatter` is an important way of creating an instant community with your customers, where you have a secure "walled garden" and a medium of communicating with customers about product issues, onboarding, and post-sales support. In most cases, `chatter` is free—so don't neglect it.

- **Salesforce for Outlook:** If you're an Outlook for PC user (32-bit versions of Office for either 32- or 64-bit versions of Windows), this freebie offers a lot of cool features. You can push emails into SFDC; synchronize contacts, tasks, and calendars; and instantly navigate from Outlook to the relevant records in SFDC. If you don't like SFDC's version, you should take a look at Linkpoint360, Riva Omni Connect, iHance, and other products. Watch out for human-factor issues before you deploy any of these products—test for at least a month with pilot users before you buy this for the whole organization, particularly when it comes to contact and schedule synchronization.

- **Mobile edition:** Designed for real-time connected use, the `mobile edition` is optimized for smartphone screens, navigation, and keyboards. Supporting iPhone, Android, BlackBerry, and Microsoft-based phones, the `mobile edition` is ideal for the road warrior who wants to be able to get at anything in the system no matter when or where. Caching of data is limited to available memory, but with most modern devices, that means several thousand records before you have to wait for the network. Of course, the navigation is limited, and reports can be challenging to read, but the `mobile edition` has good "wow" value and fits with the lifestyles of many sales reps. There is an extra-cost version offering additional features: take a look at it in addition to the freebie. It's priced by the individual phone, but at $50 per month per SFDC mobile user, the charges for this version can add up. Make this one a negotiation point. Note that on iPads and Android/Windows tablets, driving SFDC from the browser is likely to be a much better choice, particularly for data entry on the road.

- **Offline edition:** SFDC stores all of its data on its servers; nothing is stored in the user's laptop. Thus, when users are on a plane or out of Internet range, they are out of luck. For the road warrior, SFDC's `offline edition` is an invaluable productivity tool. The system caches selected data on the laptop before leaving the network and then presents a fully interactive (but limited) version of SFDC while the user is traveling. Records can be reviewed and updated through the usual browser interface, and when the user reconnects, the updates are synchronized with SFDC's master database. With SFDC's `professional edition`, this functionality is an extra-cost item that is priced per individual user, but it's very worth purchasing for your few true road warriors. If your implementation uses `custom objects`, they are unlikely to work in the `offline edition`; but that may be moot for offline users. Do an evaluation test before you buy the `offline edition` (it's free in `enterprise` and `unlimited editions`).

- **Sales Activity Dashboard:** This free app provides a number of dashboard elements and underlying reports that really help you understand what every member of your sales team is doing. Of course, this visibility comes at a price: it can induce paranoia among the sales reps. For this reason, you should introduce this dashboard—and the activity management discipline that comes along with it—gradually (wait at least a quarter before you spring it on your people). If you haven't already done so, check out the discussion in Chapter 9 on Activity Management.

- **Call Scripting:** This free add-on from SFDC provides built-in call scripting support for telesales reps. Using this app not only ensures that value proposition statements and `lead` qualification are more consistent but also automatically scores `leads` so that they can be ranked for inspection and conversion by the sales rep.

- **Videoconferencing:** WebEx, Citrix, GoToMeeting, and other Web or videoconferencing systems are ubiquitous, but only a few of them have nice integrations with SFDC that provide enriched data for `leads` and `contacts`. Make sure that the connector you use for videoconferencing or Web conferencing leverages the `campaigns` feature, as a `lead source` level of integration is a step backward. (If your IT group is sharp, they can set up an `APEX trigger` to overcome this limitation—but why shouldn't you buy this functionality straight from the vendor?)

- **Account enrichment tools:** SFDC customers that use the named account model of selling want to be able to profile companies before reps make the first call. Several commercial sources of these corporate profiles exist, and some of them have been integrated with SFDC. Of course, the granddaddy of them is SFDC's own `Data.com`, which includes data from Dunn & Bradstreet and Hoover's. `Data.com`, in its Prospecting mode, is great for reps who are trying to break in to new territories or industries. The data is accurate, generally complete (particularly for North America), and available in real time. If your reps are targeting highly specialized market segments (let's say, jet engine manufacturers) or unusual geographies (let's say, Malaysia), the best sources of data will be industry associations or other sources whose only real data are likely to reside on a CD or Web site that is not integrated in any way with SFDC. In this case, you really have two choices: first, with "gray-matter" integration, using a college intern to boil down the data and cut/paste it into the system; or second, paying an integrator to import and merge the data into your system. In either case, the total cost of this information can be fairly pricey, so make sure that you pay only for users who really use the data, the information provided is what you actually need (e.g., the source may provide the number of employees, but your reps might need the number of servers), and the individuals you're targeting show up in the database (e.g., most sales reps need connections at the VP level and below, but some databases contain only corporate officers who don't really buy anything).

- **Lead/contact prospecting and enrichment:** You can never have too much lead quality, and prospecting tools are always a hit. Again, SFDC's `Data.com` is the best general-purpose solution, with over 30 million contacts kept up to date through crowdsourcing. The tool has two modes: Prospecting and Data Quality Improvement—your team may well want both of them. You may also want to look into other tools, such as ZoomInfo and Reachable, that provide additional social-network features (such as identifying the best connection with a prospect). Inevitably, privacy laws in some countries limit the coverage, so you have to look into industry associations and other outboard databases. All the cost and hassle issues discussed in the preceding "Account enrichment tools" bullet apply here as well.

- **Sales methodology enablers:** Many large B2B salesforces use methodologies intended to make sales cycles more predictable and profitable. The core of SFDC has stayed agnostic about individual methodologies, but several third-party add-ons are available to enforce best practices of methodologies, such as Miller-Heiman, Target Account Selling, and SPIN Selling, among others. These add-ons present special screens for the `account`, `contact`, and `opportunity` objects to prompt reps about how they should move the prospect forward. These enablers can make it much easier to persuade sales reps to use the methodology consistently, but they should not be installed unless upper management is firmly committed to the methodology.[20]

- **Content and collateral enrichment:** If you are lucky enough to have a lot of quality collateral, the next complaint from your team will be, "There's too much collateral;

---

20. If upper management is undecided about which methodology to use or is trying to put enforcement measures into SFDC in a last-ditch effort to save an unpopular mandate about using a methodology, the enablers should *not* be turned on. In most cases, doing so would simply doom SFDC to the same negative attitudes the reps have about the failing methodology.

I can't find what I need." SFDC's `content edition` provides some nifty features to help customers and sales reps alike find what they need and vote on what's most useful. One of the best features is `content delivery` that lets reps construct their own packets out of approved materials and then monitor how often the prospect has looked in the packet. Some third-party products are also available to create or integrate wiki-like features for both internal and external use. When used in combination with SFDC's `customer portal`,[21] these tools can provide a nice environment for pre- and post-sales information browsing and exchange.

- **Partner management portal:**[22] SFDC has an add-on product that makes it easy to "flip" `leads` to and from partners and to jointly manage the progress of `opportunities`. SFDC's `PRM` (partner relationship management) product has become a lot more capable over time and is worth the time and effort required to fully leverage the portal on your company's Web site. The `partner portal` is being gradually replaced by `chatter communities`. At least one third-party PRM product is available, offering a different model of managing partner and value-added retailer (VAR)/distributor operations. The key issue with any PRM product is making sure that the partners are able and willing to use it. Unfortunately, large partners may rarely input data into your system (you're just not important enough for them to vary their existing processes), and Asian firms are often unwilling to share any prospect data until the deal is signed. If your partners indicate sincere willingness to use a partner portal if you set one up, these PRM products are quite worthwhile.

- **Line-item quoting:** SFDC has line-item quoting available so that `quotes` can be associated with specific line items, prices, and discounting mechanisms. The tool can be configured for approval processing so that out-of-bounds discounts or unusual configurations can be routed to management for approval before the quote is issued. Add to this DocuSign or competing digital-signature products, and the close just became that much faster. However, the user interface of the out-of-the-box features is clunky; several add-ons and consulting offerings have been created to make these features easier to use.

- **Order configurators and proposal generators:** With very complex products, particularly in B2B markets, the sales cycle cannot proceed without a semicustom proposal and a configured product quote. Before evaluating add-on configurator/proposal generation products, ask yourself these questions:

  ➥ Is there enough consistency in your proposals and orders that the process can really be automated?

---

21. If you have not yet enabled the `customer portal` or `partner portal` in your instance of SFDC, it is no longer available to you. These features have been replaced by `chatter communities`.

➥ Who will own the task of creating the content and rules for automation and modifying them over time as price lists are updated, special offers are created/retired, and marketing messages change?

➥ Is the task complicated yet repetitive enough to warrant automation?

If you have good answers to these questions, evaluate the AppExchange products in this area for ease of use, flexibility, price, and references. These subsystems are not cheap to buy or configure.

- **Integration with order management:** Out of the box, SFDC cannot start an order. In most companies, order management systems are custom coded (either in the form of a custom application or as Microsoft Word and Excel macros) because this is an area where every company likes to do things its own way. Although some AppExchange add-ons are available for quoting and order management, the more frequent practice is to integrate SFDC with your company's existing order management system. Integration companies offer several off-the-shelf connectors that hook SFDC up to order-management packages, although these products may require significant customization to really work with your company's business processes. Once the systems are integrated, SFDC's workflow features can add a nice layer of control and approval cycles that can make your firm more compliant with accounting and SEC regulations.

- **Commission and incentive management:** As B2B salesforces get larger and more complex, managing commissions and incentive programs can become a full-time job. Some poor sales operations or finance associate will have to manage the monster spreadsheets that are fed by SFDC and accounting data. A number of commissions and incentive systems in the AppExchange have nice integrations that work with SFDC. If your compensation plan is complicated enough, these automation packages can be a good investment. Watch out, though: if the compensation plan changes frequently, has product-specific commissions, or involves a lot of recurring revenue, implementing one of these standard packages can be just as monstrous as maintaining the spreadsheets that you had to build internally. Check out Chapter 9 for further discussion of this topic.

- **Forecasting and sales rep scorecards:** SFDC provides `reports` and `dashboards` to let sales managers see what's going on in the present, and most sales users are pretty happy with them. But the system cannot handle deep forecasting or performance analytics chores. External tools are required for the sales manager who really wants to understand forecasting accuracy, regional or vertical pipeline coverage, rep performance over time, and scorecarding. Although a general data warehouse or reporting engine can be configured to produce these reports, the sales manager usually wants things that the data analyst doesn't know how to produce. Check out Birst, Cloud9, Good Data, and other products. In evaluating these forecasting/performance analysis tools, do a 30-day evaluation to make sure that the product lives up to the hype. Look into the depth of domain knowledge embedded in the analytics, ease of use that ensures sales managers won't get confused, flexible configuration, and drill-down reports capabilities to satisfy the curious VP.

- **Telephony integration:** From free add-ons for Skype to high-end adaptors for PBX, ACD, and IVR systems, SFDC's ability to integrate with your company's phone system is a real plus. For outbound callers, these integrations make calls faster and more efficient and allow for their automatic measurement. For inbound call centers, these integrations make call handling much easier by pre-populating cases with basic caller information and correlating call times, number of calls per case, and other key metrics.

Essential Tools for Support

Customer support personnel—whether their duties include expediting orders, providing field technical support, or managing returns—have needs that are distinct from those of the sales and marketing folks. SFDC contains the basics needed for call center support, but there are several areas where the user experience and power of the system can be enriched.

- **Mobility support:** If you are in a field support or service organization, the ability to stay in sync with the current customer situation is fundamental to productivity. SFDC's `mobile edition` is quite valuable, particularly while a company representative is visiting the customer's site. If your company's field support personnel use laptops, iPads, or Android/Windows tablets, achieving this kind of communication is simply a matter of getting a 4G wireless card[22] for accessing the SFDC via the browser. If the field personnel don't want to lug laptops or pads/tablets around, SFDC's `mobile edition` provides real-time connected operation optimized for iPhone, Android, BlackBerry, and Microsoft mobile devices. Even though the device screen sizes limit SFDC navigation and reports can be challenging to read, the `mobile edition` fits well with how field support people work. As mentioned earlier, there's an extra-cost version of the `mobile edition` priced by the individual phone. Alternatively, SFDC's `offline edition` may be appropriate, but its requirement to prepopulate the laptop before the support rep leaves for a customer call may not be realistic for the organization.

---

22. SFDC's user interface works great with 3G and "good enough" with Edge-based communication cards that aren't much faster than a dial-up modem.

- **Call Scripting:** This free app from SFDC provides built-in call scripting support for the company's customer support agents. Using this add-on not only ensures that the correct information is collected every time but can also guide first-level troubleshooting and facilitate better consistency of support. Further, the Call Scripting app can be configured to automatically score cases so that they can be prioritized within the support team.

- **Telephony support:** Nearly any customer support operation will have a call center—whether it consists of 3 people or 300—that will benefit from some level of SFDC telephony integration. At the most basic (free) level, the SFDC screens can be configured to include buttons that automatically dial the phone numbers of people in the system, via Skype or the company's VoIP or PBX system. At more advanced levels, the integration automatically notes the time and duration of the call in the system and records phone numbers and names for inbound calls. As the integration becomes fancier, you'll want to set up more reports and metrics for tight call center management. Telephony integration is almost never free, but it can yield significant payoffs in terms of productivity and team management.

- **Email2Case:** When this free add-on is integrated with the system, SFDC gains the ability to automatically update `cases` from inbound customer emails, which eliminates a lot of copying and pasting of emails and other error-prone practices. Although the functionality is available for free, some real work is required to configure the add-on correctly for the email system and other infrastructure. Further, you'll want to set up new `case escalation rules`, `workflows`, and reports when `Email2Case` is incorporated in the SFDC system. If the necessary IT resources aren't immediately available, you'll need to set some money aside to hire a consultant to handle this task.

- **Chatter:** Of all the types of SFDC users, `chatter` is probably the most obviously useful to the support team. `Chatter` is a free feature that can be extended with free add-ons to create the best form of real-time internal collaboration for technical troubleshooting and general problem-solving, a secure form of communication between you and the customer, and communities of interest for support and knowledge exchange. `Chatter` takes a bit of getting used to, but it can dramatically decrease the amount of email surrounding cases and the support function.

- **Real-time service agent chat:** The ability to have end users chat with service agents in real time, offered through your Web site or customer portal, has been around in the best support systems for years. This feature is now available as an add-on product for SFDC, fully integrated with the rest of the system. SFDC's new `chatter communities` will make the chat feature even easier for users to get to.

- **Knowledge base and customer portal:** Although these features are available as part of SFDC,[23] they really aren't useful without significant configuration and integration into your company's Web site. When properly set up, SFDC's features provide a nice two-way communication path with customers (such as an elegant, semi-automated FAQ and `case workflow`). A number of products in the AppExchange provide more complete content management, service portals, and two-way customer communication options, such as surveys and video. The key points to consider when evaluating these products are the match of the feature sets to your company's real needs, the ease of configuring the features to your customers' needs, the amount of work required to maintain the knowledge base, and the customer and information-quality metrics produced.

- **Integration with your problem-tracking system:** SFDC manages customer issues in the context of customer complaints (`cases`) and fixes (`solutions`), which works quite well from the outward-looking perspective of a support phone person. Conversely, the inward-looking context—product defects (bugs) and upgrades (patches)—is very valuable for the support team, as it allows them to say confidently, "Nobody else has seen this bug" or "The fix will be available in two weeks." A free add-on is available that provides a lightweight bug-tracking system entirely inside SFDC, but this is really useful only if you don't have a way of tracking them already. For more serious defect management needs, connectors linking Jira, Remedy, Zendesk, and other standard products are available. Of course, general-purpose integration adaptors are also available, but these products require a significant degree of configuration and coding to be truly effective. If your company does not have the necessary IT resources on staff, you'll need to set some money aside to hire a consultant to handle this task.

- **Integration with inventory, licenses, contracts, and assets:** SFDC includes several tables that represent customer `contracts` and `assets` (historical purchases), but these tables remain empty unless they are manually filled in by order operations personnel. Even when this is done (very rarely), the process is highly error prone. As discussed in the "Integrate Rather Than Extend" section earlier in this chapter, using a two-window strategy (where your customer support reps log in to the ERP system during calls) may be a reasonable way for your team to see the serial or license numbers of products bought by a customer, the purchase dates, and other historical data. However, operational or security policies may make that approach impossible to implement. In that case, SFDC can automatically pull relevant records from the order management, distribution, and ERP systems

---

23. Historically, the `customer self-support portal` was SFDC's best path. Although that's still available on a grandfathered basis, all new portals based on SFDC should use `chatter communities`.

so they can be displayed directly within the SFDC screens. Although general-purpose integration adaptors are available to access ERP and other systems, you will almost always need to build custom code beyond those adaptors to make the integration truly useful. If the necessary IT resources aren't available, you'll need to set some money aside to hire a consultant to handle this task.

- **Entitlement/service level agreement (SLA) tracking:** SFDC provides a number of features for handling entitlements and SLAs. A couple of free apps measure effort to resolve and automatically attach SLA response times to `cases`. In addition to tracking the `entitled response time` and the `entitled resolution time`, the add-ons monitor the *actual* time parameters for each case and flag SLA violations. This functionality is very useful in both real-time escalations and end-of-quarter reporting. In addition, there are paid-for products that provide more features in this area.

Essential Extensions for Finance

In many companies, the finance and accounting organizations are among the last to use SFDC. But once the system has been up and running for a year, it has enough data to be the foundation for interesting reports and analyses that the CFO's office always wanted to do.

- **Integration with quoting and order management:** When SFDC is integrated with existing quoting and order-management systems, it can enforce much better sales behavior (e.g., preventing unapproved quotes from going out or locking down quotes and contracts once they are approved) and automatically pull relevant records from the order-management, distribution, and ERP systems. Although general-purpose integration adaptors provide access to Oracle, SAP, and other systems, you will almost always need to build custom code beyond those adaptors to make the integration truly useful. If the necessary IT resources are not available, you'll need to set some money aside to hire a consultant to handle this task.

- **Electronic document and signature management:** For the most highly integrated operations, a paperless document and contract routing system provides the fastest and most controlled way to manage approval and signature processes. Using products from Adobe and DocuSign, SFDC's `workflow` system can handle nearly every stage of this process, from quote inception to contract filing, in a paperless, digitally signed way. Implementing these capabilities is a fairly significant undertaking, but if you have to manage hundreds of contracts, it can be a boon to streamlined, standardized, controlled contract management.

- **Expense tracking:** A free add-on provides expense tracking and approval cycles for the SFDC system. Given that only full SFDC users can use this app, most companies will continue to use other expense-tracking software. However, for companies with large field forces (particularly for sales, consulting, or after-sales service), this app is a great way to link expenses to customer projects or sales cycles, so it's worth serious consideration.

- **Accounting/budgeting/payments processing:** A number of add-on products are available to help finance and accounting people do their jobs. Budgeting add-ons help develop and manage budgets, particularly for the variable expenses incurred by the sales and marketing organizations. There are even full-fledged accounting systems that can create bookkeeping and financial reports for multinational businesses. Although most companies already have accounting and financial systems fully in place, for small businesses moving up from QuickBooks or other entry-level systems, the add-on products are a reasonable alternative. In addition, there are now three accounting systems that work closely with SFDC, including one that is built entirely on the SFDC platform. The key points when evaluating accounting packages are: the match between the vendor's features and the company's real needs; the depth of support for multinational, multicurrency, and revenue recognition support; and the flexibility of the system to accommodate future changes in the organization.[24]

- **Compliance:** SEC regulations such as the Sarbanes-Oxley Act require that companies pass audits and have repeatable, documented processes for several aspects of revenue and financial management. SFDC's field history tracking provides solid `audit trails` to help the organization's personnel understand and measure processes. SFDC's security system, in combination with `workflows`—a free part of the `enterprise` and `unlimited editions`—can be configured to enforce approval cycles and lock down `opportunities`, `forecasts`, and `contracts` once they are approved by management. There is also a free AppExchange plugin called SoxRox that can automate the compliance processes, providing real-time visibility about the state of processes and approvals. Several other AppExchange products also provide support for other regulatory requirements like FINRA and HIPAA.

- **Employee management:** The AppExchange has a free app that provides a lightweight employee manager database to be stored within SFDC. When used with the fine-grained security system that's part of the `enterprise edition`, this tool provides a fine solution for small businesses or for division-level information at

---

24. Changes such as reorganizations, acquisitions, and spin-offs can be much more traumatic to the accounting system—and to SFDC in general—than simple organic growth. See Chapter 12 for further discussion of this topic.

larger companies. There are also several third-party add-ons for recruiting, talent management, appraisals, and other HR processes.

Essential Features for the Executive

Executives (particularly COOs and CEOs) will typically interact with the SFDC system mainly at—surprise!—an executive level. They need to see `reports`, `dashboards`, and scorecards for the organization so they can manage in real time and characterize organizational performance and the pipeline forecast for the board of directors. For these reports and analytics, SFDC `reports` typically are supplemented by outboard systems:

- **Data warehouse, business intelligence (BI), and reporting tools:** As mentioned earlier, SFDC has an easy-to-use yet powerful reporting engine that's great for ad hoc analysis and reporting at low levels of the organization. At the executive level, however, the questions that need to be answered are much tougher and almost certainly require an external set of tools. SFDC add-ons are available for several kinds of analytics, and some of the most popular BI tools are tightly integrated into the system. For even more complex analytics, the data must be exported to a data warehouse, and several SFDC partners offer ETL tools and integration adaptors to facilitate the most powerful analysis tools. When evaluating these products, make sure that there is a good match between what the SFDC team needs on a regular basis and the features offered by the vendor: some of the most powerful tools require extensive "care and feeding" by a business analyst who may be more expensive than the business value delivered.

- **Forecast analytics and organizational scorecarding:** As mentioned earlier, SFDC's forecasting reports and dashboards are fine for small teams but cannot answer the important questions about forecast reliability, team comparative performance metrics, or industry benchmarking. Although a general data warehouse or reporting engine can be configured to produce those `reports`, executives want easy-to-understand dashboards and metrics that capture organizational objectives. Dedicated tools that embody significant domain knowledge and "executive savvy" are much easier to use in board-level discussions. Check out Birst, Cloud9, Good Data, and other products. In evaluating these forecasting/performance analysis tools, do a 30-day evaluation to make sure that the product lives up to the hype. Look into the depth of domain knowledge embedded in the analytics, ease of use that ensures a clear boardroom conversation, flexible configuration, and drill-down reports capabilities to satisfy the curious CxO.

- **Mobility:** Some executives are very hands-on and want to quickly get contact information for customers. They also need the ability to rapidly look up the state of an account when an unexpected phone call comes in. For these executives, we recommend SFDC's `mobile edition`: it doesn't require these managers to lug their laptops on their travels, and it gives them the level of access they need on the go. Even if your executive team doesn't ask for it, it's not a bad thing to demo the `mobile edition` just for the "wow value."

GETTING THE MOST FROM **SFDC**

- Salesforce is a platform for over 1,500 add-on products. But you must not put them in all at once, and generally you want to use less than a dozen of them.
- Have a well-orchestrated sequence of featurettes that give users a reason to feel happy about the system.
- Use `email to salesforce` and free `dashboard` add-ons!
- Make sure the system administrator gets the free tools listed in this chapter.
- Make sure to get sufficient budget and staff time required for the larger add-ons—particularly if there is any data manipulation or migration required.

FOR SMALL COMPANIES

- The AppExchange provides more stuff than you'll ever use. Just pick a few items mentioned in this chapter.

FOR LARGE ENTERPRISES

- Have IT review plugins *before* you tell users about them.
- Buy and use the `sandbox`.
- Never install a new add-on without thoroughly testing it in the full `sandbox`.
- Don't buy an add-on without a 30-day evaluation period to spot "gotchas."

CHAPTER 8

Optimizing Business Processes

*If you can't describe what you are doing as a
process, you don't know what you are doing.*

—*W. Edwards Deming*

T his is the single most important chapter in the book—what really sets it apart—but it's likely to be a little abstract. Because most business users rarely think in terms of business processes, this chapter is full of concrete examples explaining how to see the big picture and optimize the way different departments work together via SFDC. The goal is to make SFDC fit into your business in the most natural way possible while upgrading the smoothness, coherence, and efficiency of your revenue and support business processes.

An SFA system could be thought of as a glorified contact manager—but if that's the way you think about the system, you're missing nearly all the value it can bring as a management tool. The whole point of a CRM system is its ability to improve the speed and effectiveness of the sales, marketing, and support teams. The larger and more complex the company, the more leverage a true CRM system can bring, because it helps manage *across* business processes and organizational boundaries.

Taking this argument a step further, SFDC gives the organization the opportunity to improve collaboration across its sales, marketing, customer service, order operations, and other departments to improve profitability and customer satisfaction at the same time. To realize this potential, however, requires thinking about and making changes to the details of how you do business—modifications to business rules, procedures, and metrics. After all, if all you do is automate, all you'll succeed at is doing dumb things faster.

One of the big lessons learned from the business process reengineering movement of the 1990s was that simply analyzing and documenting a process can expose big opportunities for business improvement, even if no automation is applied. In addition, by looking objectively at the organization's business processes, you may discover ways to dramatically simplify the requirements for SFDC. This is the secret of my consulting firm's success, and it can be yours, too.

The real potential for business improvement comes from the twin foundations of SFDC functionality and business process changes that have been "tuned" to leverage the system.

What Is a Business Process?

The term *business process* sounds pretty vague and abstract, and almost no one really understands it very well. So why use this language?

Business process is an enormously powerful concept because it allows you to see the corporation as if it were a machine or an assembly line that cranks out profits. Business process analysis helps clarify decisions and improve the way your business does business. Although abstract and sometimes cumbersome, business processes help you think about your business in a *systematic way* that avoids getting caught up in personal foibles and company politics.[1]

A business process comprises a set of interrelated tasks or activities that are done in a repeatable way to achieve a goal (typically for a customer). Business processes are supposed to be routine and predictable, but they have enough variations and exceptions that they will never be completely automated. Almost always, a business process spans more than one person's job and more than one piece of software. Most of the time, performing a business process also requires crossing organizational lines—in fact, the juiciest and most interesting ones *all* do. A typical business process takes a few hours or days and involves both automation and human judgment. But some business processes—such as a sales cycle or customer onboarding—may take months and have very little automation.

The vast majority of business processes have never been documented as such; instead, everyone knows them as a bunch of rules and steps that are "the way we do things around here." Business processes are usually embodied in habits, rules, and culture about the way to get the job done. Consequently, business processes often include several gray areas that are misunderstood by the people who *don't* do them ("You mean, we *don't* allow customers to return defective merchandise to the store where they bought it?").

Business processes can also be nearly invisible to the people doing them, because those workers are just doing their jobs the right way. For example, the department store Nordstrom has a merchandise returns policy that allows a customer to bring back almost anything in any condition and get a store credit. How does the company handle a return when it involves merchandise Nordstrom no longer carries? There's a business process covering that situation. A business process essentially tries to describe the way

---

1. Of course, like anything else that comes from consultants and business gurus, business process engineering can itself become the plaything of politics and arbitrary decision making. That's life in the big city. The goal of business process folks is to get away from politics and be objective and fair in decision making.

the company does business, as if workers were operating a giant machine, so that the individual workers can know what to do next to do an even better job.

When organizational improvements are being implemented, business process analysis helps structure arguments about resource allocation and organizational design. Business processes force members of the organization to think about disparate elements of the business (let's say, field service and the call center) in a way that's oriented around what *customers* value. Instead of getting hung up on departmental trivia, politics, and arbitrary rules, if you focus on business processes, the discussion hones in on the big things that are important—such as how the company can make more money.

In the context of SFDC, the most important reason to understand a business process is to streamline and automate it. Business processes definitions can be easily transformed into `validation steps`, `rules`, `routing`, `alerts`, `escalations`, `workflows`, checklists, and special-purpose data entry screens; further, they lend themselves to monitoring via `criteria`, `reports`, and `dashboards`. In other words, good business process definitions can drive about two-thirds of the SFDC system configuration.

Although incredibly useful, business process analysis can be time consuming. Avoid it like the plague—a business process discussion should last, at most, a few hours. It's totally self-defeating if a business process discussion lasts weeks or months, or if some knucklehead mandates documenting 300 processes before he'll[2] make a decision.

How Do Business Processes Fit Together?

A given business process should represent a "whole transaction" that is useful or meaningful from the customer's or user's perspective—for example, all the parts of taking an order over the phone and delivering it. Business processes fit together typically in an end-to-end manner, forming a cycle. Continuing the example, shipping and invoicing an order are tasks that are done right after order entry. An obvious example of a business process from an SFDC perspective would be "schedule and conduct a product demonstration," an activity that is part of the overall sales cycle.

In abstract theory, all of a company's business processes form a giant system that behaves deterministically, so it is perfectly predictable and consistent. In practice, a company that was a perfect system of business processes would be boring[3] to deal with—an inflexible robot that could never delight any customer. Real companies add the human element all the time, because that's what builds a company's reputation and customer loyalty. Think about Nordstrom, or the casual "fun feel" of how Southwest Airlines treats you before, during, and after a flight.

---

2. Although I try to be gender-neutral in this book, we know from Moses Howard that knuckleheads are always male. *Ditz* is the female form, but I haven't found a situation to use that term anywhere in this book.

3. The BPM purists are sure to object to this line of discussion, but let's face it—they're boring, too.

There's another important point to be made about business process linkages, particularly those involving the customer: you can't dictate when or how they are done. The *customer* doesn't care about your company's business processes, let alone want to fit in with their prescribed order. A customer in search of a solution may zigzag across different incomplete business process sequences—and will expect your company to deal with their random behavior. The classic frustration comes when the customer has to give an order expediter the shipping information for the fifth time today—after having jumped from the Web site, to the local store, to the warehouse, and finally into order operations. Business process designs have to anticipate and cope with this kind of possibility.

WHAT TO WATCH OUT FOR

In the early stages of any significant CRM effort, you need to look out for symptoms of process disconnects and incentive misalignments across various parts of sales, marketing, and service/support. Why? Because unifying and automating nonintegrated business processes only exposes or exaggerates contradictions. The place to look for these disconnects is in job descriptions; territory maps; sales channel rules of engagement; marketing programs; lead nurturing campaigns; and other PowerPoint, Visio, and Word documents. Here are some of the problem areas to look out for:

Unclear or Undifferentiated Processes

- Do the job descriptions in marketing (particularly the outbound side) and sales (particularly field marketing and presales) reflect highly differentiated process roles, or are responsibilities only vaguely stated? You want to see unique ownership of goals that can be independently achieved. You're looking for descriptions of cog-works in a machine, not vague statements about teamwork.
- Is there a service level agreement (SLA) between
  - ➥ Lead generation and lead cultivation?
  - ➥ Lead cultivation and inside sales?
  - ➥ Inside sales and the field?
  - ➥ Channel managers and your sales partners?
- Do these SLAs include explicit quality criteria, deadlines, and rejection rules? For example, "If a new opportunity is not explicitly acted on by sales within 4 business days, it is reassigned."
- Do you have a waterfall model that indicates each of the major phases of lead and deal maturation, with approximate times and conversion ratios for each major step?

Incentives

- Are marketing bonuses based on a balance of brand/reputation/loyalty and pipeline creation?
- Are sales compensation plans pushing people in coherent directions across all parts of the sales organization?
- Are quotas and comp plans excessively individualized in different parts of the sales team?
- In commission plans, is "a dollar a dollar," and do direct reps get commission on channel sales in their territory?

Metrics

- Are the metrics for key success factors clearly identified and enforced? You don't want to see metrics that are almost incidental (e.g., "The sales rep will make at least 10 cold calls per week").
- Are the metrics evaluating things that the individual can actually control?
  - ➥ A classic mismetric is to hold outbound marketing responsible for revenue (instead, use "number of sales-accepted leads" or "overall pipeline volume").
  - ➥ Another mismetric is to hold sales reps responsible for customer satisfaction when they don't have anything to do with product quality or service responsiveness (instead, measure "customer complaints about sales" or "number of misconfigured orders").
- Are the metrics enforced by business rules with deadlines or approval cycles? For example, are qualified leads that have gone stale supposed to be returned to marketing? Are deals that haven't moved in 60 days eligible to be closed or pulled back from the channel partner?

Terminology

- For every sales object (`lead`, `contact`, `account`, `opportunity`, etc.), is there a clear description (or even indoctrination document) of what each object means to the marketing and sales process?
- Do people say this: "We convert leads into opportunities"? Double points off if you can't explain the misconception that's baked into those words.
- For every record type and status value for these objects, are there qualification and entry/exit conditions that make it clear that all leads, contacts, accounts, opportunities, and so on, would fit into the scheme, and at least 80% of them would fit into exactly one record type/status value at any one point in time?

- For all of the status fields (for leads/contacts/accounts) and stage fields (opportunities), are the status values clearly defined, and are the entry/exit criteria unambiguous?

Channel Conflict

- Do the outside sales reps view the eCommerce system and the inside reps as diverting their commission dollars?
- Do your reps view your distributors and resellers as competition?
- Are customer renewals handled by an organization that doesn't report into sales?
- Does marketing treat channel partners as an extension of the sales force?

Which Business Processes Do You Need to Think About?

You might think, "Why analyze all this—we can just blow away the cruft that has built up over the years and replace it as we roll out the new system." And you would be wrong.

The whole point of putting SFDC in your company is to make your business processes more efficient and effective, but the changes must be well thought out and measured. It's usually easiest to incrementally improve an existing business process than to start from scratch. A poorly conceived business process will not be saved by automation—users will merely make errors faster and more efficiently. If the SFDC team pushes through an ill-conceived business process change, the credibility of both the new business process and the SFDC system will go down in flames. Business processes are not the place to do casual prototyping and quick rollout of changes.

Since these changes take planning, let's take a top-down look at business processes. At the very highest level, your entire business could be represented by a business process called "stay in business" or "grow profitably." Fine, but not very useful. At the very lowest level, a business process would consist of a checklist of all the things required to do a tiny task, such as answering the customer-support hotline. That's not very useful either.

The whole raison d'être for business process analysis is to understand the steps and actions that make your business work, and that make it work better than the competition. Therefore, there is no universal list of business processes. Instead, you need to develop the taxonomy of processes that best describes the way *your* company does business.[4] Focus on the ones that matter—nobody is going to care about the business process for procuring office supplies.

---

4. Developing a taxonomy that gets you what you need without wasting time sometimes requires the use of an external consultant.

A more useful way of working with business processes is to divide them into the activities that produce revenues—tasks that touch the customer somehow—and the activities that are carried out for purely internal support. **SFDC will add the most value to the revenue-producing business processes.** The business processes that focus only on internal infrastructure can be ignored for all but the most sophisticated and complex SFDC implementations.

Looking at the revenue-bearing business processes, the fastest way to understand them is by following SFDC's application structure.

Salesforce Automation

The core of the revenue process is—surprise!—focusing demand, making quotes, taking orders, delivering goods and services, and collecting funds. SFA includes three main business processes to cover these tasks: sales cycle, sales management, and channel management. Check out Chapter 9 for more on this topic.

Sales Cycle

The sales cycle has two major components: prospecting-to-order formulation and quote to cash. Table 8-1 shows a generic set of business processes for sales in high-technology markets. As you can see, most of the business processes have an initiator—a main actor—and an assisting organization. Once a business process is broken down to the point that it's done entirely by the main actor, it becomes less interesting because there's less interdepartmental activity involved.

Although the list format used in Table 8-1 makes it look like these business processes all follow a linear pattern, in the real world an individual customer may jump around from one business process step to another. The larger and more important the customer, the higher the likelihood that the customer will interact with several business process activities simultaneously. Because this is one of the driving reasons for having a CRM system in the first place, you need to make sure you configure and use SFDC to give all workers the visibility they need to serve the customer in real time, no matter what the circumstance.

The business process elements in Table 8-1 in boldfaced font are more likely to benefit from automation and monitoring (whether by SFDC or some other system) than the ones in standard font. Put another way, they are the processes and activities that an SFDC implementation team should examine first as the highest leverage points for the system. Interestingly, the base SFDC system actually has very few features that directly affect the boldfaced items. This is largely because many of the actual sales process steps can't really be automated—if they could, we'd make all our purchases via automats and online stores.

TABLE 8-1   Sales Cycle Business Process

Activity/Description	Main Actor	Assistant
Prospecting → Order Formulation		
Lead Generation	Marketing	Sales
Prospecting	Sales	Marketing
Qualifying	Sales	Telesales
Demo/proof of concept	Sales	Sales engineering
Focusing value proposition	Sales	Sales engineering
Order formulation/configuration	Sales	Sales engineering
Quote → Cash		
Credit check	Finance	
Quote	Sales	Sales engineering
Negotiation	Sales	Legal
Approval and close	Sales	Finance
Scheduling/expediting delivery	Sales	Distribution
Delivery/fulfillment	Distribution	Field support
Invoicing	Finance	Sales operations
Collection	Finance	
Order management	Sales operations	Distribution
Returns, exchanges, credits	Customer support	Distribution
Renewals	Sales	Sales operations
Upgrades/expansions	Sales	Sales operations

Sales Management

Sales management is the set of processes used by the company to organize its sales personnel and manage their execution of the revenue process. This business process has three major elements: setting up the organization, running it, and working with corporate headquarters. Most of the effort in sales management is in day-to-day monitoring of sales personnel to expedite sales cycles, as shown in Table 8-2.

The boldfaced items in Table 8-2 make it pretty clear that the SFDC system will be a key tool for sales management on a daily basis. Most of these activities can be facilitated by SFDC's "out-of-the-box" features, and they are made even better with add-ons and

TABLE 8-2   Sales Management Business Process

Activity/Description	Main Actor	Assistant
Setting Up the Sales Organization		
Recruiting and training	Sales manager	HR
Assigning accounts and territories	Sales manager	Sales personnel
Assigning quotas	Sales manager	Sales personnel
Designing compensation plans	Sales manager	CEO
Designing channels	Sales manager	Business development
Writing standard contract terms	Sales manager	Legal
Running the Sales Organization		
Adjusting quotas and territories	Sales manager	
Designating key accounts, account teams	Sales manager	Sales personnel
Forecasting revenue	Sales manager	Sales personnel
Monitoring sales cycles	Sales manager	Sales personnel
Account reviews	Sales manager	Sales personnel
Handling escalations	Sales manager	Sales personnel
Scheduling executive calls	Sales personnel	Sales manager
Handling splits, commissions	Sales manager	Sales personnel
Working with Corporate Headquarters		
Executive/board meetings	Sales manager	Executive team
Forecast roll-up, reconciliation	Sales manager	Finance
Budgeting and staff changes	Sales manager	Finance, HR

external system integrations. Although most of SFDC's users are sales reps and their sales cycles will benefit from the greater efficiency and speed made possible by this tool, it's the sales manager who gets much more immediate help from the system. This helps explain why many sales reps are relatively resistant to SFA system implementations and why they may view it as a tool for management spying.[5]

---

5. We put so much emphasis on featurettes and other incentives because they ensure that sales reps have reasons to use the SFDC system early on, before it becomes a deeply helpful tool to them. See Chapters 4 and 6 for further discussion of this topic.

Channel Management

Channel management is the art of harnessing dealers, resellers, and distributors to increase the reach and effectiveness of the selling function. Business processes surrounding the channel are made more difficult by the number of external interfaces—the channel typically *isn't on the company's payroll,* so your employees have little direct control over its behaviors and actions. The channel management business process has three major components: developing partners, maintaining channel infrastructure, and operations. The channel management team handles the activities shown in Table 8-3.

TABLE 8-3   Channel Management Business Process

Activity/Description	Main Actor	Assistant
Developing Partners		
Partner recruitment	Channel manager	Legal
Partner training	Channel manager	Product marketing
Channel planning	Channel manager	
Partner account management	Channel manager	
Maintaining Channel Infrastructure		
Partner communications	Channel manager	Channel marketing
Co-marketing funds	Channel manager	Channel marketing
Referral fees and splits	Channel manager	Finance
Document sharing	Channel marketing	
Channel Operations		
Lead management	Channel manager	Marketing
Deal registration	Channel manager	
Opportunity management	Channel manager	
Forecasting	Channel manager	Finance
Pricing, promotions, and discounting	Channel manager	Channel marketing
Order cycle	Order operations	Channel manager
Shipping and fulfillment	Order operations	Distribution

eCommerce Management

Strictly speaking, eCommerce management is not part of the standard sales function, and it certainly isn't part of standard SFDC. But for an increasing number of companies, the Web now represents the single largest source of transactions (maybe not the most revenues, but surely the largest number of purchases). Because the dollar value of these transactions is typically substantially less than that of transactions completed through the other channels, for profitability it is essential that as much of this business as possible be handled without human intervention. If human intervention is required, it either needs to be very short or highly likely to generate an upsell.

Depending on the organizational structure, the eCommerce workflows are handled by software that is "owned" by sales, the call center, or marketing. Irrespective of the ownership, the sequence of business processes looks like Table 8-4.

Marketing Automation

For the sales cycle to work, there have to be prospects whose interests and needs match the company offerings. In this section, we ignore the vast majority of marketing

TABLE 8-4 eCommerce Business Process

Activity/Description	Main Actor*	Assistant
Customer registration	Customer	Automation
Registration confirmation email	Automation	
Product selection	Customer	Automation
Checkout	Customer	Automation
Special pricing/discounting	Call center	
Payment/credit card selection	Customer	Automation
Special order problems	Call center	
Order confirmation + invoice	Automation	
Order status inquiry	Customer	Automation
Shipment/fulfillment	Distribution	Automation
Order cancellation	Call center	
RMA/warranty incident	Call center	
Renewal/upgrade offer	Automation	Call center

* All of the activities with "call center" as the main actor are "feeders" to dedicated business processes described in the "Call Center" section.

functions (e.g., product management, public relations) to focus on the lead generation process that directly feeds the sales cycle. The lead generation business process has three major components, as illustrated in Table 8-5: product marketing, marketing campaigns, and Internet marketing.

The marketing processes shown in Table 8-5 are embodied in both the Sales Force Automation and Marketing Automation applications in SFDC. The large number of bold-faced items indicates the degree to which marketing people need to interact with the SFDC system on a day-to-day basis. Almost without exception, marketers will need additional add-on tools (as discussed in Chapter 7) to perform their jobs according to best practices (as discussed in Chapter 10).

TABLE 8-5   Lead Generation Business Process

Activity/Description	Main Actor	Assistant
Product Marketing		
Packaging and pricing	Product marketing	Executive team
Value proposition and messaging	Product marketing	Executive team
Customer targeting	Product marketing	Sales management
Marketing Campaigns		
Event selection	Lead generation	Sales
Event execution and management	Lead generation	
Call to action and promotions	Lead generation	Product marketing
Lead collection, filtering, and import	Lead generation	
Lead scoring and routing	Lead generation	Telemarketing
Lead deduping, aging, and demotion	Lead generation	Telemarketing
Event effectiveness assessment	Lead generation	Business analyst
Internet Marketing		
Message sequences	Product marketing	Sales
List rental and merging	Lead generation	
Email blast design/execution	Lead generation	
Internet advertising campaigns	Lead generation	
Internet marketing effectiveness assessment	Lead generation	Business analyst

Call Center

The call center may perform three distinct business processes—telemarketing, inside sales, and order management—even if these processes are performed by the same individuals. Each of these business processes is fairly small but should be treated differently in your analysis. You'll notice the common thread, though: the call center functions have nearly continuous interaction with the SFDC system, and the call center personnel should be the most avid and intense group of users. See Chapter 9 for more discussion of these processes.

Telemarketing

Table 8-6 shows the key business process in telemarketing, an almost entirely outbound process that can be run at its own pace and interrupted without affecting customer satisfaction.

Inside Sales

In contrast to telemarketing, inside sales comprises a range of functions that directly support the sales process, in some cases actually taking orders over the phone. Because the specific duties of inside sales personnel are highly variable, you need to pay attention to subtleties: the inside folks might be authorized to sell only certain products, or to sell only to a certain deal size, or to sell only to a specific customer type (e.g., small- to medium-sized businesses).

The inside sales business process is typically linked with outside sales, telemarketing, and eCommerce business processes, so watch out for tricky handoffs and exceptions in this business process. Most inside sales teams handle only a subset of the functions shown in Table 8-7, but those tasks entail a mix of outbound (paced, planned) calls and inbound (asynchronous, sporadic) activities.

TABLE 8-6 Telemarketing Business Process

Activity/Description	Main Actor	Assistant
Generating scripts for target names	Lead generation	Product marketing
Collecting and distributing lists	Lead generation	Telemarketing
Lead queue management	Telemarketing	Lead generation
Calling and recalling leads	Telemarketing	
Lead nurturing	Telemarketing	Sales
Demoting uninterested/unresponsive names	Telemarketing	Lead generation
Monitoring list yield	Telemarketing	Lead generation
Monitoring campaign effectiveness	Lead generation	Telesales

TABLE 8-7   Inside Sales Business Process

Activity	Main Actor	Assistant
Lead distribution/assignment	Inside sales	
Lead cultivation and qualification	Inside sales	
Appointment setting	Inside sales	Outside sales
Lead conversion	Inside sales	
Opportunity creation	Inside sales	
Opportunity management	Outside sales	Inside sales
Initial price quotes	Outside sales	Inside sales
Order generation	Inside sales	Order operations
Close	Inside sales	Order operations
Order fulfillment	Order operations	Distribution

Order Management

In the order management business process, the call center typically handles inbound calls from customers who are having problems with placing or tracking an order (typically made on the Web) or with product delivery, as shown in Table 8-8. Because these calls

TABLE 8-8   Customer Order Support Business Process

Activity/Description	Main Actor	Assistant
Call routing	Phone rep	Automation
Special quotes and discounts	Phone rep	Marketing
Order entry/modification	Phone rep	Order operations
Order management	Phone rep	Order operations
Expediting or canceling orders	Phone rep	Order operations
Credit card or other payment processing	Phone rep	Finance
Invoicing	Phone rep	Order operations
Schedule shipping/fulfillment*	Phone rep	Distribution

*   This activity is highly variable within companies, let alone across them. Spend enough time to understand the specifics for each type of product or service you deliver, as this may be an entire business process in and of itself. You might want to use a consultant to help disentangle this area.

can happen at any time, they cannot be handled in the same routine, scripted way that outbound call sequences can. It's very important for customer satisfaction that the order management rep can quickly understand the customer situation and get access to whatever system has the most relevant information to resolve the issue.

Customer Service and Support

Personnel in the postsales call center (who are usually not the same people who handle order management or presales issues) handle inbound calls from customers who are having problems with the product. See Chapter 11 for further information on this function. The issue covered by this business function relates to troubleshooting a problem, identifying corrective action, and scheduling either a replacement product or a service call, as shown in Table 8-9.

Separate from the call center that handles first-level customer questions and resolves the "easy problems" is the technical support center that is staffed by support engineers, as shown in Table 8-10. These personnel need to have access to internal case management systems, knowledge bases, bug/fault-tracking systems, and replacement-parts inventory information. Because of contractual obligations and SLAs, the tech support business process tends to have the most complicated workflows, with exceptions, timeouts, and automatic escalations triggered by excessive delays.

TABLE 8-9 Customer Service and Support Business Process

Activity	Main Actor	Assistant
Call and email routing	Phone rep	Automation
Create incident report	Phone rep	
Problem identification	Phone rep	
Dispense customer help	Phone rep	Order operations
Issue RMA or schedule service call	Phone rep	Reverse logistics
Credit card or other payment processing	Phone rep	
Schedule shipping/fulfillment*	Phone rep	Distribution

* This activity is highly variable within companies, let alone across them. Spend enough time to understand the specifics for each type of product or service you deliver, as this may be an entire business process in and of itself. You might want to use a consultant to help disentangle this area.

TABLE 8-10   Technical Support Business Process

Activity	Main Actor	Assistant
Call and email routing	Automation	Tech support rep
Verify entitlement/warranty	Tech support rep	
Identify problem	Tech support rep	
Create/update case	Tech support rep	Automation
Case queue management/prioritization	Tech support rep	Automation
Create/update bug or fault report	Tech support rep	
Case escalation/reassignment	Tech support rep	Tech support manager
Dispense customer help	Tech support rep	
Issue RMA, software patch, or other correction	Tech support rep	Engineering
Credit card or other payment processing	Tech support rep	Finance
Schedule shipping/fulfillment*	Tech support rep	Distribution
Close case/bug	Tech support rep	
Create solution document	Tech support rep	Engineering
Update knowledge base/FAQ	Tech support rep	
Send survey to customer	Tech support rep	

*   This activity is highly variable within companies, let alone across them. Spend enough time to understand the specifics for each type of product or service you deliver, as this may be an entire business process in and of itself. You might want to use a consultant to help disentangle this area.

Analyzing Business Processes

As you can see from Tables 8-1 through 8-10, fully analyzing your company's business processes can quickly become a mind-numbing experience. Business processes are a bit tricky because they are multilevel, almost fractal in nature. According to business process experts, a large corporation may use as many as 1,000 business processes. It's the details of those processes that make your company different and better than the competition. Analyzing, understanding, and documenting any one of those business processes involves many meetings indeed. If you try to handle more than a couple of dozen at a time, you'll never get out of the woods. Instead, your goal should be to **focus your attention on a few business processes that make a difference to the customer.**

Selecting Candidate Processes

CRM projects are supposed to improve support efficiency and sales results, not reengineer the entire corporation. Don't boil the ocean; instead, focus on improving or streamlining *existing* business processes. If you set your sights too broadly, the business process work becomes a heavy-handed exercise in organizational transformation laden with politics and controversy.

So how do you determine the right number and types of business processes for improvement with SFDC? Starting with the boldfaced items in Tables 8-1 through 8-10, look for business processes that have a lot of these characteristics:

- Labor intensive

- Error prone/unreliable

- Involve paper[6]

- Involve manual data entry

- Require (and perhaps depend on) heroic acts or frequent overtime

- Visibly, irritatingly broken

- High on the "squeaky wheel" list

- Cause lost opportunities or waste

- High business value[7]

- Span three or fewer departments

- Not laden with political or organizational baggage

- Easily measured (for improvement)

- Part of someone's agenda (somebody already has a related goal or metric)

Once you identify a few hot prospects for broken business processes, you need to check what's wrong with each of them. Demote the priority of any business process where there isn't a clear idea of how the business process ought to work, where employees have wildly

---

6. Every time a piece of paper is used in a process, it costs the company something in excess of $100 in labor. While this cost may not be measured or obvious, removing the labor and delay involved with paper handling can have amazing effects on an organization's efficiency, quality, and throughput. Ironically, eliminating paper in an organization is a license to print money.

7. Business value isn't just present in items that generate big cash flows: anything that angers a customer or irritates a board member can have high business value, even if only a few dollars are involved.

differing views about the best way to fix it, or where there's major organizational trauma (e.g., no leadership or a gun-to-the-head mentality) already. Promote business processes where it's fairly clear how the process ought to work, but the precise mechanisms and specific behaviors haven't been finalized. These candidates are likely to provide the highest payoffs for your SFDC project.

Analytical Steps

The first step is to very clearly identify the start and the end of the process—that is, the inputs and the outputs of a "black box." Inputs and outputs are things that can be unambiguously measured, such as a status change or a document update. For example, the start of the quote to cash business process is a salesperson's request to issue a quote, and the end of the process is a payment from the customer. Dozens of steps may occur between these endpoints, but don't start looking at any of the details until you firmly define the inputs and outputs of the overall process.

The next step is to have incredibly clear definitions of the actors and objects of a process. An actor is a person or system that carries out an action, and objects are the things or entities that are acted upon. In the quote to cash process, the actors are the sales rep, the customer, order operations personnel, legal personnel, and finance personnel; the objects are the quote, the order, the contract, the invoice, the shipment, and the payment. Some objects go through state changes or transformations as they move from the process input to output—look for these.

These process definitions need to include the semantics for possible states or stages of the objects, such as these items:

- Draft quote

- Approved quote

- Accepted quote

- Revised quote

- Draft contract

- Amended contract

- Accepted contract

- Signed contract

- Filed contract

- Pro forma invoice

- Packing slip

- Shipment bill of lading

- Shipper tracking number

- Final invoice

- Past-due invoice

- Paid invoice

You need to describe the criteria for each of the object's stages, as well as the events, actions, or inactions (e.g., missed deadlines) that trigger movement of the transaction from one stage to another.

Once the analysis team agrees about the meaning of objects and the expected behavior of actors (this can take a while), you can start to diagram the business process. Most teams like to use a whiteboard for this purpose, but you can also use a computer and PowerPoint or Visio as well. There are only a few symbols you have to use, as shown in Figure 8-1. You can get fancier if you like, but the extra complexity of the "official markup languages" often gets in the way of communicating to a nontechnical audience.

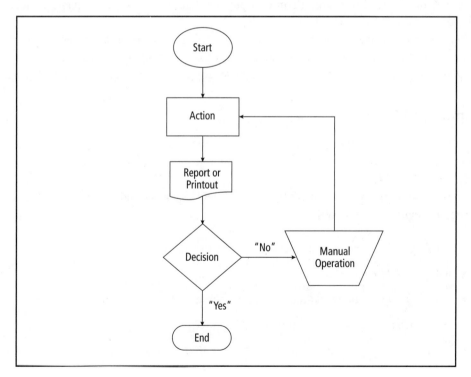

FIGURE 8-1   Essential process diagram symbols

Diagram "AS-IS"

A few diagramming rules have to be followed: the action starts at the top and moves down the page. The flow of activity is always downward unless some sort of remedial or corrective action puts things "back in process" at an earlier step. Decisions are almost always of the yes-or-no variety—and even if they are more subtle than yes or no, they must be incredibly unambiguous (like "route to correct person using the customer's ZIP code"). "Start" almost always is triggered by the ending of another business process, although a customer calling in or other exogenous event can start a business process spontaneously. "End" almost always triggers the next business process, but sometimes it signals an indefinite "wait" state (e.g., wait for customer to complain again).

If your business process is so complicated that it requires several pages to diagram, do one of three things: find a bigger piece of paper, figure out a way to draw smaller blocks, or break down the business process into several subprocesses. Almost always, multipage business process diagrams are hard to follow and signify deeper problems (such as "Why have we made this so complicated?").

The most really interesting actions or decision steps will require some explanatory notes. Keep those notes, triggers, criteria, and other details off the diagram—they'll make it unreadable. Instead, footnote them and put the details on a separate page, either in a free-text document or in a spreadsheet.

Once the team believes that the diagrams of the business processes are an accurate reflection of how things are, get them validated by people in the organization who really are in the know. Sometimes, this act alone can engender suggestions for significant improvement.

Diagram "TO-BE"

Now it's time to create another set of diagrams for how you *want things* to be. The differences between the diagrams are what will drive your business process changes—in people and in SFDC workflows.

In every process are elements that are absolutely essential and others that really don't belong anymore. Ask yourself:

- Is every part of every step really essential to completing the task?

- Are there elements that really don't add value?

- Can this process be rearranged and still achieve the same result?

- What steps could be fully automated?

- What steps could be done by the customers themselves if they had a nice Web page to work with?

- What steps could be skipped altogether?

During this process, keep your attention focused on the outcome (the "what"), not the existing procedures (the "how") and actors (the "who").

Capture the diagrams and annotations in electronic form, and store the files on the project wiki or Google Drive area. You want as many people as possible to see and comment on the workflows, as there may be things that your team didn't know about—such as "unrelated" items that ultimately affect the way the process is run. For example, an audit process may need to examine the work product of a process after the fact, and the business process may need steps or documents to support auditability. This is particularly true if you work for a public company.

Example Business Process Analysis

Let's take a look at an example business process that's almost entirely within SFDC: the lead life cycle.

Start State and End State

The starting state of the lead life cycle is the identification of one or more large groups of people who are in the company's target market. These people may be aware of the company and its offerings, but they have no stated interest in buying. The starting action of the lead life cycle is the lead's participating in a marketing campaign (such as an email blast or tradeshow) or responding to sales outreach (such as cold calling).

The end state of the lead life cycle is a set of fully qualified contacts who are handed off to sales personnel, who can create the opportunities that will form the revenue pipeline. The end of the lead life cycle is the beginning of the sales cycle.

Actors

The main actors in the lead life cycle are people in product marketing, event marketing, and marketing operations (including contractors or agencies), as well as inside sales reps, presales engineers, outside sales reps, partner marketing groups, and all the prospects in the target market.

Objects and Intermediate States

Before we can have a clear discussion about the lead life cycle, we must agree on nomenclature. There's a reasonable amount of semantics-related confusion in the lead-processing world. Here is the standard terminology this book uses as part of its best-practices recommendations:

- **Name:** The identity of someone in the target audience. You can buy names on a list (e.g., all doctors in North America or all attendees at a tradeshow), but names are of very little value because they neither know nor care about your company and its products or services. A name is, at best, a receptive ear. But the probability of names being actively interested in your company's products is so low that you should communicate with names only via automation and bulk Internet media. The point here is not that your firm should spam people but rather that it should develop a sequence of interesting, relevant material to send in a low-key "drip marketing" campaign designed to make the name more knowledgeable about your product category and increasingly interested in engaging with your company.

- **Lead:** Someone who has specifically expressed interest in your company's product or service, typically by attending an event or registering on the Web site. We know a little bit more about leads than we do about names, but typically the only thing we know for certain at the time of registration is a valid email address. If the lead has come back to your Web site or taken some other follow-up action, all of those details should be recorded in your marketing automation and SFA system so you can do some behavioral targeting and lead scoring. We urge everyone to use campaigns to cover any possible activity or response that a lead could be involved with.

- **Qualified lead:** Someone who could reasonably participate in a sales cycle, and we know this because somebody in your company has had a highly directed conversation with that individual about his or her level of interest, requirements fit, budget, and timeline. Typically, a qualified lead should be converted to a contact in a matter of hours after a follow-up call by sales personnel. If the sales conversation doesn't go well, the qualified lead should be disqualified as bogus.

- **Rejected lead:** A lead that has been rejected by sales as being unqualified, or a contact that has been identified as uninterested or incompetent to participate in a sales cycle. Rejected leads should still be given the best treatment by marketing, but they will be ignored by sales until they have done something new to prove their worthiness of human attention.

- **Contacts:** Contacts come in four flavors: a qualified lead that has been converted to initiate a sales cycle, a person who works for a company that is already in a sales cycle, a person who works in a company we've done business with in the past, or a person who works at a company we're targeting for future business. Unfortunately for zealous supporters of the named account model of selling, these definitions get very blurry. People get paid the big bucks to sort them out.

- **Dead contacts:** Contacts that have left the prospect account, have changed jobs and are no longer relevant as potential customers, or have told us to stop contacting them. Dead contacts should not be deleted but should simply be flagged as no longer relevant (this flagging will make them disappear from the sales rep's view, but they'll still be available for historical analysis).

The contact is the end state for the lead. Nevertheless, the contact goes through several subsequent status changes as part of the sales cycle:

- **Opportunities:** Indicators that a fully qualified contact should be pursued or that an existing customer is interested in some additional product. Many opportunities will be immediately closed if the sales representative discovers that there is no current sales potential. Only after an opportunity has been accepted by a rep as a genuine sales cycle candidate will a dollar amount or probability be assigned to it.

- **Customers:** Contacts who work for an account that has a contractual relationship with us and who have paid us something.

- **References:** Customers who are foolhardy enough to have their names bandied about in the press. References require special protections to prevent them from being overused by both sales and marketing personnel alike.

Lead Cultivation Workflow Narrative

Most of the early cultivation of names is focused on increasing their level of interest to the point that they really qualify to be leads. The workflows for names and demoted leads should be nearly 100% automated, using clever combinations of email blasts, Web site materials, and recorded Webinars. Your marketing automation system should be managing this communication flow for you and maintaining behavioral scores for each individual.

Once a lead is sufficiently warm to deserve human attention, marketing should almost never be involved in contacting that person. Representatives from inside sales (or telesales or telemarketing) should be doing the outbound phone calls, demonstrations, and qualification steps. In most organizations, the final decision on qualification is made by the sales rep, but the appointment for that call is made by the inside sales team. The processes involved with nurturing and cultivating a lead's interest tend to span several weeks or months, and the specific steps usually aren't worth documenting. But at some point, the lead matures and expresses deep interest in your company's products.

Once a `lead` is fully qualified, it should be a matter of moments before it is `converted` into a `contact`. `Conversion` does an amazing array of things in the SFDC system, and the user is given a few options at this time. At `conversion` time (and we recommend that this step also be handled by the inside sales group for consistency), best practices are to create a new `opportunity` (typically, for $0 at 0% probability, unless the `contact` is being attached to an `opportunity` already in progress) and to attach a `contact role` and a `campaign` to it (to support sales and marketing effectiveness analyses).

The `opportunity` is handed over to the direct sales team and serves as the input to their sales cycle process. `Leads` should never be handed directly to sales, and even after conversion to `contacts`, the real hand-off is the `opportunity` that will turn into money someday.

What if the `contact` turns out to be bogus or falsely qualified? Never, ever, ever[8] delete the `contact` or `opportunity`. Instead, set its status flag as "rejected by sales." If you are clever in your report designs, the rejected items won't mess up any operational metrics, but they will provide quantitative feedback to the marketing and lead cultivation functions.

Moving to the Workflow Diagram

The preceding narrative might be good enough for the people involved, but it contains several areas of ambiguity and interpretation. It is not detailed or precise enough to guide the SFDC development team.

The act of drawing the workflow will likely expose several ambiguous or troublesome areas, forcing the team to break down the process into further subprocesses so that it can be turned into a checklist or an SFDC workflow. Ask questions "around the edges" of the narrative to make sure that the workflow can handle all situations and exceptions. For example, the narrative doesn't mention how leads are handled internationally, how they are handled for partners, how they are processed by the marketing automation system, whether different kinds of leads are distinguished for different categories of products, and other important issues. You will often find during the diagramming process that a single narrative may require several nearly parallel workflows to handle variations that were missed while writing the narrative.

In developing the workflow diagram, it's almost always best to have a meeting of the subject-matter experts in a conference room with a *lot* of whiteboards. While developing and double-checking the diagram, do not eat doughnuts or drink a bunch of coffee:[9] people will get overly argumentative and focus too much on unimportant details. It is usually best to have a meeting facilitator with a big-picture perspective, a very analytical mind, patience, and legible handwriting. Business process consultants are a special breed, but they can save you a lot of time and frustration.

Figure 8-2 shows the lead life cycle described in the earlier narrative. Due to the space constraints of this page, the figure shows just the promotion/qualification/demotion part of the narrative. Check out www.SFDC-secrets.com to get more complete example diagrams from various business process analyses.

---

8. Not ever? Nope. Deleting records obliterates forensic information that helps identify problems in business processes and systems. The larger and more complex your system, the more damage it does to delete records.
9. Seriously, consuming this stuff can mess up team thinking and lead to contentiousness and nervous energy.

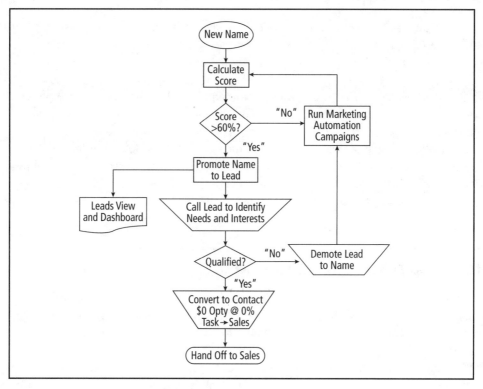

FIGURE 8-2   Example lead life cycle business process diagram

WHEN WORLDS COLLIDE

Unfortunately, in analyzing real-world business processes, the SFDC team may discover collisions of business processes—instances where two supposedly exclusive business processes appear to be triggered in parallel. This can happen in sales, order management, or support, particularly during exception handling and escalations.

This situation is never supposed to happen, so you need to figure out whether there's just a misunderstanding (a terminology, semantic, or procedural disagreement) or a logical conflict (a contradiction or a redundancy).

If a logical conflict exists, the team needs to identify and analyze the ambiguity that lies at the conflict's core. This is most quickly done in a meeting with a walk-through of the business process, looking for situations where an object's state is "gray" rather than "black or white." In cases where an object may have several valid states (as embodied in a pick list or calculation threshold), look for conditions where the object can have more than one state at a time.

Some logical conflicts are caused by frustrated customers who try to get answers by going down several paths at once, abandoning those that are unresponsive. These "dangling Inquiries" need to be resolved either through a timeout (such as "Nonresponse of customer within 48 hours closes the case with state 'resolved'") or logical cleanup (such as "If customer already has an inbound request in the Web site, close that request and move any relevant data into the call center part of the system"). These logical resolutions can be handled either as checklist items (for rare, high-value situations) or as system integration improvements (for frequent, low-value situations).

How Much Should Be Changed?

In analyzing business processes, it can be tempting to fundamentally improve things by really reworking a broken area of the business. However, redesigning from a blank slate is almost never a good idea—it's more pragmatic to make incremental changes in a business process that offers the biggest bang for the buck.

This recommendation is not just a consequence of the technical risk involved; rather, it reflects the reality that there can be a lot of politics involved with business process change. In some cases, you'll be changing the daily tasks of workers—or even changing their jobs entirely. This transformation can lead to a lot of questions, endless meetings, and user resistance even if the workers are given orders from on high. It is *critically important* to review the "before" versus "after" business process with affected managers at all levels before finalizing the recommended changes. You may want to include HR personnel in the discussion, particularly if jobs will be redesigned in a big way.

Refining or streamlining an existing business process involves a lot less uncertainty than starting from scratch. Plus, if you are upgrading something that exists, it is easier to identify valid comparative metrics (e.g., 20% fewer errors or 10% decrease in labor costs).

Improving two or three clumsy business processes by the initial SFDC go-live date is probably sufficient to prove the business case for the project. As with the rest of the project, best practices call for making incremental business process adjustments every quarter or two after the initial go-live date.

That said, sometimes larger business process changes are required. For example, there may be new regulatory requirements (like those wrought by the Sarbanes-Oxley Act or Dodd-Frank bill) or mandates from customers (such as Wal-Mart or Boeing) that must be implemented by a deadline. In these cases, you may have to make dramatic changes to existing business processes or design new ones from scratch.

Best Practices with Business Process Redesign

Although entire books have been written on business process redesign,[10] being aware of a few generalities can help keep the project within reason:

- **Maintain appropriate simplicity:** If the diagrams are to be comprehensible, they cannot cover an entire wall. Process steps in the diagram should be at the level of a single person's (or fixed group's) unwavering task, activity, or decision. Within any of the process steps on the diagram, there may be a checklist of a dozen or more items needed to complete the task items, but these actions should be documented as notes rather than being shown as discrete lower-level steps. On the other hand, there are two sure signs that a process step probably needs to be split: the activity must be handed off to another person to be completed, or the checklist for that task contains a "branch."

- **Work on processes that are naturally linked:** Assuming you will rework two or three business processes, it's better that those processes be linked in some way, rather than be disparate and autonomous. The learning curve (the effort you need to expend in surveys, discussions, and meetings) involved with really fixing a business process can represent a significant amount of the total effort, so you want to leverage your learning across teams as much as possible.

- **Focus on profitable revenue:** For an SFDC-related business process, the goal of the redesign should be streamlining the revenue generation part of the business—specifically, reducing the time and number of errors associated with that process. Although cost reductions and efficiencies almost certainly result as a by-product, don't make them the true focus of the improvement. The net result of the business process change should be happier customers and richer salespeople,[11] as these are the highest-leverage ways of improving company profitability.

- **Get executive championship:** Early on, cultivate support from a specific executive for the process change. Even the most worthwhile process improvement stands little chance of overcoming natural resistance if there isn't an executive pounding on the table about it at staff meetings. This goes double if somebody's job responsibilities are going to be changed.

- **Remove paper:** One of the deep ironies of computerization is that it has increased the consumption of paper in the office. I have nothing against the stockholders of

---

10. The author believes that these books are too dull for you to actually read.
11. This statement assumes that the salespeople are on commission. If they aren't, this sentence should be translated to "bigger and faster sales cycles," which is more accurate but won't be as exciting to the sales VP who is probably paying for this project.

Hewlett-Packard, Xerox, or Ricoh, but in business process design, paper is a sign of very poor automation. Paper is too often used as the way to transfer information from one step to another or even from one system to another. (I can't tell you the number of times my firm has discovered people rekeying data.) Although paper printouts must exist for signatures, legal documents, or reviews of really large amounts of text or data, in most cases an on-screen display of information is faster and more accurate. Be willing to "overinvest" in removing paper from business processes,[12] as this step removes a lot of hidden costs, errors, and wasted time. Replacing paper with on-screen forms also makes the workflows much easier to monitor, measure, and improve.

- **Increase information sharing:** Although some information must be carefully partitioned and protected, the goal of redesigning the business process is to increase the amount of information that can be easily shared. If both sides of a conversation have instant access to all relevant data, arguments can be resolved rapidly and fixes implemented immediately. Better collaboration also means faster identification of unintended consequences, such that problems are fixed before they have time to fester with resentment and politics. Finally, better information sharing means more meaningful measurements and a higher chance of congruent goals and behaviors.

- **Minimize manual exceptions:** Although human judgment is what sets great businesses apart from the competition, exceptions need to be handled in a methodical way in your business processes. Managing by exception—spending time on the variances and truly unusual cases—is a best practice because it forces you to systematize and streamline how you handle 90% or more of the business process. But managing by exception should still be a designed part of the process—the unusual actions should be handled as a formal branch on the business practice chart. Of course, not every step of the exception handling can be done via automation, but this activity should still be systematized and measured so that the organization doesn't spend too much time on the unusual cases. At all costs, avoid the situation where handling certain customer situations means "jumping off the chart," with a person solving the problem in a unique and undocumented way. Even if the customer is satisfied by heroic action, down this path lies gross inefficiency, inability to manage, and risk of legal problems.[13]

---

12. The investment will be in systems integration, data validation, user-input screens, and SFDC approval workflows.

13. Manual exceptions in the forecasting, quoting, closing, and revenue recognition processes make it very hard for a company to pass a Sarbanes-Oxley Act audit. Visits by SEC investigators are not happy occasions.

- **Combine individual steps:** In reworking a business process, the goal is not to speed up the execution of silly steps but to make the steps simpler, more sensible, and more systematic. As you're interviewing workers to understand precisely what they do, watch out for activities that seem clumsy, out of order, repeated (listen for red flags like "and then I have to double-check that . . ."), patchworked, or worked around (listen for red flags like "I have to watch out for . . ." or "sometimes"). Spend time investigating the root causes of these unusual activities and see if they can be made more regular by correcting problems and combining the "microsteps."

- **Validate business rules:** When your company started out, every business process was simple and straightforward: they had to be. But over time, everything became more complicated. The most complex and broken business processes are typically the oldest ones, having become gnarled messes as layer upon layer of business rules, standards, and executive mandates were added to "cover the problem" as the years went by. Business rules that were set up by long-gone managers are still in place, with new rules implemented as a patchwork. The single highest-leverage goal for business process reengineering is to eliminate obsolete, redundant, or even contradictory rules, policies, and standards. When you spot a convoluted mess, it usually exists to help the company avoid some costly mistake of the past. On further examination, you may discover that this mistake can't happen again anyway, so all the protective cruft can simply be removed. If Clayton Christensen is correct in saying that "form doesn't follow function: form follows failure," then working to expose and expunge artifacts of old failures is a noble quest. If you must keep complex rules, make sure that they provide something of beauty or value to the customer rather than just avoid some hypothetical negative.

- **Optimize globally:** This statement is fancy-talk for "Do the right thing for the company, not just your department." In falsely "fixing" a business process, you might make it much easier and faster for one department to achieve its goals at the expense of another department. The point is to make the *entire system* (the company as a whole) work better, faster, and more pleasantly *for the customer.* If you think globally, the "customer" is anyone who buys from the company, sells to the company, or invests in the company.

- **Keep it small:** Even though you should be considering the big-picture effects, do not attempt to boil the ocean. Work on a business process that's small enough to get your mind around and fix in a few weeks.

- **Bake in measurements and thresholds:** Any changes to a business process should try to establish new metrics that allow for follow-on analysis and improvement. If there is a clear metric that is meaningful to the customer (such as "how long it took the company to get back to the customer about a problem"), add thresholds and alerts to the new process so that management can see problem areas before they boil over. SFDC can be configured to send emails, set up `tasks`, and start `workflows` when thresholds are exceeded or minimum standards are not achieved. These metrics should not be viewed as micromanaging but as freeing people to apply management by exception more broadly.

- **Accommodate market-specific requirements:** Some markets have special requirements for pricing, invoicing, and revenue-handling processes. For example, sales to government agencies may involve specific approval cycles, paperwork, and discount schedules. Powerful customers may have "most-favored nation" contractual stipulations that require specific approval cycles for particular product discounts. In the delivery and services part of the business, certain requirements and SLAs may be enforced only for particular customers.

- **Understand and account for international variations:** Expect to find significant variations of business processes in different national operations in the company. The most obvious differences will relate to currency, tax, and legal regulations that affect many parts of the sales and revenue-handling processes. More subtly, the trade laws and commercial customs may be quite different and imply different `workflows`, `page layouts`, and `reports` than for domestic operations. Further, marketing processes may have to be different to comply with privacy and consumer protection laws in Europe versus North America. Finally, management in each country is very likely to have local directives that diverge from the norm—sometimes causing significant process differences.

- **Gain approval before reimplementing the business process:** Involve as many subject-matter experts as possible while you are analyzing and modifying the business process, but don't actually implement the changes until you've gotten approval from each of the organizations affected by the business process. Make sure that you are not going to eliminate an activity or decision that the business process "before you" (the one that triggers the start of the one you're working on) or "after you" (the one that starts when yours is complete) depend on. It's a good idea to perform walk-throughs of the business process, beginning two business processes before yours and ending two business processes after yours, to make sure your change will not create a new problem. These walk-throughs should be conducted in a single meeting, if practical, to make sure you haven't missed anything. The actual change approvals can be done entirely by email, but do not skip the formality of getting a sign-off.[14]

---

14. After all, your changing of a business process should itself be a business process rather than an unpredictable act.

Making the Changes

You've identified the right business processes to change, you've analyzed them and designed process improvements, you've created diagrams of the business processes (before versus after), and you've gotten explicit permission to make the changes. Now it's time to set overall metrics to use as criteria for gauging the impact of your business process changes.

These metrics need to be objective, realistic, and directly related to the business process area targeted for improvement. Make sure the metrics are achievable—at least in theory—and connected to relevant business results. Do some devil's advocate work to make sure they aren't easily gamed and do not create perverse incentives.

Following are example metrics for a business process change:

- Incremental throughput increase

- Reduction in cycle time

- Revenue increase

- Customer satisfaction improvement

- Reduction in customer or business partner complaints

- Reduction in overtime or improvement in worker satisfaction

- Reduction in error rate/rework

- Waste reduction

- Labor cost reduction

- Expenditure reduction

I can't stress enough the importance of metrics in managing change: they help justify investments, they give people meaningful goals to strive for, and they show how much better the company is doing now than it was before the change. Good metrics also let you know when you've succeeded.

Within SFDC, several areas of the system are likely to require changes. Data input changes are handled through new `page layouts`, and user-specific (or process-step-specific) input changes are implemented using `record types`. Data entries will need to be validated with new formulas and thresholds. `Triggers` will need to be established or modified and `workflows` established. `Approval processes`—both the items being approved and the approval path—will almost certainly need to be changed.

Outside of SFDC, business process changes may require changes to system integration parameters. In some cases, code in external systems will need to be written or modified.

As the system modifications are made, support for the old business process will almost certainly degrade or even disappear. For a while, the automation support that workers are used to will not exist, so they will have to handle an increasingly manual process. Consequently, it is important to get the changes made, tested, validated, and deployed quickly.

Actually implementing the "people side" of a process change consists of developing and documenting new semantics for objects, activities, and thresholds. Users need to be trained about any new wording or naming standards, procedures, rules, or caveats. To help users make the transition, the SFDC team should create new checklists or cheat sheets for the people involved.

After the Changes Are Made

Let's face it: Amazon doesn't list 16,539 books on the topic of "change management" because it can be taken for granted. The most notable failures of the business process reengineering (BPR) movement of the 1990s were largely due to change management and people issues. If you haven't already done so, you should glance at Chapter 5's discussion of the topic.

After changes have been made, the modified business processes need to be monitored for their performance against the metrics set up. Pay particular attention to error rates/rework and to the "soft side" that you won't have explicit measurements for:

- Unsolicited customer feedback (emails, Yelp, etc.)

- Company reputation metrics (talk to your marketing folks about tools to assess this)

- Internal bellyaching

- Political noise

- Number and tone of feature requests to further improve the business processes

Review sessions should initially take place on a daily basis, with corrective actions being applied as rapidly as possible to minimize rework. The frequency of these reviews should rapidly diminish as variances and unexpected consequences subside, but some of the issues won't be uncovered until you have completed an entire quarterly cycle. So do not try to start another significant business process change cycle in a directly connected area for at least 90 days, and postpone it even longer if you discover persistent errors in the business process you just reworked. If you discover errors in the new business process, validate your original business process diagram and annotations, make sure that the changes were implemented in SFDC and any supporting system, and take whatever corrective actions are required. Do not let problems persist for more than a few weeks, as they will undermine the system credibility and irritate users if they linger for too long. Even if you can't correct things quickly, make sure that users get the clear impression that there is an acknowledged problem, a plan to fix it, and a competent team working to a schedule.

GETTING THE MOST FROM **SFDC**

- Think of your entire company as a series of business processes that are linked together to achieve the corporate goals.
- Find a handful of business processes that need to be reworked to improve sales, profitability, or customer satisfaction.
- Break those business processes down into small enough chunks that can be described and diagrammed on a few pages.
- Create a "before versus after" set of diagrams that highlight the steps that need to be upgraded. Get these business process changes approved by your champions before you start to reengineer them.
- Implement the changes in SFDC and outside systems.
- Give users cheat sheets about the new way of doing things.
- Build metrics into SFDC and other systems to measure areas for improvement.

FOR SMALL COMPANIES

- Almost certainly, focus on the revenue pipeline first.
- Make sure that credible people from both marketing and sales are working on the process narratives and diagrams.

FOR LARGE ENTERPRISES

- If you already have some business process experts at your firm, get them involved with your project—at least as mentors for the SFDC team.
- Avoid using BPML, UML, or other "standard" markup languages. Keep the diagrams simple!
- Beware of politics if jobs are going to change. Tightly manage the flow of information to avoid a deluge of noise.[15]

---

15. I think it was Winston Churchill who said, "A lie gets halfway around the world before the truth gets its pants on."

PART III

Best Practices

CHAPTER 9

Best Practices for Sales

Sales reps are coin-operated.

—S. Nelson French, Sales VP

T his chapter is the centerpiece in explaining how to get the most out of your SFDC system, because the system is, first and foremost, intended for sales users, from individual reps and sales administrators up to the VP or COO.

The first word of Salesforce.com is "sales" for a reason. SFDC's corporate culture, value system, and even engineering priorities are totally focused on making salespeople productive and successful. But killer sales productivity doesn't happen just by buying SFDC. You need to put in some planning and effort.

Done right, SFDC affects every single member of your team—even your admin. To make the best practices more accessible, we've organized them by the job titles (or at least functions) of the key members of your sales team. Even if you've got a small organization or think you've already got it covered, at least skim the whole chapter: you'll find useful tips throughout even if the section header doesn't exactly match your job title.

Universal Best Practices

When it comes to sales management, there aren't too many best practices that apply across every industry and sales/channel organization. Nevertheless, there are some critical success factors that consistently hold true, even if they aren't practiced everywhere:

- Management should look at marketing and sales collectively as a single business process: the revenue engine. There's an up-front investment (e.g., salaries, programs, travel, customer dinners) and a payoff (revenue). The goal is to reduce the cost of customer acquisition while meeting the company's growth objective.[1]

---

1. This goal isn't the same as "shorten sales cycles," because the point is to obtain the sales cycle with the best business yield—which isn't necessarily the shortest one.

Management should be looking to maximize customer life-cycle profitability, not simply get more sales. The trick for both of these key success factors is to balance the investments in marketing, Web sales, inside sales, channel sales, and field sales. The classic mistake is to invest too much in direct sales without having enough real, profitable deals for them to go after. You'll definitely want to set up SFDC metrics to help you see each of your channels' performance and profitability. Then, use incentives to optimize your distribution network.

- The key for better sales productivity is to relieve the reps of busywork and overhead meetings so they can spend more time selling and working on the most promising accounts. The 80–20 rule[2] definitely applies here, and SFDC can do a lot to improve reps' productivity by helping them manage their time and focus on the accounts that will really pay off—while disqualifying the duds as early as possible.

- Although growth typically comes from getting new customers, *profit* definitely comes from repeat business. The glory and sex appeal of revenue growth may happen from hiring the most aggressive reps to break open new accounts, but that kind of selling is rarely the most profitable. Industry statistics show that upselling and expanding existing customers requires only one-third to one-tenth the cost and effort of acquiring new customers. *Of course* it is important to get new customers, but overfocusing on them just burns cash. You'll want to evaluate this area carefully with SFDC metrics (that examine both the sales and the customer support function) so you can understand the growth and health of your customer franchise. For example, SFDC reports can quickly identify the frequency of orders from a customer, the overall upsell business (percentage of total dollars, percentage of total deals, and percentage of total profitability), and the customer support renewal percentage.

- It's critically important that marketing, sales development, inside sales, and outside sales personnel are all using the same model(s) for your business. This model doesn't have to be a complex sales methodology—it can simply be a description of the life cycle of the company's pipeline, the waterfall of sales stages, and the conversion rates along the way. Things tend to fall apart when there is disagreement about the metrics, responsibilities, workflow, and semantics of the sales model. If you can't agree on what a qualified `lead` is or what triggers creation of an `opportunity`, how can you optimize and streamline anything about revenue production?

- If you have three sales channels, you are likely to have three sales models—and SFDC should be integrated so it fully supports each of them.

---

2. In most selling organizations, 80% of the revenues come from 20% of the customers. So it's important to focus everyone's effort on those one in five customers that will really make a difference to your results.

- The marketing and sales team needs to work as a lead-processing machine, with clear policies and systematic follow-up. Identify the optimal response patterns for new `leads` and repeat visitors, and enforce the right behaviors with incentives and measurements. Look for the number of untouched `leads`, the time to first touch, and the conversion ratio percentages; put in `workflows` and `alerts` so that `leads` don't go cold. A Marketing Automation System really helps with this.

- `Leads` and visibility are nice, but in and of themselves they don't put bread on the table. Focus the marketing effort on the things that start sales cycles and close deals—such as customer referencability and testimonial quotes—and pay less attention to arbitrary statistics that are easily gamed. Set up SFDC metrics that highlight sales-cycle starts that have directly resulted from marketing activity.

- `Opportunities` must be managed systematically with checkpoints and alerts to ensure that deals don't go sideways or backward. A global `forecast` should be done on a weekly basis, and the SFDC system should contain enough information so that you could do a mini account review at a moment's notice. Look for `workflows` and `alerts` that ensure key players know the state of every deal, and set up serious pipeline metrics and sales-rep scorecards. There should be no mystery about how each territory will make its quarterly number.

- The SFDC system needs to act as a public kiosk showing the current situation of all deals. It also needs to be *the* place for all people working on the `account` to find out what's going on, and where they can post updates so everyone knows the state of play. The goal is to get away from using internal email as the way to handle action items and updates. Let's face it: we're all overloaded with email and nobody can find *all* the relevant emails all the time. By using a kiosk model of `opportunity` and `account` information, all the information is available to everyone equally and at the time they *need to know* it (which is rarely the time when the typical email would be sent). SFDC makes it easy to keep the entire sales, marketing, support, and executive team in sync and to bring new resources on board without a lot of ramp-up time.

- For improved responsiveness and greater professionalism, get your field reps using mobile selling tools. On a smartphone or (better) an iPad or Android tablet, the reps will have answers at their fingertips. Beyond the "wow" value, avoiding the "let me get back to you on that" is a great way to shorten the sales cycle.

- To leverage the SFDC system most effectively, it should be configured to be a well-integrated CRM system, not just a standalone SFA system. That said, there are two things to watch out for: keep the system simple, and question the need for each external integration. There are a variety of ways to satisfy requirements, and integrations can be costly and buggy. Read the section in Chapter 7 on this topic.

- Recognize that your troops will whine that SFDC makes things harder or takes more time, even if the system actually saves them time and improves things for the company. Pay attention to negative feedback about change only if it grows over time. Have someone (e.g., a well-connected administrator) listen for scuttlebutt.

- For at least the first year, SFDC should be driven and owned by the sales organization. Not marketing. Not finance. Not IT. Although all of these departments can help with operations and expertise, only the sales department has the urgency and the firepower required to make an SFDC system work to optimize revenue.

- Unless the company is a very small, early-stage operation, you are going to need SFDC's `enterprise edition`. It's more expensive, but it is the only way to achieve the best practices described in this chapter.

- Sales reps' behavior follows the incentives that are set out for them in the commission plan. They aren't going to follow jaw-boning, artificial mandates (particularly from marketing or finance), or system rules. For a powerful commission plan, make sure it is tightly aligned with the financial goals of the corporation.[3] To make it really effective, keep the plan stable and simple—if you use more than three metrics to drive behaviors, everyone is likely to become confused. Make sure that the SFDC system is seen as being an aid to reps making their numbers!

For more exciting news in this area, check out newsletters like *The Taber Report* and *Sirius Decisions*.

People Buy from People

CRM systems do a lot to systematize the sales cycle and make it more visible so it can be optimized. Well and good, but that's all inward-looking. What about connecting with the customers?

Social media present a totally new way to access people who care about your product category—your community of interest. For example, if you make video accessories, you can find tens of thousands of enthusiasts on just a few sites. You can quickly find what's important to them, and whom they compare you to. And you can see your brand reputation in print, in real time. According to dozens of studies, customer recommendations are among the top three most powerful influencers of purchase decisions—way more credible than anything your team will ever say or do.

---

3. For even better reinforcement, make sure that marketing and customer service don't have incentive bonuses that pull in the other direction. I've seen it.

Okay fine, social media are important—but in plenty of industries (and geographies) it's not clear exactly *which* social medium will work to make selling easier and more successful. The starting point is knowing your target market and identifying which social communities they are likely to participate in. A first approximation is LinkedIn for professionals and Facebook for consumers, but you'll need to go a lot deeper than that if you want an effective social selling strategy. Do your customers pay attention to Twitter? Yelp? Google+? This is one of those areas where the marketing folks can actually give you good information.

So let's start with the simple stuff: how social media provides you with valuable clues about leads and contacts you've never met before. For example, check out a person in LinkedIn before you pick up the phone to give you a solid profile (who they are, what they've been doing) and an idea of what's important to them (from their recent posts). Of course, you have to be connected to them in the social network, but through friend-of-a-friend (FOAF) connections you should be able to get access in a day or two.

Social media can also help you solve a lot of selling problems just by listening. SFDC's `social media monitoring` system (originally Radian6) is really helpful for under-standing market sentiment—the buzz (positive or negative) about your company and its products. This can be brought even more into focus with Facebook or LinkedIn pages for your company—so if you don't already have those, you should. This can make for an early-warning system when it comes to competitive attacks, heightened price sensitivity, or even brand-reputation problems.

Moving a social media participant to a lead—well, that's mainly the job of marketing campaigns. But if you find a specific member of a community who's clearly interested in your product or service, reach out to him or her directly. **The key is to not pitch to this person in the public medium of the social community—most people will react nega-tively if you push hard.** Instead, offer relevant information via email, and try to move the community member to a private conversation.

As the lead progresses through the funnel, you should be using SFDC's free `chatter` system at every stage of the prospecting, selling, and renewal/upsell cycle. When used purely internally, `chatter` helps your team collaborate better, particularly if they work in remote offices. `Chatter` really helps with problem solving, objection handling, deal-win tactics, competitive responses, and other areas where sales and other field reps can really learn from each other's victories. `Chatter` isn't just an IM system, it's a way to identify and solve problems directly related to accounts and deal-wins, and to keep all the conversations in context, visible right from the relevant SFDC record. Unlike email, with `chatter` you can see the narrative and the opportunity data at the same time. SFDC also lets you see LinkedIn, Facebook, Twitter, and other connections for any `contact`, reinforcing the customer record with external information feeds and real-time updates.

You can take `chatter` one step further with existing customers and partners by inviting them to secure, private `chatter` groups to help them solve their problems. The ongoing conversation between support, account reps, and the customer takes relationship building to the next level—much more intimate (and measurable, and useful) than email or phone logs can ever be. (If you want to know more, check out the section "What's All This Noise about Chatter?" in Chapter 13.)

The top-line message is that commerce is a conversation,[4] so every communication your company has with prospects and clients is a chance to move the ball down the field. Effective social selling means having visibility into the social network conversations that naturally occur and harnessing those conversations to build reputation, recommendations, and purchase intentions.

Job One: Define and Document the Sales Model

Revenue generation is a business process, and it needs to be managed as one. Of course, sales owns the number, but the business process of revenue generation spans most of marketing, all of sales, a bit of finance, and much of customer service. Although some elements of the revenue business process hold true for all sales organizations, the particulars of how *your company* grows prospects into customers and customers into repeat business depends on the company and its target markets.

Before you can apply any of the recommendations in this chapter, you need to develop a model of how your company's revenue generation process works.[5] Spend a bit of time (it can be done in an afternoon or two[6] if you're serious) defining and documenting your revenue model. Involve sales, marketing, and support managers in the process, and encourage argument until the model is complete. If the model isn't realistic or consistent across the organization, each group will point to the others as the "revenue prevention department."

Start with a simplifying assumption: marketing should own names (leads that aren't good enough even for nurturing by sales development),[7] marketing and sales development should jointly own `leads`; inside and outside sales should own `contacts`, `accounts`, and `opportunities`; and customer service should own `cases`. Sales development is assumed to handle all lead cultivation, nurturing, and qualification so that the inside and

---

4. Check out the *The Cluetrain Manifesto*, the classic book on the bedrock of community marketing and social selling.

5. Just saying, "Go out and sell," is not a sales model. Developing a coherent, working revenue model and sales process is what the VP of sales is paid to do.

6. Or six.

7. Throughout this chapter, the term *sales* is used when discussing outside sales or direct field sales representatives. *Inside sales* refers to people who do sales activities entirely over the phone; these people may have job titles such as telemarketing, telesales, sales associate, or sales support. *Sales development* refers to people who do not carry a number, but whose job is to nurture leads and focus the prospect's interest to the point where they want to take a meeting—and will be a good use of the sales rep's time.

field reps can spend their time on the most highly leveraged part of their job: expanding the size of the deal while increasing the probability of winning.

It doesn't matter whether you use a drawing, a bulleted list, or a narrative to depict the model. What does matter is that your model be written down and that it answer these questions:

WHAT'S THE BOLDFACED FONT MEAN?

When an item below appears in boldfaced font, it's the best practice for most sales organizations. But your organization may not even have a functional group with that title, so adjust the idea accordingly. If there's a good reason that the answer is something else for your organization, write down the reasons in the description of your sales model.

- Who are the company's target customers? (brief written description needed for each product line or channel)

- Who is responsible for lead generation? (**marketing, sales development,** inside sales, or sales)

- Who schedules Webinars and other broad outreach events? (**marketing,** sales development, inside sales, or sales)

- Who handles inbound inquiries? (marketing, **sales development,** inside sales, or sales)

- Who makes the first call to prospects? (marketing, **sales development,** inside sales, or sales)

- How are territories defined? How are overlays defined? What are the rules of engagement (ROE) for territory conflicts within the company?

- Which kinds of channel partners does the company leverage? What percentage of the business is brought in by each type of channel?

- What kind of eCommerce and social/mobile commerce systems do you use? What are the ROE for these deals (e.g., all deals below $200)?

- What's the definition of a named account, and how many of them are there? How often are major or strategic account lists allowed to change?

- What is the organization's hierarchy for account ownership and forecast management? (SFDC really wants a clear, **unambiguous hierarchy**; dotted-line relationships and matrix organizations are a real bear to work with.)

- How are leads prequalified and routed to partners? How do partner leads get assigned within the team? (**automatic routing**, manual opportunistic process, or manual daily cycle)

- Who does cultivation, nurturing, and qualification of leads? (marketing, **sales development**, inside sales, or sales)

- How are leads qualified? What are the criteria for conversion? Who does conversion? Are these triggers *written down and used consistently*?

- Who schedules customer demonstrations or other initial proofs of value? (marketing, **sales development**, inside sales, or sales)

- How are sales teams selected (e.g., in global accounts or purchases that involve products from several divisions)?

- Who opens an opportunity, and what are the opening parameters? (marketing, sales development, **inside sales**, or sales)

- How are quotes issued? (marketing, sales development, **inside sales**, or **sales**)

- How are special orders, discounts, or contractual terms approved? Is this done through email or through an **automated approval process**?

- Who closes opportunities (both wins and losses)? (sales, **sales operations**, or finance)

- How are commissions, splits, and referral fees calculated? (case by case, **manual spreadsheet**, or automatic commission system)

- What's the waterfall model for the pipeline? (Each of the following questions should be answered for each sales channel.)

  - What's the average deal size?

  - What's the average length of the sales cycle?

  - What's the proportion of repeat/upsell deals to new customer wins?

  - How many deals does each channel need to do to make its numbers?

  - How many sales cycles have to be started to achieve that number of deals?

  - How many leads need to be collected to start that number of sales cycles?

  - How many stages are in the sales cycle? If there are fewer than four or more than eight, why?

  - What are the sales stage names, how long does each stage last, what are the required sales activities, and what are the customer actions or criteria that trigger transition from one stage to the next?

- ➡ What is the conversion (or, alternatively, the drop-off) ratio at each stage?

- ➡ What are the probabilities of closing the deal at each stage?

- How broadly is information shared, beyond the standard managerial roll-ups? Can all reps see all accounts and opportunities, or should they see only those in their own territory?

- How are divisions and subsidiaries handled? How are international sales handled?

- How are marketing, sales development, inside sales, direct sales, and the channel measured and incented?

Once you've worked through your model, compare it to the model used in this chapter and adjust the recommendations given here to fit your organization. As its ongoing example, this chapter uses the high-tech B2B sales model: a combination of eCommerce at the low end, inside sales in the midrange, and direct sales plus channel partners at the enterprise level.

Sales Development Reps (SDRs)

As mentioned previously, the sales development reps team is called different things at different companies. This book uses the term *sales development* to refer to the people who call leads to nurture them, focus their interest, and qualify them.[8] In small organizations, this team may do pretty much everything *except* selling. They may do cold calling, lead generation, lead cultivation/nurturing, lead qualification, appointment setting, and even a bit of presales customer support. In some organizations, they also make sales and assist with tricky eCommerce transactions.

No matter what the specific job title, this function needs to have *very* tight communications with both marketing and the sales reps. Almost always, best practice is to have members of this team report to the sales organization and to have them report to the appropriate geographic territory manager (e.g., the western U.S. SDR team should report to the VP of Western Sales). Typically, the SDR team is managed by a sales development pro—not a sales rep or a marketing person. The skills, pacing, and management of SDRs are just different enough that a specialist really will get more productivity out of the team. If the company does not have enough headcount to permit this organizational structure, many consultancies are available to provide really tight management of SDRs on a part-time basis. The data and features of SFDC make this kind of outsourcing or consulting help straightforward and effective.

8. Your company may call them telesales, telemarketing, sales development, account development, sales associates, or sales support.

The SDR team is the natural first audience for using SFDC. So that's the first best practice: get this team using SFDC intensively *before anyone else in sales*. SDRs spend enormous amounts of time on the phone; they already have a browser up (to hit their prospects' Web sites or find out about `leads`); and they're already using some sort of contact manager, organizer, or spreadsheet to keep track of their call-down lists.

Initial Setup

The `lead status` pick-list field needs to be modified to indicate the realistic life cycle of a `lead`,[9] as documented in the revenue model you prepared earlier in this chapter. Typically, SFDC's `lead` page will need to have a few extra fields added (such as those for the lead score, sales territory, and product interest pull-downs) for the company's unique products or target audience. If you're using the named account model of selling, add a lookup field from the `lead` to the `account`. This field[10] should appear directly below `company` on the `lead` page and will generate a `related list` for the `account` page. Resist the temptation to put in a bunch of extra fields that you know, in your heart of hearts, no one will ever fill out or use. These "great idea" fields will simply lower the system's credibility.

On the `lead tab`, configure `views` for personal call-down lists and easy navigation of all live leads.

> ### COORDINATE WITH MARKETING ON THIS IF NOTHING ELSE
>
> *Because the SDR team will be focused on* `leads`, *in addition to reading this chapter, they should check out the corresponding discussion on lead generation, collection, handling, and cultivation in Chapter 10.*

Some other SFDC features and add-ons will also benefit the SDR team:

- If you're using a marketing automation system (MAS) or email blaster with drip marketing or nurturing features, make sure to put the MAS "what's up" section on the `lead` or `contact` page layouts. These tools provide invaluable insight about the lead's level of interest and engagement.

---

9. Typically, pick lists should have between 5 and 10 items. For `lead status`, the available items may be *new, contact attempted, contact made, working, hold, qualified, bad data, no interest, lost interest, wrong person,* or *remarket.*

10. With stock SFDC functionality, this field will be manually populated. If you're using a MAS or can afford some custom code, this field can be automatically filled in by the system.

- If you subscribe to `data.com`, Hoover's, InsideView, LinkedIn, or any one of their competitors, add their info section to the lead page layout. These tools provide important information about the person and the company they work for.

- Seriously consider using `data.com`, SFDC's lead database. For North American prospects, they have probably the best database for searching leads, companies, and related demographic info.

- If your company uses Skype or Cisco IP phones, put their free[11] dialer buttons on the SFDC screen next to the phone numbers of `leads` and `contacts`. Initially, this button will save the reps a few seconds on every call while preventing misdials. But over time, the use of the button means that users will keep the phone numbers in SFDC up to date not because someone told them to but because it's in *their own best interests*. This force of gravity—using different specific natural features in each case—should be used at every turn to increase adoption across the sales team.

- Over time, the initial button can be replaced with a fancier (nonfree) one that automatically logs the time of the call, creating an `activity history` item so that the caller doesn't have to do it manually. This saves at least 10 seconds and four mouse clicks for anyone who makes a call. Of course, this fancier item is a double-edged sword: now everyone will know how many times anyone has attempted to call the prospect—a good thing to prevent double calling but a bad thing for reps who are worried about being micromanaged.

- Make use of SFDC `custom links` for things like LinkedIn search, Google Maps, Google News, and other external sources. These can be easily configured to get the user quick access to lots of industry databases.

- Make use of SFDC `consoles`. These special screens can be configured to provide everything you need to see about the prospect on one screen.

Prospecting and Initial Contact

The SDR team should point their browsers to SFDC before they even pick up the phone. Make sure that the daily `lead` flows, call-down sheets, and renewal reminder lists get to them *only* via SFDC pages—stop sending emails containing spreadsheets and lists to these reps! To implement this kind of structure, SFDC needs to be fully integrated with the company's Web site, content management system, MAS, and import/deduping tools.

---

11. There are also similar (nonfree) buttons that connect to other telephony systems and PBXs.

WHO'S DOING THE INITIAL CALLING, CULTIVATION, AND QUALIFYING?

Although this book designates the people who do the initial lead development as "SDRs," there is a counterintuitive key success factor for this function: the people who do the initial calling, cultivation, and qualification should *not* be carrying a sales quota. The existence of a commission is distracting, and it undermines the thoroughness of the (admittedly boring) process of dialing out, reading scripts, and qualifying leads. Having both a revenue target and a lead cultivation/conversion goal confuses not just the individuals on the phone but their manager as well.

Said a simpler way, don't confuse SDRs with sales.

This is a highly controversial topic that generates endless debate, but even if you disagree with the recommendation, separating SDRs from quota-carrying sales (i.e., breaking apart the function of initial qualification from selling) carries three benefits:

- You can measure each operation better.
- You remove excuses.
- You can outsource one part without affecting the other. Different kinds of firms are available for outsourcing each part, which reinforces the notion that telemarketing and telesales really are different functions.

Leads should be automatically routed to and managed in queues unless the company's sales team is very small. Queues serve as a holding tank for leads that have not been claimed or worked by someone in the queue's sales region. They provide important metrics for SDR managers, so it's important to use them properly. Typically, a queue is seen by all the SDRs in the queue's territory, and any lead in a queue can be handled by anyone on the team. As soon as one of the SDRs wants to work on a lead in the queue, that individual needs to take ownership of the lead by clicking on SFDC's change owner link to reassign it to themselves. Leads should never go from individual ownership back into the territory's queue; even if the lead owner leaves the sales team, the leads he or she is working should be explicitly reassigned to an individual, not returned to the territory's queue.

When a new lead comes in, marketing is responsible for getting it to the right queue or SDRs in as few minutes as possible. It is almost impossible for sales reps to call back too soon: prospects are always impressed with prompt responses, and a timely, relevant call says a lot about the company's customer-focused attitude. Recent studies have shown that in our fast-paced world, prospect response rates fall off dramatically within 2 hours of the initial contact. Indeed, within 48 hours most prospects will not even remember having visited your company's Web site, let alone have a clue about your value proposition or competitive advantage. Use SFDC's `auto-response rules` or MAS drip campaigns to send an email to the `lead` the instant that the potential customer registers. Best practice is to make the first phone attempt—at least leaving a voice message—on the same day that the `lead` contacted you. Some companies go so far as to have an SDR on the phone with the prospect before the `lead` even leaves the company's Web site (this advice isn't for everyone, but you can see how doing so might make a powerful impression on the prospect). This kind of responsiveness is possible only with solid automation, integration, and user indoctrination, but it pays off in higher conversion rates and cold, hard cash.

Given the variety of things an SDR needs to do, it's important to prioritize `leads` so time is spent on the most promising prospects. The default SFDC `rating` field is just a hot/medium/cold pick list, and that works out fine in most situations. Best practices are to have the lead rating automatically set by a lead scoring system.[12] Although the details of the lead score are irrelevant to the reps, the hot/medium/cold indicator needs to be completely bulletproof. By presenting only high-scoring leads to the SDR team, marketing can improve perceived lead quality, which can directly affect the effectiveness of sales overall. Move away from paper—get rid of binders and cheat sheets. Put documents that are useful to the SDR people within easy reach: right in SFDC itself. Store the scripts in the `content` section[13] and create custom links on the `lead` page so the reps can jump right to them during the call. Create other custom links to generate emails that fit the scripts. When these documents are housed in the system, there's never a risk of using an outdated version. SFDC's `Content Edition` provides a great way for marketing and sales personnel to better manage collateral documents, and it's almost essential for any sales team that has to sell a wide range of products from several company divisions. Also, use `chatter groups` and topics to make your team a learning organization, reacting to market changes in real time.

Tight scripts mean an effective SDR team. Although the company might want to experiment to find out what works best with prospects, the *only* way to get real productivity out of an SDR team is to have 80% of the calls made according to the approved formula. The other 20% can be experiments, but they need to be tightly controlled and

---

12. Scoring systems are something of a black art, but if you want to understand a bit of the magic, read the "Lead Scoring and Aging" section of Chapter 10. Of course, even the best tools require time to tune the `lead` scoring—during the first few months, the scores will inevitably be misleading (because they're based on theory rather than the behavior of your best-performing target customers). Give feedback to the marketing personnel who run the scoring system so they can steadily improve its function.

13. Only the most essential documents should actually be stored in SFDC. For storage limitation reasons, you want to store only items that are small and don't have to be individualized for every prospect or account. A few dozen pieces of sales collateral, white papers, or PowerPoint slides that everyone needs should be held in SFDC; everything else (e.g., case studies, RFP responses, quotes) should be *linked to* the relevant SFDC records but should be stored in the company's file servers (or shared directories).

measured as part of A/B split testing.[14] Evolve the scripts that achieve the best test results on a monthly basis (more frequently if things are changing radically in your market space) and *keep a log of what the changes and results have been.* It's a good idea to involve marketing personnel in this exercise, as they tend to like tracking and crunching data. SFDC dramatically simplifies the conduct of these kinds of A/B tests, and the reporting system can provide up-to-the-minute comparisons of conversion rate results. That said, it's important to not react too quickly to preliminary test data: virtually any test you run should last for more than a week, owing to daily fluctuations in user responsiveness.

If the SDR team has to deal with a lot of products or very different market segments, embed the script sequences and qualifying questions directly in their SFDC screen. (A free AppExchange plugin will get you there.) In response to the SDRs' checking boxes or selecting pull-down list items (e.g., "has budget" and "50 to 100 users"), the screens can change to reflect the script path being followed with the prospect. Further, automatic rules in SFDC can be set up to score the degree of the prospect's qualification according to the script answers. The system can even be set up to send notification emails to sales reps about the hot leads that deserve their immediate attention.[15]

Lead Cultivation, Nurturing, and Qualification

Moving the prospect from awareness to interest to desire to willingness to take an appointment is almost always done by someone in the sales team.

For marketing personnel to produce the right *quality* and quantity of `leads`—what's really required to fill the top of the funnel—they need to have a contract or service level agreement (SLA) with the SDR team covering the life cycle of `leads`. Items that need to be explicitly agreed on include how quickly `leads` get into the system, how rapidly they are contacted, how many calls or contact attempts are made, what the perishability date of a `lead` is, and the mechanics of rejecting a lead that isn't up to snuff.

In parallel with the SDR outreach (in fact, it typically starts before you get the first crack at the lead) will be drip marketing campaigns (also known as *sequential*

---

14. Split testing is a technique that compares the results of using two versions of the call script, Web page, or other marketing/sales messaging. The two versions are used randomly with prospects, but the results of the A version (typically, the baseline) are tracked separately from the B version (typically, the "new and improved" one). Following the scientific method, this style of testing can rapidly prove whether or not the B version is an improvement. As soon as a round of A/B testing is completed, the stronger version becomes the new A, and a new B version is set up as the challenger.

15. If you really want to go nuts, have your implementer write a bit of code that automatically qualifies high-scoring leads and initiates the `lead conversion` process. This strategy is not something we recommend for the first year of SFDC system operation (because too often there is disagreement about what qualifies as "qualified" or as something warranting a sales rep's attention), but SFDC technology makes this possible.

auto-responders, vertical *campaigns*, or *lead nurturing*) from the MAS. Once a prospect has registered interest, the `lead` should be sent a series of *relevant* informational emails covering their topic of interest. The sequence of emails is usually along the following lines: same day, next day, 3 days later, 1 week later, 2 weeks later, 1 month later, and so on. Each email provides a new bit of information or perspective to move the prospect farther down the learning curve about the company. The emails should contain calls to action, but they should be subtle ("find out more" is a way better link than "buy now"), and each email should *sound* different. The emails should appear to come from the relevant inside sales person, even though they are fully automated. The emails *must* have an opt-out mechanism that works, and they need to automatically stop the instant a human conversation has happened (of course, the only way for this kind of interaction to occur is for the inside and outside sales folks to actually register their calls using SFDC's `Activity` button). Check out Chapter 10 if you want to know more about automated lead nurturing.

How long should your inside folks spend on a prospect before they give up? The answer to this question varies by company and target market, but there's one cardinal rule: never, ever[16] delete a `lead` or a `contact`. Generally speaking, the timing of the lead processing should be along these lines:

- If a `lead`'s contact information is bogus (the email bounces and the phone number is incorrect), the inside sales folks should mark it as such (with a status of "Bad Data") within 24 hours of receiving the `lead`. These `leads` should be sent back over to the marketing staff so they can debug the problem (and almost certainly demote the `campaign` or source that produced the trash `lead`).

- If the prospect is a `contact`, not a `lead` (i.e., the person is a returning participant in the company's marketing activities and was already listed in the system as a `contact`), the new information about the `contact` (his or her participation/ response) should be added to the *existing SFDC record*. This is best done through the `campaigns` feature, where an existing contact becomes a member of a "new" `campaign`. If the `contact`'s contact information is now bogus, an inside sales rep should set its status to "Bad Data" within 24 hours of seeing it, and its ownership should be transferred to the marketing staff so they can investigate.

- If a `lead`'s or `contact`'s contact information is good, but the prospect is not responsive to email and voice messages for 30 days (e.g., an entire drip-marketing sequence), the `lead` or `contact` should probably be demoted and put back into the remarket or newsletter `queue` handled by marketing. Here's a surprise:

---

16. Not even if somebody dies? NOT EVER. To improve lead quality, you need to know everything about the life of a lead—including its final conclusion.

dead or disqualified `leads` or `contacts`—when properly cultivated and nurtured over time—can represent as much as one-third of a company's business. Industry statistics indicate that dead leads will buy product from *someone* in the next 18 months—it's only a matter of who gets the purchase. Conclusion: tenacity wins.

- If a `lead` or `contact` is responsive but is unable or unwilling to move forward in qualification, the inside rep should maintain ownership of the person, set the prospect's `status` to "On Hold," and create a `task` to call the person in 60 days (or whatever).

- If a prospect is responsive and can be qualified by the SDR, the sales staff should do so within 15 days of receipt. If it takes longer than that, you'll want to investigate and understand why. Of course, if a prospect is qualified before then, that person should be immediately `converted` and sent over to the relevant sales team.

It's best to create a timeline, such as in Figure 9-1, showing the sequence and timing of activities leading to a `conversion` or demotion of a `lead` in your company.

One of the key elements of the service level agreement between the SDRs and marketing is, "How do `leads` get refused or rejected by inside sales?" There should be clear criteria for this decision, and whenever an SDR rejects a `lead`, that SDR needs to set the rejection

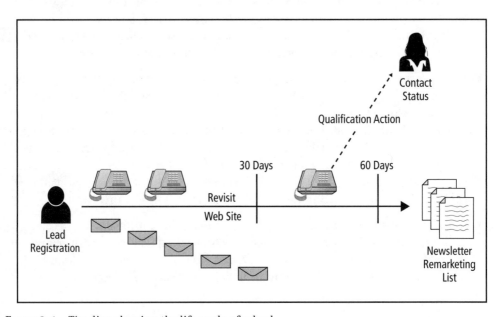

FIGURE 9-1   Timeline showing the life cycle of a lead

reason pull-down for that record.[17] Once the `lead` is rejected by the SDR, the expectation should be that the prospect will continue to receive newsletters and other electronic marketing indefinitely—forever, unless the prospect explicitly opts out of this process.

SFDC's `lead status` pick-list entries should be adjusted to fit the company's contact, cultivation, and nurturing pattern. For example, the pick list could include the following items: *new, contact attempted, contact made, working, hold, qualified, rejected,* and *bad data.* It is common practice to add a few extra fields to the `lead` record (to capture the specifics of product interest, a promotional special, or other characteristics), but keep this to a minimum. A `lead` record should be fairly brief: long `lead` pages are almost never filled in and just frustrate everybody.

The most interesting part of a **lead** record *isn't* the `lead` detail information in the body of the page; it's in **chatter** at the top and the related lists underneath.[18] The evolution of a `lead`'s interest and potential shows up as entries in `activity history`, `campaign history`, and `custom objects` such as download history. Many of these related list entries are filled in automatically by the Web site, MAS, email marketing, content management, license server, and other external systems integrated with SFDC. The idea is that *every* automated outbound touch should show up as a campaign entry, and every response (whether opening of an email, an RSVP, an attendance, a download, or a registration) should show up as either a `campaign response` or a completed `activity`. If your company's phone system is integrated with SFDC, every outbound dial and inbound callback will also be recorded automatically. With all this information, the SDRs can immediately see the profile of the `lead` and the prospect's recent level of interest. This information is particularly useful if a large SDR team shares the workload for a territory, as anyone can instantly see the state of play for any lead in the territory.

This level of instrumentation also gives sales management much clearer metrics on the SDR team, and it helps sales management determine whether their model of pipeline generation and activity management is realistic.

On the `lead` page, make it easy for the inside reps to get supplemental information from outside sources. Smart reps will want to do a little research before they call a new `lead`. Use the `page layout` tool to install links to Google Search and Google News (for general information about a prospect company), and to Hoover's, Dunn and Bradstreet, or other service (for financial and business information). For information about the individual `lead`, add links for LinkedIn, ZoomInfo, or your favorite lead database service. Of course, SFDC's own data.com service provides company digests for free and enriched `lead` data for a fee.

---

17. The rejection reason pick list is a dependent field of the lead status, so it's only after a `lead` has been explicitly rejected by inside sales that this pick list becomes visible (and in fact, mandatory). Items on this pick list might include: *bad data, no interest, lost interest, no budget, no power, no vision,* and *no competitive advantage.*

18. Actually, this general rule holds true for almost all the records in SFDC.

Outsourcing Lead Cultivation or Nurturing

Lead cultivation can be effectively outsourced, particularly if the company has a large sales operation and some of the workload can be clearly partitioned (e.g., a special promotion, a new product offering, or an uncovered territory). However, outsourcing requires careful design and monitoring—and you need to have very tight management to make this strategy work properly.

Here are the key guidelines: give the outsourced team the same tools that the inside folks have; have them be part of your team (include them in `chatter groups`); and measure them just as tightly as you do your own team. These guidelines boil down to giving the outsourced team full access to the SFDC system.

Most outsourced telemarketing/telesales teams will already be familiar with SFDC. If the team is small (or if you are buying the services of a dedicated team), it's pretty straightforward to have them use your SFDC system directly. Of course, you'll need to pay for the licenses those team members use. You'll also want to restrict their access to the system (read: you'll almost certainly need `enterprise edition`) so they can get to only what's relevant for lead processing and cultivation.

If the outsourcing firm is large, it will be managing several clients and is likely to have its own internal system for managing and monitoring calls. In this case, the outsourced team is unlikely to use your company's SFDC instance. If they use SFDC, then the `Salesforce to Salesforce` feature makes it "easy"[19] to share information across systems. If you can talk the outsourcing vendor into it, this effort is well worth the cost of setting up the feature to work as your real-time bridge.

If the outsourcing firm doesn't use SFDC, then you'll have to do things the 20th-century way. Your company sends the `leads` to the outsourced team on a daily basis (typically as a spreadsheet), and it sends the hot, ready-to-convert leads back to you pretty much in real time. Every couple of days, the team will also send the lead status information. Most of the time, you will not get any detailed call metrics from the outsourced team in the same way you would with an inside team; instead, you'll probably just receive data on the aggregate number of dials and conversations, plus the snapshot of the lead status. Pushing these updates into SFDC requires some care and use of outside tools (like the Data Loader) that really require a trained user.

While a `lead` is in process with the outsourced agency, its SFDC ownership should be changed to the `queue` or individual who's handling it. You may also want to add a `custom field` or two to the `lead` page to hold information that's relevant to the outsourcing process. For example, a `formula field` indicating "how long in this status" may provide a useful metric for monitoring the outsourcer's performance.

---

19. The quotation marks are there for a reason. SFDC2SFDC does incur an administrative burden that can be relieved only with a bunch of APEX code.

For a wide range of reasons, the best way to improve the lead cultivation and nurturing process is for members of the SFDC team to meet frequently with the marketing team. For real-time collaboration, `chatter groups` are the perfect way to do this. Supplement this with monthly checkup meetings to understand which changes are needed in terms of content, messaging, or lead production. When evaluating metrics, make sure to focus on achieving objectives and improving the number of first sales meetings—stay away from words that sound like a performance review, overmeasurement, or the assignment of blame. Outbound marketers are the natural partners of SDRs, so do everything possible to foster good communications and a tight working relationship across these teams.

Many different metrics can be implemented for SDRs. Even so, we recommend going light on these measurements for the first several months of SFDC implementation. It is important that SFDC *not* be viewed as an enforcer or a tool of micromanagers. Adoption and usage—with quality data that makes SFDC a more valuable asset to the sales organization—are the only metrics that matter for the first nine months or so of system usage. Early on, have metrics and incentives for logging in, entering complete records, and using the system's features. Leave the heavy-handed activity management for later (we discuss this topic further later in this chapter).

WHERE'D ALL THE INFORMATION GO?

For most sales models, the first contact with a prospect will be entered as an SFDC `lead`. *Initially, all the information needs to go there. But over time, the hottest, most useful information about the prospect situation should be attached to* `opportunities`. *This means that as soon as a* `lead` *is converted, all users should know that the default place to put data updates,* `chats`, `notes`, `documents`, *and* `tasks` *is in the* `opportunity` *record. The only kind of information that should be attached to* `contacts` *is information about the person (such as change in boss, location, or authority) or interactions at a personal level (such as a business lunch). The only kind of information that should be attached to the* `account` *is information that is global (stock ticker symbol change, billing address change, executive shuffling), not deal-specific items (such as "competitor" or "budget").*

For all records, use the `description` *field to put information that is more or less permanent (such as "their business rationales") and easily reportable. Information that changes as the deal evolves should be stored in* `chats` *or* `tasks` *because they are automatically dated and include an author ID. Generally speaking,* `notes` *should not be used.*

Conversion and Hand-Off to Sales

Once a prospect has been qualified, in many cases the SDR's job is nearly over (depending on how the company organizes its sales roles). It's a best practice to hand over ownership of `contacts` and `opportunities` to the inside/outside sales rep because it's not a great idea to have them looking at `leads`. Instead, he or she can focus on deals (where the money will be) and see only the relevant, up-to-date `contact` information.

The handover process is typically scheduling a follow-up call for the inside or outside rep, logging a call in the `tasks` area, and `converting` the `lead`. During the conversion process, SFDC makes the `lead` disappear and replaces it with a new `contact`, which will be attached to an `account` and a named `opportunity` that is `owned` by the responsible sales rep. If it's done right, the `contact` will have a `contact role` on the `opportunity record`. Figure 9-2 illustrates SFDC's `lead conversion` process.

Note that conversion best practices vary tremendously—your company and its business practices may need to do things in a completely different way from the "vanilla" formula described here. Check out www.SFDC-secrets.com for variations and templates that make sense for different kinds of customer and presales situations.

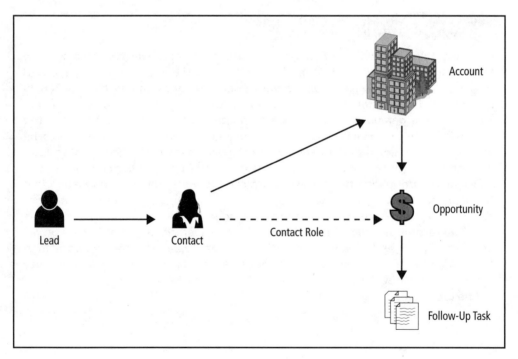

Account

Opportunity

Contact Role

Lead

Contact

Follow-Up Task

FIGURE 9-2   SFDC's lead conversion process

CREATION SCIENCE

Okay, okay: I apologize for the title. But it got your attention, right?

There really is a science to properly creating `leads`, `contacts`, `accounts`, and `opportunities` in SFDC. Do it wrong, and you end up with a bunch of duplicate records that need to be cleaned up later. Do it right, and you save a bunch of time.

The First Commandment: *thou shalt not create anything without searching for it first.*[20] Just put a short string in the search box (which should always be set up in the masthead area of your browser window). Your administrator may also have put in an automatic dupe-detection feature called RingLead UniqueEntry that warns you about `leads`, `contacts`, and `accounts` that are similar to what you've typed in. Whether by search or by RingLead, if you find an existing `contact` or `lead` record, apply your new information to it.

You have to be a little more careful with `accounts` because so many parts of the system can be affected by a change to those records:

- If you find an existing `account` that's nearly an exact match to what you want to create, use that one but don't update its information (send an email to the system administrator with the changes you think need to be made).

- If you find an existing `account` that *isn't* an exact match, create a new `account` with your information and have its "parent" field point to the existing `account`.[21]

An important corollary of this commandment: *sales shall never import lists into SFDC.* This is the devil's work and must be performed by marketing or system administrators.

The Second Commandment: *thou shalt not delete things.* The system needs to keep track of bad data, falsely qualified `leads`, and bogus `opportunities`[22]—the only way your marketing and inside sales groups will ever improve is to get concrete, quantitative feedback in the form of dead records. Identify bad records, mark them as such, and save them. SFDC has lots of ways to make bad records disappear from views and reports, but if the records are actually deleted, no one can ever learn anything from the past or measure process improvements.

The "do not try this at home" corollary of this commandment is "deduping is to be done only by professionals." They have special tools and magical methods all their own.

---

20. You don't want to create duplicate species, do you? What kind of creation would that be?
21. System administrators may consolidate these `accounts` later, but they will follow a careful set of business rules to do so.
22. To see who's been naughty and who's been nice.

Here are default best practices for the conversion and hand-off process:

- Usually, the new `contact` (and `opportunity`) should be attached to an existing `account`. If SFDC finds more than one likely `account`, the conversion wizard will allow you to select among them via a pick list. If SFDC doesn't find an `account` that is a close match to the `lead`'s `company` field, it will automatically create a new `account` upon conversion using the name from the `company` field.

- The `account` object has the standard `Name` field filled with a friendly name that people will search for (it's a nickname or "street name," e.g., Disney) and it should have a `custom field` called "Legal Entity Name" used by the accounting, legal, and other departments to indicate the formal name of the legal entity (e.g., The Walt Disney Company). Although this may seem redundant, how many people will know to search for The Great Atlantic and Pacific Tea Company when they're thinking of A&P? The friendly name needs to be free of foreign characters, accents, apostrophes, and hyphens to make searching and report filtering more reliable (e.g., if you were searching for Conde Nast or Nestle, the system wouldn't find Condé Nast or Nestlé).

- If you have a lot of `accounts` (particularly large, multinational corporations), the `account name` should be more than just the friendly, short name for the company. It needs to have some descriptive data for fast searching and viewing, particularly when you use the `account hierarchy` view. The name may include items such as country, segment, or line of business (e.g., Disney—US—Cruise Lines). The use of double dashes (or the em-dash character) is needed to distinguish the spacer from a standard hyphen (that occurs in company names like Lockheed-Martin). If you want to understand more about this issue, check out the "What's in a Namespace?" section in Chapter 2.

- For really big `accounts` (i.e., big companies, albeit not necessarily big sources of business for your company), create a master `parent account` that is named either "Company—Headquarters" or "Stock Symbol—HQ" (e.g., DISN—HQ, which is the parent of Disney Studios—US, Pixar Studios—US, and Disney Theme Parks—US). The master `parent account` is essentially a holding company for all the operations in various countries, so it has no `contacts` or `opportunities` of its own. See Figure 3-1 for an illustration of this practice.

- The `account` object should have a pick list for `type` that contains indicators for the different classes of companies with which your sales team must deal. For example, types might include *NAM*[23] *prospect, geo prospect, strategic, customer, partner, distributor, supplier, government, inactive,* and *out of business.* The `account`

---

23. See the "Named Account Model of Selling" section later in this chapter for a discussion of this issue.

object should also have `roll-up fields` to show key summaries such as "last 12 months orders $" and "total lifetime orders $" and `status` (such as "Is Customer").

- The `opportunity name` also needs to follow a naming convention, typically along the lines of account name—department/project—product—QQYY. This standard may seem time consuming to follow, but you quickly get used to it, and having `opportunity` names in this format makes it much easier to see what's going on in `forecasting`, `views`, `reports`, `bar charts`, and management roll-ups. For instance, an `opportunity` named Disney—Pixar—Film Stock—3q13 will be easy to find in a long list of `opportunities`, whereas "Disney film order" would be quickly lost.

- At the moment of conversion, the `opportunity` should be opened with a $0 amount and 0% probability, even if there are clear signs of a big deal. Until the sales rep has explicitly accepted the `opportunity` as real, it's just speculation. The SDR's intuition about the size and probability of the deal should go in the `opportunity`'s `description` text field.

- The last stage of conversion creates a follow-up `task`, which is usually assigned to the rep who needs to take over the `opportunity`. This type of task needs to be carefully monitored, as it represents the official hand-off to the field—and dropping the baton at this point is as important to results as it was for the U.S. 4 × 100 meter relay teams at the Beijing Olympics.

- Before you click that final `convert` button on the wizard, make sure that the `record owner` is properly set to the territory rep who should receive it. Although automation in this area is possible, it's add-on code that your system probably doesn't have—so just make filling it in a habit.

- Immediately after completing the conversion, open the `opportunity` record and set a `contact role` for the person who's just been converted. Assign the role that seems most likely from the sales rep's conversations with the prospect, or at least assign a blank role. If your system admin is clever, you will never have to do this step because he or she made it impossible for you to do it wrong. Ask the admin for this (if you're lucky, I might get around to doing a write-up of this on the book Web site).

SDRs need to have an SLA with the inside/outside sales reps about hot prospects, along these lines:

- It is the SDR's responsibility to contact the prospect, determine the products or services that the prospect is interested in purchasing, qualify the `lead` according to the criteria set up by sales, set up a follow-up discussion for outside sales, and convert the `lead` to an `opportunity` within 15 days of the initial connection. `Reports` and `workflows` should be set up to provide clear metrics and alerts to the inside sales team.

- It is the inside/outside sales team's responsibility to fully qualify the `opportunity`, determine whether there is a chance of a real sales cycle, and update the `opportunity` within 48 business hours of the prescheduled call. If there really isn't a deal here, the sales rep should set its stage to "Closed: Bogus Opportunity" and reassign the `opportunity`'s ownership to the SDR who generated it. It's a best practice to have a mandatory field indicating the reasons for rejecting the `opportunity`. These bogus `opportunities` should not count against the sales rep—if anything, they should be an indicator of failure for the SDRs. `Reports` and `workflows` should be set up to provide clear metrics for both the sales reps and the inside sales team.

- Once the outside rep has accepted an `opportunity`, though, it is the rep's deal to win or lose (i.e., there's no one else to blame). As a consequence, reps will be hesitant to accept opportunities unless they are *real*—and that's a good thing because it prevents them from chasing low-quality prospects, clarifies the metrics, and makes bottlenecks and shortfalls more evident.

Inside Sales Reps

We're continuing here with the assumption that the SDRs are separate from the sales team. The official start of the sales cycle is when the sales rep has accepted the opportunity (i.e., hasn't rejected it in the SLA window).

Inside Sales Opportunities

As the customer moves through the sales cycle, sales reps should update `opportunity` records with relevant notes and other information, not just bump the `stage`. SFDC should be set up with `record types` and `sales processes`[24] for the channel and customer type so that the rep gets a streamlined view of the `opportunity stage` sequence. For the inside sales team moving low-price products, the sales cycle is typically short, so they probably won't need to make much use of SFDC's `task` or `forecasting` functionality.

---

24. For example, the inside sales `stages` might be *open, fully qualified, trial, pricing,* and *closed-won.* In contrast, the outside sales `stages` might be *open, first meeting, fully qualified, demo, trial, short list, quote, selection, negotiation,* and *closed-won.* As you'll see later in this chapter, there will also be some hidden sales `stages` for legal and accounting use.

In many cases, the inside sales orders are immediate in nature: no formal quote is required, and the business rules are set up so that the inside reps can issue only valid orders. Even so, the SFDC system should be set up so that order items and discount rates are validated prior to closing the `quote` and the `opportunity`. This is done through use of SFDC's free `quoting` tool (discussed later in this chapter).

If the reps must handle complicated product structures or sophisticated discounts that can be valid only in certain combinations, the SFDC team should consider acquiring an external configure/price/quote engine via the AppExchange. Several of these engines are available for SFDC, but often they require a lot of configuration and ongoing maintenance that undercut their cost savings. Perhaps a better solution would be to simplify and streamline the company's price list so that the sales and manufacturing folks don't have as many troublesome configurations to deal with in the first place.

If the inside sales team must handle eCommerce transactions that have gone awry, the rep should enter the user's shopping cart ID and store transaction ID into SFDC's `opportunity` record so that auditors can reconcile order flows and overrides across the two systems.

Handling Order Operations for Outside Sales

Inside sales teams sometimes handle the quoting and order entry tasks for outside sales teams, particularly when the company has highly distributed field operations and complex orders. If your company has a dedicated order operations team, they need to read this section because order placement, tracking, expediting, and cancellation practices can have powerful positive effects on customer satisfaction and the speed of order flow. Through the use of `approval processes`, `record types`, and `page layouts`, SFDC can provide an iron-clad assurance of process compliance while actually streamlining the sales rep's duties. See www.SFDC-secrets.com for examples of how this process works.

Because `quoting` is a part of SFDC but actual order entry is not, best practices in this area can be highly variable—depending on the depth of integration between your SFDC system and the order management and accounting systems. Overall, it is a good idea to integrate SFDC's `opportunity` object with the company's order entry system's `quote`, `order`, and `contract` screens[25] so that order operations can see the customer's entire order history as well as the status of current "in flight" transactions. Check out www.SFDC-secrets.com for example workflows and alternative implementation strategies.

`Quotes` without controls are dangerous because they commit the company to terms and prices; if abused, this practice can trigger unpleasant customer and regulatory

---

25. These screens may be handled by the company's accounting system, ERP, distribution/warehousing system, or a dedicated order-management system. These systems are often the home-brew variety, or rickety, or both.

OFFSHORING ORDER OPERATIONS

Offshoring or outsourcing of order operations frequently happens, particularly in highly competitive, high-volume operations with overseas manufacturing. There are a few key SFDC practices to consider when customer contact functions are carried out by offshore entities.

SFDC is fully internationalized and can easily be configured to be user friendly with order operations in several countries, languages, and time zones simultaneously. The offshore personnel will need to have full access not only to SFDC, but also to any transactional systems with which the SFDC system is integrated. This means you'll want to implement fine-grained security and single sign-on to make sure that members of the order operations team can see everything they need, but *only* what they really need.

We recommend implementing `record types`, `sales processes`, `workflows`, `approval processes`, and `page layouts` for each major order entry region, as the `workflows` in these regions will probably be somewhat different from those employed in their U.S. counterpart. Using this approach allows for wording, approval cycles, special handling, and other variations to fit the sales customs in each region.

We also recommend setting the offshore order entry screen's time zone to the main time zone the offshore operation is *covering*, rather than to its local time zone. This issue can become quite important at the end of the business quarter when the last-minute order push can be quite hectic.

Although many offshore operations use VoIP phones, we discourage the use of Skype buttons in SFDC for order operations because of the marginal call quality when bandwidth is sketchy. Congestion and heavy traffic at your local Internet service provider (ISP) results in poor call intelligibility, which in turn produces a bad customer impression. Of course, if your offshore operations have dedicated high-capacity lines (e.g., T-3) for Internet service, then Skype is a fine solution.

---

problems. For example, a company may have to comply with "most favorable pricing" criteria that it has committed to in contracts with very large customers or government agencies. In this circumstance, generating even a provisional `quote` must be subject to an approval cycle. At least, SFDC should be set up so that a `quote` can't be started until an `opportunity` has reached a specified `stage`. Using SFDC to collect all the elements to generate the customer `quote`—rather than cutting and pasting fields into a Word document—can help the company streamline its quoting and approval process.

SFDC `quotes` use the `pricebook`, `pricelist`, and `line item` structure to build the `quote` from the ground up with the correct product description, pricing, and discounting information. Several other quoting and order configuration applications for

SFDC are also available, and many customers build their own quoting applications in VisualForce. In any case, best practice calls for structuring all of the company's offerings—even consulting and associated travel—as fixed-cost line items (e.g., "3 days on-site consulting" and "3 days U.S. travel") with flags to trigger revenue recognition schedules in the accounting system and renewal opportunities in SFDC.

The quote should not be printable or emailable until it is approved, and the system should check the quote for compliance with product, term, and discounting rules. If the quote is out of bounds, it needs to be sent through an SFDC approval workflow to make sure that management has approved the variances. This automation can save hours of time and sales rep hassle on every order. Once approved, the specifics of the quote record should be locked down so that it can be printed and it cannot be changed without going through another rule review/approval process. For the U.S. market, digital signatures are now commonplace, allowing legally binding commitment to contracts via DocuSign or similar add-on products. Each quote sent to a customer should be saved as an uneditable PDF file and stored as an attachment to the opportunity record (as noted earlier, to save space you may want to store this attachment in one of your file servers and merely point to it with the SFDC URL field in the opportunity record).

Once a quote has been accepted by the customer, the order operations people should mark the opportunity as "Closed: Contractual Approval," which triggers a workflow.

What About Duplicate Opportunities?

There are some tools that dedupe opportunities in SFDC. But this is not to be done lightly and should be performed only by an administrator.

To see how this works, let's assume you have two opportunities: the master and the duplicate. For the master opportunity, the quote and order numbers are stored in the record. The duplicate opportunity must be compared to it (either using tools or visually inspecting two Web browser windows), and any unique data in the duplicate should be copied into the master. All contact roles, tasks, activity history, attachments, and other related items need to be transferred from the duplicate to the master (those transfers can be done automatically).

Even after a duplicate opportunity is emptied of all unique data, though, it should not be deleted.[26] Instead, it should have its status changed to "Duplicate Opportunity" and its probability percentage changed to zero.

---

26. Deletion just isn't the right thing to do. For Sarbanes-Oxley Act compliance, and for general data hygiene, records should never be deleted because all audit trails are deleted with the record. Keeping duplicate opportunities will use an infinitesimal amount of storage, yet will provide evidence for any forensic or business process analyses in the future.

This workflow should lock down nearly all the fields in the `opportunity` so they can be changed only by finance personnel or the system administrator. (Example fields that can be changed by anyone after closure are cross-reference numbers and `comments`.)

The order operations people should then work in their order entry or accounting screens to ensure that the order is properly booked and fulfilled. Whether these other systems are fully integrated with SFDC or not, the SFDC `opportunity` number and `quote` number should be recorded in the accounting/order entry system (dedicated fields should be set aside for this information) and the accounting/order entry system transaction ID number should be recorded in a dedicated `custom field` in the SFDC `opportunity` record.

Moving the `opportunity` status to "Contractual Approval" should initiate the following `workflow`:

1. The next stage in the approval cycle should involve the legal or finance department, which should have hammered out the final details of the contract earlier in the sales cycle. Even so, legal and finance personnel need to perform final review of the `opportunity` to make sure nothing important has changed. Once they've approved it, the status should be moved to "Closed: Won," with the next approval authority set to the accounting department. At this point, the legal department should create a SFDC `contract` and attach the file of the final text and the signature pages to that record. Order operations should also attach licenses, serial numbers, and shipping bills of lading to the `contract` object (usually as a pointer to the files rather than using the file attachments themselves). Plugins are available to integrate FedEx, UPS, and other shipping services directly into SFDC.

2. Accounting issues the invoice, using the information from the approved quote; once this is done, the `opportunity` status should be moved to "Closed: Invoiced," and the next approval authority set to the finance department. A copy of (or pointer to) the invoice should be attached to the SFDC `contract` record.

3. If the product or service has an expiration or renewal period, at this point the order entry staff should create a new open `opportunity` (set to 10% `probability`) with a `close date` of one year (or whatever the period) in the future with the `line items` and `amount` reflecting the expected renewal transaction. The order entry operation should create a `task` for the sales rep (or whoever handles renewals) to remind that person of the coming renewal transaction and should set up a `workflow` that sends out a customer reminder email about the need to renew. These steps can be almost entirely automated but may require extensive expansion to the price list and custom coding.

4. Finance reviews the invoicing and any payments for recognizable revenue. When revenue recognition criteria have been met, the finance department should change the `opportunity` status to "Closed: Recognized." At this point, the `workflow`

will permanently lock the record so that only a system administrator can make changes to it.

During this entire sequence of final status changes—which most reps don't pay much attention to, as they assume the deal is closed—the records are locked down and only the back office people can change them. Following this best practice, the rep no longer completely closes the `opportunity`, which is a bit of a culture shock. But that's the only way to truly comply with requirements like those established by the Sarbanes-Oxley Act.

Outside Sales Representatives

This section assumes the company has at least a three-level organization for closing deals: eCommerce, inside sales for small deals, and outside sales for enterprise deals. If you're an SDR or an inside rep, still read this section for some tips that apply to you as well.

It may surprise you that in many companies, the outside sales reps are among the last people to embrace the SFDC system. At the beginning, the likelihood of their being happy and productive SFDC users is pretty low. There are a dozen reasons for this reluctance, but we urge you to *not* push system usage for the reps too hard because it will only generate greater resistance. Eventually, they'll be attracted to the system naturally and become avid users—once they see what's in it for them.

As described earlier, the sales reps should have an SLA with the SDRs to make sure that the field operators don't waste time pursuing `leads`. Instead, they should be spending all their time on real `opportunities`.[27]

Reps who are on the road a lot should consider using SFDC's `offline edition` because it allows them to keep things up to date on their laptops without having to be connected (sometimes a difficult task in the security-conscious corporate networks). In addition, SFDC `mobile` has great wow value but can only be seriously used on an iPad or Android tablet. The mobile app works on most smartphones, but the limited screen space and keyboard make it tough to use for anything beyond simple lookups and minor field updates. Further, if your sales reps need to have access to other systems to get their jobs done, switching their smartphone back and forth between the native SFDC client and the browser used for other applications will be hopeless.

---

27. Although I'm a firm believer in having reps develop the business in their territories by working their networks and developing business in obvious accounts, having them cold call can be demoralizing and is an expensive waste of time. In high-tech companies, the sales team represents the organization's most expensive headcount. If there aren't enough high-quality opportunities to keep them busy, you need to build up the inside sales and telemarketing team.

The opportunity screens seen by the rep should use SFDC's `record types`, `sales processes`, and `screen layouts` to achieve streamlined `profile`-specific screens tailored to the deal they are doing. The screens should be as brief as possible, using `collapsible sections` and other tricks to make the system less intimidating. Consider making the `collapsible sections` represent the major phases of the sales cycle (something like *develop, quote, negotiate,* and *close*) to bring the essentials into focus for the reps. See www.SFDC-secrets.com for examples of this kind of customization.

As soon as the rep gets a new `opportunity` from the SDRs, he or she should do research on the company and collect as much context as possible before calling the prospect. Account intelligence tools from Hoover's, Dunn and Bradstreet, and other sources are available as plugins to SFDC, providing account and industry information on almost any U.S. company. SFDC's own `data.com` provides digests of the company demographics and enriched contact information about the key players in the deal. Executive and organizational intelligence is also available from list-building and social-networking vendors such as ZoomInfo, Discover.org, InsideView, iProfiles, and others that provide information on the individuals and teams in the account. Even if your company doesn't want to invest in fancy tools, Google, Yahoo!, LinkedIn, and other Web sites can provide an amazing amount of raw data within a few seconds.[28] No matter which tool you choose, have the SFDC implementation team create magic HTML links that automatically open the outside service's record for the prospect's data.

It also helps for the outside rep to have a clear idea about the organizational politics of the customer. Although some data-mining companies publish organizational profiles (with organizational charts and solid background information) for *Fortune* 100 companies, their products are expensive and they're not well integrated with SFDC. The good news is that a couple of really nice tools are available that can quickly generate organizational charts from any data already stored in SFDC, and these plugins can be very helpful in mapping key relationships. For these tools to work well, however, it's essential to populate the `Title` and `Reports to` fields in the `contact` object, the `site` field and the `parent account` and `contact role` relationships in the `account`. With these data in place, the system can generate a very usable organizational chart diagram in just a few seconds. This output has great wow value for internal account reviews.

Outside sales reps have longer, more complicated sales cycles than inside reps do: the whole point is for the outside rep to expand the footprint of the deal and increase the order value. During the sales cycle, the customers being targeted by these reps are likely to require demonstrations, proofs of concept, executive calls or visits, special contractual

---

28. The problem with these sources is not the amount of data they provide, but rather the organization and quality of the data. It's easy to waste an hour sifting through stuff that really isn't the right information—so using only free Web sources can be a false economy.

terms, and other steps that require corporate resources. Sales reps should not be allowed to request these kinds of special resources via email or phone—over time, the company should make it a practice that requests will be ignored unless they come in via SFDC. At first, via `chatter` will be sufficient. Over time, the best practice is to create request check boxes on the SFDC screens so that these requests are made entirely through the system, are evaluated only with data entered in the system, and are escalated and approved via a `workflow`. Following this path ensures that the sales rep gets something of value—the sales assistance he or she needs—in exchange for the information that the company needs to allocate expensive resources more profitably.

Sales reps should also use SFDC `templated` emails for communications to the customer during the sales cycle. That way, everyone will be able to see the state of play for the customer relationship without having to send around a "what's up" email. Although the specifics will vary for each company, reps frequently send emails for the following purposes:

- Scheduling meetings
- Setting up demonstrations and proofs of concept
- Acknowledging a question or action item
- Following up on a question or action item
- Responding to an RFI or RFQ
- Sending a quote
- Responding to contractual issues
- Reminding prospects of deadlines for quotes or discounts
- Acknowledging receipt of a contract or purchase order

Each of these types of email should be set up as an SFDC `email template` with the messages actually being sent from the system. Not only does this structure save the sales rep time and effort; it also ensures a certain level of professionalism in interactions with existing and potential customers (e.g., the mail merge function always puts in the right name and salutation for the prospect). Further, these templates can be used in `workflows` that lend themselves to future automation that can streamline the rep's workload. Because these emails will be sent by the SFDC engine, the contents and timing of the emails will be automatically recorded for the relevant `accounts` or `opportunities`.

If your customer base still works via paper communications, the same techniques and benefits apply for automatically generating fax and postal mail from SFDC `templates`. There are a couple of nice AppExchange plugins for this.

Email and SFDC: How Cool Is That?

Of course, you can send emails from SFDC, and `workflows` can even do it for you.

But let's look at it from the other direction: how would you like to be able to send emails from your smartphone (or Mac, or Internet café . . .) to your prospect and have them automatically attached as a completed `task` to the right person and deal in SFDC? Well, you can, and it's free. It's called `email to salesforce`, and it takes about 5 minutes to set up and learn. There are a couple of setting adjustments we recommend: turn off storing attachments (they gobble up storage) and success-notification emails (they get real annoying fast).

If you want to pay for some software to be written, the feature can be extended to give you all kinds of magical powers from email without logging in to SFDC at all. But for most folks, the free functionality is great as it is.

Let's go one step further: if you're a sales manager, wouldn't you like to be able to do a `quote approval` entirely via email? You bet that's in the system. And it's free, too. Of course, it has to be tailored to your particular use cases, but that's just a few hours' work.

If you're an Outlook user and want to go nuts, there's a free plugin to synchronize `calendars`, `contact` lists, and selected emails between your PC and SFDC. This feature has some warts on it, but if you are disciplined enough to avoid them, the features can be pretty powerful.

All that, for free.

Opportunity Management

In outside sales, the length of the sales cycle may be 9 months or longer, so the reps need to make use of more parts of the SFDC system. Here's a priority list of things that the rep and others should keep in the system:[29]

1. The complete cast of characters (`contacts` and `contact roles` such as influencer, budget holder, champion, and economic buyer) should be included, along with their contact information.

2. `Files` and `content deliveries` should be attached to the `opportunity` record.

3. Deal-specific action items and ticklers should be set up as `tasks` attached to the `opportunity` record (particularly when the rep needs to leverage someone who doesn't report to him or her).

---

29. Many sales reps tend to manage information too tightly, perhaps because of their fear of being micromanaged. If you detect this attitude, you need to reread the discussion in Chapter 6.

4. `Chatter` threads should be created at least for the `opportunity` and for any hot issue that needs collaboration (such as, "How do we overcome the price objection when the competition is X?").

5. Requests for corporate resources (e.g., executive visits, on-site demonstrations, proofs of concept, and loaner equipment) should be attached to the `opportunity` record, implemented as check boxes that initiate approval processes.

6. Logged calls or emails should be recorded in the `opportunity's activity history` for each *significant* phone call or *any* on-site visit to the customer. There doesn't have to be much data in this history, but simply knowing how many times the company has been in touch with the prospect[30] is an important metric.

7. Forms and `account` profiles that fit within the company's sales methodology should be attached to the `opportunity` record. These items can be created using AppExchange plugins for specific methodologies or can be created as `custom fields` in `collapsible sections` (such as "needs assessment" or "demonstration of value") in the `opportunity` record.

STALE OPPORTUNITIES

Any `opportunity` *for new business that has not had any updates for 100 days should have its probability changed to zero, even if the rep says the deal is still alive. In contrast, renewal opportunities may be valid in the system for as long as 3 years, depending on the company's business practice. All of this auto-expiration can be handled automatically—the hard part is getting the troops to agree on a set of rules.*

Forecasting and the Pipeline

Maintaining the individual `opportunity` records for deals is the first part of any forecast. In managing `opportunities`, it's particularly important for the rep that the `amount, stage, probability %`, and `close date` reflect reality; thus, these items should be reviewed on at least a weekly basis. Assuming that the company's forecasting has a weekly pipeline-review call on Mondays, the individual reps should update their `opportunity` records on Thursday nights (you'll see why in a few paragraphs). It is *very* common to have stale `close date` entries, but they cause just as much havoc in management as having an incorrect `amount`—so reps should update *all* fields regularly (if for no other reason than that their manager will bug them about this issue).

---

30. This, of course, is the ultimate lightning rod for reps who are worried about being micromanaged. The only way to allay these fears is to clearly and consistently demonstrate that you're not micromanaging them.

For many companies, it will be necessary to break the overall `amount` field into its components (such as hardware, software, training, maintenance, and consulting services) using `custom fields`. Early in the sales cycle, neither the rep nor the customer may be certain about this breakdown, so `opportunities` will initially have only an overall `amount` attached to them. As work on the deal progresses, the rep will learn more about the underlying elements of the deal. Using SFDC's `products` functionality, the rep can enter line items that will better reflect the expected order, and the system will automatically calculate the `amount` field. If your company doesn't want to use the `products` functionality, the SFDC system can be configured with `formulas, workflow rules`, or `APEX` code to calculate the `amount` field from other system data.

The `opportunity` has a `probability` field that is automatically set by the `stage` pick list. Since most `stage` pick lists reflect where the deal is in your company's process, the probability percentage is more like "percentage we have completed our efforts in the sales cycle." Great, but that has nothing to do with where the customer is in their buying process.[31] The system does let the rep adjust the `probability` of the opportunity to reflect his or her degree of confidence about closing the deal, but this is *not the right thing to do*.[32] Instead of fudging the data (which misleads everyone), we recommend adding a `custom field` (a pull-down list, actually) to indicate the likelihood of a win so that management can really understand what's going on in the current deals. Check out the sidebar titled "Sales Stages versus Probabilities" later in this chapter.

That's it for the individual opportunity. But now let's look at the forecasting system[33] that allows each rep and manager to override the roll-ups of individual `opportunities`. The rep can exclude any deal from the `committed forecast`, adjust the total `amount` he or she believes the deal will produce, do a probability override, or move the expected `close date`. In most cases, these adjustments have comment fields that allow the rep or manager to communicate why adjustments have been made. Given that these adjustments are made by every level of sales management, this approach is a great way of increasing each manager's confidence in his or her personal forecast. The net result in a large organization is several layers of adjustment that lead to better accuracy. The reporting that is enabled by the forecasting system is pretty cool, and with add-on products you can get rep and territory scorecarding, forecasting accuracy, comparative norms—literally, more charts and graphs than you'll ever be able to explain to the board. Powerful stuff.

---

31. It's a best practice to have the `stages` defined by the customer's process, not by your activity. If you can't convince yourself to do that, at least create entry hurdles for each of your existing `stages` that reflect customer commitment rather than your team's effort.

32. There are a bunch of reasons for this, but I'm not going to go into them here. Just trust me on this one.

33. SFDC includes forecasting as part of the Sales Cloud license, but there are two versions that are quite a bit different. `Customizable forecasting` is probably what's turned on in your instance, but the better path is to go for `collaborative forecasting`. If you possibly can, go for the better path—it's the future and will be much easier to manage over time.

Quoting and Closing

Reps love the close—that is, the thrill of the win. But in this Sarbanes-Oxley world, closing an opportunity consists of a series of controlled steps involving other groups. Thus, the sales rep will initiate the close, but it will be executed by others. To find out more, see the "Handling Order Operations for Outside Sales" section earlier in this chapter.

What happens if the deal is lost? The rep closes the `opportunity`, but he or she needs to put in a `loss reason` via a pick-list selection. Many companies try to add several fields to the SFDC system to collect information about competitors and other win/loss criteria, but reps are rarely willing to fill in all those fields. Instead, keep things really simple and use a single, mandatory pick list.

Named Account Model of Selling

The lead-development model discussed up to now—in which prospects are promoted from marketing `leads` to SDR `contacts` to field `opportunities`—is popular with SMB sales organizations. With enterprise target accounts, however, more sophisticated salesforces tend to use a Named Account model. Sometimes these teams are called major account managers (MAMs), global account managers (GAMs), or strategic account managers (SAMs). Regardless of the specific name, these teams work in an entirely different way from the demand-generation, `leads`-driven geographic sales model.

MAMs, GAMs, and SAMs are not usually looking for `leads` to be discovered, cultivated, and elevated into opportunities by someone else. Instead, they are looking to increase business from existing customers or to target accounts that they *know* will be interested in the company's product or service. For example, if a MAM works for an avionics manufacturer, nearly all of the direct customers will be airframe manufacturers, such as Boeing, Airbus, Lockheed-Martin, Embraer, and Bombardier. An avionics MAM/GAM/SAM probably also knows the job titles and professional affiliations of all the prospects in these target companies. Furthermore, an authoritative list of the prospect universe, including full contact information and profiles, can be purchased for a reasonable fee.

So these account managers will identify who's a hot prospect in their own way, selecting targets from a known population.[34] These reps will also use SFDC in a very different way, but their way of using the system has to be congruent with the way the rest of the sales team uses it.

---

34. This same type of process is used by business development (BD) people who are trying to work organizations they already know. Even though BD reps typically don't work a quota the way MAM/GAM/SAMs do, they can use SFDC in a very similar way.

The SFDC best practices for named account managers include these behaviors:

- Before anything is loaded in the system related to named accounts, sales management must agree on the definition and number of named accounts to prevent poaching and hogging of big deals. Typically, there will be somewhere between 50 and 500 named accounts worldwide split among the NAM reps in a predefined way.

- The definitions and boundaries of named accounts need to be set tightly, particularly with accounts that are large conglomerates. Mitsubishi probably consists of 100 companies in Japan alone, and 200 companies worldwide—ranging from retail banking to electronics manufacturing to shipyards with operations in 89 countries around the world. So is Mitsubishi one named account or several? Sales management needs to clearly state the rules here.

- The top-level `account`—which is often a holding company or conglomerate—will rarely become an ordering customer. Even so, an `account` should be created for it in SFDC with ownership set to the NAM rep, and separate `child accounts` should be established for the operating divisions and remote offices. For example, General Electric (GE) is unlikely to be a customer, but GE Plastics, GE Jet Engines, GE Medical, and GE Leasing are likely to be. The top-level `account` should be owned exclusively by the NAM rep, and the `child accounts` should be owned by the NAM rep and shared with the relevant sales team for the territory where each division is located.

- Because the NAM rep's territory is not geographic in nature, there's almost inevitable conflict with the standard geographic territories. The difficulty comes when a small division of a big conglomerate is claimed by one of the regular territory reps, but the conglomerate is a NAM account. These internal workings can confuse the customer and lead to contentiousness inside your sales organization. It is essential to have a quick escalation mechanism that resolves these kinds of issues before they have time to fester. Once the management rules are in place, use SFDC's `sales teams` feature to properly share information about cooperative deals.

- The named accounts should be loaded into SFDC even if you've never had a `lead converted` or an `opportunity` there. Create the `account` (assuming it isn't already there; if it is, just update it) with a `custom field` check box called "Major account" (or whichever label is appropriate for you). The `account status` field should be set to `target` unless the company is already an active customer. Depending on your `sales process`, it may also make sense to create a `record type` and `page layouts` for named account managers so they don't interfere with what the geo reps use on a day-to-day basis.

Territories and Managing Ownership

SFDC was developed with the demand-generation model and geographic territories in mind. Although it has the building blocks for complex territory management, making the system automatically support overlays and nongeographic territories is an incredible chore.

In SFDC, ownership is the way the system manages visibility, access privileges, roll-ups, reporting, and dashboards. It's hard to think of one field that's more important to good operations than a record's `owner`. And pretty much every record in the system has one.

Let's say you own Disney. You'd think that all the contacts and opportunities and cases would be automatically assigned to you, right? Wrong. Every record's ownership is set independently and can be reset by authorized users. Yum.

That's the basis for one of our best practices: *don't change named account assignments often.*

If the NAM team is small, the ownership assignments can probably be managed manually. Not fun, but the automatic techniques don't scale down well.

If the NAM team is big, automation is the only way. We tend to favor using the MAS (ExactTarget, Marketo, Eloqua, etc.) to do the assignment of lead and contact ownership, and they can even be configured to do accounts and opportunities. The alternative is writing a bunch of `APEX` code or buying an AppExchange plugin. This means money, but it saves a lot of squabbling (particularly when there are partners in the mix).

One of the trickiest issues in account ownership is handling divisions of multinational companies and the use of street names (e.g., Dupont) versus legal entity names (E.I. du Pont de Nemours and Company). Doing this right involves "fuzzy lookups" that, like much of artificial intelligence, can easily go nuts. Be patient: the lookups can be tuned to behave better. But it will take time.

Which brings us back to "don't change named account lists often."

- For the people with whom your company has done business at the `account` (these are `contacts`), assign `contact roles` and `Reports to` relationships to reflect their political standing in the organization.

- The SFDC system administrator needs to add a field that relates `leads` to `accounts` and to show the `related list` for `leads` on the `account page layout`; this layout should be explicitly set up for the named account team. In the context of named accounts, `leads` are people we've never met but whom we know work at the company.

- Anybody the company has ever had a conversation with at the `account`—even if the company hasn't done business with that person—should be entered as a contact with ownership set to the appropriate NAM rep. The company may not know any more about these contacts than it would with names (see the discussion on this in Chapter 8), but it can handle that issue by setting the contact's score to a low number and setting the type to prospective target. These contacts' source field should be set to "Named Account," and the type field should be set to "prospect."[35] (Always search for these people as either leads or contacts before you create new leads or contacts—remember the Commandments given earlier in this chapter.) Make sure that the contact is associated with the *correct* account if it's part of a complex account hierarchy.

- Only after the NAM sales rep has actually talked to the individual and fully qualified that person should the contact have its type field set to "active contact."

The hallmark of named account management is a strategic account plan that outlines a series of actions that will be taken to win and grow the major/global/strategic business. Although NAM reps should be flexible enough to help with small deals at their large accounts, the core of their value comes from the proactive work that deepens the corporate relationship. Their account plan should provide a model for orchestrating the efforts of individual sales reps across the world to achieve the corporate goal. Of course, no one is really going to appreciate those kinds of personal obligations just because a written plan exists. Using SFDC's chatter, campaigns, workflows, and tasks, the NAM rep should communicate to the rest of the sales organization the specific action items in a structured way and improve the level of coordination and follow-through on plans and action items. Further, by putting this information in SFDC, pertinent dashboards and reports can be made available on a real-time basis. Finally, the account plan document files (Word, PowerPoint, or Excel) should be attached to the relevant account so that no one has an excuse for not knowing the objectives and rules of the road for each strategic account.

The other hallmark of named account management is knowing and leveraging the customer's organizational politics. It is essential for the NAM rep to know who's where in the organization, what their current account roles are, and where the political battle lines have been drawn. Anytime *anybody* in your company (sales, marketing, customer support, or consulting) makes a connection or has a conversation with someone in a target named account, they need to take the following steps:

- Make sure the person is present in the SFDC system as a contact with updated contact information.

---

35. Views and reports of contacts should be set up to filter out these named account contact statuses so that people don't get confused and metrics don't become distorted.

- Make sure that the `Reports to` field reflects the person's latest organizational status.

- Add or update the `contact role`[36] relationship at the `account`, `opportunity`, and `case` levels.

- Add `chatter` entries for the `account`, `opportunity`, `contact`, and any relevant `topics`.

- Add `tasks` on political issues and attach them to the `opportunity`.

- Keep referencability information up to date (see Chapter 10 for a discussion of this issue). These `custom fields` that marketing has set up are intended to help the company track and manage customer happiness as a resource so that references don't get burned out by sales overuse or PR abuse.

By using everyone in your company as sensors, the large-account management function can become much more effective at working customers' organizational politics and pumping out deals.

Partner Management

Most companies now must leverage several channels—direct, inside, Web, distributors, and resellers—to make revenues happen predictably and profitably. SFDC's Partner Relationship Management system and partner portal[37] can dramatically improve the indirect channel management in a big way, but most SFDC customers don't do enough in this area.

If your partner already uses SFDC, you can use a feature called `Salesforce-to-Salesforce` to share data in a systematic and continuous way. This is the über-cool solution because it provides transparency and real-time updates.

If your partner uses a different SFA system, or if it is unwilling to integrate with your company through `Salesforce-to-Salesforce`, SFDC's `partner portal` or `chatter communities` are the right solution. These provide casual access to your system with security controls that ensure the partner's employees see only their own prospects and deals. Through this portal, partners can register `leads`, add information about `contacts` and `accounts`, and update `opportunities` with the latest deal and `case` information. This means you can "flip" leads over to the partners and monitor

---

36. My firm usually adds entries to the `contact role` pick list to add some political context to the organizational chart that develops around each deal. Example items might include *champion, blocker, passive-aggressive,* and *bystander.*

37. If you have not enabled the `customer portal` or `partner portal` in your instance of SFDC, they are no longer available to you. They have been replaced by `chatter communities`.

their progress in opportunity creation and closing. Although the partner won't get any dashboards, your partner management team sure will.

Beyond these SFDC features, here are best practices to keep your company's partners as productive as possible:

- Put your company's internal document library and collateral in the `partner portal`, or give the partner access to your company's intranet content management system. They need to be part of your sales team to be effective.

- Involve your partners in `chatter groups` so they can learn from you (and hopefully, you from them). Of course, you don't want to have competitive partners in the same group, but if you manage this carefully, the partner reps really start working as allies rather than bystanders.

- Score `leads` (or at least rate them hot/warm/cold) and prequalify them *before* you send them over to the partner to help the partner manage its `lead` flow. Sending junk `leads` is bad for productivity and undermines the partnership. Make sure the `leads` are as high quality and fresh as the ones you give your own `lead`-cultivation/nurturing people.

- Send `leads` to individual reps, not just partner companies. This will improve their `lead`-response time by hours, if not days. Using SFDC `workflows` and `APEX` code, you can automatically route `leads` according to the partner's territory definitions.[38]

- Route the highest-value `leads` (the ones that appear to be the biggest deals) to the best-performing partners. Of course, it takes a while before SFDC has enough data to indicate who those best-performing partners are, but this best practice leads to even higher-performing partner relationships.

- In SFDC, mark `leads` you've sent out with the partner's name (using a `custom pick list` field or, if you have a ton of partners, via a `lookup` field).

- Do not send a given `lead` to more than one partner. Let each partner know that each `lead` you send is an exclusive opportunity for that partner. Make your `lead routing` to partners flawless to avoid creating a mess.

- Monitor the progress of the partner's lead qualification, conversion, and opportunity development. Establish a waterfall model (with norms for conversion time and percentage), and compare the partner's performance to it. If your partner's sales process requires approvals from your channel manager, make sure that

---

38. In simple situations, you might be able to use SFDC's `lead` assignment rules to accomplish this routing, but it is nearly impossible to get right for many partner situations.

approvals are handled in a timely manner using workflows and alerts to escalate any delayed approvals.

- When reviewing the partner's forecast and performance against goals, use SFDC data as the basis for all discussions so that the partner understands how important it is to keep the system data updated and clean.

- After you've got a few quarters' worth of data in the system, ask the marketing staff or perhaps a finance analyst to look at the partner productivity and to create a profile of what makes a good partner and what makes a dud. Use these analyses to guide your partner recruitment efforts going forward.

To the extent possible, leverage SFDC to make the company's partners feel like equals with the access and information they need to succeed. If they feel like they are part of your company's team, they'll be a more effective extension to your selling efforts. Provide links to documents that very clearly describe the rules of engagement and deal qualification for the partner, so the partner knows what to expect and how to "work the system" in your company.

But what about the `leads` and `opportunities` that a partner sends to *you*?

Set up a lead entry and opportunity registration system for partners that are available on a 7 × 24 basis. The `partner portal` or `chatter communities` are great for this, but some clients prefer a home-brew system that leverages the SOAP APIs instead.

Once you have the registration system in place, make a habit of accepting `leads` and `opportunities`, even if they seem a bit dubious. Nothing angers a partner more than instant rejections by your company's sales reps. If they do have to reject a partner's input, make sure the reps send the partner an explanatory email that is as polite as it is complete.

To make the partner lead and deal management process as effective as possible, follow these best practices:

- Make sure the partner `leads` are routed to the proper sales rep or product specialist on your team, using `lead assignment rules`, `workflows`, or `triggers` (for complex situations).

- Make sure that the `leads`, `contacts`, and `opportunities` are properly attributed to the individual referrer's name (a `custom field`) and the partner company (`custom pick list`), and make sure that they are included in the `campaign` that's been set up for each partner (ask marketing personnel to handle this task if they haven't done so already).

- Use `workflows` and `email templates` to send an acknowledgment email from the receiving sales rep to the partner, thanking the partner for the referral and providing full contact information for the two sides' reps to connect with each other.

- Monitor *your* progress with the `leads` and `opportunities` sent your way and keep the partner informed with reports or emailed dashboard elements. Use `workflows` to make sure that progress on deals doesn't stall and to remind accounting personnel to send referral fees when deals close. You want your company's partners to feel that information access and measurement is a two-way street.

- Drive the partner's incentive fees off of SFDC data. Although the calculation of incentive checks is always complicated (and is best done by the finance folks), make sure that all relevant data (including co-marketing funds) are stored in SFDC.

- Create `reports` and a `dashboard` for your company's partner manager to see performance for the partners he or she is responsible for on an ongoing basis.

Business Development

The business development (BD) function varies significantly across industries and channel positions (e.g., vendor, distributor, or reseller). In fact, in many companies, the BD people won't need to log in to SFDC. Nevertheless, to the extent that BD is about identifying and cultivating future customer relationships, their efforts *should* be captured and aided by SFDC. The best practices for BD are really a combination of named account management (for prospects prior to contract signing) and partner management (once the deal is done).

Many times, BD negotiations must be highly secretive, so appropriate security measures must be taken before the prospect information is entered into SFDC. These strategic BD people should be designated as direct reports to the CEO in the SFDC `role` hierarchy, even if most BD people report to the VP of sales. The reason for this structure is that many operations and analyst types will have access privileges at the VP of sales level, but they should not see the account information being developed by the BD reps. Once this `role` hierarchy is set up, use SFDC's `sales teams` features to allow the VP of sales—and only that person—to see the BD target accounts.

The BD function should probably have its own `record types` and `sales processes` for `opportunities` because they are not really conventional sales cycles and shouldn't be included in the standard forecast.

Field Sales Engineers or Product Specialists

In most high-tech firms, product specialists help the sales rep win the deal. Whether they're called sales engineers (SEs), presales support, sales specialists, or sales associates, these individuals are *involved* in the big deals, even though they don't close the sale or run the paperwork.

In most organizations, SEs are a shared resource: each specialist has to help three or more sales reps on deals. This can make their lives hellish, as reps fight for priority and SEs get jerked from deal to deal on a daily basis.

As a consequence of their jobs and their personalities, SEs are often great early users of SFDC because the system lets them rapidly come up to speed on the *crisis du jour*, update the status of action items quickly, and easily manage their backlog and workload. Better still, SFDC can help ward off artificial crises that reps may invent to pull the SE away from other deals. The best practices for SEs are outlined here:

- Set up an internal process such that requests for SEs must be made through SFDC rather than via email or voicemail. The SE manager should make it clear that requests made via the system and with more complete/informative data will be serviced sooner than requests that do not go through the SFDC system and are incomplete.

- The SE should turn each customer interaction into a `task` (open or completed, attached to the `opportunity`) so that the entire sales team can understand the state of action items and follow-ups. It's a good idea to add a `custom field` to the task reflecting hours or dollars expended.

- Any *customer* requests for technical information should be logged as a `task`, and the responses should be attached as either an email or a document to the `opportunity` record. For formal RFQ and RFI processes, the original requesting document and the company's response should be attached to (or at least pointed to from) the `opportunity` record.

- Any competitive information (such as knock-offs, benchmark results, or customer feature evaluations) should be attached to the `opportunity`.

- For very complicated products, the SE should be included in the quote's `approval cycle` to make sure that the best configuration of products has been selected.

- Finally, SEs should be among the most avid users of `chatter`. Whether it's for competitive research or troubleshooting a technical issue, `chatter` is the ideal collaboration system for people on the road.

Sales Management

This section applies to all sales managers, although some of the advice applies only at the executive level. Even if a particular item doesn't apply to you, read it so you can see what the organizational direction is—and how you fit into it.

Your first job is to make the number, right? In a similar way, the first and only job of the team working on SFDC is to get user adoption up[39] to 100% during the first few months of operation. And the only way to achieve that goal is to have high-quality, meaningful data in the system. Meaningful data means happier users who will create more good data. Success breeds more success. Without it, SFDC will just be an empty shell that won't do anybody any good.

Sales management's decisions, personal behavior, and word choices can make a big difference here. Your team knows you, and they can read what you think at from your tone of voice, gestures, and facial expressions. A few of the wrong words carelessly thrown around when you're stressed out at the end of the quarter can set SFDC adoption back by months.

Setting the Example

Show the team what to expect in terms of the SFDC system through your actions. Make sure you convey these messages both verbally and nonverbally:

- SFDC is what you'll be using to drive the boat. It's how you'll implement quota decisions, commission splits, and territory plans. It's how you'll do account reviews and precall briefings. It's how you'll run the weekly forecast meeting.

- SFDC will be the *only place you'll look* for information about customers and prospects, so anything relevant should be available and accurate in SFDC. Reps who keep "little black books" containing all the real information—whether on paper, on their blackboard, in Act, in Excel, or in Outlook—will be left out in the cold. Make it clear that you're not going to be happy if you have to look outside of SFDC for information about people, accounts, or deals.

- SFDC is how you expect the individual reps to manage their time more effectively. Field reps are business people who have been given an exclusive franchise to sell your company's product in a territory; as CEOs of their own businesses, above all else they'll need to manage their time wisely. SFDC will be optimized *for them* to increase their leverage so they can avoid the duds and close more real deals.

- SFDC is *not* a spying machine. It's not a micromanagement tool, and you will not use it that way.

- SFDC *is* a way for the reps to get more out of the resources that the company gives the sales team—people, loaner machines, travel budgets, leads, and so forth.

---

39. I know I've been repeating this endlessly, but it's a message that has to get to everyone who reads any chapter of this book.

- `Chatter` is the fastest way to find out something about the latest product, or competitor's gambit, or overcoming a new objection. Email is so last century and wastes everybody's time. Set the example by posting something relevant on `chatter` every day.

- SFDC is *not* an administrative burden. Through automation and better collaboration, it *is* a liberation from data reentry and forgotten action items. It's the fastest way to get intelligence on the customer and get through speed bumps. Tell the sales personnel to use the Outlook connector to their email system so everyone has less to type. If necessary, hire a temporary administrator (with a dedicated phone line and voicemail box) to do the reps' data entry for the first few months. *Remove all excuses for not using the system.*

THE VIRTUAL WAR ROOM

Way back during the .com bubble, I worked in a sales organization that had a war room—a physical space manned 18 × 5 during the last 10 days of the quarter to coordinate every company resource so the reps could bring in the number.

These days, a physical room isn't a good investment, but SFDC can become your company's virtual war room. Almost all the information you need for the end-of-quarter chaos is already in one place in this system; it's just a matter of getting the reps to respond quickly and without any misfires.

Use `chatter`, `tasks`, `workflows`, `escalations`, and `alerts` to make sure every action item gets done on time. Store all the sales information—customer notes, RFIs, `quotes`, and contractual terms—directly attached to the `opportunity`. Set aside a `chatter topic` (like, #win) and an email box for high-priority deals (mustwin@yourco.com is my favorite), and a voicemail box (at extension 2946[40] in your phone system) for the same purpose.

During the closing weeks of the quarter, designate an explicit "officer of the day" who receives all escalations (via SMS or voicemail to his or her cell phone), and put the duty schedule right on the home page of your SFDC home page for everyone's reference.

- SFDC is your preferred medium for communication about prospects, deals, and customers, and you consider it to be much better than email for this purpose. You want to see the number of internal emails decrease by 10% or more because the stuff that reps and others need to close deals and service customers will be available via a central, organized resource that everyone will be able to see. Tell the reps that you will give lower priority to requests made via email and voicemail

---

40. This spells "2WIN" on the phone pad.

than to requests that come in via SFDC. Emails and voicemails are fine for *alerting* people to change, but all the substantive information should be in the deal war room that is provided by SFDC. If necessary, buy the reps a new phone and SFDC `mobile edition` so they have what they need at their fingertips in real time. Take away all the excuses.

- If your team is seriously into a formal sales methodology, SFDC is the most efficient way to leverage that sales model. Buy plugins or standalone applications that interface with SFDC to streamline the use of the company's sales methodology and reduce the amount of keyboard work for their reports and forms. Some of these products can generate an account management plan at the push of a button. This step can save hours of work for the reps every week.

- SFDC usage is so important to sales team effectiveness that you'll put in place small reward systems for completeness of information and effective use of the system. Even small awards and contests can bring out competitive behavior in a sales team, so use them wisely (particularly with the company's SDRs and inside sales teams).[41]

- The adoption and extension of SFDC will occur in an *incremental and measured* way. You're not going to ram drastic changes down the reps' throats. Instead, you plan to measure the improvements (or lack thereof) to make sure that the changes really are best for everyone, and adjust the metrics and the system along the way. Training *won't* be heavy-handed full-day sessions; instead, it will be light, need driven, tailored to the company's specific operation, self-paced, on-demand, and self-scoring.

Mandates for Your Reps

To get healthy use out of the SFDC system, you need to put some mandates in place over time. Every one of the following measures is designed to steer the sales reps in the right direction, even if they want to do something that is verboten:

- `Contact` information for every person who is involved in any deal must be in SFDC. If you give the reps the `mobile edition`, the *only* place `contact` information should live is in SFDC. If you don't get the `mobile edition`, tell the reps to have a system administrator push their Outlook (or Gmail) address books into SFDC (due to data corruption issues, people must *not* attempt this feat themselves).

---

41. Make the competition relevant to the reps. Nothing is worse than a lame contest over the equivalent of office cubicle decoration.

- Sales reps must be forbidden from attempting wholesale uploads of address books or contact spreadsheets into SFDC. These data dumps cause data pollution that's painful to recover from. Instead, all (and that means *all*) `lead` or `contact` uploads must be done by the marketing staff or a system administrator. This is one of the things the marketing folks are really good at, so use them (plus, they get to take the blame if they do it wrong).

- Perhaps even more important, sales reps must not create new `accounts`[42] without searching for them first. Creating a duplicate `account` creates more damage and undermines credibility in more ways than just about any other action. Check out the "Creation Science" sidebar earlier in this chapter. There needs to be a very strict naming convention for accounts (if you want to know more about this issue, see the "Conversion and Hand-Off to Sales" section earlier in this chapter) and rules about `parent/child account` relationships.

The next big change for the reps—and they'll whine endlessly about it—is to stop them from using email or voicemail for assigning and updating internal action items. Email is just the wrong way to handle action items: if someone wasn't copied on that one relevant reply, that person is out of the loop and may make a wrong decision. Instead, use SFDC `tasks` to assign action items, follow-ups, and reminders across the company.[43] Use `chatter` for problem solving and to get information updates. In this way, everyone on the sales team will know whether an action item has been done, what the response was, and what follow-up is necessary. Managers can run reports to see which deal-oriented `tasks` are overdue, and they can spot bottlenecks before they turn into big problems around vacation time or the end of the quarter. Of course, when a communication needs to directly include the customer, you can't use `tasks`—but the email the rep sends can be attached to the `opportunity` record (using SFDC's free `email to Salesforce` feature or the Outlook connector) so that everyone can see the state of play.

There's another rep behavior that needs to change: stop using fields such as *comments, description, overview*, and *notes* to store information about the state of the deal. `Notes`, `comments`, or `description` are for information that *won't change* during the deal (e.g., "You MUST have your driver's license to get past security in this building!"). Those free-text fields are almost useless, and relying on them leads to dropped balls. Anything

---

42. The same goes for `opportunities`, `contacts`, and `leads`, although duplication of these items has somewhat less potential for damage.

43. Eighty percent of the people receiving `tasks` need to have a full SFDC license for this strategy to work properly, so make sure that key players are all working in the system. The other 20% will really be a "department" rather than an individual. The department will get an email with an SFDC link in it and then use the departmental SFDC account to see what's coming its way. Department employees will, in turn, respond through the SFDC system, so the results are visible to all members of the sales team and attributed to the responding department. For details on how to do this, visit the Web site www.SFDC-secrets.com.

transitory or sequential in nature should go into `tasks` as either an open action item or a completed call, meeting, or follow-up.

Move the reps away from issuing quotes using standalone Word or Excel documents. Move toward using the `price book`, with `quotes` generated directly out of SFDC. Have the quotes go through internal approvals for unusual discounts, and then get the customer's sign-off using digital signatures (with DocuSign or other products). Doing it right may require either a bit of `VisualForce` and `APEX` code, an AppExchange add-on, or considerable integration, but either way, the decrease in manual processing will speed up `quotes`, increase customer satisfaction, and lower error rates.

All deals—including renewals and upsells—need to be in the system as opportunities. Forecasts must be created and updated inside the SFDC system—no more external spreadsheets to manage the pipeline, the forecast, or the weekly sales call. The reps must understand that gaming the system screws things up for everyone and *will* be noticed by sales management.

Assign "ownership" of the quality of different parts of the data to different departments. For example, the marketing department and SDRs should own `leads`, and the reps should own `contacts`, `accounts`, and `opportunities`.

For *everyone* in sales, all the juiciest information should be stored in or attached to `opportunities`.

Create subtle penalties for inputting garbage data, and praise and offer small incentives for adding good data. It's pretty easy to determine who deleted something important or who created the duplicate records that everyone hates.

Tell the system administrator to remove the `merge` or `delete` buttons for most users. There are a lot of reasons why normal users should never delete anything from the system (see the "Creation Science" sidebar earlier in this chapter)—and there are ways to mark records so they'll disappear from view even though they are still stored in SFDC.

Configure the system so that the 15 or so pieces of data[44] you really want to protect and analyze in the future for each record have `history tracking` enabled. This feature is free and doesn't slow the system down, but it's an invaluable resource for future account and territory planning.

Keep your team out of the SFDC system's innards, even if they really do have the skills to change the system. Even if they were successful in modifying an `approval process`, changing a `pick list`, or tweaking an `email template` without goofing up other parts of the system, this is not the way for *sales* personnel to spend their time. They're supposed to be closing deals. Head off this behavior at the pass, so your more techie-oriented reps don't waste their time (and goof up the system at the same time).

---

44. Generally speaking, you'll want to enable the audit trails for record owner, status, stage, type, and territory for nearly every record, and the phone, email, and title for every `lead` or `contract`.

No one on the sales team (except maybe a sales operations person) should have full SFDC system administrator access. It's just a dangerous waste of time—just say no.

Now, let's look at the best ways *you* will use SFDC in the key sales management functions.

Pipeline Management

Let's just make a simple rule: the sales cycle starts when a rep creates an `opportunity` or accepts one created by an SDR. Higher up in the funnel isn't pipeline—it's just the funnel of things that could turn into deals. The start of the sales cycle means that the rep is betting his or her time, as well as other company resources, on the likelihood that this deal can close profitably. The goal of pushing this perspective is to make reps qualify harder, prioritize their time, and chase the right deals.

Once the opportunity is created, you want to see some sort of an update at least every 2 weeks (hopefully, more often than that) and very disciplined use of `sales stages`. Most sales cycles consist of four to eight stages between the creation of an `opportunity` and the hand-off of the win to order operations. As sales management, you need to publish clear entry and exit criteria for each `opportunity stage` and use `sales processes` to create subsets of stages[45] for different channels or target customers. Within the SFDC system, it's a best practice to put check boxes in the `opportunity` page so that the reps advance the deal stage by answering questions about specific buyer commitments or behaviors rather than by manually changing the `stage` pick list. You may want to take this further, creating `collapsible sections` in the page layout to help focus the reps on what they need to be doing to move to the next stage of the sales cycle.[46]

When the deal closes (either with a win or a loss), you'll probably want to have a couple of mandatory fields for the reps to collect the info while it's still fresh in their minds. You might also want to set off a `workflow alert` for the people in legal, order management, and fulfillment.

Set guidelines about `opportunity` staleness: if there hasn't been any movement in the deal, set alerts or create reports that highlight that some escalation is needed. This needs to be framed as helping reps get the resources they need to win the deal so that they don't see the system as their enemy.[47]

---

45. Sales cycles can vary by vertical industry and country, but the more consistent you can make the `opportunity stages`, the better the visibility and control you will have over the sales cycle.

46. If you really want to go nuts, you can even have a different page layout for each stage of the sales cycle. This can make for a lot less on-screen clutter, but over time leads to a fairly complex maintenance task for the system admin.

47. I've seen sales managements that take deals or even accounts away from reps if no progress has been made in 60 days. If that's where you're going to take things, please put those rules into effect for a while before you enforce them via SFDC.

Don't get too fancy with the analytics too early. Too many metrics can scare sales reps, and half the time the data aren't very good when the system is just starting up. Add a new `report`, `dashboard`, or analytic every 6 weeks or so, looking at things like time in stage, deals going backward (i.e., declining `probability`, lower `amount`, or later `close date`), the number of sales cycles in flight, and the number of customer visits required to close a deal.

THE DEVIL'S IN THE DETAILS

While everyone in sales knows about *the number,* most of the day-to-day decisions are made with your gut and communicated with your emotions.

Even if the SFDC system could provide perfect metrics—which it really can't—it's important to use reports and analytics in a genuine and productive way. It's easy to ask for reports that you won't actually use, but it's far more dangerous to ask for reports that you *will* use the wrong way.

Before you ask sales reps to enter any more data (which they'll view as another tax and an intrusion from management), figure out what *you* would *do differently* if you already had the report based on those data in front of you. Which decision would you *actually* make differently? If you're not sure what you'd do differently or are just curious, *don't ask* the reps to enter anything new. This goes double for activity management.

If you ask the reps to do something new, walk a mile in their shoes first. Top-down mandates practically guarantee attempts to game the system, particularly if the edicts have clear penalties or rewards. If you're going to lay down the law, make sure that gaming the system has the biggest penalties of all. When a rep games the system, it not only undermines SFDC's credibility (and data integrity) but also insidiously undermines *your* authority—so don't open the door to it.

Revenue Planning

The core of revenue planning is assuring that you have enough accounts and deals to make your target as a manager. If the territory isn't big enough or doesn't have enough targets, there's not much SFDC can do—so fix the territory size issue first. Implementing territory changes involves a lot of manipulation in SFDC (see the next section in this chapter), so don't put the system administrators through that stress until you have a really solid reason to do so.

To implement the revenue generation model discussed at the start of this chapter, SFDC needs to be configured with basic information: sales rep territories, inside sales territories, partner territories, named account lists, rep quotas, and so on.

When it comes to quotas, there are two schools of thought. My recommendation is to overassign the target to your subordinates, typically by 20% or so at each level of management. This is because you want to leave margin for error in the knowledge that on average about 40% of your reps won't make their individual numbers (if more than that *did* make the number, you're either setting quotas too low or being sandbagged by your reps). As a sales manager, there is nothing *más macho* than raising your target in midyear—and that's possible only if you overassigned[48] quotas in the first place.

The other school of thought is to *never* overassign quotas or even slightly underassign them. The reason: overassigning quotas simply increases the probability that reps won't make their numbers, which increases turnover, which decreases the sales department's effectiveness. Your whole team will end up spending all their time in learning curves rather than productively closing deals.

With either strategy, you have to upload or manually put quotas into SFDC, either by the month or by the quarter. For managers, calculate the amount of overassignment (or not) in a spreadsheet and enter the total quota for each manager[49] into SFDC's `user` screen. If the company has a really large sales team, have one of the system administrators import the quotas directly from your spreadsheet using the free `data loader` tool.

SFDC doesn't have anything fancy when it comes to revenue planning (such as sales rep productivity ramps, new-product introduction bookings effects, or other bells and whistles) or scorecarding (such as forecasting accuracy), so you'll have to perform all of those data manipulations in external spreadsheets or using tools from the AppExchange.

When developing your revenue plan, you'll need to create a waterfall model that takes into account the selling behavior of each of the company's major channels. This model is typically a spreadsheet, and it should include product launches, sales rep productivity ramps, quarterly timing, and the length of the sales cycle for that channel. Make sure to write these assumptions down. Faulty assumptions are the most insidious and deadly ingredients of a bad forecast, so you'll want to confirm that the model's assumptions hold up before you bet your career on them. To validate your model, ask the SFDC team to create reports that help you measure your team's performance against them on at least a quarterly basis:

- Percentage of `leads` ignored

- Time to first touch for `leads` that aren't ignored

- Percentage of `leads` qualified

- Percentage of `leads converted`

---

48. Or you were being severely sandbagged by your reps.

49. SFDC does not roll up the `quotas` of the manager's direct reports. So you need to assign the territory-level quota to each manager yourself (this allows you to do judgment calls on under- or overassignment).

- Percentage of **opportunities** rejected by sales

- Number of **opportunities** accepted by sales

- Average time for each **sales stage**

- Percentage of **opportunities** stalled

- Percentage of **opportunities** regressing[50]

- Total length of sales cycle

- Win rates for **opportunities** accepted by sales

- Upsell/renewal rates

- Average order size

Territory Management

Along with **quotas**, **territories** can be a constant source of squabbling, even if they are supposed to be stable for the year. That goes double for the Named Account model, where the NAM reps are looking for accounts to grab and geographic reps are looking for large company divisions to plunder.

The key to effective territory management is to have clear, documented roles and responsibilities for the reps, rules of engagement with partners, and appropriate commissions (splits or double commissions, depending on the situation). Territories can be really messy to manage if there are several types of overlays (e.g., new business direct, new business dealers, repeat business direct, repeat business dealers, national accounts, or special situations) and a matrix-format (or rapidly changing) organizational chart. CRM systems can accommodate all of these things, but setting the systems up to automatically do so will be painful, cost lots of money, and cause delays (due to inevitable errors and unforeseen consequences of automation). Plus, when you attempt to do historical analysis of territory productivity with territories changing all the time, your analysts will go crazy. In summary, make your territory system only as complicated as you absolutely need to—just recognize that there will be system consequences.

SFDC, like almost all CRM systems, works best with a straightforward hierarchy—where the reporting relationships form a pyramidal organizational chart with a clean "inverted tree" structure. For example, in terms of territories, California reports into the western United States, which reports into North America. You will want to add **custom**

---

50. A deal is regressing when its **amount**, **stage**, or **probability** is decreasing, or when its **close date** is moving out in time. Deals regress for lots of reasons, such as the client experiencing a budgetary cut or political upheaval, or a competitor throwing a counteroffer to keep its chances of winning the customer's business alive.

`fields` to indicate special commission or territory arrangements and set up SFDC features to handle `sales teams`, overlays, overrides, and splits. If your company depends on partners for a major portion of your revenue, you may want to set up the SFDC system to manage referral fees, cooperative selling, and two-level invoicing (one type of invoice for retail pricing for the end customer, and another type of invoice for wholesale pricing for the partner). All these can be built into or added onto SFDC, but they will all involve custom work—so set aside some budget for them.

For the purpose of evaluating the size and layout of territories, reports should show the number of target customers, the number of leads, the number of sales cycles, the revenues, and the profits for each region. The goal is to compare these metrics and make sound resource allocations. You may discover that the company makes a profit in only five U.S. states: maybe the company's sales reps should concentrate on those areas and leave the rest of the geographic regions to distributors and partner sales.

THE OWNERSHIP SOCIETY

No sales team wants to do housekeeping. But sales needs to be the owner of SFDC, and to keep things on the right track, the department needs to have a *"data owner"* for the system.

The data owner needs to be the guardian of semantics and data quality, making sure that the sales staff enter the right things into SFDC and keeping changes to the system to the absolute minimum—only things that will actually increase revenue. This data owner will work in conjunction with the marketing system administrator and the IT people to manage change in the system. In choosing this data owner, find someone who likes computers, wants to grow his or her job a little bit, and is good at foreseeing problems. Often, good candidates for the data owner will be in your sales operations group.

When you *do* need to redesign a territory, the goal is to get the most leverage out of the sales staff by balancing their workload and their opportunity to make money. You'll also want to minimize travel because it's so time-consuming and expensive. When undertaking a territory redesign, gather both the historical sales data from SFDC `opportunities` and the market sizing data from lead generation, marketing analyses, and external data sources. You'll almost certainly use a whiteboard or a spreadsheet to organize these data, but the key is to start with the best data you have from SFDC.

SFDC really works most easily with geographic territories that can be unambiguously defined by state lines, ZIP codes, or telephone city codes.[51] If you are willing to buy a

---

51. Due to telephone number-portability requirements and VoIP, area codes are essentially useless for territory definition in North America. In most other countries, city codes are still reasonably usable for the time being.

plugin product, you can use latitude/longitude or even counties to define your territories. If a more elegant way of defining territories (such as industry or customer profession) is needed, they must be defined in an unambiguous and consistent way that prevents arguments among the reps. Implementing these nongeographic territories and overlay territories will require `APEX` code in SFDC or programming in some external system. This doesn't come cheap, but it works well.

When you do redesign a territory, the following parts of SFDC need to be changed—so be ready for questions for the administrators:

- Web `autoresponse rules`, to thank clients for their interest while using the name of the correct rep in the signature/address block.

- `Lead assignment rules`, to route leads to the correct part of the sales team (this may be done outside of SFDC—in any case, the system that assigns ownership of leads needs to be adjusted).

- `Role` and `territory` hierarchies for roll-ups of forecasts and reports.

- `Filters` for `views, reports`, and `dashboards`.

- `Data access sharing rules` that allow you and your subordinates to see information in your territory, but not outside it.

- Names for the overall sales region (at least North America, EMEA, APAC, and ROW) and specific territory (e.g., Western United States) that may be used in `custom pick lists` in `lead, opportunity, account`, and `contact` records to facilitate reporting and analysis.

- `Case assignment rules` and `escalation rules`, to help route customer issues to the correct part of the support team and sales rep.

- Ownership of `leads, contacts, accounts, open opportunities, open tasks`, and `open cases` needs to be changed to the new territory owner.[52]

Historical analyses and commission calculations will be far easier if you don't make big changes to territories more than once per year[53] and if you maximize the number of customers that stay with their reps when changes do occur. Maintaining some sort of stability also enhances rep productivity, so this should be an easy best practice to follow.

---

52. Although sometimes you can just use SFDC's `mass-transfer wizard`, in the interesting cases this needs to be done with a series of data downloads and uploads. With complex `territory` overlays, this process can take a surprising amount of effort.

53. Of course, if a rep leaves or the company goes through a reorganization or merger, unplanned change is sometimes unavoidable.

> ## PERFECTIONISM STILL DOESN'T PAY
>
> *As we discussed in Chapter 3, trying to get data perfect is incredibly expensive. But there's one area where reps are incredibly sensitive—and you need to watch out for it. If 0.1% of accounts, opportunities, or tasks are reassigned incorrectly, you will hear no end of complaints about it from the reps. When just a few dozen items are wrong, it will be cheaper and faster for everyone if the reps just fix the problems themselves using the SFDC Web user interface. Although mass data fixes are best done using system administrator's tools, when there are tiny changes to be made, use of these tools carries a relatively high risk of introducing new errors in the course of fixing old ones.*

Account Planning

Account planning attempts to provide an evolving answer to these strategic questions: how can the company get more out of its existing base, how can it catch the really big fish, and how can it build its reputation to "own" the market? SFDC doesn't help that much when it comes to analyzing new markets (e.g., geographies or industries), because SFDC data are most complete for *historical* analysis. Use market research or external data (such as data from Hoover's or Dunn and Bradstreet, or hire interns from a local business school) to do this kind of analysis work. You may find that the marketing staff has some talent for this kind of forward-looking analysis.

That said, SFDC should contain incredibly valuable data about how to get more out of the company's existing customers. This is *the* strategic reason to have reps, SEs, and consultants entering information into the system, even when "the deal is already won." SFDC's most relevant data for maximizing repeat business is the sequence of campaigns, events, activities, and decisions that won deals in the past. When analyzing these data, you're looking for repeating patterns that lead to the big deals. The key information will be the patterns of tasks (as collected in the activity history) and field/state changes (as recorded in the field histories for account and opportunity records). You may also find important narrative about the wins and losses in chatter feeds at the opportunity or account level. Look for patterns that lead to repeat business and opening new departments within existing customers. To identify these patterns, you may need some help here from the quantitative folks in sales operations, finance, or marketing.

Once you have spotted the patterns, try them in some current deals and measure the results. Eventually you'll find the recipe that gives the most consistent growth results.

Account Reviews

This is the simplest section of the whole book: account reviews should move away from artificial PowerPoint presentations and spreadsheets. Most of the real discussion in an account review should revolve around the `account` page in SFDC, with the rep and the manager exploring related records (`opportunities`, `contacts`, `tasks`, and `chatter`) and updating them in real time.

As a manager, just make it a rule that if the SFDC records aren't ready to support an account review pretty much on their own, the rep isn't ready for the meeting yet. Period.

Partner Management

Although most partner interactions are handled by the individual rep or partner manager, it's important for the sales executive to get a bird's-eye view of what's going on. Achieving adequate visibility into what partners are doing—and how the partner is helping the company's overall performance—is the most commonly cited problem that executives have with channel business. Once the company has a healthy number of partners—10 companies, or representing 10% of overall sales—SFDC's `PRM module` should be used to help you assess partner effectiveness.

You will want to set up the partner with restricted access to their `leads`, `contacts`, `accounts`, `cases`, and `opportunities` using a `partner portal` or `chatter community module`. You should also publish collateral, FAQs, rules of engagement, and other sales tools there. But be realistic about how many people in your partner companies will actually use the SFDC system. A partner of significant size will have its own CRM system, so its employees will not use your `partner portal` very often. It's reasonable to expect the partner's employees to log in once or twice a week to get new `leads` or update a few `opportunities`, but their day-to-day pipeline and `lead` flow management will most likely stay in their own CRM system.

When sending `leads` to the partner, make sure that those prospects are sent to a specific *person*, not just a corporation. As many of the partner's sales reps will not log in regularly on your company's PRM portal, it's best to send every `lead` via email to the appropriate individual in the partner's inside sales team. Although SFDC's `lead assignment rules` can't handle this task, the system's `workflow` rules can be configured to send lead-alert emails automatically. It is also smart to send a weekly update report to the partner's "partner management" person so that he or she can see the lead flow on its way. These reports can be generated and sent automatically as `scheduled reports` from within SFDC.[54]

An interesting issue with channel partners is unresponsiveness: they've got lots of things to do besides responding to your new `leads`. To counter this problem, you need to make it clear to the partner that timeliness of follow-up is something you're going to

---

54. You could also generate dashboard elements that could be emailed to the partners, but that means either add-on products or extra code—which takes budget away from your partner management efforts.

measure: the better the partner's score, the greater the number of `leads` it will receive over time. The most basic measures of responsiveness are:

- Has the partner individual logged into the PRM at all?

- How many `leads` have they updated in any way?

- How many `leads` have been converted?

- How many `opportunities` have been closed?

It's best to give the partner specific goals for these metrics, as well as their overall revenue goal.

One of the best ways to encourage the partner to be more responsive is to *not* give the partner all of the information at once. For example, if you send 100 `leads` with all the details, the partner's employees are less likely to follow up than if you take one of these approaches:

- Send `leads` in small batches more frequently.

- Use page layouts that initially send only basic profile information and require a "lead-accepted" button-push to expose all the details.

- Create a leader-board report that everyone can see in the PRM portal.

- Send the partner managers a monthly update on performance versus goals.

You should also set up `workflows` to trigger alerts and escalations when a `lead` has been left untouched too long and when a partner deal is taking too long or has actually moved backward. Even if these alerts are used only by the partner managers within your company, they foster a healthy management-by-exception style.

From a management perspective, most of what you want to understand is partner performance: the number of deals closed and the total revenues. Once you have that basic data, you'll then want to go deeper. SFDC's `reports` can easily be extended to examine the partner business, so you can understand the product mix it is selling, how quickly it is ramping up on new products, the referral fees being paid, and other details.

What you *can't* measure from any `report` is channel conflict. You'll have to get that information anecdotally from your company's sales reps. You want to find out when partners are viewed as competitors, stealing deals from your reps. Then you need to drive home the idea that the partners are to be viewed as an extension of your company's salesforce—that's why you brought them on. Achieving the desired level of synergy through these kinds of partnerships requires iron-clad territory definitions, clear rules of engagement, and a commission system that encourages the reps to use the partner as a resource.

Partnerships can work really well when the company's salesforce has a high quota, tight management (e.g., "No, you won't get commissions on deals worth less than $20,000 if you go after it yourself"), and a channel-neutral commission plan. The last point causes a lot of angst for most CEOs, because it means paying out double compensation. Even so, the only way to *really* have a rep view a partner as an ally is if the rep makes the same amount of money whether the partner takes down the deal or the rep does it directly. Contrary to popular belief, double-comping doesn't rob the company of profits if the commission and accelerators are designed so that *the company pays more only if it earns more* overall revenues.

Forecasting

The forecast is the single most visible area of sales and partner management, yet it's often the least well-understood part of CRM systems. Companies large and small suffer from forecasting accuracy problems, even though they may put a significant amount of effort into creating their forecasts. Forecasting is also a risky business: if company executives make public comments based on a shaky forecast, stockholder lawsuits may not be far away.

Forecasting is inherently an unreliable process, because, well, it's about things that haven't happened yet. Industry averages indicate that more than 50% of the deals in a quarter will be forecasted wrong. SFDC can help identify *which* specific deals are most likely to be the subjects of erroneous forecasts, providing a real measure of risk mitigation for the sales VP.

The forecast is the battle of two hockey sticks, as shown in Figure 9-3. In this figure, the top hockey-stick line is the typical trend of `forecasts` during the quarter, and the bottom one is the typical trend for closed business[55] in a direct-sales organization. The gap between the two lines is the cause of a lot of stress in the executive suite.

Mechanics

Many sales managers export SFDC pipeline data to their pet Excel spreadsheets, which they email around to drive their weekly forecasting cycle. And every single one of those companies would be *wrong* in doing so. Every time the spreadsheet is modified outside of SFDC, there is increased risk of error, wasted time, and even regulatory hassle.

Although exporting the `opportunity` list to a spreadsheet is fine, inevitably that data gets modified, sorted, adjusted, and summed up. Even if you're using pivot tables and macros to do the work, using Excel is just too vulnerable to weaknesses in technology

---

55. SFDC opportunity values and forecasting are oriented entirely around bookings. By itself, it can't even approximate a shipments, revenue, or cash flow forecast. Check out the end of "The Forecasting Cycle" section later in this chapter for more discussion of this.

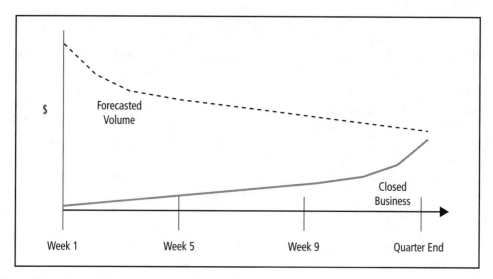

$
Forecasted
Volume

Closed
Business

Week 1   Week 5   Week 9   Quarter End

FIGURE 9-3   Forecast versus actual sales data for a typical quarter

and human nature. Do you know what modifications were made by whom, and why? Could you duplicate it next month? Could you explain why the forecast jumped around last month if the board asked you? Nah.

Even if your company doesn't have to comply with Sarbanes-Oxley Act requirements, forecasting needs to be an iron-clad process that is as consistent and objective, free from prying eyes and meddling fingers. Data entry, forecast parameter adjustments, managerial overrides, and roll-ups of forecast information must be done entirely within the SFDC system, where it is subject to a full audit trail and where it can be securely stored, shared, and locked down if necessary. Even if some individual rep's forecast is garbage, it is essential to the credibility of the sales organization that no one views the overall *process* of forecasting as unreliable baloney.

The individual rep puts the starting point for forecasting data at the opportunity level: `close date, amount,` and `stage`. It's best practice for the rep to leave the standard `probability percentage` alone: this value is set automatically by selection of the `opportunity stage`. It's an even better practice to have the sales `stage` be set by `APEX triggers` based on the status of check-box entries that reflect customer activities and commitments.

SFDC's `customizable` or (preferably) `collaborative forecast` module adds important functionality on top of these base data. The forecasting system lets the rep withhold doubtful deals from the committed forecast, and it lets every level of management override the forecast `probability, close date,` and `category` to make the forecast as realistic as possible when it reaches the CEO. For SFDC forecasting to work

SALES STAGES VERSUS PROBABILITIES

SFDC lets you set up multiple `sales processes` to reflect the sales cycles of differing channels and sales teams. These `sales processes` let you expose different subsets of `opportunity stages` and `probabilities` for different teams, all drawn from the master list of opportunity stages.

For any given sales process, the list of `sales stages` should be in two parts: four to eight stages that are directly under the rep's control and two or three that are in the paperwork departments (i.e., sales operations, legal, finance). See the "Inside Sales: Handling Order Operations for Outside Sales" section of this chapter to learn more about this issue. As discussed earlier, make sure that everyone in the sales management chain agrees on which activities need to be completed in each `stage` and on which customer behaviors trigger the transition to the next `stage`. So far, so good.

Each `sales stage` is configured with a default probability, which can be overridden by the sales reps either in the `forecast` page or in the `opportunity` itself. All too often, the probabilities that companies establish are far too optimistic. The probability *ought* to mean, "What percentage of deals that make it this far in the process actually close?" For example, if you had 10 average deals, each rated at 60%, you would expect 6 of those deals to yield revenue. If you looked back at previous quarters in almost all companies, you might find that perhaps 40% of those 60%-ers were actually won. Whoops. Adjust the percentages to reflect the *actual* close probability for deals that reach each `stage`. This usually means that the percentages for all `stages` between 40% and 90% need to be adjusted downward (sales staff being optimistic folks). As painful as it might be, reality is important to avoiding chronic overforecasting and underdelivery.

Even though `stages` and probabilities will reflect "what effort the sales reps have made," they don't necessarily reflect the customer's likelihood of buying. The sales team may have done everything right yet know that politically a competitor is on the fast track to winning the customer's business. Many reps handle this situation by adjusting the percentage up or down in the `opportunity` record, but such an approach has three problems: it's gaming the system, it doesn't convey any information to management, and the adjustment is erased the next time the `stage` value is changed.

A better strategy is to use SFDC's `customizable` or `collaborative forecasting`, which allows the rep and each level of management to adjust the `amount`, `close date`, and `forecast category` of the `opportunity`. In most of the forecast adjustment wizards, there's a place to put comments: make sure the reps do so to convey *why* the deal is being adjusted.

We also recommend putting an additional pick list in the `opportunity` record titled "probability adjustment," along these lines:

+++	Deal all but done
++	On inside track
+	Competitive advantage
<none>	
-	Competitive disadvantage
--	Severe politics
---	Deal all but lost

Although this field won't affect any `forecast` calculations, it provides warning signals that can be easily summarized in management reports.

With `history tracking` enabled, you'll be able to see signs of trouble much sooner than with just the standard fields. Eventually, you'll be able to detect sales rep overoptimism and to work on the unrealistic deals before they go completely off the rails.

properly, every rep's `quota` must be in the system on a monthly or quarterly basis (as discussed previously in the "Revenue Planning" section). The system's `role hierarchy` and `forecast hierarchy` need to correctly reflect reporting relationships so that managers can see the right roll-ups while only the executives are allowed to see the entire corporate picture. Use the `sales teams` feature to provide the right level of "dotted line" access, and use the `forecast delegation` feature to get the best possible deal information and account intelligence into the forecast.

If the system is set up properly, you will be able to run your weekly forecast call entirely from the SFDC data. For most organizations, the system's forecast reports are flexible and informative enough for most internal management meetings. When it comes to board or investor presentations, the data should be exported into Excel, which makes it easier to create nice charts and graphs.

Interpreting the Numbers

SFDC's forecast categories are counterintuitive for many sales managers, but these definitions cannot be changed[56] in the system:

- `Committed`: The total of `committed opportunities` plus the total `opportunities` that have been `closed-won` in the period.

- `Best Case`: The total of `committed opportunities` plus the total of `best-case opportunities`.

---

56. In other words, you can't create, redefine, or delete `forecast categories`, although you can *rename* the labels to suit your company's terminology.

- `Pipeline`: The total of all currently open `opportunities` except those that have been marked as `omitted` from the forecast. This means that `opportunities` that have been `closed-won` are *not* part of the `pipeline`.

Because of these definitions, the `pipeline` value may be lower than the `best case` value for a given forecast period (this can't be changed in the system's forecast views, so people will still need to be trained about interpreting the differences). In many organizations, management wants the `pipeline` to include all currently closed deals as well—if so, your external reports will need to add the `pipeline` numbers to the current `closed-won` amount.

If the company's management team and sales reps need to see the forecast along different lines, SFDC's `VisualForce` and `APEX` code will let you create metrics that are completely customized; you can even add the probability adjustment pick list mentioned earlier into your calculated totals. However, if you want serious modifications to forecasting, the required custom `APEX` and `VisualForce` code will cost several thousand dollars and will likely require rework every year or so to reflect territory and channel changes. In contrast, there are a number of third-party products that provide some better forecasting and rep scorecarding, but they aren't highly customizable.

THE BLOOD COMMIT

Many sales managers feel that the `committed–best case–pipeline` categorization just isn't solid enough. It seems that only 80% or so of the `committed` deals come in. For this reason, managers may want a more solid term that indicates the rep's deepest commitment. Depending on who you are, one of these terms will work for you:

- Worst case
- Blood commit
- Bet the farm
- Career commit

Although the labels for the standard forecast categories can be changed, the definition of the categories cannot be changed, and you can't add new categories. The workaround is to add a "blood commit" check box on the `opportunity` record. Checking this box is the rep's signal that this deal is a must-win, and he or she doesn't think management should override the rep's forecast of "committed" because the rep is doubling down on that deal.

If you implement a `custom field` along these lines, you need to tell management about what to do when they see it. You also need to modify forecasting reports so that they do the right thing when this box is checked.

The Forecasting Cycle

Best practices for forecasting in a large organization follow a regular schedule. There should be a weekly forecast for all divisions (including professional services), focused on bookings. If this weekly call happens on Mondays, the individual reps should be directed to have all `opportunity` data and individual `forecast overrides` updated and stable on the previous Thursday night. On Friday, first- and second-level managers should review the forecast numbers, understand them, and talk with reps about trouble spots. Managers should look at the `activity history` and `chatter` to see what has (or has not) changed about the `opportunity` in the last week, and they should look at reports designed to spot deals that have stalled or—worse—regressed. The managers' inputs and `forecast overrides` should all be in the system and stable by Friday night.

The sales VPs should look at the numbers on Saturday, and if there is an international roll-up of the forecast (to a COO), those discussions should happen on Sunday. The VPs should look at the deals that their managers have overridden and adjust the `forecast overrides` (either at a territory level or individual deal level) to create the most realistic roll-up at the corporate level.

The sales VPs will make heavy use of reports or dashboards generated for them by sales operations to see the big picture of the forecast, because their biggest nightmare is a rosy pipeline based on wishful thinking. Looking below the top-line numbers, the VPs should have indicators or dashboards that examine average deal size, sales-cycle length, pipeline coverage, number of deals regressing, and number of deals disappearing from the quarter altogether. If the company's revenues follow a severe "hockey-stick"[57] pattern, the sales VPs should have graphics that illustrate how this quarter's weekly revenues match the hockey-stick curve that's normal for the company. A parallel hockey-stick pattern comparison should be done for the series of weekly forecasts, allowing managers to identify weakness or upside surprises early.

SFDC's `pipeline` "as of" reports are a great place to start when conducting this assessment. The analysts should show the expected effects on revenues owing to product changes ("The company had a new product launch in week 4") and competitors' moves ("We're being attacked with a big ad campaign and discount"). Finally, the VPs should be looking at ramp effects ("We've got 10 new reps"), pipeline effects (deal-velocity metrics), and regional issues ("Five holidays in France, which is our number three market, during the quarter") to make sure that the forecast is believable and as solid as possible. A number of great sales scorecards and forecast analytics tools are also available in SFDC's AppExchange. The good ones are more expensive, but they're worth the money because they prevent embarrassment before your boss, the board of directors, and even investors.

---

57. Hockey-stick patterns occur when most of the deals happen in the last few weeks or days of the quarter. For software companies, it's not unusual to have 20% of the quarter's deals close on the last *day* of the quarter. These patterns make forecasting difficult and inaccurate.

The Monday worldwide forecast call should be run from the SFDC system, and the focus of the conversation should be on what can be done to firm up the shaky parts of the forecast rather than a mind-numbing deal-by-deal review. If the forecast for a region has shrunk or jumped, there should be discussion about why the change has occurred and what can be done to reverse the shortfall or solidify the advance.

Any modifications or amendments to the forecast as a result of this call should be made directly to SFDC records. Any follow-up items for the forecast should be sent out as SFDC `tasks` or `chatter` conversations.

To improve forecasting accuracy, your team needs to be a learning organization. Improving forecast accuracy requires providing candid (but nonthreatening) feedback to *every single quota-carrying person in sales*, including the sales VP (who is the lucky recipient of input from both above and below). After 6 months or more of forecasting data have accumulated in the SFDC system, your team should perform analytics on a quarterly basis:

- Percentage of a quarter's deals closing within 10% of the forecasted value

- Accuracy of the forecast in each of the last 4 weeks of the quarter

- Territories that chronically under- or overforecast, and the average variance

- Characteristics of deals that regress (so the company can spot those in advance)

- Characteristics of deals that are upside surprises (so the company can identify the telling factors that cause a leap in forecasted value or probability)

The SFDC forecasting system works entirely with bookings and *cannot* by itself produce a revenue or GAAP forecast. Although the SFDC system should hold "catalog level" information about all of your products' subscription prices, revenue recognition schedules, and other details, only the finance department can do a true *revenue* forecast based on revenue trigger events, inventory/shipment availability, and time. It is best practice for the SFDC system to automatically feed the accounting system[58] on a weekly basis the product and order-level information needed to drive the revenue calculations. However, the revenue final forecast is highly privileged information that should *not* be fed back from the accounting system into the SFDC system.

Commission/Compensation Management

SFDC holds a lot of data that are immediately relevant to the design and implementation of a commission and compensation plan, but the system offers no direct functionality for

---

58. If your company's accounting system is separate from its enterprise resource planning (ERP) system, SFDC should also feed data into the ERP system on a weekly basis to assist with inventory and manufacturing planning, particularly for items with long lead times.

calculating compensation amounts. If the company uses a spreadsheet or dedicated software package to calculate commissions, make sure that it is driven directly from SFDC and accounting system data.

As discussed in Chapter 7, the choice of which spreadsheet or software package to use for figuring commissions is a tricky one. If the company has fewer than 25 reps and five product lines, a simple spreadsheet is probably the right choice. Although larger sales teams or longer product lists argue for a dedicated commission software package, implementing these packages can be just as tough (or sometimes tougher) as continuing with the spreadsheet system, particularly if the compensation plan

- Changes frequently.

- Uses product-specific commissions.

- Incorporates lots of sales contests or incentives from suppliers.

- Involves a lot of recurring revenue.

- Has to deal with frequent territory changes.

- Has to deal with lots of temporary promotions or product changes.

Activity Management

The ability to see what people have been doing—to really see the blow-by-blow events that have shaped an `account` or `opportunity`—is something that was never possible before the advent of CRM systems. Salesforce has upped the ante on this with its `email to Salesforce` and `chatter` features. Activity management helps the company understand what's really involved in closing business and to develop realistic models for the sales team. It can mean fairer quotas and better resource allocations for assets such as presales engineers, travel budgets, and loaner systems. It can also provide early warning signals that pipeline formation isn't going fast enough, long before the problem shows up in the formal forecast numbers. Activity management is a particularly powerful tool in the first month of the quarter, when the pipeline may be sketchy.

Unfortunately, too-aggressive attempts at activity management are also a major reason for user resistance, low adoption, and failed CRM implementations. People are suspicious of activity management because they're afraid of how *you,* the manager, will abuse the information. Further, most reps will simply see activity management as a tax— that is, as a burden that offers no direct benefit to them.

Clearly, before you start using activity management, you have to make people comfortable with the idea that the information they put into the system will not be used against them. You also have to persuade them that putting information into the system is *for their own purposes*, to make *their* job easier, and to ensure that nothing falls through the cracks. When everyone uses the SFDC system to hand off and track action items, provide ticklers for follow-ups, and record customer interactions, the system will be full of information that's useful to everyone on the sales and support team. Although it's true that sales personnel will have to enter data into SFDC, they *won't* have to write anywhere near as many emails to get things done.

The core of activity management is monitoring and evaluating the sequence of `chatter` posts and `tasks` (including attached emails and phone notes) recorded in the `activity history` of `accounts` and, preferably, `opportunities`. Early on, you'll be looking only at gross measures such as "the total number of activities per rep" without paying any attention to exactly what those activities are. The first milestone is to get the reps to enter almost any relevant action as an activity. The next milestone is getting them to use the `type` field on `tasks` to categorize the ones they've completed.

Once you've gotten beyond the basics, activity management requires you to develop a model of the activities required to close a sale, and the best way to do that is with real data from successful sales cycles. Of course, you will need at least a couple of quarters' worth of data before you can really see anything valuable in activity management; early on, there just won't have been enough sales cycles to make reasonable generalizations. You may discover that the average sale requires four on-site visits and six phone calls. You may figure out that pilot projects or proofs of concept are involved in 80% of sales amounting to more than $50,000, but that they indicate a 70% chance of *losing* deals worth less than $20,000. These kinds of discoveries can help you dramatically increase your forecasting accuracy or avoid low-probability deals altogether. But it will take you a while to get there.

Generally speaking, SDRs and inside sales reps will be much more comfortable with activity management than the outside sales staff and partner management organizations, because they are more used to being closely monitored. Ironically, the biggest payoff from activity management comes for the outside sales team, even though those reps are usually the most wary of it. The principles for activity management should apply to everyone, though: start with a baseline model of how workers should be optimally spending their time, measure, and then look for odd patterns. Sometimes the patterns mean an individual is doing the wrong things—but be wary of cases where the "oddball" is the *right* behavior and you need to adjust your model. Know that the specific patterns will probably vary significantly across groups: be willing to look at different details and to measure and evaluate teams in different ways.

The output of activity management is guidance for all of the salespeople. Your first foray into guidance should be done at the group level, showing new discoveries that are good for everyone. For example, you might be able to show that at week 4 of the quarter, successful reps (the ones who consistently make their numbers) are making 30 prospecting calls and 4 on-site visits per week. Show the correlation between certain activities and building a healthy pipeline. If you can show reps quantitatively how they *ought* to spend their time in the last month of the quarter, you'll be telling them how to invest their time to make a ton more money—a message that they'll certainly listen to.

Invite debate from the team. They may have good reasons for disagreeing with your suggestions, and their input will make your model more realistic for everyone.

After providing guidance a few times at the group level, you can start giving feedback to the individual sales reps—usually the most junior ones, or the ones who are having consistency problems. This feedback must be given in private, and it should be delivered in a collaborative environment where the rep can see you are trying to make him or her even more money. If you deliver the advice in the form of punishment or criticism, the rep will soon stop entering activities or will put in fake information to game the system—which is actually worse.[59]

Performance Management

SFDC records an amazing array of information that can be used as the basis for performance management of sales personnel. With `chatter`, you get a lot of narrative information to supplement the metrics you've been using for the annual review cycle.

SFDC has added a new `social performance management` option to the system to facilitate better performance, not just the annual review cycle. The idea is to build real-time recognition, goal alignment, and motivation right into the system. By intermeshing the feedback and reward mechanisms right into the work at hand, the system can become an online coach. Pretty powerful stuff if your organization is ready for it.

However, as with activity management, being too assertive with performance management can be dangerous medicine (particularly early on in your team's adoption of the system). It is imperative that sales leaders follow three key guidelines in this area:

- Do *not* make SFDC the center of attention during the formal performance review process. To the degree that the reps believe that the system will be used as Big Brother, the ultimate spybot, they will try to hide information from the system, undermine management visibility, and game the measurements.

- Do not measure the wrong things—and make sure to temper the measurements you do make with "reality factors" such as the quality of a territory and the loyalty level of existing accounts. Identify the right things to measure by evaluating the beliefs, behavior, and activities of the top 20% of your reps (because they probably deliver 60% or more of the company's revenue and profits). Ask *them*

---

59. The fake data will corrupt the results of the real stuff, making the situation look too uniform and positive. Fake data that look real are very hard to expunge from the system.

what makes them different and better: how they spend their time, how they evaluate which prospects have the biggest potential, and which activities and tactics help them close deals more reliably.

- Make sure there's a good cultural fit between the measurement system, the people, and the way the team works. Generally speaking, activity management and `social performance management` work a lot better with younger, more distributed personnel.

GETTING THE MOST FROM SFDC

- Make sure everybody who touches `leads` and `contacts` is working with a common set of semantics and has the same model of the funnel and the `opportunity` pipeline. This is crucial, yet often way out of alignment.

- Make sure there are clear SLAs between marketing (`leads`), sales development (`contacts` and unqualified `opportunities`), and the field (`opportunities` and revenue).

- Make sure there is a "rules of engagement" document (even if one page) that describes how your field deals with each of your channels and customer situations.

- For everyone in sales: if it isn't in SFDC, it doesn't exist. Stop using outboard spreadsheets, Word documents, and emails to manage your accounts and your business.

- Managers: lead by example. Show that you are going to drive the ship using only SFDC data, and make sure nobody believes you're just going through the motions. Finally, show that you're not going to use SFDC to micromanage the troops.

- Use `chatter` for internal collaboration and to get closer to your customers.

- The SFDC system should probably be owned by sales, at least for the first year.

- Check out "Essential Features for Sales Management" at the end of Chapter 7.

FOR SMALL COMPANIES

- Your team may be small enough that every rep does "everything." Configure SFDC `leads`, `contacts`, and `opportunities` so the evolution is continuous and crystal clear at every stage.

FOR LARGE ENTERPRISES

- It's best to organize your people as dedicated SDR, inside, outside, and partner selling teams. Each team needs its own set of metrics and SFDC screens.

- Get the SDRs, sales engineers, inside reps, and sales operations on SFDC first. Get the field reps on only after the system is already full of useful data.

- Make approval cycles for needed sales resources (demos, POCs, SEs, etc.) only through SFDC. After a while, ignore requests over email.

- Use approval cycles for big discounts and digital signatures for the contract.

CHAPTER 10

Best Practices in Marketing

Half the money I spend on advertising is wasted.
The trouble is, I don't know which half.

—*John Wannamaker*

This chapter is for every member of the marketing team, because every part of the Salesforce.com system holds data and tools that can make your job easier. No matter what your role in marketing, you need to skim every part of this chapter. Zero in on the things related to your job, but read up on what the boss will be looking at as well!

For most companies, the marketing department is usually the first or second organization to adopt and effectively use SFDC. But the marketing team almost always makes mistakes in how they set up and use SFDC because they haven't really looked deeply enough at their business process—what can be called "the life of a lead." Consequently, marketing looks bad—and undermines system credibility—when SFDC reports are misleading. But that's just the beginning. For marketing to be more data-driven and more measurable, to be accountable, and to hold others accountable, marketing teams need to dramatically up their game and gain CRM and analytical skills. This chapter is designed to start you down that path.

Marketing Organizations

Across the range of company types and industries served by SFDC, the marketing operation is organized in very different ways. Sometimes it reports to engineering, sometimes to sales, sometimes directly to the president—and sometimes the marketing function is split across several departments. So there's no way to organize this chapter around marketing *job titles*. Instead, it is structured around *job functions*, which may or may not report to the marketing organization.

The First Order of Business

Most of marketing's interactions with SFDC surround the early stages of pipeline formation—lead generation, processing, cultivation, nurturing, and qualification. This is the early part of the revenue generation business process, which is owned by sales even though it's started by marketing.

Although I'm a card-carrying marketing guy, my first bit of guidance is that the marketing group should almost never be the owner of the SFDC system. This system is called *Sales*force for a reason, and you have to admit that the sales animal is a lot different from the marketing wonk. The SFDC system should be owned by the team that owns the revenue number—almost always, that's the sales department.

That said, marketing *must* be very actively involved in the design, usage, and analytics of SFDC. The core of many marketing functions will live in SFDC records. Marketing must own `leads` and `campaigns` and should have control over several policy areas in the system. Marketing personnel play a critical role in creating some of the fanciest reports and spearheading several of the key integrations between SFDC and supporting systems, such as the Web site, the marketing automation system (MAS), the content management system, the license management system, and the eCommerce system.

Further, marketing will design the database characteristics that lie at the core of closed-loop marketing[1]—where every customer touch, from first mailing to customer support to PR, is logged and monitored through SFDC. Closed-loop marketing focuses on the feedback loops between the target market sentiment, marketing message, sales activities, and customer response. Because SFDC will be used by advertising, marketing, external service bureaus, sales, customer support, and professional services, the system can hold *all* the data about a customer relationship and be the touch point for all customer-facing activities. Add the elements of listening to customer input and adjusting your messaging, and you have closed-loop marketing. Such a seamless operation means huge wins in conversion, loyalty, and profitability.

Developing a Model of Sales and Marketing Interactions

Before you can apply any of the recommendations in this chapter, you need to develop a model of how the company's revenue generation process works and how sales and marketing need to interact. The goal is to create a service level agreement (SLA)—that is, a contract between sales and marketing about who does what to make revenue happen.

---

1. To find out more on this topic, check out "The CMO Strategic Agenda: Automating Closed-Loop Marketing" (www.neolane.com/usa/pdf/200804_AutomatingClosedLoopMarketing.pdf), published by the Aberdeen Group. Several wonderful consultancies will also help you implement closed-loop marketing systems for a nominal fee (nominal as long as you sell expensive stuff).

Read the section "Job One: Define and Document the Sales Model" in Chapter 9, and participate with the sales team to get the details of this model nailed down and documented.

This task can be achieved in an afternoon if you're serious, but it's one of the most highly leveraged things you can do to ensure that the marketing staff is on the same page with the sales team (as well as to help marketing personnel get on the same page with each other!). Don't forget the channel here: marketing to and through partners is a key success factor in many industries.

Yes, it's true, developing this model takes time (mostly meetings) and can involve some politics. But the politics are there anyway—if you want to improve things, you're going to need a model to argue over anyway.

Social Marketing and Social CRM

To say that social media is important to marketing is to belabor the obvious—but only if it's obvious to *you*. There are still plenty of industries (and geographies) where it's not at all clear how to leverage social media for the marketing and sales function.

Even in the most evolved markets, the rules of the road are still evolving rapidly. It's not entirely clear how soon they will stabilize, so the best rules of social marketing are as follows:

- Listen to the audience.

- Be prepared to learn new techniques.

- Don't dig in your heels.

The term *social CRM* was coined (and immediately overhyped) by the vendor community to signal the new capabilities that are required to execute an effective social media marketing campaign. None of the CRM vendors has a complete offering yet, but SFDC is clearly the leader among the major CRM players.

The broadest area of SFDC's social functionality is `chatter`. As discussed in Chapters 6 and 13, `chatter` provides a rich and secure medium for internal collaboration, with use cases in marketing, sales, customer support, and elsewhere. Because it's a threaded communication medium baked right into nearly every SFDC record, it is much more efficient than email. But of course, it requires behavioral changes from the user—so don't expect that overnight.

`Chatter` makes it much easier to set up a "sensor array" for your company's early-warning system: marketers may start seeing new messaging, sales may start hearing new competitive objections, and support may detect a growing sense of resentment from unhappy customers. `Chatter`'s ability to create subject-interest `groups` on the fly and to auto-suggest new `topics` from trending `keywords` make it a very helpful, intelligent listening system.

What most marketers don't realize is that this functionality can be extended (in many use cases, without charge) to your customers, partners, and even prospects. `Chatter` provides a secure environment to a walled-garden community, where conversations and collaboration could begin almost from the first touch of the sales cycle. Let's not get trapped in Fantasy Land, though. Most prospects already have enough IM clients, thank you, and other prospects may not be permitted to use any IM at work. Prospects also have no interest in following whatever rules you have in your collaboration community (and trust me, you will need to develop a solid set of chattiquette guidelines).

To set expectations reasonably, you might be able to get some of your (smaller) part-ners and (closest) customers to participate in `chatter`. But to succeed at this, they have to have an intrinsic reason to do so. You'll definitely need to come up with a credible WIIFY[2] statement.

Check out www.SFDC-secrets.com, www.salesforce.com/chatterguide/start-here/practices.jsp, and www.facebook.com/Chatter—or just Google "chatter best practices" for lots more articles all over the Web.

Moving to more specialized areas, SFDC has three big offerings in its Social Marketing Cloud: `social media monitoring` (neé Radian6), `digital marketing auto-mation` (neé ExactTarget), and `social media messaging` (neé BuddyMedia). All of these offerings have solid (and very different) uses cases for B2B and B2C markets. Unlike `chatter`, these offerings are not automatically integrated with the rest of the SFDC object model. That's why it's imperative to collect the social media handles (at least for LinkedIn and Facebook) for all `leads` and `contacts` as early as possible in your marketing cycle.

`Social media monitoring` is probably the most broadly applicable feature, as every company needs to know about its standing on the Web and the sentiment of its audience. In addition to assessing unaided awareness, `social media monitoring` can be used to measure message effectiveness, advertising campaigns, and product repu-tation. This ability to listen objectively—not just to friendly customers but to people who have decided to purchase from others—is the foundation for closed-loop marketing.

Although this nirvana beckons, it is not easily achieved. Most marketing staff and agencies don't have deep skills to leverage social media monitoring, and doing it right requires some serious analytical tendencies. Further, a social listening engine can only give you great metrics, not great execution (of the Web site, email blasts, calls to action, etc.). Most of the great examples of closed-loop marketing are in the B2C space, particu-larly with virtual goods and impulse-buy items. If your business is staid or B2B, getting the positive effects requires way more than just a good social listening engine.

---

2. What's In It For You—WIIFY.

SFDC's `social media messaging` features are the flip side: publishing to your community. The idea is to have tightly coordinated messages go out, tailored to different elements of your community (on Facebook, Twitter, LinkedIn, Google+, and other "channels"). By focusing the relevance of messages going to these communities, your team can increase audience engagement. If commerce is a conversation,[3] social media marketing optimizes it. But, like marketing automation systems (see the "Marketing Automation" sidebar later in this chapter), effectively using social media marketing requires significant attention by at least one of the marketing staff. Make sure that you have that person identified (and the level of effort budgeted) before making promises to upper management.

SFDC's digital marketing system has a wide array of features for email blasting, vertical campaign management, lead nurturing, SMS push messaging, and ongoing customer communications. Because SFDC's acquisition of ExactTarget and Pardot won't be fully integrated until well after this book is published, it is impossible to know exactly what feature mix will be integrated into the system. However, SFDC's Agile product engineering makes it pretty clear that the integration will take several release cycles. Expect some features to remain on the horizon until 2014.

Lead Generation and Collection

Before any `lead` generation starts, it's important to have a common understanding with sales about the life of a `lead`—how `leads` evolve, who handles them at various stages, and how the `workflow` triggers the `conversion` or demotion of `leads`. Read the discussion of this topic in Chapter 9 if you haven't already done so. Also check out the articles on www.SFDC-secrets.com for further discussion and tricks.

Some issues need to be argued through in detail. One of the critical decisions is, "Which information should we collect at the start of the prospecting process?" Almost always, marketing wants to collect a lot of information about the customers' demographics and the competitive products they are considering. Sales typically wants to collect the customer's title, purchase timeframe, and other qualification questions. These are all valid requests, but it's not wise to collect all these data at initial registration time, for three reasons:

- The collection form isn't always under your control, particularly for tradeshows and videoconferencing services that allow the collection of only their minimum-standard fields.

- In almost any collection medium (but particularly the Web), the more information you ask for, the higher the likelihood of user drop-off. Typically, having more

---

3. From the classic *The Cluetrain Manifesto*.

than five fields causes a significant reduction in the number of leads and an equal increase in bogus responses (such as emails of asdf@asdf.com).

- Many target audiences get really irritated by nosy questions about purchase intent or budget. In market segments where prospects hate sales calls, asking these questions can *dramatically* lower the quantity of `leads`.

In debating which data to collect, always ask what the information will *really* be used for, who is going to take the time to enter it and validate it, and whether the information could be inferred from some other data that can be purchased or obtained in the public domain. For example, in a Web form there is no reason for you to ask the registrant's location: 90% of the time you already have it from the IP address. You'll probably get to ask the registrant for only five items up front, so make sure they're the best five. The answers should provide the minimum information needed to route/process the next step for the inquiry. The rest of the information that people would love to have should be collected during the subsequent steps of the qualification and lead-nurturing process.

On every version of your registration forms, put the logos for the social networks that are most likely to be relevant for your audience (hint: B2B == LinkedIn, B2C == Facebook). Even if you have no intention of doing social CRM, these networks provide some single sign-on (SSO) and avatar unique identifiers that make your site easier for the user and provide keys that are super-valuable for analytics. Best practices are to offer some small incentive (a *tchotchke* or some virtual points) for registrants to reveal their social network identifier.

The next issue that needs to be argued about is, "What constitutes a lead?" Best practices are to focus more on lead *quality* than on lead *quantity*. Low-quality leads are simply a waste of everyone's time and money. Why market or try to sell people who don't have genuine interest? The first step to lead quality is to distinguish leads from "names":

- A *name* is merely the contact information for a person believed to be part of the target audience. Names are typically purchased from lists or are obtained from outside but have not explicitly indicated they want to know more about the company, its products, or its services. Names are the lowest-quality leads and should almost always be relegated to mailing-list status and excluded from the telesales call-down list. Read the discussion of this topic in the "Example Business Process Analysis" section of Chapter 8.

- A true *lead*, who is a respondent to marketing efforts, has explicitly requested more information about the company or its products. These leads should immediately be scored (a topic discussed later in this chapter) and put on the telesales call-down list in order of "hotness." Check out the discussion on this topic in Chapter 9.

Once these basics are agreed to (and documented in the project wiki or Google Drive area), the SFDC screens and variables need to be customized to fit the company's model. Almost always, a few `custom fields` (such as a calculated field for the `sales region`) need to be added to the `lead` object, and pick-list fields for `status`, `industry`, and `rating` should be replaced by custom ones. `Field history tracking` should be turned on to provide an audit trail for the 20 most interesting fields in the `lead` object (including, in particular, `owner`).

In addition to the SFDC modifications, it's important to modify the user registration screens on the company's Web site. Use drop-down pick lists for as many fields as you can (e.g., country, state, and job title), and use multiple landing pages to obviate the need for entering certain items (e.g., product interest area or vertical industry). Don't use a `lead source`, but instead populate the relevant `campaign` for the action the user has taken (more on this topic later in this chapter). If you decide to collect phone numbers, do so after you've collected the country information (so the user doesn't need to enter the country code for the phone number), and have a field for city/area code separated from the actual number. To avoid the infinite variety of misentered phone numbers, put example formats in small font immediately under the fields in the Web page. These tricks can dramatically increase both the data quality and the form-completion rates on your Web site.

Even if your company doesn't use email for marketing, it is *imperative* that your Web page forms collect the user's email address and validate it. Email addresses are essentially the *only* universal identifier that exists on the Web (and even they aren't completely reliable), so collect this information and validate it as early as you can. The strong form of validation is to send the user an email at the address the user provided, with the mail containing a unique URL[4] that must be clicked for the user to get access to the desired information, download items, or other goodies. A weaker form of validation is to simply send the user an email including the links to the documents or other goodies they've requested. This technique has become less effective as more users learn to block HTML mail, and each new release of Outlook raises filters to higher and higher levels. Either way, you need to let the registrant know what will happen when the user clicks "submit" (typically with a splash page on the Web), so he or she knows what to do next. Inevitably, some people will employ "single-use" email addresses for their registration, but in most markets they usually constitute only a tiny percentage of the total audience, and you still know that the registrant is a human rather than a Web bot.

If you want to get really fancy, create an "account" page on your Web site where users can select and maintain their preferences. When a user registers, your Web server software creates the account and drops a cookie on the user's system so you can track all of that person's actions on the site going forward. Every few months, when the user returns

---

4. By making this URL unique, you can measure which individuals follow through and when their actions occur. This information can be used to trigger some detailed lead scoring or assist in Web site redesigns.

(assuming you have a highly informational site or lots of short-term offers), you ask the user for just a bit more information. Such a request is typically couched in terms of "Our records aren't quite complete . . ." and asks for only one or two new items each time. This progressive registration technique allows you to collect quite a bit of information about visitors without irritating them. See more on this in the "Marketing Automation" sidebar later in this chapter.

Of course, you need to make sure that all this information is completely integrated with the company's eCommerce site so that users don't ever have to reenter any of their information when they actually buy. As discussed in Chapter 2, do *not* collect or store highly personal financial information (credit cards, Social Security numbers, health ID numbers, or the like) in SFDC.

Special attention needs to be given to email opt-in/opt-out preferences. For a good discussion of general principles of user privacy and email preferences, check out www.SFDC-secrets.com. The key point is that the lead-capture page should really be a *user account creation* page so that when users come back to the site in the future, their information and personal preferences will be remembered. On the registration page, give visitors clear guidance about what registering will do, which kinds of communications they can opt in/opt out for, and how they can change their preferences later.[5] Typically, you want to have at least three different levels of opt in/opt out. A new CAN SPAM requirement mandates that opting out must be achievable from a single Web page, so keep the design simple. What you *don't* want is to have a single opt-out check box, as offering just one choice greatly increases the probability that users will tell you to leave them completely alone—and you would then have to honor that overly broad request.

The following sections describe best practices surrounding typical lead generation activities. For all tactics, make sure to read the "Lead Capture and Insertion" section later in this chapter.

Tradeshows and Conferences

At tradeshows and conferences, you have almost no control over the data the show operator will collect. The data are usually provided in one or more spreadsheets or CSV files, and you need to watch out for and fix the following problems: states and countries that are misspelled and do not conform to ISO standards,[6] phone numbers with erratic formats (particularly with international attendees who forget to include their country codes), and foreign character sets that become garbled (particularly for individuals' names and street

---

5. These choices are typically implemented as short HTML links that point to help/FAQ pop-up pages.

6. When importing or entering data into SFDC, it's a good idea to *not* spell out country and state names but instead to use ISO-standard two-character country and state codes. Using these short codes makes it much easier to develop and maintain lead routing rules, formulas, triggers, reports, and other SFDC features. You can find references to this best practice at www.SFDC-secrets.com.

addresses). Often, the data are not made available to sponsoring companies for several days after the event: get them in the system immediately thereafter!

Tradeshows and conferences sometimes deliver a bunch of information you didn't ask for and probably won't get from any future venue. For example, questionnaires may ask attendees, "By what percentage will you be expanding your office/operations in the next 12 months?"—this could be great background information, but you don't collect this kind of thing for everyone. Nevertheless, don't throw this information away! You can either store it verbatim as a `note` associated with the `lead`, or you can abbreviate it in some way and put it in the `lead`'s `description` field (in the preceding example, the information might be shown in narrative form as "Growth in next 12 months: 8%").

POSTMORTEMS AS A WAY OF LIFE

For any marketing event, activity, or campaign, make sure to schedule a postmortem as part of your overall checklist. At the start of the event/activity/campaign, set metrics of success—and make sure they're realistic for the type of thing you're doing. If it's just a branding or visibility campaign, impressions or click-throughs are all that's relevant. If it's a loyalty campaign for the existing customer base, signups for the call to action are all you should be measuring. These metrics should drive inputs you make to target fields for the `campaign` record (all the objectives should be documented at least in "description" or "notes" fields).

The postmortem meeting should be brief—15 minutes—with at least the following three people: the marketing event "project manager," a marketing tactical person who knows what actually went on, and a person from sales who received some of the leads. Discuss the things you were able to measure, understand the things you weren't able to measure, and identify the lessons learned for future events (including "don't do this one ever again"). As always, document the findings briefly in your marketing Wiki or Google Drive area (that should be accessible to any interested salespeople), and put a pointer to this entry in the `campaign` record. By doing this, you'll be setting yourself up as a learning organization, and it's likely you'll improve SFDC's overall data quality as well as your lead quality over time.

Webinars

Webinars—whether recorded or live—are typically conducted through a service such as WebEx or GoToMeeting. These services collect relatively fixed types of attendee data. The spreadsheets (XLS or CSV files) they send to sponsoring companies have all the same problems as the data collected at tradeshows and conferences, but at least these services provide the data more quickly. Get these data cleaned and put into the system right away. Write a standard import template with macros in the spreadsheet that prep the data quickly and in a repeatable fashion.

Events

Seminars, meetings, dinners, and other lead generation events can deliver much better data quality for leads, particularly if attendees are required to register for the event on your company's Web site. If your registration page follows the guidance given earlier in this section, you're good to go. Plus, the leads will be entered into the system immediately, thanks to the Web-service automation; thus, your lead response times can be very short.

Banner Ads, Site Sponsorships, and Other Internet Advertising

Banner ads and their brethren typically generate traffic to your company's Web site without providing intrinsic lead or other tracking information. The only lead-related data that can be gleaned from this traffic is anonymous (unless users happen to have a browser cookie you're tracking) and of no real relevance to SFDC. If, however, there is a referring user ID embedded in the URL (as happens with big ad networks), use this to infer a `campaign` record for each visitor.

Of course, if the site visitor is interested enough in your offerings to fill out a registration form, you now have a `lead` to which you should attach all the "anonymous" information that HTML traffic provides. It is a best practice—although fairly complex—to correlate the lead's information with his or her page-visited history (using Web analytic software) so you can understand more about the nature of the prospect's interest. Pass this user-profile information into SFDC via hidden fields so that your `lead` records are as rich as possible. Note that the better MAS offerings do all this for you.

Google AdWords

Like other online ad media, Google AdWords can generate traffic for a company's Web site. Unlike more primitive online ads, AdWords traffic can be tightly correlated with SFDC `campaigns` and tracked through the conversion and sales-cycle process.

To increase lead quality[7] for AdWords' ads, follow these guidelines:

- Organize your `campaigns` around your product's *use cases* or *target segments*. If you sell a database accelerator, create `campaigns` around online transactions versus data warehousing, or financial versus telecom comparisons.

---

7. Even though lead quality is king, many advertisers focus instead on the bid value for AdWords. While doing so can make your budget go farther, it's much *less effective* than most people think, and it will do nothing to improve the company's lead quality and will likely lower pipeline yield. Focus on these issues—that is, on the revenue potential—rather than fixating on lowering lead generation costs.

- Once you've focused your messages on these use cases or segments, create coherent content for the AdWords keywords and ad text. Keep that coherence going throughout the landing page content and the call to action.

- On the landing page registration area, encode the `campaign` name in `hidden fields` that will be transferred into SFDC along with the rest of the registration details.

- Tune the entire set of content (keywords, ad text, landing page text, graphics, and landing page call to action) as a whole, trying to optimize for *the total number of converted clicks.* There is no point in trying to increase just the number of clicks or the conversion ratio in isolation—those statistics aren't meaningful. First, optimize the click-through rate by matching the keywords to the ad copy. Next, optimize the conversion rate by matching the keyword/ad to the landing page content. Collect at least a week's data for each tuning cycle (shorter periods of data are misleading because of the variable nature of Web site traffic).

- Do end-to-end A/B "split testing" of the entire content set: the keywords, ad copy, and landing pages as a coherent set (for this testing, do not use Google's ad-rotation feature). Keep a log of all the changes you've made and the results of the "new in-test" set versus the baseline set. These comparisons will help you systematically analyze the effectiveness of the content and improve the results; do it right, and you can double your high-quality lead flow at no extra advertising cost.

- For every $1,000 you spend on Google, someone should be spending an hour tuning the keywords/ads/landing pages and analyzing what's going on with the people who *do* click through. If you spend $100,000 per year on ads, that would mean you'd need a half-time person (or an agency) focused on getting the ad yield up. Sounds expensive, but it really isn't—it's actually the only way to get serious return on your AdWords investment.

- Review the content sets on at least a quarterly basis, and preferably biweekly. Your competitors will be making improvements to their ads when you aren't paying attention, and lead flow (measured in terms of both quality and quantity) can degrade rapidly in highly competitive situations. For better or worse, keeping the ads tuned for peak performance is a source of job security for marketers.

Search Engine Optimization

Despite all the justified excitement about Google AdWords, getting results in the *left* column (the natural search results, as opposed to ads) is more effective (and far more *cost* effective) than the brute-force advertising in the right column. A number of search engine optimization (SEO) tools, services, and books are available, although none of them is specifically targeted at SFDC usage. Follow these guidelines to get the most out of SEO techniques in conjunction with your SFDC system:

- Invest a small amount of time almost continuously (rather than doing big bursts of effort infrequently).

- Examine what the competitors are doing on their Web sites, and copy what works in their strategies. (You don't want to copy them verbatim, but learn from their results and do them one better.)

- Drop cookies as early as possible in the Web visit, and analyze the visitors' page-view metrics carefully.

- Start to use landing pages for visitors who fit certain profiles, and tune the landing pages for best results.

- Pass visitor profile data into the SFDC lead record when the user completes a registration (or information-request) page.

- Know that you'll need to retune your SEO tactics at least every 90 days, as competitors' tactics and search-engine algorithms change frequently and may degrade your search position. It's another case of never-ending job security for marketers.

Lead Generation Services and Products

Several lead generation services have sprung up with a variety of models and price points. The big thing about using any of these services is carefully negotiating your service level, lead quality, and qualification criteria *before* you sign the contract. Set up criteria by which you can reject leads without penalty (they'll want a cap on this, but make the initial cap quite high, so you don't pay excessively for their learning curve). Lead price point or volume per se are meaningless without nailing down these issues! In fact, before you even call the services for quotes, think through the following:

- What is your target market? What 5 to 10 list selection criteria can you set?

- What are your sales folks' lead qualification criteria? They have to be black-and-white, with 5 to 10 items.

- Do your reps actually need to qualify the leads themselves? Would they trust anyone else to do this? If not, you probably can't afford the "pay-per-appointment" model.

- How many leads can your team actually handle? If each rep really got 5 new leads per week that were all worthy of follow-up and sales calls, could they keep up (or would they start to ignore many of them)?

- What's your threshold of spending before you start a sales cycle? "Cost per lead" isn't meaningful–use "cost per first meeting." Create a model with a budget showing the cost of leads at various stages of development.

Generally speaking, the leads that are produced by these services should *not* go directly to sales. Almost inevitably, you have to put in work in a telesales/telemarketing function to nurture and grow the leads. The good news is that you *can* rent that kind of service–you don't have to hire personnel. But no matter what you do:

- Find out if their service or product has an SFDC add-on.

- Manage them tightly. Set up specific reports, views, and alerts in SFDC for the lead generation service metrics.

- Push them to use SFDC on every call so you can measure them (they will probably resist this, but hang tough). It's best if they actually work the leads in your system, not just drop them in at the end–that way, you know the nature of the contacts and conversations they have had along the way. This helps you score the quality of the lead.

- If they have their own SFDC instance and don't want to log into yours all day, use the free `salesforce to salesforce` feature to bridge them so you can see what they're doing without interfering with their normal way of doing business.

Email Marketing

As for SEO, AdWords, and other online marketing techniques, dozens of books have been written about email marketing. None of these tomes focuses specifically on SFDC, and there are some specific tricks you need to learn. There are two main methods of email marketing relevant to SFDC: the broadcast ("mass email blast") and the vertical campaign ("individual drip sequence"). No matter which of these approaches your company employs, the same key success factors apply:

- Use an email marketing tool that integrates with SFDC's `campaign`, `campaign member`, `task`, `contact`, and `lead` objects and that presents useful information on the system's screens. Several companies have done a great job in creating such tools, with new entrants and product upgrades happening all the time. Because these products come with a wide range of features and price points, there is no universal best choice–but it is imperative that you use the email system on a trial basis for at least a month before buying to make sure that its features and concepts fit tightly with your company's needs.

- Make sure the content the company is sending out via emails is relevant to your list. If you don't know whether the prospect would be interested, you're not ready to send the email yet! Sloppiness here is the root of most spam complaints (which could cost you $10,000 in fines per incident).[8]

- Recognize that the best list to email to is the one you already have—the one you've been nurturing and cleaning all along. You can buy email names by the millions, but most of them will be virtually worthless, and emailing those addresses puts your company at risk of spam complaints. Leverage partners' and industry associations' lists, but do a full opt-in cycle before you add those prospects to your list of blast names.

- Depending on your audience, as many as one-third of the emails will be read on a mobile phone. For this reason, keep the emails brief, clean, and "upper-left-corner optimized" so the readers can get the point without panning or scrolling. Make the subject line compelling and keep it to less than 50 characters!

- Make sure that any links in the email point to a unique URL or pass a hidden field into the registration process for identifying where the lead came from. Make sure all the landing pages feed data directly into SFDC.

- Don't use images for anything important in the email—they should just be decoration for those email clients who let images through. In some audiences, more than 50% of the recipients will not see any images in the email—or may never receive the email at all because the embedded images trigger spam filters.

- Don't email the entire list at once. Instead, roll out emails in phases (separated by a day or so) to catch errors in your copy and make minor improvements as you do. You don't want to burn your list out with too-frequent mailings (monthly seems to be the de facto limit unless you've *really* got fast-changing information or temporary offers). Mail to your list too often, and you risk a dramatic surge in unsubscribe requests and complaints.

- Use your partial-list mailing strategy to support A/B split testing of format, content, and calls to action. *You can't know* what will be effective with your audience: you will find out only through testing and tuning for better email response rates.

For drip marketing campaigns, there's a big twist: the recipient has declared interest in a topic, which means you can have a much more relevant and frequent email conversation

---

8. Even though the FTC has chosen to leave this regulation nearly unenforced, such a law actually makes good business sense. Sending email to people who don't care about the content is a *waste of your brand* as well as your time. Just say no.

with this prospect. Instead of consisting of just one generic email per month, a drip marketing sequence should be highly specific, with a series of messages that move the customer along the learning curve for the company's product.

Drip marketing entails an additional best practice (which involves an email system feature). If the individual target is contacted by anyone in the company (presales, sales rep, or postsales support) during a drip sequence,[9] the sequence should be terminated. If a human conversation has occurred, the robot-generated emails are rarely appropriate and can be quite confusing. This "halt email" `status` is set by a `trigger` that evaluates a newly created `task` on the SFDC `contact` or `lead` record. Users need to be briefed on the importance of putting even an empty `task` into the records of the `leads` or `contacts` with whom they talk.

Drip marketing campaigns can be the core of automated `lead` cultivation and nurturing, and the fancy systems provide dynamic `lead` scoring based on recipient behavior and click-throughs to the Web site. Marketing automation systems such as ExactTarget (now SFDC), Eloqua, and Marketo provide solid solutions on which to build closed-loop marketing campaigns. But these systems are content engines in disguise, and they require a set of skills in addition to mastering SFDC. Successful MAS implementations require *dedicated* marketing staff who create and orchestrate the sequence of emails and content deliveries that cause the target audience to respond.

MARKETING AUTOMATION

SFDC provides a solid platform for streamlining sales and marketing processes. It plugs into email blasters and SEM/PPC advertising. It has a content edition, and it has a customer-ideas forum. It helps manage and analyze campaigns. It has social media advertising and monitoring. Until very recently, it was in no way a MAS. But with its ExactTarget and Pardot acquisitions, SFDC has a very serious MAS offering.

If you're already an ExactTarget/Pardot customer, the obvious path is to follow SFDC's guidance on migrating from the version you have into the fully integrated version they'll be offering "real soon now."

If you're already running a different brand of MAS, or plan to buy one, some of its data (at least "scoring events") must be integrated or synchronized with SFDC (check out the "Split Brain" sidebar later in this chapter).

The best answer for the standalone MAS is to get one that comes pre-integrated with SFDC, as most of the modern ones do. Although their integration is never perfect, they

---

9. Typically, emails are sent out on a sequence of days after the initial registration, such as on days 1, 3, 5, 7, 10, 15, 21, and 30. Different audiences and industry preferences may make the sequence more or less frequent.

definitely pass the "good enough" test. If you don't already have a MAS, implementing one is very similar to what we recommend for SFDC:

- Before you start, make sure you have enough content to drive prospects toward desired behavior. If you don't have the white papers, videos, demos, or other calls to action—or the talent available to write great email copy every week—stick with a simple email blaster.
- Get executive championship, budget, and a minimal set of measurable goals.
- Think through the usage model and organization impact (see Chapter 1).
- Understand and align the data models (see Chapter 2).
- Design reports and analytics to fit your organization (see Chapter 2).
- Clean and deduplicate data (see Chapter 3).
- Start small and deliver incrementally, with quick wins (see Chapter 4).
- Analyze and rationalize business processes (see Chapter 8).
- Quantify new skill and organizational requirements (see Chapter 8) and the political implications on your team (see Chapter 6).
- Identify and train a MAS administrator (probably not the same person as the SFDC administrator) for managing the campaigns, policing list usage, creating meaningful reports, and managing MAS usage.
- Engage users, and get the good news out about how much the MAS is making SFDC an even stronger system and boosting overall ROI.

If you are stuck with a MAS that does not have an SFDC plugin, you'll have to do some level of integration as a development project. It is critical to keep this as minimalistic as possible: these integration projects are classic budget busters that don't really deliver on schedule, due largely to wishful thinking and scope creep.

Campaign Management

The power of marketing comes from repetition—a series of prospect communications that gets increasingly more relevant and effective over time. The whole point is to carry out a series of touches that educates the lead and moves the prospect closer to purchasing the company's offerings. SFDC provides a simple `lead source` field (a pick list) to indicate the origin of each lead. Unfortunately, `lead source` is a "training wheel" that rapidly gets in the way. If you create a `lead` and use `lead source` when that person responds to a second outreach from your company, what are you supposed to do with the original `lead source`? Ignoring the new `lead source` or overwriting the existing one destroys information. Conversely, creating a duplicate `lead` to hold the new `lead source` is even worse, causing confusion and lowering data quality.

The solution: don't use `lead source` at all.[10]

SFDC's `campaigns` feature[11] allows you to capture much better information about target audiences, respondents, and activities for your marketing efforts. If you've been using `lead source` until now, your data can be converted to `campaigns` with no data loss.

Once a `campaign` is set up, SFDC tracks which `leads` and `contacts` are target participants (e.g., they are sent email invitations) and respondents (they replied via email or HTML links) and stores the sequence of all participation and response. When `campaigns` are configured properly, looking at `lead` or `contact` pages reveals the entire history of every prospect touch the company has attempted or completed. Further, SFDC's `campaign influence` feature lets you identify all the campaigns that had some impact on each of the `opportunities` in the company's pipeline. This capability makes it easier than ever before to calibrate the ROI of marketing activities.

The `campaigns` feature is really a management and reporting facility, not an execution tool. It is used in conjunction with third-party MAS tools to organize, monitor, and report on the company's outbound marketing activities. This magic requires some planning and careful execution. The good news is that after the first few weeks, working with this feature will be second nature. The bad news is that the vast majority of SFDC customers are *not* using `campaigns` correctly—so some explanation is in order here.

Naming Campaigns

Before you start using SFDC's `campaigns` feature, you have to examine all the ways you collect leads, whether directly generated by marketing activities or not. All of these `lead` streams—even cold calls and customer referrals—need to be represented as `campaigns`. It's best to create a list of every way that customers may contact the company (and every vehicle that the company uses to find them). The list is best organized on a spreadsheet that looks like Table 10-1.

Most of the information in Table 10-1 is self-explanatory, but the `campaign` naming convention needs some special attention. You will want to be able to look back over `campaigns` years after they were done without getting them confused with one another (if you want to understand more about naming issues, check out "What's in a Namespace?"

---

10. Actually, `lead source` is a system field that you can't delete anyway, so it's okay to store some interesting information there—but it will be a redundant field whose semantics you need to manage carefully. It's particularly important to *not* use `lead source` in reports unless you *really* know what you are doing.

11. Included in the `enterprise` and `unlimited editions`; it's an extra-cost item in the `professional edition`.

TABLE 10-1   Campaign Summary Information

Type	Name	Description	Start/End Date	Audience	# Leads	Budget
Ad	08q3--Goog--NA--Svcs	Services promo	Sep 08/Jan 09	USA execs	200	$ 2,000
Event	00q1 Dinner NYC	Exec dinner	Oct 08/Oct 08	NYC execs	50	$ 5,000
Show	08q4--GGSymp--USA	Symposium expo	Nov 08/Nov 08	USA execs	300	$30,000
Email	08q4--Email--upgrade	Upgrade promo	Dec 08/Dec 08	Customers	50	$ 500

in Chapter 2). You should think of a naming convention that is intuitive, with all names between 25 and 80 characters, and easy to identify even if you weren't involved with running the `campaign`. Your names probably should be case-insensitive so they can be easily read into a phone conversation. The exact parameters of this namespace will depend on your company's marketing and target markets, but generally the names should look something like this:

> <year+qtr>--<event/activity abbreviation>--<geography>--
> <product line or message>

The year+qtr (note the format in Table 10-1) should be at the head of the name so that you can rapidly sort `campaigns` by year in HTML or Excel list views. The double dashes are needed in the name so that they can be unambiguously parsed[12] by reporting software. The overall name may seem long, but it ensures that humans can rapidly identify the `campaigns` that they're looking for in reports or other long listings.

You will need to create a `campaign` name for every single `lead source` you use in the system today, and every lead generating activity you can conceive of using in the next few years. Expect your list of `campaigns` to be somewhere between 50 and 500 lines long—even more if your company does a ton of highly variable or experimental `campaigns`. This amount of data sounds daunting, but summarizing this list actually goes pretty quickly once you put your mind to it. Besides, this list simply represents a reality that is already complex.

In addition to the traditional outbound activities marketing explicitly does, make sure that your `campaigns` list includes items for things that go on indefinitely, such as natural searches, newsletters, customer referrals, employee referrals, press articles, analyst recommendations, call-ins, word of mouth, and other data streams. These never-ending `campaigns` should be named with the year field as "20XX."

---

12. This is fancy talk for "filtered, sorted, or interpreted."

Setting Up Campaigns

You already do some planning before you execute a marketing campaign. It's important to extend this planning a bit and put the information into the SFDC system, as it will become the system of record for all `campaign` information.

First, you will probably need to add some `custom fields` to the `campaign` page to hold the following data items:

- The business unit, target market, or product line benefitting from the `campaign`

- The value proposition, message, or call to action

- The geographic reach

- The media channel

- The Web site landing page URL or other registration vehicles

- The offer or promotional item

- Venue, timing, and logistics

- The organizations and agencies involved

You'll also almost surely want to expand the `campaign response` pick list to reflect the expected response `workflow` surrounding the `campaign`.

When preparing for a `campaign`, identify the qualitative goals and quantitative metrics for it. Summarize the costs (include internal labor allocation as well as external agency/materials costs). Identify the call to action for the `campaign`, and think through any special actions that might be required. For example, a `campaign` for a local prospect dinner would need specific action to deal with the restaurant for headcount and a reminder call-out activity for the telesales group. These special actions should be embodied as either SFDC `tasks` or `workflows` associated with the `campaign`.

Enter the `campaign` information into the SFDC system, and make sure to set up appropriate `campaign sharing` rules so your colleagues have visibility into the `campaigns`. Also set up `campaign hierarchies` to reflect relationships among `campaigns` (such as geographic, product line, or target market groupings) for easier analysis and roll-ups over time. Make sure to fill out the `description` field with as much relevant information as possible about the target audience, goals, and call-to-action sequence. At the time, all this information will seem completely obvious and boring—but 6 months after the `campaign` ends, no one will be able to remember any of these details that make the `campaigns` relevant to generating real business.

Add all of the creative pieces (whether a Web page or an email or a PDF file of the paper deliverables) to the `campaign` record as `attached files`. If any coupons or discount offers were made available, make sure that they include an expiry date, were reviewed by the legal staff[13] before they were sent out, and are attached as a PDF to the SFDC `campaign` record.

If the `campaign` has experimental or innovative elements, you should set up a `chatter group` to collaborate around the topic. This way, the team discovers more about what works—and what doesn't—and everyone learns much faster. The telesales group will also need tools for follow-up to responses. Include scripts and pointers to follow-up `email templates` and `content deliveries` (relevant collateral packs) in the `campaign description` field. SFDC has a free AppExchange call-scripting feature that makes it easier for your phone jockeys to say the right things to `campaign` respondents, no matter how new the messages or offers might be.

You might also store ideas about best responses to certain situations (e.g., competitive objections or unable to travel to your event) as `attachments` to the campaign.

A HISTORY LESSON

`Campaigns` are *the* way to handle the full variety of prospect interactions. But in many cases, `campaign membership` records prove unwieldy for workflows or formulas. So here's a trick: create a download history as a single ASCII field (in `leads` and `contacts`) that grows indefinitely. The history field has brief codes that you can use in `filters`, `formulas`, `workflows`, and `reports`. Here's an example:

> Product download = P
> Subsequent product download = p
> White paper download = W

So your download history field might look like this:

> P12.10.08-p01.05.09-W01.07.09-. . .

Note the use of "." rather than "/" for date separators and "-" as an event separator. Using these characters makes it easier when doing Regex and string processing in your scripts, spreadsheets, `formulas`, and `workflows`. Also note the use of leading zeroes on days and months to facilitate parsing and character counting (each download uses exactly 10 characters).

How is the history field created and updated? Through either an **APEX trigger** in SFDC or a **Web service call** from your content management system. The history field can get arbitrarily long, but if its length gets unwieldy, you can have a `workflow` formula that truncates the field to remove any history over 2 years old.

---

13. Of course, these bits of advice are not unique to SFDC. But I can't tell you the number of times I've discovered illegal or unethical elements accidentally included in marketing offers.

Running Campaigns

The first step is to make sure the system administrator has set up the `campaign member` report[14] as a `custom` `link` in the `campaign`, `contact`, and `lead` pages. This AppExchange freebie is worth its weight in gold and will make it much easier to see what's going on with the `campaign` in real time.

The next step is to set up a `campaign`-specific landing page (for registration, confirmation, or download) on the company's Web site. Add the `campaign` ID value (the last 15 digits of the URL for the `campaign` page in SFDC) as a hidden field in the appropriate Web registration page, email link, or name-import spreadsheet template for the respondents.

Make sure that you've set your `campaign` to `active` status before you do any test runs of the registration and other user interactions. Unless the `campaign` is activated, no data will be recorded in SFDC.

Test the `campaign` by sending out a test email and following the response system (typically, a Web landing page or two) before you fully implement the outbound elements of the `campaign` to make sure that all "sent" and "responded" data end up in the right buckets. The whole point of `campaigns` is to keep these data properly separated, so make sure that everything works correctly before you go live.

Before you push the `campaign` offer out, send an email to the relevant sales reps, telesales people, and product marketing folks to notify them that the `campaign` is about to begin. Include the URL for all collateral, "hot tips," objection-handling, and promotional documents (these documents should be placed on your internal wiki so that any partners' sales reps can get to them as well). Also send out the URL for reports. You'll want to train everyone to look in the SFDC system first for all the real-time information about `campaigns` because, well, that's where the information will appear first.

The larger the `campaign`, the more appropriate it is to send out the `campaign` offer in batches. Batching allows you to do tests that compare the wording of emails, layout of Web landing pages, and a dozen other details that can dramatically improve response rates. Using A/B testing on every part of a `campaign` will help you discover what works best for your target audience so that you can improve `campaign` designs while the `campaign` is in progress. But you must track your A/B tests very carefully, and ideally you should manage each batch as a separate sub-`campaign` (with a common `parent` but with all the change details recorded separately). Although this involves some effort and complexity, over time it can easily double the effectiveness of your `campaign` dollars.

Once you've reached the end date of the `campaign`, you must manually deactivate it. There's no real harm in leaving it `active` beyond the scheduled end date, but it's good housekeeping (for reporting and other analytics) to turn `campaigns` off once you don't expect any more responses. If you want to get all ambitious, you can set up a workflow

---

14. Make sure your administrator sets up the special link for campaign membership reports, as shown by SFDC at
https://www.salesforce.com/appexchange/detail_overview.jsp?NavCode__c=&id=a0330000000j5OdAAI.

that automatically deactivates campaigns when they reach their end date. Because this kind of automation can backfire, you should have the auto-deactivate occur a few days after the expected end of the campaign and send out an email to the campaign owner that the campaign is now over.

Lead Handling

One of the areas ripe for the highest leverage by marketing people, which can help them enhance their own credibility as well as that of the SFDC system, is proper lead handling. Although managing leads properly does not involve any additional effort, it *does* require preparation and discipline—which is why lead handling is all too often done wrong.

Read the "Creation Science" sidebar in Chapter 9 right now.

First, Make Sure It's a Lead

As discussed in Chapter 8, the best operating definition of a *lead* is an individual who has asked for information or some level of contact from the company. Job one is to make sure that the data you've been handed really are `leads`.

The first thing to watch for is names purchased from industry associations, memberships, or attendee lists. Unless the list is brand new, it will contain substantial information rot: typically email addresses and phone numbers degrade between 1% and 10% per month. Info-rot is just the beginning: the names you bought have not expressed any interest in your company or its offerings, so the unsubscribe (or worse, spam complaint) rate will be quite high when you try to contact them. Consequently, this category of names should not be imported into SFDC at all. The bad data will merely muck up the database, produce misleading metrics, and lower the credibility of the system.

Instead, we recommend that names be entered into the hopper of your email blasting system or MAS (see the "Split Brain" sidebar), where their quality can increase over time until they eventually graduate to being real `leads`. Although mailing to names is risky, you have to start somewhere when you're going after a brand-new market.

First, select a list that has a decent chance of being interested. For example, if your company sells a dental laser, you would look at the membership list of the American Dental Association—but not of the American Association of Orthodontists. You would go to a list broker and rent email addresses for a blast, and deliver information or an offer that was *specifically* interesting to dentists (such as a case study about how dental lasers improve the patient flow through dental offices). Design the call to action so that the email recipients go through an opt-in process so that the respondents become legitimately part of your ongoing list. Typically, if you don't have any connection with the members of

SPLIT BRAIN

At first blush, you might expect the SFDC database to hold everything having to do with prospects and customers. In reality, sophisticated organizations often use a split-brain approach that separates the *marketing* database from the *sales* database. There are three reasons for this separation. First, the marketing database contains a large number of low-quality leads (really, they're little more than names) that aren't relevant to the sales folks. Second, sophisticated MAS tools need to operate from their own copy of the data. And finally, mixing the two databases together slows down reporting for everyone.

If you're already using a tool such as Eloqua, Marketo, Vertical Response, or ExactTarget, you're on the split-brain path. You don't really have a choice.

If you aren't using this kind of tool, you do have an architectural choice to make: do you need to have all of your leads—regardless of quality—in one place, or do you want to create a category of leads that are of such low quality that they're handled externally? Although there's no overwhelming cost or operational advantage to going in either direction, changing the path you take after deployment will involve considerable one-time costs. So choose wisely, grasshopper.

a list, there's little point in hitting them more than three times (typically a month apart), and the costs of list rental can make it too expensive to go even that far.

The next category of names to look out for is sales reps who have used SFDC's Outlook connector to import their entire contact list into the system. These data are really dangerous (which is why we recommend that no one except the marketing staff ever be allowed to import `leads` or `contacts` into the SFDC system) because the information is of unknown quality, provenance,[15] and age. Expunging these kinds of mass imports from the system isn't especially difficult (with careful use of SFDC's free `data loader` or `Excel connector`), but it's a chore you would rather avoid, and the bad data can mess up reports for a while. Many of these imported contacts will show up as "private contacts," but some may not and (through deduping) may corrupt data already in the system.

Some quite messy symptoms can occur if the contacts are synched from two different reps' Outlook address books. Life becomes even more fun when different versions of Outlook are involved or when they are using different synching technologies. Obviously, this area requires some careful thought and testing before you try to establish a federated (i.e., shared yet distributed) contact management system. A couple of articles discussing this issue in more depth are available on www.SFDC-secrets.com.

---

15. Are these names even legal for your company to have? If the rep's list "fell off a truck," you might have a customer privacy issue on your hands, as well as the legal issue of using some other company's confidential information.

Lead Capture and Insertion

From the moment a lead has been collected, it is already starting to go stale. Recent studies have shown that in our fast-paced world, prospect response rates fall off dramatically within hours of initial registration. Indeed, within 48 hours most prospects will not even remember having visited a company's Web site, let alone have a clue about its value proposition or competitive advantage. Use SFDC's `auto-response rules` or your MAS to send an email to the lead the instant that they register.

The "freshness date" of `leads` is calibrated in hours! Depending on your location[16] and industry, even 1 hour of delay will measurably impact conversion rates. Add automation at every step to get `leads` into a MAS drip campaign or over to the inside sales teams right away. But the sense of urgency needs to be about accuracy, because a junk lead delivered quickly is just an annoyance. It is much easier to fix data before they are entered into the system than afterward, and it's worth an extra couple of hours to really get things right before distributing `leads`.

Part of accuracy is that "the `lead` is routed to the right person." SFDC provides automatic `lead routing`, but some `lead` entry points (particularly manual ones) don't automatically trigger the system's `lead assignment rules`. If a large proportion of your leads are not being routed properly, ask the SFDC development team to create an **APEX trigger** to catch the exceptions and route them in real time, or use the MAS to do clever routing.

The system's `lead assignment` rules are easy to set up—and even easier to set up incorrectly. The rules are similar to the email filter rules used in Outlook: they're simple Boolean matches, with only **and** and **or** operators. The rules are evaluated one at a time, and as soon as the first rule fires, the `lead` is routed to the individual **user** or **queue**.[17] All subsequent rules are ignored for that `lead`. Most companies can live with a few dozen well-structured rules, whereas other companies might have 150 of them. Rule sets this large almost always have bugs, and they're basically unmaintainable. If your sales organization is really *that* complicated (with lots of overlays, national accounts, special markets, and other sources of complexity), you might do better using a bit of **APEX** code, a MAS smart list, or an external assignment module to do the routing. This is particularly necessary with the Named Account model, as `territories` and `lead ownership` are nongeographic.

Now, let's take a look at the various sources of `leads` that need to be inserted into the system.

---

16. The urban areas of the United States seem to have the shortest attention span, and impulse-purchase items obviously are more time critical than other product categories. But this Short Attention Span Theater is not limited to consumer markets: B2B customers are impatient and under time pressure as well.

17. See the discussion of `queues` in Chapter 9.

WHAT'S A PERSON ACCOUNT?

SFDC in its default mode is set up for the business-to-business (B2B) marketplace, where all the `leads` and `contacts` work for an organization. But if you sell to consumers (B2C), the notion of an "account" doesn't really make much sense: you're selling to the individual, and you neither know nor care who their employer is. `Person accounts` were created to handle exactly this situation.

`Person accounts` are a `record type` that can be enabled by submitting a support case in the system. The detailed description of how `person accounts` change system behavior is very well explained in SFDC's help system, so there is no need to reiterate it here. But beware: once you've turned this feature on, it can never be turned off, and the special `record types` can never be deleted from the system. Never.

Why is this a problem? If you have both B2B and B2C customers, `person accounts` can cause some confusion. This goes double when you discover your `person account` consumers also work for your business customers. There are also some minor irritants in SFDC's UI and reporting engine when working with mixed customer types.

Unless you absolutely must have `person  accounts`, we recommend that you not turn them on. Instead, have all your consumer customers be "owned" by a dummy `account` (called something like "###Consumer###" or "###Individual###"). Many of our clients actually have several of these dummy accounts to reflect the market segment of the consumer, such as "###SOHO###", "###Student###", and "###Amazon###".

Manual Data Entry

It's hard to believe that anyone types in `leads` anymore. But it does happen, particularly when reps collect business cards at cocktail parties. Fortunately, there are only a few things to look out for when entering data manually. First, never enter a `lead` without searching for it first, or use a duplicate preventer such as DupeCatcher (free) or UniqueEntry (not free, but well worth it). A business card may already be in the system as either a `lead` or a `contact`: if it's there as both, go to the `contact` record and update the data there. For the state and country fields, best practices state that these items be presented as pull-down pick lists[18] of two-character ISO codes[19] that minimize typing. For the person's employer, search for that business name (using multiple browser tabs is really helpful for this kind of thing)

---

18. SFDC is just releasing the ability to have pick lists for state and country on `account`, `lead`, and `contact` objects. If you're starting from scratch, use these immediately! For existing customers, the conversion is a little hairy—but we're all going to be on the pick-list path during 2014.

19. These codes are found in ISO standard 3166. In most cases, a two-character code is all you need. However, if the company has a worldwide operation that does business in really obscure places, you might need to use the three-character versions of these codes. If you have to make that switch, make sure you enforce it everywhere, and normalize the existing two-character codes to their three-character versions.

before you enter it; don't forget to search for both the friendly name (discussed later in this chapter) and the formal one (just in case). Creating duplicate `companies` or `accounts` is even less amusing than creating duplicate `leads` or `contacts` in the system.

`Leads` also come in via inbound voicemail or email. Enter them and get them assigned immediately: conversion rates start to drop within the hour if someone doesn't have a conversation.

Web Leads

With `leads` that come in over the Web (from one of several registration pages on your company's Web site or elsewhere), the `lead` entry is automatic and nearly instantaneous. Unfortunately, the basic `web2lead` functionality in SFDC is satisfactory only for very small companies. Most SFDC customers use a third-party Web entry application from companies such as RingLead or CRMfusion. These AppExchange add-ons confirm that the Web registrant isn't already in the system as a `lead` or a `contact` and update existing records rather than create duplicates.

More highly sophisticated marketing operations may want to develop their own code to create multiple `campaign` memberships per registration, call a `lead` enrichment service to validate and extend data, create an `activity` for the user's download history, create a "friendly" version of the company name (see the sidebar on this topic later in the chapter), create `custom object` record entries for users' page-view sequences, update a "last campaign date" field in the `lead/contact` record, or append topic-interest strings to fields in that record. These are all best practices for preventing duplicates while assuring full visibility into the customer's behavior, both in real-time views and in reports. Implementing these capabilities requires a bit of code in the company's content management system or Web page logic to push the data properly into SFDC, and a bit of retry and logging logic to handle the times (typically 1 hour per month) when SFDC is down for scheduled maintenance. High-quality MAS systems can be configured to do all this for you if your IT shop doesn't want to code.

Spreadsheet Imports

Virtually all SFDC customers need to deal with external `lead` flows that are presented only via spreadsheet or CSV files. It is best practice to allow only a few individuals (all of them in the marketing department) to perform imports because of the number of steps involved in doing an import correctly. Before the spreadsheets are imported into SFDC, the marketers need to complete the following tasks:

1. Avoid all the foibles of Excel when working with CSV files. Check out "The Joy of Regex" sidebar in Chapter 3.

2. Fix the individual entries to correct spelling problems, number format problems, foreign character sets, data in the wrong fields, and other issues.

3. Normalize the data (particularly state, country, and phone numbers) so they are in the correct format and match the system's pick-list values.

4. Add columns for fields that can be inferred from the source of the spreadsheet (e.g., this spreadsheet came from WebEx; therefore, the product-interest field should be filled in with the topic of our most recent Webinar), and create a friendly name for the company.

5. Add a column with the list's relevant `campaign` ID.

6. Remove duplicates from within the Excel list.

7. Change the column headers to fit with SFDC's template.

Create a standardized template including Excel `macros` to streamline and automate as much of this process as possible. You need to get the import done in minutes, not hours or days.

FRIENDLY NAMES

The company names that appear in `leads` (and will eventually be propagated into `account` records) typically start out as "whatever the user typed on the registration page." But sometimes the user types stuff that's meaningful to them but useless to you. A user might have typed in "GMAC," but the company name is really "Ally Bank." With some companies, foreign or domestic, the names may not be recognizable (e.g., E. I. DuPont de Nemours) or may have characters that make search difficult (e.g., Nestlé). This goes double for companies whose names are also acronyms (e.g., Badische Anilin und Soda-Fabrik [BASF] or Bayerische Motoren Werke [BMW]).

A best practice is to use the system-standard `company` field on the `lead` (which becomes `account` on the contact record and `name` on the account record) to hold a "friendly" name that people will easily search for and recognize (such as "Disney"). Initially, this `company` will consist of whatever the user originally typed in, but over time your lead cultivation people should change it to the form (usually an abbreviation) that is most likely to be searched for. Friendly names are *always* in the native language of the headquarters office of your company, and they need to be free of foreign characters, accents, apostrophes, and corporate suffixes (e.g., "Inc.," "Pty," "Ltd").

In addition to the friendly name, create a `custom field` called "Legal Entity Name" on the `lead`, `contact`, and `account` records that is initially filled in (via workflow) with the user's original entry. Over time, the accounting, legal, and other departments will change the legal entity name to indicate the formal legal name for the customer (e.g., "Pixar Animation Studios division of The Walt Disney Company").

During the import of these spreadsheets, it is imperative to use a deduping tool such as RingLead's or CRMfusion's tool,[20] as SFDC's deduping feature for spreadsheet imports is too basic. As mentioned earlier in this chapter, using `lead source` is really for amateurs, so *don't* use that field. Instead, once you've imported or updated the `leads` with the deduping tool, you import the entire list (*without* deduping) as a set of `campaign members`, using the wizard within the `campaign` main page.[21] Your spreadsheet importer tool or MAS may have more straightforward ways of getting this done.

The import procedure should be set up to route new `leads` to the proper `queues` or `user`. But what about registrants who were already in the system as `leads` or `contacts`? The SFDC system will not send emails to the appropriate salespeople to indicate that one of the people they are tracking has participated in a new campaign. However, there are several approaches that the marketing staff can use to provide appropriate cues to the salespeople:

- Modify all `lead` and `contact views` that the sales folks use to set "recently modified" (rather than "recently created") as the filter criteria.

- Modify any reports that the sales folks use to filter on `modified date` rather than `created date`.[22]

- Create a `workflow` that automatically sends an alert email to the `owner` when one or more of that person's existing `leads` or `contacts` are `modified by` a marketing employee.[23]

- Manually create a `task` for any salesperson whose individual records have been modified or who has received new `leads`. This approach is more time consuming for marketing but is a best practice because it sends *a single alert to each salesperson*, irrespective of the number of new or modified `leads` that individual has received.

Be careful about email overload: make sure that the approach you use won't generate dozens of emails or tasks a day, particularly when you do a big lead import.

---

20. These are different products but use the same kind of fancy-shmancy logic as the companies' `web2lead` dedupers.

21. Different deduping tools will import these `leads` in different ways, so it's not possible to describe a universal procedure here. What you are trying to achieve is (1) a set of `leads` that is truly new, (2) a set of updated `leads` and `contacts` for people already in the system, and (3) all the individuals (new or updated) added to the `campaign member` table for the marketing `campaign` in question.

22. When a record is first created in SFDC, the `created date` and the `modified date` are the same—so there won't be any apparent change to the views. But when a record is updated, only the `modified date` changes—so only the modified views will work properly.

23. Be careful in designing this `workflow`, as it can generate hundreds of annoying emails if not set up properly.

Lead Scoring and Aging

By default in SFDC, `leads` can hold a `rating` of A/B/C or hot/medium/cold. There is no built-in automation to set the rating, so the field is often ignored. Further, the SFDC system doesn't have a corresponding `rating` field for `contacts` to indicate their current level of interest.

Prioritizing `leads` and `contacts` (to answer the sales rep's inevitable question, "Which ones do I call first?") really needs to be automated as much as possible. The last few years have taught the industry several lessons about scoring. The bottom line: getting high-precision scoring (say, 0 to 100) to work credibly requires a surprising amount of work, so do calculate scores, but present to sales only a hot/medium/cold rating that is *derived from* bands of scores (say, less than 60 is cold, more than 80 is hot, and in the middle is warm). The hot/medium/cold rating should be used to sort and filter `leads` and `contacts` in views, reports, and dashboards.

The numerical scoring should be recalculated with each significant update to the `lead` or `contact` record. There are three important things to look for in a `lead` scoring system:

- **Profile scoring (or explicit scoring):** This score assigns a static number based on "who they are": the individual's demographic or descriptive information, such as job title, company name, industry, department, or product interest. Points are typically added for "more fields filled out on the page"[24] and are subtracted for data that are contradictory (the ZIP code doesn't match the state), irrelevant (the person says he or she is from a country your company doesn't sell to), or unattractive[25] (e.g., a student, or someone who only gave you a Yahoo! email address). Profile scores should be adjusted to reflect where the company is strong (competitive superiority, more references, or a better track record with sales). Profile scoring is a good start but is subject to a lot of faulty assumptions that can be found only when you have a lot of other data.

- **Behavioral scoring (or implicit scoring):** This score yields a dynamic number that results from "what they've done": the individual's choices, behaviors, and patterns in interacting with the company. Points are added for *any* desired action taken by the individual (e.g., responding to an email, registering for a Webinar,

---

24. It doesn't matter where the information comes from—whether manually entered by the prospect or imported from a reference database. In the case of `contacts`, most of the information will have been entered by employees. Of course, any `contact` who is a customer receives an instant and permanent score of 100.

25. Sales reps will be happy to give you very clear guidance on what they believe will make for a likely conversion candidate. If you're lucky, the guidance will be consistent across reps and sales management, but even then it's likely to be right maybe 55% of the time. So don't tune the advantages/penalties in the scoring formula so severely that viable but "unattractive" leads get a ridiculous score.

or attending that Webinar), and special points are added for highly indicative behavioral sequences (e.g., viewing the demonstration video and requesting a trial download within the same week). Points are deducted for behaviors that indicate "tire kickers" or other low-yield people (such as students or job-seekers). In many markets, behavioral scoring is *way* more effective at predicting the most interesting `leads` than profile scoring is. However, setting the point values and triggers requires a lot of experimentation, configuration, and even coding.

- **Decay scoring (or time-based scoring):** This score yields a dynamic number that results from "when did they do it": the behavioral score is lowered by lack of subsequent activity. Every week or so, inactive leads are demoted, thereby moving stale `leads` farther down the priority list over time. After 30 or 45 days, inactive `leads` or `contacts` should disappear entirely from the sales view because of these scores. The ultimate in decay scoring is moving unresponsive leads to the "marketing queue" where the MAS system will use the lowest-cost efforts possible to revive and nurture them. This system is fairly simple to implement with `APEX` code or external scoring applications, or a MAS system.

A number of free, simple, `lead` scoring tools are available from the AppExchange. In any event, SFDC's `formulas` and `validation rules` can set you fairly far down the path for pure profile scoring. If you are just starting out, begin with those features.

Fancier `lead` scoring algorithms are often embedded in MAS products. Even though using one of these packages is simpler than coding the algorithm yourself, configuring these off-the-shelf systems is relatively complicated and can cause buggy interactions with other systems. Each product is a little bit different, but the best practice is to have all scoring processing (and the `lead assignment` or `contact ownership` logic that feeds off of it) in one system, not spread across two.

Even the best tools require quite a bit of time to fine-tune the `lead` scoring. During the first few months, the scores will almost certainly be misleading because they're based on theory rather than the behavior of the actual target customers and sales folks. Put time into understanding your target customer behaviors, working closely with the sales team to steadily improve the realism and accuracy of the scores. Expect that tuning and enhancing the `lead` scoring system will be an ongoing responsibility of the marketing staff, and recognize that the scoring factors and thresholds will need to be updated on a quarterly basis. The more competitive the market space you're in, the more effort will be required for this tuning and tweaking of scores.

In addition to sliding-scale scoring, several helpful tools do filtering to immediately eliminate garbage `leads` from view. These `lead` garbage collectors range from free standalone plugins to features available in more sophisticated add-on products.

DIAGNOSING BAD DATA

A best practice is to not allow users to delete SFDC records, because allowing deletion will merely mask a process problem. Instead of deletion, the record should be marked to reflect its problem for further investigation in the fullness of time.

Whenever a record is marked as bad data, somebody needs to do some data forensics to understand which process, system, or individual is causing the bogus records. It is not uncommon to have hundreds or thousands of bad records pile into the SFDC database every month, particularly when external systems are inserting data into the SFDC system.

There are two major classes of bad data: duplicate records and spurious field values. Duplicate records are dangerous because they rapidly confuse people and can be very difficult to root out. Work on those first. Duplicate records most commonly derive from the following sources:

- Incorrect importing procedures
- Untrained or sloppy users
- Incomplete or poorly implemented external logic or integration
- Poor naming standards or semantics

The most prolific and dangerous sources of duplication are those that you cannot control, such as feeds from an eCommerce system, a partner's database, or an internal accounting system. One SFDC customer's external integrations systematically created hundreds of duplicate `accounts` *every day*, and the company cannot turn the source system off. This way lies madness.

The only real solution for this kind of situation is to create a message buffer system that takes in the external "new record" requests, runs deduplication logic, and properly updates the existing SFDC records. This kind of message buffer is needed in any case to handle the times when SFDC is down for planned maintenance. Unfortunately, creating this "holding pen" requires some fairly expensive custom code.

The problem of spurious fields can be interesting as well. Look for patterns: when are the fields correct, and when are they bogus? Common issues are mishandling of foreign characters, coding errors, and mishandling of spreadsheet data (particularly when somebody sorts only *some* of the columns of a spreadsheet).

When you've identified the needed data corrections, it's usually better to update existing records than to delete trashed ones and reinsert new records. Using updates preserves history and provides important clues for future data forensic analysis should it be needed. Be sure to document the process problem and put it into the system wiki or Google Drive area.

When Leads and Contacts Need to Disappear

As discussed earlier, `leads` and `contacts` (like `accounts` and `opportunities`) should never be deleted from the SFDC system. But there are plenty of situations where you want individual records to disappear from view. For example, a record that holds bad data and a `contact` that will never go anywhere should be removed from the marketing and telesales lists.

The mechanisms for hiding records are `ownership` values of the `lead` or `contact`, in conjunction with the `roles` and `sharing settings`. By setting a `lead`'s `owner` to a `queue` named "Remarket" or "Newsletter," the `lead` will disappear from view except for the marketing department users.[26] If the `lead` *doesn't* disappear for some users, that's because that user's `profile` is set with the `view all` privilege for `leads`. In that case, adjust the filters on users' `views` and `reports`. Using the `status` or `type` pick-list values for the `leads` or `contacts` can just as effectively cause disappearance, but of course the specifics are a little different.

What about `leads` and `contacts` that haven't been touched in years? I have to confess that I'm an information packrat. It is very rare for `leads` or `contacts` to cause real problems or excessive storage use in the system. At some point, of course, there's a limit: even the IRS doesn't care about information that's more than 7 years old. `Leads` that are far too old can be archived (into a CSV or MDB file—Excel can't handle large data sets as well as other tools can). Note that your MAS will probably have its own mechanisms for archiving ancient leads—make sure to look at their help system for guidance on how to do this. Because `contacts` are linked with many other records in the system, it's much more complicated to extricate them: it's probably not worth the effort to create a `contacts` archive.

Opt-Out

As discussed earlier, it's essential to company credibility—and common sense—to comply with CAN SPAM email requirements. You may be fairly aggressive about allowing people to opt *in* to your email campaigns, but you need to provide them *several* ways to opt *out,* including email response, Web links, personal profile editing, and even phone calls. Once the opt-out request has been made, you need to service it quickly and thoroughly.

Most email blasting systems handle this task automatically, and they should be used as the system of record for opt-outs. But these systems can only know about opt-out requests

---

26. Unfortunately, the `lead` or `contact` may also disappear from view of your MAS (check with your vendor's support people to know for certain). If your MAS has this problem, you cannot use SFDC `queues` at all (because the MAS will create a duplicate lead when someone in a queue responds to a campaign). Instead, you need to have your remarket/nurturing/newsletter `leads` or `contacts` owned by a person in marketing (such as the VP) who is high enough in the `role hierarchy` to keep them effectively hidden.

made from within their emails or opt-out pages. You'll need to import opt-out requests from your external systems and sources on a regular basis.

Further, you'll need to make sure that the opt-out requests in the email system make it into SFDC. Even if the email system doesn't perform this task automatically as part of its SFDC integration, the export/import cycle can be completed in a few minutes via spreadsheets or CSV files using the Data Loader or other tools.

An additional step is needed to do things really right. SFDC maintains an email opt-in flag, and it enforces the right behavior—but only for emails that are sent from within the SFDC system. What if a sales rep runs a report from SFDC and uses it to drive a mail merge, or uses the Outlook sync to grab contacts out of SFDC `contact` for mailing? In these cases, the opt-in flag will be ignored, and the email will go out to customers who specifically asked you to stop contacting them this way.

To protect against this possibility, create a `workflow` for the `lead` and `contact` records that automatically corrupts email addresses of opt-outs. These addresses are guaranteed to bounce, yet still preserve the original email information. Check out www.SFDC-secrets.com for a checklist that explains how to create the email address auto-corrupter in your own system.[27]

Lead Enrichment

In many cases, the only thing you know for certain about a `lead` is an email address, which you can (should!) validate through an email-response cycle. Depending on your target audience, many of the other data entries may be empty or clearly bogus—but that doesn't mean you should throw all of the `leads` into the remarket bucket.

Several services are available to enrich, correct, or supplement `lead` and `contact` records in SFDC. Salesforce offers data.com, which combines `account` information from Hoover and Dunn and Bradstreet with `contact` and `lead` information that has been crowdsourced. Using data.com's `cleanse` mode is probably the best available strategy, although competitive offerings change rapidly. In any case, don't expect much more than a 50% match rate on individuals with corporate email addresses, and a significantly lower rate when you have a "commodity domain" (e.g., gmail, hotmail, Comcast) email address—or no email at all. Enrichment of B2C leads/contacts is even more sketchy. Due to privacy issues, you will find that there is little data to enrich with for contacts in several European countries. If data.com does not provide the information that you want, look at other services, such as iProfiles, ZoomInfo, DiscoverOrg, EmailAppenders, and others that provide supplementary information about individuals and companies.

---

27. Yes, the address auto-corruption will undo itself if SFDC's `email opt-out` check box is unchecked to reflect a "re-opt-in."

The bottom line: the best information you can get applies to the people already in your database, and the best way to improve this information is to get it directly and voluntarily updated by those individuals. Use the nurturing and progressive-registration techniques discussed earlier in this chapter to get "just a little more information" in exchange for providing the user with some relevant information or a small incentive (it's surprising how much information people will give you in exchange for a chance in a sweepstakes contest). Hit your entire database with progressive-registration requests at least once a year so the core information is as complete and up to date as possible.

Lead Handling in the Named Account Model

Generally speaking, there is very little for marketing to do with leads in the Named Account model (NAM) of selling, because this model doesn't use the traditional `lead` generation and nurturing process. If you get a `lead` that is owned by a NAM rep, the typical path is to `assign` the `lead` to him or her, instantly `convert` it to a `contact` (see "Lead Conversion" later in this chapter) without creating an `opportunity`, and send the rep an email indicating the new contact to be worked.

In addition, at least once a year the NAM reps will come to you asking to import new `contacts` into their `accounts`. Read the section "Named Account Model of Selling" in Chapter 9 for the specific things you need to help the NAM reps with.

Lead Cultivation and Nurturing

Although MAS tools that assist in `lead` cultivation are best owned and run by marketing, the manual process of `lead` nurturing—moving the prospect from awareness to interest to desire—is almost always done by someone outside of marketing. Even if the team that handles this duty is called a tele*marketing* group[28] in your company, that group usually doesn't report to the marketing department. Because of this natural hand-off, the success criteria and SLA between marketing and the sales development rep (SDR) team must be clear and detailed. Make sure that your MAS is finely tuned to the needs of the SDR team—collisions in this part of the business process are very wasteful.

If you haven't already done so, read the section on `lead` cultivation and nurturing in Chapter 9. Pay particular attention to the discussion of the "life of a lead" timeline.

On the `lead` page, make it easy for the SDRs to get supplemental information. Smart reps will want to do a little research before they call a new `lead`. Use the `page layout`

---

28. This is the team that does calls to leads for initial assessment, nurturing, and even appointment setting for the sales reps. They may be called telesales, telemarketing, inside sales, account development, sales development, or other things. For clarity, this book calls them sales development reps (SDRs).

tool to put links to Google Search and Google News for general information about the company and to Hoover's, Dunn and Bradstreet, or some other service for financial and business information. For information about the individual lead, put in links to LinkedIn, ZoomInfo, or your favorite `lead` database service. There are dozens, some quite specialized by geography and industry.

In the `lead` cultivation and nurturing process, marketing is responsible for creating a significant amount of content: email campaigns, special offer response Web pages, call scripts, qualification questions, objection responses, and competitive FAQs. These content elements should all be stored in SFDC, both as `content` and as `attached files` to `campaigns`.

For a wide range of reasons, the best way to improve the `lead` cultivation and nurturing process is to meet frequently with the SDR team. Understand their challenges, find out what's working in the real world, and measure every part of the process. Set up a `chatter group` focused on nurturing so the key players can collaborate about it in real time. When evaluating metrics, make sure the focus is on achieving objectives and improving the number of first sales meetings—stay away from words that sound like a performance review, overmeasurement, or the assignment of blame. SDRs are the natural partner of outbound marketing, so do everything to foster good communications and a tight working relationship between the two groups.

Lead Qualification and Conversion

Marketing isn't directly involved with the `lead` qualification and conversion process. Nevertheless, it should be involved with setting the criteria and the process steps involved, because these elements are the materialization of the target market description, value proposition, and messaging that are the results of marketing work.

Some companies talk about having a "marketing qualified `lead`," in the sense that MQLs are good enough to deserve starting the manual `lead` cultivation/nurturing process. In my professional opinion, it's a bit dangerous for marketing to claim a lead is qualified: if you have to use that term, always use "MQLs" and never spell it out. Real qualification means that the company has a communication cycle with the prospect where the SDRs determine the match of needs and values and assess the prospect's readiness to have a serious discussion about purchase. What marketing *can* do is screen and score `leads`, and pass only high-scoring `leads` to the inside sales team.

The real qualification conversation should be *scripted* by senior people in marketing and sales. Typically, there will be 5 to 10 qualification questions with yes-or-no answers, and a `lead` is qualified when 80% of the answers are yes. Some companies use a sliding scale (high/medium/low or 1 to 10) and set a composite score as the qualification criterion. Even if members of the sales team actually write all of the scripted questions, the marketing guys and gals need to know what's being said about the product. The marketers also need to see where prospects are falling out of the funnel, and why, so they can quickly identify areas for improved retention and conversion. So put in metrics and feedback loops, and use `chatter groups` to collect narrative information in the most natural way.

Once the qualification criteria and scripts are stable, they should be built into the SFDC `lead` screens. SFDC offers a free AppExchange plugin to facilitate call scripting, but you may want to go beyond its baseline capabilities if your company has multiple product lines with different target markets and qualification criteria. With clever use of `dependent fields`, `record types`, `page layouts`, and `VisualForce`, the system can become a good prompting system for the reps. Even though this solution is certainly elegant, don't overdo it: if your messaging isn't stable (because it's not mature, or because the competitive environment is changing too fast), the benefits derived from perfect screen sequences may be too short-lived to be worth the effort.

Once a `lead` is fully qualified, it is usually converted to a `contact` almost instantly. Several details of conversion need to be nailed down from the beginning:

- How will the `custom fields` be mapped from the `lead` to the `account`, `contact`, or `opportunity`? Will you need to clone certain standard fields so that their information can be sent to more than one object?

- Who does the conversion process, and under which conditions?

- What are the naming standards for `accounts` and `opportunities`?

- How will duplicate `accounts` or `opportunities` be flagged or handled if discovered during the `conversion` process?

- When do you create an `opportunity` at `conversion` time? Under what conditions do you not do so?

- How are you going to ensure that every `opportunity` has at least one `opportunity contact role` defined? This can be solved through training, but we actually recommend enforcing it with system configurations or plugins.

- What are the default `stage`, `amount`, and `close date` values for the new `opportunity`?

- What is the `task` resulting from creating a new `opportunity`, and who receives it?

- Under which conditions can a sales rep reject an `opportunity`? How does the SDR learn from the rejected `opportunity`?

These details are discussed in the `lead` conversion section of Chapter 9. The SFDC system should be set up so that `field history tracking` is turned on to provide audit trails for the 20 most interesting fields in the `lead`, `contact`, `account`, and `opportunity` records (in particular, always check the `owner`, `status`, `stage`, `record type`, `type`, and `industry` fields for any object that has them). Doing so will help you see what's going on and allow the marketing staff to base improvements on data from real sales cycles—instead of folklore and urban legends.

DEMOTING A CONTACT

As discussed in the "Split Brain" sidebar earlier in this chapter, `leads` can be effectively demoted to names but can later be promoted back to being a `lead` when their behavior indicates a rekindled interest. The same logic can be applied to `contacts` as well, but the mechanics are quite different. Maintaining `contacts` in the database in some fashion is worth doing because industry sources estimate that half of all `leads` in the "remarket" or "dead lead" area will be viable purchase candidates—you just don't know when or what will trigger them to become motivated to buy your company's product or service. You can't afford to send these prospects all of your high-cost marketing items, but you can't afford to ignore them either.

`Contacts` are not as easy to demote as `leads` are, because the `lead conversion` process is a one-way street: once a `lead` is converted to a `contact`, several changes are made that cannot be undone. Even so, it makes sense to have `contacts` go stale if they are unresponsive for a year or more.

Demoting a `contact` in a way that preserves all history requires the following procedure:

1. Change the `contact's` `type`, `status`, or `ownership` fields so that it disappears from view. Be particularly attentive to the views and filters used by your deduping tool so that the `contact` is truly invisible to the deduping process.

2. Create a `lead` from the `contact's` information, with a score that's low enough that the prospect falls into the remarketing process. Record the `contact's` universal object identifier (UOID)[29] as a hidden field of the cloned `lead`.

3. Create a `trigger` that fires when leads are converted. If that newly converted lead has a hidden UOID that's not empty, the trigger will bring the hidden contact back into view by reversing the `type`, `status`, or `ownership` value changes you made in step 1. During the next deduping cycle, the deduping tool will automatically merge the two contacts, and all history will be preserved.

---

29. SFDC has been pretty clever in that the UOID is the last 15 characters of the record's URL. If you look at your browser URL field when looking at any SFDC record, most of the time it will show something like this: https://na1.salesforce.com/001000054UxeyTER. The UOID is "001000054UxeyTER."

Partner Marketing

The marketing team is rarely the true owner of partnerships, either on the technology side or on the revenue side. Nevertheless, the company's marketing staff must interact with partner marketing folks and supply their sales teams with collateral, information, and leads.

As discussed in Chapter 9, the way to get the most out of partners is to treat them as an extension of the company's own sales team as much as possible. This means giving partners access to the sales tools, testimonials, product training, and other documents that are in the company's marketing arsenal. Set up some `chatter groups` for the partners. You also want to send partners leads and monitor their development through the pipeline. This is most effectively done through SFDC's `partner portal`[30] but can be done in a variety of other ways. Make sure to create `dashboards` that summarize the partner's use of your materials, so you have a top-down view of what's working. Since the portal doesn't give partners access to `dashboards`, if you want partners to see them, you'll have to set up a `scheduled refresh` that emails the dashboards to them on a regular basis.

If your company does cooperative marketing with its partners (e.g., joint advertising, shared tradeshow booths, or cooperative Webinars), make sure that each partner's information is included in the `campaign` description in your SFDC system. Depending on your lead-sharing arrangements, you will want to create `campaign member` reports with special filters for each partner.

Customer References

Customer references are the most essential ingredient of company credibility and are required elements for many marketing deliverables. Analyst relations, PR, Web marketing, and the sales team all depend on quotes, reference customers, and testimonials. It has always surprised me how many marketing departments seriously lack aggressiveness and discipline in collecting and managing this key resource.

Before discussing ways to handle references in SFDC, we need to consider how customer happiness and usage information are collected. The main problem with most reference marketing programs is that they jump too quickly to "Can we get your quote?", thereby scaring off the customer. It's far better to develop a large population of customers who have provided a small amount of core information about their businesses and the way they use your company's product or service. Once these people have told you something

---

30. If you have not enabled the `customer portal` or `partner portal` in your instance of SFDC, they are no longer available to you. They have been replaced by `chatter communities`.

about themselves, it's easy to extend the conversation with very specific requests based on who they are and how they benefit from your product. It's the same idea as progressive registration, but you have a lot more to work with.

To build this pool of customer information, several processes need to be tapped to collect the highest-quality reference information:

- **Customer support, technical support, training, and consulting staff:** These folks are the most tragically underutilized sources of customer reference information. These people are on the phone (or even on site) with the customer base more than anyone else in your company, and they should be finding out as much as they can about how the customer is using your product. While they're helping the customer, they can be asking subtle questions that can reveal interesting information about the number of users, the business impact, and factoids about the customer's business and how it has benefited from using your company's product. When done correctly, this kind of data collection won't feel like prying, yet it will gather at least one "gee whiz" story each week. This information should be added to `opportunities`, as it is relevant to the project or purchase, rather than the individual `contact` or the `account` overall. Marketing should write these questions and format them as prompt screens for the support and consulting teams, using the free call scripting plugin from the AppExchange.

- **Product marketing personnel:** Product marketers and product managers may conduct periodic customer surveys that collect great demographic and usage profiling information. The key is to ask the right questions and provide an incentive for the customer to respond. Use an embedded URL with a unique identifier so you automatically know who generated each response. This advice applies equally to customer satisfaction surveys sent out by the customer service department and even to warranty registration cards. There are a number of survey engines that plug right in to SFDC. Check out the AppExchange for the latest on this.

- **The company's PR team:** The PR agency or internal folks may conduct customer phone surveys to collect quotes and testimonials, and they should be designed to collect customer usage information even if customers are totally unwilling to have their names published. Set these surveys up with subtle incentives to provide information that will be kept private, as the majority of customers will be unwilling to have any contact with reporters or analysts. These survey results should be attached to the `contact` record for the individual involved.

- **The account management team:** The account manager contacts customers at product or service renewal time (assuming your company has some sort of ongoing service element). Have the renewal cycle begin with an "application" that collects demographic and usage information. While this information is useful for the support organization, it's pure gold for the marketing team. Attach these data to the `opportunity` that is being renewed.

• **The Web team:** The people who build your Web site, blog, online forum, or Web-based user community should be requiring users to register (only with a valid email) to get to the content located on your properties. When users want to post or add to the comment trail, ask them for further registration information that gives you a better profile of who they are and how they use your company's product. This progressive-registration information should be attached to the person's `contact` record in SFDC.

Once you've thought through this issue, the key is to add—in a disciplined way—specific information from these sources to the relevant `contacts`, `accounts`, and `opportunities`. Of course, you can attach surveys and emails to the records, but they will not very easy to search, manipulate, or report. Instead, the essential elements of "referencability" should be added to the records as `custom  fields` or `custom objects` that answer questions such as the following:

• Which product is the customer using? How long has the customer been using the product, and which departments are using it?

• Which other products did the customer evaluate? Why did the customer decide to go with your company's offering?

• How many users are there, and how many *non*users benefit from the product?

• What are the economic benefits of the product? How soon did the product pay for itself, and what's the long-term ROI?

• What is quotable about the customer's experience, and what are the names and titles of people who would be willing to talk about their experiences?

• How happy is the customer? Would the customer buy again?

• Would the customer be willing to take a call from a prospect? An industry analyst? A reporter?

The exact design of the reference management system will depend on how the company wants to use the references, but the guideline is to store the information as close to the user or project as possible. Use `page layouts` or `collapsible sections` to keep clutter down. To make the information easier to see from a top-down perspective, use `roll-up fields` or `workflows` to provide referencability indicators (e.g., "total potential references") at the `account` level. You should definitely set up a `chatter` topic or two about referencability so that people can collaborate around things that work in special customer situations.

All of this implies that everyone in sales, marketing, customer support, and PR has an SFDC login and uses the system to store the customer data. This is the way life should be anyway, but proper customer reference management turns SFDC usage into a requirement.

Customer references are coveted resources, so sales reps will try to hide the good ones. To prevent anyone at the company from burning out a reference through overuse, it's important to track every time the reference has been used. Either use SFDC's `case` object (with a special `record type` and `page layout`) or create a `custom object` that records when references were used, who used them, and what the purpose was. To protect the customer's trust level, it's a best practice to handle customer reference requests through SFDC as an `approval process` and to have the reference marketing person be the unbiased decision maker who approves and allocates usage of this precious resource. Generally speaking, using a reference more than once per quarter will probably irritate the individual, and it may get the reference in trouble with his or her company's PR department.

Advertising and Messaging

The starting point for any messaging efforts—paid or otherwise—should be the target market definition and prospect/customer data. So these functions should be using SFDC as a source of their "raw materials." Unfortunately, the operative word in the previous sentence is *should*, because advertising and messaging teams are seldom CRM-data-driven. This leads to some pretty random[31] thinking.

Where to start? Read the following sections of this chapter (feel free to skip the omitted ones), looking for sources of data about the market, the prospects, and the customers:

- "Develop a Model of Sales and Marketing Interactions"
- "Social Marketing"
- "Google AdWords"
- "Search Engine Optimization"
- "Lead Handling"
- "Lead Scoring and Aging"

---

31. Creative types will call it "creative" or "inspired." That only works on "Mad Men" in an era that ended decades ago. Too often, messaging that is not based on data just means sloppy thinking—and leads to battles that are politically dangerous for the marketing team.

- "Lead Qualification and Conversion"

- "Partners"

- "Customer References"

- "Public Relations"

- "Product Management/Product Marketing"

For market sentiment analysis, message formulation, message testing, advertising testing, campaign analytics, and ROI, it is hard to imagine a richer source of information than the CRM system. SFDC has features that go way beyond traditional CRM and are particularly relevant for the messaging and advertising function: `chatter`, `social media monitoring`, and `social media marketing`.

Entire books are published on how best to leverage each of them, so this chapter doesn't attempt a deep discussion on this. The key is to understand that each of them requires marketers to learn new behaviors and new ways of creating and managing content. Although the features are plug and play, the results take quite a bit of ongoing effort on your part. Make sure that upper management does not set expectations too high, too soon.

Public Relations

Most PR departments wouldn't dream of having an SFDC login. Most PR departments are also behind the times.

In addition to the reference marketing functionality described in the preceding section, PR departments need to know how SFDC can help them in their day-to-day tasks. PR departments are in touch with reporters, editors, and industry analysts, and they need to manage their contact information. They need to track action items. They launch campaigns and want to track their results. Sounds sort of like the SFA functionality with a twist—right?

SFDC developed a free add-on for the AppExchange designed around the needs and workflow of PR teams. This add-on provides the basics for the PR function, and it can be easily extended to match the workflow of nearly any PR team. Assuming the company uses a PR agency to supplement its internal team, SFDC's Web-based functionality is a great way to coordinate all of the organization's PR efforts.

The PR Manager plugin works well if what you are really trying to do is replace shared contact and task lists in Outlook. As always, SFDC does a great job of handling shared `tasks` and exposing the history of action items and conversations across a distributed user base. `Chatter` makes the back-and-forth about positioning and marketing issues much more natural; correctly used, it dramatically improves the effectiveness of your marketing/PR collaborations. The integration via SFDC's `Outlook connector` is a bit clumsy, and the scheduling[32] of repeating events (such as conferences or meetings) is ugly, but it works.

In using the PR Manager plugin, there are a couple of things to think about. First, the PR agency (or agencies) used by your organization may have its own in-house systems and may not be willing to keep the blow-by-blow details in SFDC. Although this proprietary attitude is understandable for the senior partner in the agency or specialists who are not dedicated to your company's account, the account manager or the dedicated underling should be able to use your company's SFDC system without any double entry or interference with the agency's system.

The second issue is keeping the reporters, editors, and analysts separate from your customer contacts. This segregation is most easily accomplished by setting the owner of the contact[33] to someone in the PR group and by setting the record type or type to be "reporter," "press," "analyst," or another appropriate indicator. Make sure the PR team's role is in the hierarchy so that the sales team cannot see the PR contacts. If you set up the filters in views and reports properly, the PR targets will be kept totally separate from your prospects and customers. Do the same thing with accounts for the publishers or analyst firms that the PR function works with.

Once the basics are under control, use SFDC campaigns to monitor the pitches, events, and outreach you have done to all reporters, as well as the responses they have given to your pitches. Of course, you need to keep these PR campaigns separated from the standard prospect campaigns, but that's why God invented record types and campaign hierarchies.

You'll need to adjust pick lists to reflect the status of reporters and editors, as opposed to evaluators and buyers. You'll almost certainly want to use record types and page layouts to customize the look of SFDC for the PR users.

A key resource for PR and marketing teams is the social media monitoring brought to SFDC by their acquisition of Radian6. This tool is a powerful way of monitoring market sentiment, measuring the effectiveness of messaging, and intercepting the growth of Internet fire-storms. The metrics and alerts made possible by social media monitoring are a must for any sophisticated digital PR efforts.

Another consideration is the handling of press citations, blog threads, and other reporters' content. If what you *really* wanted was Vocus or a custom PR database, you'll need to adjust your expectations downward a bit. Because document attachments aren't searchable in SFDC, this kind of content is typically stored in a file server (using a plugin such as FTP Attach), with a pointer to it from within SFDC's reporter (contact) record. Although this structure means that content searching must be done entirely outside of SFDC, it also means that searchers don't need to have SFDC licenses.

---

32. You may find that SFDC's integration with Google documents really helps with calendar management.

33. There is absolutely no reason to use leads in the PR function. While you're at it, ignore the opportunity and case objects as well. That way, you can use the much less expensive single-application force.com license for the PR wonks.

Product Management/Product Marketing

The product manager, vertical market manager, and product marketer roles are classically held by people who love the product and have no problem writing. Typically, they are also starved for real data about customers, prospects, and markets. SFDC is an amazing resource to help these personnel ply their trade in the following areas.

Marketing Collateral and Documents

SFDC's `content` functionality acts as a central store for all of the company's marketing collateral. You can create `libraries` by topic and vertical market, and the system manages the evolution and delivery of collateral packages. Although there are other interesting document management stores in SFDC (most notably, the `files` area that works with `chatterbox` and the `knowledge` area that works with the `customer support portal` and `communities`), populating `content libraries` is going to be job one for the product manager or product marketer.

`Content` provides a mechanism for sales reps to create their own bundles of collateral by assembling individual pages from different documents. These `content deliveries` allow highly customized collateral out of approved materials, and each `content delivery` measures the number of times the prospect has read the materials. Content even includes a voting system that allows readers to rank which are the most relevant documents. We also encourage setting up `chatter groups` and `topics` to cover the hottest areas of the collateral tree. For the product manager, these features provide essential feedback regarding which documents should be enhanced or retired.

Analytics and Business Intelligence

SFDC is a godsend to the numbers-driven marketer, provided that the data are clean and properly organized.

Let's start with a simple and nearly universal problem: analyzing the life of a `lead`. Every marketer wants to know the cradle-to-grave behaviors of the `leads` that come in. But in the vast majority of SFDC instances, this is not possible, because `leads` don't go to the grave: they are put in suspended animation before the sales cycle even begins. So you can't do your analysis unless the linkage from `lead` to `contact` to `opportunity` is always there. And the name of that linkage is the `opportunity contact role`. If it doesn't exist on *every* opportunity, all the marketing reports will dramatically understate your pipeline and sales influence. Check out articles on www.SFDC-secrets.com for more on this.

The other simple and nearly universal problem: dupes. Pay the money to get (and get trained on) a proper deduping tool before you try doing anything fancy with analytics. Do it the other way around, and you're just wasting your time and credibility.

As discussed in Chapter 2, the most advanced reporting and analytical requirements will involve an external reporting system. Of course, the data must be entered into SFDC in the first place, which is why product marketing needs to be involved early in the design process.

That said, it is imperative to keep screens simple and data entry as unintimidating as possible. Customers and sales folks alike get annoyed when they are asked to enter too much data.[34] If the product marketing folks say that they will require a bunch of data, always ask yourself, "Who's going to type in and validate all that data?" Also ask, "What's the likelihood that half of these records will be empty?" If there's a fair chance of empty records, *do not* ask people to manually fill the desired information in—get the data some other way.

This recommendation goes double for competitive information. In theory, your sales reps should know who the competitors are and what messages they are using against your company. In practice, it's rare for reps to really have this knowledge base and even rarer for them to fill in more than one field in the SFDC database with the relevant information. That said, it may be very easy to get system integrator, consulting, or customer support personnel to provide detailed competitive intelligence. Use `page layouts` and plugins like FormsAssembly to facilitate this data collection without annoying users with clutter.

You may be asked by the finance people to help with product profitability analysis. If so, make sure to read that section in Chapter 12.

Price Lists

The price list is the most basic marketing deliverable: every rep needs to use it, and every product manager needs to contribute to it. Price lists don't have to reside in the SFDC system, but they should. Maintaining the price list in the system enables `line-item level quotes`, product-level `forecasting`, and integration with your order entry and accounting systems.

SFDC's price lists are fairly simple SKU-based tables; the `Price Books` and `Product` tables contain a single level of SKU, so bundled products are simply handled as new SKUs with no hierarchy or pointers.[35]

---

34. Too much can be as few as five fields per page. Keep it simple!

35. Bill of material (BOM) structures are creatures of a manufacturing system, not an order entry system. It's not possible to create BOMs in SFDC.

SFDC doesn't handle discount schedules natively. Most companies simply store the discount level as a `custom field` for each SKU in the price list (perfect for per-product discounting), or they create different SKUs for different volume levels. Other companies create a SKU called "discount" with a negative value that is applied to the entire order.

Renewal and upgrade products can get very hairy, particularly if your company has bundles and temporary specials. As much fun as it is to create the Christmas package, it's a nightmare to manage the upgrade paths from it. Almost all of these situations are handled with batches of new SKUs and `custom fields` on the `product` table. With highly configurable hardware or heavily versioned software suites, your price list may rapidly grow to thousands of items. This is not fun and is not easily managed in SFDC. Most customers with this situation either write loads of code or purchase a third-party product to manage it over time.

International `price lists` are simple yet profound data structures. SFDC's standard operation is single-currency, and most companies start by creating foreign price lists that override the home-country price, expressed in the company's home currency. This works fine if your `quoting`, `contracts`, and accounting is all done in dollars. If you have to operate in multiple currencies, things get more sophisticated. First, you have to enable SFDC's `multi-currency mode`[36] (you'll definitely want to use the advanced option), which gives the foreign price lists their own currency (£, €, $, ¥, and so on) while leaving the home price list in the company's home currency. The translation across currencies occurs at both `quote` time and `opportunity close date`, using the then-current exchange rate. `Reports`, `forecasts`, and `views` of orders will show all information in the local currency of the individual who's viewing the data. Pretty fancy stuff.

Polling, Customer Feedback, and Product Planning

Out of the box, SFDC gives you solid information on `leads` and `contacts`, but no direct interaction with *customers*. Over time, as the system is configured with more and more options, it will likely begin to include touch points for several kinds of customer interaction:

- Does your product or service already have a "call home" feature that periodically reports back technical or statistical data to your servers? Even better: do you offer a cloud service? If so, *drop everything* and spend a few minutes to spec some customer instrumentation into the next version of the product. Why bother customers with polls and emails? Instead, put in passive monitors so you can know what the

---

36. Turning on the `multi-currency` feature in SFDC is a one-way street: once it's on, it can never be turned off. Turning it on will also break some of your `reports`, `calculated fields`, and other customizations. For this reason, it's best to leave this feature off for as long as you can and then have a carefully planned transition project when you can no longer postpone it.

customers are doing and how they are using your features in a completely non-intrusive (and statistically valid) way. While you're at it, put in "send feedback" buttons in tricky areas and offer incentives for the best feedback every quarter. Salesforce.com does this with its own products—why not learn from the leader in Agile product management?

- `Chatter` is a completely free way of interacting with customers and prospects in a walled garden. Although nobody needs yet another IM protocol, the ability to have threaded conversations, spontaneous topic creation (synthesized from trending words), document collaboration, real-time voting, and direct linkage of personas to specific CRM `contacts` makes `chatter` an invaluable feedback mechanism.

- The partner relationship management (PRM) module includes a `Partner Portal`[37] that can provide good metrics on the company's interactions with its intermediary "customers." If the marketing group owns some of the partner relationship, add a survey link to the portal page so that marketers can get feedback from the partner on a continuous basis.

- The `Customer Self Service Portal`[37] provides an obvious place for interaction with those customers who are actively using the company's support services or are covered by warranty periods. Add a survey link to this page as well. In addition, it's smart to have the Web-tracking analytics engine inspect traffic through the `Knowledge Base`; this setup enables you to quickly spot troublesome areas related to the product and its documentation.

- SFDC's `Ideas` module is an ideal way to get narrative feedback and voting from customers about new feature ideas and priorities. If you plan to use this module, make sure to prepopulate the `ideas` list with items that you suspect could be killer customer issues—even if the customer has yet to discover them. Also, add `idea` items for product attributes that the customer might reflexively ignore:[38] reliability, performance, fit and finish, documentation, international issues, level of support, pricing options, and features to *remove*.

- For market sentiment analysis (and particularly for assessing the people who are not your prospects), it is hard to imagine a tool more useful than SFDC's `social media monitoring` system. It's not cheap, it's not super-easy—but it is extremely powerful, particularly in highly volatile consumer markets.

- As discussed in the "Customer References" section earlier in this chapter, SFDC should be configured with several `custom fields` to track and manage

---

37. For new customers, this feature has been replaced with `chatter communities`.
38. If these items are omitted from the list, all the feedback statistics will be misleading and overfocused on bells and whistles that *aren't* critical to customer satisfaction.

customer happiness and testimonials. By using these data carefully, you survey your customer base to help guide the company's product development roadmaps and strategy exercises. If you are trying to set up a customer review board, this effort should be tracked through SFDC as well.

- A few of the popular survey engines have plugins that support SFDC, and you should strongly favor using them. Be willing to sacrifice a few advanced features to get the data fully integrated into the "customer system of record." The pain of trying to keep data synchronized between SFDC and an unintegrated tool will quickly overwhelm any advantage that some other "perfect" survey tool might have.

- Rally Software offers an Agile requirements collection/management tool that plugs in to SFDC. If your internal product development team is focused on Agile practices, this tool can be a huge asset for both marketing and engineering personnel.

Marketing System Administrator

As discussed previously, a common mistake among SFDC customers is to give full system administrator privileges to too many people. Best practice calls for having two or three administrators, unless the company has a huge SFDC installation.

We recommend that someone in the marketing department be one of the administrators, because marketing personnel typically are intimately involved with new-product launches and understand what's coming in the next several quarters. Marketers can make

---

THE DATA ADMINISTRATOR

Someone in marketing needs to be the God of Data. This person must be an SFDC system administrator (or at least be trained up to that level) so that he or she can make good decisions about data standards, new fields, expanded pick lists, and lead-handling processes.

There is no universal best practice for data management, because there are just too many market and company variances. Even so, *somebody* has to set your company's standards and enforce the rules. *Somebody* has to be the owner of data definitions. *Somebody* has to play referee in internal arguments about data ownership. The best kind of *somebody* will be involved with lead handling, cultivation, or nurturing; they will know people in both sales and marketing; and they will be systematic and detail oriented.

Check out the discussion of the data architecture review board in Chapters 3 and 4 to understand the duties a little better.

Although this role could theoretically be outsourced, it's typically not economical to do so. The good news is that it's nowhere near a full-time job, even in the largest company.

pretty good guesses about what the sales folks will need in the future—and they have the most analytical thirst for numbers.

The marketing-based SFDC administrator should coordinate his or her efforts with those of the administrators of other marketing tools (such as the Web site, MAS, email blaster, content management system, eCommerce, customer portal, and customer data warehouse products). As these systems become increasingly integrated over time, these administrators will need to interact fairly frequently.

Privilege Restriction

Some of the decisions related to privilege restriction are policy issues that can have political overtones, but the following really are best practices:

- `Delete` and `merge` buttons should be hidden from all standard users, including most marketing folks.

- API and import-wizard access should be turned off for all standard users except for those marketing individuals who handle `leads`.

- Report creation should be turned off for all standard users (but not managers).

Chapter 13 describes a number of general best practices related to permissions, which should be reviewed by marketing's designated SFDC administrator.

Report and Dashboard Logistics

One of the biggest problems with SFDC's reporting capability is the huge pile of prefabricated reports found in the system. It is so easy to get lost and overwhelmed. The first order of business is to create the reports report, which shows you when the last time every single report in the system was run. Don't be surprised if 70% of your reports haven't been run in the last year. Check out www.SFDC-secrets.com to get the metadata for the Reports Report.

The next order of business is to clean out the "unfiled public reports" that come with the system and put them in folders meaningful to you. If a particular report doesn't seem especially meaningful, create a report folder called "Ignore Me" and put it there. I do not recommend deleting reports from the system: you never know when one will provide a good idea for solving a future reporting problem.

Create another new folder called "<Company> Special Reports" and put this folder on the top of the list. Make this folder read-only so users can't accidentally mess things up. For any reports that are really important, create duplicate copies and put them in a new read-only folder called "Backups."

Create yet another read-only folder called "Dashboard Reports—DO NOT TOUCH." Put the reports that feed dashboards there.

Check out the AppExchange for prebuilt reports and dashboards. Dozens of freebies can be found there, and they can save you a bunch of time when you are trying to set up your own SFDC system.

There's some good news on the report logistics front: the Force.com Eclipse tool includes ways to view, archive, and upload report definitions. It's a much cooler way to get the job done and avoids the tedium of mouse driving that SFDC users have had to endure for the last 12 years. Even better: using Eclipse lets you search through all the report metadata, so you can see how many of your reports use the foobar field as a filter.

Ongoing Tasks

The marketing SFDC administrator needs to become very comfortable with the deduping tool that your company has bought. Because these tools typically need to be run on at least a weekly basis, the administrator needs to understand all of the chosen tool's detailed settings (e.g., fuzzy logic fields, thresholds) and the workflow of deduping a large batch of `leads`. Note that, generally speaking, accounts should not be deduped. Check out the "Instead of Deduping Accounts . . ." section in Chapter 3.

Although SFDC runs continuous backups on all system data, recovery of data is neither free nor fast (it requires a small consulting project). The marketing SFDC administrator should take a weekly system "snapshot" of the system's entire contents. This task can be carried out as an automatic scheduled event through the system itself,[39] or the administrator can use an external batch-oriented tool from Informatica or another vendor to do the job. Although the snapshots can get really large with all the attachments, it is not necessary to back up absolutely everything every week. Anyway, disk space is cheap, and the peace of mind that comes with having your own backup will more than compensate for the 10 minutes per week devoted to this chore.

Before attempting any significant amount of data manipulation in SFDC, it is always best to take an immediate "before" snapshot of the data object(s) you're working on. This is most easily done with SFDC's free Data Loader plugin, but you need to be trained before you use this software. For more on this topic, check out the sidebar titled "Backups and Snapshots and Replicas, Oh My!" in Chapter 13.

---

39. The data exports are free but limited to once a week. So if somebody else is already taking a snapshot, just make sure you can get access to it if needed. If they can't share it with you, well, you're going to have to use another of the available backup strategies.

Marketing Executives

SFDC provides the foundation for many important improvements in the way marketing works. Its use requires behavioral changes of the marketing team, but it can mean dramatic improvements in marketing's effectiveness, your relationship with sales, and overall corporate reputation.

Many SFDC best practices immediately translate into marketing best practices. Further, SFDC brings into focus the real cost of customer acquisition and the importance of repeat business—the most profitable revenue that any company can have. By aligning the marketing effort with the most profitable revenue sources and by improving sales cycles, the marketing team will automatically align itself with the goals and objectives of the sales team and the stockholders.

After a few months of proper use, the SFDC system should be able to screen out low-quality leads, identify low-yielding sources, and help tune marketing messages so that they yield the biggest bang for the buck. It will take a few months longer to lower the cost of lead generation (or at least increase the bang for the buck) and increase the sales pipeline. Because of seasonality effects, SFDC will likely continue to reveal new opportunities for marketing improvements more than a year after it goes into production. However, the only real cost reductions that most companies will find are in eliminating "dud" marketing vehicles; do not expect the SFDC system to reduce the company's headcount. In fact, to leverage SFDC and marketing automation will require new skills of your staff and may increase headcount.

The best practices for marketing team members have been discussed throughout this chapter. As a marketing executive, you need to reinforce marketers' behavior with incentives and pep talks:

- Don't ask for data items that you won't really use or that won't fundamentally change the outcome of any decision.

- Add instrumentation to as many customer points of contact as you can, including customer-facing individuals in support, service, and consulting.

- Involve the customer in as many marketing processes as you can,[40] and record the data in SFDC so that the information becomes a shared resource.

- Strive for closed-loop marketing, where you can track a single customer's interactions through every "touch" by your company. That said, don't bite off more than

---

40. If you haven't already done so, read *The Cluetrain Manifesto* by Christopher Locke (Basic Books, 2000). You can also read it online for free at www.cluetrain.com/book/index.html.

you can chew: work incrementally, starting with email and click-through behaviors. Test messaging and refine it with email threads for specific customer segments. Add behaviorally targeted offers as you learn more about the customer's preferences and responses.

- Use `campaigns` for every single `lead`. Period.

- Insist that `contact roles` be attached to every `opportunity`. Period.

- Use `chatter`—it's the best way for marketing to know what's happening in the field and provide them support. It's an invaluable listening tool and keeps marketers in the loop on the latest info about prospects and customers.

- Integrate as many marketing systems as you can afford to with SFDC. This seamless operation reduces errors and dramatically increases visibility into the customer's behavior.

- Use SFDC and other systems to conduct A/B split testing at every level of the customer interaction. From word choice in messaging and scripts to the design of the purchase button in the company's online store, testing can significantly improve the results and power of the marketing effort. There is simply no substitute for real-world testing with the company's own prospects and customers.

- Use `workflows` and `alerts` to support management by exception. SFDC can streamline the majority of marketing processes while giving you better data for more solid decisions.

Read the last few pages of the Executive Summary in this book to find out about the general behavior changes and mandates you personally need to make—they're all quite pleasant, actually, but it's important for the troops to hear and see coherent behaviors directly from you.

Marketing Best Practices

When it comes to marketing in general, several critical success factors seem to be ignored all the time—often because of internal politics, board-level beliefs, and company culture. Here are the things that are most often *missing* in marketing management:

- Lead quality is *much* more important than lead quantity. It is very easy to generate tons of low-quality leads that will waste a lot of everyone's time. What's the point of handing over to sales a stack of leads a foot high if there's an infinitesimal chance of those leads being converted to a sale? Focus on *reducing* the total number of leads while increasing the number that convert and start sales cycles! You'll definitely want to set up SFDC metrics and incentives to bring this issue into focus.

- Lead response time can be *much* more important than branding, persistence, and lead scoring. It is almost impossible to be too quick in responding to a lead, and recent studies by Professor James Oldroyd of MIT[41] indicate that lead response rates drop dramatically within *minutes* of a Web registration. Providing a professional response to a lead in near real time *really* sets companies apart. Statistics show that a prospect's attention moves on to other things very soon, and the vast majority of Web site visitors will have no recollection of a company within 48 hours of visiting its site. Make sure that leads get into SFDC very fast and that an automated drip marketing sequence starts the same day. Set up SFDC metrics, escalations, and incentives to optimize "first touch" response times. Jump on the marketing automation system bandwagon if you haven't done so already.

- Generally speaking, field sales reps should not touch `leads`. Marketing and sales development reps should be converting the `leads` before they are ever handed over to the field. The field reps should be focused first on `opportunities` and any `contacts` and `tasks` associated with them.

- Although leads are quite perishable, paradoxically they don't have a real "expiration date." Generally speaking, leads that are unresponsive or uninteresting should be moved from the active working list into the "remarket" list within 30 to 45 days. But with the right kind of newsletter marketing, a lead that first signed up with the company 2 years ago may come to life and be immediately ready to purchase.[42] You can never know which specific lead will prompt this reaction or when the prospect will be ready to make a purchase. So the only times you should give up on a lead is when all of the contact information is no longer valid or the lead has explicitly asked you to go away and die.[43]

- The match of your marketing message to the target audience is much more important than the inherent power or uniqueness of that message. *Of course* you want to have a unique, powerful, and eloquent message, but if it really isn't all that relevant to the target audience, why should they care? Properly segmenting your target audience is job one, and it's almost exclusively a marketing

---

41. Check out the resources at the LeadResponseManagement.Org Web site—there's a ton of cool, free research posted on the site.

42. One of my favorite clients came to me after 3 years, saying "Taber and his incessant marketing have finally worn me down."

43. Okay, so they rarely ask for this exactly. But unsubscribe requests and opt-outs *must* be immediately and permanently honored.

responsibility. SFDC's data will be the foundation for that segmentation, and as a marketing executive you should demand that any target market analysis be based on customer and prospect data in the system.

- Related to the previous point is the importance of the company's Web site design: the first page a visitor lands on may disqualify your company from further consideration. Web visitors will rarely get to the proof points and the company's value proposition if they weren't motivated by the landing page they first saw. Use A/B split testing to optimize every step of the prospect's click path.[44]

- Marketing rarely focuses enough on customer loyalty and upselling. Marketing to customers really is like shooting fish in a barrel: although these customer-oriented `campaigns` will never generate a single lead, they'll generate plenty of revenue. It is sublimely important to set up metrics and standards for marketing to the installed base, because it is an area where the marketing department can truly shine. It also is the most profitable kind of revenue your company can have.

- Customer reference information is the highest-value data the SFDC system can possibly hold. Marketing should spearhead the collection, updating, and management of customer references so that the company gets the highest marketing impact from them and the references are not burned out from overuse.

- It's critically important that marketing, inside sales, and outside sales agree about the company's sales model. Get the following things right: the `leads`-to-`opportunity` workflow, the division of labor, the number of contact attempts to be made, the stages of `lead` development, the criteria for qualifying and `converting` leads, and the semantics of the SFDC data fields. If you can't agree on what a qualified `lead` is or what triggers the creation of an `opportunity`, how can you possibly optimize or streamline anything?

- SFDC should become an important point of collaboration between marketing and sales. Improving the quantity, quality, and usability of the customer information in the system is one of the critical ways marketing can show how it's adding value to the sales process.

- Get your team on `chatter`, and have them be thought leaders in modern collaboration.

- If you've got a heavy social media focus and have some budget, look seriously at what SFDC's social media monitoring and `social media marketing` can do for you.

---

44. It's okay if you don't understand this sentence—but somebody in your organization must, and must be in a position to actually follow the recommendation!

- As you get some serious data in the CRM system, you'll be able to look at timing and sequencing effects of marketing campaigns, nurturing, and lead flow. You'll want to look for situations where a territory has too many or too few opportunities, particularly considering calendar effects (Chinese New Year, Japanese fiscal year, U.S. Government fiscal year, etc.).

For more exciting news in this arena, there are over 90 marketing-oriented articles at www.SFDC-secrets.com.

Metrics and Analytics

I've worked at the VP level in marketing for more than 10 years, and a lot of things have changed this century. But in high-tech marketing, some bad habits seem to be evergreen. Much of the time, marketing is measured (or measures itself) by metrics that aren't very meaningful to the business. SFDC, when properly configured and used, can move companies to much better behaviors.

Here are some measurements that are simple to ask for, quick to measure, easy to fake or game, and almost pointless:

- Number of activities

- Number of `chatter` posts

- Number of mailings

- Number of new collateral/creative pieces

- Number of attendees and size of lists

- Visibility, buzz, and attitude indicators about your company

- Number of press releases

- Number, reach, and CPM of ads

- Number of click-throughs and Web site visits

- Number of registrations or downloads

- Number of leads

- Cost per lead

The last two items on the list are sacred cows in many companies, but unless you measure something about the *quality* of the lead, its convertibility, and its readiness to be qualified—well, these aren't sacred cows, they're just a bunch of bull.

> ### WATCH OUT FOR MULTIPLE REPORTS AND DASHBOARDS
>
> It is very common for organizations to inadvertently create several versions of a report or dashboard. This is almost always dangerous, because SFDC makes reports really easy to create and even easier to create incorrectly. There are too many ways to filter and sort data incorrectly and too many assumptions that can differ. Contradictory reports become a big source of politics when sales, marketing, support, and the executives are looking at "the same metric" with very different numbers. See "How to Blow Up Two Careers at Once!" in the Introduction.
>
> The only antidote is to use one officially blessed folder of reports that are designed and implemented by a single team. Using the requests from sales, marketing, and the executives, a business analyst (typically in the marketing or finance department but perhaps on loan from IT) should create the company's official management reports for lead generation, pipeline, and forecasting metrics. All other report versions should be deprecated and hidden from users.

Instead, match your measurements to the prospect's evolution and depth of attention in the pipeline/funnel—visibility and awareness are relevant only at the start of the relationship between customer and company. Use your revenue model (described at the beginning of this chapter) as your guide about what to measure, and when. Here are example metrics that can be quite meaningful (and hard to achieve):

- Time to first touch
- Percentage of unsubscribes and Web site "bounces" (indications of relevance)
- Accuracy of lead scores
- Number of converted leads
- Average time to convert
- Proportion of leads rejected by, and neglected by, sales
- Conversion ratio
- Number of fully qualified leads accepted by sales
- Number of sales cycles started due to marketing efforts
- Value of sales pipeline started due to marketing efforts
- Value of sales pipeline influenced by one or more campaigns (SFDC's `campaign influence` feature makes this much easier to measure)
- Profitability of new customers due to marketing efforts

- Marketing cost of acquiring a new customer

- Loyalty of new customers

- Percentage of repeat business

- Ability to segment customers and predict behavior

Each of these metrics can be analyzed on a per-`campaign` basis, so you can identify which activities really drive the business. The same items can also be analyzed by region, by industry, and by product line so you can determine which parts of the marketing message are working in different geographies. There are usually some great surprises on this front.

Most of these reports can be generated entirely within SFDC's reporting system, although some will likely require some external help. For example, a "time to first touch" report requires either clever use of SFDC's `custom report types`, exporting of SFDC data to a spreadsheet with a bunch of `VLOOKUP` functions, or using `join` processing in an external database engine.

The "jewel in the crown" of marketing is strategic analysis. Naturally, you'll want to team up with executives in sales, engineering, customer support/services, and finance to look at the big picture and answer questions such as these:

- What are the company's most profitable products, and why? What are the correlations among product purchases, and which "loser" products actually help move the winners? What are the most likely situations for upsells and repeat business?

- What are the characteristics of the most profitable customers? What are their behaviors and growth patterns? What can the company do to find more likely candidates and stimulate their purchasing patterns?

- How is the competitive battlefield changing? Does the company need more product, better promotion, or a pricing or packaging change? How are the company's brand and reputation faring in the marketplace?

- What are the inflection points during the sales cycle? Is there a key success factor or a failure pattern we need to fix?

- Which customers seem to be more trouble than they're worth, causing huge costs and rework in customer support? Can the company identify product or sales problems by understanding the situations involving whiners and troublemakers?

- Which marketing tactics are paying off, and how are they helping sustain the company's products and ease the sales cycle? What's the profitability of the marketing promotions?

- Which channels and partners are working, and which are just a waste of time?

Answering these kinds of questions will take solid analysis and almost certainly use of a multidimensional business intelligence tool. But the fanciest tools in the world will do no good if the source data are incomplete or misleading—and that's why it's imperative that the marketing team invest in making SFDC the authoritative source for "all things customer."

Getting the Most from **SFDC**

- Use `chatter` to help sales win some deals.
- Use `leads` and `contacts` the way God intended.
- Get `leads` into the system in hours, not days or weeks. That said, get the data quality up before you do: no point in importing junk and duds.
- Make sure that every `opportunity` created has a `contact role`.
- Keep the information you initially collect on `leads` to the essential minimum. Use progressive registration.
- Make sure everybody who touches `leads` and `contacts` is working with a common set of semantics and has the same model of the funnel and the pipeline. This is crucial, yet often way out of alignment.
- If you aren't on the marketing automation system bandwagon, ask yourself why.
- Do not imagine that the SFDC system should be owned by marketing. This is a rare exception indeed.
- Check out "Essential Add-Ons for the Marketer" in Chapter 7.

For Small Companies

- It's okay to use `lead source` for now.
- It's okay to just add a couple of fields to the `opportunity` to reflect partners.
- Do all your analytics in SFDC and Excel.

For Large Enterprises

- Use `campaigns` instead of `lead source`. Period.
- Use SFDC's PRM features and the `partner portal` or `chatter` communities to manage partner `leads`, `opportunities`, and `cases`.
- You're almost certain to need external analytics tools to span SFDC, the MAS, and your other marketing systems.
- You'd be surprised how many folks on the marketing team need to be on SFDC. Look at this chapter!
- Get your act together! You really need to create a detailed model of how marketing contributes to the revenue generation. For a large, multichannel enterprise, this can take weeks. But without it, you won't have solid ammunition for discussions with sales.

CHAPTER 11

Best Practices in Customer Support

> | | |
> |---:|:---|
> | *Waiter:* | *"Tea or coffee, gentlemen?"* |
> | *First customer:* | *"I'll have tea."* |
> | *Second customer:* | *"Me, too—and be sure the cup is clean!"* |
> | | *(Waiter exits, returns)* |
> | *Waiter:* | *"Two teas. Who asked for the clean cup?"* |
> | | *—Anonymous* |

The customer service and support team are often the most avid early users of SFDC. But most training and professional services teams can benefit from using the system as well. This chapter discusses how to set up and use the system to maximum advantage, which will seed the system with credible data that benefit everyone.

Many SFDC customers miss the opportunity of having their support personnel working in SFDC nearly from day one. Of course, the system is called *Sales*force, but service and support staff can rapidly leverage the system and fill it with data that become immediately valuable—and therefore attractive—to the sales and marketing organizations.

The members of the support organization are on the phone or in the room with customers nearly all day long, and their jobs already require good data hygiene—recording data with accuracy and good organization. Further, support people are in contact with the company's riskiest asset: upset customers. Making a customer happy one hour sooner, or with one less error, has payoffs in repeat sales and an annuity of profits. SFDC helps not just with CS productivity and cost structure—it helps turn the support and service team into a strategic asset for the company.

Support Organizations and SFDC

Service and support are frequently in contact with the company's most valuable asset: happy customers who could be turned into references. The business value of a happy customer is so high because they not only bring the most profitable revenue (repeat business), but they also bring the easiest new business (referred customers). More than a few marketing consultancies are based on the premise that "how likely are you to recommend our product to others?" is the only question that matters.

The company's support, training, and professional services personnel also have a good perspective on who are mission-critical customers and who are noisy poseurs and wannabes. They can provide context and input on `contact roles`, product usage, customer politics, and organizational dynamics. Encouraging the support and services people to adopt the SFDC system early pays for itself with dramatic reductions in cost and internal errors, measurable improvements in customer satisfaction, and increased renewal and re-up rates for customers—which collectively spells higher profits. Enough said?

But even that's not the whole story: support and service organizations have a lot of internal reasons to be in SFDC. The system has a dazzling[1] array of features that can make support teams more responsive, more effective, and (frankly) a more fun place to work. Support organizations, roles, titles, and responsibilities vary greatly across the SFDC customer base. Nevertheless, five types of service and support teams should be leveraging the system on a routine basis for both B2B and B2C companies:

- **Order operations:** This team handles inbound calls from customers or sales reps needing assistance with getting the order right. Most of their time is spent on tricky order configurations; problems with eCommerce; and handling discounts, promotions, and service contract renewals. These personnel must have tight interactions with both SFDC and the order entry system, and they may also need to get information from the eCommerce engine and the accounting system. Ideally, they will spend their quality time on big customers, but the goal in using SFDC is to streamline *all* of their order entry interactions.

- **Order expediting, distribution, and shipping:** This team handles inbound calls from sales reps and customers needing assistance with orders once they have been placed to make sure those orders are fulfilled as quickly and efficiently as possible. Things get tricky when products are on allocation, when products are bulky or difficult to ship, and when the customer has particular partial-shipment needs. This team needs direct interaction with the order management and warehouse/distribution systems, as well as SFDC, to resolve issues as smoothly as possible.

- **Help desk:** Large and consumer-oriented companies may have a group of employees who act as a lightweight ("Level 0") customer support team. Because this call center is focused on getting quick answers to customers, members of this team don't need access to many systems beyond the knowledge base and online documentation, because they don't actually file cases or troubleshoot technical issues. However, their work can be dramatically streamlined via interaction with SFDC,

---

1. Confusing.

and management needs to closely monitor them to assess their productivity and to detect troubling patterns in customer calls.

- **Technical and warranty support:** This team handles inbound calls from customers who are having difficulty with the product or who need to arrange for a warranty return or out-of-warranty service. Because this team is *always* dealing with unhappy customers, they need quick access to answers, resources, and escalation paths. They will need access to the case management system and knowledge base, and they will almost certainly need access to engineering's trouble-ticket and the factory's return merchandise authorization (RMA) system from SFDC. This team will also find `chatter` and `live-agent` IM facilities invaluable aids in responsiveness and open communication.

- **Professional services and training:** Unlike all of the previously mentioned teams, this group has no call center duties. Instead, their job is to plan and execute training and consulting projects for customers. Members of this team use SFDC in preparation of proposals, customer responses, statements of work, and project progress reports. SFDC acts as a central, accessible repository of reusable content, templates, and project histories. In addition, because the professional services team has personnel on site at customers' locations and is intimately involved with customers, the team can be a *very* effective sensor for customer satisfaction issues, product ideas, and upsell opportunities that should be documented in SFDC. `Chatter` and `ideas` will be invaluable aids to their projects and for fostering the customer relationship.

Universal Support Best Practices

If you haven't already done so, definitely check out the support and professional services business process diagrams on SFDC's Web site.[2] These brief PowerPoint presentations are a great starting point for discussing and designing your support organization's activities.

No matter which part of the support organization your team is in, several SFDC essentials almost always apply:

- Anyone who is in any service, support, or call center role should be on the SFDC system all day. There is just too much leverage to be cheap about this!

- Any size support organization should be using `chatter` internally to collaborate on identifying and solving customer problems. Check out the sidebar "What's All This Noise about Chatter?" in Chapter 13 if you want to know more.

---

2. SFDC keeps moving these diagrams around, so I can't give you the URLs here. Just Google "Salesforce support business process diagrams".

- If your company has long-lasting customer and partner relationships, customer support teams should also be using `chatter` in the external use case that provides a secure "walled garden" for communications. Don't push too hard on this one, though, as many companies will not let a new IM client into their networks.

- While SFDC can handle large, centralized call centers, for most companies a decentralized virtual call center provides significant cost savings and a better match for local languages and commercial customs. SFDC is designed from the ground up to support the virtual call center. Because it runs in the cloud, its performance is essentially identical from anywhere in the world. SFDC also facilitates offshore and multilingual agents for "follow-the-sun" 7 × 24 customer support and service. So exploit this strategy, already. (But first, make sure you have nailed down solid rules of engagement, policy, and people issues!)

- Integrating telephony into SFDC makes life much easier for nearly any size call center. All computer–telephony integration (CTI) tools can automatically document the basics of the call (call wait time, calling number, time of day, and length of call). The best tools automatically display a pop-up with the customer's name and most recent `case` on the screen before the call is even answered—an important consideration for call center people who are measured on the number of calls handled per hour. Although a few free CTI tools are available in the AppExchange (e.g., for Skype and Cisco IP phones), the more advanced tools are well worth the price when the call center is staffed by more than a dozen people.

- Due to the time-sensitive nature of customer support, call center personnel should make extensive use of SFDC's `case queues`, `case teams`, `alerts`, `workflows`, and `approvals`. Email `auto-responses`, `templates`, and `workflows` should be used to provide frequent customer updates.[3] Set up `entitlements`, `escalations`, and `SLAs` to ensure that `cases` are responded to within time-specified windows of the customer's `business hours`, or else automatically pushed to the next level via `escalation rules`. The system's `web2case`, `email2case`, and `case assignment` features should be configured from day one to speed interactions and responses. `Tasks` should be used to handle action items, and `attachments`[4] should be used to hold log files and other troubleshooting information. SFDC has a number of great features that can help streamline the cycle time for any person in support or consulting.

---

3. These emails need to be in plain-text format and should be informative and specific enough (using mail merge techniques, including embedded links to the customer's case record) to escape spam filters and provide the customer with a sense that progress is being made.

4. SFDC's allocation of free storage space is becoming more accommodating and useful, particularly for the `enterprise` and `unlimited` editions. If your company has a huge document library, however, you'll probably want to check out one of the document manager plugins available in the AppExchange.

- Special attention should be given to the `Service Cloud Console`, which provides a consolidated view of customer and support information. In addition to saving screen real estate, the `Console` can decrease the number of call center personnel clicks by 50%. This is a big deal for more than just carpal tunnel syndrome—it improves the responsiveness and error rate of your support agents.

- It is almost impossible to spend too much on systems integration for the customer support function. The agents should be able to at least see (if not manipulate) data from any customer-facing system and should be able (at least through an internal service ticket) to update incorrect records. The agents should also be able to see the key systems (e.g., enterprise resource planning [ERP] or inventory) that hold customer and shipment data.

- In most industries, the actual time to resolve or remedy a customer problem is *not* the determining factor for customer satisfaction. In fact, a support team that resolves issues more slowly, yet more smoothly and completely, will score much better than a team that resolves issues quickly but leaves customers in the dark. Most customers are happiest if the support team responds quickly with initial (partial) information and then sets expectations correctly about when the next level of response will come. Use `live agent`, `chatter`, `email templates`, `auto-response rules`, and `escalations` to keep the conversation moving. SFDC can be the cornerstone for optimizing smooth and complete support communications.

- At the conclusion of any customer interaction, the support person should survey the customer about the experience, even if the transaction was not successful. The SFDC system should be configured to initiate an email-based survey engine, Web-based survey, or phone-based set of questions to be answered. This information should be stored in the relevant `opportunity` or `case` record.

SURVEY, SCHMURVEY

Most customer service metrics of "customer sat" are usually relatively primitive. Think about it for a second: marketing scores their work product (lead "hotness"), sales scores their work product (the forecasted probability of close), but most support organizations are not scoring their work in process. Maybe they'll run a customer happiness survey once a year.

There's nothing wrong with an overall annual survey of customer satisfaction. Attach that data to the account record. But B2B and B2C companies alike also need to do very brief surveys at the end of every customer service or support transaction, collecting info on the timeliness and effectiveness of the problem-solving as well as the general "willingness to recommend" your product or company. (Full disclosure: here's a card-carrying marketing guy who believes that willingness to recommend is *the only question that matters* in marketing.) Attach that data to the case and contact record. Only after a few months, start analyzing them to determine the data quality (% of wild points), distribution (average is nice, but quintiles are better), and clustering (divide them by product, geography, and customer type and look for modalities). You may find some interesting trouble spots in your sales, product, and service groups just with that analysis.

But let's dig a bit further, as surveys are almost inevitably flawed in four big ways:

- **Surveyor bias:** The questions are focused on things the surveyor cares about, inevitably omitting things that are relevant to the customer. Resolve these by including optional text fill-in areas on every question, plus a question at the end: "Is there anything else you'd like to tell us?"

- **Semantic bias:** The questions are worded in a way that makes sense to the bureaucratic needs and language of the surveyor rather than using the language and context of the customer. Resolve these by pretesting the surveys themselves with neutral outsiders.

- **Sample bias:** The only answers you get are from the people with the time and inclination to answer surveys, omitting key members of the audience (like the ones who are busiest and most important). Resolve these by providing tchotchkes and other incentives for people to answer.

- **PITA skew:** There's a wonderful book whose title says it all: *Don't Make Me Think* by Steve Krug (New Riders, 2006). In the Short Attention Span Theater that is modern business, customers won't spend time on surveys. Resolve this by keeping your survey to five multiple-choice questions, answerable from an email optimized for a smartphone. Provide a link to your Web site for those who want to wax poetic, and thank your lucky stars if more than 5% of respondents go there (even if you offer a prize for doing so).

Surveys are essentially medieval.[5] You'd think with cloud computing we could do better. For the purposes of assaying customer happiness, what we really want is to measure the propensity to re-up (buy more), renew support, and recommend to others. Although this score has lots of components, the aggregate score should best be thought of as an *at-risk index*, with a lower score being better. (For those screaming, "But higher always has to be better for my executives," too bad: the scientific method says you can't prove the positive here, only absence of the negative.) The at-risk index should be collected at the contact level in the CRM but must be aggregated to the opportunity record (as this is typically your closest proxy to a "project" or a "purchasing entity").

---

5. Don't believe me? Check out the *Domesday Book* of 1086 (http://en.wikipedia.org/wiki/Domesday_Book).

What are the measurement points for this at-risk score? The good news is you already have a lot of them in your CRM system:

- **Direct indicators:** The number of SLA violations, long-open cases, unsuccessfully closed cases, complaint emails, non-renewed contracts, non-upgraded products, negative course evaluations, and so on

- **Implicit indicators:** The number of "case notes" that indicate an unhappy customer and the number of posts in your online document commentary area ("How can we make this page better?") and in your ideas area ("How can we make the product better?")

- **Occluded indicators:** A customer negative-sentiment index as measured by a social media monitoring system that's evaluating posts in your online community and (if you know the person's handles) in social networks

If you are lucky enough to have a product with usability monitoring built into the UI, or if you deliver your product as SaaS, you can collect click-by-click metrics on "where this customer is getting stuck." Although this data should really be collected and used to improve the product (that's how Salesforce itself uses these data), they can be aggregated to discover "here's a customer that is frustrated." This data is unlikely to be in your CRM system now, but best-in-class companies are all going that direction.

Scoring systems may be a pain to set up, but it's even harder to get really good results from them. But seriously, it's worth it. Technology is not the problem here: scoring must be based on a model and a set of assumptions. And nobody has a really solid model for how individuals decide they are happy or unhappy about a purchase or a company. The modeling errors from a single bad assumption or weak relationship easily overwhelm the predictive power of a dozen good elements.

So expect to be tuning your scoring models for many months, if not quarters, before the results are credible. Because of this break-in period, it is critical to set expectations low, particularly with executives and sales people who will really give you only one chance.

A key caveat: analytics will inherently magnify any problems you have with data quality. Be sure about your semantics and data filtering before you make critical decisions based on analysis of these scores.

- In most industries, providing a well-executed customer self-service portal can achieve higher customer satisfaction scores than having "more people on the phone." Particularly in high-tech industries, customers are very comfortable interacting with portals. Many can use these portals to get the information they need into or out of the system much faster than they could through a phone person.

- However, *do not implement a self-service portal as a "slash cut"* in which phone support is eliminated—you will face a customer revolt! Further, do not introduce a portal solution without doing end-to-end usability testing first—the tiniest glitches will cause huge customer irritation. Introduce the new ideas gradually, and have customers naturally drift over to your customer self-service portal as it becomes more attractive and useful. As more of the support volume shifts to the portal, you'll get suggestions for refinements to make it even easier and faster for customers. Implement these suggestions! Once 80% of the "call volume" is handled through the portal, you can provide some incentives (such as lower costs or better service levels) to cement the "portal first" customer behavior.

CUSTOMER SELF-SERVICE PORTAL[6]

A well-executed customer portal lowers the company's costs, giving customers 24 × 365 access to the information they need and reducing the error rate[7] associated with support information. It doesn't come cheap, but the payoffs can be remarkable. Ideally, the portal should include access to the following information:

- Customer name, address, phone, and account information (Do *not* include credit card numbers here!)
- Order history, invoices, and shipment history
- Warranty information and support entitlements
- Licenses or serial numbers
- Frequently asked questions (FAQs)
- Product documentation and manuals
- `Solutions` and a `knowledge base`[8] with really good categorization and full search capabilities
- IM with a support person or chat bots
- `Case` (problem or incident) submittal, tracking, and updates
- Field service appointment schedule (set, view, and edit)

---

6. SFDC's `portal` offerings have recently been replaced with `chatter communities`. Although the technology has changed dramatically, the essential features and user model are the same.

7. A customer is much less likely to misspell his or her own name than a phone service rep would be.

8. SFDC's `knowledge base` is a great place to start when implementing this feature, but it can be supplemented with document libraries and blogs that should be fully searchable by customers.

- Support contract renewals or warranty extensions
- Ordering information for accessories, parts, and upgrades
- Training and certification options
- SFDC's `ideas` application, which provides a great way to capture and prioritize customer suggestions
- Survey/feedback center
- User preferences for items like time zone, business hours, language, currency, email format, and newsletter selection

The support personnel will need access to lots of information that's outside the purview of basic SFDC, so you will almost certainly need the `enterprise edition` to facilitate integration with external systems. If your company has been able to stay at the `professional edition` level up to now, support will be *the* compelling reason to upgrade to a higher SFDC level. Ideally, the support organization will need to have access to the following items in SFDC:

- `Opportunities`
- `Accounts`
- `Contacts`
- `Products/Price Book`
- `Contracts`
- `Assets`
- `Cases`
- `Chatter`
- `Content`
- `Knowledge`

Support should also have integrated information from the following systems:

- **Marketing:** Call scripts, suggested renewal/upsell packages, and short-term promotions
- **Order management:** Current orders, pending fulfillments, licenses, serial numbers, etc.
- **Accounting:** Order history, invoices, and payments
- **eCommerce:** "Shopping cart" status, order details, and credit-card payments (some of this information won't be available in real time from your own accounting system)

- **Manufacturing/ERP:** Shipments, serial numbers, inventory, backlog, replacement parts availability, RMA numbers, reverse-logistics information, and warranty information

- **Support internal systems:** Appointment scheduling, training class scheduling, consulting project management, and professional services automation (PSA) information

- **Engineering:** Defect reporting/tracking, technical bulletins, patches, resolutions, licenses, and repair/rework status

- And now the caveat: be aware that external integrations will add significant costs and (potentially) delays to the project. Budget accordingly. Further, do not attempt such integrations before you've solidified the basic functionality of the SFDC system and brought your key customers into it. There are a variety of strategies for handling integration requirements, so make sure to read the relevant section in Chapter 7 before you make any firm decisions in this area.

- Focus on measuring the customer experience—and how that affects their satisfaction. Extend Salesforce CRM to bake in as many measurement points of the *customer's behavior* as you can. For example, click-path analysis in the customer self-service portal tells you a lot about things to improve in your operation. In addition, online surveys (keep them short!) at the end of every customer interaction help you develop a holistic picture of your customer relationships as they evolve.

TOP 10 WAYS TO RUIN THE CUSTOMER EXPERIENCE

Customer support and service are often at the receiving end of several not-so-brilliant Great Ideas that almost guarantee an unhappy customer. You don't have any control over those, but there are several service decisions that are under your control—and you don't want to head down the path of any of these:

- Setting up really deep, convoluted interactive voice response (IVR) navigation trees.
- Having the leaf node of your IVR navigation tree a dead line, a continuous busy signal, or a full voicemail box.
- Going purely single-channel for customer support—and then not doing an end-to-end test of that channel.
- Using low-quality phone lines, cheapie headsets, and people with heavy accents or subpar language skills.

- Publishing too many documents and having none of them be task-oriented. On top of that, using a crummy search engine for your knowledge base (because zero results is better than lots of irrelevant ones).

- Skimping on systems integration, so that neither the customer nor the customer support agent can see the whole picture.

- Requiring users to register before they file a ticket about the impossibility of getting into the system (because registration failed).

- Not performing usability testing of your service portal with an outsider.

- Setting up a ticket echo-chamber that opens up a new ticket every time an old one is updated.

- Being overzealous in license enforcement, making the customers' productivity stop dead in its tracks whenever there's a malfunction in your systems.

- Don't measure operational things too narrowly. Of course you want productivity and service level agreement (SLA) metrics, but the SFDC system can provide a lot deeper and richer information about customer interactions. Spend some time optimizing the company's operations by figuring out the characteristics of failure: Who are the most troublesome customers? What are the most likely cases to be delayed? Why are certain situations more likely to result in multiple callbacks? Identify the trouble spots, and you may be able to fix underlying product, service, or "attitude" issues that can radically improve the cost, effort, and excellence of the company's services.

UNDERSTANDING SFDC's SERVICE CLOUD

Salesforce has offered basic case management for more than 5 years and has made significant engineering investments to dramatically extend its offering. The basics of case management, content management, solutions, and collaboration are free with the `enterprise edition`, but that's not the serious stuff that they market heavily.

When you purchase a service cloud license, you're turning on a wide range of features focused on the enterprise, with features targeting both B2B and B2C support relationships. There are several optional extras (such as live-agent IM support for your Web site), and the most serious call center operations will involve considerable custom code to leverage the SFDC platform.

Separate from that is RemedyForce, which is one of several third-party products that SFDC has promoted to bolster its help desk functionality.

And separate from that is Desk.com, which is SFDC's own offering targeted at SMB customer support operations. Desk.com is much easier to set up than the rest of the service cloud but it doesn't try to solve all the enterprise's problems.

All of the content of this chapter is based on SFDC's Enterprise Service Cloud offerings. If you've bought less than that, you're going to have to ignore the guidance about features that aren't enabled in your system.

So now for the fun part: although all these offerings can be used together, they have different data models, use different operational concepts, and don't really share detailed data. Sure, the accounts and contacts are going to be the same everywhere—but the service incident, the fix, and, most importantly, the knowledge bases are essentially different worlds. For example, `solutions` are part of the `enterprise edition`, but that is a separate technology from `knowledge`. Although these feature sets could *in concept* be integrated with each other with custom code, in practice they almost never are (at least not yet). That goes double for relevant documents.

So in evaluating SFDC's service cloud offerings, for any one service and support team, it's a one-or-the-other choice. If your company decides to pursue more than one of these paths (which is a perfectly reasonable choice for multiple business units or different target markets), we recommend that you partition the service load so that no individual *customer* has to deal with more than one of these product families—even if your service and support team does.

Developing a Model of Support and Service Interactions

Before you can apply any of the recommendations in this chapter, you need to develop a model of how your company's service and processes work, including how your teams interact with sales and other internal organizations. The goal is to create an internal SLA—that is, a contract between the various teams about who does what to ensure customer satisfaction. This model needs to cover all aspects of postsales customer contacts— including service order correction/expediting, customer onboarding, technical support, training, and consulting—and have unambiguous semantics around details such as the following:

- Who's a customer?

- What constitutes a trial/pilot?

- What's an incident/case?

- What's an upsell for service or consulting, and how is the transaction handled?

- Who gets revenue credit for all support, service, consulting, and training transactions?

- How are service, consulting, and training partner transactions handled?

- What's an auto-renewal, and who handles the exceptions?

As you can imagine, developing this model requires some meetings with the sales team (and maybe with the eCommerce team) to get the details nailed down and documented. This task can be achieved in a couple of afternoons if you're serious, but it's one of the most highly leveraged things you can do to prevent crossed wires and confusion. Don't forget the channel here: providing support to and through partners may be a key success factor in your industry.

Yes, it's true, developing this model will take time (mostly in meetings) and can involve some politics. But the politics are there anyway—if you want to improve things, you're going to need a model to argue over.

Social Service and Support

Depending on your company's customer base and market situation, customer service and support may be the single most "social" business function. There are two sides to this: people in customer support are on the phone or communicating via email/IM all day long, and the customer probably has more contact with customer service and support than any other part of your company. So social media and social CRM are natural tools for your team.

The term *social CRM* was coined (and immediately overhyped) by the vendor community to signal the new capabilities that are required to execute an effective social media marketing campaign. None of the CRM vendors has a complete offering yet, but SFDC is clearly a leader in this area.

The broadest area of SFDC's social functionality is `chatter`. As discussed in Chapters 6 and 13, `chatter` provides a rich and secure medium for internal collaboration, with a bunch of use cases in the call center, technical support, professional services, and training. Because it's a threaded communication medium baked right into nearly every SFDC record, it is much more efficient than email. But of course, getting the most from `chatter` requires behavioral changes from the SFDC user—so don't expect that overnight.

`Chatter` makes it much easier to set up a "sensor array" for your company's early warning system: marketers may start seeing new messaging, sales may start hearing new competitive objections, customer service may detect a growing sense of resentment from unhappy customers, and technical support may start hearing about a product defect long before it's obvious. `Chatter` lets you create subject-interest `groups` on the fly and auto-suggest new `topics` from trending `keywords` to make it a very helpful intelligent listening system.

You can take `chatter` even further with your customers and service partners by setting up a walled-garden community, where conversations occur in a secure environment. If you're lucky, customers and service partners will be able to add `chatter` IM in their network. Make sure to have an *onboarding* process for external `chatter` users, as they will need to be indoctrinated in your community's chattiquette[9] guidelines.

Let's not get overzealous here: You may be able to get only your (smaller) service partners and (closest) customers to participate in chatter. But to succeed at this, they have to have an intrinsic reason to do so. You'll definitely need to come up with a credible WIIFY[10] statement. Check out www.SFDC-secrets.com, www.salesforce.com/chatterguide/start-here/practices.jsp, and www.facebook.com/Chatter, or just Google "chatter best practices" for lots more articles on this topic.

When it comes to serious IM, though, you really have to pay attention to Twitter, Facebook, LinkedIn, Google+, Yelp, and the other established social networks. Particularly for B2C markets, you want to communicate with customers where they already are[11]—not force them to switch media in order to get the support they need. SFDC has connectors available for these social networks so that you can link avatars to customer records as soon as they have identified themselves. For obvious reasons, you want to work with marketing to collect the social media handles (at least for LinkedIn and Facebook) on every registration form they have.

It is a best practice to survey your customers after every service/support transaction, so you can measure and continuously improve. But what about the service opportunities that haven't taken place—how do you survey the customers who are just steaming mad but haven't contacted you? `Social media monitoring` is the best way to quantify market sentiment about your company and its products. In addition to assessing unaided awareness, SFDC's `social media monitoring` can be used to measure product reputation, service satisfaction, and likelihood of renewal.

While this nirvana beckons, it is not easily achieved. Most service and support staff really don't have deep skills to leverage `social media monitoring`, and doing it right requires some serious analytical skill.

Community management is, unfortunately, in the same boat for most service and support organizations. But if you look at open-source software vendors, you can see how they have dramatically improved mean time to resolve (MTTR) while lowering costs through community self-support. The cornerstone for this is the community management

---

9. It's been conclusively proven that `chatter`'s signal-to-noise ratio is pretty low unless there are clearly defined use cases and rules of the road for communicating and collaborating in this threaded-IM environment.

10. What's In It For You—WIIFY.

11. This is the same rationale for the instant-IM presented within your Web site: catch clients on the page they're wondering about, and IM them before the focus of their attention changes. SFDC's `live agent` is very effective for both customer and partner interactions.

engine, which up until now has been provided by companies such as Lithium. Salesforce is in the process of rolling out `chatter communities`, which will be used for customers, sales partners, and service partners. The feature set will roll out over several quarters and gradually replace the `customer` and `partner self-service portals`.[12] For obvious reasons, it is not yet possible to provide best practices in this area. However, SFDC's `ideas` feature is invaluable in identifying customers' hot buttons and getting the user community to prioritize bugs and product improvements. Work with product management and engineering to prepopulate the `ideas` list with items that you'd like customers to vote on, and make sure that you tell customers on every phone call about their ability to influence the product evolution. Check out the discussion on this in the "Product Management/Product Marketing" section of Chapter 10, and definitely look at how SFDC uses its community input for its own product (`ideas` can be found at https://success.salesforce.com/ideaHome).

One area of significant community innovation is gamification—using small competitions and real-time rewards to get more engagement and participation from your community. Actionale, Badgeville, Bunchball, and others offer gamification plugins to SFDC for both internal and external use cases. These systems not only have a great coolness factor, but they can be kind of fun.[13]

If you fast-forward 5 years, there can be little doubt that the economics, if not the daily operations, of all leading service and support operations will be significantly changed. At the core of this will be increased automation, higher levels of cross-system integration, and dynamic participation of the user community in support. Essentially, that's the definition of social service and support.

The Customer Order Support Center

The ordering component of customer support may be a shared responsibility with inside sales because of the nature of the work: helping customers get their orders into the system the right way. This job is focused on order entry, order configuration, and order correction. If you haven't already done so, read the "Handling Order Operations for Outside Sales" section in Chapter 9.

Everyone who touches an order in SFDC needs to be working with coherent rules, business processes, and controls to ensure that orders are not corrupted or mishandled. Nothing angers customers more than incomplete or inconsistent "assistance" when they call in for help.

The first challenge in most order-support implementations is making a correct and complete order history available to the customer support reps. This is particularly true

---

12. If you haven't enabled these portals in your SFDC instance, they can no longer be enabled.
13. Okay, so I lead a dull life.

if the call center must handle orders from several business units, channels, or countries. In some cases, several systems and databases may have to be integrated before they are presented to SFDC users at all. The results of these integrations can initially be presented as read-only data, but even this lightweight integration can entail a significant amount of work.

In most cases, the phone representatives need to go further than just reviewing the customer's order history. The order support center may also be involved with selling service items that other company representatives don't sell, such as support renewals, warranty extensions, manuals, and replacement supplies or parts. For this reason, they'll need full access to the `products` and `quotes` functionality of SFDC, order-configuration systems that you may use for more complex products, and your order management system. For example, these reps need access to "internal only" order capabilities, such as partial shipments, co-terminating contracts, special-order items, adjustments, and special discounts. They also need access to the contract signature engine (e.g., DocuSign), invoicing system, and they may even need access to parts of the ERP system to see shipment schedules. Ensuring this kind of across-the-board access can represent a significant investment, but it doesn't take long to pay for itself with lower costs, reduced error rates, and increased upsells.

In addition to following the best universal practices discussed in the previous section, the order support center should leverage SFDC to help with the order handling and warranty/service renewal cycle in these ways:

- If the order has come in through the eCommerce system (or if it wasn't properly processed there), make sure that the customer information (particularly phone number and email address) and transaction information (particularly the credit card tracer number) are properly recorded on the `contact`, `account`, and `opportunity` records before you hang up the phone. As discussed in Chapters 2 and 13, it is a best practice to *not* store credit card numbers, bank account numbers, Social Security numbers, or other personal financial information in SFDC.

- During the `opportunity` close process, a `contract` object should be created within SFDC, recording the appropriate warranty, license, and serial number information in `custom fields`. Contractual terms, signature pages, licenses, and invoices should be stored in the `contract` object. Warranty service periods and SLA terms should be stored in the `entitlements` object. SFDC should be set up to lock down fields and records so that only members of the finance department can modify `opportunity` and contract `records` once the deal is signed.

- As soon as an `opportunity` is won, a new `opportunity` should be automatically opened for the anniversary of the purchase date or whatever time is appropriate for renewals or support contracts. Most of the fields of the new `opportunity` should be prepopulated with data from the existing opportunity, and the `opportunity contact role` should be cloned as well to streamline the renewal sales process. Further, at least one `task` should be created to remind the appropriate renewal rep to start calling the customer 60 days before the end of the warranty or support period.

- Automatic reminder emails should go out to customers about support or warranty expiration, starting 60 days before the expiry date. This communication should be done via ExactTarget (or your existing email blasting system if it is tightly integrated with SFDC `campaigns` and `activities`).

- Because the order support reps will have to handle tricky orders that may include upsell `opportunities`, the team should use `call scripting` features (a free AppExchange plugin) to guide them through the order-handling call.

- The `opportunity` record should include a `custom field` to indicate customer problem areas. It should consist of a `pull-down list` with the 10 most common problem areas, supplemented by `tasks` regarding specific instances. These fields should be populated manually and via survey engines.

- The order support reps should create new `contacts` for people with whom they interact in purchasing, legal, or other customer departments. They should also set `contact roles` for `accounts`, `opportunities`, or `cases` they are working on, to help everyone understand the political structures in its customers.

Order support teams should be measured along the following lines, with reports and dashboards being created for managers:

- Number of calls handled per rep per day

- Average wait time or call queue length

- Average call time

- Number of order fixes (e.g., reconfiguration, repricing) processed per day

- Number and value of returns or exchanges per day

- Number of upsells or renewals closed per day

- Value of orders fixed per day

- Value of eCommerce, upsell, and renewal orders processed per day

- Number of orders escalated per day

- Survey results regarding call satisfaction (percentage of customers satisfied or very satisfied)

Order Expediting, Distribution, and Shipping

Due to the nature of the order expediting, distribution, and shipping work, this part of customer support may be a shared responsibility with the manufacturing planning, distribution, or shipping functions. The focus here is on allocating inventory to achieve the best results in revenue recognition, customer satisfaction, and profitability. This role is most critical for products that are in short supply, have high shipping and storage costs, or carry very high price tags.

The first challenge in most SFDC order expediting implementations is to make the current orders list and inventory commitment/routing information available to the expediting representatives. This is particularly true if the customer support center has to handle orders from several business units, channels, or countries—in some cases, several systems and databases may have to be integrated before they are presented to SFDC users at all.

In most cases, the phone representatives need to go further than just seeing the orders and inventory. Specifically, they need to be able to edit records so they can expedite shipments, reallocate inventory to orders, or arrange for partial shipments. Achieving this goal requires two-way integration with order history, ERP, distribution, and other systems, along with appropriate controls and security. This level of integration entails significant custom work.

In addition to the best practices discussed earlier in the "Universal Support Best Practices" section, the order expediters should leverage SFDC in these ways:

- SFDC should be set up with `alerts` and `time-dependent workflows` to remind order expediters and the shipping departments of overdue orders. This consideration is particularly important for products coming in bulk shipments from Asia, where the exact contents and timing of a shipment may not be known until it is about to arrive in-country.

- The expediting and shipment information should be attached to the `opportunity` or `contract` record in SFDC—*not* delivered via an internal email. Given that sales reps will often have to manage customer expectations, they need to be able to see the best and most complete information available, all in place.

- If you use FedEx or UPS for product shipments, use the AppExchange plugins for these shippers for a much smoother customer experience.

Order expediters should be measured along the following lines, with reports and dashboards for managers:

- Number of calls handled per rep per day
- Average wait time or call queue length

- Average call time

- Number of orders resolved per day

- Value of orders resolved per day

- Number and value of returns or exchanges per day

- Number of orders escalated per day

- Survey results regarding call satisfaction (percentage of customers satisfied or very satisfied)

Customer Help Desk

Large companies—particularly those with consumer products—need a customer assistance center to provide the first line of defense for confused customers. Their job is to help customers who haven't read the manual, need basic questions answered, or aren't sure whether they even bought the right product. Consequently, the focus of this team is assistance and quick information access, not heavy transactions or deep problem solving. Its goal is to immediately help the customer with the problem or quickly identify problems that must be escalated to tech support.

Some innovative companies have developed software systems using chat bots, email, artificial intelligence, and IVR technologies to dramatically decrease the human element of the help desk function or eliminate it altogether. Although few—if any—of these systems are currently in production with a high level of integration to SFDC, that trend is certainly on the horizon.

In addition to the best practices discussed in the "Universal Support Best Practices" section, the help desk should leverage SFDC in these ways:

- `Chatter` is perhaps the single most important tool that the help desk should use to discover and troubleshoot emerging customer problems. As the "first responder" for customer issues, the help desk is most likely to be hit with surprises.

- The help desk team should open (and rapidly close or escalate) `cases` and `tasks` with annotations from phone or IM conversations. They should also update `contact` and `opportunity` records as appropriate.

- The help desk should have access to the SFDC `knowledge base`, particularly `ideas` and the `chatter community` (if they are set up). But mostly, help desk personnel need access to product documentation, service bulletins, and FAQs held in document management systems, Box.com folders, wikis, or plain old "shared disk" areas outside of SFDC.

The customer help desk management needs nonintrusive measurement systems to make sure the call center is running smoothly:

- Number of calls handled per day per rep

- Average wait time or queue depth

- Percentage of hang-ups (abandon rate caused by excessive wait times)

- Average call time

- Number of cases escalated to technical support

- Top 10 problem categories

- Survey results regarding call satisfaction (percentage of customers satisfied or very satisfied)

Technical and Warranty Support

The technical and warranty support team spends more time dealing with unhappy customers than anybody else in the company and provides a shield for engineering, sales, and product marketing. Members of this team need to respond quickly and courteously to deal with customer problems, so they need access to systems that can move the resolution process along as quickly as possible. Some customers will have an SLA or other support-response guarantee, with contractual penalties if time limits are exceeded.

This team will benefit the most from a `customer self-service portal` or `chatter community`. Spend money on these features to improve customer satisfaction and reduce support costs at the same time.

Although the tech support team rarely needs to edit the `contact`, `opportunity`, `account`, or other SFDC data, they may need to edit `assets`, `contracts`, and `entitlements` (to determine support entitlement or warranty eligibility)[14] and create or update `cases` throughout the day. They also need access to the SFDC `content` and `knowledge` areas, as well as a couple of systems that other SFDC users almost never use: bug/defect tracking system and fix/upgrade database.

The first challenge in most SFDC tech support implementations is making a correct and complete `case` history available to the reps. This is particularly true if the customer support center has to handle products from several business units or countries—it's not

---

14. If the company has chosen not to implement `assets`, these data should be attached to `contracts`. In B2C companies where there aren't any `contracts`, eligibility or entitlement data must be attached to `opportunities`.

MOBILITY AND THE SERVICE TEAM

If your organization provides field service or on-site professional services, the team should be taking SFDC with them with each truck roll. The system will make their jobs easier, improve collaboration, and leave a better impression with the customer. In most situations, there is no extra charge for accessing SFDC out of the office—so what's not to like?

If the field people use a laptop and have network connectivity while on site, they should simply be using the browser-based UI and perhaps the `chatter` app that they use in the office. These apps run well enough even if all you've got is 1G Edge connectivity, and they run quickly on 3G, 4G, or WiFi connectivity.

Some of your customers won't allow network connectivity while you're in their buildings. This is an ideal use case for SFDC's `offline edition` that allows updating of records in the browser and resyncs the records as soon as network connectivity is available.

If your field support people have iPads or Android tablets with 3G/4G access, they should simply access SFDC with the browser that's native to their device. If their mobile device has a small screen (such as an iPad mini or a smartphone), they should use SFDC's `mobile edition`. Accessing data is free, but updating some SFDC data requires a mobile license that may carry a charge. Of course, the limited screen space and keyboard make it hard to use for anything beyond minor field updates.

unusual for several systems and databases to need to be integrated before they are presented to SFDC users at all. Expect to spend some money here.

In addition to following the best practices discussed in the "Universal Support Best Practices" section, the technical and warranty support team should leverage SFDC in these ways:

- SFDC should be configured to show SLA requirements and response times as part of the `account`, `opportunity`, and `contract` records. The system should be configured so that `cases` automatically inherit the SLA deadline information from the appropriate `contract` or `entitlement`.

- The technical and warranty support reps should create `contacts` for all new customer personnel with whom they interact. Even though most of the fields on a closed `opportunity` should be locked down, the tech support reps should update

---

15. `offline edition` is free for `unlimited edition` and may carry a nominal charge on `enterprise`; its functionality is limited, and it's not clear how much longer SFDC is going to continue updating it to work with the latest browser updates.

opportunities with information about the way the customer is using the product, including any custom referencability fields or custom objects that are appropriate there. They should also set contact roles for cases they are working on, thereby helping the company document the political overtones that exist in its large customers. They may also set contact roles for accounts or renewal opportunities if they should discover them during calls.

- SFDC case records should be expanded with custom fields for cross-reference information to bug/defect databases, service bulletins, RMA numbers, license/serial numbers, warranty/shipment numbers, and related information. If your company's products are heavily regulated, additional information about lot numbers and distribution channels may have to be recorded as well, in either the case, opportunity, asset, or contract record.

- A push-button timer should be added to the case page layout, so the service agents can easily record the time spent on each case. These plugin timers are available on the AppExchange.

- The SFDC system should be integrated with the company's defect or bug tracking system, using plugins or general-purpose integration tools from the AppExchange. For the technical support rep, these systems need to look like a seamless part of SFDC. That said, for the rest of the engineering department (which will almost certainly *not* have SFDC access), the defect/bug tracking system's records need to contain complete details of the customer situation.

- If your company sells hardware, SFDC should be integrated with its RMA and reverse-logistics system so that shipping authorizations and related warranty paperwork can be issued on the fly. For post-warranty repairs, the technical support rep needs access to the repair work-order system. Implementing these custom integration projects will require the use of the general-purpose integration tools found in the AppExchange.

- If your company's products or services require fulfillment or "onboarding" projects to make customers successful, SFDC should be integrated with the service scheduling and task management system used by the field service agents. In some product/service categories, the onboarding process may take a month or more, so the tech support rep needs to be able to see the "state of play" and scheduled next events from within the SFDC pages.

- Because the technical and warranty support reps are trying to solve customer problems in real time, they need to troubleshoot, run diagnostics, and provide advice on the fly. With products or services of any complexity, each rep should have access to highly scripted question/response sequences throughout the call.

The free plugin from SFDC should be used to handle the "first pass" questions that are posed to all customers by tier-1[16] support. Soon after that initial volley, however, the rep will need to switch to more detailed information. Depending on the company's style, these data may be provided as a set of PDF documents, intranet pages, or wiki articles. No matter which format is used, the tech support reps will need to be able to rapidly search by topic and keyword. This kind of functionality is usually kept in totally separate systems but is best accessed via its own `tab` in SFDC. Reps need to *rapidly* navigate across the functional areas they need to use.

- `Cases` should be configured to use `record types` and `page layouts` for different product lines and service types to keep screen content as uncluttered and relevant as possible under each situation.

- As much information as is relevant should be attached to the `case` record. In some product categories (particularly software), however, the attached information may be several megabytes in length. Instead of using the `file attachment` feature in the SFDC system, the reps should store these large files in standard file servers and put the path to a specific file in a `task` attached to the relevant `case`.[17] In this way, engineering or other personnel can access the diagnostic file even if they don't have SFDC user accounts.

- The `case` record should include a custom field to indicate customer problems. This field should take the form of a pull-down list with the 10 most common problem areas, supplemented by `tasks` regarding specific instances. These fields should be populated manually and via survey engines.

- If your company uses field service technicians (either your own or through a service partner), the `case` record should include custom fields to indicate the field service technician's name, any parts or equipment required for the visit, the scheduled time of the service appointment, the actual time of the visit, and the length of on-site time. These fields should be synchronized with your appointment scheduling system and your customer portal.

- The technical and warranty support system should also be configured to present real-time alerts (e.g., emails and pages) to line managers, allowing them to avert brewing problems such as excessive wait times, pending escalations, imminent

---

16. In high-tech industries, this is typically called front-line, tier-1 or level-1 support, but the terminology varies across product and service industries. See http://en.wikipedia.org/wiki/Technical_support#-Multi-tiered_technical_support for an explanation of this jargon, and use that to translate it into your industry's standard terms.

17. There's a nice AppExchange plugin, FTP Attach, that allows files stored in standard file shares to be displayed as part of the SFDC pages. There are also plugins for file-management solutions like Box, if you don't want to fill up your servers with these files.

SLA violations, and other trouble spots before they boil over. Using SFDC work-flows and automatic report generation, multisite technical support operations can do load shedding to maintain high levels of customer service despite large varia-tions in support load.

- Finally, the system should issue a brief support-satisfaction survey when each case is closed.

Technical support should be measured along the following lines, with reports and dashboards being made available for managers:

- Number of calls handled per day per rep
- Average wait time or queue depth
- Percent of hang-ups (or "abandon rate," indicating that the customer gave up because of the wait time)
- Average call time
- Average number of calls required to resolve an issue
- Number of cases by severity
- Average time spent by severity
- Number of cases opened per day per rep
- Number of cases closed per day per rep
- Number of cases escalated per day per rep
- Average wall-clock time to resolve
- Average total effort to resolve
- Top 10 problem categories and their total costs to resolve
- Top 10 escalation categories
- SLA compliance percentage
- Customer loyalty percentage
- Customer re-up percentage
- Survey results regarding call satisfaction (percentage of customers satisfied or very satisfied)
- Customer satisfaction (likely to buy again, recommend, and so forth) percentage

OFFSHORING SUPPORT CENTERS

Offshoring or outsourcing parts of customer support is a continuing trend, particularly in highly competitive, high-volume operations with manufacturing overseas. There are a few key SFDC practices to consider before the company makes the decision to offshore its customer support functions.

SFDC is fully internationalized and can be easily configured to be user friendly for support operations in several countries, languages, currencies, and time zones simultaneously. The offshore personnel will need to have full access not only to the SFDC system but also to the support-relevant systems you have integrated with SFDC. For this reason, the company should implement a fine-grained security plan to make sure that the support people can see everything they need to, but only what they *really* need. The company will also need to set up a virtual private network (VPN) and limit access so that only those inside the VPN can log in to SFDC.

We recommend implementing `record types, support processes, sales processes`, and `page layouts` for each major customer region (such as the Euro Zone or Asia), as the case-handling `workflows` and `escalations` within these regions will probably be slightly different from their U.S. counterparts. Using this approach allows spelling and other variations to fit the sales and support customs in each area. The company may also need to develop different approval cycles to fit local management chains—a need that goes double if the company uses distributors or channel partners in some countries.

We also recommend setting the offshore system's time zone to the main time zone of the customers being covered, not the reps' local time zone. This consideration is important when trying to manage tight SLA deadlines across support centers, and it can be critical during the end-of-quarter rush, when the last-minute order push can be very hectic.

`Case escalation rules` and `workflows` need to be flawless and to fit with the realities of the local workforces.[18] Set up `email approvals` and `delegated approvals` to facilitate weekends and holidays in different countries. It is particularly important that escalated cases be smoothly handed off at the end of the local workday so that those cases move to the top of the list of the remote "morning shift." It can be quite difficult to create reports that accurately capture these cross-site performance metrics.

Although many offshore operations use VOIP phones, we generally discourage the use of Skype buttons in SFDC for support operations because of marginal call quality. When network bandwidth is uneven, distortion or skipping of Skype calls will waste time and leave a bad customer impression. This warning goes double for technical support operations that need to access and transfer large amounts of data to headquarters' engineering staff. Because SFDC's screens depend on low latency and infrequent "lost packets," the last thing the team needs is more competition for Internet bandwidth.

---

18. For example, if an escalation will occur during the lunch hour in Spain or France, the escalation needs to be triggered before the support team leaves the office.

Professional Services

The professional services teams that provide training and carry out consulting projects are often ignored in SFDC planning, but there are very good reasons to include them. These personnel see customers for longer periods than anyone else in the corporation, and they can act as early warning sentinels for both beneficial and damaging trends.

Training

Courses should be included in the SFDC system as standard price-list products, and their order history should be maintained along with the rest of the products in the `opportunity` and `contract` records. As customers subscribe to the courses, a `custom field` in the `opportunity` record should be updated to indicate the number of course tickets remaining. The certificates of course completion should be kept in `custom fields` and `tasks` for the individual `contacts` who have completed the course; it's also a good idea to annotate them as `tasks` attached to the relevant `opportunity`. If you want to get fancy, a `workflow` and some `APEX` code could be set up to keep a tally of the available course chits remaining at the `opportunity` level.

For custom courses (which are typically delivered on an on-site basis for major customers or partners), a price-list item should be created with a "standard" price and description that are modified for each situation. Even though the product roll-ups will be somewhat misleading, the `opportunity` records will indicate the number of companies whose employees have taken custom courses.

When it comes to online ordering and scheduling of courses, SFDC almost always needs to be supplemented with an eCommerce system that has a calendaring and confirmation engine. Whichever system you choose needs to have a plugin that properly synchronizes with `contact`, `account`, and `opportunity` records in SFDC. Check in the AppExchange for the current offerings.

Invite students in your courses to join the `ideas` community, both for future course expansion and product improvements. Also invite them to join `chatter` groups focused on the topics of your courses, as engagement typically leads to additional course purchases.

Consulting

Although some consulting projects can be sold as fixed-price packages, most consulting work is done as custom projects. Typically, the consulting organization will create `price list items` such as "Senior Consulting Day" or "Business Analyst Day," and the `opportunity products` for each order will show the total number of person-days

SERVICE AND SUPPORT PARTNERS

Increasingly, large support operations are leveraging partners for providing all elements of support—from initial call centers to field technicians to training organizations. These can become fairly complex intermediary relationships, particularly if you use several vendors to cover your worldwide customer base. Although SFDC clearly is flexible enough to accommodate any complexity needed for your support channel, out of the box there are no features for this.

SFDC's `partner portal` and `PRM features` are focused on the sales aspect of partners, and if you haven't enabled them yet in your instance, they are no longer available anyway. So you have to focus attention on `chatter communities` as your way of communicating and collaborating with your service partners. Unfortunately, SFDC is only gradually rolling out these `chatter` features, so the service partner best practices surrounding them are anything but clear.

What is clear is is the need to integrate SFDC with other systems (including your partners') and create custom code to provide any significant level of automation for service and training partners. This can represent a serious IT project—perhaps bigger than your internal service cloud project—so make sure to allocate the time and budget before you set any executive expectations. If they use SFDC and `chatter` themselves, the integration and automation work can be made easier by `workflows, outbound messages, salesforce to salesforce`, and other free features of the `enterprise` and `unlimited editions`.

required for each category of consultant. The statement of work, signature pages, NDA, acceptance criteria, and other consulting artifacts should be attached to the customer's `opportunity` or `contract` record.

Once a project has been brought under contract, large consulting teams need to use a project management and consultant-time management system. PSA systems are typically standalone products, but @task, Open Air, QuickArrow, and others have good integrations with SFDC[19] that reduce the amount of redundant information. If you don't have a PSA system and use Microsoft Project and Excel to manage consulting teams, seriously consider Clarizen's cloud-based project collaboration system. If that's too much for you, create a projects `custom object` that hangs off the `contract` record, and put these project management files as `attachments` to the projects object. Search for "project management" in the AppExchange to find free modules that can get you started down this path.

---

19. Although adaptors are available for systems like Basecamp, Confluence, and Jira, they are very limited and do not provide sufficient information to coordinate a serious project.

Given the nature of consulting projects, it's important that action items be visible to all team members. Consequently, consultants should not use personal calendars for project action items and deadlines; instead, they should use SFDC for this purpose. Consider[20] using `Salesforce for outlook`, Linkpoint 360, iHance, or Riva to synchronize consultants' Outlook or Google calendars. Using `tasks`, `workflows`, `alerts`, and `escalations`, SFDC can do a lot to coordinate the work of the consulting team and ensure that deadlines and milestones are not missed by individuals or upper management.

Typically, at least one `chatter topic` should be created for each project. Project progress reports (e.g., progress versus milestones, budgets, variances, and consultant's time-card summaries) and engineering documents (e.g., specifications, code, tests, and final documentation) can be evolved as `files` attached to `chatter feeds`. `Tasks` for action items and follow-ups can be created directly within the relevant `feed`. Given that these documents have a tendency to multiply rapidly, it's a good idea to archive down-rev versions of documents using one of the document offloading plugins available in the AppExchange to avoid running up against SFDC's storage limits.

As the project comes to completion, the consultants need to update as much `contact` information as they can. They will also have the latest insights about `account contact roles`, project politics, customer satisfaction, and referencability information associated with the `opportunity` that spawned the project. These updates will be invaluable to both sales and marketing personnel in their pursuit of renewal and upsell business.

Project management systems typically have their own metrics for budget, schedule, and process compliance. These "final scores" should be copied over to the project record in SFDC. In addition, consulting projects should have their own metrics in SFDC:

- Project budgeted and actual expenditures

- Projected and actual schedules

- Number of projects abandoned or terminated prematurely

- Number of consultants used on the project

- Number of cases related to the project (if any)

- Survey results regarding project satisfaction (percentage of customers satisfied or very satisfied)

- Overall customer satisfaction (likely to buy again, recommend, and so forth) percentage or score

---

20. Take the word *consider* literally: *do not* implement these tools without first running a 30-day evaluation with a few pilot users. These tools may work fine for the way your users work, or they may lead to disastrous calendar corruption. Test before using!

Service and Support Executives

SFDC provides the foundation for many important improvements in the way service and support works. Achieving these improvements will require behavioral changes from the team, but it can mean dramatic improvements in effectiveness, efficiency, cost structure, and—most important—customer satisfaction.

Many SFDC best practices immediately translate into service and support best practices. If you haven't already done so, at least skim the "Universal Support Best Practices" section earlier in this chapter. Further, SFDC brings into focus the real value of service and support to your company's overall profitability. However, do not expect the SFDC system to reduce your team's headcount: you'll be able to achieve more with the same staff, but some of their skill levels will need to be raised.

The best practices for service and support team members have been discussed throughout this chapter. As an executive, you need to reinforce their behavior with incentives and pep talks:

- Don't ask for data items that you won't really use or that won't fundamentally change the outcome of any decision.

- Add instrumentation to as many customer points of contact as you can, including customer-facing individuals in support, service, and consulting.

- Provide incentives so that, in the course of normal conversations with customers, your staff is collecting information that will be valuable for references.

- Strive to track each customer's interactions through every "touch" by your company. That said, don't bite off more than you can chew: work incrementally, starting with email and case-filing behaviors.

- Insist that `contact roles` are attached to every `case`. Period.

- `Chatter` is the best way for support personnel to alert the company about what's happening in the field and with customers. It's an invaluable listening tool, and it keeps everyone on the team in the loop on the latest info about prospects and customers. So . . . set the example by posting something relevant to `chatter` at least once a day.

- Integrate as many service, support, and training systems as you can afford to with SFDC. This seamless operation will reduce errors and dramatically increase visibility into the customer's behavior. To understand more about SFDC integration strategies, check out the discussion in Chapter 7.

- Use dashboards for the people working in your call center. The ones available in the system are a great start, but if you want to get really fancy, you can export the underlying reports via the `office connector` and drive some impressive Excel charts. In most situations, customer support and service will not need to use data warehousing tools to drive day-to-day operations. But if you want to know more, check out "Reports–Inside versus Outside" in Chapter 2.

- Use `workflows` and `alerts` to support management by exception. SFDC can streamline the majority of service and support processes (in particular, escalations, approval cycles, and SLA management) while giving you better data for more solid decisions.

You may be asked by the finance people to help with product, service, support, or training profitability analysis. If so, make sure to read that section in Chapter 12.

Read the last few pages of the Executive Summary in this book to find out about the general behavior changes and mandates you personally will need to make–they're all quite pleasant, actually, but it's important that the troops hear and see coherent behaviors directly from you.

WATCH OUT FOR MULTIPLE REPORTS AND DASHBOARDS

It is very common for users to inadvertently create several versions of a report or dashboard. This is almost always dangerous, because SFDC reports are really easy to create and even easier to create incorrectly. There are too many ways to filter and sort data incorrectly, and too many assumptions that can differ. Contradictory reports become a big source of politics when marketing, sales, service, support, and the executives are looking at "the same metric" with very different numbers. See "How to Blow Up Two Careers at Once!" in the Introduction.

The only antidote is to use one officially blessed folder of reports that are designed and implemented by a single team. Using the requests from service, support, professional services, and executives, a business analyst (typically one of your team or someone on loan from finance or IT) should create the company's official management reports for order handling, case, trouble-ticket, productivity, and other metrics. All other report versions should be deprecated and hidden from users so they can't mess them up.

GETTING THE MOST FROM **SFDC**

- If you're serious about customer service and support, you need to be using SFDC's `enterprise` or `unlimited editions`.

- Understand that SFDC is a platform, not just an application. There are literally dozens of add-ons you will want to add for service and support.

- Essentially, everybody in service and support should be on SFDC, pretty much all day long. That goes double for `chatter`.

- Your on-site field technicians, trainers, and consultants should be using SFDC's `mobile` or `offline editions`. There's just too much to be gained, and for most service cloud customers, it is free.

- Support is the new sales: you need to start thinking of your service and support team as the foundation for customer loyalty and upsells.

FOR SMALL COMPANIES

- Seriously consider using `desk.com`: it's easy, and it was designed for customer support!

- Focus on the basics of service and support—just the stuff to make customers happy and keep them that way.

- If you try to leverage community self-support, assign somebody on your staff to the key role of community manager.

FOR LARGE ENTERPRISES

- The best service and support systems are built, not bought. SFDC will need to be integrated with several other enterprise systems, so make sure to budget the time and money needed. It will be substantially more than what you spend on SFDC.

- Invest seriously in customer self-support through a portal or a `chatter community`.

- Use SFDC `ideas` to help prioritize your product and service roadmap.

- Make sure to survey all customers with every service and support transaction, and use call notes to keep track of customer referencability.

CHAPTER 12

Best Practices in Finance and Legal

It's accrual world.

—*Anonymous*

S FDC should be the hub of a comprehensive system for managing and storing the legal and contractual artifacts of the customer relationship over time. Like it or not, somebody in finance and legal is going to be involved with SFDC from the very beginning. If the system is the least bit successful, it's going to be a whole bunch of somebodies. So no matter what your function in the finance organization, you need to read the sections that apply to your job title and skim the rest.

Why is this enterprise system not like all other enterprise systems?[1]

If you think about your accounting system, the setup and ongoing maintenance is pretty straightforward. No politics. Business rules that change only over years. Indisputable right answers. In contrast, CRM systems are—must be—chaotic. The users are highly variable, work in organizations that live and breathe politics, and the business rules may change every quarter. Really.

So CRM systems are never "done," and if ongoing investment isn't needed . . . well, that's a sure sign that the system is not being used properly.[2] Of course, every company's situation is different, but look at Table 12-1, which compares CRM cost functions with traditional enterprise software.

You might wonder why the follow-on customizations are so much more than for traditional enterprise software. You don't ever *have* to do customizations, so the number could be zero. But SFDC is a platform disguised as an application, so its out-of-the-box feature set is just enough to get you going. But what about all the tricky things that make your sales, marketing, and support organizations really excel? Those features get added later.

---

1. Best said in an Eastern European accent while holding a glass of wine over a candle-lit dinner with the family.
2. Of course, the reverse is not true. In fact, explosive project costs and continuous rework of the same functional area is another sure sign that the system is not being developed and used properly.

Table 12-1   Software Cost Comparison

	Most Enterprise Software	CRM
Initial procurement (incl. add-ons)	$$$	$$
Initial customization	$$$$	$$
Data migration*	$$$	$$$
Integration†	$$	$$$
Training	$	$
Ongoing fees (incl. add-ons)	$	$$
Follow-on customizations	$	$$$

*   Data conversion and migration fees vary directly with the amount and quality of data migrated. Watch out: migration may be your single biggest cost item in the first year. See Chapter 2 for more on this topic.

†   Although small CRM systems are essentially standalone (so integration costs are zero), serious CRM implementations generally need to touch more areas of the business and therefore need to be integrated with more systems than any other category of enterprise software. Even though SFDC is probably the easiest system in the world to integrate with, system users will need more integration points (and broader data visibility)—particularly for the customer service and support function. Budget accordingly.

(In fact, we strongly recommend that you *not try to build it all at once*—that just doesn't work, and it wastes money.) For more on this, please read Chapter 4.

Driving the Investment Decision

For companies large enough to have a CFO—and most SFDC customers do—the investment decision about whether to adopt CRM, convert CRM systems, or expand the company's existing system deserves finance's attention.

The good news is that SFDC is the most popular cloud application for a reason: it has done a huge number of things right, and the company does well by its customers. The SFDC infrastructure is strong enough to comfort even the most curmudgeonly IT department, the security is solid, and the business model is proven. SFDC also has staying power, with over 100,000 customers and 1.5 million users providing a revenue annuity. That's all very nice, but you want to make sure that your company won't be contributing excessively to SFDC's annuity.

SFDC and nearly all of the third-party products geared toward SFDC are sold using a recurring revenue model, so the ROI evaluation will look different from what the finance team might be used to when dealing with hardware and enterprise software products. Nevertheless, it's important that they understand *the* key advantage of the cloud: no shelfware. Enterprise software sales teams are famous for providing terrific "discounts" on their products because they know that the day after the purchase is done, the customer will consider it a sunk cost. There will be little direct incentive to actually *use* the software, and many traditional software companies have made their fortunes by selling software for which 80% of the purchases sit collecting dust on the shelf. One of the most spectacular cases of this involved a State of California purchase of Oracle products—a $130 million transaction, yet only a few dozen users ever implemented the product. With recurring-revenue products, this kind of falloff doesn't happen. Because it's a pay-as-you-go model, if your users don't like the software or if your company decides not to use it, you simply turn those users off, or discontinue the system altogether.[3] This strategy provides a built-in insurance policy for the purchaser, providing protection against bad sales behaviors and changing internal priorities.

In evaluating the ROI for the SFDC decision, try to keep the big picture in mind. Financial personnel will have solid figures on procurement and operational costs as well as the potential for savings from cost avoidance and reduced labor. The more interesting value from SFDC comes from subtler benefits:

- **Sales effectiveness:** Shortening the sales cycle; increasing the win rate; increasing the upsell/resell/renewal rates; increasing the number of transactions a representative can handle without errors; reducing unnecessary travel; and improving forecasting accuracy.

- **Marketing efficiency:** Increasing the number of fully qualified leads; decreasing the number of dud leads; identifying and decreasing the use of poor-performing campaigns; understanding the true cost of customer acquisition; targeting profitable market segments better; and methodically prioritizing features.

- **Better customer support:** Lowering the cost of customer support; improving responsiveness, resulting in higher customer satisfaction numbers; increasing customer renewal/retention rates; improving visibility into repeat purchase patterns; and increasing sales profitability (seriously!). *Do not skimp on this area*, as a well-executed customer self-service portal can yield dramatic improvements in both support costs and customer satisfaction.

- **Better executive decisions:** Driving executive decisions more with facts and less with opinions, thanks to a 360-degree view of the customer and much better metrics on sales, marketing, and customer support; allocating more rational resources for items such as sales travel, loaner equipment, and proof-of-concept projects; and improving real-time visibility.

---

3. If you do cancel, you might as well wait until the end of the year because the cloud vendors won't let you out of your contract or provide any refunds. This is, after all, the software industry.

- **Streamlined internal operations:** Improving measurability and executive visibility; decreasing the amount of paper generated by and handled in the organization; eliminating wild goose chases caused by misplaced documents; decreasing search time for legal, financial, or marketing analysts; decreasing email volume by 20% or more; and shortening organizational learning curves.

- **Compliance:** Automating workflows, escalations, and alerts; auditing forecast changes; and preventing (or at least managing) service level agreement (SLA) violations.

The project team should be able to provide good estimates for the 3-year costs, expenses foregone, and revenue potential associated with adopting an SFDC system (as described in Chapter 1). Of course, you'll need to help the team members organize the spreadsheets so they fit with your standard model for evaluating investments, but the raw materials for your business case should be there already.

When it comes to negotiating the deal with SFDC and any third-party vendors, know that they won't offer the discounts with which you might be familiar. Of course, if you're buying 10,000 seat licenses for SFDC's `unlimited edition`, you can get a heck of a price. Most customers represent a much more modest deal, and SFDC can't afford to bend over backward for a 50-seat transaction. To get the best deal, try these tactics:

- Negotiate for the aggregate number of seats you'll need a year from now, but at the end of the day enable only those seats you need immediately and gradually add the new ones in real time.

- Know that SFDC is happy to do a pro-rata upgrade at any time but will not do downgrades except at renewal time (and may not allow downgrading even then).

- Use the standard end-of-quarter tricks, but know that SFDC's quarters are one month off from standard fiscal quarters (even for medium-sized deals, end-of-month effects can shave a point or two off the price).

- Find out if your company is eligible to use `single-application seats` to supplement `enterprise seats`, as they can significantly lower your average per-seat charge.

- Be willing to prepay fees for the first year or more, and be willing to contractually commit for 3 years or more (longer than that doesn't seem to make much difference).

- If you are converting from a system offered by one of SFDC's big competitors, negotiate some favors in exchange for their using you as a public reference.

- Try to get them to commit to continuing your first-year discount into *all* future renewal contracts. Almost certainly, the SFDC rep will balk at this—but then "back off" to a commitment for the next renewal contract. You may have trouble getting even this, but you'll never get it if you don't negotiate.

Cloud vendors have changed the formula for product costs, but the implementation can easily cost your company more than the licenses in the first year or two during which you run the system. The real cost of your SFDC implementation may take the form of consulting fees if users have lots of requirements for integrating the SFDC system with existing systems across the enterprise. Watch out for excessive requirements for integration and data migration,[4] as these are typically big components of the total project.

Once the initial investment in the SFDC system has been made, we generally recommend that extensions and improvements to the system be charged to the main user[5] department's budget. It's too easy for users (particularly in the sales department, which is often the leading user of the system) to ask for things when they are free. When their "great ideas" are paid for out of their department's own budget, they will magically become a bit more conservative.

Keeping Expectations Reasonable

The SFDC project is likely to be championed by the head of sales, the head of marketing, the head of customer support, and maybe even the CEO. This kind of clout is essential to ensuring the system's credibility and success, but it also tends to lead to overoptimism. One of finance's most valuable roles in the SFDC development process is to keep expectations reasonable so that people and departments do not become overtaxed.

Here are the key issues to consider when guiding executive expectations for the SFDC project:

- **Your company's risk tolerance:** SFDC should not be used simply as a way of automating existing processes and practices; its whole value lies in the ways it can improve business processes and change the rules of your business, both internally and competitively. But with this opportunity comes uncertainty. You may discover that some departments want to limit their risk, which means that some of the more aggressive expectations must be toned down.

---

4. Make sure to read the sections in Chapters 4 and 7 that cover these topics.
5. Typically, the biggest users of SFDC are the sales, marketing, and customer support departments. The easiest way to identify the big users is the number of seats the department has active in the system. Apportioning the budgetary "hits" should be based on either the number of users or the functional benefit that will be realized by each group. For example, an improvement to quoting should be paid for by sales and perhaps operations, not marketing or customer support.

- **Your company's agility and change-management abilities:** Some companies thrive on change, using alacrity as a competitive weapon. Other organizations view change negatively. The better your organization is at adapting to and profiting from change, the better it will be at managing business process change. These "type A" organizations can set more aggressive SFDC goals.

- **The intransigence of existing business processes:** In some organizations, customers, suppliers, and partners will enforce constraints on the organization's business processes no matter how good your company might be at internally adapting to change. If your supply-chain partners' "business rules" are inextricably tied to your organization's business processes, you need to tone down the more aggressive goals for SFDC. Here are some questions to calibrate the impact of these external entanglements:

  ➥ Which business processes could be radically simplified through automation? Which processes must stick around no matter what?

  ➥ Where could you simply remove paper and human intervention from a business process? Who would be upset if you did?

  ➥ How many trading partners insist on *not* changing the mechanisms and checkpoints of transactions? How many of them unilaterally mandate standards and dictate changes that impinge on your company's internal business processes?

  ➥ Which regulations or compliance issues can be satisfied only in a narrowly prescribed way? Where do you have freedom in the details of *how* to comply?

Once you've reined in the wilder expectations, it's time for triage. Sort business processes into three buckets: the ones you are trying to replace/eliminate/automate, the ones you are trying to extend/optimize, and the ones that must be left totally alone.

It's also a good idea to shepherd the creation of a set of specific success metrics at the executive level. For an SFDC project metric to be meaningful, you need an "as is" (before) measurement and a "to be" (after) metric of success. Don't let people fudge on defining these metrics—if it can't be quantified realistically, it's a "desirable goal" rather than a "success criterion."

The Path to Project Success

Although the SFDC project team will span many departments, it's important that members of the finance department play the role of referee in the politics that may develop around the project. This warning goes double if the IT organization reports into finance.

Once the decision has been made to undertake an SFDC implementation, three critical "soft factors" determine project success:

- The consistent enthusiasm and support of the executive champion(s). Raise red flags if the champion isn't engaged or has delegated too far down in the organization.

- The choice of project lead. This person needs to have a passion for CRM, a good understanding of the company's business, some political credibility, and experience in how to manage an ambitious project that spans several departments.

- Unswerving focus on user adoption. Focusing on features implementation is fool's gold, because without users, the system is just an empty shell. The only way for the system to have its positive impact is with enthusiastic users.

Accounting and Ongoing Operations

Once the SFDC system is up and running, there are some things personnel need to do across the company to ensure clean, consistent operations in finance.

The Quote to Cash Cycle

The most involved interactions between finance and sales personnel occur during the quote to cash cycle, and you should be pushing for controls as early as possible in this business process. As discussed in detail in Chapter 9:

- Special requests—for features, consulting, discounts, or contractual terms—should be requested via the SFDC system rather than through ad hoc emails. Putting these requests in the system lets finance personnel apply `approval cycles` to make sure that the right management reviews have been done before any commitment is made. More importantly, by attaching these requests to SFDC `opportunities`, it becomes straightforward to analyze the effect of approved "specials" on the win rate, deal size, and profitability. Setting up these `approval cycles` takes a few days' time but can make a big difference in the amount the company spends on variances.

- `Quotes` should be generated and rendered entirely within the SFDC system, and they should not be available for printing or emailing until they are complete and have gone through an SFDC-enforced financial or legal approval cycle. Quotes should be saved in a read-only format such as PDF that can't be edited by mischievous sales reps.

- Once a `quote` has been approved, it should not be editable without another SFDC automatic screening for discounting and terms (if the screening fails, another approval cycle will be automatically initiated).

- Once an order has been received, parts of the `opportunity` and `contract` records must be locked down to prevent meddling. The administrative part of the deal-closing process (legal confirmation, posting of the contract, and generation of the invoice) should be handled through SFDC's automatic `workflows`, with an increasing proportion of fields being locked down at each step.

- The company may want to have `contracts` be automatically generated from the SFDC system (in conjunction with Word or another application) to minimize the labor and error rate associated with data reentry. SFDC has very powerful templates and external-system interfaces, and it can be integrated with nearly any external application.[6]

- Using products from Adobe, DocuSign, and EchoSign, the entire `contract` generation and `approval process` should be configured to be automated and paperless. The cost savings can be dramatic, particularly if financial personnel have to manage hundreds of contracts. Further, at least in the U.S. market, postal or fax signature cycles add delay and have an antiquated, unprofessional appearance.

- At the end of the close cycle, the `opportunity`, `contract`, and associated detail records should not be editable by anyone except auditors or system administrators.

If you want to perform detailed searches or create `alerts`, `reports`, or `workflows` about a piece of information, the information needs to be stored in an SFDC field. As mentioned previously in this book, attached documents stored in SFDC are only partially searched. Thus, even if three documents show a contractual milestone date, if you need to see or search for that date from within SFDC, you'll need to add the data item as an explicit SFDC field. For example, renewal dates, price expiration dates, and renegotiation windows would need to be explicitly entered into SFDC's `contract` object.

Out of the box, SFDC provides very few roll-up views or fields. Instead, details about each `contract` are visible only from the `contract` record. For `account` management (such as when dealing with a customer who has a history of payment problems), it is very useful to create custom `roll-up fields` at the `account` level that summarize the overall situation, such as the following elements:

- Total number of orders

- Total value of orders

- A flag indicating in arrears

- Date of last order

---

6. All it takes is time and money.

To help manage the quote to cash cycle (particularly if you've integrated SFDC with the accounting, invoicing, order entry, and order management systems), you'll want to design several SFDC workflow `approval processes`, as well as `views`, `reports`, and `dashboards` to see items such as these:

- Discounts by product line

- Discounts by sales rep

- Discounts by region

- Billings by size

- Invoices by customer

- Days' sales outstanding

- Top 10 customers

- Top 10 in-arrears customers

- Top 10 non-renewing customers

Once an order is received, SFDC offers several areas of functionality that help record and organize information that accounting, finance, customer support, and legal personnel will want to see over time. SFDC can act as a centralized repository for the following items:

- RFI, RFQ, and quote information

- Statements of work (SOWs), schedules, milestones, and work-breakdown structures

- SLAs

- Licenses, authorizations, certificates, and serial numbers

- Contracts, exhibits, non-disclosure agreements, and addenda

- Engineering change orders (ECOs)

- Purchase orders

- Invoices

- Call notes

- Payment history

- Follow-up or callback tasks

Integrating SFDC with Financial Systems

Here are several important best practices regarding financial information and SFDC, which are particularly important if you integrate the system with your order entry, order management, or accounting systems:

- SFDC has a standard `account name` field, which should be used as the "friendly name" that most users would tend to search for (e.g., "Du Pont"). The system should be extended with a `custom field` that holds the customer's legal entity name, which should match the name used by legal and finance personnel (e.g., "E. I. DuPont de Nemours, Inc.").

- SFDC's `account` object should have `custom fields` pointing to the corresponding customer records in the order entry, order management, distribution, and accounting systems.

- The accounting and order entry systems (and the order management system if it is yet another system) should have pointers to the SFDC record. SFDC's `account` record identifier is an 18-character alphanumeric[7] value that is *case insensitive*.

- SFDC's `opportunity` object is the parent of all `quotes`, and the `opportunity` is where the most interesting customer data are found. Consequently, the pointer to the accounting system's order record should be stored there. SFDC's `opportunity` record identifier (again, an 18-character case-insensitive alphanumeric called a UOID) should be stored in the accounting system's order record.

- SFDC's `account` and `opportunity` objects need to follow a fairly strict naming convention. This name should be used in the accounting/order entry/order management system as the start of the "description" or "comments" field to make it easier to track customers and reconcile orders.

- If you use Excel extensively, watch out for its auto-mangling features for numbers, particularly if your company uses the CSV format for its data exchange. Read "The Joy of Regex" section in Chapter 3!

- SFDC should be left in single-currency mode unless you have an explicit need for `multi-currency` operation. Once you have determined you need multi-currency reporting and forecasting, the switchover must be carefully executed

---

7. Some SFDC reports and views present a truncated 15-character case-sensitive version of the UOID. These identifiers work, but it's better (for compatibility purposes) to always use the full 18-character version.

because it is disruptive to many parts of the system (particularly system integrations) and can never be reversed.[8]

- SFDC has settings for `fiscal year` and `business hours`. Make sure they agree with the settings in the other systems your company uses! Note that lots of historical records get wiped out if these are changed at some later time.

- SFDC provides a sophisticated and robust `forecasting` system, but it works only at the level of bookings. Although the system's `products` and `price list` functionality can be used to hold flags and schedules for revenue recognition at the stock-keeping unit (SKU—that is, line-item) level, you should not attempt to manage revenue-recognition events or calculate schedules within SFDC. Instead, use SFDC reports or outbound messages to send the needed data to your accounting system to enable a proper GAAP forecast of products and services.

- SFDC can store all of the company's products, orders, and all the other "raw data" needed for calculating commissions. However, the system does not offer any internal incentive or compensation management functionality, and you should not attempt to build this yourself in the system. It is surprising how often simply exporting SFDC data to spreadsheets is the right answer. Several powerful and elegant third-party incentive management systems plug in to SFDC or can be nicely integrated, but they are expensive and can be hard to manage. Check out Chapter 7 if you want to know more about these products.

- SFDC is very easily extended to accommodate new fields and new kinds of records. Before you attach new data to the system, however, make sure the data are in the right place so they will be well behaved over time. This means a bit of analysis prior to taking action—check out "A Guided Tour of the SFDC Object Model" in Chapter 2.

- SFDC also has a wide range of features (e.g., user data entry screens, email alerts, reports, dashboards) that should be leveraged by other applications. SFDC is one of the most easily integrated applications on the market, but it should not be used in place of an integration server or data warehouse. If you want to know more about what's possible, check out the discussion on integration in Chapter 7.

---

8. Note that switching on `multi-currency` is fairly straightforward before SFDC is integrated with the accounting or other financial systems. It is much less so once the accounting system has been integrated. Further, once `multi-currency` has been turned on, it can never be turned off in SFDC. So careful testing using SFDC's `sandbox` is urgently recommended.

- If you integrate SFDC with the accounting, order entry, or order management system, it is essential that `accounts` can be created and updated in SFDC long before they appear in your financial system(s). Your integration logic needs to allow for this functionality and should not attempt to create a customer record in the financial system(s) until a valid order has been placed in SFDC.

- If your company has grown through acquisition and has several CRM and financial systems, double-check any integration logic that may create `accounts` in SFDC or customers in the financial system(s). In consulting engagements, we have discovered nightmarish situations in which duplicate `account` (customer) names are created on a daily basis due to poor business process integration.

Profitability Analysis

The company's transaction history is the bedrock of product and service profitability analysis. But just using sales and cost data paints an incomplete and sometimes misleading picture of the company's success. Product profitability can be distorted by politically driven cost allocations,[9] and customer behaviors like upsells and repeat business are completely masked by conventional product sales analysis. Since repeat business is typically more profitable than initial customer acquisition, sequential analysis of sales is critical to understanding profit dynamics.

The whole point of a CRM system is to be able to track and analyze patterns of customer interactions over time. Work with the marketing team to identify

- Correlations among purchases (such as "80% of the time when we sell profitable product A is when we sell unprofitable product B")

- Profiles of customer profitability (such as "Our highest-profit customers are never our highest-volume customers")

- Inflection points in the sales cycle (such as "70% of the time when we do a free proof of concept [POC], we win the deal—but only if the POC is done before stage 5")

- Impact of references and referrals on sales (such as "70% of the leads that died noticed our negative references on Yelp")

Marketing people love to analyze and discover trends, and the real pros are more objective than either engineering or sales personnel when it comes to product or promotion investment decisions.

---

9. Dave Taber's theory: Whenever you have cost allocations and transfer pricing, you have politics.

The sales management team could help you with territory and channel profitability analysis, which can be seriously important given the cost and efficiency of many sales organizations. Unfortunately, because of political and budgetary self-interest, it is rare for them to be objective about it, even when they do help. But the CRM system has no political agenda, and if you have a careful data analyst with good SFDC skills, you can make serious headway in a hurry. Some significant data filtering or correction is almost always required, though, because of poor data quality practices:

- Incorrect territory assignments

- Empty partner assignment fields

- Incomplete or inaccurate addresses (needed to infer the previous two issues)

- Empty `contact role` records

- Undocumented meetings, loaner equipment, or POC costs

- Empty or inaccurate `amount` fields, even on closed `opportunities`

Note that none of these data quality issues is inherent to SFDC—but most sales organizations are pretty far away from best practices in their usage patterns (see Chapter 9 for guidance on the right way to get things done).

The management of customer service and support are typically more inclined to do cost or effort analysis on their own, because they are typically a cost center and want to be as efficient as possible. As natural problem solvers, they tend to have the needed Excel and math skills to provide you a solid starting point for your profitability analysis. Typically, the customer service and support people will have metrics for call center pipeline and throughput, time spent per case, percentage of cases handled via self-service, customer satisfaction surveys, renewal rates, and other objective measures.

Workflows and Streamlining

When properly implemented, SFDC is a great way to streamline a company's marketing, sales, order, and customer support operations. Its workflow system can be extended to go even further. If you're interested in the business process streamlining that's possible with SFDC, check out Chapter 8 for more information.

Even if you're not interested in workflow, a few principles should be followed as SFDC is implemented:

- Centralize as much sales, marketing, and support information as you can. SFDC provides worldwide, secure access via a Web browser, and the simple act of making information more consistently accessible can translate into a big difference in internal efficiency.

- Set an explicit goal to reduce your company's internal email by 10%, because each piece of information stored in SFDC should be able to save a couple of last-minute "Anybody know what's going on?" emails. If you use `chatter` correctly, you can set the goal at 20%. SFDC pushes companies toward a "kiosk" model of information—where anything users need to know is available on demand, in a consistent, reliable place—freeing them from the tyranny of email (which lowers productivity due to its "interruption model").

- Try to eliminate paper from at least 25% of business processes relating to sales, marketing, and customer service. You should also try to eliminate at least one external spreadsheet from a business process each quarter. Aside from adding costs, external spreadsheets and paper are painful to audit, because there are no formal access controls, approval cycles, or process-enforcement mechanisms. SFDC's built-in security and process controls take you a long way toward regulatory compliance.

- Move quickly down the path from SFA (which is focused just on sales) to true CRM functionality, as that is where the biggest payoffs happen. SFDC makes it very easy to move incrementally and is among the easiest applications in the world to integrate with. Unifying sales, marketing, support, order operations, and other groups' customer information can be the basis for obtaining a true 360-degree view of the customer—whether you're an executive or a worker bee who needs to know the state of play.

Cost Containment

Although your company probably already has an expense-tracking system, SFDC has a free add-on application that makes it easy for sales and field support personnel to put in expense claims and attribute their expenses to individual customers, projects, or contracts. For the field force, adding this functionality to SFDC is ideal for three reasons:

- These reps are already in the system, so they have no excuse to not enter a bit more data there.

- The add-on minimizes the amount of data entry and automatically correlates costs into the right buckets.

- Using SFDC's reporting engine allows for easy export of the expense data and, therefore, for integration into the company's standard expense-tracking application.

Process Controls, Security, and Compliance

SFDC has very fine-grained security, and it can be set up so that users can see or edit only the things they need to for that stage of the business process. In addition, most objects can be set up with full audit trails, so you know precisely who did what and when. SFDC also supports locking down records and approval cycles that ensure process compliance. Although configuring and maintaining all these controls can be tiresome, that's what security's all about, right?

Here are recommendations for SFDC's security system:

- As a matter of company policy, no one should be allowed to delete anything in the SFDC system. Users may be able to flag records as bad data or a dead deal, but the organization can never improve (or really comply) if users can autonomously expunge records from the system. By prohibiting deletion for everyone except system administrators, you'll have an extra measure of process assurance.

- For auditability, `field history` should be turned on for all objects in the system. These audit trails are free, and they can be turned on for as many as 20 fields per SFDC object, but they do have to be activated manually.

- For auditability and "data insurance," it is imperative to back up all the system data weekly. These free backups need to include all the `field history tables` and `documents`, so they can be big. But disk drives are even bigger, so you can store several backup cycles on almost any laptop. In addition, there needs to be a quarterly backup of the `login history` and `setup audit trail` tables,[10] which aren't included in the weekly backup. Task your IT team with this 5-minute weekly chore.

- `Data-sharing rules` should be relatively lax initially but should gradually tighten up so that reps and customer support users can see only the `accounts`, `opportunities`, and `contacts` that are within their purview. If other people need to see the `opportunity` records, consider using a `page layout` that hides the total order amount from them. The gradual tightening is needed to ensure that the security policy is not getting in the way of revenue generation. In addition, we recommend that the `view all forecasts` option be turned off to maintain a strict need-to-know hierarchy.

- For access control, `password policies`—including `login hours, allowed IP ranges,` VPN-only access, `auto-logout, account lockout,` and `password aging`—should start out a bit lax and then tighten up after the first few weeks of SFDC use. The reason for this guidance is system adoption: you don't

---

10. These are just CSV files.

want to provide *any* excuse for people not to use the system. Once they've become familiar with SFDC, make access controls a bit tighter after having notified the users of this plan (and given them a cheat sheet for when things go wrong). You'll know the policy is too strict if people are constantly getting locked out of the system because they forgot their password for the twelfth time this month.

- As a matter of policy, the number of people with administrative privileges should be kept to a bare minimum—typically between two and six people total. Because system administrators have complete visibility into every user, every significant action, and all the data managed by the system, this must be a highly trusted role. As with any IT system, never let an administrator become a disgruntled employee (or let a disgruntled employee become a system admin)—they can become a serious security and compliance risk.

- Leverage the system as an aid to regulatory and standards compliance. SFDC's `workflow` system, in conjunction with `record types` and conditional `page layouts`, can provide the core for an auditable process control system. Several companies have used this system as the basis for compliance with Sarbanes-Oxley Act (SOX) Sections 404 and 409. There are a couple of SOX modules available in SFDC's AppExchange.

HIDE THE REPORTS?

SFDC has a powerful and easy-to-use reporting system that gives users visibility into all their data.

That's the problem. Anyone who can access the reporting system at all can access pretty much *all* of it—and there isn't even an audit trail to indicate who has run which reports. A disgruntled or soon-to-depart sales rep can pull all of his or her contacts and contracts onto a paper, PDF, or Excel report that can walk out the door tonight. (SFDC's security lets them pull out only the specific data that they need to do their jobs—not *everyone's* data—but even that is a source of concern.)

Unfortunately, there isn't much subtlety in the choices for dealing with this issue: either let users have access or turn reports entirely off for certain types of users. Turning reports off isn't that draconian: those users can still receive standardized reports by email on a daily basis.

While you're at it, you need to think about Outlook synchronization. This feature is both useful and secure, but it means that employees can download all of the company's contacts at the click of a button. Again, this is an all-or-nothing decision.

These are judgment calls but ones you and the IT team should explicitly make. Check out Chapter 13 if you want to know more.

- Explore the AppExchange for add-on products for more general compliance around email, SFDC record content, `chatter` conversations, and attached files. These are all subject to legal discovery, so you need to make sure there is as much solid automation and reporting around this as possible.

- Because users frequently misunderstand compliance requirements, set up a `chatter group` about standards and practices. You can also use the system to publish PDFs of process manuals, but there's nothing like `chatter` to get real-time response to people who are curious or confused.

Investor Relations

Wall Street analysts, private-placement firms, and other investors are a valuable constituency that must be skillfully managed. Although most SFDC clients do not have a full-time person dedicated to investor relations (IR), larger companies (particularly *Fortune* 500 conglomerates) will have not only a full-time IR person but an entire IR agency. If your company is large enough to have these functions, or if it runs an investors' conference, SFDC can be configured to help.

The idea is to improve collaboration inside and outside the company. Outlook and Excel are the lingua franca of finance, but they are quite clumsy when it comes to cross-company collaboration (e.g., between a company and its IR firm). SFDC's Web-based functionality is a great way to coordinate and collaborate on your IR projects. `Chatter` allows you to confer in a secure way that is much more organized than email.

SFDC has developed a free add-on (available in the AppExchange) designed around the needs and workflow of the PR team, as discussed in Chapter 10. This add-on provides all the basics for the PR function, and it can be easily modified and extended to match the workflow of nearly any IR team.

After you've read Chapter 10's description of the free PR add-on, here are some extra considerations for managing investor relations:

- Keep all the detailed personal information on `contacts` in Outlook (or your favorite contact management or email tool). Don't try to synchronize this database with SFDC—this effort will be more trouble than it's worth in the world of IR. You will need to create IR `contacts` in SFDC, which can easily be done as a one-time import of a CSV file dumped from the main `contacts` database. All that really needs to be imported into SFDC is each person's name and email address. These IR `contacts` will be a different `record type` so that they can have special `fields`, `page layouts`, and `workflows` that other records don't have.

- Run the investor bulk mailings from within the SFDC system (its functionality works well with lists containing as many as 200 emails per blast). Typically, there's no point in setting up a `campaign` to track responses from individual mailings, but if you have the energy to do so, knock yourself out.

- Make your IR team's position in the `role  hierarchy` such that nobody outside of finance can see their records.

- For the SFDC `contacts`, create one or two new values for the `type` pick list so you can identify the main roles your IR targets have (e.g., analyst versus mutual fund manager).

- Put investor firm names in the SFDC system as `accounts`. Again, create a `record  type` and `page  layout` for investors and one or two new values for the `type` pick list to keep these `accounts` separate from your company's prospects and customers.

Mergers, Integrations, and Divestitures

The topic of mergers, integrations, and divestitures has two sides: the strategic work of identifying and developing the mergers and acquisition (M&A), spin-off, or carve-out, and the operational work of actually making the change in corporate structure.

The Strategic Side of M&A and Divestitures

If your firm does an acquisition or divestiture only infrequently, SFDC will not add a lot of value to your corporate development group. However, if the company is constantly being pitched deals, needs to evaluate several candidates at a time, or does an acquisition or divestiture several times per year, SFDC can make life much easier for the folks charged with managing those deals. Indeed, hundreds of venture capitalists and private equity firms use SFDC all the time for managing their deal flows and capital calls.

SFDC provides a free template for M&A operations that creates several `custom objects` that are relevant for tracking and evaluating candidates over time. Features such as special records for quarterly financials, sources of referrals, intermediary fees, funding sources, and valuations can be quickly enabled. Due to the confidential nature of this information, it is imperative that you implement the `role  hierarchy, record types`, and `page  layouts` to keep this strategic information safe from prying eyes. That said, the centralized nature of SFDC—and the fact that most executives will have logins to the system already—make it an ideal way to share information among the people with a need to know.

With a small amount of `VisualForce` development, specially formatted screens can be created for the corporate development team. `VisualForce` and outboard tools can even generate deal-summary one-pagers at the click of a button for strategic review meetings.

The Operational Side of M&A or Divestitures

The operational aspects of mergers, acquisitions, and divestitures comprise a big topic requiring some special attention with respect to SFDC, particularly when the system is highly integrated with other systems across the enterprise.

Any large structural change in the sales, marketing, or customer support departments will necessitate significant reworking of the SFDC system. Do not underestimate the effort required to cope with a merger—updating SFDC as the result of such a deal can be just as a big a project as the initial system implementation. Further, administrative and policy implications of mergers can be quite thorny, even if the system implementation is straightforward.

If you need to integrate another company's data with your company's existing SFDC system, there is an easy path: if both companies use SFDC already, you can use the `Salesforce to Salesforce` feature (it's free) to span the two instances. If, however, the other company has a different CRM system, it may be less disruptive to convert that company's data to its own SFDC instance (the plan being to run two instances indefinitely, spanned by `Salesforce to Salesforce`) than to bring those data directly into your company's existing SFDC instance. Talk with your SFDC sales rep and your favorite consultant for the latest guidance on this issue.

If you're going in the other direction and the company plans to divest itself of a division, there's some real work to do—but it's a lot simpler than integration. The basic approach is to buy a second SFDC instance, do a full dump of the existing instance's data, clone its configuration (using `packages` and the force.com Eclipse add-on), filter out only the things that are relevant to the divested division, and load all of the relevant data in the instance. I've made this process sound much easier (and weeks shorter) than it really is, but from a purely SFDC perspective, it's a straightforward project. That said, dis-integrating SFDC's connections to external systems can involve much more serious work.

Fundraising

Whether you work for a pre-IPO (initial public offering) company looking for your next round of funding, a public firm planning a secondary offering, a VC or private equity firm doing a fundraiser, or a not-for-profit organization looking for institutional grants, SFDC can be a very helpful tool for executive staff. SFDC can be used in three distinct contexts:

- As a standalone tool for investors (typically the `professional` or `enterprise edition`)

- As a standalone tool for fundraisers (typically the `professional edition`)

- As a fundraising tool in conjunction with SFDC's normal roles in sales, marketing, and customer support (must be the `enterprise` or `unlimited edition`)

SFDC provides a couple of free configurations tailored to the needs of venture capitalists, private equity, and nonprofit organizations, with a series of prefabricated `custom objects`, `relationships`, and `record types` that can be further customized to your organization's operational needs. Due to the subtle nature of long-term relationship management that's part of the investment banking world, you'll need to do *very* careful analysis of your deal flow, business processes, and information-sharing model before any implementation work is done. In my firm's investment banking engagements, just discovering and understanding these factors can account for 20% of the overall SFDC implementation effort.

If you work for an investment firm, the "later stage" your investment focus is, the more important historical data will be. This means a more complex object model and a much higher cost of migrating the existing database to the SFDC system. If your historical data are really a mess, cleansing and enriching the data can be twice as expensive as most CRM data—and this can amount to several dollars per record. So evaluate the business value of migrating each batch of historical data.

If you work at a nonprofit organization, and particularly one that targets individuals with large numbers of postal mail, email, and phone campaigns, the cost of migrating the existing `contact` information is relatively small (typically, the `contact` information consists of just the target's name, mailing address, email address, and phone). However, if you need to import the donation history and discussions with donors, the cost of properly migrating the data can reach several dollars per record (even more if there's substantial information on paper). So do the cost–benefit thing before you start on a giant historical import.

Legal

In most companies, the legal function works closely with finance, particularly on contractual and policy issues. Here are the things that legal personnel should know about working with SFDC.

Information Retention

SFDC is a cloud application that delivers all functionality from Salesforce.com's computation centers. SFDC stores essentially no information on any of your company's computers—it's all stored "in the cloud" of the Internet. SFDC has implemented very tight internal security, has duplicated its data centers, and runs continuous backups of all client companies' data.

On a practical level, this means that anything put into a cloud system will be stored indefinitely. Even if your company's personnel delete data, that information resides in the cloud's archive somewhere and can be recovered as part of a discovery process (although recovery of that data would be anything but free). For this reason, legal personnel need to extend their company's information storage retention policy to cover SFDC (and to cloud vendors in general).

The good news is that SFDC's parametric records are relatively benign from a legal point of view (take a look at the screens and you'll see what's in the record). It is a best practice to forbid the storage of personal financial or health-oriented information (such as Social Security, credit card, bank account, and insurance numbers) in SFDC. Go ahead and forbid with my blessing.

The less-good news is that SFDC allows the storage of arbitrary files as record attachments, which means "you don't know what's in there." You should encourage storing PDF files containing things like signature pages and installation diagrams in SFDC, but it's a good idea to forbid users from uploading photos, videos, or other large files to the SFDC system.

Back to the good news department, there are a number of add-on products that make it easy to store documents on your own file servers or in file services such as Box, but the links to the files are presented within SFDC pages. This means that you can have the centralized management of information with the underlying file and information retention issues managed within the four walls of your company. Check out Chapter 7 for more on this.

Privacy and Personal Information

SFDC has a hard-earned reputation when it comes to securing and protecting its customers' information, and they are quite proactive when there is even a hint of breach issues. They are TRUSTe certified, SysTrust audited, and have passed ISO 27001 and SAS 70 Type II testing.

But the real privacy and personal information issues in CRM are on your side of the fence: in your policies, practices, and people. Throughout this book, we give guidance on best practices for the marketing, sales, and support people: our general tack is always "avoid the problem in the first place," as many security issues are caused by "great ideas" that weren't all that desirable even if they'd been executed right.

The specifics?

- Don't store personal financial, educational, or medical information in SFDC at all unless it is absolutely unavoidable.

- If you have to store personal information in the system, encrypt those fields (the overall system is already encrypted, but this is a second layer of protection).

- For citizens of the European Union, store their information in an instance of SFDC running in Europe (one of the "EU" clusters). See Chapter 7's "Who Owns the Data Now?" section for more on this.

- If you work for a large company, get Safe Harbor certified for EU, German, Swedish, and UK Internet privacy requirements.

- Make sure to have users explicitly acknowledge that you are storing their personal information *before they give you the data* in Web forms.

The coolest thing in the CRM world right now is also the most problematic from a legal standpoint: social media. There is unquestionably a lot to be gained—both revenue increases and lower costs—from social media in marketing, selling, and supporting your products. But the standards and practices are not well evolved, and most of the practitioners are not "process people." So make sure that the privacy policy, terms of use, and related verbiage shown to your community pages properly reflect what you will actually be doing. Of course, this is not an SFDC-specific concern, but the data from those social media activities will be stored in the system, so you need to be aware of this.

Contract Generation

SFDC can be configured and integrated to feed customer and order information into your existing contract generation system (of course, it won't do so until the final approvals are in place, but the mechanism for all this is there in SFDC). This strategy works equally well with full legal content management systems or with simple Word templates (if your organization is a small company).

If you want to exert better control over contracts, SFDC can be configured to generate contracts from standard boilerplate without resorting to an external Word document. The system generates an uneditable, digitally signed PDF document, so you have solid control over exactly what the customer receives. Any of the options mentioned here can be configured with a few days' consulting work.

Contract Storage

As discussed earlier in this chapter, it is a best practice to store customer contracts as PDFs in SFDC, attached to the system's `contract` record.

Once you've gotten your mind around this idea, you'll discover that SFDC is equally useful for storing and tracking your partner and supplier contracts. Although a bit of extra customization is required to implement this process, the leverage it provides for both the financial and legal functions can pay for the consulting work in just a few months. Of course, if your company already has a legal content management system, it makes more sense to leave all of the contracts where they are and simply provide pointers to the contract locations from within SFDC's records.

Human Resources

In many companies, HR works closely with the legal and finance departments and sometimes reports into the CFO. SFDC isn't a tool that HR personnel typically use very often, but there are still some considerations for the HR function when this system is implemented:

- It's a good idea to put internal contact information for all employees into the SFDC system. This database is secure, and having everyone's internal phone number, mobile phone number, location, and email address available is helpful for any SFDC user. If your company has a global employee directory (such as an LDAP database or Exchange GAL), it should be integrated with SFDC's `user` record.

- It is *not* a good idea to put employees' personal information in the SFDC system, such as home address, home phone, or any compensation or financial information. If these data are stored in SFDC, you should lock down those fields with `field-level security`, `record types`, and `page layouts` to keep prying eyes away.

- SFDC is not particularly appropriate for a general HR management system. Of course, SFDC could be configured to do nearly anything—and there are a number of add-ons that are helpful for recruiting and other HR use cases. Under most circumstances, HR applications shouldn't be built from scratch in SFDC; instead, buy them in the AppExchange.

- If your company has a nearly continuous talent identification and recruiting need (particularly in professional services or high tech), you should think about the recruiting process as similar to a sales process. Take a look at one of the many AppExchange add-ons that configure SFDC to match almost any recruiting process, providing a central repository of opening and candidate information with interview and offer approval cycles, nice reports, metrics, and management dashboards.

- Set up `chatter groups` for hot topics in the recruiting and HR areas. You can always use the system to publish PDFs, but there's nothing like the responsiveness of an IM channel focused on a topic to get people engaged.

- If you are looking into continuous performance feedback systems such as gamification or 360-degree input, take a look at SFDC's `work.com` feature. It provides a cool mechanism for collaborative performance appraisals and is particularly appropriate for sales and support personnel.

GETTING THE MOST FROM **SFDC**

- Work closely with the SFDC implementation team to help them prepare the business case for the project. The ROI usually comes from revenue upsides and greater company throughput, not cost control.

- SFDC will be most obviously beneficial in the revenue-generation business processes.

- Cloud computing and Agile project management mean an incremental style of development and deployment. SFDC is surprisingly flexible and, when done right, will stay that way. But these advantages require some behavior modification when it comes to decision making and resource allocation over time. You're missing out if you treat this like "traditional IT."

- You will want to put in process controls and approval cycles to make sure that quotes and contracts can never make it to the customer without proper management, finance, and legal reviews.

- SFDC will provide you a whole new level of data about purchase patterns (or . . . lack of purchase patterns) that will transform the way you think about and analyze product profitability. Work closely with the analytical types in marketing and support to understand the correct way to interpret the CRM data.

- SFDC also contains a range of new security, workflow, and compliance functionalities. These features need to be configured to really work for your business, but they're all part of the platform.

- Check out "Essential Extensions for Finance" in Chapter 7.

FOR SMALL COMPANIES

- SFDC provides more stuff than you'll ever use for finance and legal. All the real goodies require configuration and tailoring.

- If you're a startup, consider using SFDC for your next fundraiser.

- Invest, but don't overinvest, in SFDC.

FOR LARGE ENTERPRISES

- In evaluating the business case, don't neglect the subtler benefits listed in "Making the Business Case" in Chapter 1.

- Don't let executive expectations for the system spiral out of control. There is cool stuff that's free, but the bright shiny objects are usually expensive.

- If you work for a public company, consider using SFDC for investor relations or PR.

- You might find SFDC useful as a recruiting database.

- If you're merging or acquiring another company, the upgrades to the CRM system will not be trivial. Make sure CRM is on the integration team's agenda.

CHAPTER 13

Best Practices in IT

The three most dangerous things in information technology are a programmer with a soldering iron, a manager who codes, and a tech support guy who gets ideas.

—Anonymous

This chapter is for everyone who works in information technology—whether employee or consultant. Most IT people already have most of the skills, knowledge, experience, and attitudes they need for a smooth, successful implementation of Salesforce.com (SFDC). But if you've never worked with SFDC or been part of an Agile project before, there are a few critical twists. This chapter explores three key issues for IT personnel: policy, data quality, and administration.

Before we start on the details, it's important to get one point across: SFDC is unique among cloud applications in that it is not just an application—it's a real development and deployment platform. In addition to over 1,500 add-on applications, over 1 billion lines of code have been deployed into production by over 100,000 developers. At peak times, SFDC is now running well over 1 million transactions a minute serving customers' custom APEX[1] code, plus over 250 billion total transactions a year. So even if the current plan is for SFDC to be "just another app" in its initial deployment, if it's successful in your company, it will grow to be much more than that. If the old saying is true that the best CRM applications are built, not bought, then your SFDC instance can grow into being one of the best CRM applications around. But that grandiose possibility will never happen without the help of the IT team.

---

1. APEX is a Java-esque language used for business logic and database queries/searches. It's not clear from SFDC's data whether the number claimed is database queries or class calls—but it's a million of something a minute, served by over 2,000 Intel processors spread across 15 clusters.

Level of IT Engagement

Although SFDC sales reps might say that IT does not need to be involved with the SFDC system, if your company is large enough to have an IT department, it's a safe bet that your team should be involved with the system at least on an advisory and oversight basis. Although SFDC is "just an application," it's pretty far-reaching. IT folks will quickly notice global ramifications of application decisions that users and business analysts are bound to miss.

If you've never deployed or worked with a significant software as a service (SaaS) application before, there is a bit of a learning curve, because the cloud changes a lot of the rules for applications software. Here are the key things you need to look out for:

- Initial decision making is different, because the cost functions and benefit streams have different timing. The up-front payment is low because there's no hardware or software to procure, and there are no upgrade fees for new versions. Payments are steady and predictable, not lumpy—but the fees continue forever. On the benefits side, a basic system can be operational in 6 weeks, so time to value is much quicker than with on-premises software. Consequently, don't try to apply the "standard decision template" for Enterprise, on-premises software to SFDC.

- SFDC tends to stay much more malleable over time than most applications. Making a change to the system a year from now will cost almost the same as it would to make the change now, unless there are data implications to the change. Consequently, there is no advantage to traditional waterfall project management—in fact, there are economic and technical disadvantages. SFDC is ideally suited for incremental improvements and the Agile model of development. It is inadvisable to try to deploy all the required features during the first year of use. SFDC stays malleable over time *except* in the areas where custom code has been inserted: in those areas, it becomes just as inflexible as the systems you're used to.

- SFDC is almost always paid for and run out of the sales, marketing, or customer support department. Although IT personnel may be called upon to work on the system occasionally, the expenditures rarely hit the IT budget directly. In fact, we recommend (for the clearest decision making) that the budget for any work IT does on the SFDC system be a transfer *into* the IT budget rather than a drain on it.

- In many parts of the SFDC project, there isn't that much for the IT team to actually deploy, particularly in the first year. However, your team will need to fill some important roles:

  - ➥ Oversight for security, policy enforcement, compliance, and asset protection

  - ➥ SSO, VPN, firewall, and related access control/security issues

➥ Guidance on architectural issues and ramifications of decisions

➥ Helping the users understand and specify what they want in reports (errors here cause no end of trouble later in the project—more on this later in the chapter)

➥ Access strategies for data in other systems, mashups, migrations, or integrations

- Many SFDC development, extension, and integration projects may be completed entirely without the assistance of central IT, because the required resources and interfaces are entirely in the cloud. SFDC also has over 1,500 add-on products that extend and integrate the system, and half of them are free. (See Chapter 7 to find out more about these applications in SFDC's AppExchange.)

- Almost every truly successful SFDC implementation will need to integrate with existing software in the company's network. The IT team must be intimately involved with this process, and integration usually involves just as much effort for SFDC as it would any packaged enterprise application. Keep your eyes open for the "signal flare" represented by an SFDC upgrade to the `enterprise edition`, as this is the minimal version for any real external integration.

- After deployment, user departments can be almost entirely self-sufficient. For example, users will never call the IT department and ask for help in rebooting a machine because of SFDC issues (although they will call the help desk when they lock themselves out of the system because they forgot their passwords). Further, users can call consultants in to make system modifications or extensions without needing to call IT, because the changes are usually entirely in the cloud, not in the company's internal systems.

- System administration can be largely delegated to user groups (assuming, of course, that they are adequately trained). Many SFDC systems are largely stand-alone entities, so there's no intrinsic need to involve IT in their administration. Of course, once SFDC has been integrated with the company's other systems, you'll need to have a federated model for administering the systems in tandem. SFDC, fortunately, makes it pretty easy to create this model.

- Performance and operations for cloud applications are mostly out of IT's hands, because the vendor takes care of all aspects of its application's uptime and performance. SFDC has a very good record indeed of operational continuity, and the company provides several weeks' notice for planned downtime. Most of the time, the SFDC servers respond to user interactions within 250 milliseconds, and they publish real-time statistics on their Web site (http://trust.salesforce.com).

In most cases, however, the *perceived* performance of SFDC in your headquarters building will be somewhat slower than what you'd get with an on-premises application due to network latency. Conversely, SFDC will be perceived as much faster in other buildings and remote offices (particularly those located outside the United States). Perceived performance really takes a hit if your network has latency problems or drops a lot of packets during busy hours. SFDC has several Web 2.0 features that make for fairly large page sizes, and interrupted refreshes make the system look very slow. These problems are particularly noticeable on marginal WiFi links. If you measure a lot of packet drops, SFDC will give you a good excuse to upgrade to those new base stations you wanted anyway.

- Another wrinkle on operations and performance occurs when cloud applications are integrated with one another. There will be no end of amusing finger-pointing among the vendors about performance, incompatibilities, and bugs, particularly if their products compete with each other. Be wary of this, and run performance and latency tests of each cloud system before you jump to any conclusions about which vendor is at fault.

- Because the company's IT department doesn't deploy much,[2] if anything, for the SFDC functionality, the IT personnel have basically no involvement in, or control over, patches and upgrades: they simply appear, and the users *can't* stick with the old version. Fortunately, SFDC's quality and compatibility have been very high, and the company gives plenty of advance notice regarding upcoming changes.

- Security and disaster recovery are also largely out of the IT department's hands. SFDC has a very solid security track record, and it has invested millions in establishing highly available, distributed data centers for disaster recovery. The company performs continuous replication and online backup, and its servers have proved very resilient to attack and compound hardware failures.

  However, security and disaster recovery issues become complicated with the addition of third-party add-ons (which are typically running in entirely separate cloud data centers). If your company's internal IT teams have tough standards, make sure that they notify everyone on the SFDC team that all third-party SaaS products and integration adaptors must be screened and tested prior to purchase.

- Information leak protection (ILP) is always a hot topic, particularly when the information is customer records, leads, and transaction history. Throughout the book we have urgently advised that highly sensitive customer information—credit

---

2. In a vanilla SFDC deployment, everything is in the cloud. But there are several AppExchange add-on products (for things like email synchronization, document storage, or SSO) that do require deployment of software on the user's PC. And there are some integration engines that require installation on VMs or servers. These are almost always simple MSI packages that install COM or .Net libraries and an add-on or two to extend existing apps. If you decide to use any of these add-ons, they'll need to be vetted in your labs and installed with your standard administrative infrastructure.

card numbers, Social Security numbers, bank account numbers, ACH/SWIFT routing numbers, FEIN or state corporation numbers, and health-related information—*not* be stored in the SFDC database at all. SFDC has done a good job of protecting information with fine-grained field-level access, role-based privileges, field encryption, and audit trails for logins and changes. Nevertheless, if a user is authorized to see a piece of data, he or she *will* be able to pull it out of the system as an Excel spreadsheet or print it as an HTML page. It will be important for IT personnel to set up their company's ILP system to recognize SFDC .csv or .xls files and block them from being attached to emails or downloaded to external storage media. Of course, because SFDC is available to any authorized user machine,[3] your ILP software would need to be installed on users' home machines and laptops before they can be permitted to log in to the system.

What's All This Noise about Chatter?

It's not like the world needs yet another instant messaging service. But don't worry, that's not what `chatter` is.

The whole promise of `chatter` is that it's *not* a general-purpose IM or social media platform. Its use case is focused on collaboration within a defined, self-selected community. And its user personas are in departments all over the enterprise (and outsiders can be invited in, for free).

The whole point of `chatter` is about collaborative problem solving, something that even the smallest organization has trouble with. But as an organization gets larger, more geographically diverse, and more virtual, problems with simple visibility and coordination can become acute. The old days of solving a problem by "running into Joe in the coffee room" are over, because the virtual office is any Starbucks or airport lounge.

Sales and service functions in particular have grown increasingly virtual, with many reps having no office at all. For sales, service, and marketing organizations, the natural center of gravity is already the CRM system. So having a collaboration medium baked into the CRM is a natural way to improve effectiveness. CRM is the virtual coffee room.

I'm now in my 30th year of using email in business, and I'm increasingly irritated by the inexorable increase in volume—even with spam filtering. As was reported in a study about office PC usage,[4] email and similar interrupting technologies lower IQ by more than 10 points (nearly a full standard deviation). I, for one, can't afford that.

---

3. Yes, the SFDC system has IP range restrictions, time-of-day restrictions, auto-logout, and strong password and authentication mechanisms. But once users are in the system, they're in.
4. http://www.cnn.com/2005/WORLD/europe/04/22/text.iq/.

The problem with email isn't just its interruptive nature (which can be solved with time management techniques): it's the ad-hocracy of how people organize information and communicate about it. How you might organize things for yourself may well confuse me. Threaded emails help, but those email threads aren't linked to any other structured information. So no matter how well organized your email box is, it's at best a bunch of sticky notes—not a library. Worse, nobody else can reap the value you've created in your private email box.

The model behind `chatter` is to thread the conversations within structured data, so when you're looking at either the database record or the conversation, you have a more complete picture. Done right, it turns your system into a library that everyone can see, saving a bunch of time for everyone who even looks at the record.

One of the metrics of success for `chatter` deployments is "How much internal email can be eliminated?" Ten percent is definitely achievable, and really disciplined deployments could do better than 20%. So ask yourself: how much would you like to increase your organization's collective IQ?

`Chatter` is on by default in SFDC. If you turn it off, you lose access to some nifty features (particularly in document storage and search). Sometime soon, parts of SFDC (notably `notes`, `tasks`, and `attachments`) are going to be replaced or significantly altered by extensions to `chatter`. Further, many areas of the UI will be reorganized around `chatter`, so Luddites will not be able to access the latest functionality.

It might be only a matter of time before the "off" switch for `chatter` is removed entirely from the system. With that planning assumption, the issue at hand is "How do we get ready for that day?" This is less an issue of technology than of organizational sociology around communication, security/access control, and netiquette. Because, just as with the transition to email 20 years ago, the fundamental issues are change management and improving the signal-to-noise ratio. If you're old enough to remember those days, that wasn't an instant transition for most businesses. A key success factor in `chatter` adoption is to identify clearly articulated use cases that fit naturally and intrinsically into the business processes, and don't try to force-fit `chatter` into every situation.

It's time to get ahead of that train.

Skills IT Will Need

There's a continuum of SFDC usage, from simple SFA to comprehensive CRM. On the pure SFA end of this continuum is standalone sales, marketing, and customer support functionality. IT won't need to learn very much here. The system has extensive online documentation, and it would be hard to take more than 2 weeks of classes. A couple of IT people could attend these educational sessions and then do mini "train the trainer" sessions for the few things that the help desk and system administrators would need to be ready to handle once the SFDC system is implemented.

In the middle of the spectrum are simple system extensions and customizations, which consist of either internal SFDC wizards or external file sharing, Excel macros, or Access queries. Again, there's almost nothing for IT personnel to learn beyond the SFDC object model (discussed in Chapter 2) and the report wizards. The most common external application integrated in this part of the spectrum will be an email blasting system (also known as *marketing automation*), which is itself a cloud application; this integration/ configuration task should almost always be handled by the third-party vendor.

At the CRM end of the spectrum is custom coding and integration of SFDC to systems that IT personnel are typically already familiar with. Integration of the IT applications with SFDC typically follows this functional order: quoting, order entry, eCommerce, accounting, inventory/distribution, bug tracking, professional services automation, content management, and analytics/business intelligence (see Figure 1-3 for an overview of the SFDC application landscape). Even though off-the-shelf adaptors are available for most standard applications and SFDC has a superb Web services API, the work to merge the data models that underlie the various systems can take several months and should involve the IT team. Even if your company uses consultants for this purpose, IT people need to determine the architecture, the rules, and the business process implications of changing data. Your team will likely already have most of the skills needed for this effort. But if you've never used Web services, there are some things to learn—and learning to use SFDC's API will require some homework.

There are many cases where real code needs to be developed and deployed into SFDC. This code is typically written in CSS, JavaScript, `VisualForce` (an HTML/XML derivative), `APEX` (a Java derivative), and SOQL (a SQL subset). You'll need classic development and testing skills for creating and implementing this code. As with most cloud development, you'll need to become adept at working in three to five languages at once and coping with debuggers that just don't help much. For further discussion of this topic, read the "IT and Web Team Organizational Readiness" section in Chapter 5. Also read the discussion of tools, and particularly "Essential System Administrator Tools" section, in Chapter 7.

One final area in which IT skills are needed is project management. SFDC lends itself to Agile project management techniques. Even though your company may have solid program or project managers, few of them will understand software project issues and almost none of them will "get" Agile techniques. At the very least, IT people should help train the project managers for the SFDC implementation and upgrade cycles so that they apply the right judgment calls for a smooth project deployment.

Training Wheels versus Racing Bikes

SFDC provides a wide array of features that are essential "training wheels" for early, quick implementations. The features are easy to understand, require zero coding, and are more or less user friendly. They are also dead wrong for anything sophisticated. An easy example is using multiple lookup fields on the same object (e.g., board member, attorney, and advisor on an `account`, all pointing to external `contacts`) because it's easier to understand and report on, rather than using a `junction object` ("external VIPs") that allows for an arbitrary number of people to be added to an `account`.[5] Other very common examples are using `lead sources` instead of `campaigns`, or sending lots of emails from `workflows`. Bad ideas all the way around.

The most critical training wheels for IT to examine are `validation rules`, `workflows`, and `flows` because these bits of automation will seriously conflict with custom coding. The two big issues with these technologies are the inability to fully control sequencing (leading to race conditions) and erroneous or misleading error messages (leading to panic attacks). I won't go into the specifics; just know that when you bump into these issues during debugging, you will start swearing.

The solution is this: as soon as you start doing any juicy `APEX` and `VisualForce` code, you'll want to replace all the logic from workflows and validation rules with `APEX` classes. This, along with all the test code you'll have to write, is a major undertaking. But it is in your future if you do serious development.

Take it one step further: SFDC's best practices guidance is that for any one object there be only one trigger, and all the work of the many triggers you may have written gets moved into supporting classes. This leads to a major refactoring exercise that Eclipse will help with somewhat. As you curse the hours you'll spend, just know that this is a "pay me now or pay me later" situation.

Now for the coup de grace. Remember error logs that were actually useful in debugging production problems that happen in the middle of the night? In cloud applications, those logs are just a fond memory unless you build code to capture error conditions and generate them yourself. SFDC, like nearly all cloud applications, has training-wheel logging: for performance and storage reasons, the logs are recorded only when they are explicitly requested, and they stop after a few transactions. Let's think about this: since the most important log events are issued during error conditions, the logs should really be stored outside of the system, pushed out by some nice Web-service classes. I've been looking for an SFDC add-on for this, but I have yet to find it.

You knew the job was dangerous when you took it.

---

5. You may know that there already is a junction object on the `account`, `opportunity`, and `case` objects to serve just this purpose. It's the "`contact roles`" object, which is typically all you need for this specific example.

Certification for the SFDC technologies is not required, strictly speaking, for any IT people. Perhaps ironically, taking a bunch of SFDC classes and getting certified won't prepare you for the real world, because you're likely to forget key things you learned in the class before you use them in a project. That said, being able to pass the certification exams without taking the classes is an important indicator of the depth of your experience and knowledge about SFDC. So passing the certification exams is a worthwhile milestone. SFDC has added a lot of new certifications lately. The one that most IT people should shoot for is Administrator (it's a prerequisite for many of the others anyway). The next step would be either Sales Cloud or Service Cloud—but unless you are a consultant, there's no point in doing both of them. Surprisingly, the Developer certification has nothing to do with coding: it's more about the object model and configuration. The more advanced certifications are a serious mark of distinction, but they are a PITA[6] to pass. Unless you have a penchant for test-taking, don't bother.[7]

THE SKILL OF ACCESSIBILITY

Because most SFDC users (and their management) will be organizationally very far away from the IT group, it's doubly important that IT personnel be approachable and accessible for help with SFDC projects. The non-IT people who will be making decisions probably don't know the right questions to ask about SFDC's technical details and won't realize the implications of their assumptions and wishful thinking.

To help the SFDC newbies, create a FAQ about IT's involvement and put it on the project wiki or Google Drive area. Set up a `chatter group` or two. Have an outreach phone conference with the project leaders (ideally, before they've signed any contracts) and get in the loop early to help the non-IT people avoid problems and bureaucratic delays. If your review boards meet only once per quarter, make sure to tell project managers about deadlines well in advance.

Planning for the Implementation

Although the SFDC sales rep and the users will want to rush into implementation yesterday, SFDC is an IT system: unplanned actions have untold consequences. If you haven't already done so, read Chapters 2 and 3 carefully. Read the "Who Owns the Data Now?" section in Chapter 6. Also, at least skim the Introduction and Chapters 1, 7, and 8 to get some context and expectations management tips for SFDC.

---

6. It's a kind of bread.
7. In fact, I didn't bother.

Here are some specific issues that only IT can think through and make sure fit well with your company policies.

Data Quality and the Continuity of Information

SFDC is destined to be the system of record for the customer master, so it is important that customer records be as meaningful and complete as possible. Here are some of the constraints and cross-currents IT personnel need to consider when developing standards for both data quality and continuity:

- Customer data should be complete for a horizon of 2 years, maybe a little longer. While "more is better," it also increases costs and delays of migration geometrically. Apply value engineering on the topic of data history: it is very unusual for anyone to care about orders or other customer interactions that are more than 5 years old. Even the IRS and the courts won't care what happens beyond 7 years.

- The company will need to develop policies for how much historical information will be brought into the SFDC system as part of the initial implementation and for the conditions under which information should be archived. While the goal is to keep information intact as much as possible, SFDC's storage costs (beyond the few gigabytes provided for free) can become an annoyance.

- The rule of thumb for customer-oriented data must be, "If it's not visible in SFDC, it doesn't exist," because that is the reality from an end user's perspective. Decisions will be made long before anyone has time to unpack and process an archive file, so keep the important stuff within a couple of mouse clicks.

- Despite the users' gotta-have-it-now focus, there must be a standard of quality for data to be allowed into SFDC: the new data must result in increased credibility and better ease of use for the system. Thus, if a data set contains a lot of duplicates, mismatches, or noise, it's better to keep those data out of the system until they can be brought up to snuff. The rationale here is the need to reinforce the virtuous circle: more confidence in the system means more users of the system, who bring in more data, which results in more visibility, which builds further confidence in the system. Bad data cause this cycle to run in reverse, causing a general degradation of the system's value. For most of the system's data, the data quality responsibilities fall on the marketing department. But for the data that is migrated or integrated from other sources, data quality is in your lap.

- Naming conventions and data standards will be critical for any level of scalability, particularly if SFDC is going to be extensively integrated with other systems. **The user community will not understand the importance of namespace design,**

so help them. Check out Chapter 2's section "What's in a Namespace?" because nobody else will get it.

- Unique external keys are fundamental for any hope of record matching and data quality when SFDC is integrated with external systems. The best candidates for universal keys are the email address, Facebook/LinkedIn handle, and cookie ID (for `leads` and `contacts`); the D-U-N-S number, Web site address, and main phone number (for `accounts`); and the transaction ID (or time stamp) for `opportunities`, `contracts`, and `cases`. Since you should not store Social Security numbers, credit card numbers, or other financial account numbers in the system at all, so do not recommend them as a matching key. Of course, SFDC generates its own unique UOID for every object in the system, but make sure to use the 18-character version of the UOID that is case insensitive.

- Certain SFDC features cannot be turned off once they are activated, and some records and objects cannot be deleted once they are created. Specifically, `user IDs`, `forecast hierarchies`, `person account record types`, `divisions`, `partner relationship management (PRM)`, `partner portals`,[8] `email to case`, `customizable forecasting`, `territory management`, `custom fiscal years`, and `multi-currency` can never be removed once they are instantiated. Although some of these items can be renamed, it is best that obsolete records and artifacts not be recycled because this practice is likely to confuse historical analytics and comparisons.

- Integrations need to be tolerant of system change, as most cloud system updates are compulsory and not under your control. The more systems with which the SFDC system is tightly integrated, the higher the likelihood of updates causing data corruption and duplicates. In a perfect world, these problems wouldn't happen—but in the real world, the tiniest revisions to integration code, upgrades to external applications, evolution of business process workflows, or even changes to pick-list values can cause new bugs to appear over time. Use an integration strategy that is as *loosely coupled* as possible to satisfy the company's business requirement, as a read-only mashup is far safer for the data in both SFDC and the external system than a "full-duplex" replication or synchronization scheme.

Once you've established those policies and standards, it's important to identify the owners of data quality for every phase of the SFDC project. During the initial construction and deployment, the implementation team (including the external system integration people) will own the problem: identify those individuals and assign them the tasks

---

8. If you have never enabled `partner portals` in your instance of SFDC, they are no longer available to you. They have been replaced by `chatter communities`.

of developing metrics and meeting objectives. After the system is live, the data quality problem will be owned mainly by the system administrators and architectural review team (see Chapter 4).

Be sure to read the "Backups, Replicas, and Snapshots" sidebar later in this chapter.

GO INSTANTIATE YOURSELF

SFDC's multi-tenant architecture creates an independent instance of the system for each customer org or instance. These instances are hosted in a pod or node (e.g., "na1.salesforce.com") comprising about 50 clustered multiprocessor servers running Oracle on Solaris and Linux. If you're new to SFDC, your instance will be created on one of the high-numbered pods, but they're all essentially the same.

For many large customers of SFDC, however, a new group of users may warrant a new instance of SFDC. Although I don't have an example of a single customer with more than 80 instances, I wouldn't be surprised to hear of one with 100. The issue isn't user count or performance;[9] it's flexibility and ease of administration. As with any server-intensive application, the more use cases you have in a single system, the more intricate the coding and security details become. Beyond a certain point, adding a new group to the system will degrade the ease of use and administerability for the existing users. Further, there are per-instance limits and governors[10] that increasingly come into play as the user base is scaled.

Of course, a multiple-instance strategy will present its own complexities, but they are only visible to IT. In a CRM application, simplicity for the users trumps having a weekend for you. It's never a simple decision, and sometimes users will not sit idly by while you think through the complexities—they simply get a new instance of SFDC turned on before you know about it. The new instance won't necessarily be on the same pod as the ones you already have. That's really not an issue, and there are several strategies (some free, some with third-party products and code) for keeping the multiple instances of SFDC in sync.

Architectural and Data Model Decisions

Even in the simplest SFDC project, there are decisions to be made about the data model and system architecture that will have far-reaching consequences—which many members of the implementation team will miss. Although most of these data model issues are fairly

---

9. Most SFDC instances have less than 1,000 full CRM users, and I dare you to find a single instance of SFDC with more than 35,000 users (mail me the factoids at users@sfdc-secrets.com and I'll send you a nice gift). Performance on these big instances scales just fine, but even small companies legitimately elect to spin up additional instances when the use cases and access controls of new groups are nearly contradictory.

10. Check out the latest version of the "Salesforce Limits Quick Reference Guide." It's fastest to just Google that name, as the URL for the PDF keeps changing inexplicably.

simple and reversible when the folly is discovered, some decisions are very painful to fix if you change your mind. So it's almost always a better idea to avoid the following three choices unless there is absolutely no alternative: `master/detail` records, standard `state` and `country` fields,[11] and `person-accounts`. There are some other areas where, if you change parameters, significant quantities of historical data get wiped out: `custom fiscal years` and `product schedules` are examples. There are also a bunch of other areas where things that seem similar are actually very different, so an inappropriate choice will cost the project (the more data put in before the change, the more painful the conversion will be later):

- `Notes` versus `tasks` versus `chatter posts`
- `Attachments` versus `documents` versus `content` versus `files`
- `Solutions` versus `knowledge`

Finally, there are a number of system features that can "never" be turned off once they are instantiated, so you'd better really mean it when you activate them (as these can add cruft and complexity even if you never use them again): `record types, person-accounts, forecast hierarchies, divisions, quotes, partner relationship management (PRM), partner portals, email to case, customizable forecasting, territory management, custom fiscal years, multi-currency`, and (the granddaddy of them all) `unlimited edition`.

Support and Administration

During the planning phase, it's a good idea to specify administrative policies and think through how help desk and administrative tasks will be handled during each phase of the system life cycle. Here are recommended best practices:

- Although duplicates and noisy data are annoying, best practices call for disabling the `delete` and `merge record` functions for all standard users. Although these users should be *flagging* records for deletion or consolidation, their flags should simply hide the bad data. System administrators need to do the data fixes promptly, but they won't be able to identify or solve root causes if users have "papered over" the problem by spontaneously deleting the errant records.

---

11. Always use the pick lists for a new instance, as the conversion from free-text fields to pick lists is a combination of root-canal and podiatry surgery: pain now, pain for weeks to come. If you have an existing system, assess the costs of conversion carefully before you start in.

- User login IDs (typically, this is the user's email address) must be unique for all users forever. For example, if a user's ID is joe@shmoe.com, the system must never let that ID be used again in any SFDC instance—even if that instance is in your company, and it's been years since the original "joe" left. This requirement is not especially onerous, but if your company has a lot of employees and some of them have common names[12] before the @, you'll want to develop some sort of a standard for these SFDC login IDs before assigning system IDs.

- Setting a policy for the user alias in SFDC is surprisingly important, particularly if you want to develop reports that automatically filter for an individual's perspective (e.g., "Show all tasks generated by Fred"). The aliases need to be unique, so a scheme based on first and last initials works only in the smallest implementations—even a three-initial strategy tends to fall apart after a few hundred users.[13] For larger user bases, we recommend assigning user aliases based on a nomenclature of first initial, middle initial, and last name. If overlaps still occur, we recommend adding a single digit at the end of the last names for the overlapping users. Another clever approach is to have the user alias be the first three characters of the department name, followed by a hyphen, followed by the three initials of the user (e.g., "SAL-ABC" or "FIN-JBS").

- The number of administrators should be kept to the bare minimum (to avoid data corruption and system misconfiguration problems) while satisfying the needs of users. In operations with one site and fewer than 100 users, a single SFDC administrator (with a backup who has privileges but rarely logs in) is sufficient. Even in large, multilocation operations, one administrator per "shift" (one for the Americas; one for Europe, Middle East, and Africa [EMEA]; and one for Asia/Australia) can be enough. I can't conceive of a situation requiring more than six administrators for a single instance of SFDC.

- Irrespective of the number of administrators, each of them needs to take a week's worth of SFDC training before he or she is allowed on the system. Even if "they've worked with SFDC before," the claims of competence are too often exaggerated. Besides, every 3 months, the administrative tasks become increasingly complex, and administrators regularly make visible, annoying mistakes when configuring

---

12. Bill Gates's email address was bill@microsoft.com for more than a decade, despite the size of his company. According to industry lore, Microsoft had more than 6,000 employees before the company hired another "Bill." Most companies will not have this level of discipline about email addresses and common names, so you may need to develop a standard whereby the user ID is not the same as the email address.

13. Even though the namespace for three alphabetic characters could theoretically cover 17,576 individuals, the distribution frequency of letters is by no means linear with names. In an Irish or Chinese company, a large proportion of the names will converge to only a few initials, and the three-character namespace will soon be exhausted.

the `security` and `access` privileges, `lead assignment rules`, `case assignment rules`, `escalation rules`, `workflow approval processes`, and other items that ought to be black and white. An undereducated administrator who wants to do a quick data import or cleanse and dedupe data can cause an amazing amount of damage in short order. SFDC has solid administrator certification tests and classes, and it's a great idea to send at least your main administrators to these sessions.

- Generally speaking, very few nonadministrative users should have access to importing tools and API access. This is an area where self-service is absolutely the wrong strategy.

- SFDC supports a number of administrative models, thanks to its very flexible role-based privileges. Although a "follow the sun" (shift-based) administrative model is easy to think through, it may not be flexible enough for the company's real needs (particularly at the end of the quarter, when everyone is stressed). Consider a delegated model (where power users local to an office can do some administrative actions and offload "administrivia" such as resetting passwords). In highly complex implementations with a lot of external integration points, it's a best practice to use a federated model, where individual administrators become subject-matter experts in particular areas of the system. To make any delegated administration model work, IT personnel will need to apply some sort of change-control aid. See Chapter 7 for more on the tools needed by system administrators.

Accessibility Features

SFDC has done a lot to make its system as friendly as possible to people with disabilities, and the "Section 508" features (required by the Americans with Disabilities Act [ADA]) may be particularly relevant if your company is a nonprofit organization or a government contractor.

As good as the SFDC system is, however, there's only so much that can be done with browser-based applications. The basic data entry and interaction pages are fairly accessible with keyboard shortcuts and "hooks" for readers and voice synthesis. To work well, the reader application must be able to handle frames, CSS, and JavaScript. Unfortunately, turning on accessibility mode inevitably disables some of the more advanced Web 2.0 features of SFDC. Further, some parts of the system—`calendars`, `dashboards`, more advanced pages, wizards, and administrative setup pages—do not meet accessibility standards. Although `VisualForce` pages that you build yourself can be made more ADA friendly, many of the third-party plugins found in the AppExchange are not likely to be up to snuff.

SFDC is likely to enhance the accessibility of the system over time, but people with special accessibility needs are unlikely to be productive in the current system beyond basic sales, marketing, and call center activities.

Security

Security is always a tradeoff. When I used to consult for the U.S. Department of Defense, the agency had A-level-compliant computers that were secure but nearly useless. B2-level-compliant computers were better, but it was still easy to get in irritating security catch-22s.

Of course, SFDC is not nearly as restrictive (indeed, the default configuration is very open), but it is based on Secure Sockets Layer (SSL) and carries an SAS 70 type II certification. SFDC can be configured for single sign-on (SSO) through the Lightweight Directory Access Protocol (LDAP) or OAuth. The system can be set up to achieve a high level of commercial security, using a wide range of controls that should be thought through prior to implementation and deployment. Indeed, a large SFDC instance may have over thousands of independent controls that cover, among other things:

- Field-level CRUD controls by user profile
- Field-level audit trails
- User role hierarchies (for data visibility)
- User profiles
- Profile-specific record type visibility
- User profile–level activity controls (e.g., reporting)
- Profile-level screen layouts and views for each object
- Conditional "lockdown" of data
- User-level sharing of records and forecasts
- Delegation of approvals
- Delegation of administrative privileges
- Login hours
- IP range restrictions
- Machine authorization
- Session auto-timeout
- Account lockout (after N unsuccessful login attempts)
- Password strength and aging

The proper security tradeoff seems to be where everyone can get their jobs done, 80% of users never have a problem, and 20% are occasionally irritated. For example, password settings should be tight enough so that one person forgets his or her password once a week and gets locked out of the system. In contrast, if dozens of users get locked out during the closing week of the quarter, the security policy has probably gone too far.

An important prerequisite for good security is having the support of the boss. The boss has to show that he or she cares about protecting company information, protecting the privacy of customer information, phishing, and information leakage. The boss has to authorize the budget for end-user training on security (only about 30 minutes—but for *every* user) and set up some sort of HR policy for identifying and dealing with the security risk posed by disgruntled employees.

An important area of security planning is developing policies for on-boarding new employees and off-boarding old ones. This process requires an explicit link from the HR function, and these policies should take immediate action as soon as the HR people know that an offer letter has been accepted or an employee has given notice.

Compliance

Given that SFDC has been deployed to over 100,000 companies around the world, it's a safe bet that it complies with any relevant regulations and standards. Of course, if your company has special requirements, check with your friendly SFDC sales rep. (Also, check the SFDC blogs and forums to see if there's been any chatter among the cognoscenti.)

Keep the SFDC data policy simple: any highly confidential or risky data should not be stored in the SFDC database. Even if some users need access to confidential data as part of their "SFDC activities," those data can be stored in an existing system of record and accessed via a read-only mashup or a pop-up window. Check out the discussion in Chapter 7 for more on this topic.

On the flip side, SFDC can help with compliance, thanks to its built-in workflow system and ability to lock down records (from writing or even reading) under conditions specified in the use case. The core facilities are in the system, and typically no coding is required to use them. There are also compliance add-on products for financial services and other industries, as noted in Chapter 7.

Integration

SFDC is one of the easiest systems in the world to integrate with. It has a well-documented and rich API, and its solid Web services architecture supports both inbound and outbound messaging via SOAP, ReST, JSON, and other mechanisms. Off-the-shelf adaptors are available from several companies (see Chapter 7) to link the SFDC system to hundreds of application packages or nearly any database you are using internally.

Integration with Microsoft Outlook is available as part of a free add-on from SFDC, but it is really suited only for one-way "synching" of emails, contacts, tasks, and events. The add-on runs inside the Outlook executable on the client PC. Although it can sync in two-way mode, the practical implications (in ease of use and risk of data duplication) of this mode may result in many wasted hours for users. This replication issue becomes even more obvious with Microsoft Exchange and shared folders. If your company needs ambitious and sophisticated integration between SFDC and Outlook, there are several alternatives from vendors such as Linkpoint 360 and Riva. Test before deploying!

Integration with Microsoft Office[14] (Excel and Word) is also available for free from SFDC, and these add-ons have worked well in most customer engagements. If you need to do some fancy stuff, the Excel connector is available as an open-source version. Of course, Office's .Net compatibility libraries let you do anything you want over Web services' SOAP calls—it's a simple matter of VB.net coding.[15]

Integration with IBM/Lotus Notes is also available as an AppExchange plugin for client PCs and Macs. I have no idea exactly which Lotus products are actually covered (probably only Mail and Organizer, versions 7 and 8), and I have not seen this add-on used in production. But it almost certainly works for someone—SFDC wouldn't have created the add-on if the company weren't on the hook to a big customer for this integration. If you look at SFDC's site, however, it's pretty clear their main purpose in integrating with Lotus Notes is that they want to migrate users away from it.

Integration with LDAP and OAuth is available from several sources, providing SSO capabilities for users. These adaptors typically run on one of your company's servers, but the best way to understand their deployment and configuration options is to do a trial evaluation of the software before the implementation starts in earnest.

There is a wide range of integration approaches and strategies, and every major integration and ETL vendor has an offering for SFDC. Read the section in Chapter 7 on this topic, as it's important for cost and security reasons to eliminate any marginal integration "requirements." As discussed in Chapters 1 and 4, it's important to do some "value engineering" analysis before committing to an ambitious integration program. The ongoing costs of integration can be just as significant as they are for custom application development.

Internal Safeguards

SFDC has a number of internal defenses against common Web and browser exploits. Their two-stage authentication is the most visible one, but they add new protections in

---

14. 32-bit versions running on the PC. Mac users pretty much get *bubkes*, unless they're impressed with running Windows in a VM on their lovely hardware.
15. And localization. And testing. And documentation. And maintenance. And the help desk.

the UI and `APEX` every couple of releases. For example, SFDC has implemented filters that screen out harmful characters in most output methods to block cross-site scripting (XSS) attacks. As long as you stick with standard `formulas`, `APEX` classes, and output methods, the threats of XSS flaws have been largely mitigated.

Further, all Web applications are vulnerable to cross-site request forgery (CSRF). Salesforce has specifically engineered protections in the language and executable framework, so applications built in `APEX`, `Visualforce`, and `Touch` platforms are protected by default. That said, the parts of your application that are built in JavaScript and other languages that interact directly with the SFDC platform still need to have protections explicitly written by the developer.

Implementation

If you haven't done so already, read all of Chapters 4 and 6 and their guidance on project management, deployment cycles, and the political side of user adoption. Even if members of the IT department aren't directly involved with all the topics described, knowing how the SFDC team works will help the IT professionals and SFDC mavens collaborate better.

Before you even start the implementation, set up a few `chatter groups` covering key players where conversations with the implementation team will need to happen. In addition, you should set up `chatter topics` for key areas of controversy: #data model, #user access, #security, #code, #add-ons, #data semantics, #business process, #triage, and so on.

During the SFDC implementation, the IT team may not need to do much directly in the system. Usually, SFDC's own professional services team is used or a specialist consultant is brought in. The reason: the core implementation is surprisingly short, and it's often not worth IT's time to gain the knowledge required. However, IT's assistance will be needed in the data import cycle described in Chapter 3.

IT personnel also need to be involved to make sure that key requirements and standards are being taken care of—and to make sure that "nice to have" features aren't being assigned an ridiculously high priority. The biggest enemies of a tight implementation project are

- Spurious requirements

- Anything that detracts from system credibility (in particular, unneeded fields or "feature-itis")

- Anything that causes scope creep

Here are some specific things to watch out for so as to keep the implementation team on track:

- Keep pages as sparse as possible. Use hidden fields, `page layouts`, `record types`, `collapsible sections`, and maybe `VisualForce` or JavaScript.

- Remove buttons that are ill-advised or "training wheels" options, such as `delete` or `merge`.

- Use `typed` fields, `pick lists`, and `lookup` fields as often as possible. Avoid `long-text` and `rich-text` fields.

- Use field `validation rules` (or, better, `VisualForce` pop-ups) for manual entry; auto-populate as many fields as possible with `formula fields`, `rollup fields`, `workflow rules`, and JavaScript or `APEX` code.

- Use `matrix reports` to quickly find data exceptions and problem trends; use Excel pivot tables to find even more data anomalies before they become problems.

- Prune the number of reports and report folders. The initial set of reports that comes with the SFDC system is overwhelming.

- Work closely with users in designing reports, views, and alerts at every stage of system implementation. As discussed in Chapter 2, many SFDC users do not know anything about the system's object model and aren't able to state their requirements in any other way than "I need a report that lets me see this by that" (you'll be lucky if they are even that clear). It will surprise you how many cases of "I need an alert when this happens" can mean fairly big changes to the object model. And most of the time, these hidden details are exposed late in the project. Hence the recommendation for an iterative, Agile style of deployment.

ONLY THE PARANOID SURVIVE

Andy Grove was right, but when it comes to SFDC security, paranoia is expensive.

It's easy to ask for security exceptions, complex logic, and special situations that will make for a manageability nightmare. SFDC provides very fine-grained control of user access and privileges, using a deceptively small number of fundamental control points. Every record in SFDC has a single `owner`, and every user has a single `role` and `profile`. The system uses a `role hierarchy`, which is used to exclude `users` from read or write access, and `sharing rules`, `sales teams`, `account teams`, and `manual sharing` (ACLs) that override the `role hierarchy` to add reinclusions.

The system supplements this with `profile`-level privileges that define what a user can create and see for each kind of record. But since the field-level access control is done as a combination of field, record type, profile, and CRUD setting, the stage is set for a combinatorial explosion. It's not at all uncommon to have the security settings composed of 1,000 Booleans plus 100 pick-list items in even a modest system. As a rule of thumb, you will need to get the users (and the risk management department) to streamline requirements when there are more than 100 of any[16] of the following: `roles`, `profiles`, `sharing rules`, `sales teams`, `account teams`, `public groups`, `queues`, `record types`, `page layouts`, `assignment rules`, or `mobile configurations`.

- Avoid frivolous use of JavaScript, `APEX`, and `VisualForce` code. If the features are really required, go for it. But for every function or page built using these technologies, there will be operational consequences, decreased flexibility, and diminished self-maintainability.

- Make sure that all the item-level, `user-defined help` items are populated with information that's comprehensible by real users. The system is self-documenting if you use it properly. Also make sure that user cheat sheets are written and stored both in the system's `documents` area and in the project wiki or Google Drive area.

- Implement the `Ideas` application for internal users. This free SFDC application is a great way to collect user feedback and understand ongoing priorities.

COMPLEX CALCULATIONS

SFDC has built-in math functions that can be used in formulas (`custom-field definitions`, `data validation`, `workflows`, `reports`, etc.), so virtually any simple calculation (à la Excel formulas) can be easily handled. The precision of calculation is greater than most calculators, which is more than enough for any business math. Although simple conditions can be handled (nested "if/then"), these formulas are simple functions, not algorithms. Anything that requires procedures, interim variables, fields from unrelated objects, queries, flow control, branching (`SWITCH` or `CASE` statements), or recursion (`FOR`, `WHILE`,

---

16. In a very large organization, you can take this "acceptable" number up to 250.

or loops) is off limits. For those, you'll need to use the APEX language (and then, users will not be able to modify the formulas at all).

In some situations, calculations have to be done outside of SFDC. For example, a license-key generator may need to manipulate variables of 100 significant digits and lookup data from a Web service. These are typically done via an external service (e.g., an Amazon Web Service [AWS] node), and the call out/return cycle is handled by an APEX class. It's an SMP.[17]

In a more common example, people may want to do some number crunching on SFDC data for ad hoc analytics. These are typically done with one of four strategies:

- File exchange (batch CSV files)
- Manual record "pull down" via the `Excel connector` or `data loader`
- Manual report "pull down" via the `Office adaptor`
- Real-time query using Excel's .net or SFDC's Office VBA library

A crafty VB developer can make an amazing number of things automatic and seamless in Excel or Access.

Implementing Data Quality

During the architecture and design phase, the most highly leveraged step the IT team can take is to remove unnecessary data items and restructure the data model to match the company's business processes. Left to their own devices, users tend to make several classic errors that contribute to the degradation of data quality:

- Too-lax security settings

- Too many system administrators

- Too many `roles` and `profiles` (one for every user)

- Confusing `roles` with `profiles`, and believing that they don't need to use both of them

- Confusing `record types` with `page layouts`, and believing that they don't need to use both of them

- Confusing the `role hierarchy` with the `forecast hierarchy`, and believing that they don't need to use both of them

---

17. A Simple Matter of Programming.

- Making the `role hierarchy` or the `forecast hierarchy` a direct reflection of the org chart

- `Custom fields` attached to the wrong objects

- Incorrect `custom objects`

- Sloppy or ill-conceived data imports

- Misconfigured data synchronization tools

- Erroneous formulas and Booleans used in `field changes`, `filters`, `assignment rules`, `autoresponse rules`, `workflow criteria`, `formulas`, and `data validation`

- Bogus `reports` and `dashboards` (particularly using the wrong join or filtering on the wrong field)

The good news is that fixing these issues is typically a one-time job. There won't be a lot of ongoing need for system fixes caused by users—particularly if you severely limit the number of system admins and lock most of the system down so that they can't hurt themselves.

During the construction phase, the team needs to build in as much data quality as possible (particularly using human-factors engineering) and invest in self-corrective mechanisms (particularly in system integration interfaces). For example:

- Building a `customer self-service` Web portal or `Chatter communities` page with an "account maintenance" page will enable customers to fix data quality problems and make updates on their own. Even though the customers and prospects will be updating only a few fields (e.g., contact information), the cumulative effect of all those data fixes can be amazing. Portals are the *only* economical way to do things if your company is a consumer-facing business with millions of records.

- Using an email-validation loop for new `lead` creation, cookies to identify return registration (as discussed in Chapter 10), and `campaigns` are great ways to cut down on the number of low-quality `leads` and `contact` duplication—perhaps by as much as 50%. That said, Captcha or similar bot-deflection techniques are usually overkill[18] for most customer communities. Clever use of `workflows` and internal filters can usually divert most of these.

---

18. The techniques work but are usually considered a hassle by the registrant. This leads to a simultaneous decrease in lead volume and lead quality (here the users retaliate to the implied insult of Captcha with bogus entries).

- Developing "query first" code for all external system integrations (particularly the Web site) can prevent the creation of duplicate `leads`, `contacts`, `accounts`, `opportunities`, and `cases`. As these records are typically the most visible data in the system, preventing duplication in these areas can yield a dramatic improvement in data quality.

- Implementing a data-enrichment service (such as SFDC's data.com `cleanse` mode) for `leads`, `contacts`, and `accounts` can mean important improvements in perceived data quality and completeness. These services, which can be implemented as a Web service in real time or on a nightly basis, can automatically validate data, correct typos, and provide expanded address and corporate demographic information.

- For external system integrations, using a data-queuing mechanism to handle SFDC timeouts or busy periods.

- Improving the data import and cleansing/enrichment processes will make a big difference in the value of the data, particularly for `leads`. Spend time developing templates, macros, scripts, and checklists that turn the `lead` preprocessing cycle into a repeatable, bug-free process. See Chapter 10 for more discussion of this topic. Note that the best marketing automation systems (MASs) provide a lot of automation in support of these process improvements.

SKY WRITING

So if your system is in the clouds, where should you be looking for the documentation? There's never been a good excuse for not commenting code or documenting systems, even though these practices are every bit as helpful to cost and quality as test-driven development are. But let's face it: documenting systems isn't exactly macho, and besides, it doesn't give you the ugly job security of unmaintainable code.

Working in the clouds, unfortunately, can give developers a new excuse: "I don't have any access or control over that (public-cloud) service, so I can't document anything about it."

Uh-huh. So, call their bluff this way: all consumers of a (public or private) cloud service need to document what the service does, how it's used, and what behaviors (including bugs and error conditions) the consuming side uses or depends on. Immediately, the whine will come: "But that means we have to document the same cloud service in every module we use it." To which your response should be, "Put your documentation info in a wiki, a Google Doc, or other collaborative system that the entire development and integration team can access."

This pushes everyone toward the best practice for the external interfaces and dependencies of modules and services: a centralized repository whose content is created and maintained by every member of the development team—as distributed as developers may be. In my experience, the alternative of having a centralized team responsible for creating and maintaining data dictionaries, entity-relationship models, business-process descriptions, or interface documentation produces only two things: an excuse for not doing documentation or, at best, obsolete or often incorrect tomes.

But is a wiki or Google Doc the best place to document the internals of a module or the administrivia of a variable? It's not a bad idea, but most of the time developers just won't be in the documentation area while they're hacking code or tweaking a variable inside an app. When they're working in their code, in-line commenting must not just be encouraged: it must be *measured*. For the code my firm develops, we don't allow any module to be checked in to the system unless at least 10% of the lines are explicit comments and another 10% of the lines have in-line remarks. The inline code requirement goes double for test modules, as it can be difficult to guess what a particular method is testing for and where to look in the module under test when there is a failure. Your code integration system may already have counters and enforcement mechanisms for this, but if they don't, you can typically script it so that it does.

In most parts of the system, SFDC supports commenting in code and even formulas, but even where they don't there's almost always a way to plant comments via inoperative code fragments containing the documentation message (e.g., `IF 0=1`,"The comment goes here—maybe as long as 80 characters,").

So there are no excuses for not commenting code. In modern cloud-based applications, though, much of the action isn't in code: it's in declarative programming and custom fields/objects/relations. Here, too, document-as-you-go must be explicitly measured with incentives for both the developer and administrator. In systems like SFDC, every new field has two opportunities for self-documentation: the description area and the help-bubble information area. Both should be used, with different information in each. If a cloud system doesn't have this, use dummy fields with names that shadow the real field, adding metadata information in a human-readable way. For example, for the numerical field "Salesteam," add a text field "▼Salesteam" and set the default value to descriptive text. If your system doesn't support extended ASCII in the field name, use a punctuation mark like "{" or "¡" that forces the variable name to come at the end of any alphabetized list. If your system doesn't support default values for text fields, you'll have to embed as much intelligence as you can into the dummy field name.

What about self-documenting the messages that go between modules? With WSDL or other XML dialects, you can put lots of metadata into the XML itself or into supporting DTDs. Although these can be verbose and lead to arguably slow system response times, most of the time the extra overhead is barely noticeable. When you're making a call to the cloud directly from your code, the libraries that actually form the ReST or SOAP messages typically won't let you control much of what goes over the wire. In this case, sending an extra information-only text variable or two in the outbound request will make both troubleshooting and learning curves a lot easier in the long run.

The bottom line: even though the cloud doesn't enforce any documentation or make it any easier to enforce, there are clever ways to use cloud app features and Web service protocols to make modern systems more self-documenting. Call it "sky writing," and mandate it.

Even before the SFDC implementation team creates user reports and dashboards, its members should create data quality reports, dashboards, and monthly metrics. In addition to using SFDC's data quality dashboards, create reports that can measure the following items:

- Number of incomplete records (to identify fields that are habitually left blank)[19]

- Number of records marked as "bad data" (particularly `leads`)

- Number of new unread/neglected records (particularly `leads`)

- Number of `accounts` with no child objects (i.e., `contacts`, `contact roles`, `opportunities`, or `cases`)

- Number of records with "data bounces" (where a single field is repeatedly changed back and forth[20] between a couple of values)

- Number of records with contradictory data (e.g., states that don't agree with countries, postal codes, email domain country identifiers, or phone city codes)

- Number of records with out-of-bounds values (e.g., 12-digit ZIP codes), silly input (a 2,000-character text entry or a 2-character `notes` record),[21] or data in the wrong field (look for email addresses or phone numbers in text fields)

- Number of records that appear to be duplicates (particularly for `leads` and `contacts`, but also for `accounts`, `cases`, and `opportunities`)

- Number of records that are out of date (particularly open `opportunities` and `cases` that haven't been updated since their deadlines)

---

19. Also, definitely plug in the free FieldTrip tool from the AppExchange to help in this area.
20. This problem is most easily quantified by enabling `field history tracking`, and it usually indicates faulty code, buggy integration logic, or contradictory automation in external systems such as MAS or pricing/configuration engines.
21. SFDC's internal reports cannot "see" the `notes` object. Reports on `notes` must be done via the `Excel connector`, `data loader`, or another API-based data access tool.

SFDC Project Areas Needing Direct Involvement by IT People

Even the most independent system implementation team will need assistance from central IT in a number of areas. For example, they'll need assistance with policy standards, review boards, and infrastructure configuration (e.g., the SFDC team may need IT to open a port in a firewall).

The SFDC team will also need assistance with any data that are to be imported or migrated: they need to get the schemas and metadata, understand the semantics, and be informed of any unusual behavior associated with the data. They'll need data samples to run pilot migrations and the full data set to do the final import. They may need some assistance to properly placate external systems at certain points in their deployment.

The SFDC team will also need assistance in coding and configuring some external systems, particularly the company's Web site and eCommerce system. Some trivial work (a few lines of HTML) is required to set up the `web2lead` and `web2case` functions. In implementing the `partner portal` and `customer self-service portal`, the SFDC team will need to integrate IT's HTML, CSS, and JavaScript code with templates provided with the SFDC components. If someone builds a `Sites` application—using `VisualForce` and SFDC's deployment platform—the application will need to be linked into the company's main Web site. This effort may require writing a trivial amount of HTML and JavaScript, but somebody has to build that application and push it into the main site infrastructure.

If your company plans to use the `support` module in SFDC, some work must be done in the company's mail server to fully integrate the `email2case` functionality. Some integration is typically also done between SFDC's `case` object and the defect reporting system (such as Jira or BugTraq).

If your company operates a significant call center (inbound or outbound), integrating SFDC with its phone system will require a bit of IT time. Several computer-telephone integration (CTI) adaptors are available as off-the-shelf products, but they still require some configuration and setup. For all the really fancy stuff, the CTI framework requires some real programming support and, of course, security and deployment assistance.

As users make requests for add-ons found in the AppExchange (see Chapter 7), at least some setup work will be required to evaluate, test, and install those programs. Usually, this amounts to an hour or so of IT time to implement simple features, but it can be significantly longer for some of the complex external applications. The rule of thumb: the more expensive the add-on is, the more IT will need to be involved in its setup and configuration.

If you decide to develop some custom code—either as internal `VisualForce` or `APEX`, or in the language of your choice as external Web-service functionality—the IT department will almost certainly be called upon to use the Eclipse IDE with the SFDC add-ons. They really work! They're only partially buggy! They have user interface "features" that could only have been created in Eastern Europe!

Seriously, Eclipse is a very solid IDE, particularly when plugged into a version control system. Its weakness—endemic across cloud applications—is in debugging. Error messages are ugly, brutish, and short. Worse, they are often misleading because the best code you write will be operating across six languages at once: CSS, HTML, JavaScript, `Visual-Force`, `APEX`, and `SOQL`.[22] There is no debugger in the world that can handle that mess. Pile on top of that the goblins that live within the interpretive stack inside your Web browser. There are literally hundreds of bizarre rendering and behavioral bugs unique to Firefox, Internet Explorer, Safari, and Chrome—and the bugs seem to change with each bug patch of the browser. You might wish that these issues were merely a faded memory, but an amazing array of anomalies continues to occur with code that looks legal. The bottom line: leave lots of time for testing any browser code you deploy, and reserve the right to limit your users to a narrow range of supported browsers!

AVOIDING TEMPTATION

In IT, coding is second nature. And SFDC is a well-thought-out platform for building business apps. So knock yourself out—*for features that are absolutely required.*

Pay attention to the word *absolutely* in that sentence, because you'll be tempted to add some features that are really cool but really aren't critical. In the land of SFDC, features aren't as important as data quality. Features aren't as important as flexibility. Features, unless they are explicitly requested by a lot of users, get in the way of success.

A critical success factor in CRM is ongoing flexibility, so the system can accommodate the inevitable changes in requirements over the years. Every feature that you code in SFDC will reduce its flexibility in the objects you touch and perhaps in related objects. Too much code means the users can't even add pick-list values without a complete coding, testing, and deployment cycle. If you don't build your code in some really clever ways (using lots of introspection and dynamic techniques), the tiniest changes can have big consequences.

Even if you are coding in the best possible way, the code from third-party products may not play nice. Every time they upgrade, and every time you make a change, there may be hundreds of test failures and new anomalies to troubleshoot.

So don't overdo it.

It's very common for users to need help in creating some of the fancier reports and dashboards. You may well need to help them bolt on a BI tool or have SFDC feed records into your data warehouse. If you haven't already done so, read "Reports—Inside versus Outside" in Chapter 2.

---

22. Not to mention the libraries like jQuery, extJS, or SenchaTouch that you might be using.

The biggest single area requiring IT effort will be any integration of the SFDC system with external systems. Even if your company can use the pure off-the-shelf adaptors, IT personnel will need to be involved with defining the business process activities and triggers for the integration, aligning the data items, and testing for corruption-free, duplicate-free operation. This analysis can entail a significant effort. If you haven't already done so, read the section on integration in Chapter 7. Unfortunately, the juiciest integration problems almost always involve external code and very tricky data manipulations. Although external consultants can help in these areas, in the long run the highest-quality and most economical integrations will happen because of dedicated internal IT resources. As Chapters 9 through 11 suggest, executives may demand a dozen integrations for the fanciest CRM implementations, so budget accordingly (or better yet, get them to budget accordingly).

Project Management and Deployment Issues

Even if members of the IT department aren't asked to handle the project management for the SFDC implementation, you should know what the project managers are doing and which project management model they are using. As discussed in Chapter 4, we highly recommend an Agile project management style. Although SFDC rarely involves extensive development, Agile's incremental delivery style, user focus, and iterative testing are essential to ensuring the success and controlling the costs of SFDC deployments. The larger the project, the more essential Agile management and phased deployments will be.

Finally, in setting up security features and access controls, err on the side of laxness (at least initially) to maximize early adoption, collaboration, and information sharing. Over time, the controls can be easily tightened, but at the beginning do everything you can to *not* intimidate or frustrate users.

Ongoing Usage

Given Agile project management and quick deployment cycles, "ongoing usage" of the SFDC system will probably start within weeks of system procurement—even as development continues. Although only a few users may be actively on the system, in the words of Emperor Palpatine, it will be a "fully armed and operational battle station."

As users are set up and activated, it's often best to log in to their accounts before you hand them over, so you can configure things for the users before they dip a toe into the water. To make things easy, file a case[23] with SFDC to have them turn on login privileges

---

23. Like all good things, cases take time. Unless you are on `unlimited edition` or have SFDC's highest level of support, always allow 5 working days for the simplest case to be completed.

for admins, a feature that allows you to impersonate anyone in the system without ever knowing their password. Unfortunately, there are a few settings in the account that can be tailored only if you log in as the user:

- `Grant login access` for administrators; this date can be up to a year in the future.
- Set the `application` for the user (assuming that it needs to be one of the non-default applications).
- Set the default `dashboard` for the user.
- Set the `report` lists (folder contents and ordering) for the user.
- Tailor the `UI options` for the user (e.g., should the user see hovering items?).
- Collapse or expand `collapsible sections`.

One little issue that is a bit irritating is SFDC's user authentication system. The first computer and network that a user logs in from doesn't need to be authenticated, but all new computers or network addresses for that user do. The authentication drill can be done in 60 seconds via email or phone, but it sometimes generates an amazing amount of static from users. So here's a trick: set the system's `network security` feature to whitelist all computers within your company's IP address range. You'll find this feature in SFDC's `Administrative Setup` area, and it's largely self-explanatory. The address range you put in can consist of two major address increments (e.g., 66.0.0.0 to 68.0.0.0), but don't set it wider than is needed to cover all of the business's locations (as this would unduly weaken login security).

Encouraging Adoption

Users will be coming on to the SFDC system in waves. The goal from day one is to get people using the system, filling it with the data they need to complete their own tasks. It is essential that users not be asked to put in data that "would be great," because they will view this request as a bore unless it helps them directly in some way.

Entering good data is the number one way to improve adoption and the level of utilization for the SFDC system. If you implemented the data quality and enrichment features discussed earlier, turn them on as early as practicable. Make sure that people are trained in how to use the data quality features. Set expectations properly, and then please the users with how much better things get every few weeks.

Start using the data quality reports as early as you can. Look for trends in the data to understand where problems are occurring. When an obvious data entry problem crops up,

---

THE VIRTUAL HELP DESK

Help desks are important to users, yet most SFDC implementation teams don't have a help desk function.

The first line of defense is the SFDC system itself: fully populated "bubble help" for items on the screen, a `content library` full of cheat sheets, a FAQ, and helpful links within each of the major page types.

The next line of defense is the project wiki or Google Drive area, which should include reference documents, cheat sheets, podcasts (5-minute training sessions), and ScreenCam tutorials (keep them to less than 15 minutes in length).

Even with all of this documentation available at users' fingertips, you have to be ready for people who won't read this material or who are clever enough to discover problems you didn't anticipate. To do so, you need some sort of virtual help desk.

The help desk won't really be staffed, and it's not really a desk. Rather, it's a `chatter persona`, a set of `chatter groups`, an email address, and a voicemail box at which users can report problems. Someone in IT needs to check these sources *very* frequently—ideally, twice an hour. Most of the time, they'll be empty, but you never want to have users hanging in the wind for more than 30 minutes.

---

use (or tighten up) field validation rules to prevent the problem from spreading. Whenever you discover data pollution from outside sources, don't fix the records until you have also fixed the external source of the pollution.

The SFDC project team will be focusing on "good news" generation and politics. At the same time, it is essential to have solid metrics on how groups are adopting the system. SFDC's built-in `adoption dashboard` isn't a bad place to start. You can then go even further by creating some weekly reports that provide a bit more detail:

- Number of logins and length of login per user

- Number of `lead`, `contact`, `account`, `opportunity`, and `case` records created and updated

- Number of fields changed per user, as indicated by `field history tracking` entries

- Number of `chatter` posts

- Number of `tasks` created and updated

EXPERIENCING OBJECT HYSTERESIS

Hysteresis is a term used to describe hardware and signals that have nondeterministic behavior, for which outputs are time dependent. Let me be the first to introduce you to this phenomenon as it applies to software.

SFDC is a SaaS application that is delivered as a set of Web services. Most of the time, results from instantiating or modifying things appear (essentially) instantly to all users of the system.

However, because of SFDC's loosely coupled services and replication delay within a pod, some complex objects may not appear to all users and services at the same instant. For example, if you have successfully created a new report, it may not show up instantaneously when you search for it. Updating `custom objects` and clicking some buttons (e.g., setting up the `forecast hierarchy`, recalculating `object sharing rules`, pushing updates to the `sandbox`, and updating `dashboards`) may generate a "We'll send you an email when we're done" message. These updates may take several minutes to be available to all users, even if they appear available to the individual making the change.

While the object update is being propagated across your cluster, the system will pretend to have performed the update even though it hasn't completed. For example, SFDC's search engine may take a minute or more to notice new data entries. For the hysteresis interval, the system will demonstrate uncertain behavior. These effects can be quite annoying to developers who are trying to debug some problem.

The best antidote for this problem is to chill out, work on some other detail, or just grab a cappuccino. Make it a decaf. Sometimes the bugs are due to hysteresis; at other times they occur because you've made a minor punctuation mistake and you can't see it. Either way, why sweat it? The system may go back to behaving properly in a couple of minutes.

Administration

Even though much of the SFDC administration may be done by people who don't work for the central IT department, this section pulls together guidelines for all administrators.

For small- to medium-size operations, SFDC administration is usually a part-time job. It's nowhere near as challenging or specialized as the administration of SAP, Oracle, or even Microsoft applications. Real training is required for the admin to be effective, but most of the time this is a job that makes sense for people who have a technical bent but *not* real IT depth.[24]

---

24. Of course, if your company has 1,000 users and has integrated SFDC with SAP accounting and outsourced payroll and distribution applications, at least one of the SFDC system administrators will need to be an IT professional.

The first order of business for administrators is to create a virtual help desk to handle the most basic questions. Create and collect as many cheat sheets as you can for users and post all of them in SFDC's documents area. Also publish these documents, as well as FAQs and other helpful documents (e.g., user guides for the Outlook add-ons), in the project wiki/Google Drive area. Obtain any needed training materials (including audio tracks for podcasts and WebEx sessions for Web replay) and post them, along with links to SFDC's online tutorials, in the project wiki/Google Drive area as well. The joy you'll get from the first time you say the administrator's mantra—"RTFM"[25]—will make it worth all the effort.

One topic deserves special mention. You will most likely receive calls from power users who claim to need system administrator access. Almost invariably, adding a "cowboy" system administrator is a serious mistake. Just say no.

The following sections cover example "administrative duty roster" items that you may well have to work on.

On-Demand Activities

You will occasionally need to resolve user problems in real time:

- Unlocking user accounts or resetting passwords due to user forgetfulness

- Adding new whitelisted IP addresses

- Troubleshooting email campaigns or auto-responders that generate excessive bounced mails

- Expanding or refining `sharing rules` so records can be properly manipulated

- Fixing data records that have somehow been set with `record types` or `ownership` that make them inaccessible to users

Weekly Activities

SFDC's typical administrative duties seem to follow a weekly cycle. A lot of things will go wrong Monday morning (don't ask me why), and a couple of tasks need to be done once a week on the day of your choice. These cyclical duties include the following tasks:

- Running and storing the weekly snapshot (`data export`) of the system data and attachments

- Running deduping tools such as RingLead or DemandTools[26]

---

25. In a book such as this, I'm not allowed to spell out this acronym. All you need to know is that R stands for "read," T stands for "the," and M stands for "manual."

26. These things are dangerous if not used correctly, and their UIs are clunky at best. Actually read the user guide for your deduping tool, as well as the how-to guide that's on www.SFDC-secrets.com.

- Running adoption dashboards

- Deactivating `users` (either due to departure from the company or transfer to a new job that does not require SFDC access) or reassigning their `roles` and `profiles` to reflect their new duties

- Transferring record `ownership` due to changes in job responsibility or territory coverage

- Modifying roles or record-sharing rules

- Importing leads and contacts

- Modifying price lists (particularly if your company does a lot of promotions and limited-time offers)

- Changing delegation and escalation paths to account for absences or extended travel

Monthly Activities

There are a few activities that can only be done once a month but need to be done more often than quarterly:

- Running data quality reports to identify any new sources of data pollution:

  - ➥ If you find fields that are consistently blank more than 30% of the time, consider removing them from page views.

  - ➥ If you find a set of bad data records, don't delete them; instead, quarantine them until you've been able to troubleshoot the problem and fix its root cause.

- Before you refresh the `sandbox(es)`, using Eclipse to make a complete metadata backup of the `sandbox` images and your main system image. You'll thank me when somebody comes back to you and asks for a report they deleted 2 months ago.

- Refreshing the `sandbox(es)`.[27]

- Navigating to `Setup>App Setup>Develop>Apex Classes` and pushing the `Run All Tests` button. It may take an hour or more for this to complete, but if you find any new test failures, log them in the system wiki/Google Drive area and troubleshoot. Some of the failures may go away if you push the `Options` button and click the `Disable Parallel Apex Testing` box. The causes of new test errors are typically new `validation rules` that fire; changes to `workflow`

---

27. Make *sure* to coordinate the timing of these updates with the work of any developers who are using the sandbox, lest you blow away some of their work.

rules, particularly when they change `field values` or generate `outbound messages`; modified `pick-list` values or `record types`; changes to the security model that make some things inaccessible to code; and changes to the software modules that blew up. You may have to file a case with third-party vendors (check `Setup>App Setup>Installed Packages`), but that usually starts a finger-pointing exercise—so make sure you have your act together first.

- Reading about high-priority fixes that SFDC has come up with. Note that these fixes will be installed by default within a few weeks, but it's better if you do the patch installs at a time of your choosing (where you have time to react to and fix any problems you discover).

- Installing the "high-priority updates" that may have been pushed into your instance by SFDC. It's best to rerun the "run all tests" exercise after enabling the updates—and if something goes wrong, disable that update and notify the relevant vendor(s) of the issues.

- Creating an archive copy of any error logs kept in your integration server.

- Running a full system backup (data, metadata, and error logs, if possible) on any system or application that is integrated with SFDC.

Quarterly Activities

Although there are a lot of items in the following list, the first two are mission critical, with the resulting files being kept *forever* (you'll thank me someday when a pesky plaintiff attorney goes into a discovery process on SFDC data):

- Downloading the CSV from the user login history.

- Downloading the CSV from the system administrator setup audit log.

- Running the Force.com IDE to get a copy of the full system metadata. (Create a new "project" every time, and archive them for at least a year—you'll thank me.)

- Running the `Reports Report` (get it from www.SFDC-secrets.com) to identify reports that haven't been run in 6 months (hide—don't delete—them from users).

- Examining any new `validation rules` and `workflows` that have been added to the system to make sure that the Boolean conditions have been set correctly. Fix them so they don't cause new `APEX` errors to be thrown.

- Examining any new pick-list values that have been modified or added to any fields in the system, and using the Force.com IDE to identify the impact of those changes across all the Booleans, `formulas`, and `APEX`/JavaScript/`VisualForce` code in the system. Correct any elements that have been impacted.

- Running `FieldTrip` and `EasyDescribe`, two free tools that give you an overview of the health of your system's object model.

- Reading the release notes for the upcoming version of SFDC to see if any of your existing features or APIs you depend on are being changed significantly. If so, you will need to do some testing of the pre-release features in your `sandbox` and do the "run all tests" exercise there. It is getting increasingly common that code, formulas, and buttons need to be reworked to accommodate version changes.

- If you are a certified SFDC administrator, studying for (hours) and taking (minutes) the admin recertification test (this is typically a 15-question multiple-guess online test).

- Attending at least one local SFDC user group meeting.

- Archiving (or maybe deleting) weekly data snapshots that are more than a quarter old.

Annual Activities

The main responsibility here is to capture data that will fall "over the horizon" or need to be archived for compliance reasons:

- Creating an archive of all the system's field history tables (typically spanning no more than 18 months) to ensure that you have an audit trail that goes beyond a year.

- Archiving or purging `documents` (all four forms),[28] `emails`, and `tasks` to reduce the storage charges in your system or to adhere with your document/email retention standards.

- Archiving chatter histories for audit, compliance, or regulatory reasons.

- Attending DreamForce!

A bit of elaboration is required regarding the mass-record transfers that are needed whenever a new `user` starts in the system, a `territory` is split, or new `assignment rules` are established. Generally speaking, the `accounts, leads, contacts, open cases`, and `open opportunities` should be reassigned to the new user. `Closed opportunities`, however, should not be transferred to the new user, as this change could lead to erroneous calculation of commissions (and may propagate problems to the accounting system or data warehouse). Further, `closed opportunities` should be

---

28. Aren't you glad to know that SFDC stores BLOb files in four separate areas in the object model? I know I am.

BACKUPS AND SNAPSHOTS AND REPLICAS, OH MY!

SFDC performs continuous replication and online backup, and it's a background process that is free (even in the cheapest SFDC editions). That's great for disaster recovery and SFDC error recovery, but not so great for you. Because the backup is analogous to a continuous database log, restoring a system based on the SFDC backup data will always entail a fairly involved consulting project (which will cost you unless you can prove the data loss was SFDC's fault—good luck with that one). Read those words again, and take heed. These things can get expensive in a hurry.

That's why it's essential for you to make a complete `data snapshot`—including `attachments`—at least once per month, and really, it should be weekly. This kind of backup requires only a few link-clicks, so there's no excuse not to make these copies. You can also use SFDC's `data loader` tool to perform a scripted data dump to your company's own servers.

Keep several months' worth of archives on a company-owned disk. Storage is cheap, so use it to lower the cost of mistakes. You'll thank me for this advice someday.

In addition to backing up data, you also need to keep backups of the system configuration, metadata, screen designs, and code. This is best done through creating a `developer sandbox` (you get one of these for free with `enterprise edition` and 20 of them with `unlimited`), because you get a coherent replica of the entire system configuration in a very navigable form. Be careful when updating your `sandbox` replica: any data or system changes that may have been done in the replica will be wiped out by the updating process. Having these data available can also be very helpful for cloning your system if you need to set up a second instance for debugging or other operational reasons.

You should also consider investing in a data replication tool such as those available from Pervasive, RelationalJunction, and Informatica. These tools can be used to create replicas of your company's SFDC data set on your own servers for disaster recovery, real-time data warehousing, or other purposes.

completely locked down so that neither the new rep nor the old rep can modify them. If the new rep wants to see old `opportunities`, use the `sales teams` function to give him or her visibility into the records. To perform these reassignments, if just one or two changes must be made, use the wizards found in the SFDC system. By contrast, if the entire salesforce is being redesigned, it's usually better to use the `data loader` tool and Excel to make all wholesale changes.

If you have implemented significant add-on applications to SFDC (such as an email blaster, document management system, or commissions/incentive management system), these third-party products will likely have administrative needs of their own. Some of those administrative controls will be in SFDC, but for the more ambitious applications they will have their own administrative portal outside the system. There are too many issues to cover here, but typically the users will not be able to properly handle these cross-cloud duties properly—so someone in IT will probably have to. This means taking the vendor's class in configuration and administration,[29] and setting aside time for the care and feeding of the third-party application on a weekly or at least monthly basis.

Dealing with Dupes

Duplicate records seem to be a never-ending problem in CRM systems because of the number of data sources and proportion of records that are entered by hand. Dupes irritate and confuse users and are among the top three causes of data quality problems in CRM systems. But dupes are a whole lot easier to create than they are to properly fix, and in extreme cases you can't rid the system of them. Do not naively start on a dedupe adventure without doing your homework, testing your strategies before using them on production data, and devoting enough time to get the job done.

Let's start with the simple situations. If only a small number of records needs to be merged, use SFDC's `merge lead` button. `Contacts` are a little bit harder, but the `merge contacts` wizard is accessed from the `account` page (note that the `contacts` you're trying to merge must "live" in the same `account`—if not, move one of them).

SFDC's internal features dedupe using a fairly simple matching algorithm. For more sophisticated deduping, you will need to use deduping tools provided by CRMfusion, RingLead, or Cloudingo. They provide some very advanced features (such as fuzzy logic) to find a wider range of candidate duplicate records. However, harnessing the power and speed of these tools requires some real discipline and craftiness on the administrator's part, because there isn't an effective undo mechanism that you can employ after performing a false merge. (As always, do a full backup of all potentially affected records before you start the deduping tool.) Do the deduping in several passes, starting with the strictest matching criteria, merging those records, and gradually loosening the criteria. Once your match criteria produce more than 20% spurious matches, stop using the tool for this cycle. In most SFDC implementations, anything less than 5% duplication is perfectly acceptable (and anything less than 3% seems almost unattainable).

`Accounts` should sometimes be merged if they really are the *same* entity. Before you go there, think about whether the `accounts` should be merged in the first place. Although there is an easy-to-use `merge accounts` function (available at ./merge/accmergewizard.jsp), if you have any external integrations, it's bad juju. Why? Because in SFDC the account is at the top of the data model, with many objects hanging off of it. If you merge

---

29. Beware the applications that end users think are "super easy" to administer. Some of these easy UIs are in fact bears to control. Although SFDC provides good audit trails of administrative action (and there are several ways to get yourself out of trouble), some of the add-on apps have no auditing, no undo, and little in the way of warnings when you're doing something dangerous. So, even more than with SFDC, take those third-party administrative classes.

accounts, there are lots of repercussions to the relationships underneath. If your instance of SFDC is integrated with outside systems, lots of pointers will be lost—and in some cases your integration logic will cause phantom accounts to be recreated within minutes.

So examine these `accounts`. Are they related in some way—do they have a parent, child, or sibling relationship? SFDC's `parent account` relationship was specifically designed to create `account hierarchies`, which can be very helpful for understanding company politics and purchasing department behavior. If the two `accounts` in question are siblings (say, GE Jet Engines and GE Medical), create a parent `account` (in this example, GE HQ) with nothing in it (for the time being) and have both of the existing `accounts` point to it as the parent. Populating the `parent account` field provides much more information and context to the customer relationship, so don't merge `accounts` until you understand this issue.

If you are using a mass deduping tool, there are some special procedures you need to go through to avoid big headaches and rework. **Find the (long) checklist at www.SFDC-secrets.com.**

Archiving Data

SFDC provides a reasonable amount of record storage for free, but there are several situations where it gets overfilled by external integrations or internal code. And then SFDC storage charges mount up in a hurry. If your company's SFDC system is overflowing with data or it's time to archive old records, here are guidelines of how to prepare for the archiving:

- Only archive records if you know they are the cause of storage problems, as archiving is a task you'd generally like to avoid. Most SFDC records are quite small; it's the attached files and emails that typically fill up the system.

- You can't delete an object from the system unless its dependent objects are removed first. Tracking all of these relationships down can be time consuming, so don't plan on completing even a small archive operation in 20 minutes.

- You may be able to archive just `notes`, `tasks`, and `attached files` to free up all the space you need. Because `notes`, `tasks`, and `attachments` are always attached to another record, make sure to capture the UOIDs of the objects they are attached to, to facilitate future searches and joins. Check out the Case Detachifier add-on found in the AppExchange, and use the `view top files by size` feature in the `storage management` area of SFDC `setup`.

- It's usually okay to archive `chatter` conversations, but do not forget to first archive any `files` or other data artifacts attached to the chats. Note that some compliance add-ons, `triggers`, or `reports` may have some noisy reactions to mass deletion of chats, so do some testing in your `sandbox` before you do anything fancy.

- **Leads** are typically never deleted from the system, because doing so will obliterate metrics on marketing and **campaigns**. Normally, **leads** are merely transferred to queues that render them invisible to most users. If you plan to remove **leads** from the system, make sure to archive **activities, notes, attachments,** and **campaign membership** tables that point to each of the archived **leads**.

- **Accounts** should almost never be deleted from the system. These records are tiny, but they are the top level in an information pyramid that cannot be safely removed. If you need to have old **accounts** disappear from view, use **ownership** or the **type** pick list to create **filters** for **views**, **reports**, and other user touchpoints.

- **Opportunities** should follow the same rules as **accounts**. Never let a sales rep convince you to remove an **opportunity** because it's irrelevant.

- **Quotes, line items, contracts, and assets** should follow the same rules as **opportunities**.

- **Contacts** should follow the same rules as **accounts**, unless a **contact** has been created in the system with no updates to data or related lists. These still-born **contacts** can be safely archived.

- **Cases** should never be deleted, unless they were spuriously created by an errant piece of software. Even then, make sure that the software bug has been resolved before you remove the case.

- **Campaigns** should never be deleted or archived.

- **Users** can never be deleted or removed from the system. They can, however, be renamed to indicate that they are deactivated. In addition to deactivating idled users, change a name like Joe Blow to {Joe Blow} and the alias to {JBlow}, as this puts the name at the bottom of alphabetized lists and provides an easy way to filter these names in reports and views. Do *not* recycle individual **user accounts** (by changing the name entirely), as this will corrupt all kinds of historical analyses. Once you have deactivated the **user**, his or her license will be available for use with a new **user** account—so just leave the old user there.

Management of the Administrative Function

Once the SFDC system is up and running, the administrators should set up and review a user suggestion box forum using either **chatter**, the project wiki, the Google Drive area, or SFDC's **Ideas** feature. By engaging users to come up with solutions, and polling them on their preferences, the administrative staff can be much more responsive to the users' real needs. This wins big points for the IT department as well as for SFDC itself.

As discussed in Chapter 4, SFDC administrators need to act as (or deputize) a set of data architects who make decisions about which additions or corrections to the system object model (particularly custom objects and relations) are necessary, which reports should be removed from the system, which AppExchange goodies should be added to the system, and how to best implement user requests.

At least one of the SFDC administrators should be designated as the data steward, who looks out for the health and cleanliness of system data by controlling design changes and external data inputs. This role includes tactical responsibilities (designing deduping rules and running data cleansing tools) and strategic goals (maintaining the integrity and relevance of the data dictionary, ensuring that data elements are denormalized only for good reason, and developing data update strategies for denormalized data).

In a large, multidivisional company, the administrators should also set up a change control board (CCB) to review the list of user requests and allocate resources for the requested changes. If the users are really asking for something big (like a new subsystem or an additional system integration), the CCB would be the vehicle for arbitrating and formalizing budget requests. Figure 13-1 illustrates an example CCB process. The CCB

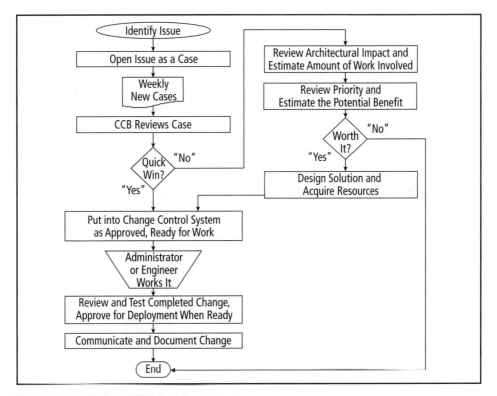

FIGURE 13-1   Change control board review process

should definitely form a `chatter group` and establish `chatter topics`. The CCB typically meets on a weekly basis when the system is first being deployed but eventually can move to monthly meetings once the system is stabilized.

Every few quarters, the system needs "meta-administration"—the management of system management. The administrators need to think through how they'll work as a team, whether they should use a federated model of administration, and which kinds of privileges should be delegated to power users.

Getting the Most from **SFDC**

- Understand that SFDC is a platform, not just an application. The more successful SFDC is in your company, the more serious the administrative, security, and control functions need to be.

- Cloud computing and Agile project management mean an incremental style of development and deployment. SFDC is surprisingly flexible and, when done right, will stay that way. But these advantages require updated skills and some behavior modification when it comes to decision making and resource allocation.

- SFDC doesn't require a lot of effort from IT. In fact, you'll be surprised by how little may be involved with bringing the system up.

- IT's highest leverage comes in the design and process-architecture phase, because you can see ramifications and best practices much more easily than the user and implementation teams can.

- IT may not be involved with ongoing SFDC administration or operations at all, but you should make sure to reach out to the administrators to make sure they are making the right judgment calls.

- It bears repeating: user adoption is everything. At least for the first year, focus on making the system as easy as you can for the users, so it becomes valuable and self-sustaining. Features don't matter anywhere near as much as data quality, because credibility and lack of wasted time are what will draw users to the system.

- Check out "Essential System Administrator Tools" in Chapter 7.

For Small Companies

- You probably don't have an IT department, so whoever your sysadmin is needs to at least skim this chapter and take ownership of the relevant duties.

For Large Enterprises

- The SFDC teams will need help with review cycles, approvals, and IT committees. So help them, already.

- Help the SFDC teams understand the regulatory compliance or legal standards that must be maintained.

- Avoid the temptation to overcode. Every line of code you add to the system is going to cost in terms of time, rework, and loss of ongoing flexibility.

Index

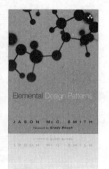

FREE
Online Edition

Your purchase of **Salesforce.com® Secrets of Success, Second Edition,** includes access to a free online edition for 45 days through the **Safari Books Online** subscription service. Nearly every Prentice Hall book is available online through **Safari Books Online**, along with thousands of books and videos from publishers such as Addison-Wesley Professional, Cisco Press, Exam Cram, IBM Press, O'Reilly Media, Que, Sams, and VMware Press.

Safari Books Online is a digital library providing searchable, on-demand access to thousands of technology, digital media, and professional development books and videos from leading publishers. With one monthly or yearly subscription price, you get unlimited access to learning tools and information on topics including mobile app and software development, tips and tricks on using your favorite gadgets, networking, project management, graphic design, and much more.

Activate your FREE Online Edition at
informit.com/safarifree

STEP 1:   Enter the coupon code: HGSPXAA.

STEP 2:   New Safari users, complete the brief registration form.
Safari subscribers, just log in.

If you have difficulty registering on Safari or accessing the online edition,
please e-mail customer-service@safaribooksonline.com